We Americans

. . . among democratic nations each new generation is a new people.

ALEXIS DE TOCQUEVILLE
Democracy in America

A TOPICAL HISTORY OF THE UNITED STATES

Consulting Editors

PAIGE ARTZT
Miami-Dade Junior College

G. PORTER EWING
Los Angeles City College

MYRON A. MARTY
Florissant Valley Community College

LEONARD PITT

California State University, Northridge

We Americans

VOLUME II   1865 TO THE PRESENT

SCOTT, FORESMAN AND COMPANY   Glenview, Illinois

Dallas, Tex.   Oakland, N.J.   Palo Alto, Cal.   Tucker, Ga.   Brighton, England

Dedicated to
the Tricentennial Generation.
May we Americans leave them
a cleaner environment,
a more just society, and
a world at peace.

Copyright © 1976 Scott, Foresman and Company.
All Rights Reserved.
Printed in the United States of America.

Library of Congress Cataloging in Publication Data
Pitt, Leonard.
   We Americans.

   Includes bibliographies and indexes.
   CONTENTS: [1] From colonial times to 1877. — [2] From 1865 to the present.
   1. United States — History. I. Title.
E178.1.P55   1976b   973   75–35845
ISBN 0–673–15002–X (v. 2)

   678910-RRC-908988878685848382

Acknowledgments and Credits for maps, charts, and illustrations appear on the following page.

CREDITS AND ACKNOWLEDGMENTS

The author and publisher acknowledge with gratitude permissions to reprint or adapt the following materials. The numbers shown below refer to the pages of this text.

Literary Permissions

818c: Poem, "For Brother Malcolm" by Edward S. Spriggs. From *For Malcolm: Poems on the Life and Death of Malcolm X*, edited by Dudley Randall and Margaret G. Burroughs. Copyright © 1967 by Broadside Press. Reprinted by permission of the author. 818d: Fragment of poem, "Back to/Back to" by Victor Hernandez Cruz. From SNAPS, by Victor Hernandez Cruz. Copyright © 1968, 1969 by Victor Hernandez Cruz. Reprinted by permission of Random House, Inc.

Maps, Charts, and Tables

504: Map, Where the Buffalo Roamed. Adapted from J. A. Allen, "The American Bison, Living and Extinct," *Memoirs, Museum of Comparative Zoology*, Vol. 4, No. 10, Harvard University Press, 1876. 505: Maps, Virgin Forest, 1620, 1850, 1926. Adapted from *The Influence of Geography on Our Economic Life* by Ridgley & Ekblaw, Gregg Publishing Co., 1938, pp. 528–529. Used with permission of McGraw-Hill, Inc., Gregg Division; and of the Department of Agriculture. 524: Chart, Mass Communications, 1929–1945. Adapted with permission of *Editor & Publisher*; and the National Broadcasting Company.

Illustration Credits

PART III 341: Carnegie Library of Pittsburgh. 357: Byron Collection, Museum of the City of New York. 359: Library of Congress. 361: Courtesy of The New York Historical Society. 365: Photo by Lewis Hine, George Eastman House Collection. 371: Brown Brothers. 374: Courtesy of the Caterpillar Tractor Co., Peoria. 379: From the Collection of R. L. Dodd, Kosciusko, Miss. 383: Library of Congress. 384: Culver Pictures. 386: Underwood & Underwood. 392: *Harper's Weekly*, October 20, 1877. 395: U.P.I. 399: National Archives. 400: U.S. Signal Corps. 406, 408: Library of Congress. 413: National Archives. 415: U.P.I. 416: National Archives. 421: Library of Congress. 425: Montana Historical Society, Helena. 426: National Archives. 427: Jack R. Williams. 434: Library of Congress. 437: History Division, Natural History Museum of Los Angeles County. 441: Courtesy, The Bancroft Library. 445: The Bettmann Archive, Inc. 446: George Eastman House Collection. 447: Museum of the City of New York. 451, 455: Brown Brothers. 459: Natural History Museum of Los Angeles County. 463: The Bettmann Archive, Inc. 464: American Telephone & Telegraph Co. 466: David R. Phillips. 468: Courtesy of The Chicago Lawn Historical Society. 474: Brown Brothers. 475, 481: Library of Congress. 482: Library of Congress. 484: Montana Historical Society, Helena. 486: Photo by Jacob A. Riis, The Jacob A. Riis Collection, Museum of the City of New York. 487: Photo by Lewis W. Hine, George Eastman House Collection. 489: Frederic Lewis. 491: Culver Pictures. 493: Library of Congress. 499: The Darius Kinsey Collection. 500: Collection of Robert E. Cunningham. 503: Library of Congress. 506: The Huffman Pictures, Miles City, Montana. 512: Photo by William Henry Jackson, Metropolitan Museum of Art. 513: Denver Public Library. 514: Courtesy of The Sierra Club, Photo by Joseph Le Conte. 353: Mark Twain Memorial, Hartford, Conn. 510: M.I.T. Historical Collections.

PART IV 521: Brown Brothers. 535: U.P.I. 542, 546: Brown Brothers. 548: *Collier's*, October 10, 1936. 552: Wide World. 554, 557: U.P.I. 559: Brown Brothers. 562: The Bettmann Archive, Inc. 563, 570: Brown Brothers. 573: Wide World. 578: National Archives. 584, 585: U.S. Coast Guard. 586: Underwood & Underwood. 589: Margaret Bourke-White, Time-Life Picture Agency, © Time Inc. 592: Energy Research and Development Administration. 595: Dorothea Lange/National Archives. 598: Photoworld. 602: Duncan Schiedt Archive. 607: Wide World. 608: Culver Pictures. 613: Underwood & Underwood. 616, 618: Brown Brothers. 619, 622: Wide World. 627: U.P.I. 628: Franklin D. Roosevelt Library. 633: Culver Pictures. 635: Underwood & Underwood. 637: Culver Pictures. 641: Photoworld. 644: U.P.I. 648, 652, 657: Brown Brothers. 653: Library of Congress. 659: Underwood & Underwood. 665: Mrs. Henry Rhoades. 666: Frederic Lewis. 541: U.P.I. 566, 591: Photoworld/FPG.

PART V 671: Donald C. Dietz/Stock Boston. 681: Bill Owens. 686: Cornell Capa/Magnum. 693: Charles Harbutt/Magnum. 696: Burk Uzzle/Magnum. 699: Marc Riboud/Magnum. 704: Nicholas Sapieha/Stock Boston. 714: Lawrence Fried/Magnum. 719: Cornell Capa/Magnum. 727: Wide World. 729: Robert Phillips/Black Star. 737: Photri. 732: Wide World. 739: Charles Gatewood. 744: Charles Moore/Black Star. 749: George Ballis/Black Star. 759: George Gardner. 763: Karen Preuss/Jeroboam. 771: Charles Gatewood. 775: Jeanclaude Lejeune. 778: Bill Owens. 782: Ellis Herwig/Stock Boston. 789: Arthur Tress. 793: George Gardner. 796: Archie Lieberman. 803: Burk Uzzle/Magnum. 808: Larry Keenan, Jr./Nest. 812: Optic Nerve/Jeroboam. 813: Elihu Blotnick/BBM. 743: U.P.I.

Photographic Essays

CHRONICLE: THE WILDERNESS 338a: (top) Library of Congress; (bottom) Collection of The Oakland Museum, Gift of Miss Marguerite Laird in Memory of her parents, Pinkston Wade Laird and Flora McCloskey Laird. 338b–338c: U.S. Department of the Interior, National Park Service. 338d: The Berkshire Museum, Pittsfield, Mass.

CHRONICLE: A HARD LIFE TO SWALLOW 527: (top) Dorothea Lange Collection, The Oakland Museum; (bottom) Library of Congress. 528: (top, right) Dorothea Lange Collection, The Oakland Museum; (bottom) Library of Congress; (left) Library of Congress. 529: Dorothea Lange Collection, The Oakland Museum. 530: (top and bottom) Dorothea Lange Collection, The Oakland Museum.

CHRONICLE: MUSEUM OF THE STREETS 818a: (top) Alex Webb/Magnum; (bottom) "La Raza de oro" by Jose G. Gonzalez. 818b: (top) Peter Menzel/Stock Boston; (middle) Elihu Blotnick/BBM; (bottom) Jerry Sloan; (center page) Erich Hartmann/Magnum. 818c: (top) Gianni Tortoli/Photo Researchers; (bottom) John Running. 818d: (top) Frank Muller-May/Magnum; (bottom) Elihu Blotnick/BBM.

Foreword

As the United States begins the third century of its national existence, Americans of all ages are looking back to the past in an effort to evaluate just where we as a people are today. Perhaps from this study of the past will come a firmer sense of purpose for the future. No one can deny that the rate and scope of change in all spheres of life have been remarkable. For example, the early English colony at Jamestown in Virginia was almost wiped out during an acute period of want, the so-called starving times. Yet today America is a land of vast wealth, and it recently became the first nation in history to reach an annual Gross National Product of $1 trillion.

The growth in the number of our inhabitants is also a striking development—from the 3.9 million Americans recorded in the census of 1790 to the 214 million citizens estimated in 1975. And the change in our pattern of living has been equally great. In 1790, for example, the vast majority of Americans were descendants of white immigrants from the British Isles. Their language, laws, and customs were derived from England, and they were overwhelmingly Protestant in religion. Today Americans are of different races, creeds, and cultural backgrounds. This book traces the contributions of all the groups who have met and interacted throughout our history: the descendants of the original colonists; the offspring of later immigrants from Europe; and our four large racial minorities—Indians, blacks, Chicanos, and Asian Americans.

We Americans offers a thematic, or topical, approach within a strong chronological organization. This format provides a clear, interesting, and fresh approach. It allows for a wide selection of topics including the role of women in American life in society at large as well as in the family, the search for an ideal community, the rise and growth of towns and cities, the shift from a rural to urban life style, and the ways whereby America's development has affected our natural environment. This is a sound and solid appreciation of the American past—one having an appeal both to instructors and students of the basic survey course.

Vincent P. De Santis
University of Notre Dame

Preface

On the eve of the American Revolution Patrick Henry told the Virginia Convention: "I know of no way of judging the future but by the past." An English contemporary, Sir Edmund Burke, wrote a few years later: "You can never plan the future by the past." These statements present a paradox to anyone who studies history. This paradox is especially confusing to young people, who sense that their nation's history is vitally important to an understanding of the times in which they live. But when events accelerate, as they now seem to be doing, history's pattern is blurred.

I hope that this book, by its thematic approach, will help link the past and present and eliminate some of the confusion. With the aid of my students I have identified eight important themes that have special contemporary meaning and can be traced back into the American past. These themes run like threads through the fabric of the book. They are Wealth, Power, War, Race, Nationality and Religion, Women and the Family, Community, and Environment.

In addition to its thematic, or topical, approach, the book offers a strong chronological framework. It is divided into five chronologically arranged parts that correspond to distinct periods of American history. Each of the five parts is introduced by two features: (1) a brief listing of important dates for the period; and (2) an overview that clearly ties together the events and developments relative to the eight topical chapters that follow. I believe that this organization will help clarify the pattern of history in the minds of students.

It is my expectation that both the students and instructors in the basic survey course will find the organization of *We Americans* more appealing than the more conventional organization of other texts. The emphasis on themes of enduring importance as well as on the role that all Americans have played in our national life is meant to personalize the story of the past and make it more interesting.

Instructors have many options in using *We Americans*, depending on the type of course they offer. Some will follow a strictly chronological approach, dealing with all chapters in Part I (Beginnings to 1789) before moving along to those in Part II (1789–1865). Others may want to assign all chapters on a given topic (Wealth, for example) before progressing to the next topic (perhaps, Power). Still other instructors can find their own variations by combining these two approaches. In any event, it will be found that the organization lends itself to greater flexibility.

To meet the needs of schools offering different types of courses, *We Americans* is offered in a single-volume clothbound version that covers American history from its beginnings to the present and in two paperbound volumes. Volume I covers from colonial times to 1877, and Volume II from 1865 to the present. An Instructor's Resource Book has been prepared by G. Porter Ewing, and a Study Guide by Robert Ellis and Tommie Jan Lowery. I am most appreciative of their work, which should enhance the use of the basic text.

It is impossible to write a book of this size and scope without incurring many debts. My gratitude and apologies, first of all, to the many unnamed scholars whose works I have consulted; limitations of space have prevented my citing more than a few of them by name. In particular, I am indebted to the editorial consultants for the work—Paige Artzt, G. Porter Ewing, and Myron A. Marty—whose thoughtful comments, suggestions, and advice helped and encouraged me through various stages of the manuscript. Vincent P. De Santis' detailed criticisms for Parts I, II, and III were most helpful. Then, too, I have benefitted from the advice and criticism of friends and colleagues. Those who have read sections of the work, made valuable suggestions, and saved me from careless errors include Ronald Schaffer, Rena Vasser, Ronald Davis, Gay Hayden, Paul Koistinen, Joseph Ernest, and Roy Merrens. Walter Smith and Kathryn Dabelow were also helpful. I am grateful as well to David Lash, an extremely resourceful research assistant. None of them is responsible for any of the faults that may remain in the book.

The Scott, Foresman editorial, design, and production staffs extended themselves greatly on the project. Most notably I want to thank Robert J. Cunningham for his patience and encouragement. The creative thinking and insight of David R. Ebbitt and Robert Anderson were equally valuable. I am grateful for the cooperation of Marilyn Reaves, Susan Houston, Mary Ann Lea, Barbara Frankel, Michael Werthman, Douglas C. Mitchell, Marnie Lynde, Robert Johnson, Robert Gruen, and Walter Dinteman.

I have also been helped by Norman Pitt, Sharon Smith, David Halfen, William A. Sommerfield, William Doyle, and the late George Vlach.

Members of the secretarial staff of my department at California State University, Northridge, who helped prepare or type the manuscript exhibited great forebearance. They are Mary Alvarez, Margaret Ball, Nancy Meadows, and Selma Rosenfeld.

Finally, I owe thanks also to my immediate family. My children, Marni, Adam, and Michael, put up with many inconveniences while their father was in the throes of "The Book." To my wife, Dale, who patiently researched, edited, typed, listened, and advised at every stage of this long project, I owe my very special love and gratitude.

Leonard Pitt
Los Angeles

Contents

Carnegie Library of Pittsburgh

Brown Brothers

Donald C. Dietz / Stock Boston

prolog
Beginnings to 1865

Indian civilizations before Columbus

The earliest immigrants to North America arrived between 25,000 and 50,000 years ago. These first humans to inhabit the continent probably crossed from Siberia to Alaska during an ice age which exposed a natural land bridge that is now covered by the Bering Sea. These people were Stone Age hunters. For thousands of years they fanned out over the Americas. By the end of the last ice age—about ten thousand years ago—many of their larger prey were extinct. The hardy wanderers, who had spread from the Arctic to the tip of South America, now turned to hunting smaller animals and learned to grow crops. Their descendants are the many peoples known as American Indians.

Between 7000 and 2000 B.C. Indians began growing corn, beans, squash, and other foods in Central America (sometimes called Middle America or Mesoamerica). Farming provided a food supply they could depend on and eventually enabled them to begin creating settled communities. From as early as 1200 B.C. to about 400 A.D. the Olmec civilization grew and flourished in the lowlands of Mexico's Gulf coast. From 300 A.D. the Maya culture developed on the Yucatán peninsula, reaching its peak around 900 A.D. The Aztecs of the Mexican highlands built an empire that lasted from about 1300 until its destruction by the invading Spaniards in the early 1500s. In Peru the Incas ruled their empire for almost five centuries before they too fell before the conquistadors.

When the land area of what became the United States was populated only by Indians, there were about six hundred separate tribes. Some two thousand languages and dialects were spoken, many as different from one another as Chinese is from English. The Northeast was occupied by forest hunters and farmers. The most prominent of these were the Iroquois, a remarkably stable alliance of tribes centered in what is now upper New York State. In the Southeast lived an agricultural people, whom the Europeans called the Five Civilized Tribes—Cherokee, Creek, Chickasaw, Choctaw, and Seminole. They were noted for their flat-topped burial mounds and for the open plazas in their villages, both of which show influences from Mesoamerican Indian civilizations. Their arts included decorated pottery, flint beads, and copper ornaments. In the arid Southwest were the Hopi, Pueblo, and Zuñi Indians. Strongly influenced by the culture of the Mexican highlands, they built cleverly designed apartmentlike dwellings of stone and adobe (sun-dried brick), some high on the faces of steep cliffs, and they used irrigation to grow crops in that harsh, dry land.

It is not certain how many native Americans there were around 1492. Estimates range from 6 million to 60 million, with 1 to 8 million living north of Mexico. What is certain is that in 1900, when the whites had spread over the whole continent, there were only 237,000 Indians left in the United States.

Explorers of North America

The voyages of Columbus opened the New World to centuries of exploration and settlement. During the fifteenth century European traders were seeking new routes to the Orient. Precious cargoes from India, China, and the Spice Islands (the East Indies) had always reached western Europe through the Mediterranean and the Near East. But the powerful Ottoman Turkish Empire controlled the Near Eastern routes, and the practice of using Italian merchants as middlemen was becoming too costly. Cheaper, more reliable routes had to be found. The western Europeans, whose ships were the most advanced in the world, sought an all-water route. It was Columbus who tested the idea that such a route could be found by sailing west across the Atlantic.

Christopher Columbus (1451–1506), a sailor from Genoa, had a deep, almost overpowering sense of personal destiny and limitless faith in his own ideas. The Spanish rulers Ferdinand and Isabella sponsored his project and gave him the title Admiral of the Ocean Sea. On August 3, 1492, the newly named admiral sailed from Palos, Spain, with ninety men and three ships. They reached San Salvador (today's Watlings Island) in the Bahamas on October 12 and established a colony in Santo Domingo. Columbus returned to Spain fully convinced he had reached Asia by a new route. Three more trips, exploring the Caribbean and touching parts of Central America, failed to persuade him that he had discovered a whole new hemisphere.

The news of Columbus' discovery caused other explorers to set sail. John Cabot, a Genoese serving the English king, anchored off Newfoundland and New England in 1497 and may have sailed as far south as Delaware in 1498. Amerigo Vespucci, sailing first for Spain and a second time for Portugal, scouted the northeast coast of South America (1499–1500). His place in history is assured because the Americas were named after him. Pedro Cabral claimed Brazil for Portugal in 1500. In 1513 Vasco de Balboa crossed Panama and discovered the Pacific. The final proof that Columbus had actually found a New World was supplied by the Portuguese explorer Ferdinand Magellan, whose Spanish expedition sailed around the world between 1519 and 1522. France entered the hectic contest to claim parts of the New World with the voyages of Giovanni da Verrazano to New York Harbor (1524) and Jacques Cartier to Canada (1534 and 1535).

In a single generation Spanish conquistadors swept through the Caribbean and Central America. They quickly subdued the Aztec empire in Mexico (1519–1521) and the Inca empire in Peru (1531–1533). In search of new conquests and wealth, the Spanish government sent explorers farther north to claim land in what is now Florida, Texas, New Mexico, California, as well as other territory west of the Mississippi.

France sent adventurers into Canada, through the Great Lakes, and down the Ohio and Mississippi rivers. Quebec became the capital of New France. In the seventeenth century the French empire included eastern Canada, the Great Lakes, and the Mississippi Valley, as well as islands in the Caribbean. The Dutch briefly held a toehold around New York until the English pushed them out.

England in the New World

During the expansion of Spanish holdings in America, England was a poor and disunited country. Because it came late to the colonial feast, it had to settle for what was then considered the crumbs: the Atlantic coast from Maine to Georgia. Queen Elizabeth I, who ruled from 1558 to 1603, supported overseas colonization as part of her effort to make England economically self-sufficient.

The first English colony was founded by Sir Walter Raleigh in 1585 on Roanoke Island, off what is now North Carolina. A few years later it mysteriously disappeared. The English made their first permanent settlement at Jamestown, Virginia, but only after overcoming great hardships. Colonists numbering 104 arrived in May 1607 after a five-month voyage. They were soon joined by 400 more. Yet by 1610, disease, famine, hostile Indians, and mismanagement had reduced the colony to a mere 60 people. In 1620 the *Mayflower* carried English Pilgrims to Plymouth, on the rocky New England shore. The Massachusetts Bay Colony, settled by Puritans in 1630, was a more successful enterprise.

Most of the earliest English colonies were planned as business ventures under royal charters. Investors and government officials back in England made the rules for settlers, who had little or no say in how their colonies were run. This awkward system slowed economic growth and political development for a time. When greater flexibility was allowed, or when the colonists themselves got charters to settle new land, the colonies grew and prospered. A good example is the Massachusetts Bay Colony, which attracted more than ten thousand people between 1630 and 1640. It was largely self-governing because the original settlers had formed a joint-stock company (an early sort of corporation) and had brought with them a charter directly from the king. Their experience in organizing their own company and then in managing their own colony helped create an American tradition of self-determination.

Black Americans never shared in this tradition. The first black Africans were brought to Jamestown in 1619, one year before the *Mayflower* reached America. It appears that most of this party became bond servants, who had to work a certain number of years for their employer. Later arrivals from Africa came as slaves. As tobacco became a more popular export crop by the mid-seventeenth century, more slaves were brought here to work the fields. For the next two centuries the institution of slavery continued to grow in America. In 1789, when Washington (himself a slave owner) became president, many Americans defended slavery with the argument that the Africans were barbarians who needed to be civilized. Whites in Europe and America looked on blacks as inferior, even subhuman, and the fact that civilizations had flourished in black Africa for six centuries, or perhaps even longer, was unknown to them. Unfortunately, even if whites had understood African history, they probably would have behaved much the same toward blacks. Little effort was made to abolish slavery in the colonies because too many whites either benefited from slave labor or the slave trade or mistakenly believed that the institution would just disappear when it was no longer useful and profitable.

Because English colonization followed in the wake of the Protestant Reformation, it continued to be shaped by religious issues. Henry VIII, England's king from 1509 to 1547, had challenged the supremacy of the pope and created the Church of England (the Anglican church), which most of his subjects joined. But the establishment of a state church produced numerous splinter groups. The Pilgrims (known as Separatists in England) broke completely with the Anglican church because they felt it could never be reformed. They were persecuted and fled to America. The Puritans (or Nonconformists) tried to stay within the Church of England and purify it. But they too were hounded and many were forced into exile. They founded the Massachusetts Bay Colony as a model Puritan state and a place where they could practice their religion in peace.

America as a colony

The Puritans in England overthrew the Stuart king, Charles I, in the English Civil War (1642–1649) and established the Puritan Commonwealth, which lasted until 1660, when the monarchy was recalled to power. The restored Stuart rulers began to expand England's colonies and to organize them into a unified empire. After 1660 charters for *new* colonies were granted to proprietors rather than to joint-stock companies.

The economy of the British empire was based on the theory of mercantilism, a system that prevailed among many European nations in the seventeenth and eighteenth centuries. Mercantilism meant, among other things, strict government control over trade and manufacture and a reliance on colonies for resources to enrich the motherland. To these ends, the English Parliament passed a series of Navigation Acts (1651–1767) which required the colonies to supply those raw materials not produced in England. All manufactured goods had to come from England or, if from other countries, first had to go through English ports and pay duty there. All cargoes had to be carried by English or colonial ships so no foreign nations could profit from colonial trade. England in turn promised to provide military and naval protection for the colonies.

North America was both a battleground and a prize in a great game of empire in which the European powers competed for raw materials, land, and markets. In the 1600s and 1700s rivalry between England and France caused four major wars that were waged in Europe and India and on the high seas, as well as in North America. The struggle that decided the future of North America was the French and Indian War (1754–1763), which spread to Europe in 1756 and was called there the Seven Years War. The conflict ended in almost total victory for England. The French lost nearly all their American colonies, including Canada. These gains, along with territory won elsewhere in the world, made Britain the leading imperial power of the day.

The American Revolution

America's struggle for independence can be traced in part to Britain's stunning victory over France in 1763. Large war debts had to be repaid somehow, and the English thought the colonists should pay their share. After all, British troops had fought in America and protected the colonists from the French and their Indian allies, so why should the colonists not be taxed for administering the new empire? Thus Parliament tried to raise new revenues in the colonies, in two ways. 1) New taxes would be imposed. 2) Old taxes that had been avoided through bribery and smuggling would now be collected under strict enforcement of trade regulations. The plan was bound to anger many colonists.

In March 1770 there was a bloody encounter between redcoats and Bostonians. It began when a crowd of laborers taunted and threw rocks at British soldiers guarding the customs house. The soldiers finally opened fire. Five civilians were killed, including Crispus Attucks, a runaway slave. A dramatic trial followed, in which some of the soldiers were found guilty but were let off with light punishments. Sam Adams used the outrage caused by the Boston Massacre to spur radicals from other colonies to unite against British policies.

When Parliament imposed new taxes on tea, the colonials responded by dumping British tea into Boston Harbor (the Boston Tea Party of 1773). Parliament struck back hard in 1774 with what came to be known as the Intolerable Acts. The port of Boston was closed; the colonial courts were shackled by a rule allowing soldiers and royal officials to be tried in Britain; and an even stronger Quartering Act permitted British troops to be housed in private homes.

These serious attacks on colonial rights provoked Americans to take strong countermeasures. They convened the First Continental Congress in Philadelphia in 1774. Its furious members urged the people to arm themselves. In Massachusetts British troops tried to arrest the rebel leaders in early 1775. On April 19, at Lexington and Concord, British redcoats and colonial Minutemen exchanged the first shots of the Revolutionary War.

The Second Continental Congress met in May 1775 to deal with the growing crisis. It voted to establish a Continental Army and appointed George Washington commander in chief. Meanwhile, the hostilities continued. Rebel forces besieging the British in Boston inflicted over a thousand casualties on the redcoats in the Battle of Bunker Hill (June 17). There was also fighting in the South and in Canada.

The Declaration of Independence, written by Thomas Jefferson with the aid of Benjamin Franklin and John Adams, was issued on July 4, 1776. Many of the noble ideas in the Declaration can be traced back to the writings of the seventeenth-century English philosopher John Locke. Locke believed that society was created to protect people's natural rights and that a just society was based on a social compact between the people and their government. If a government violated those rights, the people had the right to overthrow that government. The Declaration of Independence was intended to unite the rebels and strengthen their cause by forcing people to take sides. It was also meant to gain foreign support, particularly from France, which was anxious to break the links holding together the British empire.

The Continental Congress faced serious difficulties in opposing the British army. Many of the colonists still could not bring themselves to renounce their loyalty to the crown. Because the colonists were beset by local fear, distrust, and jealousy, Congress was hard-pressed to finance the war, obtain supplies, and organize a reliable army. Colonial soldiers would not enlist for long periods of service because they knew they would be needed to care for their farms. And the rebels had few professional officers. Fortunately, Congress found a remarkably capable commander in the Virginia planter George Washington—the single most important figure in the Revolutionary War.

From June 1778 until late in 1781 the war was in a stalemate, which worked to the advantage of the rebels. Washington went on the defensive and avoided fighting any conclusive battles with the redcoats. In the end, his policy of patience and caution was rewarded. The British troops were trapped in a vulnerable position on the Yorktown peninsula, with their backs to the sea. On October 19, 1781, the British laid down their arms.

When the Treaty of Paris took effect in 1783, after months of negotiations, the Americans had won a generous settlement. Britain recognized the rebels' independence and granted them title to land as far west as the Mississippi River. The Americans had liberated themselves not only from Britain but from the European social system—the new nation was a republic without kings or nobles. The birth of the American Republic was without doubt a great moment in the history of human freedom. The question now was whether the baby could survive infancy.

The Articles of Confederation and the Constitution

The Continental Congress ran the Revolutionary War, but it was not really a national government. At first the rebels operated under state constitutions, most of which were drafted during the Revolution. A national system of government, called the Articles of Confederation, was adopted in 1781. Since the aims of the Revolution included independence and the overthrow of Britain's centralized monarchy, it is understandable that the rebels wanted power divided among the various state governments. So under the Articles the national government was quite weak. In time, many people grew concerned over this situation and began to press for a new structure of national government.

The Congress of the Confederation responded to the pressure by arranging for a convention to revise the Articles of Confederation. At Philadelphia, in the sweltering summer of 1787, fifty-five delegates debated the reshaping of the American Republic. The discussions brought to light the intense conflicts between big states and small ones, northerners and southerners, slave owners and those who owned no slaves, farmers and merchants, westerners and easterners, debtors and creditors. But the delegates did not give up until they had forged a new constitution. It severely limited the powers of the states and elevated those of the central government. It provided for a two-house federal legislature, for a president chosen by a college of electors appointed by the states, and for separate executive, legislative, and judicial branches. It did not just revise the Articles of Confederation; it totally replaced them. After many searching debates the Constitution of the United States was finally ratified and became the law of the land in June 1788.

The following February, in the first national election, General Washington received all sixty-nine electoral votes to become the first president. John Adams of Massachusetts was chosen vice-president. Washington was sworn in April 30, 1789, on the balcony of Federal Hall on Wall Street in lower Manhattan. New York City, with its Dutch gabled roofs and cobbled streets, became the first capital of the new United States.

Setting a new government in motion

During Washington's presidency the new government was organized. Washington chose such able men as Thomas Jefferson (secretary of state) and Alexander Hamilton (secretary of the treasury) to serve as his department heads and to be members of his "cabinet"—a body of presidential advisers not mentioned in the Constitution. He sent his own program of laws to the Congress instead of waiting for Congress to spend proposed laws to him, and he sent only *signed* treaties to the Senate for approval. He also supported the Federal Judiciary Act (1789), which organized the Supreme Court, circuit courts, and district courts, created the office of attorney general, and made it possible to appeal decisions of state courts to federal courts.

Disputes over the basic nature of the new government had begun during the struggle to ratify the Constitution and adopt the Bill of Rights. During Washington's administration such disagreements grew more heated. One of the stormiest disputes was over Hamilton's proposals for handling the national debt, national revenue, banking and currency, and tariffs. Their purpose was to give the new nation economic respectability, thereby winning it the support of the wealthy and powerful, and to create favorable conditions for the growth of commerce and industry.

Jefferson, on the other hand, believed that America's future depended on its being largely a nation of farmers, whose freedoms had to be preserved. He detested Hamilton's efforts to push America in new directions away from his own agrarian ideal. Jefferson argued that Hamilton's proposal for a national bank was unconstitutional. He championed "strict construction" (narrow interpretation) of the Constitution in an unsuccessful attempt to block Hamilton's scheme.

Political factions and Jefferson's election

Soon America was divided into two political camps: Federalists and Democratic-Republicans, or Republicans (later to be called Democrats). The first signs of the split occurred at the time of the ratification of the Constitution but became more pronounced in the 1790s with the emergence of the Hamilton-Jefferson disputes during Washington's administration. The partisans of Hamilton's financial program (the Federalists) were strongest in commercial towns, in New England, and in the southern Tidewater region. They won the 1796 election with John Adams as their first presidential candidate. Opponents of Hamilton (the Republicans) supported Jefferson. This faction gained strength among farmers and artisans in scattered areas of the nation and was able to win a narrow presidential election in 1800.

Though some Federalists expected him to govern as an extremist, Jefferson in power was remarkably conservative. He did not undermine the Hamiltonian financial system or destroy the national bank. He did lower internal revenue taxes, including Hamilton's unpopular whiskey tax, and he did cut federal spending, including expenditures on naval construction and showy public functions. His purchase of the Louisiana Territory (1803) from France for $15 million was a far-reaching action which he knew to be unconstitutional (or at least not explicitly provided for anywhere in the Constitution). It directly affected the lives of fifty thousand Americans in the Ohio and Tennessee valleys and indirectly affected the entire nation—then and thereafter. Jefferson sent Meriwether Lewis and William Clark up the Missouri River to explore the new territory, and between 1804 and 1806 they trailblazed their way to the Pacific Ocean and back.

The War of 1812

In 1809 James Madison, who inherited Jefferson's headaches along with the presidency, supported a variety of restrictions on commerce as alternatives to America's being pulled into the war between Britain and the expanding France of Napoleon. But Madison's efforts to keep the peace were in vain. Because of British seizures of American ships and seamen he asked Congress, on June 1, 1812, for a declaration of war against Britain.

American sentiment in favor of the War of 1812 was far stronger in the West and South than along the North Atlantic Coast. In fact, there was a threat of rebellion in New England because the war further damaged the ocean commerce on which the New Englanders depended. In December 1814 powerful Federalists in New England called a meeting, the Hartford Convention. They demanded basic changes in the structure of government, both to protect their interests and to bring an end to what they called the "Virginia dynasty" that had dominated American political life since the Revolution. By the time they ended their discussions, in January 1815, British and American delegations meeting in Ghent, Belgium, had signed a treaty ending hostilities. But the news did not reach the United States until after Andrew Jackson had won an amazing victory over the British at New Orleans. This ended the War of 1812 on a note of triumph for Madison's Republican administration, whose fortunes had been sagging throughout the conflict. Madison and Jackson became national heroes overnight, and the Federalist party was left with little prestige and few followers. By 1824 all the major candidates for the presidency were called Republicans.

The westward movement

In the decades following the War of 1812, millions of settlers poured westward across the Appalachians to make permanent homes on new land. New farms, new towns, and even new cities arose. Indian tribes were forced out of the Old Northwest and the South. New states were created to swell the Union: Indiana (1816); Mississippi (1817); Illinois (1818); Alabama (1819); Missouri (1821); Arkansas (1836); Michigan (1837); Texas and Florida (1845); Iowa (1846); Wisconsin (1848); California (1850); Minnesota (1858); and Oregon (1859). In 1810 fewer than 300,000 settlers lived in the Old Northwest (the territory west of the original states, north of the Ohio River, and east of the Mississippi). By the Civil War there were more than seven million people there. In the popular mind the West had become a "safety valve" to ease the pressure of growing social problems in the older, more settled parts of America. In theory, if not in practice, the availability of free land would save Americans from class conflict and urban strife. So Americans "hitched their wagon to a star" and rode west.

The Jacksonian era

Until Andrew Jackson was elected in 1828, American presidents came from either Virginia or Massachusetts, and all Washington's successors had worked their way up through the cabinet. Jackson ended his "aristocratical" pattern and "toppled the Virginia-Massachusetts dynasty." Around the hero of New Orleans there formed a coalition of western farmers, city laborers, small bankers, tradespeople, and others who saw him as God's gift to the common people. They hoped to put him in the White House in 1824, and in the election of that year he did get the largest number of popular votes. But as Jackson's supporters saw it, a "corrupt bargain" between candidates John Quincy Adams and Henry Clay gave Adams the most electoral votes and the presidency.

Adams then made Clay secretary of state.

Jackson—Old Hickory—succeeded in 1828 and was reelected president four years later. Jackson made good on the slogan "to the victors belong the spoils" by giving patronage jobs (positions filled by appointment) to his backers. He became the symbol of democracy at a time when the number of voters was expanding rapidly and when mobility—both social and geographical—was the keynote of American life.

Jackson waged two fierce contests as president. In one he tried to limit the activities of the federal government; in the other he greatly strengthened federal power. First, he destroyed the Bank of the United States, which had enjoyed special powers and privileges, and he placed its funds in state and local banks (1833). This pleased his backers, who wanted trade and finance to be free of central government control, but it helped cause a harsh economic depression in 1837. Second, he resisted South Carolina's attempt to "nullify" a tariff law that state disliked (1832–1833). This pitted him against Senator John C. Calhoun, a spokesman for the Old South and for the idea that the states could declare federal laws unconstitutional. Jackson's victory in this nullification contest was a victory for centralism and the Union over "states' rights."

During Jackson's term the removal of Indians to the West became official government policy. The president ordered the Civilized Tribes of the Southeast moved to the "permanent Indian Frontier" beyond the Mississippi. Some went peacefully, making new treaties and getting some payment for giving up their homes. Others resisted, like the Cherokees, who took their case all the way to the Supreme Court, and the Seminoles, who fought on until 1843, inflicting many casualties on the U.S. Army. By 1839 the military had removed most of the southern tribes, but the cost was enormous—both in wasted human lives and in the growing moral burden created by such acts. For example, forced marches over the "Trail of Tears" killed about four thousand Cherokees and subjected the survivors to intense suffering from hunger and exposure.

American expansionism

Regionalism—divisions and differences between commercial North and agrarian South, between settled East and frontier West—was a constant factor in shaping the new nation. But so were nationalism and the American dream of expansion. John Quincy Adams, while secretary of state (1817–1825), had a vision of the U.S. stretching from ocean to ocean. He conducted a series of brilliant negotiations with Spain, which brought Florida under American control and gave the U.S. a clearer claim to lands bordering the Pacific north of California. And he helped write the Monroe Doctrine in 1823. There was a possibility that the great continental powers of Europe would seek to win back for Spain the Latin American republics that had established their independence, and Russia represented a threat to American ambitions in the Pacific Northwest.

In the Monroe Doctrine the U.S. proclaimed that Europe must not try to take back old colonies or grab new ones in the Americas. In turn, the U.S. would not take sides in any wars in the Old World. An important point about the Monroe Doctrine was that Britain also feared the intervention of the continental European powers in Latin America and lent its support to the newly stated policy of the United States. By its official words and actions, America seemed to be taking the stand that if there were to be any expansion in this part of the world, the U.S. would do the expanding. America was building an image of itself as a proud national state eager to grow larger.

By 1845 American expansionism was going into high gear. The press, politicians, and ordinary citizens had begun talking about the right of the U.S. to spread over the whole continent. Some saw American expansion as a plan of God or Nature and called it Manifest Destiny. Such a mystical idea suited a country whose population was growing fast and whose citizens were moving out to settle beyond the national boundaries. The U.S. tried to fulfill its Manifest Destiny by taking more and more land—some by annexation, some by peaceful agreements, some by war.

Texas, formerly a part of Mexico, had been an independent republic for a decade when, in 1845, it was annexed to the U.S. and quickly made a state. Next year the U.S. and Britain ended their joint occupation of the Oregon Territory by dividing it at the present Canadian-American border. The annexation of Texas led to the Mexican War (1846–1848), which not only settled the Texas issue but resulted in the American acquisition of what is now New Mexico, Arizona, Nevada, Utah, part of Colorado, and all of California, with its very valuable harbor at San Francisco. In only a few years the idea of Manifest Destiny had become the reality of an America stretching from sea to shining sea.

Slavery: the great debate

At the time America won its independence, it seemed possible that the institution of slavery would gradually die out. But after the invention of the cotton gin, in 1793, southern agriculture was revolutionized. By the turn of the century production had increased nearly tenfold. After the War of 1812 great new territories were opened up that could be profitably worked by slave labor. The Missouri Compromise of 1820 prohibited the further expansion of slavery into the Louisiana Territory above the line of 36°30' north latitude. But the spread of slavery into the West became an issue that was more and more difficult to settle through political compromise. Crisis piled on crisis as southerners supporting slavery and northerners opposing it argued an issue on which they could never agree.

After 1830 the South began thinking of itself as almost a separate nation based on slavery. Southern whites defended the system by saying it was economically necessary. And they argued that their way was better than that of the North, where white workers who could be hired and fired at will were free in name only. They claimed that many slaves in the South lived better, happier, more secure lives than poor whites in the North. The abolitionists disagreed violently and the ever harsher debate went on. The South reacted by denying freedom of expression to abolitionists. Those who spoke out were whipped and beaten. Schools, colleges, public forums, and the mails were denied to abolitionists. In 1836 southern congressmen even imposed a "gag resolution" that prevented the House from receiving anti-slavery petitions.

At no time did the abolitionists become a dominant political force. They remained a minority up to and during the Civil War. There were two camps. One, led by William Lloyd Garrison, founder of the Anti-Slavery Society, called for immediate abolition. The other would accept a slower, more gradual ending of slavery.

Compromise and crisis

Texas had been admitted to the Union as a slave state. But the vast territories acquired in the Mexican War raised again the whole issue of whether or not slavery would be allowed in new areas. Senator Henry Clay of Kentucky worked out the Compromise of 1850. This series of laws was supposed to bring about a peaceful and reasonable settlement of all disputes between pro-slavery and antislavery forces. It offered something for both sides. California was to join the Union as a free state; the settlers of New Mexico and Utah were to decide the slavery question through "popular sovereignty"—dealing with the issue locally, by and for themselves. The sale of slaves was to end in the District of Columbia, and there was to be a new fugitive slave law so that runaways could be seized in the North and returned to their southern masters.

Senator Daniel Webster of Massachusetts thought slavery was wrong, but he believed "the preservation of the Union" was the supreme issue, and so he favored the Compromise. Senator William H. Seward of New York opposed the Compromise because, to him, slavery was such a great moral wrong that any compromise would be equally wrong and vicious. Opinions were so sharply split on the matter that the Compromise of 1850 soon increased existing differences. The Fugitive Slave Act was openly violated in some northern cities, and the South felt deeply betrayed.

The next major crisis over slavery came in 1854 when Senator Stephen A. Douglas of Illinois proposed a bill that would allow the settlement of the last sections of the Louisiana Purchase under the system of "popular sovereignty." That is, the people of Kansas and Nebraska would assemble in convention and decide whether or not they wanted slavery. But slavery in these territories was forbidden by the Missouri Compromise of 1820. To many people this ban had become a fundamental constitutional principle. Nevertheless, Douglas pushed his bill through Congress. His personal objectives were to win support for a transcontinental rail line across the northern United States and to increase his own chances for the presidency. But the Kansas-Nebraska Act, with its built-in repeal of the Missouri Compromise, tore apart the Democratic party in the North. And violence soon broke out in "Bleeding Kansas," as proslavery and antislavery forces fought to gain control of the territory before it was admitted to the Union.

The slavery issue split such important American institutions as political parties and churches. The largest church denominations divided along sectional lines. The "Conscience Whigs" joined with those Democrats who had been outraged by the Kansas-Nebraska Act and formed a new Republican party. In 1856 it ran the western explorer John C. Frémont in a losing bid for the White House against the Democrat James Buchanan. In 1860, with the Democrats hopelessly divided, the Republican candidate was Abraham Lincoln, a former Whig congressman who had always taken a moderate position on slavery.

With four candidates running, Lincoln was able to win the presidency with northern electoral votes alone, though he received less than 40 percent of the popular vote. The South, believing that Lincoln would not compromise on the slavery question and fearing his strong views on preserving the Union, would not accept his election. Southern states seceded and formed the Confederate States of America. Outgoing President Buchanan made ineffective efforts at compromise, and by the time Lincoln was inaugurated on March 4, 1861, civil war was unavoidable. On April 12, 1861, Confederate guns fired on Fort Sumter, a federal installation in Charleston Harbor. The Civil War had begun.

Civil War

The North had several advantages. In the course of the war some two million served in the Union forces, compared to about 750,000 for the Confederates. The Union's railroads, ships, and shipyards, its weapons production, farm output, and financial resources, and its civilian population all far outweighed the South's. But the Grays (the soldiers of the Confederacy) were fighting in defense of their homeland and had the advantage of shorter supply lines. And the Blues (the Union soldiers) had to defeat the South completely, while the Confederacy could win just by gaining a stalemate.

Early Union attempts to seize Richmond, the Confederate capital, failed, but Union armies fared better in the West. Under Ulysses S. Grant, they advanced along the Tennessee and Cumberland rivers from 1862 on, finally capturing Vicksburg in 1863. This opened the Mississippi River to Union ships and cut the Confederacy in two. But it took more than two years and some of the bloodiest warfare in history before the final northern victory. The gallant southern general, Robert E. Lee, finally surrendered the main Confederate army to Grant at Appomattox Court House, Virginia, on April 9, 1865. Five days later, an actor named John Wilkes Booth shot President Lincoln as he sat watching a play in a Washington theater. Lincoln died the next day.

The Union was preserved and the slaves were freed, but the price was awesome: 600,000 dead soldiers and many, many more gravely wounded, large portions of the South ravaged, the president slain, and a bitterness between the victorious and the defeated that would last for decades. The prayer of the fallen president for reunification was realized. He had hoped also, in his eloquent Gettysburg Address, "that this nation, under God, shall have a rebirth of freedom." Insofar as this referred to black Americans, achieving such a true rebirth of freedom would test the American Republic for generations—and tests it still.

CHRONICLE: THE WILDERNESS
. . . the early conservationists

The first to record the splendors of the unexplored West — photographers like William Henry Jackson, artists like Albert Bierstadt and Thomas Moran, and, above all, naturalist John Muir — reported scenes of unsurpassed majesty and wonder. Each in his own way contributed to the decision to set aside areas of particular beauty and natural importance for the benefit of future generations — so they too might wonder and rejoice at Nature unspoiled.

Right: Theodore Roosevelt and John Muir in Yosemite, photograph by William Henry Jackson

Yosemite Valley, by Albert Bierstadt (1868)

The Yosemite . . . looks like an immense hall or temple lighted from above. Every rock in its walls seems to glow with life. . . . Down through the middle of the Valley flows the crystal Merced, the River of Mercy, peacefully quiet, reflecting lilies and trees and the onlooking rocks . . . into this one mountain mansion Nature had gathered her choicest treasures, to draw her lovers into close and confiding communion with her.
                                                                    JOHN MUIR

The Grand Canyon of the Yellowstone, by Thomas Moran (1893–1901)

When I first visited
California, it was
my good fortune to
see the "big trees,"
the Sequoias, and
then to travel down
into the Yosemite,
with John Muir. The
first night was clear,
and we lay down in the
darkening aisles of
the great Sequoia grove.
The majestic trunks,
beautiful in color and
in symmetry, rose
round us like the
pillars of a mightier
cathedral than ever
was conceived. . . .
I shall always be glad
that I was in
the Yosemite
with John Muir.

THEODORE ROOSEVELT

The Giant Redwoods of California (Sequoias), by Albert Bierstadt

The centennial celebration of steamboat navigation in inland waters; Pittsburgh, October 31, 1911.

Chronology

1865
Civil War ends. President Lincoln assassinated.

1865–1877
Era of southern Reconstruction.

1869
Completion of first transcontinental railroad.

1870
Standard Oil Company organized.

1886
American Federation of Labor (AFL) formed.

1890
Formation of National American Woman Suffrage Association (NAWSA).

1892–1896
Agrarian revolt. Defeat of William Jennings Bryan in 1896 presidential election.

1898
Spanish-American War.

1901–1917
Progressive era. Theodore Roosevelt president, 1901–1909. Woodrow Wilson president, 1913–1921.

1909
Henry Ford starts producing Model T automobile.

1914–1918
First World War. U.S. declaration of war, April 1917.

America has been another name for opportunity, and the people of America have taken their tone from the incessant expansion which has not only been open but has even been forced upon them. . . . Movement has been its dominant fact. . . .

FREDERICK JACKSON TURNER   (1861–1932)
American historian

overview
An Industrial Nation

The United States experienced more drastic changes from the end of the Civil War to the end of the First World War than in any other five decades in its history. A nation of farms, small towns, and small businesses became a nation of great cities and booming industries. A vast railroad network reached out to every corner of the land. Thousands of smoke-belching factory chimneys signaled the fact that America was the world's foremost manufacturing nation. Cities teemed with immigrants who had come from all over the world in the hope of sharing in the promise of America. Labor organizations were emerging to struggle with the owners of industry for decent working conditions and a larger share of the wealth.

The United States had become an imperial power with island possessions in both the Atlantic and the Pacific. Its industrial might and its critical role in helping win the First World War ensured it an important place in world affairs.

By 1918 American cities had begun to take on a modern look: electric lights bordered streets paved for automobile traffic; airplanes soared overhead; and some of the world's tallest buildings created new and distinctly American skylines. The nation had moved into the twentieth century at a headlong pace.

Reconstruction under the Radical Congress

Although the fighting was over in 1865, many serious problems caused by the Civil War remained to be solved. The nation's most pressing concern became Reconstruction: how to restore the Confederate states to a normal role in the

Union and what rights and status to assign to newly freed blacks. For twelve years the South's fate was a matter of public debate. The form Reconstruction would take—and thus the fate of the South—was in the hands of northerners who themselves disagreed on how to deal with the defeated Confederates.

At this turning point in history, when a decision had to be made about how the South could be restored to the Union, the nation sorely missed its most skillful political leader, assassinated only days after Lee's surrender. Abraham Lincoln's humanity and his practical, down-to-earth style would have been most useful. He had outlined a moderate program of Reconstruction, and Andrew Johnson, who succeeded him as president, tried an even more generous approach. But the Radical Republicans who controlled both the Senate and the House of Representatives refused to accept the political reorganization of the South that would have taken place under Johnson's plan. It seemed to them that the same men would be leading the South who had led it against the Union and that blacks there would be subject to many of the same restrictions and injustices they had endured during slavery.

The disagreement between Johnson and Congress became a pitched battle after the president vetoed a bill prolonging and increasing the activities of the Freedmen's Bureau, which gave help to freed slaves, and a civil rights act that guaranteed certain rights of blacks as *citizens*. Congress not only overrode the veto of the civil rights bill but then proceeded to go over the heads of both the president and the Supreme Court by incorporating black citizenship in a proposed amendment to the Constitution. The Thirteenth Amendment, which outlawed slavery, was ratified in 1865. The Fourteenth, proposed in 1866, offered federal protection to citizens whose rights to "life, liberty, and property" were not upheld by the states. While it did not say that every adult male must be allowed to vote, it penalized a state that deprived any group of that right by reducing that state's representation in Congress. Some northerners were concerned less by the fate of the freed slaves in the South than by the political strength the South would have if all its blacks, rather than three fifths of them as in antebellum days, were counted in determining the number of representatives it could send to the House.

The Fourteenth Amendment also said that any person who had taken part in the "rebellion" after previously holding office within the Union was to be denied state or federal office until pardoned by Congress. The southern states rejected the amendment, which therefore remained unratified. So the Radical Republican majority in Congress set out to impose its own form of Reconstruction. In 1867 the South was divided into five military districts. The voters—including black adult males but not those white males whose activities under the Confederacy made them ineligible—were to elect representatives to state constitutional conventions. When constitutions that incorporated the voting clauses of the Fourteenth Amendment were adopted, and when the states ratified that amendment, they could reenter the Union. The amendment was ratified, and the first southern states returned to the Union in 1868.

In the same year the House of Representatives impeached President Johnson on eleven charges, including violation of the Tenure of Office Act. This act had been passed by the Radical Congress in 1867 specifically to limit Johnson's power by prohibiting a president from dismissing high civil officials without the consent of the Senate. When Johnson was tried in the Senate on these "high crimes and misdemeanors," the vote was thirty-five to nineteen to remove him from office, only one short of the two-thirds majority needed. Johnson stayed president for the remaining months of his term, but Reconstruction continued to be directed by the Radical Republican Congress.

The end of Reconstruction came right after the disputed presidential election of 1876. Democrat Samuel J. Tilden had received more popular votes than Republican Rutherford B. Hayes, but it was clear that in several states there had been election fraud, by one side or the other or even by both. A special commission voted eight to seven to give the election to Hayes. But resistance to his becoming president was not overcome until there was an understanding that he would remove federal troops from the South, see that federal grants were made for a new southern railroad and other internal improvements, and choose at least one southerner for his cabinet. These agreements were part of the so-called Compromise of 1877 between Republicans and southern Democrats. And although not all could be kept, Hayes did pay the principal price demanded by those who helped him gain the presidency—Reconstruction was ended. By this time white supremacy had already been permitted to revive in the South, and the movement to guarantee the full rights of citizenship to blacks would remain dead for many decades.

Industrial growth and big business

Civil rights did not begin to command the attention and energy that America devoted to industrial growth in the years after the Civil War. Industrial growth was rapid before the war and became much more so in the coming decades, so that by the end of the century the U.S. was the world's leading manufacturing nation. The rail network expanded from coast to coast. Production of copper, coal, oil, iron, and timber increased rapidly. Steel became the backbone of the industrial economy. With the continued application of machinery to farming, agricultural output continued to soar. Industrial corporations took a commanding lead in much of this economic activity, which was aptly termed the "Industrial Revolution."

During this era of growth, wealth and power tended to become concentrated in the hands of relatively few people and organizations. Powerful individuals took command of various areas of the economy: John D. Rockefeller in oil; Andrew Carnegie in steel; Collis P. Huntington, Cornelius Vanderbilt, and others in railroads; Jay Cooke and J. P. Morgan in finance. They were known as "kings," "barons," or "captains" of industry and finance. These men and others like them built corporate empires based on centralized control, partly because of a personal desire for power.

Big business dominated the economic front. Ruthless competition among many small companies had been making it increasingly hard for most of them to earn a profit. This situation encouraged the creation of various kinds of combinations. Some were called pools, others holding companies. Many were known as trusts (a term often applied to all such corporate groupings). All had the same goals: to reduce or end competition and to control markets, prices, and profits. The result was that entire industries were monopolized by one or two organizations. For example, the original Standard Oil Company, the first trust, at one time controlled virtually all of the American petroleum industry. U.S. Steel, organized in 1901 as the largest industrial company in the country, remains the major force in the steel industry to this day. There were many similar monopolies—in everything from the manufacture of locomotives to the production and distribution of sugar, leather, tobacco, and even whiskey.

At first these enormous businesses had considerable freedom from government regulation. American tradition allowed private enterprises to operate with a minimum of government interference. Then the Supreme Court strengthened the new corporate system by saying that under the Fourteenth Amendment a corporation was a "legal person" entitled to "due process" and "equal protection of the laws." This made it very hard for state governments to regulate large corporations that did business nationally, because the corporations, as "persons," could go to court and claim that regulation of their affairs was depriving them of their right to freedom of action and of their property (profits). It soon became obvious that only the federal government could limit the growing power of the corporate giants.

Attempts at federal regulation began with the Interstate Commerce Act of 1887, involving railroads, and the Sherman Antitrust Act of 1890 (strengthened by the Clayton Antitrust Act of 1914). But limiting big business was no easy matter. If a particular form of organization was found to be illegal and was ordered dissolved, the corporation merely regrouped or found other ways to maintain its domination of some sector of the economy. Corporations seemed able to stay one step ahead of laws meant to regulate them, and the laws themselves were seldom enforced vigorously. So concentration of wealth and power continued. (By 1910, 200 of the 200,000 nonbanking corporations controlled at least 40 percent of U.S. corporate assets.) A tiny group of eastern banking and financial houses, including J. P. Morgan and Company, also controlled enormous wealth.

The last frontier

The western frontier opened wide after the Civil War. Thousands upon thousands, native-born and immigrant, rushed in to seek fortunes, put up new homes, build a richer future. Some came to raise cattle, others to cut timber or work mines, some to start businesses and establish towns. Nearly all came in search of a better life. For most that meant a chance to farm their own land somewhere on the vast, sometimes rich, often harsh and dangerous, plains and prairies. Opening or "taming" the frontier could not be completed until the U.S. Cavalry forced the last of the "wild" Indians onto reservations. But some of the western tribes resisted fiercely. A high point of their resistance came in 1876 when the Sioux and Cheyenne—responding to treaty violations and invasion of their sacred Black Hills, where gold had been discovered—wiped out Lieutenant Colonel George Armstrong Custer and all 264 men under his command at the Battle of the Little Big Horn in Montana. The cruel massacre of Sioux Indians at Wounded Knee, South Dakota, in 1890 is sometimes taken as the last Indian "war."

By the 1880s, however, the Sioux, Cheyenne, Arapaho, Apache, Navajo, and Nez Percé had all been defeated. With the Dawes Act of 1887 Congress tried to improve the situation of Indians by breaking up the reservations and granting land to individual families. But this attempt to Americanize the Indians only speeded up the destruction of their tribal life and customs and left many of them even more dependent on the government. Perhaps the most graphic example of the way white Americans made it impossible for the Indian way of life to survive was the extermination of the buffalo. Between 1867 and 1883, thirteen million buffalo were killed. These magnificent animals, which for centuries were the main resource of many Indians, were driven to the edge of extinction—and with them the ancient tribal ways.

Hundreds of thousands of farmers took advantage of the Homestead Act of 1862 by going west to convert public land to private use. They opened more new farmland during the several decades following the Civil War than in all the previous history of the Republic. During the 1860s, cattle were driven from Texas to Kansas to meet the railheads that were pushing westward across the Great Plains; from the railheads the cattle were shipped to midwestern slaughterhouses. Later herds were fattened on open range as far north as the Dakotas. Actually, the cowboy frontier immortalized by Hollywood only existed for two short decades from 1865 to 1886, after which most of the open range was fenced in. Eleven new states were formed in the West between 1867 and 1912. In 1890 the census bureau declared the frontier officially closed, although the westward movement of Americans has never really ended.

Following the "close" of the frontier Americans became more aware of the need to prevent the unnecessary waste of forests, wildlife, and natural resources. The Forest Reserve Act of 1891, which established government-protected forests on public land, was the first major conservation law. Theodore Roosevelt did more than any previous president to promote conservation.

The rise of organized labor

Americans had always felt that the Atlantic Ocean was a wide enough barrier to protect the U.S. from the social and political problems that plagued Europe. Such problems had produced the French Revolution in 1789, and during the following century much of Europe had experienced class warfare. In the 1870s and 1880s some of the same problems seemed to be coming to a head in America. There was considerable unrest among working people. Some faced losing their jobs because new machines made them unnecessary. Most resented having to work for long hours at low pay, often under unhealthful and even dangerous conditions. And business panics in the late nineteenth century meant frequent layoffs and unemployment. Strikes and labor violence shocked middle-class Americans into a realization of how desperate many working people were.

The only way workers could improve their situation was to organize. Several new labor organizations emerged during the second half of the nineteenth century, the largest being the National Labor Union (1866), the Knights of Labor (1869), and the American Federation of Labor (1886). While some unions had ambitious social goals, the fundamental objectives were shorter hours (eventually calling for an eight-hour day), higher pay, abolition of child labor and foreign contract labor, workmen's compensation (to protect workers injured on the job), and collective bargaining, in which representatives of management and labor would negotiate contracts. Labor's most effective weapon was the strike. From 1880 to 1900, the nation experienced some 24,000 strikes involving 6.6 million workers.

There was a nationwide railroad strike in 1877, which left scores of people dead and made many Americans think a labor revolution was at hand. The Haymarket Riot, an outgrowth of a strike at the McCormick Harvesting Machine Company in Chicago in 1886, resulted in the bombing deaths of seven policemen. Seven men were arrested and tried as anarchists, and four executed on flimsy evidence. It seemed clear that America would have to deal with its labor problems or face the same sort of social turmoil that had been disrupting Europe.

Few strikes in this period were successful. In fact, the two major strikes of the 1890s, at the Homestead plant of Carnegie Steel (1892) and the Pullman railroad car factory (a strike that spread through much of the railroad industry in 1894), were both lost by labor. Organized labor was set back temporarily by these failures and by the fact that a large segment of the public believed unions encouraged dangerous radicalism and anarchism. But despite the use of troops against strikers by both governors and presidents, the labor movement continued to grow until it became a major force in twentieth-century America.

The capitalist ethic

A major reason why both the government and the general public tended to side with management against labor was the belief that the capitalist industrial system was a good and right way of organizing the economy and even the society. Already deeply ingrained in American thought was the so-called Protestant Ethic; it held hard work and thrift to be prime virtues and profiting from one's efforts to be a sign of God's grace. The Gospel of Success also had a strong influence on Americans' ideas and attitudes. Its various forms during the late nineteenth century included the immensely popular Horatio Alger stories, accounts of how poor boys gained fame and fortune through a combination of honest effort and good luck. The Gospel of Youthful Endeavor was an uplifting notion used to justify child labor.

The doctrine of laissez-faire held that the greatest progress would take place if government interference in private business was kept to a minimum. Laissez-faire found strong support during the late nineteenth century in Social Darwinism, a new philosophy based very loosely on discoveries that the English naturalist Charles Darwin had made about the evolution of animals. Its advocates maintained that "the survival of the fittest" and "natural selection" were at work in the marketplace—that is, if the weak and poor fell by the wayside, so much the better for society in the long run. Social Darwinists claimed that winnowing out the unfit—the failures—ensured progress and strengthened the human race.

Darwinian theory caused a stir throughout American life and thought in the late nineteenth and early twentieth centuries. Darwin's ideas served to strengthen both conservatives who wanted to justify keeping things as they were and liberals who demanded change—it all depended on how the ideas were interpreted. Darwin's theory of the evolution of life challenged the biblical account of the Creation in Genesis. While many churchgoers and theologians were able to adjust their thinking to allow for his biological discoveries, fundamentalists (people who took the Bible to be the word of God and the literal truth) rejected the idea of evolution completely.

Immigration and urbanism

Post-Civil War immigration increased steadily, reaching a peak from 1905 to 1914, when more than ten million people entered the United States. After 1895 most of the immigrants came from eastern and southern Europe, and most were Roman Catholic, Eastern Orthodox, or Jewish. To a nation whose population was largely Protestant, with roots in Britain and northern and western Europe, these newcomers seemed truly foreign. Often they were treated with suspicion and hatred by American "patriots" who feared they would "pollute" the native stock and by American workers who feared they would lower wages and steal jobs. The fear of "bomb-throwing anarchists," "papal conspirators," and "Christ-killer Jews" became an obsession. Some "nativists" even talked of America's committing "racial suicide" by allowing so many immigrants in. They demanded that immigration be sharply reduced. This came to pass in the period after World War I.

As industrial activity expanded and immigrants poured onto these shores, cities mushroomed. Between 1860 and 1900 the fastest growing cities were Minneapolis (whose population increased seventy-nine-fold), Omaha, Kansas City (Missouri), Denver, and Chicago. In 1890 greater New York City was the largest immigrant center in the world. About 20 percent of all city dwellers in 1890 were of foreign birth. Clearly, in urban America, at least, there was little "pure" native stock to "save."

With the rapid growth of cities came the problems well known to modern city dwellers: increased crime, problems of waste disposal, housing shortages, slums, and an ever growing need for programs to help those unable to help themselves. The government of cities was marked by great corruption. But at the Chicago World's Fair in 1893 more than 27 million people glimpsed a sparkling vision of city life. The imposing structures, waterways, and electrified streets of the "Great White City" ushered in a renaissance in urban architecture and planning that lasted several decades.

Politics in the Gilded Age

From 1876 until the turn of the century presidential elections were won by very narrow margins—and by men of less than memorable character. Personalities rather than basic policy differences were usually the issue. Politically, the Gilded Age is notable for its corruption—at the local, state, and national level—and for its lack of impressive leaders. With the possible exception of Grover Cleveland, who at times during his two separate administrations at least demonstrated considerable independence, the presidents held a narrow view of presidential power. They were usually quite willing to let Congress play the more active role in running the government.

Just how close the elections of this period were and how petty the issues could be is seen in the campaign of 1884. Cleveland (the only Democratic president in this GOP era) beat Republican James G. Blaine by fewer than thirty thousand votes out of a total of nearly 10 million cast, and a major issue was that Cleveland had once fathered an illegitimate child. Some Republicans, during campaign demonstrations, had the poor taste to shout: "Ma, Ma! where's my Pa? Gone to the White House, Ha, Ha, Ha!"

The outstanding political event of the 1890s was a movement sometimes known as the Farmers' Revolt. Farmers in the West and the South had long been complaining about the excessive power of railroads, middlemen, speculators, and bankers. To them it seemed that eastern-based interests were intent on driving farm prices down, cutting farm income, monopolizing farm land, and, in general, denying the producers of the nation's food a fair return for their labors. To help their struggle against the financial-industrial forces lined up against them, the farmers formed numerous organizations. The Patrons of Husbandry (or the Grange) in the 1860s, the Farmers' Alliances in the 1880s, and the Populist (or People's) party in the 1890s were the largest and most important vehicles for expressing agrarian discontent. In the elections of 1890, candidates supporting the farmers' cause had great success in a number of farm states and won many congressional seats. In the presidential election of 1892 the Populist candidate got more than a million votes. But the true test of the strength of Populism came in 1896, when William Jennings Bryan ran for the presidency as candidate of both the Democratic and the Populist party.

Bryan campaigned mainly on the issue of free silver. It was believed by many, particularly in the West and South, that if enough silver coins were minted, the nation's economic problems could be solved, because with more money in circulation it would be easier for farmers and others to pay their debts. Although Bryan got as much mileage as possible out of the silver issue, it was not enough to win him the election, and he was afraid to support some of the more radical ideas of the Populists, which included nationalization of the railroad, telephone, and telegraph industries, and a graduated income tax. This did not stop the Republicans from claiming that Bryan was a radical whose election would ruin business, cost workers their jobs, and bring disorder to the country. William McKinley, the Republican candidate, was elected with the first popular majority in twenty-four years. It was a crushing defeat for the Populists. Not only did they fail to get much support from labor and the middle class but midwestern farmers voted Republican. Clearly, many American farmers and workers believed that their interests and the interests of big business were closely intertwined.

America's new role in international affairs

In 1898 the United States fought a "splendid little war" with Spain to free Cuba from Spanish oppression. The war was "splendid" in that the United States won a quick and relatively cheap victory. Fewer than four hundred Americans died in battle, although many more died from disease and food poisoning and the death toll rose in the postwar years while America was consolidating its gains. For winning the war, the U.S. gained possession of Puerto Rico, Guam, and the Philippines, as well as effective control over Cuba—all former Spanish holdings. The formerly independent kingdom of Hawaii also became an American possession in 1898, through annexation, after years of agitation by American sugar planters on the islands. Another Pacific outpost, Samoa, was obtained in 1899 through negotiations with Britain and Germany. (See map, p. 404.)

The U.S. was also commercially involved in China and eager to prevent the European powers from dividing that country up among themselves. To do so, it proposed an "Open Door" policy whereby all foreign nations would trade freely with China without interfering with one another or with China's right to collect tariffs. When Chinese nationalists known as Boxers sought to drive out foreigners in 1900, American troops joined European and Japanese forces in putting down this Boxer Rebellion.

That America had become an imperial power was vividly demonstrated in the Philippine Insurrection of 1899–1902. Although the Spanish-American War had been fought to free people from Spanish colonial rule, the Americans, in the eyes of many Filipinos, were merely replacing the Spanish as foreign masters of the islands. The result was bloody fighting between Yanks and Filipino guerrillas, with heavy casualties on both sides before the insurrection was finally put down. Seemingly good American intentions had involved the U.S. in a war thousands of miles from home and cast Americans in the uncomfortable role of imperialist oppressors of a people who wanted to rule their own country. But the drive for overseas expansion would not be denied and America took its place as a world power.

The Progressive era

The first decades of the twentieth century—or at least the years from Theodore Roosevelt's inauguration in 1901 to Woodrow Wilson's war message in 1917—have been called "the Progressive era." It was a time of liberal domestic reforms. The Progressives tried to humanize the industrial system and overhaul those parts of the democratic process that had been rusted by arrogance, greed, or corruption. The movement voiced the ideas of older, nineteenth-century reformers that only a few years before had been considered dangerously radical. Progressives included clergy, social workers, physicians, editors, teachers, lawyers, and businessmen. Although unorganized and with no specific platform, the movement became a force in both major political parties. Progressives expressed strong hostility against big business, although once installed in power, they often hesitated to move vigorously against business combinations. Some of the new liberals rejected the Jeffersonian ideal that "that government governs best which governs least" and looked to government as a tool for progress. In so doing, they helped move America closer to a Jacksonian principle—"Equal rights for all, special privileges for none"—by widening and strengthening the democratic and humanitarian foundations of the Republic. Public support of Progressivism increased as crusading journalists known as "muckrakers" exposed business greed and political corruption.

The reform movement found a leader with remarkable energy, personal appeal, and political abilities in Theodore Roosevelt (1858–1919), who became president in 1901 when McKinley was assassinated. Though philosophically a political conservative, he led the GOP toward enacting legislation to regulate big business. His influence brought about the Hepburn Act (1906) for the federal regulation of railroads (and later telephone and telegraph companies) and the Pure Food and Drug Act (1906). On the other hand his reputation as a trust buster is exaggerated, since he actually considered big business a positive force, not to be harmed until it committed some overt illegal act. A nature enthusiast since boyhood, Roosevelt was personally committed to improving the conservation of rare wildlife and natural resources.

Roosevelt's friend William Howard Taft was elected president in 1908. But Roosevelt, still a very young and vigorous person, thought the Taft presidency was too conservative and became a candidate again in 1912. He ran on the Progressive (Bull Moose) party ticket, thereby splitting the Republican vote and assuring the election of the Democratic candidate, Wilson.

Woodrow Wilson (1856–1924) was one of the most highly qualified men ever to occupy the White House. He was a scholarly author, a lecturer on political science, president of Princeton University, and governor of New Jersey before defeating TR and Taft in 1912. He was not particularly liberal; but the pressure of the Progressive movement made itself felt, and he campaigned in 1912 for the "New Freedom," which promised to restore competition in the business world. During his first term a considerable amount of reform legislation was passed. As president he helped enact many laws valued by Progressives: child labor, antitrust, regulation of banks, lower tariffs, and the eight-hour day for railroad workers.

Many Progressives supported women's suffrage as a way of improving the democratic process and humanizing the competitive economic system. After the 1890s feminists worked painstakingly, state by state, to bring women the vote. Finally they were able to prevail on Congress during Wilson's administration and received the right to vote by a federal amendment in 1920.

Progressives showed a real interest in social justice for workers, women, and children but not for racial minorities. The blacks had been abandoned by their liberal white allies before the end of Reconstruction. Not even the reform spirit of Progressivism seemed able to overcome America's long history of ignoring or mistreating nonwhites. Wilson allowed an increase in the segregation of federal offices in the District of Columbia.

Literature in the Gilded Age

New directions of American life were reflected in literature. One of the famous writers of his time—some consider him the greatest of all American writers—was Samuel L. Clemens, better known as Mark Twain. In his personal life Twain combined a hunger for wealth and fame with an increasingly bitter attitude toward human nature and society. With Charles Dudley Warner he wrote *The Gilded Age* (1873), from which the period took its name. Twain also represented a school of writing known as the "local color movement" that celebrated the distinct flavor and custom, the humor and dialect, of a locale. His short story "The Celebrated Jumping Frog of Calaveras County" (1865) had as its setting the mining region of California where Twain had been a reporter. In *The Adventures of Huckleberry Finn* (1884) Twain described childhood life in the Mississippi Valley with such skill and verve that the book has become a classic.

Realism was a trend in the arts that tried to put aside romanticism and concern itself with commonplace events and ordinary people. The writings of Twain and of his friend William Dean Howells exemplify this trend. A movement related to realism was naturalism, which came into vogue around the turn of the century. Under the influence of Darwin, this literary trend portrayed people as the victims of natural forces beyond their control. Stephen Crane, Frank Norris, and Jack London represented the style of naturalism. So, too, did Theodore Dreiser in *Sister Carrie* (1900), a novel which described the corruption and misery encountered by a young girl in the big city. His *The Financier* (1912) dealt with the career of a ruthless businessman. Frank Norris condemned the Southern Pacific Railroad in *The Octopus* (1901) and the operation of the Chicago grain market in *The Pit* (1903). A literature of protest

Mark Twain (1835-1910)

THE GILDED SAGE

His most popular book was *Tom Sawyer*, and his masterpiece was *Huckleberry Finn*. But Mark Twain's first novel, coauthored with Charles Dudley Warner, was *The Gilded Age* (1873). Twain (whose real name was Samuel L. Clemens) became a celebrity, the nation's favorite humorist. The book that gave its name to an era was uneven, mixing Warner's sentimentality with Twain's satire and clowning. It attacked the robber barons, crooked politicians, the vulgar new rich, and the public which tolerated all evils. It also introduced a character named Colonel Beriah Sellers, an endearing wheeler-dealer-get-rich-quick dreamer, who was always just missing the brass ring.

Mark Twain had much of the modern-day huckster in him. Even as his attacks on the frenzied greed, corruption, and graft of the post-Civil War years sharpened, he fell victim to the speculation fever that he was debunking. He saw potential fortunes in almost all the gadgets brought to his attention and invested time and money in over one hundred of them, including a synthetic food for invalids called "plasmon." He wrote later, "All through my life I have been the easy prey of the cheap adventurer. He came, he lied, he robbed and went his way, and the next one arrived by the next train and began to scrape up what was left." The humorist was not just interested in possible earnings but also in the creative thought and adventurous spirit being poured into the new machinery of the nineteenth century. He believed that machines would ease the burdens of people and stimulate great wealth and happiness.

Unfortunately Twain's instinct for business left much to be desired. He turned down Alexander Graham Bell's earnest pleas to invest in a new gadget that would transmit the human voice over an electric wire. Instead the humorist poured $300,000 — his own life savings and most of the inheritance of his wife — into an invention called the Paige typesetter. This was an unsuccessful machine with thousands of parts that never seemed to operate all at the same time. The panic of 1893 swept away what was left of his wife's money and dried to a trickle receipts from the sale of Twain's books. His once prosperous publishing house went bankrupt the following year, and Twain and his wife were faced with debts of $100,000. But he was confident that he could raise money by himself from lecture tours and future book earnings. In fact, he was able to settle the last of his debts by 1898.

Although Twain admired success and the comforts that wealth could buy, he continued to denounce the worship of money and the destruction of human lives and values that often accompanied the amassing of great fortunes. His attacks on the Vanderbilts and Rockefellers were funny, but beneath the humor readers felt the author's outrage. Twain was both the unsuccessful gambler who lived to strike it rich and the successful author who saw through sham and exposed it. Perhaps Twain expressed the paradox best: "Let us consider that we are all partially insane. It will explain us to each other."

helped alert the public to the evils that Progressives sought to overcome. In the most famous protest novel of the Progressive era, *The Jungle* (1906), Socialist Upton Sinclair described the frightful conditions of the immigrant working class of Chicago, including the putrid conditions in the meat-packing industry.

New directions in American thought

The philosophical movement known as pragmatism was to some degree also an expression of liberal thought and faith. It was a reaction against Darwinism and related theories that held that existence was predetermined by natural laws. It was an attempt to liberate human thought and will without denying the validity of natural science. William James' *Pragmatism* (1907), *A Pluralistic Universe* (1909), and other works argued that ideas were merely "instruments" to be judged not as eternal truths but according to their practical success or failure in concrete situations. To James, truth was always relative and ideas should always be measured by their consequences. John Dewey, the founder of "progressive education," advanced a theory of experimentalism in government and education. His influential *The School and Society* (1899) emphasized the growth and development of the child as a good citizen of a democratic community.

Pragmatism understandably appealed to Americans, who liked having a practical, common-sense philosophy that called for testing ideas through action. And pragmatism neatly fit the needs of Progressivism, because it supported the notion that social realities could be altered—reformed—by the application of ideas that could be proved right by being made to work.

From Dollar Diplomacy to World War

Roosevelt, Taft, and Wilson all continued American involvement in international affairs. Roosevelt, concerned about the international balance of power, was determined that the U.S. should be dominant in the Western Hemisphere. The Roosevelt Corollary to the Monroe Doctrine asserted that the United States could intervene in Latin American affairs to exercise an international "police power" when necessary. TR made sure that an American canal could be cut through the Isthmus of Panama by encouraging a rebellion in Colombia, which owned that valuable strip of land. Taft's economic imperialism in Latin America, nicknamed "Dollar Diplomacy," was intended to oust European investors and tie the economies of the "banana republics" to that of the U.S. in a way that would favor American business and political interests. United States marines landed in Latin America several times to protect American investments. In 1915 Haiti joined Cuba as an American protectorate. Driven by a missionary zeal for liberty, Wilson sent troops to influence the outcome of the Mexican revolution in 1916. This effort accomplished very little, though, except to anger the Mexican people.

Beginning in 1914 the Wilson administration had to deal with a crisis brought on by the outbreak of the First World War. Not unlike John Adams, Jefferson, and Madison a century earlier, Wilson tried to insure the neutral shipping rights of the United States. He faced overwhelming odds, because both sides in the European conflict depended on control of the sea and both the British and German navies interfered with American ships. Wilson's response was not consistent: although his position was that America should remain neutral, he seemed to support Britain.

Wilson continued to try to keep the U.S. out of the conflict and to help the Europeans find a way to achieve peace. In January 1917 he presented his idea of an international organization to prevent war. He asked the warring nations to accept "peace without victory," but neither side was willing to give up the chance of winning. In February and March 1917 German submarines sank six American ships. Wilson broke diplomatic relations with Germany. In March the start of the Russian Revolution made matters worse for the forces allied against Germany, and on April 2, 1917, Wilson called for America to join in the war because "the world must be made safe for democracy." Congress voted to declare war on April 16.

Wilson hoped that the Great War would be a "war to end all wars," that it would secure freedom of the seas, permit national liberation of colonial peoples, and bring about universal acceptance of liberal democracy. He expressed these and other lofty aims in January 1918 in the Fourteen Points of his plan for peace. The Allies won the war, but the peace Wilson sought remained a noble dream.

Wilson was unsuccessful in his attempts to get the United States Senate to ratify the peace treaty worked out at Versailles as a final settlement of World War I. The Senate and the American people were split on the issue of membership in the League of Nations, which was tied to acceptance of the treaty. Wilson was so convinced he was right about the League that he refused to compromise on it, and so was unable to overcome his opponents, even though he had many supporters—perhaps a majority of the public. America never signed the treaty, and without the U.S. as a member, the League was probably doomed from the start. After playing a major role in winning and settling the greatest war in history to that time, America returned to its more traditional isolationism, trying to avoid "entangling alliances" that could lead to involvement in foreign wars.

World War I was the first great international war in a century. For the United States and Western civilization generally, it marked the end of an era of optimism about the material and moral progress of humanity and the start of a period of international instability and self-doubt. Some historians consider it the most important turning point in modern history.

wealth

Dinner given for New York bankers by Harrison G. Fiske, 1900; photograph by Byron.

We can have democracy in this country or we can have great wealth concentrated in the hands of a few, but we can't have both.

LOUIS D. BRANDEIS (1856–1941)
Supreme Court Justice

17

17

The Triumph of Industry

Germany's Chancellor Bismarck once said, "Providence watches over drunkards, fools, and Americans." Like many Europeans he envied America its amazing economic growth in the late nineteenth century. By 1890 America's factories were producing more goods than those in England. It had taken the U.S. only half a century to catch up and pass the world leader in industrial production. The nation was blessed by vast untapped natural resources, generous boundaries, deep harbors, and free-flowing rivers. Yet luck and nature alone cannot be the answer, for other well-endowed countries (China, for example) have not grown as rapidly or in the same way. Nor does luck alone explain Edison's electric dynamo, Ford's Model T automobile, the Wright brothers' airplane, or America's large railroad network, which reached from coast to coast and was more extensive than that of all Europe.

How wealthy was America? And how well off were its people? A rough indication can be found in the Gross National Product, which rose from about $9 billion at the start of the Civil War to about $37 billion at the turn of the century. And while the GNP quadrupled, the population only doubled— thus the country gained in *per capita* wealth as well as in *overall* wealth. Over the long haul the per capita economic growth of the U.S. has increased at a healthy 1.6 percent since the 1860s.

As stated before, three factors—technology, efficiency, and skilled people—are essential for economic growth. One or another may dominate, but all three must be present. In America all three were. Stupendous technological change occurred from about the 1870s to the end of World War I. Equally dramatic was the improvement in the efficiency factor as expressed in the rise of big business. Not all giant businesses were efficient, of course, but size alone usually provided an enormous plus factor to the growth of business activity.

Orville and Wilbur Wright launched the first successful flight of a motor-driven airplane on December 17, 1903. General opinion held that the airplane would be used for "sporting purposes," but the Wrights claimed that the principal market for flying machines would be for war purposes—where cost is no object.

The Rise of Big Business

The heroic age of invention

In its first seventy years of operation the United States Patent Office issued 36,000 patents. In its next thirty years, after the Civil War, it gave out 440,000. Many of the inventions turned out to be useless, but their very number indicates that science and technology had triggered a new era. In the late nineteenth century steel and electricity were the mainspring of the new industrialism, and, by the early twentieth century, the automobile contributed enormously. Building, transport, manufacture, and the life style of ordinary people would never again be the same.

America's love affair with machinery was celebrated at the Centennial Exposition in Philadelphia in 1876. The theme of the fair was mechanical power. Thousands watched on opening day as President Grant threw the lever on the world's biggest steam engine. It powered hundreds of machines at the fair and lighted huge Machinery Hall. Viewers were fascinated by a steam hammer that could crush steel with a blow of 125 tons or tap the glass of a pocket watch as lightly as a feather. Alexander Graham Bell demonstrated his amazing telephone. New-fangled contraptions called typewriters and vacuum cleaners were displayed. A favorite exhibit, a

Pullman Palace sleeping car, sported gold and silver trim. Nearby a carpenter with a band saw carved wooden curlicues for furniture and house trim. A rock drill and other compressed-air tools, already in use in cutting tunnels and mining coal, playfully blew hats and skirts into the air. George Westinghouse exhibited his air brakes, which stopped *all* the wheels of a railroad train at once. These new brakes meant that trains could be made longer and heavier and yet be safer. A high-speed press printed 25,000 sheets of newsprint every hour. Machines to make machines—metal-turning lathes—were also shown.

In the years before World War I other wonders appeared: the incandescent light bulb (1879), the Wright brothers' airplane (1903), George Eastman's Kodak camera (1884), the wireless telegraph, and cars.

I want none of the rich man's usual toys.
I want no horses or yachts—
I have no time for them.
What I want is a perfect workshop.

THOMAS A. EDISON (1847–1931)

Not the least important was the assembly-line method for making cars. The greatest credit for assembly lines goes to Henry Ford. He opened a factory in 1909 to make the Model T, a twenty-horsepower, four-cylinder automobile that sold for $360. By setting up his plant as a long production chain, Ford was producing one complete car every three minutes by 1916. The Model T, or Tin Lizzie, gave American families an undreamed-of mobility. Applied to the manufacture of other items, the assembly line created a vast array of new products for the consumer market. Soon America would be called the consumer society.

The cleverest inventor of the age was Thomas Alva Edison (1847–1931), the "Wiz-ard of Menlo Park." In 1881 he and Stephen Field put together an electric dynamo that powered New York City's streetcars, thus opening the Age of Electricity. Working tirelessly at his inventions-made-to-order laboratory in Menlo Park, New Jersey, Edison developed a carbon microphone for the telephone, a phonograph, a practical light bulb, and a movie camera. He even held the first important radio patent. And he noted the strange leak of current in a vacuum tube, the "Edison effect," which later provided the basis for television. In all, Edison held 1093 patents. He and Ford became national heroes.

Besides the celebrated geniuses—Edison, Orville and Wilbur Wright, and Henry Ford—the heroes of the technological revolution were the unknown mechanics, engineers, and laboratory assistants. At first most of the skilled workers in American industry were self-trained, a product of the family toolshed or of the assembly line or foundry. Often they were the jacks-of-all-trades who worked with simple tools and equipment and displayed a knack for solving practical problems. Increasingly, though, laboratories were replacing the haphazard development of new technology. Edison, for example, relied heavily on a well-staffed laboratory. Many of the skilled technicians in industry were now college trained and able to conduct experiments that built upon the scientific work of theoretical investigators in America and Europe.

But the country's investment in private and public education was also beginning to make its contribution to industrialism. By 1900 most states insisted that children go to school. Five times as many students went to high school as before the Civil War and all but 11 percent could read and write. Manual training schools and vocational high schools were supported by industry. Mechanics' institutes that offered advanced technical training were well attended. Federal land-grant colleges, as well as private colleges, turned out specialists in mining, engineering, and farming. America was recognizing its need for skilled workers and technicians.

The ruthless power of big business

Natural resources and technological ability alone would probably not have made America the leading industrial nation. Big business was a vital link. America's new wealth came primarily from manufacturing. Most impressive were the advances in railroads, steamships, farm tools, and the steel and chemical industries.

The railroad was the first to leap ahead. In the spring of 1869 at Promontory Point, Utah, a golden spike was driven into the rail that completed the first transcontinental line. Chugging across flat plains and through high mountain passes, scattering the buffalo in their paths, railroads could now carry goods and passengers from coast to coast.

The new east-west rail line did more than mark the finish of the first railroad to cross the continent. It also opened the Age of Big Business. The railroads were the first of the giant corporations that were to assume such a commanding place in American life. Their owners—the empire builders whose vision spanned the continent—needed more capital and labor than ever before. Banks and financial syndicates sprang up to lend them money. Construction companies were organized to carry out their plans. New and bigger unions were formed to organize railroad workers. The government set up the first regulatory agencies to control the lines. As their finances increased, the railroads organized their own subsidiaries to store grain, drill oil, cut timber, or mine coal and ore on their own land. They spent millions in lobbying—and graft—to get grants of money and land from federal and state governments. And they also sold and leased the land on a huge scale.

A caricature of railroad monopolies, entitled "The Scourge of the West" (1885), pictures a railroad robber baron astride his locomotive brandishing six-guns labeled "land grants," "U.S. Congress," and "U.S. appropriations." The hold-up victims are western workers and merchants. "Justice" and "industry" have perished along the way.

It will be a great mistake for the community to shoot the millionaires, for they are the bees that make the most honey, and contribute most to the hive even after they have gorged themselves full.

ANDREW CARNEGIE (1835–1919)

The era gave rise to a new type of business leader. Called "robber barons" or "tycoons," they were known for their ruthless competition and their indifference to the needs of either their workers or the public. "The public be damned!" Cornelius Vanderbilt once exclaimed. Vanderbilt and Collis P. Huntington in railroads, Andrew Carnegie in steel, John D. Rockefeller in oil, Phillip D. Armour in meat packing, Cyrus McCormick in farm machinery, and Jay Cooke and J. P. Morgan in finance controlled enormous chunks of money and power. They considered themselves rugged individualists. A few rose from rags to riches, but most worked their way up from moderately comfortable surroundings.

While the new tycoons were thought of as self-made men, it is misleading to ignore the help they got from Uncle Sam and from state governments. Some of the largest fortunes in railroads, oil, timber, water power, coal, cattle, and land were made from the public domain. The federal government granted 131 million acres of public land to the railroads, and the states added another 40 million acres.

Andrew Carnegie, who emigrated from Scotland with his poor parents in 1848, amassed a fortune in iron and steel. In 1872 he began using the new Bessemer process to make steel for railroad tracks. Seven years later he had virtually cornered the market on steel production. His own barges and railroad cars carried mountains of iron ore and coal to his giant mills in Pennsylvania. The secret to his success, Carnegie said, was to control the resources:

Two pounds of ironstone mined upon Lake Superior and transported nine hundred miles to Pittsburgh; one pound and one-half of lime, mined and transported to Pittsburgh; a small amount of manganese ore mined in Virginia and brought to Pittsburgh—and these four pounds of materials manufactured into one pound of steel, for which the consumer pays one cent.

Some tycoons built their fortunes by ruthlessly destroying the competition. A classic example was John D. Rockefeller. He organized Standard Oil in 1870 and in 1882 formed the Standard Oil Trust—the first trust ever organized—which represented a combination of 77 different oil companies. A master of cutthroat competition, Rockefeller also organized the South Improvement Company, a transportation business that has been called by Stewart Holbrook "the boldest, most naked attempt at dry-land piracy" in all of history. It contracted for special rebates with leading eastern railroads that shipped its oil. From them it got in exchange secret information about competitors, as well as secret rebate payments for shipping the oil of competitors. In effect it was getting some of the profit of competing firms. When necessary, the early Rockefeller companies used hired goons to dynamite the refineries of competitors and bribed various elected officials in New Jersey and Pennsylvania. Six U.S. senators were on the company payroll (one received a salary of $100,000) and were expected to favor Standard Oil with special laws. The company contracted with more than a hundred Ohio newspapers to print only stories that put Standard Oil in a favorable light. By these methods—and through new technology and efficient management—Rockefeller amassed a personal fortune of $800 million and created a billion-dollar industrial corporation. A devout Baptist, Rockefeller felt convinced that "God gave me my money" and that the South Improvement Company was "right between me and my God."

When the captains of industry retired or died off, many of the major corporations they had formed remained in existence. These large corporate organizations were not dependent on a single leader nor limited to the time span of one life. They took advantage of a simple fact: the bigger the output, the cheaper the unit cost. By gaining nationwide and, when possible, worldwide markets, they magnified profits. Even greater profits could be earned if competition could be cut out. Sometimes competing companies agreed to limit production or to charge the same prices. These agreements were not legally binding, and the "pools," as they were called, broke down when one member pulled out.

A lawyer for Standard Oil invented a stronger device—the trust. Competing companies were "invited" to have their securities administered by a common board of trustees while keeping the profits for themselves. In this way they coordinated their operations instead of competing with one another. Soon there were trusts controlling petroleum, cottonseed oil, whiskey, sugar, lead, and other products. When the trusts were attacked by state and federal govern-ments, they reorganized into holding companies. A corporation was formed to hold a controlling interest in a group of related companies. These arrangements were legal. The simple merger, where one company bought out another, was yet another route. In the late 1890s a wave of mergers hit the manufacturing and mining industries.

So strong was the trend toward concentration that in a number of industries it looked as if one company would completely dominate the field by the end of the century. In 1870 there were nineteen locomotive makers; thirty years later there were only two. Standard Oil of Ohio refined 80 to 90 percent of the oil in 1879. At first bigness resulted in lower prices for the consumer. But when a producer established a monopoly, consumers had to pay any price the company set.

Say what one will of the "robber barons" —that they were crude and ruthless and exploited their workers mercilessly—it is also true that they contributed in a revolutionary way to the creation of new material wealth. They did so by bringing together labor power, resources, and intelligence at a particular moment in time when they could make a lasting mark on American history.

BUSINESS ACTIVITY 1870–1920

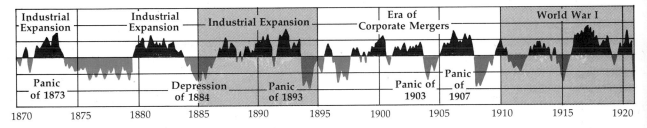

The vast expansion of the nation's railroads after the Civil War sparked a massive industrial expansion. However, it was also a time of economic instability, with periods of expansion and depression following in rapid succession. Just prior to World War I the United States seemed to be entering the first stages of a depression. But Europe's requirements for food, war supplies, and raw materials led to a boom economy in America that lasted until late 1920, when the boom ended and a new downturn began.

Poverty in the Midst of Progress

The other side of the tracks

"Life [in America] in the last forty or fifty years," wrote E. L. Godkin of the New York *Nation* in 1882, "has grown easier, pleasanter, and more luxurious. Life in the United States to the average man is a sort of paradise." Considering the abundant production of food, the availability of creature comforts, the opening of new land, and the economic opportunities for ordinary people, many readers would have agreed with Godkin. Yet why was there, in the words of Henry George, "the shocking contrast between monstrous wealth and debasing want"? Why must poverty go hand in glove with progress? George spent years in pursuit of the question. His work entitled *Progress and Poverty* (1879) was one of the most influential works of social criticism ever published in America.

Certainly nagging social and economic flaws persisted. Big business trampled small producers. Factories exploited women and children. Immigrants struggled to survive in squalid slums. Then there was the business cycle which brought periods of high prosperity, expansion, and speculation, followed by financial panic or depression. Downturns occurred in 1873, 1893, and 1907. Bank failures destroyed the savings of millions of hardworking Americans. The unemployed lived "lives of quiet desperation." Thousands of small businesses went bankrupt, and farmers lost their farms to bankers.

The gulf between the rich and the poor was widening. In 1892 a New York newspaper counted 4047 millionaires in the country. John D. Rockefeller was worth over $800 million. Carnegie's income averaged $7.5 million yearly, and he added $250 million to his fortune in 1900 when he sold out to U.S. Steel. Eighty-one-year-old Cornelius Vanderbilt boasted of earning one million dollars for every year of his life. No income taxes existed to limit these giant fortunes.

The working class read about the wealthy in the newspapers. They followed accounts of the building of luxurious mansions and knew who had gone abroad to buy paintings and sculpture for their estates. They scanned the guest lists of fancy-dress balls and read which gentlemen had lit their cigars with dollar bills.

Meanwhile the highest paid coal miner earned $560 a year in 1902, which barely covered living costs. In a third of the working-class families in Massachusetts the husbands' wages had to be supplemented by what the wives and children could earn. In the coal mines eleven-year-old slate pickers got 39¢ for a ten-hour day. Thousands of railroad workers, cotton-mill hands, and shoemakers averaged less than $460 a year. At the end of the "Gay Nineties" about 10 million out of 73 million Americans lived in poverty.

The weak shall succumb

The theory of rugged individualism took a new twist in the last half of the nineteenth century. The ideas of biologist Charles Darwin were dressed up to explain the accumulation of wealth by some people and the poverty of others in an industrial environment. Darwinian concepts were translated into a social philosophy by the English thinker Herbert Spencer, who lifted phrases like "survival of the fittest" and "natural selection" out of context to justify trusts and big business on the one hand, and slums and low wages on the other. Life was a jungle, Spencer wrote, in which the strong and the wise became industrial leaders who prevailed over the weak and the ignorant. Supporters of the theory held that the "captains of industry" should be free to lead the nation

In 1870, the first year child labor statistics were compiled, 750,000 children between ten and fifteen years of age were employed. Their numbers continued to increase until effective child labor laws were enforced. These young slate pickers remove slate from coal at a breaker, then sort the remainder into various sizes for different uses.

forward. To critics this "Social Darwinism" seemed a slick justification for greed and plunder, but to the business community it was a godsend. Thus John D. Rockefeller described the growth of a huge company as "merely a survival of the fittest. . . . The American Beauty Rose can be produced in the splendor and fragrance which brings cheer to its beholder only by sacrificing the early buds which grow up around it. This is not an evil tendency in business." The other side of the coin for these Social Darwinists was that the unfit should be allowed to fail, for public assistance would weaken their self-reliance and interfere with "natural law."

A more optimistic note was struck in the novels of Horatio Alger, whose 135 books fed the dreams of 50 million readers. Alger popularized the rags-to-riches success story. *Luck and Pluck, Bound to Rise, Brave and Bold, Sink and Swim,* and the rest all told the same story.

Through good fortune and good character, a poor boy rises to great wealth.

Some Americans believed, with Andrew Carnegie, that experiencing poverty early in life could be a virtue. Said the once-poor Carnegie, "The millionaires who are in active control started as poor boys and were trained in the sternest and most efficient of all schools—poverty." God, he wrote, had temporarily entrusted him, Andrew Carnegie, with great wealth but intended him to hand it over to society. He wanted to build libraries, universities, schools, and museums to improve society. After retiring, Carnegie endowed over 2500 libraries and set up foundations and trust funds that gave away more than $350 million. Ten percent of his fortune was still left when he died. Earlier he had written, "The man who dies rich . . . dies disgraced."

Sympathy for the victims

Toward the end of the century some middle-class Americans developed a greater awareness of poverty and a sympathy for its victims. Social workers, journalists, painters, and fiction writers drew attention to conditions among the poor. Socially conscious reformers around the turn of the century who called themselves "progressives" attacked the industrial system for needlessly wrecking so many lives. They proposed humanitarian reforms to improve the lot of the lower classes. This search for social justice became part and parcel of the progressive political movement early in the twentieth century. New York City police reporter Jacob Riis examined the immigrant slums of Manhattan in *How the Other Half Lives* (1890). He estimated that 20 to 30 percent of New Yorkers lived in squalor.

Frank Norris' *McTeague* (1899) and Theodore Dreiser's *Sister Carrie* (1901) depicted middle-class people struggling to stay above the poverty line. As "naturalists" these authors expressed in a literary way the theories derived from Darwin that life was a struggle for survival. As "realists" they were concerned with the details of everyday existence among the middle and lower classes. Upton Sinclair's realistic novel *The Jungle* (1906) portrayed the immigrant workers of Packinghouse Town (Chicago) surviving under terrible conditions.

Paralleling these literary realists, painters of the "Ashcan School" showed people sitting in dingy gaslit rooms, sunning themselves on tenement rooftops, and working in factories. Lewis Hines' camera exposed the shocking working conditions for women and children in industry.

The liberal analysts of wealth and poverty scorned the notion that poverty came from personal moral failure, bad housing, or drink. They pointed a finger at the ruthless businessmen who paid starvation wages and brutally exploited their workers. They blamed government for not protecting the weak against the strong. These "progressives" outlined various programs of government help for the lower classes. The reforms included proposals for higher wages, reduced work hours, public housing, an end to child labor, safety controls for dangerous work, workmen's compensation for job injuries, more public health clinics, recreational facilities, aid to the handicapped, unemployment insurance, old age pensions, and government medical care. The super rich would foot the bill for these reforms through a graduated income tax and an inheritance tax. The scheme was ambitious and in some ways contrary to the American principle of free enterprise. In modern terms the reforms added up to the "welfare state." Similar programs already existed to some extent in Germany and England.

Theodore Roosevelt once wrote to Jacob Riis that he wanted to "avoid the extremes of swollen fortune and grinding poverty" by shifting wealth from the very rich to the very poor. Nothing of this sort came to pass in his time. The first obstacle in the path of such reform was strong public resistance to an income tax. After the Sixteenth Amendment, which legalized an income tax, was passed in 1913, the redistribution of wealth became technically possible. But in the end it took the depression of the 1930s to justify it on a large scale. Even now the U.S., of all developed nations, has one of the weakest welfare programs, and it is the middle class, not the super rich, that supports the poor.

As of 1914, both liberals and conservatives were hopeful that the worst effects of poverty could be alleviated. Growth and welfare both seemed possible in America. Farmers were producing more food than they could sell, so no one need starve. Jobs in industry were fairly steady after the recovery from the panic of 1893. Progress in medicine was increasing the span of life. Future prospects were exciting. In 1914 the young journalist Walter Lippmann wrote, "Rebellion against misery is at last justified, and dreams have a basis in fact." Overcoming poverty had become a part of the American Dream.

Unions as Underdogs

The worker's lot

Violence exploded in 1877 that probably had no match in our history. It started in West Virginia in the midst of a depression that had caused great suffering. When the Baltimore and Ohio Railroad announced its second wage cut in a short time, local railroad workers struck. Their demonstration spread to all the major railroad centers from coast to coast, tying up about two thirds of the railroad mileage. Federal troops, local police, and state militia clashed with rioters. In Pittsburgh twenty-five were killed and in Reading, Pennsylvania, thirteen died and forty-three were injured, while in Chicago there were nineteen killings. Rails were torn up, stations burned, and freight cars smashed and looted. Steel workers, coal miners, and canal boatmen struck in sympathy. The official report of the Pennsylvania legislature determined that the riots "were the protests of laborers against the system by which his [sic] wages were arbitrarily fixed and lowered by his employer without consultation with him and without his consent. . . ." Unhappily the violence produced no corrective to this injustice. The scope of the strike and the physical destruction that it caused left middle-class Americans in a state of shock and fear.

It is true that in a general way industrial workers in the nineteenth century shared in the benefits of industrial growth. Industrial workers shared the overall rise in living standards. After the depression of the 1870s real wages increased, more food and consumer goods appeared on the market, and a long-term decline in prices improved the life of the average worker. As the president of the Cigar Makers Union testified before the United States Industrial Commission in 1890: "Today you can go into the average workingman's house and find several carpets on the floor and a piano. I never saw many pianos in workingmen's homes when I was a boy. . . . I want to say, and I am frank enough to really admit, that we can live better today. . . ."

Yet the complaints of industrial labor were many, and the Industrial Revolution brought with it extreme labor unrest. The most frequent grievances were low pay, dangerous work, long hours, sudden layoffs, competition from foreign contract labor, lack of recognition for unions, and violent repression of strikes. So bitter was the fight between organized labor and capital that some observers feared a full-scale social revolution.

In part, labor's discontent came in response to the growing rift between working people and employers. In 1883 a brass worker recalled that fourteen years earlier labor and management were "as one happy family . . . but now the boss is superior. . . . The average hand growing up in the shop now would not think of speaking to the boss . . . the boss would not recognize him either." Another workingman complained: "The employer has pretty much the same feeling toward the men that he has toward his machinery. He wants to get as much as he can out of his men at the cheapest rate. . . . That is all he cares for the man generally."

There were more tangible causes for dissatisfaction. The policy of open immigration in America created a large and fluid labor pool that held wages down, and in some industries the new technology displaced skilled workers. To justify investments in new labor-saving machinery, employers actually increased work hours. By 1880 the average workweek reached seventy hours. Wage earners were hurt by poor management practices, business slumps, and job competition. They could be fined heavily for minor infractions of company rules, and even in good times factory workers were laid off part of the year without notice or severance pay. Pensions did not exist.

OCCUPATIONAL DISTRIBUTION, 1870–1920

By 1920 the number of workers engaged in agriculture and such basic industries as mining, manufacturing, and construction remained high. At the same time there was over this half century a rapid increase in the percentage of persons engaged in services, especially trade, finance, and professional work.

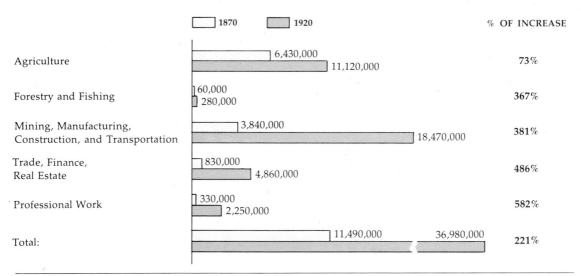

	1870	1920	% OF INCREASE
Agriculture	6,430,000	11,120,000	73%
Forestry and Fishing	60,000	280,000	367%
Mining, Manufacturing, Construction, and Transportation	3,840,000	18,470,000	381%
Trade, Finance, Real Estate	830,000	4,860,000	486%
Professional Work	330,000	2,250,000	582%
Total:	11,490,000	36,980,000	221%

SOURCE: "Industrial Distribution of Gainful Workers: 1820 to 1940," *Historical Statistics of the United States, Series D 57–71,* p. 74, *Statistical Abstracts to 1957*

At a time when compensation for job injuries was meager or totally absent, some industries had terrible accident rates. One out of every 150 Pennsylvania coal miners suffered injury in the pits in the 1890s, and one out of every 400 was killed. One out of every ten railroad workers was burned, mangled, or otherwise injured on the job. Upton Sinclair's novel *The Jungle* exaggerated very little in its accounts of packinghouse workers who disappeared forever into the sausage vats.

Nationwide unions

Unions of the early nineteenth century were city-wide or regional in scope. But the rise of national corporations created the need for larger unions. Two years after Appomattox, ten national unions were organized, and by 1870 there were thirty such bodies. The first was the National Labor Union formed by William H. Sylvis. It championed the eight-hour day, repeal of the contract labor law that allowed Chinese cheap labor into the country, and establishment of producers' cooperatives to compete with big corporations. It became the National Labor Reform party in 1872. During the depression of 1873–1877 its membership shrank from 300,000 to 50,000, and it soon expired altogether.

A new organization, the Knights of Labor, emerged in 1869 and reached its stride between 1879 and 1887. Under the leadership of Terrence V. Powderly, the Knights planned a network of cooperatives. The organization was open to all "legitimate producers" or "honest toilers," including factory hands and farmers. Only lawyers, stockholders, liquor dealers and physicians—"the exploiters of honest labor"—were barred from membership. The Knights shied away from strikes and collective bargaining. Nor would they deal directly with bread-and-butter issues like wages, which seemed too narrow and temporary a concern to solve labor's problems. Yet their smashing victory in a strike against Jay Gould's railroad network in 1884 catapulted their membership from 52,000 to 700,000 in two years. It was the Knights' role in the disastrous Haymarket Riot that did much to destroy them.

In Chicago's Haymarket Square on May 4, 1886, a dynamite bomb was tossed at a group of policemen who were breaking up a labor demonstration sponsored by social revolutionaries. The demonstration was to protest the killing of a striker at the McCormick plant and other strikebusting activity there by the police and to favor the eight-hour workday. Seven policemen died and eight prominent anarchists were arrested. Four were executed and one committed suicide in jail. So enflamed with prejudice was the court that Illinois Governor John Peter Altgeld eventually freed the three remaining prisoners. The tragedy radicalized some working people. But it also created immense fear among conservatives, and many people associated anarchist violence with the labor movement. The Knights of Labor, which had no part in the violence, soon suffered a tailspin decline in membership, partly in consequence of it.

The AFL under Gompers

In 1886 a group of craft unions formed the American Federation of Labor (AFL), the most enduring American labor organization. Its guiding genius and president until 1924 was a Jewish-English immigrant, Samuel Gompers of the cigar makers. After a youthful flirtation with Marxism, Gompers rejected socialism, even the mild collectivism of the Knights. Under his leadership the AFL renounced long-term social reforms in favor of immediate gains for craft workers, most of whom were native born. "More, now," was his slogan.

Gompers rejected welfare reforms like public housing, compulsory health plans, unemployment insurance, and minimum wage laws as schemes that would destroy the independence of labor unions. He dismissed any suggestion that the Federation form a labor party. Instead Gompers plugged for higher wages and shorter hours and also for the union shop (where all employees had to be union members). Other objectives backed by Gompers included job seniority, grievance boards, arbitration, and negotiated contracts (collective bargaining).

The AFL was designed to help the "aristocrats of labor," the skilled and semiskilled native-born white male workers. But it offered far less to the unskilled factory hands—the women, immigrants, and racial minorities, who made up the largest part of the work force. Out of a total nonfarm work force of 18 million in 1900, fewer than 800,000 belonged to unions, and less than half of these belonged to the Federation.

We struck at Pullman because we were without hope. We joined the American Railway Union because it gave us a glimmer of hope.

Statement of Pullman strikers
June 15, 1894

The sharpening contest between labor and management

At the end of the nineteenth century the struggle between capital and labor in the U.S. was the most violent of any industrial nation. More heads were broken and more time lost in strikes here than in Britain, Germany, or the other advanced nations of western Europe. Nearly 24,000 strikes occurred between 1880 and 1900. About 700,000 workers struck in 1894 alone. Many employers still thought unions, even the rather tame AFL, a criminal conspiracy. They saw unions as an assault on their profits and a challenge to their authority. Employers reared in the tradition of rugged individualism tried quite openly to destroy unions altogether. They

used blacklists to identify troublemakers (such as union organizers) and deny them jobs. Some companies forced workers to sign "yellow-dog" contracts swearing that they were not, and would not become, union members. Many workers considered unions their only defense against inhumane employers. The worst violence broke out when "scabs" backed by police tried to break strikes and thereby destroy the unions. When pickets met scabs, blood often flowed.

The Homestead strike was typical of the labor unrest in the 1890s. In 1892 the Carnegie steel mill in Homestead, Pennsylvania, installed new machinery and then announced a wage cut and a seventy-hour workweek. When the union struck, management hired Pinkerton detectives to protect strikebreakers. In a twelve-hour siege on July 6, a number of detectives and workers were killed. Strikers lost popular sympathy when an anarchist shot and nearly killed the plant manager. The strike and the union were broken. Steel, the major target of organized labor, stayed nonunion for another generation.

Another crucial strike began in 1894 in the Pullman Company near Chicago. The Pullman workers walked out when management cut wages without cutting rents in company housing. In a sympathy strike, the American Railway Union, led by Eugene V. Debs, tied up all western railroads. The strikers were willing to handle the U.S. mails but not Pullman cars. Since management was intent on breaking the union, it insisted on hooking Pullman cars to mail cars. Claiming that the strikers were "in restraint of trade," President Cleveland secured a federal labor injunction under the Sherman Antitrust Act. Two thousand federal troops were ordered to Chicago to "protect" the U.S. mails. Thousands of railroad cars were destroyed. Debs ignored the injunction and was jailed for contempt of court. The strike was broken. Over the next 25 years labor injunctions were used 200 times against strikers.

Clothing workers strike for an eight-hour day and the right to a closed shop. Clarence Darrow defended the closed shop by arguing that "the workman has the same right to choose the companions with whom he associates in labor as to choose the friends with whom he will spend his pastime; and the employer has no more right to force the society of another upon him during his hours of toil than during his hours of recreation."

Socialists, anarchists, and Progressives

After serving his six-month term for contempt of court Eugene V. Debs emerged from jail a confirmed Socialist. He had been visited by Socialists who brought him theoretical works to read. "I am for socialism," he would later explain, "because I am for humanity." The cause of humanity demanded that private property be abolished and the competitiveness among people laid aside. Under socialism they would not be so alienated from each other or from their work.

Most Socialists hoped to create a new social order in America, which would include state ownership of all industry, but they wanted to do so through peaceful political reform, not violence. They hoped to channel labor's rising militancy in the 1880s and 1890s into constructive reform.

But the Socialist reformers failed to overturn the old order. Socialism had great appeal among European workers but the immigrant Socialists had relatively little success spreading their gospel in America. Whether with justification or not, Americans continued to think of class lines as temporary and fluid — a person could move from one class to another. And racial and ethnic divisions in the U.S. destroyed the working-class solidarity that was needed for radical reform.

Another radical group wanted to destroy not only capitalism but all government. In the 1880s anarchists in Europe and America turned from pacifism to violence. They drilled with rifles, devised homemade bombs, and nursed the delusion that killing prominent businessmen or policemen would topple government everywhere. The American public did not distinguish between anarchist revolutionaries and Socialist reformers. Anarchist violence produced savage reactions against all radicals. Since most anarchists were immigrants, the violence also rebounded against European immigrants generally, who were feared as dangerous radicals.

The Progressive movement from about 1901 to 1917 helped the labor movement in certain ways. Though the Progressives were of the middle class—physicians, teachers, clergy, lawyers, small merchants, and social workers—and though they feared the power of big labor as well as of big business, they sympathized with labor's humanitarian goals. While the Progressives opposed strikes and collective bargaining, they worked with the unions and the moderate Socialists to pioneer various labor laws on the state level. Maryland's workmen's compensation law (1902), Oregon's maximum-hour law for working women (1903), and Massachusetts' minimum-wage law for women and children (1912) were new concepts in labor law.

More legislation emerged from the ashes of the Triangle fire in 1911. A fire that swept through the Triangle Shirtwaist Company, a New York City sweatshop, killed 146 garment workers, most of them women. Many of the victims jumped to their deaths because the building lacked fire escapes. A new union, the International Ladies Garment Workers, demanded reforms. An investigation conducted by New York's Progressive

legislature disclosed widespread building-code abuses. Some sixty safety laws were passed.

The Wobblies

In 1905 the Socialist labor movement was revived under the leadership of the Industrial Workers of the World (IWW). This organization was formed by two men: Eugene V. Debs of the railroad union and William "Big Bill" Haywood of the militant western miners. The IWW (or "Wobblies") appealed mainly to unskilled and unorganized workers: western miners, lumbermen, stevedores, itinerant farm hands, and New England textile workers. With their militant speeches and stirring labor songs, the Wobblies attracted the discontented and alienated, including European immigrants who had followed the American Dream up a blind alley.

The IWW favored a variety of socialism known as labor syndicalism. According to the Wobblies' theory, workers had a right to seize the privately owned factories, mines, forests, and corporate farms where they worked and run them for the nation at large. The IWW considered capitalists useless parasites and labeled Gompers and his associates class collaborators. Wobblies dreamed of "One Big Union of Toilers" that would one day paralyze the nation with a general strike and achieve the final triumph of the working class.

But they were better at organizing strikes than building a permanent organization. Their top membership of 250,000, realized during the Lawrence, Massachusetts, textile strike of 1912, was a far cry from One Big Union. Nevertheless, they demonstrated the potential of *industrial unions* in which all the workers in an industry, both skilled and unskilled, were part of a single bargaining unit. This system contrasted with the AFL, which was made up of a number of *craft unions*.

The IWW fell victim to an internal split and

to government prosecution. The split came over the question of whether or not to engage in conventional politics. The government prosecuted the organization for opposing the First World War. In 1918 the Wilson administration convicted 101 IWW leaders, Eugene Debs among them, for subversive activity, causing the organization to crumble. The movement died, but its stirring, class-conscious songs lived on.

Wilson as a friend of labor

President Wilson personally sympathized with many of labor's goals. He was the first president to address a labor convention (that of the AFL, in 1917). He refused to use federal injunctions in peaceful labor strikes. He also signed the Clayton Act of 1914, which included a provision that antitrust laws could not be applied against labor organizations. The AFL hailed the Act as "labor's Magna Carta." Gompers patriotically supported Wilson's war effort, and was appointed to sit on a government board that shaped wartime labor policy. In exchange for a no-strike pledge from labor, the president gave labor the right of collective bargaining during the war. Wilson also agreed to give wage increases in war industries. These accommodations were an enormous boon to big labor, and union membership soared.

Raising "Less Corn and More Hell"

The shift to commercial farming

Almost a quarter of a million farms spread out over the grasslands of Kansas, Nebraska, Minnesota, and the Dakotas in the 1860s and 1870s. The Homestead Act, plus encouragement from railroad companies and state and territorial governments, lured easterners and immigrants to the West. The expanding population, swelled by European immigration, meant millions more mouths to feed. The world market for grains was rising. From 1860 to 1900 farm acreage in the U.S. more than doubled.

The Industrial Revolution created turmoil in American agriculture. Farming had started to become a complex business enterprise in which specialization was a main objective. Commercial farmers could have a higher standard of living than subsistence farmers (still about 25 percent of American farmers in 1920) who grew primarily for their own consumption or for barter with merchants. But to compete successfully, commercial farmers had to have more capital, better machines, scientific training, and market information. If they could expect greater monetary rewards, they also faced greater risks of failure.

Modern farm machines encouraged big farms. The gangplow, the reaper, the twine-binder, and the harvester-thresher combine, among other inventions, multiplied farm productivity. Most stages of growing wheat, a durable, saleable crop, could be handled by machines. In some places on the Great Plains in the 1880s, steam engines were hooked up to huge threshing machines. Just before World War I tractors replaced steam engines, causing even more dramatic change.

Commercial farming raised new problems even as it solved old ones. Machinery was a necessity, but it was costly. How many machines to use, what kind, and whether to rent or buy them were crucial decisions that

On the big wheat farms of the Great Plains and the far Northwest, mechanical combines converted the open spaces into "America's breadbasket." Pulled by gangs of as many as forty horses, the huge machines joined the work of binding and threshing into one operation which required the labor of only a few men. The animals were soon replaced by steam power; by 1912 gasoline-powered combines began to appear.

farmers had not faced before. Many went bankrupt paying for their new gadgets. Buying machines, land, feed, and supplies required credit, especially in the first years of building a house and barn, fencing in cattle, and planting and harvesting crops. Farmers on the frontier also had to worry constantly about drought, animal diseases, prairie fires, and insects. In 1866 a winter blizzard and summer drought wiped out many pioneers. "In God We Trusted, In Kansas We Busted" was painted on some wagons moving *east* by the end of that year.

Farmers, like all business people, wanted a fair return on their investment. This meant fair prices for their crops, fair freight charges for storing and shipping their produce to market, fair interest rates on money they bor-

rowed, and fair terms for the machinery they bought. Above all, farmers hoped some day to own the family farm free and clear of debt. If they could realize this dream, or help their children do so, they would endure any hardships.

To succeed in business, farmers had to keep track of agricultural prices and freight rates. But the farther west they lived, the poorer their marketing information was. Besides, from 1866 to 1900 farm prices kept inching downward, reaching their lowest ebb in 1894–1896. More and more farmers went into debt. By 1900 one third of all U.S. farms were mortgaged. Farm tenantry increased from 26 percent of all farms in 1880 to more than 35 percent by the turn of the century.

The farmers' complaints

In explaining their plight, farmers found plenty of villains. Railroads topped the list. When it came to buying or leasing land, or storing grain in silos and shipping it, farmers were at the mercy of the railroads. As monopolies, the railroads could charge high rates. They favored the large shippers, who supplied them with more profitable business. Freight rates sometimes ran so high that, rather than ship their grain, farmers let it rot or used it to stoke up potbellied stoves on cold winter nights.

Moneylenders, especially eastern moneylenders, were also high on the enemy list. Bankers charged as much as 25 percent for desperately needed mortgage loans. Besides, the banks seemed to keep the money supply scarce, which hurt debtors trying to make payments. Thus, a farmer who took out a thousand-dollar mortgage in the 1860s that could be paid off by selling twelve hundred bushels of wheat, had to sell almost twice as much to settle the same debt in the 1880s. Farmers demanded not only cheaper interest rates for mortgages but also a greater flow of credit to the West. They also wanted more money in circulation as a way of bringing on inflation, for they felt that inflation would help them pay off their debts more easily.

Farmers also cursed the speculators who set the prices in the major commodity exchanges of the world: Chicago, New York, and Liverpool, England. Men who had never milked a cow or stacked hay haggled in the pit of the exchanges. They speculated on the wheat, corn, pigs, and cotton grown by hardworking farm people. Wheat prices fell from $1.60 per bushel in 1866 to $.49 in 1894. Cotton plummeted from $.31 per pound in 1866 to $.06 in 1893. It almost did not pay to farm.

Farmers found the land laws far from perfect. The Homestead Act (see p. 202) was supposed to favor pioneer farmers at the expense of land speculators. But railroads and land syndicates found enough loopholes to acquire large chunks of public land in the West. Even worse, foreign capitalists, especially British investors, bought up American ranches, mines, and forests.

Tariff laws also hurt the farmers. American growers sold their crops in an open world market but had to buy high-priced finished products in a national market. The prices were high because duties on goods manufactured abroad protected American manufacturers against competition from foreign imports.

The farmer's miseries were most acute in the South, where cotton was the big crop. Poor farmers, both blacks and whites, found it hard to own their own land. Hundreds of thousands were tenants and sharecroppers. In 1880 not more than one percent of the black farmers in Georgia owned their own land. By 1900 half of all the farms in Dixie were run by tenants. Like all commercial farmers they needed credit for seed and supplies. It was often provided by the local merchant or landlord in exchange for a lien (first claim) on the harvest. This forced the cropper and tenant to divide his crop with the lender. Blacks and whites alike entered into debt peonage (bound to work for their creditors until their debts were paid off), a way of life with a distinct resemblance to slavery. Beset by illness and ignorance, they handed down their debts and their poverty from one generation to the next.

The railroad executives, brokers, and bankers who were attacked by farm leaders were likely to reply that the "hayseeds" were exaggerating. Railroad rates, though higher west of Chicago, were generally declining. Because westbound freight trains usually ran empty ("dead head"), their operating costs had to be applied to charges on eastbound runs. Interest on a mortgage did not exceed 35 percent of its value, with a time limit of three to five years. And this did not seem to bankers to be an intolerable burden for the farmer—unless he suffered a catastrophe like drought or locusts. In spite of arguments to the contrary, however, farmers were getting a smaller profit than many others engaged in business, and their anger was basically justified.

In the final analysis commercial farmers suffered from too much competition. Growers from all over the world were competing for the same market. American wheat growers were competing not only with each other but with the farmers of Canada, Australia, Argentina, South Africa, and all other wheat-exporting nations.

Organizing for farm power

At the time of Appomattox, farmers felt they were still the backbone of the Republic. Within a few decades their economic standing was deteriorating and they felt as if they were the nation's doormat. In an attempt to improve their position, they began to organize. Farmers established clubs and cooperatives and pressed for reform legislation. Finally they plunged into politics, sometimes joining with labor or other groups sharing common grievances.

The first successful farm organization, the Grange, was founded as the Patrons of Husbandry in 1867 by Oliver Kelley, a government clerk. It was intended to bring together isolated pioneer families of the western prairies at picnics and other social occasions and to spread information about scientific farming. Soon the Grange set up consumer cooperatives, co-op banks and fire insurance companies, and even co-op marketing organizations to sell wheat in the big cities. Encouraged by success, its members entered politics, electing governors and winning control of numerous western and southern state legislatures. There the Grangers helped hammer out laws to control railroad rates and combat the stranglehold of business combinations like McCormick Harvester Company. They won a victory in *Munn* v. *Illinois* (1877)

when the Supreme Court upheld the right of states to regulate railroads.

At its peak the Grange boasted 1.5 million members. But as its co-ops expanded, they were plagued by bad management, pressure from middlemen, and private competition. And by the 1880s the Supreme Court had begun to reverse itself, denying the power of the states to control the railroads. Grange membership began to shrivel, and the organization lost its muscle. In the 1870s many farmers also sought a solution in monetary reform and joined the Greenback movement to force inflation (see Chapter 18).

When hard times descended again upon the South and West in the late 1880s, new and more militant farm groups sprouted. The most organized of these, the Farmers' Alliances, pressed for legislation to control financial and industrial power. The rhetoric of discontent blossomed during the 1890s. "It is no longer a government of the people, by the people and for the people," declared the Kansas farm leader Mary Elizabeth Lease in 1890, "but a government of Wall Street, by Wall Street and for Wall Street. . . . What you farmers need to do is to raise less corn and more *Hell*."

In 1892 the Alliances and the state parties they had formed fused into a new national political organization, the People's party, or Populists. Its purpose was to use the government as a counterweight against the powerful corporate interests. It sought government ownership of transportation, telegraph, and banking, as well as currency inflation to help the many farmers who were deeply in debt. The defeat of the Populists in the presidential election of 1896 took the starch out of the agrarian rebels (see pp. 393–394).

Then suddenly the farmers' doldrums vanished. In 1896–1897 the worldwide depression ended, and prices for American staples improved. Rainfall increased in the United States. The gold discovered in the Klondike put more money in circulation and brought about inflation. Mortgage money flowed west. In 1914 the outbreak of war in Europe cut off wheat farming in France and Russia and gave a lift to American grain growers. New farmlands opened in Kansas and other areas. By 1918 farmers were beginning to look back over the previous twenty years as "the golden age of American agriculture."

Review

By the end of the nineteenth century the U.S. was the world's leading industrial nation. Big business, science and technology, and a force of skilled workers had created an economic revolution. The joining of a coast-to-coast railroad in 1869 symbolized the scope of big business. Captains of industry amassed great wealth and power. Often they founded giant corporations that outlived both them and their era. These corporations expanded nationally and internationally, sometimes wiping out their competition.

Despite the overall economic growth of the country, the gulf between rich and poor widened. At the end of the 1800s journalists, social workers, and novelists called attention to conditions of poverty. The elimination of poverty became a goal of reformers in the Progressive era. But the growing awareness of the problem brought little change.

While the standard of living for workers improved, labor unrest increased. The spread of national corporations led to national unions. The AFL, a relatively conservative federation of craft workers, was the most enduring. Most American workers approved of capitalism. Only a very small minority hoped for socialism, and the Socialists' dreams were dashed by World War I. The AFL, by supporting Wilson in the war, improved its own position and gained respectability for labor organizations.

As commercial farming spread westward, acreage multiplied and new agricultural methods and machinery increased productivity. But rising expenses, declining prices, and continuing natural disasters plagued farmers. Farmers had valid grievances against railroads, bankers, and brokers. And there was a surplus of produce, here and abroad. More and more farms were mortgaged, and tenantry rose. In a rebellious mood, the farmers banded together to form the Grange, the Alliances, and then the militant Populist party. But the agrarian rebellion subsided after the defeat of the Populists in the election of 1896.

Questions

1. Explain how technology and business efficiency contributed to economic growth after the Civil War.
2. Choose either A or B:
   A. Identify and describe briefly: the "Wizard of Menlo Park," captains of industry, Standard Oil, Jacob Riis, the Homestead strike, and the Pullman strike.
   B. What are the differences between pools, trusts, holding companies, and mergers?
3. How did Social Darwinists, Horatio Alger, Andrew Carnegie, and the Progressives view poverty? To what extent do you believe people still hold these views today?
4. Trace the development of unions during this period, beginning with the National Labor Union. What were the goals of the various unions, and how did they differ?
5. What forces prevented commercial farmers from prospering more during these years? Detail the attempts they made to solve their problems.

James K. Vardaman, atop a lumber wagon drawn by oxen, campaigns for the Mississippi governor's seat in 1903.

Oh, the candidate's a dodger,
yes, a well-known dodger,
Oh, the candidate's a dodger,
yes, and I'm a dodger, too.
He'll meet you and treat you
and ask you for your vote,
But look out, boys,
he's a-dodging for a note!
             "THE DODGER,"
             Late nineteenth-century jingle

18

18
Corruption and Reform

The Founding Fathers feared the concentration of power. A knowledge of history had convinced them that too much power in the hands of an individual or a single group or one social class posed the gravest danger to liberty. The Constitution expressed their experience and concern. It divided power among the three government branches and created checks and balances to prevent any one branch from becoming dominant. For two generations this method functioned well, and even after the outbreak of civil war no one doubted its essential wisdom. Yet with each passing year after that war, power increasingly concentrated in a few hands. While their activities stimulated economic growth, the major industrialists and financiers were threatening to control the nation.

Industrialism helped build vast urban centers, opened up new territories to farming, and established the U.S. as a world power. Through the jobs it created, the goods it produced, and the philosophy it represented, it affected family life, reinforced the spirit of individualism, and altered the life style of millions of people. It created a small elite class of business leaders who owned the means by which millions had to make their living. Whether the captains of industry hired or fired workers, raised or lowered prices, borrowed or loaned money, bought or sold stocks, to a great degree they affected the national economy and also the welfare of many Americans.

Inevitably industrialism also affected government and politics. The new industrial elite presented a bold challenge to government by the people. In a broad sense, democracy was expected to insure that no one class would rule another and that every vote cast would count the same. But quite plainly the super rich had far greater power than ordinary citizens to manipulate politicians and influence legislation.

In looking at power during the decades between the Civil War and World War I, this chapter deals first with the way that industrialism altered social structure and then with the link between business and government and the effort to control big business through regulatory agencies. Lastly, the chapter examines the shifts in politics from Reconstruction to the period of Populist revolt and finally to the Progressive era.

Captains of Industry in Command

Social change

Not least of the changes brought on by the Industrial Revolution was a redistribution of the labor force according to occupations. A noticeable drop occurred in the proportion of farmers between 1870 and 1920—from about 56 percent to about 30 percent. Almost as impressive was the increase of the proportion of blue-collar workers (urban laborers and industrial workers) in the same period. They rose from about 33 percent to 50 percent of the work force. Though the overall proportion of professionals remained small, it doubled from about 3 percent to 6 percent (see chart, p. 368). Most new blue-collar workers were semiskilled or unskilled, performing a few steps in the production process. Clerical workers served mainly in large corporate concerns and government; the majority were women.

By far the most dramatic change in American social structures was the rise of the new industrial elite. First came the captains of industry—Jay Cook, Jay Gould, Andrew Carnegie, J. Pierpont Morgan, John D. Rockefeller, and others. Later came the less spectacular but equally influential directors and upper-level management of industrial corporations. The new industrial class swiftly replaced the older agrarian and mercantile elites in the seats of power, though not in public esteem. Before the Civil War the economic elites tended to be provincial: the *Tidewater* planters, *New England* merchants, or *Pennsylvania* Quakers, etc. To a much greater degree the new captains of industry were free of local attachments and had a nationwide perspective. They were the first national elite.

The facts in the rise of the new elite of wealth and power demonstrate that the rags-to-riches myth, so popular in the Gilded Age, was based largely on wishful thinking. To be sure, a few, like Henry Ford, traveled from the family farm to the pinnacle of success. But by 1900 over half of the most prominent businessmen had attended college, and another one quarter had been to high school. Two thirds came from families with business or professional backgrounds, and a disproportionate number were Protestants of British ancestry with native-born parents. In fact, according to one study, 86 percent of the business leaders in 1870 came from families that had been in America since colonial times. By 1900 the sons of the men who had risen above the middle ranks of industry were beginning to take over their fathers' positions. Throughout the nineteenth century fewer and fewer business leaders came from farm families or from the class of craftsmen. At no time did a significant number come from laborers' families.

Although class lines were fluid in America as compared to European nations, claims about working-class mobility in the U.S. are not borne out by research. Stephan Thernstrom's *Poverty and Progress* (1964), a study of Newburyport, Massachusetts, shows that *occupational mobility* was limited in the nineteenth century. The son of an unskilled Irish immigrant laborer often became a semi-skilled or skilled worker. Less often he became a clerk or supervisor, for these jobs required schooling. He almost never joined the ranks of businessmen. *Property mobility* was much more common. Laboring families often had $600 to $1000 in property holdings—perhaps a home or an income-earning building—or in a savings account. Even during depressions working-class families owned substantial amounts of property. Sometimes this success depended on rigid economies or on sacrificing the education of the children. As a result, the next generation might be unable to move up the class ladder.

Moving west and pioneering a farm continued to be a possible path to success in America. Even more important, education was then, and remains now, the surest means of social mobility. Many working-class and farm families found it a hardship to take their children away from work and send them to schools. Higher education was, of course, still out of their reach. But by 1910 most industrial states maintained tax-supported public schools and had laws requiring at least some school attendance. Achieving a high-school diploma was becoming more prevalent.

When I want to buy up any politician I always find the anti-monopolists the most purchaseable. They don't come so high.
WILLIAM H. VANDERBILT (1821–1885)

Political connections of the super rich

Stockholders and corporate managers wielded more than their share of political power, directly and indirectly, legally and illegally.

In a sense the new elite had narrow political interests. Their goals included free access to public land and natural resources and protection from foreign competition but freedom from government "interference"—that is, from regulation of the way they ran their businesses. When they had to work within the political system, they found it easy to do so. Broad philosophical questions, including questions of ethical conduct and responsibility, barely interested them. As one wealthy man, Frederick Townsend Martin, confessed:

Among my own people I seldom hear political discussions. . . . We are not politicians or public thinkers; we are the rich; we won America; we got it, God knows how; but we intend to keep it if we can by throwing all the tremendous weight of our support, our influence, our money, our political connection, our purchased senators, our hungry congressmen, our public-speaking demagogues into the scale against any legislation, any political platform, and Presidential campaign, that threatens the integrity of our estate.

Martin's statement was not fanciful. When it suited their purposes, forceful business leaders plied politicians with gifts or special investment opportunities, lent money to legislators, and at times enlisted their company sales representatives to serve as political ward heelers. Standard Oil agents, for example, occasionally worked for the GOP.

Outright bribery was a typical mode of operation during the Gilded Age. In a six-month period Ohio Senator Joseph Foraker pocketed $44,000 from the Standard Oil Company while he sat on various Senate committees and prepared the antitrust plank of the Republican party. The most famous congressional scandal concerned the group that promoted the Union Pacific Railroad. They gave stock to Ohio Congressman Oakes Ames to distribute to his House colleagues at half its market value in order to hush up a potentially embarrassing investigation of their construction company, the Crédit Mobilier. When the scandal leaked out in 1872,

Ames stated that Congress was like an auction block where legislation went to the highest bidder.

California railroad baron Collis P. Huntington in 1877 explained his philosophy of bribery: "If you have to pay money to have the right thing done, it is only just and fair to do it. . . ." By following this philosophy, Huntington and the Southern Pacific Railroad successfully controlled governors, senators, congressmen, judges, labor leaders, reform politicians, delegates to both major party conventions, state legislators, mayors, and city councilmen. In fact, until 1911 "the octopus" controlled California government from top to bottom and assured itself a virtual monopoly over all major forms of transportation in that state.

Financier Andrew Mellon once observed that "it is always a mistake for a good businessman to take public office." Yet at the turn of the century there were twenty-five industrial millionaires in the Senate, including Leland Stanford of the Southern Pacific and Chauncey Depew of the New York Central Railroad. The Senate jokingly called itself the Millionaires' Club. Many of the super rich who did not seek office involved themselves in politics from the sidelines. Midwestern industrialist Marcus Alonzo Hanna retired from business and devoted himself to getting GOP Senator William McKinley elected president in 1896.

The power barons

The industrial elite held powerful sway over the country by controlling the job market for millions of workers and the business opportunities of thousands of small businessmen. As the century drew to a close, the power of financiers seemed to grow. In 1895 President Cleveland summoned banker J. P. Morgan to an urgent White House meeting to consider ways of stopping the flow of gold reserves from the federal treasury. The Wall Street financier swiftly organized a syndicate to sell some $62 million in gold bonds here and in Europe and thereby stemmed the flow and helped save the country from bankruptcy.

In 1889, shortly before debate began on the Sherman Antitrust Bill, Joseph Keppler's "The Bosses of the Senate" appeared in Puck. *The combined circulation of such picture weeklies was huge. During this period political cartoonists probably had greater influence on public opinion than any time before or since.*

J. Pierpont Morgan was a born aristocrat, renowned art collector and sportsman, and head of a colossal financial and industrial empire. He also loathed publicity. Here he lunges after a photographer with his cane, but the photographer sidestepped Morgan's charge to make off with this picture.

That a handful of bankers, and one banker in particular, could have such a grip over the U.S. treasury (and earn a small fortune in commissions on the side) was a frightening notion.

Several years later Morgan bought out Andrew Carnegie and reorganized various other steel firms into the U.S. Steel Corporation, the first billion-dollar corporation. From his office in the House of Morgan at 23 Wall Street, he manipulated industrial corporations like pawns on a chessboard. He also found time to sail around the world on a destroyer-sized yacht, the *Corsair*, meeting with kings and heads of state. The newspaper humorist "Mr. Dooley" (Finley Peter

Dunne) imagined Morgan instructing his butler, "James call up the Czar an' th' Pope an' th' Sultan an' th' Impror Willum an' tell thim we won't need their services afther nex' week."

Morgan took power for granted. When Theodore Roosevelt threatened to break up a Morgan-controlled monopoly, he asked TR, "If we have done anything wrong on that one, why can't you just send your man [the U.S. attorney general] to see my man [a lawyer], and we will work something out." Testifying before a congressional committee in 1913, Morgan expressed astonishment that anyone feared his power. He explained that although the House of Morgan controlled numerous boards of directors, each representative of his organization cast an independent vote. The reply left some of his listeners unconvinced. Until the Great Crash of 1929, J. P. Morgan and Company was undoubtedly the single most influential firm in the country. It controlled hundreds of companies involved in finance, railroads, shipping, electricity, and other industries.

Beginning in the 1880s, decisions of the judicial branch particularly backed the giant corporations. In 1886 the U.S. Supreme Court gave a curious twist to the Fourteenth Amendment, declaring that legally a corporation was a person and that therefore no state could deprive it of its property without "due process" (*Santa Clara Company* v. *Southern Pacific Railroad*). If a state attempted to regulate a corporation, lawyers for the company would claim that its property (profits) was being threatened. The court would then examine the merits of the charge and usually bar the state from taking action. In this manner the Fourteenth Amendment, which did practically nothing to protect blacks against discrimination—the purpose for which it had been created—became a foundation stone of the corporate system.

By no means did the new elite hold complete power over government. While big businessmen used politicians in a variety of ways, they were also used by the politicians, who had power to sell or to withhold, to increase the industrialists' profits or to reduce them. And besides those in government and their associates in business on the outside, there were other influential groups: lawyers, newspaper editors, local business leaders, physicians, and clergymen. Even intellectuals like John Hay, a friend and confidant of Theodore Roosevelt, were influential in public affairs. It was from groups like these that the challenge to the political and economic elites came.

> *Our government, national and state, must be freed*
> *from the sinister influence or control of special interests. . . .*
> *We must drive the special interests out of politics.*
>
> THEODORE ROOSEVELT   (1858–1919)

Curbing the Power of Big Business

The regulatory agencies

In a corrupt era with politics and big business closely allied and the public interest largely ignored, radicals and reformers groped for economic and social answers. Short of abolishing capitalism or nationalizing industry, how could corporate power be dealt with? The two most popular ideas were the establishment of regulatory agencies and breaking up the trusts. Both approaches appealed to farmers and small merchants. In response to public pressure, Congress began groping in the 1880s toward antitrust laws and started setting up federal agencies to control private enterprise.

The first federal regulatory law was the Interstate Commerce Act of 1887 which dealt with railroads. A five-man Interstate Commerce Commission (ICC) was established. Rebates to big shippers and short-haul overcharges were prohibited. Railroads were to charge "reasonable and just" freight rates. But precisely what this meant was left up to the courts to decide, for the ICC lacked the power to fix rates. The Supreme Court ruled for the carriers in fifteen out of sixteen cases.

Thus the railroads had no reason to oppose the Commission, which brought a certain tidiness to an industry plagued by harsh competition.

In 1894 the U.S. attorney general wrote to an angry railroad company president advising him not to oppose the ICC. That agency, he argued, "satisfies the popular clamor for a government supervision of railroads, at the same time that the supervision is almost entirely nominal. Furthermore, the older such a Commission gets to be, the more inclined it will be to take the business and railroad view of things." His advice proved correct.

The Progressive era renewed the pressure for regulatory legislation. (For a general definition of Progressivism see Overview, p. 351.) In 1906 Theodore Roosevelt wrested from Congress the Hepburn Act, a landmark regulatory law. For the first time the ICC was allowed to examine corporate account books and establish effective maximum rates. And for the first time the Commission's rulings were binding without a court order.

Three other federal regulatory agencies

were founded before World War I. Meat packers were notorious for distributing rotten or contaminated meat doctored with dyes and artificial preservatives. Upton Sinclair's realistic novel *The Jungle* (1906) exposed shocking conditions in the Chicago meat-packing industry. That same year the Pure Food and Drug Act was passed into law. It established the Food and Drug Administration which helped bring modest changes in the consumer marketing industry. The Federal Reserve Act (1913) set up the Federal Reserve System, the first central banking system in the U.S. since Jackson's time. The Federal Trade Commission (1914) could investigate corporations suspected of monopo-

ly practices and issue cease-and-desist orders to prevent unfair business practices.

The public naturally believed that regulatory agencies would function in the public interest to limit the concentration of wealth and to regulate unfair competition. In practice, however, federal agencies were often quite helpful to big business. The biggest and most successful meat-packing companies actually welcomed government curbs on smaller packers, who threatened to bankrupt the entire industry by selling poisonous foods. In reality the regulatory agencies rarely hindered the concentration of wealth. The FDA did improve meat inspection, but it was almost totally ineffective against the drug industry which continued to sell poorly labeled and harmful products.

The Federal Reserve System proved helpful to bankers, especially when depositors made panic withdrawals, but it showed extreme weaknesses as far as the general public was concerned, especially in time of depression or inflation. Regulatory agencies blunted public outcry, but whether they really prevented abuses was often hard to determine.

Clamping down on the monopolies

By the 1880s small business people, farmers, and labor were aroused to such a fever pitch against monopolies that conservatives feared a social upheaval. Several states passed antitrust laws but these had limited scope in controlling businesses selling goods over state lines. To quiet the public outrage, Congress in 1890 passed the Sherman Antitrust Act. It declared "every contract, combination in the form of trust or otherwise, or conspiracy in restraint of trade . . . illegal." However stern sounding, this measure was actually a weak compromise. Instead of creating a special agency to regulate the trusts, Congress turned over enforcement of the law to the Justice Department and the courts. They

Teddy Roosevelt, always a dynamic speaker, campaigns in the West in 1904. In order to drive an oratorical point home, according to one contemporary account, "His teeth snap shut between the syllables, biting them apart . . . a sharp forward thrust of the head . . . seems to throw the word clattering into the air."

were poorly equipped for the job. Besides, the law provided for only slap-on-the-wrist penalties.

The Justice Department moved slowly against the trusts, and the Supreme Court let even the most blatant monopolies off the hook. In *U.S. v. E. C. Knight Company* (1895) the Court ruled that the sugar trust, though it controlled 98 percent of sugar refining in the United States, was not in restraint of commerce, and that only the government may control commerce. This decision made a shambles of the Sherman Act. The trusts that were dissolved by court order formed holding companies and mergers, which were declared legal. The courts dealt gently with violators. All but the most arrogant corporations were allowed to conduct business as usual. However, the attorney general attacked the unions in the courts as monopolies in restraint of trade. Meanwhile the number of trusts multiplied rapidly with relatively little government opposition. From some 230 trusts in 1894 the total rose to 1730 by 1913: hence a cynic once called the Sherman Antitrust Act the "mother of trusts."

The new rash of mergers intensified the public fear that combinations were grabbing too much control over labor, markets, and materials, and were gouging the public with high prices and inferior goods and services. Muckraking works like Ida Tarbell's *History of the Standard Oil Company* (1904) exposed the evils of business combinations. The Progressive era then brought renewed demands by small manufacturers, farmers, and railroad shippers for clipping the wings of the trusts. President Theodore Roosevelt, the first president to identify himself with Progressivism (see pp. 395–396), acquired a popular reputation as a trust buster, but his reputation rests more on bold speeches than on bold actions.

Roosevelt did not actually oppose all big corporations, but only "bad" ones—those that crudely violated the law. He initiated

forty-four suits against large corporations. The most famous was against the Northern Securities Company, a giant, railroad holding company, which the courts ordered dissolved in 1904. But Teddy Roosevelt believed that big business generally was rational and systematic and benefited the country if controlled by big government, especially a strong president. This desire for controlled monopoly was part of the doctrine of the New Nationalism, which he enunciated in 1910 and again in 1912. TR's successor, William Howard Taft, though less associated with Progressivism, prosecuted many more trusts than Roosevelt.

While campaigning against Roosevelt in 1912, Woodrow Wilson advanced his philosophy of the New Freedom, which proposed to limit the rise of new combinations, though not to destroy existing ones. He was concerned with "predatory" trusts that prevented the rise of small business people through free competition. Wilson wanted no partnership between big business and big government. After Wilson's victory, the Clayton Antitrust Act and the Federal Trade Commission Act in 1914 tried to close up the loopholes of the Sherman Act. A regulatory agency was set up, and court injunctions ended unlawful practices. The Clayton Act specifically exempted unions from restraint-of-trade suits. On the other hand, during the First World War Wilson suspended the antitrust laws as an aid to the war effort.

After the dust had settled, it turned out that the government had actually busted few trusts in the forty years after 1890. Combinations that were broken up found new ways to survive. While the Standard Oil Company was broken up in 1911 as a holding company, its thirty-two fragments functioned with about as much coordination as before. Concentrated economic power continued.

The number of business mergers and combinations leveled off after the Progressive era. This owed less to trust-busting than to the new objectives of the managers who succeeded the original captains of industry as heads of large corporations. These professional executives were salaried employees while the former owners had been gambling to increase their personal fortunes. The new managers were more interested in making steady profits for the stockholders on a long-term basis than in going after chancey big killings.

Stagnation and Reform in Politics

Reconstruction: Radicals in the North and South

In the Reconstruction period after the Civil War the nation faced two major problems. The first was how to bring the southern states back into the Union—as former partners returning to the fold or as defeated enemies deserving punishment. The second problem concerned civil rights for the freed slaves. The bitterness revolving around these questions was heightened by the fact that both Congress and the president expected to dictate the solutions. (See also Chapter 20 on Race.)

Congress was thoroughly dominated by Republicans, who after 1866 commanded a two-thirds majority in each house of Congress. Moreover the leadership of the House and Senate was wielded by Senator Charles Sumner of Massachusetts and Representative Thaddeus Stevens of Pennsylvania who had been stern abolitionists before 1865. The Radical Republicans refused to restore the South to its former status until it granted full civil and political rights to black males. They looked upon the Democratic party as the party of treason—nothing more.

President Andrew Johnson, a loyal Union man but a southerner and Democrat, hoped to be lenient with the Confederates and to increase the rights of blacks as little as possible. He vigorously opposed adoption of the Fourteenth Amendment by which the Radicals hoped to ensure full equality to all citizens regardless of race. In the election of 1866 Johnson carried his fight to the country by personally campaigning against Radical congressional candidates. His effort was a dismal failure. Nor did he succeed in blocking some of the Radicals' major legislation. They passed a civil rights act and the Reconstruction Acts of 1867–1868 over his vetoes. The Reconstruction Acts gave black men the right to vote but took the vote away from Confederate leaders. They also placed the Confederate states temporarily under martial law. These severe terms would prevail until new state constitutions were drawn up. Before a state could resume its place in Congress, its legislature would have to ratify the Fourteenth Amendment, guaranteeing civil rights to all its citizens, regardless of race.

In the southern state governments organized by Congress, power was shared by a loose political coalition. One element consisted of white "carpetbaggers," northerners who had gone south (whether out of idealistic or selfish motives) to take part in education, business, or politics. Another element was the "scalawags," mostly southern Democrats or former Whigs of the planter or merchant class, who had decided to help the Republicans. And finally there were the blacks, men who were newly enfranchised and elected to office as Republicans. Though occasionally involved with scandal and corruption, the southern Radicals accomplished certain reforms on the state level by expanding needed social services. This was the first time that black men participated as citizens, although the black politicians had far too little influence compared to the size of the black population. Racial prejudice and opposition from the majority of whites doomed these governments to eventual collapse.

To impose their plan of Reconstruction, the Radical Republicans had to clip the wings of both the president and the Supreme Court. In July 1866 Congress reduced the number of Supreme Court justices to seven in order to prevent Johnson from appointing two justices favorable to him. Then a law was passed denying the Court the right to hear appeals in habeas corpus cases. In practical terms this meant that the Supreme Court could not undercut the military rule which Congress' Reconstruction Acts had imposed on the South.

Johnson's impeachment

On May 16, 1868, the Radical Republicans came within an eyelash of removing President Andrew Johnson from office. The impeachment grew out of conflicting theories of Reconstruction. It also involved a dispute over Constitutional power. Most Congressmen believed that the legislative branch should be more powerful than the executive. For the first time in history Congress had passed many important laws over presidential veto. The members were determined to push for more authority.

The showdown turned on a relatively minor point—whether the president could fire a cabinet member without Senate approval. The Radical Congress knew that Johnson hoped to rid himself of Secretary of War Edwin M. Stanton, a leftover from Lin-

SOUTHERN STATE GOVERNMENTS DURING THE RECONSTRUCTION

Between 1865 and 1877 the southern state governments went through three phases.

Phase 1. (1865 and 1866)
The legislatures were dominated by white ex-Confederates. Black Codes were passed restricting the rights of blacks to own property and move about freely.

Phase 2. (1876—early 1870s)
The state governments were governed by Republican legislators, both white and black. After one to three years of military rule, the southern states were readmitted to the Union. Dates of readmittance were

1868 Alabama, Arkansas, Florida, Louisiana, North Carolina, South Carolina
1870 Georgia, Mississippi, Texas, Virginia

Phase 3. (Early 1870s to 1877)
Black and white Radical Republicans lost power. White Democrats regained control of the southern legislatures in the following years:

1869 Virginia (before state was readmitted)
1870 North Carolina
1871 Georgia
1873 Texas
1874 Alabama, Arkansas
1875 Mississippi
1877 South Carolina, Louisiana, Florida

coln's time who was sympathetic to them. In 1867 it passed the Tenure of Office Act, forbidding the president from firing high officials without Senate consent. Believing that this law was unconstitutional and should be heard before the Supreme Court, Johnson fired Stanton.

Three days later the House voted to impeach the president. The eleven articles of impeachment focused on his violation of the Tenure of Office Act. The trial in the Senate for "high crimes and misdemeanors" was presided over by the Chief Justice of the Supreme Court and lasted for eleven weeks in an atmosphere of confusion and frenzy. More attention was paid to lining up votes than to sifting the evidence. Senators who had not yet made up their minds were insulted and threatened by colleagues and constituents. The chief prosecutor was Benjamin F. Butler, an intelligent but tactless congressman who, as a Union Army general, had earned the nickname "butcher of New Orleans."

Johnson, who never appeared in person, was ably defended. In the end the vote to convict was thirty-five to nineteen, one vote short of the necessary two thirds. Seven Republicans broke rank and voted against conviction. One of them, Senator Edmund G. Ross of Kansas, is among the heroes in John F. Kennedy's *Profiles in Courage*. He had refused to divulge his vote in advance and as a result came under heavy pressure. Ross cast the swing vote against conviction because, in his words, "If . . . the President must step down . . . a disgraced man and a political outcast . . . upon insufficient proofs and from partisan considerations, the office of President would be degraded, . . . and ever after subordinated to the legislative will." Removal of the president would have revolutionized the American constitutional system, he feared.

Had Johnson been convicted and removed from office, future presidents might have served only as long as they could muster a majority in Congress. The U.S. might then have moved toward the British system, in which the prime minister must leave office on a vote of no confidence.

Scandal and weakness in the White House

A marked trend in post-Civil War politics, starting with the administration of Ulysses S. Grant (1869–1877), was greed and corruption. Grant thought that a president must approve and administer the laws passed by Congress, but nothing else. He ran his administration as he had run the army, giving great power to his "generals." Although honest himself, Grant appointed cronies to office who took advantage of his confidence.

An instance of greed was the "Salary Grab," a law passed by Congress (1873) and signed by the president which doubled his salary and gave each congressman a handsome raise.

On Black Friday (September 24, 1869) the stock market took a deep plunge as financiers Jay Gould and James Fisk, in cahoots with Grant's brother-in-law, tried to corner the market on gold. In another example of corruption Grant's personal secretary Orville E. Babcock assisted the "Whiskey Ring," a conspiracy to defraud the government by avoiding payment of millions of dollars in tax revenue. Still another example was Secretary of War William W. Belknap, accused of taking bribes in exchange for the appointment of posts to government agents who were on Indian reservations. The greatest scandal of all involved a construction company, known as Crédit Mobilier, which was set up by the managers of the Union Pacific Railroad. The company bilked the government of some $23 million, bribing key members of Congress with railroad stock to hush up the details. Such scandals on the part of congressmen and businessmen were repeated in many state and local governments. Audiences laughed knowingly when Mark Twain said, "It could probably be shown by facts and figures that there is no distinctly native American criminal class except Congress."

The disputed election of 1876 was a major turning point in postwar politics. Democrat Samuel J. Tilden won the popular vote, but corruption and fraud clouded the balloting in several states, including three southern states where federal troops were stationed. A fifteen-man commission established by Congress looked into charges of irregularity and gave the edge to Republican candidate Rutherford B. Hayes. Angry southern Democrats threatened a filibuster to prevent Hayes from being officially certified. Democratic and Republican leaders worked out an informal deal known as the "Compromise of 1877," whereby Hayes would become president if he agreed to withdraw federal troops from the South, appoint a southerner to the cabinet, and encourage the construction of a southern railroad. After his inauguration Hayes ordered the Yankee soldiers withdrawn. So ended Reconstruction along with the power of the Radical Republicans.

Politics returned to more familiar patterns. The Democratic party surged back strongly. In the South elections took place according to the old formulas. Black males were slowly disfranchised, and conservative whites took over politics. Immigrants began to play a more vital role in northern politics, which had been essentially a WASP game. The millions of immigrants pouring into the country were swiftly naturalized under lax regulations and became voters in the major cities. Democrats had always found it easy to manipulate the "great unwashed masses," and now the GOP was beginning to do so as well.

Between 1876 and 1896 Republican and Democratic presidential hopefuls ran neck-and-neck at the polls. Garfield won over Hancock by fewer than 10,000 votes out of 9 million cast in 1880. Cleveland squeaked by Blaine in 1884 by about 23,000 votes out of a total of 9.9 million. Harrison's victory over Cleveland in 1888 and Cleveland's over Harrison four years later also balanced on a few thousand votes. Four presidents—Hayes, Garfield, Cleveland (twice), and Harrison— were elected with a minority of the popular vote. In the six elections only McKinley received a majority.

Neither party had the least desire to confront the hard issues created by industrialism, such as collusion by big business, the exploitation of children and women in industry, and the rigging of freight rates by

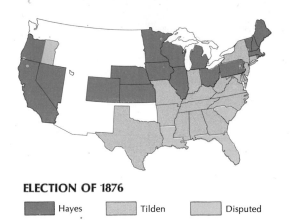

ELECTION OF 1876

■ Hayes   ▨ Tilden   ▨ Disputed

railroads. The parties' positions on such issues as tariffs, trust regulation, collective bargaining, civil service, women's suffrage, monetary reform, and overseas expansion were almost identical. But the Republicans were luckier. In thirteen elections from 1868 to 1916, only Cleveland and Wilson managed to win the White House for the Democrats. As presidential candidates studiously avoided fundamental issues, the electorate was forced to choose on the basis of character and personality. In 1884 James G. Blaine's alleged corrupt dealings and Cleveland's illegitimate child were the most heavily debated questions.

From Ulysses S. Grant to William McKinley all presidents, with the exception of Cleveland, saw themselves as figureheads who were to interfere as little as possible with Congress. After their elections they stayed out of the way of the bureaucrats and congressmen who ran the government. As a result, the Speaker of the House and the Majority Leader in the Senate had more to say about legislation than did the president. Congressional leaders had access to party funds and could give out or withhold committee assignments. Through these handy tools they were able to manipulate even the most independent senators and representatives.

The seeds of civil service reform

As the country expanded in the postwar decades, so did the bureaucracy. Armies of clerks, bookkeepers, tax collectors, internal revenue agents, inspectors, and supervisors ran the government day in, day out. These posts, as well as higher federal appointments, were looked on as the spoils of office, and they were often filled by "spoilsmen" — party bosses who gave jobs to the highest bidder. In order to keep their jobs, many federal employees had to "kick back" part of their salaries to their bosses and do precinct work for the party, whether they wanted to

Six years before the Civil Service Commission was created, President Hayes had issued an executive order to institute civil service reform measures. This cartoon shows "Sentinel Hayes" standing in the way of influence peddlers whose banner reads, "The Vultures — To the Victors Belong the Spoils."

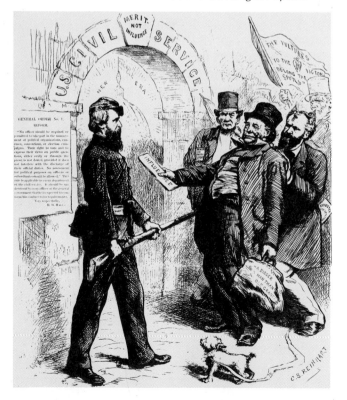

or not. Promotions often went to those who made the biggest contributions to the party treasury.

In 1881 a disappointed office seeker shot and killed President Garfield. About the same time, Republican candidates in the Northeast lost heavily, because of growing voter resentment over the spoils system. These events prompted a group of editors, lawyers, and other professionals to found the National Civil Service Reform League. Among the failings of the spoils system in their eyes was that it put incompetents in offices that now demanded skilled professionals, and that the turnover in government damaged efficiency and continuity. The League forced GOP congressional candidates, sometimes against their own leanings, to endorse civil service reform. Garfield's successor, President Chester A. Arthur, signed the Pendleton Act (1883), which set up a three-member Civil Service Commission. This reform measure outlawed federal assessments on federal employees. Applicants for office had to take competitive tests to prove a knowledge of penmanship, arithmetic, and elementary bookkeeping, plus a smattering of English, geography, history, and government. Also, federal office holders would keep their jobs on the basis of merit. As this reform applied to only about 10 percent of federal jobs, it had little effect, but gradually it was extended to an increasing number of government workers (today it applies to about 85 percent). Eventually political parties could not hold their power through the spoils system alone.

Third parties

American politics heavily favors a two-party system. The winner-take-all provision of congressional districting and the electoral college in presidential voting discourages small parties with the prospect of never winning representation in government. And yet the major parties, to attract as many voters as possible, have generally tried to shy away from basic issues or ideology. So the partisans of basic political reform or of clear-cut ideology often form third parties to make their voices heard. The first such party following the Civil War was the Liberal Republican party in 1872 which tried to defeat Grant by calling attention to the corruption in his administration. It brought together proponents of civil service, as well as of women's suffrage and tariff reduction. It nominated Horace Greeley for president. As the candidate of the Democrats as well, the maverick newspaper editor received less than 44 percent of the popular vote, giving Grant a smashing reelection victory.

Several farmer-labor parties came upon the scene prior to World War I, demanding government intervention to curb the power of the new industrial elites. Though most of their demands were rejected initially, a great many were subsequently backed by a major party and enacted into law. The National Greenback party, founded in 1876, was the first radical agrarian party. It called for currency inflation to help debt-ridden farmers and for shorter working hours and restrictions on foreign immigration to appeal to factory workers. In 1878 the Greenback Labor party won fourteen congressional seats. But two years later Greenback presidential hopeful James B. Weaver of Iowa garnered only about 300,000 votes, while the two major candidates each polled over 4.4 million. After 1884 the party was defunct.

The next important farmer-labor organization was the People's (Populist) party, founded in 1892 as a coalition of two major farm organizations, the Northern Alliance and the National Alliance, as well as Knights of Labor, Prohibitionists, and Greenbackers. Although started by farmers, it took in discontented city workers and radical intellectuals. The Populists included a small bloc of conservative western silver miners, who hoped to force the government to use more silver in coins.

The 1892 Populist platform called for lower tariffs, government ownership of railways and telegraph and telephone lines, a graduated income tax, a system of postal savings banks, and an expanded monetary and currency program to ease the plight of debtors, including free and unlimited coinage of silver. The platform also favored government loans to farmers with stored crops as security. One of the most remarkable features of Populism was the attempt by its white southern members to restore the civil rights of blacks. In fighting the Democratic establishment of the Old South, the radical white farmers teamed up with black farmers. The Populists attempted to attract labor's support by calling for an eight-hour day and immigration restrictions. Although Cleveland was reelected president in 1892, Populist candidate James B. Weaver won twenty-two electoral votes. The party also stunned political pros by electing five senators, ten representatives, and three governors.

When the 1893 depression struck, the Populists attacked Cleveland as a tool of wealthy interests. In the 1894 elections they made a much more impressive showing in the popular vote and prepared for the next presidential election with great gusto. The Populist onslaught caused the Democratic party in 1896 to drop both Cleveland and the gold standard. After William Jennings Bryan of Nebraska made his electrifying "Cross of Gold" speech in defense of free silver, the Democrats nominated him and supported silver. The Populists also gave Bryan the presidential nomination. The free silver campaign was an attempt to secure federal law to coin silver at a ratio of 16-to-1 of gold. Silver miners pushed it and some farmers saw it as a panacea to bring about inflation. But it had little relevance to a large segment of voters and it diverted attention from other, more basic, planks sought by the farmer-la-

You shall not press down upon the brow of labor this crown of thorns.
You shall not crucify mankind upon a cross of gold.

WILLIAM JENNINGS BRYAN   (1860–1925)

bor alliance. Even in 1896 the Populist leaders split over policy, and the organization began to crumble. Still, many of its planks were subsequently adopted by the major parties.

The GOP named as its presidential candidate Ohio's handsome and popular governor, William McKinley. He had the backing of the wealthy industrialist and political genius Marcus Alonzo Hanna. Since the Republicans held firm to the gold standard, high tariffs, and other conservative planks abandoned by the Democrats and Populists, the campaign issues were, for the first time in a generation, sharply drawn.

The 1896 election campaign was unprecedented for its bitterness. For the first time in living memory, wrote Kansas editor William A. White, the entire creditor class was arraigned against the entire debtor class. New York City Police Commissioner Theodore Roosevelt believed the Populists were plotting revolution and proposed lining up twelve of their leaders against the wall and "shooting them dead." Although Bryan was a pious fundamentalist and a firm believer in property rights and the homely virtues of middle-class life, he was denounced as "an apostle of atheism . . . and anarchy."

Bryan, the Democratic and Populist candidate, suffered a crushing defeat. The returns showed that his vote came almost exclusively from the plains, mountain, and southern states. These were the wheat and cotton regions, hardest hit by the depression. He ran poorly in the cities. Even the farmers of the older and better established agricultural centers of Minnesota, Wisconsin, Iowa, and Illinois turned to McKinley.

So ended one of America's most radical political movements. The Democrats ran the

"Great Commoner" Bryan in 1900 and again in 1908, with ever worsening results. In 1900 McKinley won the first presidential majority since Grant. With the exception of Wilson's two terms, the GOP would reign triumphant in the White House for the next thirty-six years (1897–1933). Moreover, from 1896 on, rural America took a political back seat behind the forces representing the urban and industrial sectors.

The Socialist party

German immigrants had established in the U.S. in the 1870s a Socialist party which never became more than a radical sect. The official founding of the Socialist party occurred in 1901 with the blessings of Eugene V. Debs, who was to become its most famous leader.

Debs believed in the American democratic process. "There is nothing in our government [the ballot] cannot remove or amend," Debs wrote. "It can make and unmake presidents and congresses and courts. . . . It can sweep over trusts, syndicates, corporations, monopolies and every other development of the money power." By 1912 the platform of American Socialists urged nationalizing the country's railroads, mines, banks, and grain elevators. They wanted workmen's compensation and a curb on labor injunctions. Like the Progressives and Populists, the Socialists supported the initiative, referendum, and recall of federal officials. Their own proposals included a one-term presidency, an end to the presidential veto, an end to judicial review by the Supreme Court, and complete abolishment of the United States Senate as an antidemocratic body. Debs himself ran for president several times. In 1912 he polled almost 900,000 votes against Wilson's 6.3 mil-

Eugene V. Debs, five times a presidential candidate for the Socialist party, makes an impassioned appeal to his audience. In accepting his party's nomination in 1908, Debs declared: "The Rockefellers have the dollars, but we have the votes; and when we have sense enough to know how to use the votes, we will have not only the votes but the dollars for all the children of men."

lion, Theodore Roosevelt's 4.1 million, and Taft's 3.5 million. In 1920, when he was still in prison for having opposed American participation in World War I, he received a slightly larger vote. Socialist policies would also influence the major party platforms in later years.

The Progressive movement under Roosevelt and Wilson

Progressivism was an urban, middle-class reform movement of the early twentieth century. The Progressives tried to stop the political corruption and social injustices of the industrial era and to curb the power of busi-

ness combinations. They never intended to destroy the social order. Their movement cut across both parties. Thus the Republican Theodore Roosevelt and the Democrat Woodrow Wilson were both Progressives in their own way. These men, one a Republican and one a Democrat, revived the dying tradition of strong presidential leadership. Both believed that the president should lead a coalition for moderate reform and act as the prime mover in Washington. Roosevelt's basic instincts were conservative; he greatly feared a rebellion and hoped to head it off by Progressivism. TR has been characterized as a "party regular with a conscience." From 1901, when he succeeded the assassinated McKinley, to 1908 he slowly steered the GOP away from "stand-pattism" and toward reform legislation like the Hepburn Act and the Pure Food and Drug Act. In 1912, after four years of retirement, he again announced for the presidency, a decision that split the Republican party and led to the formation of the Progressive or "Bull Moose" party. As standard-bearer for the new party, the charismatic Roosevelt was considerably more liberal than before.

Progressives conducted a crusade for cleaner and more responsible government. To halt greed and corruption by big business and city bosses in politics, they proposed a number of specific political reforms. They gave high priority to the Seventeenth Amendment (1913), which provided for the direct election of senators, as a means of changing the membership of the Millionaires' Club. (Under the Constitution U.S. senators were chosen by the state legislatures.) At the state level Progressives also favored the initiative (legislation introduced by the voters), referendum (popular vote on laws passed by a legislature), and recall (removal from office by popular vote). They pressed for changes in state primary laws to give voters a greater choice of candidates and to reduce the importance of nominating conventions and closed-door nominations. Since they saw no sense in city candidates identifying themselves with national parties, the reformers pressed for nonpartisan urban elections. In a few states they made "cross-filing" a possibility, so that a candidate could seek nomination in more than one party. They also advocated the secret ballot, women's suffrage, and civil service.

Such measures made some progress in cutting down the worst forms of narrow political control and bossism. At the same time, they also made it more difficult for any party to maintain discipline. A decline in voter participation and in party loyalty began in 1896 and lasted until at least 1924. Political pros found it harder and harder to predict voting behavior or to command voter loyalty.

Wilson, the leader of Congress

Although the candidate of a minority party, elected to office in 1912 because of the split in the Republican party, Democrat Woodrow Wilson enjoyed the rare advantage of having a Democratic Congress and knowing how to manipulate it. A former professor and university president, Wilson was a keen student of political science. He blasted the Washington lobbyists, conferred often with party chiefs, exploited the Democratic caucus, threatened to veto bills he disliked, mobilized the backing of influential party leaders (like Secretary of State William Jennings Bryan), and appeared in person before Congress to present his legislative program. By these efforts he reduced tariffs, instituted the Federal Reserve System to centralize banking, and pushed for new income tax legislation. Wilson urged creation of the Federal Trade Commission and pushed for the Clayton Antitrust Act. He also wanted a Farm Loan Act which enabled western and southern farmers to borrow money at low interest rates. When his Democratic majority dwindled in 1914, he wooed the Bull Moosers in Congress. Progressive legislation, including workmen's compensation, a child-labor law, and an eight-hour day for railroad workers, was passed. Like Franklin D. Roosevelt who served an apprenticeship in the Wilson administration, he was one of the most skillful presidential strategists of this century.

The war put an end to domestic reform. Progressives had cleansed government of some of its worst abuses. Social justice had penetrated to some of the darker corners of American life. But with respect to curbing the political power of big business, it is hard to argue that the Socialists, Populists, Progressives, or any other party critical of big business had been very successful.

Review

The Industrial Revolution changed America's social structure. It enlarged the size of the industrial working class proportionately, and reduced the portion of farmers. It also produced the captains of finance and industry, who became the first national, rather than regional, elite. Contrary to myth, most of them came from comfortable backgrounds. The new elite had narrow political interests. Mostly, they preferred to coach from the sidelines rather than seek office. They exerted great control over the job market and the fate of small businesses. The Supreme Court shifted the focus of the Fourteenth Amendment from blacks to big business when it declared that a corporation was a person and therefore entitled to "substantive due process." Regulating big business became a major goal of social reformers. They prevailed on Congress to police and control free enterprise through federal regulatory agencies. But the new agencies offered little threat to the corporations' power or wealth. Public anger led to the Sherman Antitrust Act, which also had little effect. Concentration of corporate ownership leveled off finally, largely as a result of the professional attitudes of the corporate managers who succeeded the captains of industry. Public intolerance of big business increased.

Congress was the major power center in the federal government after the Civil War. At first it was controlled by Radical Republicans. In their attempts to humble the old southern planter elite, they clashed with the moderate President Johnson. They instituted impeachment proceedings but failed to convict him by a single vote. After the election of 1876 Reconstruction ended, and politics reverted to older patterns. The federal bureaucracy expanded. Charges of corruption in the "spoils system" led to the founding of the civil service system.

Third parties often raised issues the two major parties chose to ignore. The Populist party grew rapidly, only to collapse after the 1896 election. Before World War I, however, the Socialists were a viable political party. Both Theodore Roosevelt, a Republican, and Woodrow Wilson, a Democrat, were strong presidents who responded to the reformist demands of the Progressive movement. The specific reforms enacted by Progressives to get more responsible leadership at the state and local level served to decrease party loyalty and discipline. Voter participation continued to decline.

Questions

1. What were the political interests of the new corporate elite? How did they achieve their goals in the Gilded Age?
2. Describe the following presidents' attitudes toward big business and government: (a) Grover Cleveland, (b) Theodore Roosevelt, and (c) Woodrow Wilson.
3. How effective was trust busting, beginning with the Sherman Act?
4. Describe the way the Republican party maintained its power after the Civil War. Do you think the country would have been better or worse off if the Senate had found President Johnson guilty? Why?
5. Why were the elections of 1876 and 1896 the most important political battles of the post-Civil War era? What parties and issues were involved, and what effects did the election results have in each case?
6. Discuss the role of third parties in American politics from Reconstruction to World War I. What did they want, and what did they accomplish?

war

Trench warfare, World War I.

The world must be made safe for democracy. Its peace must be planted upon the tested foundations of political liberty.

WOODROW WILSON   (1856–1924)
War Message, April 2, 1917

19

19
World Power and World Conflict

Just before the turn of the twentieth century the United States achieved the status of a world power. Between the time of the war with Spain in 1898 and the world war in 1917–1918 the nation achieved a hemispheric and global reach. Those wars, and the intervening events in international affairs, shaped the course of American history down to the present.

The rise of America as a world power is easy enough to describe. The *how* and the *why* are harder to establish. Some claim that America entered the charmed circle in a fit of absentmindedness, picking up the pieces of empire that Spain hastily left behind. Others argue that expansion was deliberate and inevitable. One school stresses ideology; another, economic causes. In any case, this country's debut on the international stage can be studied in four phases. From 1865 to 1898 were years of preparation. From 1898 to 1900 the Spanish-American War and its aftermath took place. From 1901 to 1912 the policies of Theodore Roosevelt and the balance of power dominated the scene. Finally, from 1913 to 1918 Woodrow Wilson stood as a beacon of international morality.

The first section of this chapter centers on the growth of global interests in the United States, the Spanish-American War, and what was probably the most crucial event of the twentieth century, the First World War. The second section of the chapter discusses changes on the domestic scene resulting from the U.S. effort in World War I.

The Global Reach

Growing pressure for overseas expansion

A tradition has it that the United States embarked on a course of empire more or less accidentally in 1898. There is some truth in this, since the consequences of going to war with Spain that year were not thoroughly considered until later. Britain and Germany plunged into Asia and Africa in search of markets for surplus capital and manufactured goods and sources of raw materials. Such pressures were minor in this country. The U.S. still enjoyed abundant natural resources, and expanding national markets. President Grant in 1869 developed an obsession to seize the Dominican Republic for its naval base. To Congress this had the earmarks of grubby materialism and the effort was resoundingly defeated by Congress despite the president's intense lobbying. Secretary of State James G. Blaine's attempt to intervene in Latin American affairs during President Garfield's administration (1889–1893) was similarly turned down. As late as Harrison's administration, imperialism was looked on as a form of greed that appealed only to a small segment of society.

Nevertheless it is well to remember that since the days of Jefferson and John Quincy Adams America had been an expanding nation. Even in the quiet period between 1865 and 1898, the United States gained significant pieces of overseas territory. Alaska, considered by Secretary of State Seward as a bridge between the New World and Asia, was purchased from Russia in 1867. The Midway Islands were acquired in the same year. In 1887 the United States established a naval base at Pearl Harbor by signing a treaty with Hawaii. At about the same time, resident Americans and naval officers were beginning a long campaign to win total control of the Hawaiian Islands. Samoa became the protectorate of the United States, Great Britain, and Germany by an agreement made in 1889. Ten years later the islands were divided between Germany and the U.S.

The nation underwent a revival of imperialist fervor in the 1890s such as had not been seen since the clamor for Manifest Destiny in the 1840s. The pressure for trade expansion, if not for territorial gain, came from a variety of quarters. Factory owners and workers alike were alarmed by the depression of 1893, which seemed to threaten political and social upheaval as well as economic collapse. The demands of unemployed workers for jobs, mingled with other social protests, frightened the middle class. New overseas markets could not only guarantee the profits of business people but could also quiet discontent and assure social stability at home. Nor was industry alone in feeling an economic squeeze. American farmers, afraid of growing surpluses and falling prices, looked anxiously overseas for new markets. Army and navy commanders hoped to try out their new weapons and strategies, and Social Darwinists hoped to apply the doctrine of survival of the fittest to a contest among nations. In addition, the Reverend Josiah Strong urged the country to conquer the "barbarians" of the world and instill in them the love of liberty and Christ. Missionaries dreamed of millions of heathen Chinese and Africans flocking to Christ, and called for the Stars and Stripes to lead the way for the Cross. Some intellectuals believed that a war could be an ennobling experience, restoring a sense of patriotism, valor, and honor. It could be a moral tonic for a nation that was becoming too materialistic, they felt.

The official government announcement of the closing of the western frontier in 1890 teased the nation's appetite for overseas possessions. "Up to and including 1880 the country had a frontier of settlement," the Census Bureau reported, "but at present the unsettled area has been so broken into isolated bodies of settlement that there can hardly be said to be a frontier line." Since Americans had long defined freedom in terms of the frontier, this announcement came as a severe psychological jolt.

The search for new worlds to conquer was aided by naval expansion. Admiral S. B. Luce of the Naval Academy deplored the "cankers of a calm world and long peace." The Naval Appropriations Act of 1883 started the ball rolling. The notion of a strong navy owed much to Admiral Alfred T. Mahan, president of the Newport War College. The author of *The Influence of Sea Power upon History* (1890), Mahan urged that the U.S. have a navy that could go on the offensive. The key to industrial expansion as well as to domestic security, he felt, was a distant line of "defense." This meant a flotilla of steel-clad, steam-powered battleships capable of escorting American merchant ships in all waters of the globe. To be fully effective such a fleet would need coaling stations and repair docks

Commerce follows the flag. The great nations are rapidly absorbing for their future expansion and their present defense all the waste places of the earth. . . . The United States must not fall out of the line of march.

HENRY CABOT LODGE   (1850–1924)
Public official, author

in the Caribbean and on far-flung Pacific islands, as well as a canal across Central America to let the ships pass from one ocean to the other. The government must also subsidize the merchant marine, a vital element to America's prosperity.

That Mahan could sell such ideas to a nation at peace is testimony to his brilliance. Kaiser Wilhelm II said he "devoured" Mahan's book, and both Queen Victoria and members of the imperial Japanese court were Mahan enthusiasts. Theodore Roosevelt, soon to become Assistant Secretary of the Navy, studied Mahan avidly, as did members of Congress.

President Cleveland, though a foe of territorial imperialism, nevertheless agreed to naval expansion. With widespread unemployment in 1893, union spokesmen and industrialists urged him to continue an ongoing naval armament program to prevent additional layoffs in the steel industry. A year later he authorized new naval armament contracts. "If no new contracts were given out," he explained, "contractors must disband their workmen and their plants must lie idle." By the time of the Spanish-American War, the U.S. Navy ranked fifth in the world. In 1907 President Roosevelt sent the "Great White Fleet" on a world cruise to display America's naval might. The American navy was second only to Britain's.

In 1893 American sugar growers in Hawaii engineered a plot to overthrow native rule and annex Hawaii to the United States. The United States tariff of 1890, which favored homegrown sugar, had threatened Hawaiian sugar growers with ruin. That year a native queen, a strong nationalist, tried to dump the white-dominated Hawaiian legislature and restore native rule. U.S. sugar growers staged a rebellion forcing her to abdicate. President Harrison sent American marines to Hawaii and the U.S. minister there recognized the American revolutionary regime. But the newly elected President Cleveland firmly opposed the take-over in Hawaii and rejected a Senate treaty of annexation.

In the midst of the Spanish-American War, the Senate reconsidered annexing Hawaii. Popular sentiment had changed dramatically since Cleveland had vetoed the annexation treaty five years earlier. In July 1898 Hawaii became a U.S. territory.

While it is true that many Americans assumed they had moral and cultural superiority over other peoples and a civilizing mission to perform, it was assumed nonetheless that America's mission would be executed mainly through the expansion of trade rather than the acquisition of territory. The country's trade horizons, it was felt, would be enlarged by mostly peaceful means, not by war. The main prizes of commerce and diplomacy were to be China and Latin America.

The Spanish-American War and the Filipino uprising

By the start of McKinley's term in 1897 opinions about foreign affairs had changed drastically from what they had been ten to thirty years earlier. Manifest Destiny and the pressures for overseas expansion were much greater. In 1895 Cubans had revolted against Spanish rule and asked for American help. Spanish soldiers herded large numbers of civilians into concentration camps, and the New York newspapers carried screaming headlines announcing their atrocities. Such reports evoked great sympathy for the Cubans. Also, American sugar planters in Cuba felt particularly distressed by the rebellion, since they suffered a loss of investments because of recurrent fighting. President McKinley explained to the Spanish foreign minister that the disturbances there affected all Americans. In the United States the popular slogan of the election campaign, "Free Silver!" was replaced by "Free Cuba!"

The Cuban crisis coincided with disturbing news from the other side of the globe. In 1894 several European nations had invaded China, carving out spheres of influence and dividing up China's railroads, mines and ports among themselves. This particularly angered American traders, who reversed their previous position against military intervention in the Far East. Assistant Secretary of the Navy Theodore Roosevelt pinpointed the Philippines, a Spanish possession and a gateway to China, as the ideal place for an American power play in 1898.

The "yellow press" fueled a growing war fever when in early February 1898 William Randolph Hearst's New York *Journal*, eager to beat out Joseph Pulitzer's *World* with lurid information about Spanish Cuba, printed an indiscreet letter by the Spanish minister to the United States that characterized President McKinley as a weak politician and a demagogue. Days later, on February 15, the U.S. battleship *Maine* blew up mysteriously in Havana Harbor, killing 260 American seamen. The slogan now was: "*Remember the Maine!* To hell with Spain." Roosevelt ordered Commodore George Dewey to prepare to attack the Spanish Philippines in case of war.

In April, reluctantly giving in to powerful pressure, President McKinley asked Congress for the power to use armed forces to end the fighting in Cuba and to establish the island's independence. The leading anti-imperialist in the Senate, Henry M. Teller of Colorado, agreed to vote for the declaration with the proviso that the U.S. disclaim any intention of annexing Cuba. So the Senate adopted a formal war declaration on April 25, whose purpose was to boot Spain out of Cuba. As has frequently happened in American history, congressional debate on the war declaration was less than thorough and not entirely grounded on facts. Actually Spain had agreed to suspend fighting on the island and abide by an armistice when McKinley asked for power to intervene.

The Spanish-American War lasted one hundred days, of which only one, July 1, 1898, was a day of pitched fighting. On that occasion Teddy Roosevelt and the Rough Riders stormed San Juan Hill, though far

GUANTANAMO BAY
1903
(*Leased from Cuba*)

PUERTO RICO
1898

VIRGIN IS.
1917

Caribbean Sea

Gulf of Mexico

UNITED STATES

CORN IS.
1916
(*Leased from Nicaragua*)

CANAL ZONE
1904
(*Leased from Panama*)

ALASKA
1867
(Admitted as a
state 1959)

Bering Sea

HAWAII
1898
(Admitted as a
state 1959)

MIDWAY IS.
1867

JOHNSTON IS.
1858

JARVIS IS. *1857*

HOWLAND IS.
1857

BAKER IS.
1857

AMERICAN SAMOA
SWAIN'S IS. *1925*
PAGO PAGO *1872*
TUTUILA *1899*

WAKE IS.
1899

MARSHALL
IS.

U.S. MILITARY
OCCUPATION
1945

BONIN IS.

MARCUS IS.

VOLCANO
IS.

MARIANA IS.

TERRITORY
OF THE
PACIFIC ISLANDS
CAROLINE IS.
1947
'U.S. trust territory)

RYUKYU
IS.

GUAM

PHILIPPINE IS.
1898
(Granted
independence
1946)

**THE CONTINENTAL UNITED STATES AND PRINCIPAL
OVERSEAS STATES AND TERRITORIES**

Dates of acquisition appear below place names

heavier fighting was encountered at El Caney and Siboney on the same day. Two days later U.S. warships destroyed a Spanish fleet as it sailed from Cuba, killing over 400 seamen. Two months earlier, on May 1, Dewey had destroyed a second Spanish fleet in Manila Bay and seized the Philippines without the loss of a single American. Only 379 Americans were killed in battle during the Spanish-American War, but about 5500 died of disease.

The war was immortalized by Secretary of State John Hay: "It has been a splendid little war; begun with the highest motives, carried on with magnificent intelligence and spirit, favored by that fortune which loves the brave." Under the Treaty of Paris, Spain gave the United States the Philippines (for $20 million), Puerto Rico, and Guam and relinquished all title to Cuba. Senate antiimperialists came close to blocking annexation of the Philippines.

Heated debates over the Treaty of Paris took place during the presidential campaign in 1900. Antiimperialists argued that taking control of territory whose people could not be granted complete equality within the Republic represented a completely new policy for the U.S. Empire would lead to militarism, they warned, and would necessitate a standing army, which also violated American tradition. Furthermore, the repression of liberty and the brutality usually involved in imperial rule would dishonor America. On a practical level, the new empire would cost more to administer than it would yield in resources or markets. A big navy would be very expensive to maintain, and new battleships would become obsolete before they were launched. And empire building in the Far East would certainly provoke wars with Japan and Russia. Also the antiimperialists charged that it was cowardly for the United States to pick on a small and weak nation. Finally they noted that the Filipinos were of the "wrong" (nonwhite) race, and there-

fore could not be fully assimilated into the American mainstream.

The imperialist argument was generally stated in terms of the "white man's burden" and the civilizing mission of America. McKinley hoped to "educate the Filipinos, and uplift and civilize and Christianize them." He explained that he had received divine guidance to the effect that it "would be cowardly and dishonorable" to let them fall into the hands of France or Germany but that they were "unfit" for self-government. He was merely reflecting a widespread sentiment in favor of holding on to the Philippines. The islands seemed quite useful as a base for trade with Asia and as a field for missionary and humanitarian efforts. The Senate ratified a treaty with Spain in February of 1899.

The war against Spain was no sooner over than the U.S. Army became involved in a new and bloodier fight—the Philippine insurrection. The Filipino patriots, who had been fighting to overthrow Spanish rule in 1898, now turned against their new masters, the Americans. For three years, from 1899 to 1902, as many as 100,000 American soldiers fought guerrillas in nearly 3000 separate battles in the jungles of Mindanao and Luzon. It resembled the worst border wars of the West against American Indians. American soldiers tortured rebel captives to extract information, forced civilians into "reconcentration camps" of the type used by the Spaniards in Cuba, and occasionally killed women and children while attacking guerrilla fighters. The U.S. government "managed" the news from the Philippines in an effort to keep from the public the extent of the violence.

The Filipino uprising triggered angry public debate. William Vaughn Moody penned an acid poem, "To a Soldier Dead in the Philippines," complaining of the injustice of suppressing a people struggling for freedom. Mark Twain wrote and lectured actively against American overseas adventure. The Filipino insurrection was finally crushed in

A group of Filipinos taken prisoner in the Philippine insurrection. Filipino patriots who were fighting against Spanish rule at first supported Admiral Dewey and the Americans, believing that the U.S. would grant independence to the islands. But President McKinley, siding with American expansionists, decided otherwise: "I sent for the chief engineer of the War Department (our map-maker), and I told him to put the Philippines on the map of the United States. . . ." The Filipinos tried to overthrow their new rulers in a bloody rebellion that lasted three years.

1902. The U.S. Army suffered 7000 men killed and wounded. Over 16,000 Filipinos were killed in battle, and 100,000 more died of famine and disease. The dollar cost to the U.S. was around $800 million. The fighting was followed by a long and costly colonial administration. This experience helped sour America's taste for territorial conquest: American statesmen now sought less costly alternatives.

The Open Door in China

By 1898 Britain, Japan, France, Russia, and Germany had secured spheres of influence with special trading privileges and immunity from Chinese law within their spheres. This infuriated Chinese nationalists. It also irritated Secretary of State John Hay who wanted an entrance into China for trade, but without military force. In 1899 Hay discovered a new way to skin the cat. He notified Britain, Japan, France, Russia, and Germany

that the United States was requesting that all nationals be recognized equally in all spheres of influence in China. They responded indifferently. But Hay announced to the world their acceptance of America's "Open Door" policy. In 1900 a weak and divided China was wracked by the Boxer Rebellion, a nationalist uprising against foreign influence. U.S. forces invaded China as part of a joint international army dispatched by western powers to help liberate foreign legations and Christian missions that had been placed under siege by Chinese nationalists. In a second series of messages Hay added that the United States would protect China against a complete take-over by any foreign power.

The Open Door notes did not claim an actual American sphere of influence on mainland Asia, but they did put a foot in the door to preserve future American interests there. While they hinted vaguely at protecting China through forcible means, no actual guarantee of military protection was intended. In such a case the U.S. would have had to risk military defeat in a land war in Asia, against which the best military minds had already issued strict warning. Yet the notes cost nothing. Without the disadvantages of annexation, invasion, long-term occupation, or administration, they had enlarged the perimeter of American commercial interest.

America tried to press its advantage in China, but without too much success. In 1904 the "Open Door imperialism" of the U.S. was threatened by the Russo-Japanese War. Fearing that a complete victory by either side in the war could lead to a take-over in China, Theodore Roosevelt mediated a settlement at the Portsmouth Peace Conference. Nevertheless, in the coming years Japan gained control over the Manchurian trade and Korea. The fabulous China trade of which American merchants had long dreamed, continued to elude the nation's grasp. Financiers, business people, and diplomats disagreed on further initiatives in Asia. By 1917 the U.S. had pretty well lost influence in China.

Theodore Roosevelt and the balance of power

The country fully expected Theodore Roosevelt to steer the United States to new territorial conquests. But the public misunderstood his concept of world power, which involved military activism but not conquest. He was the first American president with global vision. Those who favor power politics and who consider themselves realists in foreign affairs still revere his memory. TR saw the globe as divided into spheres of influence among the major powers—Germany, Britain, Russia, Japan, France, and the United States. He believed that great nations must respect each other's spheres and that minor powers must realistically recognize the distribution of power in the world. TR, in other words, ac-

If a nation shows that it knows how to act with reasonable efficiency and decency in social and political matters, if it keeps order and pays its obligations, it need fear no interference from the United States. Chronic wrongdoing, or an impotence which results in a general loosening of the ties of civilized society . . . may force the United States . . . to the exercise of an international police power.

THEODORE ROOSEVELT (1858–1919)

cepted the reality of power politics (in German, *Realpolitik*). The United States would help keep peace by maintaining an international balance of power. Where one power or group of powers was becoming too strong, the United States would support the opposing nation or alliance of nations. In danger zones like Africa, where new colonies and spheres were in the process of being carved out, the big powers must compromise. For arbitrating the Russo-Japanese War in 1905 Theodore Roosevelt won a Nobel Peace Prize.

In TR's eyes the U.S. had a legitimate sphere of influence in Latin America. In the nineteenth century this had been Britain's sphere, but now, whether the British liked it or not, Cuba, Haiti, the Dominican Republic, Nicaragua, and even Mexico, were dependencies of the U.S. Throughout the Caribbean, "the American lake," the strategic and economic needs of the United States were to prevail.

TR spelled out his Latin American policy during the Venezuelan crisis of 1902. When Venezuela defaulted on its debts to Britain and Germany, those two powers sent warships steaming into the Caribbean, where they blockaded and shelled Venezuelan ports. TR sympathized with the foreign financiers for wanting their money but disagreed with the display of naval power in the Western Hemisphere. He countered by sending part of the Great White Fleet into the area, which forced out the European warships. At the same time, he made Venezuela

Shortly after Panama won its independence from Colombia in 1903, it authorized the U.S. to build a fifty-mile canal through Panama. President Roosevelt publicly defended the United States' role in the Panamanian revolution: "Our course was straightforward and in absolute accord with the highest standards of international morality." Privately he confessed, "I took the canal zone and let Congress debate, and while the debate goes on the canal also does."

arbitrate the problem before an international tribunal. In 1904 Roosevelt announced that the Monroe Doctrine, as interpreted by him, gave the U.S. the right to police Latin American nations that engaged in "chronic wrongdoing." Then he added his memorable advice that the U.S. must "speak softly but carry a big stick." This was soon called the Roosevelt Corollary to the Monroe Doctrine. Whereas the original Monroe Doctrine opposed the intervention by Europeans in Latin America, the Roosevelt Corollary supported the notion of intervention by the U.S. in Latin America. Earlier, the Dominican Republic had also defaulted on debts to European creditors, and in 1905 the United States took over all Dominican customs houses. Having rejected European intervention in the hemisphere, the United States took responsibility for seeing that hemispheric countries paid their debts.

The Roosevelt Corollary meant wielding military power in Latin America without permanent conquest or annexation of territory. From this time forward the United States landed troops more or less at will in the Caribbean — in Cuba, Colombia, Venezuela, the Dominican Republic, Haiti, Nicaragua, Guatemala, and Mexico. In 1903 TR plunged directly into the internal affairs of Colombia to manage the outcome of a rebellion in Panama, then a Colombian province. He ordered a navy cruiser to prevent Colombia from putting down the Panama rebels. The gunboat diplomacy succeeded, and the U.S. was quickly granted permission to build a canal through the new republic. The Panama Canal would not only help U.S. commerce but it would also allow the Great White Fleet to deploy rapidly on two oceans.

After several years of military government, American forces were withdrawn from Cuba, and in 1902 the island officially became self-governing. The United States retained naval bases, however, and had the right to intervene to protect Cuba from external danger or internal disorder. Under the provisions of the Platt Amendment, United States troops landed on the island in 1906 and ran a provisional government for three years.

While President Taft lacked TR's sophisticated global vision, he vigorously pushed American interests in Latin America. With a candid and unshakable belief in capitalism and the civilizing mission of the United States, he tried to integrate the economies of the Caribbean republics into the economy of the United States. Taft encouraged replacing European capital with American capital and sent in troops to intervene at the least sign of "instability" to American investments. He mixed in the internal affairs of Latin American nations as energetically as Roosevelt had. Troops were sent to Nicaragua in 1910 and 1912 and into Cuba that same year. Called "Dollar Diplomacy," Taft's Latin American policy did little to improve the image of the "Yankee Colossus" among Latin Americans.

Latin American nationalists and anti-imperialists in the United States charged that the dependent countries created by such policies generally developed one-crop economies, producing a raw material needed by U.S. industry; that class distinctions sharpened; that native culture eroded; and that the self-determination so eloquently celebrated in the Declaration of Independence was trampled under foot. That the birthplace of colonial liberation had embraced political and economic imperialism was considered a supreme irony south of the border.

Yet Yanks who returned from Cuba, Puerto Rico, and the Philippines proudly called attention to positive achievements—to hospitals and sanitation systems, to control of yellow fever and other tropical diseases, to schools, industrial plants, roads, and harbor installations. The United States, they said, must get credit for building railroads, opening new plantations and mines, tapping hidden resources, and bringing law and order to

backward provinces formerly under the thumb of "bandits."

Woodrow Wilson and the First World War

Woodrow Wilson shared with Taft, Roosevelt, and McKinley a belief in Anglo-Saxon superiority and America's civilizing mission. And yet in theory at least, Wilson held different views about American foreign policy. The balance of power and power politics made little sense to him, and he rejected Dollar Diplomacy as naked aggression. In his view all nations should try to settle their disagreements by arbitration. Foreign trade could be arranged by mutual agreement, not by force. "Cooling-off" periods and disarmament should be used to prevent war. Ultimately he hoped to create an international peace-keeping agency, a league of nations, to solve serious world problems. Thus, if Theodore Roosevelt was the great realist in foreign affairs, Wilson was the idealist.

The first test of Wilson's beliefs came in Mexico, where in 1912 a counterrevolution overthrew the reformer Madero and replaced him with General Victoriano Huerta. Wilson refused to recognize the take-over, and in 1914, on a very slight pretext, he sent the fleet to occupy Veracruz. They withdrew only when Huerta abdicated. In 1916 Wilson again intervened in Mexico by sending General John J. Pershing and six thousand volunteers south of the border in hot pursuit of guerrilla leader Francisco (Pancho) Villa, who was thought to have raided Columbus, New Mexico, and killed nineteen Americans. This force stayed in Mexico until 1917 and accomplished nothing. Wilson finally recognized a regime that he mistrusted, thereby admitting that his efforts to impose a political solution had failed. In some respects he had merely repeated the policies of his predecessors. Yet this was the first instance in which the United

I can't keep the country out of war. They talk of me as though I were a god. Any little German lieutenant can put us into the war at any time by some calculated outrage.

WOODROW WILSON (1856–1924)

States intervened against a revolution in an underdeveloped country.

The First World War, or the Great War, as contemporaries called it, put Wilson's moral diplomacy to its most difficult test. Like the rest of the country, he found it hard to believe that all of Europe would be engulfed in a war over the assassination of an Austrian archduke by a Serbian nationalist. He hoped to remain neutral and mediate the struggle; instead the country was drawn into a state of belligerency.

During the "Century of Peace" general wars had been avoided through a balance of power involving nearly equal alliances. In 1914 the major alliances were the Triple Entente linking Britain, France, and Russia, and the Triple Alliance joining Germany, the Austro-Hungarian Empire, and Italy. These two camps managed to settle their differences peaceably until June 28, 1914, when a Serbian nationalist assassinated Archduke Ferdinand, heir to the Austrian throne. A pistol shot demonstrated how unstable the balance of power was. An international holocaust resulted from which the world has never fully recovered. It is not exaggerating to say that the unsolved problems of World War I led to another world war and are related to the unceasing international friction since 1945.

When the war began, Wilson announced America's neutrality and stated that the war was one "which cannot touch us." He offered to mediate between the great powers. (Italy had remained neutral, leaving Germany and Austria-Hungary as the Central Powers versus the Allies.) Since both sides were confident of victory, they rebuffed his offer. As late as January 1917 Wilson called for "peace without victory," and the U.S. remained technically neutral. Yet the United States found it difficult to stay neutral, for freedom of the seas was at stake. So America entered the war in April 1917. Whether intervention could have been or should have been avoided has been debated ever since.

When the British declared a blockade of Germany, the Royal Navy searched U.S. merchant ships, allowed them to travel only in certain sea lanes, denied them access to specified ports on the continent, and seized cargoes it considered helpful to the enemy. It was nearly as meddlesome as it had been during the War of 1812 and acted in direct violation of international law, a matter of importance to Wilson. He protested and threatened to retaliate.

When the British blockade began strangling Germany's lifeline, the Kaiser's high command in 1914 resorted to a new weapon—the submarine. These U-boats often struck without firing the customary warning shot across the bow and then disappeared without picking up survivors. This made them appear particularly barbaric. Nevertheless, Germany faced starvation unless it broke the blockade. In May 1915 a U-boat torpedoed the British liner *Lusitania* off the coast of Ireland killing 1200 passengers and crew, including 128 Americans. Anti-German sentiment in the U.S. soared. Wilson warned Germany that the U.S. would hold it to strict accountability unless the attacks on passengers ended. For fifteen months the Germans complied, hoping to prevent American involvement. In February 1917, when U.S. involvement seemed unavoidable, the

410 An Industrial Nation: 1865–1918

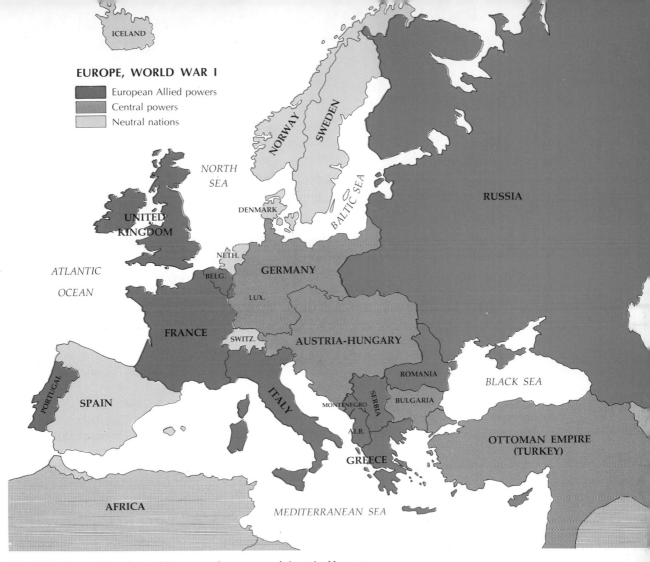

ICELAND

EUROPE, WORLD WAR I

- European Allied powers
- Central powers
- Neutral nations

NORWAY
SWEDEN
NORTH SEA
DENMARK
BALTIC SEA
RUSSIA
UNITED KINGDOM
ATLANTIC OCEAN
NETH.
BELG.
GERMANY
LUX.
FRANCE
SWITZ.
AUSTRIA-HUNGARY
ROMANIA
BLACK SEA
PORTUGAL
SPAIN
ITALY
MONTENEGRO
SERBIA
BULGARIA
ALB.
OTTOMAN EMPIRE (TURKEY)
GREECE
AFRICA
MEDITERRANEAN SEA

World War I pitted the Central Powers—Germany and Austria-Hungary—against Britain, France, and Italy. Later Bulgaria and Turkey joined the Central Powers, while Italy (originally an ally of Germany and Austria-Hungary) entered the war on the side of the Allies in 1915.

Kaiser resumed the unrestricted use of submarines. U-boats torpedoed six American merchant ships in February and March.

Both major powers violated Wilson's concept of freedom of the seas and both were verbally blasted by him. But Germany appeared more threatening. Allied propaganda depicted the Kaiser's soldiers as despoiling the liberty of independent nations. Their invasion of Belgium was portrayed by British propagandists as the "rape of Belgium."

Despite America's neutrality, American bankers had a vested interest in an Allied victory to the tune of $2.3 billion in loans for the purchase of war goods. The Wilson administration encouraged the loans and the manufacture of weapons. This would later support the argument that "the merchants of death" had pushed the country into war. The loans and sales to the Allies were so great that they reversed the traditional flow of capital from Europe to America and made the

We are going into war upon the command of gold. We . . . run the risk of sacrificing millions of our countrymen's lives in order that other countrymen may coin their lifeblood into money.

GEORGE W. NORRIS   (1861–1944)
Lawyer and legislator

U.S. the world's leading creditor nation. They also gave a tremendous boost to the economy.

This country's ties to Britain and France predisposed it in favor of the Allies. Wilson himself revered British culture. His attorney general quoted him as saying in a quiet but determined way that the ordinary rules of conduct about neutral rights must be disregarded, for "the Allies were standing with their backs to the wall, fighting wild beasts." Great Britain, he believed, was fighting for the very survival of civilization. Many Americans shared this belief.

Germany's resumption of submarine warfare in the spring of 1917 was the major argument for America's war declaration, but two other events drew the country closer to fighting. Germany's Foreign Secretary Zimmermann secretly suggested to Mexico that if it joined the Central Powers it could look forward to reclaiming Texas, New Mexico, and Arizona from the United States. When the message was intercepted by British intelligence and its contents divulged, the American public was outraged. Also, Russia's czarist regime collapsed and a short-lived liberal democratic government took power. At this point most of the Allied nations had governments that were more or less democratic, whereas those of the Central Powers (now including Turkey and Bulgaria) remained autocratic. For the time being it was easier to speak of the democratic objectives of the war.

On April 2, 1917, Wilson delivered a war message asking Congress to help make the world "safe for democracy." After a brief, bitter debate Congress declared war on April 6. Most Americans were deeply convinced, as Wilson was, that the country was going to war for a highly moral cause.

In the fall of 1917 the Russian Bolsheviks, led by Nikolai Lenin, seized control of the government of Russia. They made peace with Germany and brought home the Russian troops. In the spring of 1918, with the Russians out of the picture and the American Expeditionary Force (AEF) not yet ready to fight in France, the Germans tried to encircle Paris. By May they had advanced as far as Château-Thierry, less than 40 miles from the French capital. They were stopped there by an Allied force that included the first American combat troops. The AEF, soon to number 4.4 million Yanks in all, was led by General John J. ("Black Jack") Pershing, a veteran of fighting in Cuba, the Philippines, and Mexico. The AEF would make a small but important contribution to the fighting.

In July and August an Allied counteroffensive that included 270,000 Americans turned the tide in the Second Battle of the Marne. In September an American army of 500,000 repelled the German troops at Saint-Mihiel. The enormous and decisive Allied offensive in the region between the Meuse River and the Argonne Forest in September and October involved 1.2 million troops. The Yanks alone suffered many of the 120,000 casualties.

Wilson described the war as a utopian struggle, a "war to end all wars." In a moving speech to Congress in January 1918, he presented his Fourteen Points. He called for "open covenants of peace, openly arrived at," a reference to his distaste for secret diplomacy. Other goals included freedom of the seas, the removal of all possible economic barriers between nations, and a reduction of armaments. Wilson suggested giving more rights to colonial peoples and creating independent nations for the long-oppressed

American troops in France, on their way to the front, 1918. General Pershing, leader of the AEF, refused to allow American soldiers to serve as reinforcements in French and English fighting units. He insisted that the U.S. forces "are a distinct and separate component of the combined forces, the identity of which must be preserved."

minorities of central and eastern Europe. His Fourteenth Point proposed a "general association of nations" for peace-keeping purposes. This idea would give rise to the League of Nations. Some of these points were included in the Versailles Treaty of 1919, although others were altered or eliminated, and the U.S. Senate refused to sign that treaty.

In November the Kaiser was overthrown and the German Republic established. On November 11 the new German leaders ac-

cepted Wilson's Fourteen Points as the basis for an armistice. More than 1.8 million Germans had been killed. France counted 1.3 million dead, Britain 947,000, and Russia 1.7 million. Losses for the U.S. were comparatively small: 112,500 killed in action and through disease, and 237,000 wounded. Altogether the Great War caused 35 million casualties. As the former enemies assembled in the great hall at Versailles to sign a peace treaty, the world wondered what kind of settlement could justify such a catastrophe.

A Managed Society at Home

Except for the Civil War, the First World War affected the life of civilians and increased the power of the national government more completely than any other conflict in which the U.S. had been involved. (By contrast, the war with Spain in 1898 caused few changes in civilian life.) The government took extreme measures to repress dissidence and insure loyalty, to recruit soldiers and mobilize production.

Opposition to the war

A large and respectable peace movement had administration backing until 1917. While at first Wilson applauded the opponents of intervention, after the war declaration his administration became increasingly preoccupied with putting down all types of dissidents. Until he resigned in 1915, William Jennings Bryan was the only pacifist ever to serve as a secretary of state. The war's opponents, real or potential, were of varied background. The American Peace Society had many members, fat revenues, and influential backers, including Henry Ford and Andrew Carnegie—despite Carnegie's having made a fortune selling armored plate to the navy. Many pacifists were politically conservative, but a few were radicals. The Socialists denounced the war as a capitalist perversion. Millions of immigrants from Germany and the Austro-Hungarian Empire, as well as descendants of such immigrants, were reluctant to have their sons fighting kinsmen. Irish Americans supported Ireland's rebellion against Britain and opposed any alliance with England. American Poles and Jews opposed participation in any alliance that included Russia. Scandinavians retained strong pacifist tendencies. Antiwar groups were at the height of their power in November 1916 when Wilson was reelected on the slogan, "He Kept Us Out of War!" and Americans were singing, "I Didn't Raise My Boy to Be a Soldier."

When Wilson asked Congress to declare war in April 1917, fifty congressmen and six senators voted against the declaration. The administration feared that antiwar socialists, labor radicals, pacifists, and ethnic minorities would disrupt industry and the draft. Resistance to the war effort was looked on as a dangerous threat to its success. Patriotic zeal had to be guaranteed.

The government's loyalty campaign

With a zeal that turned out to be excessive the government set about to insure loyalty. The "battle for the American mind" was directed by a new government agency, the Committee on Public Information (CPI). Its head was George Creel, an able journalist, who supervised the biggest advertising campaign the nation had yet seen. He worked through the national news services (United Press and Associated Press) which agreed to a government request for self-censorship of news. All ages and classes of citizens—adults, children, professors, laborers, and aliens—were bombarded by filmed, printed, spoken, even sung messages that were intended to make them not only comprehend but *feel* the beastliness of the Hun, the justice of the Allies' cause, and the necessity for sacrifice on the part of loyal Americans. The Pledge of Allegiance was for the first time used commonly on public occasions. Associated with bravery and personal sacrifice on the field of battle, this patriotic observance became a permanent addition to

American mass culture.

Wilson shelved his pacifism for the duration and endorsed the mind-bending loyalty campaign. The 1917 Espionage Act provided penalties of up to twenty years in jail for those who disclosed information to the enemy, abused the flag or military uniforms, advocated treason, or interfered with the draft. The Sabotage and Sedition Acts of 1918 were intimidating. Eugene V. Debs was arrested, tried, and imprisoned for a speech to a Socialist party convention that included these words: "I am opposed to every war but one; I am for that war with heart and soul, and that is the world-wide war of social revolutions. In that war I am prepared to fight in any way the ruling class may make it necessary, even on the barricades." The legislative program of the Progressives stopped short in its tracks, although their optimism and crusading spirit carried over into the war mobilization.

The government actively prosecuted approximately fifteen hundred Socialists and pacifists, and vigilantes pursued the cause out of court. The Justice Department moved against the IWW with a series of prosecutions and jailings. Some Wobblies were beaten and lynched. Leftist publications were denied mail privileges. The entire organized peace movement was scattered, and conscientious objectors who resisted the draft were severely punished.

The trend toward vigilantism was particularly intense against all things German, including Americans of German extraction. High schools dropped German literature and language courses. Sauerkraut was rechristened "liberty cabbage," and dachshunds became "liberty pups." German Americans suffered numerous personal indignities from superpatriots who questioned their loyalty. Thousands of aliens from Germany were arrested and detained in internment camps during the war.

One of the major causes for the loyalty

program was the government's concern about recruiting soldiers. In reviewing recruitment policies since the Civil War, military planners concluded that the demands of the war would be enormous and that a volunteer army was about as useful as a contingent of medieval knights. During Wilson's moves against Mexico and his preparedness campaign of 1915, the Army envisioned enlisting 400,000 recruits in three years. To their dismay only a small group volunteered to follow General Pershing on the trail of Francisco Villa. General Leonard Wood, a top military planner, rated voluntary enlistments a "tragic failure." The memory of the 1863 draft riots in which a thousand persons died on the streets of New York City haunted the war planners. Nor did they relish the prospect of arming and training thousands of citizen-infantrymen at army barracks scattered throughout the nation.

The Army's decision to rely on the draft

The men of New York's 69th Infantry making their farewells. The Selective Service Act of 1917 required all men between twenty-one and thirty years of age to register for the draft. The law was changed a year later to extend the age limits to eighteen and forty-five. Under the lottery system used, 2.8 million men were called up for duty.

was, therefore, a reluctant one, though it proved more successful than anticipated. Drafting independent men with a nonmilitary tradition was a hard task, but there was little choice in the matter. The Defense Act of 1916 shifted the National Guard from state to federal control, thereby breaking down the long-standing difference between the state militia and the regular army. The Selective Service Act of April 1917 authorized drafting young men into the National Guard. Twenty-five million men registered for the draft, and 2.8 million were sworn in. There was little open resistance to the draft law, though 250,000 draftees simply failed to report for induction. By and large, the manpower problem was solved with amazing efficiency.

The War Industries Board

It proved no easy matter to create a war economy in a capitalist democracy. Natural resources, capital, transportation, and labor that were more or less freely allocated in peacetime had to be strictly managed. Snarls caused by labor strikes in sensitive industries, by mishandling of railroad freight, and by a scarcity of ships for ocean commerce, had to be straightened out. The various branches of the military vied with each other to see how many supplies they could hoard. War Secretary Newton D. Baker discovered one day that typewriters were stacked from floor to ceiling in the cellar of the War Department. The Army adjutant general was laying in an infinite supply simply to keep them out of the hands of the surgeon general, the Treasury Department, and the Navy.

By the summer of 1917 the economy was in a state of utter confusion and an extraordinary degree of government planning and centralized control was needed. In July 1917 Congress created the War Industries Board (WIB) and gave it broad powers to regulate production and consumption. The WIB, a form of "guided capitalism," was dominated by representatives from the biggest industrial firms. In 1918 Wilson appointed as head of the WIB Bernard Baruch, a successful financier and stock speculator, who in effect became America's economic wartime czar. Under the WIB the antitrust laws were suspended for the duration. Trade associations representing various industries got free rein to set prices, priorities for resources, production standards, and wages. The Board compiled extensive data on the potential of 28,000 factories and helped convert many of them to war production. In streamlining production, for example, the WIB reduced buggy wheels from 232 varieties to 4.

Government control over the private sector varied from one industry to another. The railroads and merchant shipping fleet were simply nationalized for the remainder of the war. But in general, Baruch and the WIB opposed this sort of commandeering as undemocratic. Baruch appealed to the patriotism of manufacturers or threatened to oppose uncooperative companies. Priority controls were a favorite lever. If a company failed to grant a government request, the WIB could cut its quota of coal, electricity, or other resources. On the positive side the WIB promised high profits for those who cooperated with the government. Some lumber companies cleared 17 percent profit. The average rate of return for steel manufacturers was 20 percent, and ten small steel mills made from 30 to 319 percent. Big industries were given other bonuses. For example, the government allowed the American chemical industry to take over highly profitable German chemical patents.

Production levels were sometimes disappointing. Although $7 billion was spent for weapons, the AEF had to use French artillery and ammunition most of the time. The output of ships, tanks, and aircraft fell far below initial estimates. The most spectacular production accomplishments were in agriculture. Under the direction of food administrator Herbert Hoover, American farmers produced a superabundance of food. Hoover set high wheat prices to boost farm production, and he requested that consumers observe "meatless" and "wheatless" days during the week. Such actions helped save Britain and France from starvation.

The Army brass were jealous of the WIB. Only grudgingly did the generals accept civilian leadership in wartime. Finally they admitted that they knew less about production and supply than the industrialists. The top-ranking role in the home-front effort went to industrialists, not generals. This shotgun marriage created what later would be called the "military-industrial complex" that was to loom so large on the American scene.

Mobilization caused further changes. Wartime leadership made the business community seem more attractive than it had during the Progressive era. Some men directly associated with the mobilization effort later made use of their World War I experiences during the depression of the 1930s. Among them was Franklin D. Roosevelt, Wilson's assistant secretary of the Navy. Production incentives and controls during the First World War provided a working model for the emergency economic measures used by the New Deal in the 1930s. The same basic formulas were also applied to home-front production in World War II.

Review

During the 1890s pressure for U.S. expansion mounted. Among the contributing factors were a desire for new overseas markets for American industry and agriculture, domestic unrest in the wake of economic depression, the closing of the country's western frontier, and the concept of America's civilizing mission in the world. In 1898 the U.S. embarked on a course of overseas empire when the country went to war against Spain. The fighting to free Cuba lasted only a hundred days. The treaty ending the Spanish-American War gave the U.S. possession of the Philippines, Puerto Rico, and Guam. Spain also gave up all title to Cuba. In the same year the United States annexed Hawaii. The country was soon embroiled in another military conflict, the Filipino insurrection. U.S. forces crushed the revolt, but the bloody contest, plus the heavy cost of administrating the Philippines, began to sour America's taste for territorial conquest. The nation's leaders sought less costly ways to assert U.S. power and extend American economic interests in Asia. In 1899 the secretary of state announced the Open Door policy in China.

Theodore Roosevelt believed in an international balance of power, which meant, among other things, that the U.S. had a legitimate sphere of influence in Latin America. Without resorting to annexation or conquest, Roosevelt wielded U.S. might to intervene in Latin American affairs. President Taft pursued American economic and political interests in the Caribbean through his Dollar Diplomacy. Although Wilson renounced the foreign policies of Roosevelt and Taft, he nonetheless intervened with military force in the domestic politics of Mexico.

World War I put Wilson's philosophy of pacifism, neutrality, and mediation to a severe test. His offer to mediate between the warring nations of Europe was rejected. And violation of Wilson's concept of freedom of the seas, especially the belligerent actions of German submarines, made it impossible for the U.S. to remain neutral. In 1917 the U.S. entered the war on the side of the Allies, sending General Pershing to lead the American forces in Europe. By the war's end, a staggering 35 million casualties had been tallied, although American losses were relatively light. Wilson thought of the struggle as a war to make the world safe for democracy, a war to end all wars. In 1918 he announced his Fourteen Points, which served as a basis for an armistice. The Fourteen Points included a proposal for a world peace-keeping organization that would eventually become the League of Nations.

On the homefront, the government had to manage strong antiwar sentiment and mobilize industry for wartime production. Until shortly before the U.S. entered the war, most Americans supported neutrality, and a large peace movement was at work. The government opened a massive patriotic campaign to assure loyalty and smother dissent. The administration's concern over manpower recruitment under the new draft program was one reason behind the "battle for the American mind." Government planning and control over the economy reached new levels during World War I. The War Industries Board was created to regulate production and consumption, and leadership roles in the WIB went to industrialists rather than the military. The most spectacular success was achieved in agricultural output. World War I became a training period for planning and production methods that would be employed during the Great Depression and the Second World War.

Questions

1. Identify (a) Alfred T. Mahan, (b) Open Door policy, (c) *Realpolitik*, (d) balance of power, (e) spheres of influence, and (f) Dollar Diplomacy.

2. What political, social, and economic forces moved the U.S. onto a course of empire in the late 1890s? Do you see any parallels between America's involvement in the Spanish-American War and the Filipino uprising and its role in Asia in the 1960s and 1970s?

3. How did Theodore Roosevelt apply his "big-stick" policy in Latin America?

4. Why did the U.S. swerve from its course of neutrality to enter World War I? Why did it join the war on the side of the Allies?

5. What means did the government use to mobilize industry and control production during World War I? What role did industrialists play in the mobilization effort?

Following the Civil War, urban blacks were restricted primarily to the unskilled trades and menial service. In this photograph, dockworkers in Jacksonville, Florida, take a break for lunch. The lure of the city proved to be more glitter than gold and blacks suffered from low wages and high costs of living.

20

20
One Nation, Divisible

Racist thinking gathered new force in the Western world in the nineteenth century. In America the belief in the superiority of the white race acquired a "scientific" status between 1880 and 1920. The popularization and distortion of the theories of Charles Darwin had much to do with it. The subtitle of Darwin's *On the Origin of Species by Means of Natural Selection* was *The Preservation of Favoured Races in the Struggle for Life.* While this referred solely to animals, racial thinkers made an easy carry-over to humans. They reasoned that those peoples with the *highest* material culture, namely whites, had the strongest genes. In a racial "struggle for existence," the "fittest" race would survive and the "inferior" ones would disappear. For a time in the 1890s both blacks and Indians were said to be "vanishing races." Racial thinkers believed that the English-speaking and Teutonic peoples were superior and that Anglo-Saxon Americans were the cream of the crop. Senator Albert Beveridge declared:

God has not been preparing the English-speaking and Teutonic peoples for a thousand years for nothing but vain and idle self-contemplation and self-admiration. No! He has made us the master organizers of the world to establish system where chaos reigns. He has made us adepts in government that we may administer government among savages and servile peoples.

Racism achieved popularity partly because it had the ring of "scientific truth" about it, which Americans greatly appreciated. Intellectuals in all disciplines supported it. Anthropologists and other scientists, historians, and economists spread the gospel of race. Professor Herbert Baxter Adams of Columbia University offered graduate seminars in political science and history which "proved" the superiority of the white race, and of the Anglo-Saxons in particular. One student who agreed with him was Theodore Roosevelt.

Perhaps the most popular of all "scientific" works on race was Madison Grant's *The Passing of the Great Race* (1916), which warned of the hazards of free immigration and racial mixture. The blond, blue-eyed, long-headed peoples of northern Europe (the "Nordic race") were the most inventive, industrious, artistic, and socially organized. The Nordics, Grant believed, had assured America's greatness. By allowing the free immigration of Jews, Slavs, Italians, and others, Anglo-Saxon America was committing "race suicide" (see also Chapter 21).

Racism has always served social ends. Prior to 1865 it was used to defend the conquest and removal of Indians and to defend slavery as a social institution. Late in the nineteenth century it was employed to keep the freed blacks "in their place" and to keep the defeated Indians in a state of subjection. It was also pressed as an argument to restrict immigration and to encourage America's overseas adventures. Importing cheap Mexican and Asian labor and limiting the flow of European immigration were also supported on racist grounds.

The Indians: From the Battlefields to the Reservations

Wiping out the "savages"

The Indians' long struggle to hold their lands reached its final stage after the Civil War. Their fight for survival started out on the field of battle and ended twenty years later on the reservation. The spreading network of railroads, the stepped-up traffic in beef cattle, the movement of miners and farmers to the West, and the presence of a federal army and war veterans all pointed to renewed hostilities between whites and Indians on a larger-than-ever scale.

The Apache and Navajo fought for a time and then, in 1865, made their peace with white soldiers by agreeing to settle on reservations in the Southwest. The Sioux of Wyoming and Montana agreed to stop fighting in 1868 and to settle in Dakota Territory, the site of their sacred Black Hills, if the whites would leave them alone. Indians were to stay in a given area, receive government annuities, and be Christianized and trained as farmers. At the same time, whites agreed to keep off the reservation lands.

Until 1871 Indians were legally considered separate nations that could negotiate treaties on the best possible terms. But a law passed by Congress in 1871 put a stop to new treaty making with Indians. After that, the federal government dealt with the Indians by executive agreement only. This was a less favorable position for the Indians. The four hundred treaties already concluded would be enforced by the president and by the Bureau of Indian Affairs without consulting the Indians.

In some respects the repression of Indian peoples by a nation as expansive as the U.S. was inevitable, but the subjugation of Indians could never have been so brutal without white society's belief in the "red savage," an image which clung beyond the 1880s. Custer wrote that the Indian was "savage in every sense of the word" with "a cruel and ferocious nature [that] far exceeds that of any wild beast of the desert; he need not be judged by rules or laws [of warfare] applica-

> *What treaty that the whites have kept has the red man broken? Not one.*
> *What treaty that the whites ever made with us red men have they kept? Not one.*
>
> SITTING BULL   (1831–1890)

ble to any other race of men." The Topeka *Weekly Leader* in 1867 characterized Indians as "miserable, dirty, lousy, blanketed, thieving, lying, sneaking, murdering, graceless, faithless, gut-eating skunks as the Lord ever permitted to infect the earth, and whose immediate and final extermination all men, except Indian agents and traders, should pray for." Even Theodore Roosevelt, an educated man, said: "I don't go so far as to think that the only good Indians are the dead Indians, but I believe that nine out of every ten are, and I shouldn't inquire too closely into the case of the tenth. The most vicious cowboy has more moral principle than the average Indian."

In 1868 the Sioux of Dakota Territory had agreed to allow the whites to cross their land in exchange for being left in peace in the Black Hills. The Sioux encountered further trouble in 1874 when whites discovered gold in the Black Hills and white miners and farmers clamored for Indian removal. Some leaders of the Sioux (Lakotas, as they called themselves) counseled peace. Others, like chiefs Crazy Horse and Sitting Bull, believed that the choice was between freedom and death and urged their braves into battle. These chiefs led their warriors in the most famous encounter in Plains warfare: Custer's "Last Stand." In the spring of 1876 the U.S. Cavalry was trying to clear the Indians off land on the northern plains which had been guaranteed them by treaty. Lieutenant Colonel George A. Custer, a headstrong man who was overanxious to fight, underestimated the Indians' strength. Feeling that the time had come to make a last desperate stand, Crazy Horse and Sitting Bull took up the fight with the battle cry, "Come on Lakotas, it's a good day to die!" On June 26, 1876, Custer (called

"Yellow Hair" by Indians) and 264 men of the crack Seventh Cavalry were wiped out by 2500 Sioux and Cheyenne warriors on the Little Big Horn River. News of Custer's debacle broke into the headlines in the East on July 5, 1876, the day after the nation's centennial celebration. Thereafter the Sioux were broken up, and those that were not killed off either moved onto reservations or crossed the Canadian border. Crazy Horse, killed while a captive, is today remembered by the Sioux as their greatest patriot chief.

The next year the cavalry moved against the Nez Percé Indians in the Northwest. In seventy-two years of contact with whites (from the Lewis and Clark expedition in 1805), no Nez Percé had ever killed a white person. But provocations by white farmers, miners, and government officials broke the peace in 1877. Rather than submit to the U.S. soldiers, who were about to drive them from their homelands, the Nez Percé under Chief Joseph's leadership decided to seek sanctuary in Canada. They fled through the northern Rockies, covering a thousand miles in four months, meanwhile conducting a superb military campaign. Very near the Canadian border, U.S. soldiers outflanked them and forced a surrender. "Hear me, my chiefs, I am tired; my heart is sick and sad. From where the sun now stands, I will now fight no more forever." With these words, Chief Joseph swept his blanket across his face in a sign of mourning and surrendered. The Nez Percé, a mountain people, were sent in boxcars to a flatland reservation in Indian Territory (Oklahoma). There within a year Joseph's own six children and one quarter of his nation died of malaria and other diseases.

Then began the mop-up stage of the conflict with the western Indians. The Utes of

Mass burial of Wounded Knee victims. Black Elk, an Oglala Sioux, later recalled the scene: "I can still see the butchered women and children lying heaped and scattered all along the crooked gulch as plain as when I saw them with eyes still young. And I can see that something else died there in the bloody mud, and was buried in the blizzard. A people's dream died there."

Colorado, a peaceful people who were goaded into a brief uprising, succumbed in 1878. Chief Geronimo and thirty-six other Apaches still held out against the army. This tiny band kept five thousand soldiers occupied in the deserts of New Mexico and Arizona. It cost the U.S. government about $1 million dollars for every Indian killed. Geronimo's band resisted until 1886 when they were taken to a Florida reservation.

The final "battle" with the Plains Indians occurred at Wounded Knee, South Dakota, December 29, 1890. Some one hundred men and two hundred women and children of the Sioux tribe were on their way to a holy place of the Ghost Dance religion. This creed originated with a Paiute prophet named Wovoka, who preached that those who would wear a "ghost shirt" and dance the "ghost dance"

would be immune to the white man's bullets and would see the buffalo run again. A Christlike redeemer would come to them, and the whites would disappear. Although basically a pacifist cult, the Ghost Dance religion worried the military. Custer's old cavalry unit confronted the band of Sioux led by Big Foot that had camped at Wounded Knee Creek in the Badlands. The soldiers completely disarmed the Sioux and ringed the camp with Hotchkiss guns. When a hidden weapon was accidentally discharged, the nervous soldiers opened fire at point-blank range, killing practically every Indian in sight and some whites as well. The cavalry felt it had avenged Custer. Congress gave special medals to the soldiers in this "military engagement," but today Wounded Knee is remembered as a shameless butchery.

While tribal chieftains signed treaties, individual Indians often refused to be bound by them. These members of the Crow nation were taken prisoner in 1887 after a skirmish in Montana. The prevalent white attitude was expressed by General W. T. Sherman: "We have provided reservations for all, off the great roads. All who cling to their old hunting grounds are hostile and will remain so till killed off."

Life on the reservations

By the time of Wounded Knee most surviving Indian tribes had moved onto reservations. In some respects this was the Indians' most difficult period. There were some twenty-five reservations in Indian Territory (eastern Oklahoma today) and about seventy-five scattered throughout the country, mostly in the West. The attitude of the white administrators is spelled out in this statement by Indian Commissioner Francis Walker. Whites who dealt with Indians were to respect the "superior rights of civilized men. . . . There is no question of national dignity . . . involved in the treatment of savages by a civilized power. With wild men as with beasts, the question whether in any given situation one shall fight, coax, or run, is a question of which is safest."

As fighting gave way to reservations, the Bureau of Indian Affairs (BIA), a branch of the Interior Department, came into its own. The BIA ran the reservations through a network of agents, teachers, clerks, traders, and supply contractors. At agency headquarters on the reservations, the BIA handed out annual benefits, blankets, food, education, and religious guidance to dispirited Indians. Young braves sometimes escaped to hunt game and roam free, but they were usually recaptured. Whites who dealt with Indians continually scolded them for "laziness." They must stop waiting for government handouts and must not expect the buffalo to run again. They were urged to turn to farming, abandon old superstitions, and send their children to school.

In the 1880s Congress voted money to hire Indian police. On the Sioux reservations they were told to spy on those who still observed "pagan" religious ceremonies, practiced polygamy, consulted medicine men, engaged in bootlegging, or encouraged their children's truancy from school. In 1883 Courts of Indian Offenses were established in which the Indian police sometimes doubled as prosecutors and judges. This, of course, made them thoroughly despised by other members of the tribe.

Whites considered education the key to Indian assimilation. By 1899 the government was subsidizing 148 boarding schools and 225 day schools that taught some 20,000 pupils. The Indians received mainly vocational and "moral" training. Generally, the government favored off-reservation schools over day schools, reasoning that the farther away

Sioux schoolchildren pose for a group portrait at Rose Bud, South Dakota, in the 1890s. Booker T. Washington, who early in his career had served as a teacher on a reservation, once observed that "no white American ever thinks that any other race is wholly civilized until he wears the white man's clothes, eats the white man's food, speaks the white man's language, and professes the white man's religion."

young Indians moved from "backward" tribal influences, the swifter would be their acceptance of white ways. Destroying tribalism was considered the first step to "Americanization." Younger Indians were made to feel profoundly alienated from the older, "blanket" Indians. Some teachers, doubling as missionaries, tried to suppress religious ceremonies like the Sioux Sun Dance, which they thought particularly barbaric. The BIA, like most expanding bureaucracies of the later nineteenth century, was shot through with corruption. Contractors connived with agents to supply Indians with shoddy blankets and contaminated beef. They skimmed the fat from government appropriations into their own pockets. Moreover, many reservations were situated on infertile or arid land that would have frustrated the most experienced white farmers. As a result, reservation Indians, called by one of Geronimo's warriors "America's prisoners of war," frequently suffered from malnutrition and a variety of illnesses, including extreme depression.

Toward the end of the century white reformers came to the aid of the Indians who were complaining of the shabby and inhumane conditions on the reservations. Indian delegations went to Washington to ask the Great White Father for better treatment and spoke before attentive white audiences. Journalists and literary figures joined in denouncing reservation policy. Some BIA agents, teachers, and army officers worked hard and remained honest and humane.

Among whites who urged better treatment for Indians, the best known was Helen Hunt Jackson, author of *A Century of Dishonor* (1881). Her book was an exposé of reservation conditions on the Great Plains. Like *Uncle Tom's Cabin*, published thirty years earlier, the book awakened the public to the hardships of a racial minority. But it was bitterly denounced by those who looked on Indians as "savages"—Theodore Roosevelt called the new breed of Indian reformers "foolish sentimentalists." Three years later Jackson's novel *Ramona* depicted the miseries of the California mission Indians. It, too, became enormously popular.

The ravages of the Dawes Act

The reservations appeared in a poor light to whites who hoped to convert the Indians totally to white ways and also to those who wanted the Indians' land. The "final solution to the Indian question" was the Dawes Severalty Act of 1887. Under the terms of this law, sponsored by Senator Henry Dawes of Massachusetts, communal lands on the reservations were to be broken into small parcels and distributed to individual Indians as private property. The purpose of the Dawes Act was to dissolve tribal unity and civilize the Indians. Each family head would receive 10 to 160 acres of reservation land plus a certificate of citizenship. (The citizenship clause was soon removed.) "Excess" reservation lands would be put up for sale, with the proceeds to be used for "civilizing" the Indians.

To prevent real-estate sharks from fleecing Indians out of their new property, the law appointed the BIA to act as the Indians' trustee for twenty-five years. During this time the individual land parcels could be leased but not sold. (The trusteeship arrangement was usually renewed.) It was assumed that somehow the Indians would turn into successful farmers, livestock growers, and Christians. The Dawes Act was never applied to the Pueblo, the Zuñi, or other Southwest Indians whose arid desert villages seemed forbidding to white farmers. At first the Five Civilized Tribes were exempt because of their loud protests, but six years later Congress also subjected them to the Dawes Act.

Probably the single most striking difference between white and Indian societies was the private property of the former and the communal property of the latter. It was the firm intention of whites to bridge that gap through the allotment scheme, which in a sense imposed the white man's "dream of success" on the Indians. As Theodore Roosevelt proclaimed:

The [Dawes] Act is a mighty pulverizing engine to break up the tribal mass. . . . We should now break up the tribal funds . . . they should be divided into individual holdings . . . we should definitely make up our minds to recognize the Indian as an individual and not as a member of a tribe.

In a period of laissez-faire it was hard for even the most well-meaning Americans to recognize that Indian contentment depended on group identity and that destruction of common landholding meant destruction of the tribe and inevitable alienation. Indians were first and foremost a tribal people. Weakening tribal loyalties and assets only reinforced their sense of loss.

The new "reforms" eventually proved a total disaster. When the Dawes Act became law, the Indians possessed some 138 million acres of land; four decades later they were left with 48 million acres. Moreover, their physical health was deteriorating. In 1910 the U.S. government estimated that only 250,000 Indians survived in the U.S. compared to at least 800,000 in the days of Columbus. The major physical problem was communicable diseases. Even the most careful and sympathetic observers agreed that the Indian was literally a "vanishing race." (This idea, of course, was narrow and misleading, for 13 million Indians lived in other North and South American countries in the early twentieth century.)

In 1911 an emaciated Stone Age man was found in northern California. He was the sole survivor of a small band of Yahi Indians, the last Stone Age people in America. For years he had lived on the fringes of white settlement, pilfering what he could but never daring to emerge in the open. Ishi's people had been decimated by whites over the previous half century, and he finally came forward out of desperation. He became an informant and friend of University of California anthropologists, one of whom, T. T. Waterman, considered him the most remarkable individual he had ever met. Ishi regarded his scholarly white friends "as sophisticated children — smart but not wise." Waterman wrote of Ishi, "He was kind; he had courage and self-restraint, and though all had been taken from him, there was no bitterness in his heart."

Blacks During Reconstruction and Accommodation

After slavery

When the Civil War ended, blacks expected "forty acres and a mule" or some other way to rise above poverty, an idea implanted by northern forces in the final months of the struggle. Black leaders who met in conventions hoped to find a niche within the democratic process. "We are part and parcel of the great American body politic," declared a convention of Kentucky blacks immediately after emancipation. "We love our country and her institutions and we are proud of her greatness." The most useful political tool was to be the vote. This would give blacks a voice in government and protection against any attempts to reenslave them. The widespread white fear that blacks would, when freed from slavery, rise up and destroy their former masters was dispelled by the restrained conduct of former slaves after 1865.

To blacks, emancipation had a bittersweet taste. A former Tennessee slave recalled: "When freedom come, folks left home, out in the streets, crying, praying, singing, shouting, yelling, and knocking down everything. Some shot off big guns." But, he added, "Then came the calm. It was sad then. So many folks done dead, things tore up, and nowheres to go and nothing to eat, nothing to do. It got squally. Folks got sick, so hungry. Some folks starved nearly to death. Ma was a cripple woman. Pa couldn't find work for so long when he mustered out."

Although the Thirteenth Amendment prohibiting slavery went into effect almost without a hitch in December 1865, it did not give civil equality to blacks or prevent former slaveowners from using labor practices closely resembling slavery. The southern states set up Black Codes which modified the old apprentice and vagrancy laws in order to tie the freed black laborer to the soil. While these provisions varied in severity from one state to the next, they convinced the Radicals in Congress that the South as a whole was trying to sneak slavery in through a back door. The South's resistance to the Fourteenth Amendment, which recognized blacks as citizens and sought to protect their civil rights, reinforced the message that it opposed civil equality for blacks. The formation of the Ku Klux Klan in 1866 made it clear that "uppity" blacks — those who sought political equality — would be dealt with violently. In that same year 37 blacks were killed and 119 wounded in a New Orleans riot over racial equality.

The economic future of ex-slaves remained a key question. Colonization to South America or Africa still had some backers but seemed less practical than ever. Moving blacks from the South to the West to open new farmland was possible but might create competition for white farmers. Most blacks, it seemed, would remain in the South.

"There they were born," said Horace Greeley, "there they have lived; there they mean to live and die." During the war, Union officials temporarily confiscated some Confederate plantations and turned them over to blacks. With considerable success blacks operated cotton plantations as a cooperative enterprise on the Sea Islands off the Carolina coast. But this experiment ended within two years.

Federal protection and aid for blacks was tried for a time. The Freedmen's Bureau, established by Congress in March 1865, provided short-term relief for ex-slaves. It issued them rations and clothing and supervised work contracts to prevent white employers from reenslaving blacks by unfair contracts. Temporarily and in a small way the Bureau even redistributed land taken away from Confederate officers. It established more than 4200 schools and employed 6300 teachers, who taught 247,000 pupils, both white and black. Despite inefficiency, corruption, and inadequate funding, the Bureau accomplished much of what it set out to do. It ended because the public was not ready for a permanent program of federal care for blacks.

Negroes were expected to conform to the American tradition of self-reliance. "Freedom and opportunity—these are all that the best Government can secure to White or Black," the liberal newspaper editor Horace Greeley asserted. "Clear away the wreck of slavery, dispel the lingering fear of a return to it, and we may soon break up our Freedmen's Bureaus and all manner of coddling devices and let negroes take care of themselves."

Racial thinking about blacks changed very little in spite of the Civil War. Most whites would have liked to forget about the ex-slaves altogether. At best, they considered blacks simpleminded, docile, and affectionate; at worst, dangerous animals. Even abolitionists and idealistic Radical Republicans questioned the intelligence of blacks. Whites who favored giving them legal equality and a fair chance still could not conceive of them as being *socially* equal. The most generous point of view was that blacks should be given a chance at freedom.

Reconstruction programs and governments

Representative Thaddeus Stevens of Pennsylvania wanted to give civil rights to blacks in the South as a matter of simple, straightforward justice, a natural extension of the Declaration of Independence. Radical Republicans who did not believe in racial equality agreed that it would be necessary to give blacks the vote in order to keep their party in power and to prevent the planters from regaining political strength. It was also important for Radicals to make blacks content in the South, so that they would stay there and not move away to bother *northern* whites.

The Radicals' civil rights program had to be forced on southerners and required changing the Constitution. The most significant act was the Fourteenth Amendment. It provided that "all persons born or naturalized in the United States" were citizens of the country and of the state in which they resided. No state could "abridge the privileges" of any citizen or "deprive any person of life, liberty, or property, without due process of law." The amendment recast the relationship between the states and federal government, throwing cold water on the South's old claim to states' rights. And as the courts later interpreted it, the amendment also gave corporations special privileges as legal persons. As a result, it became the most important amendment ever added to the Constitution. When, on President Johnson's urging, the South refused to approve it, Congress passed the First Reconstruction Act of 1867, which placed the South under martial law and enforced black suffrage.

The Fifteenth Amendment, making it illegal to deny black men the right to vote on account of race, was ratified in 1870. The Civil Rights Act of 1875 was intended as a follow-up to the Fourteenth Amendment, but it proved toothless and unenforceable. Equally weak were the Force Acts of 1870–1871 which tried to prevent southern whites from terrorizing blacks and sabotaging the Reconstruction. Congress drafted bills providing for equal education for Negroes, but these did not pass.

In 1867 and 1868, under the eyes of 20,000 federal troops, black and white voters went to the polls, held constitutional conventions, elected new legislatures, and established "Black Republican" regimes in the southern states. Some 150,000 white Confederates remained disfranchised while 700,000 Negroes voted. But while black voters outnumbered whites in South Carolina, Mississippi, and Louisiana, only in South Carolina did they have a majority in the legislature. Still, the most radical feature of the new southern regimes was that they gave blacks a political voice. Blacks were represented at many levels and branches of government, though not as fully as they deserved, considering the size of the black vote. Twenty-two black men sat in Congress between 1868 and 1901. The most prominent was Senator Hiram Revels of Mississippi. They also served as state legislators, lieutenant governors, secretaries of state, state court justices, and sheriffs. About half of these officeholders were ex-slaves, while the rest were ministers or lawyers who had been free blacks. They did not fit the vicious stereotype featured in the more lurid anti-Reconstruction literature, nor were they vindictive toward whites.

Angry white southerners described Black Republican governments as the most corrupt and despotic regimes in the history of Christendom. "Scheming carpetbaggers" (northerners who went to the South) and "traitorous scalawags" (southerners who collaborated with the blacks) were manipulating "ignorant, vengeful Negro puppets." Together they were heaping indignities on honest whites and lining their pockets with cash. Graft and corruption did exist in the Black Republican governments, but white conservatives benefited almost as much as scalawags and carpetbaggers. Nor was the criminal mismanagement of public funds any worse there than in the North.

In fact, the new southern governments scored many positive achievements. They built badly needed roads, asylums, railroads, and other public works. They also started public schools and improved the system of poor relief. These were comparatively costly programs. Taxes rose, but not excessively, for they had been too low before the war. Under Black Reconstruction, state expenditures were higher, but they went mainly for needed public projects.

Already slowing for some years, Reconstruction finally ground to a halt in 1877, when President Hayes removed the army from the South one month after his inauguration. Actually, most of the Black Republican regimes had already ended. Terrorist groups like the Ku Klux Klan had unleashed a campaign of night riding, beatings, and

Our main and fundamental object is the maintenance of the supremacy of the white race in this republic.

Oath of the Knights of the White Camelia

lynchings that frightened many black voters away from the polls. Sumner and Stevens and other key Radicals in Congress had died or retired. Those still in office expressed disappointment at the "excesses" of Black Republican governments. Many white liberals had abandoned their former black allies. The GOP discovered that it had enough northern votes to stay in power without the aid of southern blacks. The new breed of Republican politicians was more interested in tariffs, railroad expansion, currency, and finance than in civil rights. Without opposition from northern businessmen and politicians, the former southern ruling class resumed authority in the South through a resurgent Democratic party. They called themselves the "Redeemers."

We consider the underlying fallacy of the plaintiff's argument to consist in the assumption that the enforced separation of the two races stamps the colored race with a badge of inferiority.

HENRY B. BROWN   (1836 – 1913)
Majority opinion, *Plessy* v. *Ferguson*

Keeping southern blacks "in their place"

After the whites returned to power, blacks were kept "in their place" by physical terror, segregation, and disfranchisement. In the 1880s and early 1890s about a hundred were lynched each year, mostly in the rural South. With rare exceptions, the police, the courts, the Congress, and the president all closed their eyes to this violence.

In the late nineteenth century more and more blacks experienced the humiliation of "Jim Crow" policies, the common expression for the systematic segregation of Negroes. Before the Civil War, segregation in transportation or public places had been more common in the North than in the South. Under slavery it had been both unnecessary and impractical to separate whites completely from the blacks. The caste system was so strong that whites had not felt the mere physical presence of blacks as a threat. In the postwar South segregation started informally and gradually became legalized. By the 1890s

there were Jim Crow churches, trains, streetcars, schools, beaches, jails, toilets, parks, benches, hotels, water fountains, and even Bibles for swearing in court witnesses. Blacks were forbidden to testify in court against whites, to serve on juries, or to enter most professions. Worse yet, they were replaced by whites in skilled trades as well as unskilled work.

The U.S. Supreme Court helped undo civil rights reform. In 1883 it declared the Civil Rights Act of 1875 unconstitutional. Under the Fourteenth Amendment, it said, Congress could outlaw discrimination by the states, but not by individuals. In the celebrated case of *Plessy* v. *Ferguson* (1896), it ruled that "separate but equal" public facilities were consistent with the Fourteenth Amendment. This opinion held for the next fifty-eight years. In 1898 the court upheld the South's use of poll taxes and literacy tests to disfranchise black voters. The court found reasons to deprive blacks of the "equal protection" promised them in the Fourteenth Amendment, which was originally designed to grant them the full rights of citizenship.

Some racial moderates in the South tried to prevent the repression of blacks. Henry W. Grady, editor of the *Atlanta Constitution*, popularized the idea of "The New South." He believed an industrialized South with a strong rail network and a healthy agriculture could rise from the ashes of civil war and reconstruction. He saw no need for terror and violence against blacks. Another moderate, Confederate hero Wade Hampton, elected governor of South Carolina in 1876, promised that no blacks would lose their civil rights in his regime. The moderates were grateful that slavery was ended. They felt convinced that blacks were "perfectly peaceable and harmless," especially when not stirred up by radical whites. Many of these moderates were old-fashioned aristocrats who had little patience with "red-neck" Dixie racists who replaced them in the 1890s.

Southern states effectively nullified the Fifteenth Amendment in the late 1890s. Earlier the whites found it more convenient to manipulate the black vote than to eliminate it. But in the 1890s the Populists threatened to create an alliance of white and black farmers to challenge the Democratic establishment. At this point, white supremacists moved against the black voters by introducing grandfather clauses (a voter had to be a direct descendent of someone who had voted in the same state before 1867), literacy tests, and poll taxes. These laws effectively barred most Negroes from voting. Near the turn of the century disfranchisement proceeded swiftly. In 1896 over 130,000 Negroes were registered to vote in Louisiana. Four years later enforcement of new regulations reduced the eligibility lists to about 5000.

During Reconstruction, blacks joined the American body politic for the first time. Reconstruction failed because it tried to impose a solution from the top down, from the outside in. While giving blacks the vote, it disfranchised many whites, thus alienating those whose compliance was essential for success. The Radicals pushed for *legal* equality but never came to grips with the underlying poverty and social inequality of blacks. From Reconstruction until the 1950s blacks—and other racial minorities—made little progress in acquiring civil rights. Lincoln's "new birth of freedom" had yet to materialize.

Booker T. Washington and accommodation

Reacting to violence and to Jim Crow restrictions, abandoned by liberal white friends, and ignored by Congress, the White House, and the courts, the black community turned in upon itself, looking for solutions through self-help. Now that their civil rights were dead, blacks hoped that accommodating the whites would save them.

There is hope for a people when their laws are righteous, whether for the moment they conform to their requirements or not.

FREDERICK DOUGLASS (1817–1895)

Booker T. Washington (1856–1915), an educated ex-slave, became the oracle of moderate black America. Washington believed in full equality, but for the time being, Jim Crow was a reality that had to be lived with. As long as Negroes remained poor, ignorant, and unskilled, they would be despised by whites. They must turn to vocational education, hard work, and thrift in order to improve themselves. Washington warned that it was unwise for blacks to leave the rural South for the cities or for the North. "Cast down your bucket where you are," he urged in a famous address at Atlanta in 1895. On the other side of the coin, he held that whites should give blacks a hand by hiring them rather than European immigrants whenever possible. Washington also worked actively with southern Negro merchants who were attempting to gain the good will of southern whites. Privately he fought segregation and took a vital interest in politics and patronage, although in public he urged Negroes not to use these tactics.

Washington had graduated from Hampton Institute, Virginia, a Negro vocational school founded in 1865, and was convinced that Negroes trained in farming, handicrafts, home economics, carpentry, and other manual careers would advance farther in the world than those who might try to elbow their way into white-dominated professions. In 1881 he founded Tuskegee Normal and Industrial Institute in Alabama to train Negroes as teachers, farmers, and skilled workers. The school's success was due in part to the work of George W. Carver, an agricultural chemist who joined its faculty in 1896. He

Among the black population over ten years of age, 80 percent were illiterate in 1870, but by 1900 the illiteracy rate had dropped to less than 45 percent. Meanwhile, the doctrine of Tuskegee Institute criticized classical education for blacks as unsuited to the needs of the race, favoring "industrial education" in its place. Several "little Tuskegees," like Snow Hill Institute (above), sprang up because of the influence of Booker T. Washington's school.

developed numerous by-products from the peanut, sweet potato, and soybean. Carver's work with the peanut had particular impact in diversifying southern agriculture, which had become too dependent on a single crop, cotton.

A man of great charm and eloquence, Washington had the ear of prominent whites. Philanthropists Andrew Carnegie and George F. Peabody generously endowed Tuskegee. President Theodore Roosevelt invited him to lunch at the White House. His autobiography *Up From Slavery* (1901) became a classic of Negro American writing. Many whites considered him the "chief spokesman for his race."

Yet Washington led his people down a fruitless path. Few trained Negro craftsmen could find decent jobs. Even the best trained black farmers could seldom escape debt or

sharecropping. Often they drifted away to the cities, even northern cities, against Washington's advice. Northern white employers preferred white European laborers to blacks. Meanwhile, accommodation by blacks seemed to inflame rather than calm southern whites. Racist mobs continued to lynch blacks—nine hundred were lynched between 1900 and 1910.

Stereotyping of blacks reached its most vicious extreme during the era of accommodation. Nonwhites had always been portrayed as children or savages (or both), who required the civilizing example of whites. Minstrel shows carried on the image of happy-go-lucky, banjo-playing Black Sambo (impersonated by whites in "blackface"). But this picture of blacks was only one side of the coin: whites were increasingly obsessed by the "black brute." He was dangerous precisely because he was not under white control. He "did not know his place," stole jobs from white men, and raped white women. Running for governor in Mississippi, James K. Vardaman in 1903 assured his audience that the black was a "lazy, lying, lustful animal which no conceivable amount of training can transform into a tolerable citizen. We would be justified," he claimed, "in slaughtering every Ethiop on earth to preserve unsullied the honor of one Caucasian home." *The Klansman* (1905) by Thomas Dixon Ryan, Jr., became the basis for D. W. Griffith's classic movie *Birth of a Nation*, which included several scenes of the "black brute" during Reconstruction.

The beginnings of militancy

The realities of lynching and discrimination mocked Booker T. Washington's blueprint for improving the status of blacks. Whites seemed to take advantage of accommodation. This made Washington suspect to young blacks. His most articulate black critic was William E. B. Du Bois (1868–1963), a northern-born, Harvard-trained scholar. Du Bois insisted that blacks must stop waiting for white charity and seek full equality. A professor of sociology at black Atlanta University, Du Bois had little regard for Washington's philosophy of vocational training. He wanted the "talented tenth" of blacks to assert racial pride and independence and seek the best education available.

Du Bois and other militants founded the Niagara Movement in 1905. In a flaming manifesto they protested the denial of the vote, civil rights, economic opportunities, and higher education to blacks. Booker T. Washington sensed a threat to his leadership. Fearing that white philanthropists would stop supporting black schools, he pulled strings to deny the upstarts access to the press. Soon the Niagara Movement ceased to function.

We claim for ourselves every single right that belongs to a freeborn American, political, civil and social; and until we get these rights we will never cease to protest and assail the ears of America.

W. E. B. DU BOIS (1868–1963)

Yet time was on the militants' side. They helped form the National Association for the Advancement of Colored People (NAACP) in 1909, which became the first line of legal defense for victims of race riots, lynchings, and Jim Crow policies. By now most black leaders rejected Washington's leadership. The NAACP lobbied for antilynching laws and sued in the courts to eliminate grandfather clauses, white primaries, segregated schools, discrimination in housing, and other infringements on the Fourteenth Amendment. It won its first major court victory in 1915, when the U.S. Supreme Court agreed to nullify Oklahoma's grandfather clause.

The Progressive era as a whole produced no great benefits for blacks. Few white Progressives believed in racial equality. Even those who did usually found it expedient to compromise with white supremacist politicians. Woodrow Wilson refused to end black segregation in the Post Office and other federal agencies.

During the First World War the emerging northern ghettos began to attract attention. Wartime jobs opened up for blacks in northern factories. By the war's end 500,000 southern black men and women had moved north of Dixie. A great migration of blacks from southern plantations to northern cities was under way. In the cities poverty and housing discrimination were creating large black ghettos. On the fringes of these ghettos racial violence flared. A serious clash occurred in East St. Louis, Illinois, in 1917. This prompted a silent march of blacks along New York's Fifth Avenue, the first such protest.

Meantime 200,000 blacks entered the armed services. Two Negro divisions served overseas. While most were placed in non-combat positions and labor battalions, many others fought. Some blacks were decorated by the French government. But almost none rose above the rank of captain. Discrimination against black troops was common. In Houston in August 1917 black infantrymen rioted against repressive action by police. Seventeen whites were killed and thirteen blacks executed. Nevertheless, the war created new black voters, industrial workers, and community leaders. World War I also gave nationwide scope to racial issues formerly identified as strictly southern.

Mexican Americans: One Thousand Miles of Conflict

A new minority

Mexican Americans became a minority not by migration to the U.S. but by conquest. This occurred, first, when Anglo-Americans overthrew Mexican rule in Texas (1835), and when the United States subsequently fought and defeated Mexico (1846–1848) and purchased a further slice of Mexican territory (1853). Mexican Americans lived in relative isolation, almost exclusively in the border states and territories of Texas, New Mexico, Arizona, and California. Here they were reduced to subordinate status. For decades the borderland from Brownsville, Texas, to Santa Fe, New Mexico, and as far west as San Jose, California, seethed with trouble between the Anglos and the Spanish-speaking. There were relatively few Mexican Americans until about 1900, when a new and large-scale labor migration moved north from Mexico. They came in response to the expansion of irrigation, agriculture, and railroads in the Southwest. The Mexican laborers took their place as a vital factor in the developing economy.

Violence in Texas

South Texas was the scene of considerable violence in the late nineteenth century, especially in the region between the Nueces and Rio Grande rivers, where the Mexican War had started. Here Anglos rapidly acquired most of the old Mexican-owned land titles, and around 1875 proceeded to fence in the open range. This blocked out smaller ranchers and created deep resentments. At the same time, outlaws of both nations roamed unchecked. An American general reported in 1875 that "there is a considerable Texas element in the country bordering on the Nueces that thinks the killing of a Mexican no crime . . . [and numerous] Mexican thieves and cut-throats who . . . think the killing of Texans something to be proud of." Angry Mexicans took up cattle rustling. Old grudges were settled by pistols and rifles in every sunbaked village. Bandidos from Mexico raided Texas ranches to "collect grandfather's cattle," as the expression went, and the ranchers retaliated. One of the raiders, Juan Cortina, to the Anglos a vicious murderer but to the Mexicans a folk hero, declared, "Our personal enemies shall not possess our lands until they have fattened it with their gore." Cortina for a time held a high political office in Mexico and cast a shadow over South Texas for twenty years.

By 1890 only 10 percent of the population of California consisted of Mexican Americans, and of these, only a handful were rancheros who had managed to retain their ancestral lands. Here, members of Southern California's Lugo family—typical upper-class Californios—pose for a group portrait in 1887.

El Paso witnessed the "Salt War" of 1875. At issue was whether Mexican Americans could continue to dig salt from a mine they considered public property and Anglos considered private. The population of El Paso County was about twelve thousand, all but eighty of them of Spanish-Mexican background. The Anglos controlled the local government. When they tried to monopolize the mine, enraged Mexicans seized the town and killed several Anglos. The retaliation was almost as bloody. It is said that President Hayes considered going to war with Mexico to pacify the border area. Not even the most fearless Texas Rangers could assure the safety of Anglos in the border region.

Mexican decline in California

In California old scores were settled more often with a lawyer's brief or a tax lien than with pistols. For a time some Californios, the original Mexican families, continued to hold key positions in California society as assemblymen, tax assessors, mayors, and the like. In 1871 Romualdo Pacheco of Santa Barbara was elected lieutenant governor and even occupied the governor's chair for a few months. But in general the Mexican Americans lost ground numerically, economically, and politically. An unprecedented drought in 1862–1864 killed huge numbers of cattle throughout the state and hastened the end of the old way of life based on the rancho. Payment of heavy property taxes, loans, and lawyers' fees spelled financial ruin for many Californios. By the century's end approximately sixty Spanish-surname families still owned land on ancestral holdings in the southern part of the state; perhaps half that many were left in the northern part. While the second generation of upper-class Californios discarded ponchos and rebozos in favor of Edwardian coats and hoopskirts, the poorer ones crowded into "Sonoratown," or "Spanish town." Here in the *barrios* they mingled with newcomers from Mexico, immigrants who helped keep the old culture alive in California. The lack of real border control led to the constant renewal of Mexican traditions.

The Spanish-speaking in New Mexico

The scene in New Mexico was considerably different from that in Texas or in Mexican communities on the West Coast. There were no border wars or bandido raids from Mexico. Since far fewer Anglos settled there than in California, the proportion of Spanish-speaking people was larger. There were perhaps as many as sixty thousand in the 1880s, two thirds more than in California. Moreover, the Indian and mestizo heritage of the Southwest remained strong, owing to the presence of Zuñi, Hopi, Pueblo, and other Indian tribes.

As the U.S. cattle frontier extended into New Mexico in the 1880s, conflict flared. Cattlemen, who hated the "woolies" and the sheepmen, considered the entire West as open range. They insisted on grazing their cattle on all "unoccupied" land. Fights broke out over grazing rights, land titles, and water holes. In many cases the Spanish-speaking owners held valid land claims under Spanish or Mexican grants, but their legal titles were still unsettled. Some Anglos bought land outright or purchased grazing or water rights. The less scrupulous resorted to legal loopholes or to pistols. In any event, Anglos managed to consolidate their holdings.

Around the turn of the century the federal government withdrew considerable acreage in New Mexico for homesteading, railroads, and national forests. All of this compelled the Mexican American ranchers and farmers, whose grazing rights or land tenure dated back to Mexican and Spanish days, to retreat to isolated pockets of land or to become wage laborers. The way the Anglo ranchers and the federal government pushed out the Mexicans is a basis for discontent in New Mexico to this very day.

A handful of wealthy Spanish dons continued to own considerable land and sheep and to employ numerous Mexican workers. One aristocrat ran one million head of sheep and kept a thousand shepherds on his payroll. The landed families maintained the old caste system. The dons who could deliver the votes of their ranch hands became involved in politics. Miguel Antonio Otero II, for example, was appointed territorial governor by President McKinley. Otero was a strong advocate of statehood and an able administrator. He and his family and their associates ran a well-oiled GOP machine. At New Mexico's constitutional convention at Santa Fe in 1910, one third of the delegates were Spanish-speaking. In the state constitution the bilingual heritage was preserved. All laws were to be printed in both Spanish and English, and both languages were to be used in the schools.

A wave of immigrant laborers

Early in the twentieth century more Mexicans found jobs in the Southwest. Federal reclamation projects brought water into the lower Colorado River basin beginning in 1901, making large-scale agriculture possible for the first time in southern California deserts. Irrigation farming requires a large labor force, and Mexicans or Mexican Americans provided cheap labor. American growers needed armies of workers to dig irrigation ditches and to cultivate the sugar beets, cotton, and other crops of California, New Mexico, Arizona, Colorado, and Texas. New mines and new railroads also called for cheap labor. The labor problem was especially acute because Chinese immigration had been cut off by the Exclusion Act of 1882 (see p. 441). Mexico supplied a large part of the Southwest's labor. The Mexican Revolution sent about one million persons fleeing north across the border between 1910 and 1920. Many of these exiles who considered themselves temporary visitors remained to work permanently in the fields and mines and on the railroads.

About 700,000 persons of Mexican background lived in the four southwestern states by the end of World War I, and an additional seventy thousand resided east of the Mississippi. Many served in the U.S. Army and Navy during World War I. In fact, their enlistment rate was proportionately higher than that of other ethnic groups. With cotton in great demand for use in military uniforms and automobile tires, thousands of acres of desert land were opened to cotton planting in Arizona and New Mexico. Sugar beet growers in Colorado, desperate for laborers, tried to lure workers away from New Mexico, Texas, and Arizona. By 1918 Chicanos lived in widely dispersed and isolated communities: farm labor camps, mining towns, and urban *barrios*. The majority stayed near the Mexican border and kept in close touch with Mexico. The language, religion, and customs of the Old Country remained stronger among Mexican Americans than among most other immigrant groups. Economically they depended almost entirely on the corporations and labor contractors who hired them. Because they often lived in remote rural communities, and moved from one agricultural job to another, they were not absorbed into the political mainstream of American society.

Living in a region remote from the farthest centers of population, this Spanish-speaking minority was only vaguely understood by most Americans in the early twentieth century. The local-color stories of Bret Harte or of Helen Hunt Jackson produced vignettes of the Hispanic Southwest as "a picture, a romance, a dream, all in one." The overall impression of Mexican Americans in this literature is that of a picturesque and childlike people, charming and lazy, colorful and humorous — and occasionally nasty. They are presented as the opposite of their Yankee neighbors, who lived by the Puritan Ethic, although these writers were usually quite critical of Anglo arrogance. Even though they opened the eyes of Anglo readers to the older Indian and Hispanic culture, they left them in the dark about the real people who now occupied the land.

As a progressive people we reveal a race prejudice intolerable to civilization; as Christians we are made to blush beside the heathen Asiatic; as just and humane men we slaughter the innocent and vie with red-handed savages in deeds of atrocity.

HUBERT H. BANCROFT (1832–1918)
American Historian and Publisher

Confronting the "Yellow Peril"

White opposition to Chinese labor

Those whites who feared and resented Asians did so for a variety of reasons, but job competition was a common denominator of organized prejudice against the Chinese and Japanese. In 1868 the United States, in response to lobbying by manufacturing and railroad interests, negotiated the Burlingame Treaty with China. It allowed an unlimited number of Chinese laborers to be imported by contract. To white workers, these so-called coolie slaves seemed every bit as dangerous as black slaves or freedmen. More than 10 percent of California's total population in the 1860s was Chinese. In the next decade one out of four persons in that state's labor force came from China. At first, the Asians worked principally at gold mining, or washing laundry for the miners. From the 1860s on they worked also at railroad construction and fruit picking—in other words, in California's most important industries. They also made up a large part of the work force in cigar making, textile production, and shoe manufacturing.

The depression of the 1870s convinced many white Californians that their economic salvation depended on Chinese exclusion. Some considered the Chinese subhuman. As one witness testified before a congressional committee in 1876, "The Chinese are inferior to any race God ever made. . . . I think there are none so low. . . . I believe that the Chinese have no souls to save, and that if they have, they are not worth saving." "The Chinese must go!" became the credo of rabble-rouser Denis Kearney and the Workingman's party, an organization that rose overnight from complete obscurity to become a major force in California politics. Anti-Chinese feelings unified organized labor and helped mold San Francisco into a union town. Every California politician attached himself to the anti-Chinese crusade, and Denis Kearney began to consider himself presidential timber. Along the Pacific coast, Tacoma and Portland also joined the crusade.

On the other side was a small but influential minority that favored Chinese immigration. Wealthy families valued their Chinese houseboys. Big industries, the Southern Pacific Railroad, and major fruit growers prospered from the cheap Chinese labor. Protestant missionaries also tried to hold the door open to the Asians.

But bigotry prevailed, working its way deeply into the grain of the law. The legislature voted in a tax on foreign miners, a head tax for Asian immigrants, a special tax on Chinese laborers, and many statutes against Chinese prostitutes. State authorities also established special segregated schools for Asians. The first zoning ordinance anywhere in the U.S. was used to restrict the location of Chinese laundry establishments in San Francisco. A queue ordinance forced Chinese prisoners in the city jail to have their hair cut Caucasian-style. In denying Chinese the vote, the California constitution of 1880 classed them with idiots and infamous criminals. Furthermore, an act of the legislature ruled that anyone ineligible to vote could not be granted a business license. The state constitution also prohibited Asians from competing for all public jobs desired by

We declare that white men . . . cannot live as the people of the great republic should and compete with the single Chinese coolie in the labor market. . . . To an American, death is preferable to life on a par with the Chinaman.

DENIS KEARNEY   (1847–1907)
Political agitator

whites. However, the federal courts struck down the discriminatory sections of the state constitution as violations of the Fourteenth Amendment.

As the germ theory of disease became more widely understood in America, it gave whites a new reason to fear Asians. It was charged that contagious diseases were drifting in from the Far East. They were incubating in the brothels and shops of West Coast Chinatowns, threatening to destroy the good health of the entire Anglo-Saxon race. To quarantine the "filth" of the Chinese became a mania in itself.

Finally Congress obliged the anti-Chinese crusaders. The Exclusion Act of 1882 halted all Chinese immigration for ten years. This was the first federal law limiting free immigration to the U.S. The California Oriental Exclusion League and other pressure groups saw to it that the Exclusion Act was renewed in 1892 and made permanent in 1902.

Anti-Chinese racism seemed to work like a lightning rod for other ethnic groups in California. Because of the presence of the hated Asiatics in the Far West, the Irish Catholics, Germans, Italians, and Jews were spared the usual ration of bigotry they received elsewhere.

Harassment of Japanese immigrants

As the Chinese "threat" eased, racial hatred on the West Coast was transferred to the Japanese, who by 1910 numbered more than 72,000 in the United States. Japan's surprising victory in the Russo-Japanese War in 1905 sparked West Coast fears of a new "Yellow Peril." California's first anti-Japanese meeting was held that year. The San Francis-

A Chinese immigrant in nineteenth-century San Francisco could find a home away from home. In Chinatown he was surrounded by people who spoke his language, dressed in traditional manner, and understood his ways. The public letter writer, above, was one of many institutions imported from the cities of China.

co *Chronicle* featured such scare headlines as "The Japanese Invasion," "Japanese, A Menace to American Women," "Brown Men an Evil in the Public Schools," and "Crime and Poverty Go Hand in Hand with Asiatic Labor." Vigilantes beat and harassed Japanese nationals in San Francisco. In 1906 the San

Those we have injured we hate. . . .
HUBERT H. BANCROFT   (1832–1918)

Francisco school board transferred ninety-three Japanese children to a segregated school for Asians. The Japanese Imperial Government protested strongly. Hoping to avoid a nasty diplomatic incident, President Theodore Roosevelt intervened personally with the board, persuading it to reverse its policy by promising to end Japanese immigration. Patriotic groups and organized labor persisted in their attacks. In 1907 the California legislature drafted several bills curtailing the importation of Japanese labor, and again TR stepped in to negotiate a "Gentlemen's Agreement" (part of the Root-Takahira Accords). The Japanese government agreed to refuse passports to Japanese laborers seeking work in the U.S.

Attacks on Japanese on the West Coast continued. By 1910, of the 72,000 Japanese in the U.S., 40,000 were in California. The traffic in "picture brides" angered the state's anti-Oriental organizations. Japanese bachelors in the U.S. married women in the Old Country whom they had only seen in photos. They then signed legal papers that made their brides eligible for immigration to the U.S. The number of women involved was greatly exaggerated in the press. Japan put a halt to this minor furor by changing its emigration regulations in 1920.

More serious was the apparent threat from Japanese landowners. Unlike the Chinese, who had no great passion to own land, Japanese immigrants hoped to acquire their own farms. Successful farmers, they were expert at growing rice, lettuce, and other crops. White farmers resented the competition and pressured the California legislature to prohibit Japanese aliens from owning land. When such a bill was drafted in 1913, the Japanese government sent an official rebuke to Washington. Now it was Wilson's turn to plead with California. He convinced the state legislature that it should water down its proposed law. Similar legislation was passed in Oregon, Idaho, and other western states. California's Alien Land Law partly limited the right of the Japanese to lease and own land, but it left some loopholes. Japanese landowners could evade the full effect of the law by registering their property in the names of American-born children or relatives.

Review

A dominant belief in white supremacy during the half century following the Civil War affected all of the nation's racial minorities. The Indians' struggle for survival shifted to the trans-Mississippi West. Warfare followed the coming of the settlers, climaxing with the "battle" at Wounded Knee. By this time most Indians had been forced onto reservations run by the Bureau of Indian Affairs. Many whites thought that tribal culture had to be abandoned before Indians could assimilate successfully. The Dawes Act of 1887 was an attempt to impose individual ownership on Indians, whose native culture had flourished on tribal and communal living. As their lands shrank and their health deteriorated through malnutrition and disease, the Indians indeed seemed to be a vanishing race.

After a short period of hope during Reconstruction, blacks found that they were not about to achieve equality with whites. The most radical feature of the Reconstruction regimes was that blacks were given a political voice and were elected to public office. But despite the Fourteenth and Fifteenth Amendments, blacks were deprived of the vote, and Jim Crow became institutionalized in the South by the end of the century. When Booker T. Washington's program of accommodation failed, more militant leaders like W. E. B. Du Bois demanded justice. In World War I black men served in a segregated army. The jobs made available by the war greatly increased the northward migration of southern Negroes. By the 1920s the black ghettos in northern cities made racism a national rather than a strictly southern issue.

Racial conflict between people of Mexican background and Anglos flared along the Mexican-U.S. border. In California, Mexican Americans (now known as Chicanos) soon lost ground financially and politically. While the second generation of Mexican Americans became more acculturated, continuing migration from Mexico maintained the Old Country culture. In New Mexico conflict increased as white cattle ranchers moved into the area. Although much land slipped from old family holdings to new Anglo owners, the Spanish-speaking culture stayed strong. Local-color writers romanticized the "Spanish" tradition and contrasted it with the Puritan Ethic. In the twentieth century Mexican Americans became an important labor source in reclamation and agricultural projects in the Southwest, but they were not absorbed into the nation's mainstream.

Job competition was the greatest cause of discrimination against Asians. California had an especially high ratio of Chinese in its work force. In 1882 Congress passed a law halting all Chinese immigration for ten years. As hatred of Chinese eased, resentment was directed against the Japanese, whose numbers were increasing and who were successfully competing with white farmers. Western states passed laws prohibiting Asians from owning land. Except for the short period of Reconstruction when blacks in the South had some opportunity for political growth, the years from the Civil War to World War I saw little advance for the country's racial minorities.

Questions

1. Why was the belief in white superiority especially strong in the late nineteenth century? How did white racism affect the different minority groups?
2. Describe the reservation policy that developed after the Civil War. What role did the BIA play?
3. It has been said that if Reconstruction had lasted longer, the history of blacks in America could have been very different. What differences do you think might have been possible? Knowing what you do today, what programs would you have kept, changed, or added to make Reconstruction more successful?
4. Describe how the Mexican Americans became a minority. Do you think this helped or hurt them in the U.S. during these years?
5. What were the major grievances Caucasians had against the Chinese and Japanese?

Group portrait of an immigrant family; they pose in new quarters.

Some came for love of money
and some for the love of freedom.
Whatever the lure that brought
us, each has his gift. . . .
All have come bearing gifts
and have laid them on the Altar
of America.

Secretary of the Interior
FRANKLIN K. LANE (1864–1921)
himself an immigrant

21

21
The New Immigration

This chapter is concerned with changes in immigration patterns at the end of the last century. These changes—which drastically altered the country's earlier ethnic composition—resulted from the so-called new immigration from southern and eastern Europe. The offspring of many of those immigrant newcomers are today's "white ethnics." The rising consciousness of the white ethnics in the 1960s has given the study of immigration and nationality new meaning. Until the '60s many Americans presumed that assimilation had virtually wiped out ethnic identity among whites. Their belief in the melting-pot idea was shaken by the protests of whites claiming to be victims of prejudice on the basis of nationality and religion, and perhaps on the basis of class as well. Assimilation is indeed a powerful force, as this chapter shows, but it also produces pains and scars that tend to linger, even from one generation to the next.

Changes in the religious climate also arose at the end of the last century. Religion generally was unsettled by the growth of industrialism and materialism and by the spread of scientific attitudes. Protestantism had to face a massive influx of people of "foreign" religious affiliation, and had to adjust to rapidly increasing urbanism, class conflict, and poverty. Protestant Americans of Anglo-Saxon cultural background had taken their pre-eminence for granted. Now, more or less suddenly, the Anglo-Saxon Protestant consensus seemed to vanish, and a new ethnic and religious mix appeared in its stead.

Immigrants on their way to America in 1893, aboard the S. S. Pennland. Most of the "new immigrants" from southern and eastern Europe left the Old Country to escape hardship and poverty. One Polish peasant explained in a letter, "I have a very great wish to go to America. I want to leave my native country because we are 6 children and we have very little land. . . ."

The "Pull" of America

Newcomers from southern and eastern Europe

Early in the 1890s officials at Ellis Island, the reception center for immigrants in New York Harbor, began noticing a striking change on their registration sheets. Newcomers from southern and eastern Europe (Italy, Russia, Poland, Greece, the Balkans, and Austria-Hungary) were outnumbering those from northern and western Europe (Germany, Ireland, Britain, and Scandinavia). (See maps, p. 452.)

The old immigration peaked at 600,000 a year in the early 1880s and then gradually fell, while the new immigration reached over 1.2 million people in 1907 and remained high until the outbreak of World War I. Most of the new immigrants settled in the Northeast, in urban, rather than rural, areas. Few of them went to the South.

The new immigrants were both "pushed" from Europe and "pulled" toward America. A combination of social and economic factors drove the peasants, laborers, and small merchants out of southern and eastern Europe at the end of the century. Better food supply, a declining death rate, and a rising birth rate had caused overpopulation. For every son who inherited his father's property in 1750, there were two or three by the time of World War I. Southern Italy was periodically wracked by cholera. As the citrus industry blossomed in California and Florida, the Italian industry shriveled. Croatian vineyards suffered from blight. In many nations the peasant faced falling agricultural prices and rising taxes. The institution of conscript armies in many countries imposed a special hardship on poorer families by calling up for service those males who had the highest earning power. In czarist Russia and in Poland pogroms (massacres and persecutions) drove out the Jews. So a variety of reasons—escape from economic hardship, and from religious persecution and military service—propelled the southern and eastern Europeans outward.

Then there was the "pull" of America as the promised land. However downtrodden, the poor of Europe had one hope—that of achieving a better life in the United States. In hundreds of European villages the same dream was enacted. A family would receive an "American letter" describing the wonders (and sometimes the difficulties) of the New World. A decision was made to depart. Adults and older children tore themselves loose from family and friends, from all that was familiar. They promised to write often and to send for their next of kin as soon as possible. Then came the tearful farewells. Finally they streamed across Europe by foot or cart or railroad to port cities and booked passage on steamers to America. For ten days or more they endured the filthy, crowded conditions of steerage. Eventually they sailed past the Statue of Liberty, whose torch had become a beacon of freedom. On its base was inscribed a poem by Emma Lazarus, an immigrant: "Give me your tired, your poor,/ Your huddled masses yearning to breathe free,/ The wretched refuse of your teeming shore./ Send these, the homeless, tempest-tost to me,/ I lift my lamp beside the golden door."

Debarking at the immigrant depot on Ellis Island in New York Harbor, they were quarantined and examined by doctors and tagged by inspectors. Immigration clerks bobbed their names to fit the English language. Eventually those who passed muster boarded a ferry to New York City or Hoboken. They groped their way to the neighborhoods of the relatives or friends who had written the "American letter." Many remained there, speaking the old language and retaining close ties with the old culture.

Crowding into city ghettos

Until 1890 many newcomers headed west. Most of these immigrants dreamed of owning small farms in the new land. Following the Civil War, German, Swiss, Scandinavian, and Czech settlers streamed onto the Great Plains by the hundreds of thousands. They were a hardy bunch. But farming in the West involved difficult and unusual conditions. The sod was tough, the machinery unfamiliar, and the marketing techniques unfamiliar. Truck farmers near big cities usually fared better than those who raised staple crops on the remote prairies and plains.

After 1890 the major pull was to the industrial cities of the Northeast (although many reached the industrial cities of the Midwest as well). Most immigrants settled in the first city they saw—New York or Boston, for example. Many became construction workers, repairing railroads, paving roads, or hauling brick and lumber. Still others became miners, stevedores, domestics, peddlers, porters, street cleaners, shoe blacks, seamstresses, and ditch diggers or other kinds of day laborers. Two thirds of the workers in the major industries at the turn of the century were immigrants. They were sometimes recruited by employers who wanted to maintain a large labor pool and thereby keep wages as low as possible. Factories in New England, for example, recruited workers in Portugal who arrived with company labels tied in their lapels. Andrew Carnegie, among others, deliberately encouraged "free trade in men"—that is, he discouraged restrictions on immigration and paved the way for thousands of immigrants to come to America and work in his mills and mines. By constantly hiring new arrivals, Carnegie prevented the growth of unions in his plants. Employers also used "greenhorns" as strike breakers. The complaint of native-born workers that immigrants were undercutting wages and standards was in the short run often true. Yet by coming in at the bottom, the immigrants pushed some of the native-born into better jobs that provided a better income.

Each "homeless, tempest-tost" immigrant acquired a new identity based on nationality, language, and religion. In the Old Country identity was by status or occupation (peasant, merchant, etc.) and by village or region. Neither point of reference was quite as useful in America. The Poznansker or Lubliner was now simply a Pole, the Bavarian or Saxon a German, the Tracian or Athenian a Greek. And Anglo-Americans could easily lump newcomers by their language and religion.

Native Americans expected adult immigrants to retain their own language, even if they picked up a smattering of English. By the same token, teachers and school officials expected immigrant children to speak English exclusively. They saw no other way to run the schools. Stamping out the "babble of tongues" was essential for promoting patriotism. The offspring of immigrants found little reward in speaking their parents' language, and gradually they lost that ability. The possible educational advantages of being bilingual were not appreciated until years later.

In most immigrant homes the children's welfare was the prime concern. The educational and social attainments of the younger generation were a source of bursting pride among their parents. In some families the children even taught their parents the lessons they had learned at school. But the newly acquired customs, manners, and language of the young also created a gulf between the generations. In many households the distance between the two generations could not be bridged.

While necessity forced most immigrants to settle in a poor and crowded "Hunkytown," as an immigrant ghetto was sometimes called, they often found positive advantages in those ghettos. Here they could search out and live with Old World friends and relatives, sing, dance, and worship in the traditional way, buy foreign-language papers, eat Old World foods, and play familiar games like soccer or bocci. And they could join organizations to help their less fortunate countrymen. Mutual-benefit associations flourished in every ghetto, offering group insurance with sickness and death benefits and supporting programs for education and civic advancement. Sometimes they sent money home to help bring over relatives or to support political causes. In 1910 Springfield, Massachusetts, with 2915 Italian residents, had twelve different Italian organizations.

By the late nineteenth century the foreign-born were an integral part of American politics. Many gave their votes to native-born political bosses in exchange for a variety of benefits. Politicians attended weddings, confirmations, bar mitzvahs, and church picnics with the hope of winning the backing of immigrants for the straight party ticket. They landed jobs for newcomers, intervened with the police and judges in criminal cases, brought Christmas baskets to poor widows, and generally made life easier in the "foreign" quarters of the city. The peasants-turned-citizens knew little about democracy at first, but they did value the help of city bosses and they had a deep respect for authority. As a result, they became part of the political system.

Those of the old immigrant stock stood a

better chance of being elected to office. The most renowned foreign-born politician of his time was John Peter Altgeld, a naturalized German, who became governor of Illinois in 1892. Displaying a particular knack for city politics, the New York City Irish managed in 1885 to elect an Irish-born mayor. The Irish vote was very large there. Still, this was an important achievement, considering the fact that signs reading "No Irish Need Apply" were still common in other cities. But in New York City attacks on parochial schools tapered off, and the Irish suffered less job discrimination.

The Progressives were divided in their attitudes toward the foreign-born. That dedicated Anglo-Saxonist Theodore Roosevelt feared that free immigration would finally spell "race suicide" for the original Anglo-Saxon stock. Many reformers looked on foreigners as the tools of corrupt politicians. The one nativist law introduced during the Progressive era was a result of McKinley's assassination; it barred anarchists from entering the country. Others took a more liberal view. Lincoln Steffens tried to prove in his muckraking articles that the true source of urban political corruption was the business community and that the naturalized voters were only scapegoats. Jane Addams and other social workers staunchly opposed nativism and listed the cultural contributions made to America by immigrants.

Nativist pressure to restrict immigration

New immigrants often faced discrimination. And their problems increased when an organized nativist movement arose in the 1880s and 1890s in the wake of a depression, labor troubles, and anarchist violence. It intensified after the Haymarket Riot of 1886 in which foreign anarchists were convicted of murdering Chicago policemen.

In 1887 the American Protective Association (APA) was formed to halt the supposed spread of Catholic power. The APA blamed the labor unrest and the depression of the 1890s on an international conspiracy of Catholics, led by the pope himself. Terence V. Powderly, the American-born Catholic leader of the Knights of Labor, was accused of being an archconspirator.

Nativism generally rose in periods of economic hardship. The Immigration Restriction League was organized by wealthy old-line Bostonians after the panic of 1893. It urged Congress to restrict immigration and to insist that immigrants could read and write. Such a bill did pass both the House and Senate in 1897, but President Cleveland vetoed it. Populists blamed the scarcity of money on an international conspiracy of Jewish and British bankers. Some gave anti-Semitic and nativist speeches during the 1896 presidential campaign. McKinley backers feared that "dangerous classes of foreigners" might vote the "anarchist" William Jennings Bryan into the White House. They were wrong. Most of the foreign-born cast their ballots for the solid, middle-class candidate, McKinley. This, coupled with a return of prosperity, temporarily squelched the movement to restrict immigration. It also reduced anti-Catholicism.

Organized labor as represented by the AFL favored restrictive immigration laws. In 1885 it finally won a long-fought battle to end hiring contract labor in Europe. At its 1902 convention Federation delegates voted 1858 to 352 in favor of a literacy test for incoming foreigners. Samuel Gompers, himself an immigrant, expressed the view that "cheap labor, ignorant labor, takes our jobs and cuts our wages." By contrast, employers on the whole still favored free immigration.

During Theodore Roosevelt's administration, Congress set up the Dillingham Commission to investigate the impact of immigration. Its forty-seven-volume report

(1907–1911) contained ammunition for those opposed to the new immigration. The conclusion of the report was that, to a much greater degree than before, recent arrivals to the United States were filthy, diseased, and uneducated and a burden on their communities. They preferred ghettos to farms. They competed in the job market with native-born Americans. They abetted political corruption and encouraged anarchy. Those who made their fortunes in America often returned to the Old Country to spend them. Furthermore, the immigrants had many children

Reckon each as a pound of dynamite—
surely a modest comparison. . . .
Not all these enemy aliens are hostile.
Not all dynamite explodes.

SAMUEL HOPKINS ADAMS   (1871–1958)
Journalist and author

and worshiped God in strange and alien ways.

The First World War brought nativist activities to a new high. Again Congress passed a bill requiring immigrants to pass a

Immigrant laborers frequently worked as dockwallopers. Workers of the same nationality and even from the same home town in the Old Country tended to team up together. One Italian-born immigrant observed that "in this country, immigrants of the same town stick together like bees from the same hive and work wherever the foreman or boss finds a job for the gang."

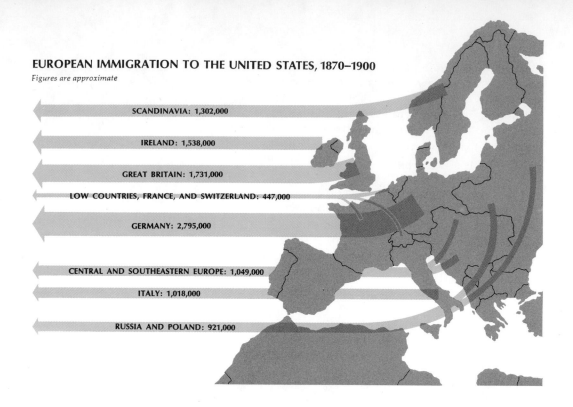

EUROPEAN IMMIGRATION TO THE UNITED STATES, 1870–1900

Figures are approximate

SCANDINAVIA: 1,302,000

IRELAND: 1,538,000

GREAT BRITAIN: 1,731,000

LOW COUNTRIES, FRANCE, AND SWITZERLAND: 447,000

GERMANY: 2,795,000

CENTRAL AND SOUTHEASTERN EUROPE: 1,049,000

ITALY: 1,018,000

RUSSIA AND POLAND: 921,000

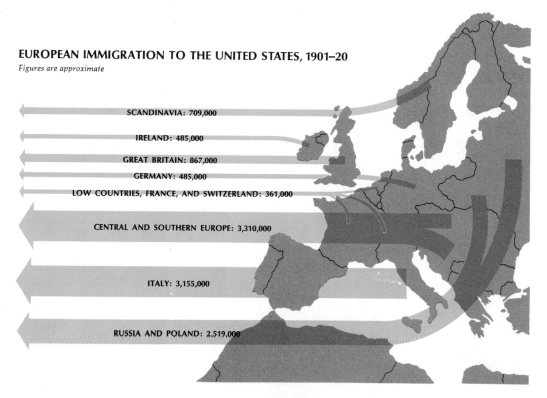

EUROPEAN IMMIGRATION TO THE UNITED STATES, 1901–20

Figures are approximate

SCANDINAVIA: 709,000

IRELAND: 485,000

GREAT BRITAIN: 867,000

GERMANY: 485,000

LOW COUNTRIES, FRANCE, AND SWITZERLAND: 361,000

CENTRAL AND SOUTHERN EUROPE: 3,310,000

ITALY: 3,155,000

RUSSIA AND POLAND: 2,519,000

literacy test and sent it to the president. Again the president vetoed it, but this time the veto was overridden. Now newcomers had to prove their ability to read and write a language. When the literacy test had little effect in slowing the postwar immigration of "inferior racial stocks," nativists started to clamor for even more restrictive legislation, which was enacted by Congress in the 1920s.

Immigrant contributions

There were many success stories among the immigrants, from Andrew Carnegie, the captain of industry, to Samuel Gompers, leader of organized labor. Scientist Charles Steinmetz came from Germany. Composer Irving Berlin was a Jew who emigrated from Russia. Football hero Knute Rockne was originally from Norway, and Father Edward Joseph Flanagan, founder of Boys Town, arrived from Ireland. Actress Mary Pickford, America's Sweetheart, came from Canada. These were only a very few of the immigrants who enriched the life of their adopted land.

But most immigrants did not achieve the American Dream. As a Norwegian settler in South Dakota explained:

[There was] the sense of being lost in an alien culture, the sense of being thrust somewhere outside the charmed circle of life. If you couldn't conquer that feeling, if you couldn't break through the magic hedge of thorns, you were lost indeed. Many couldn't and didn't and many were lost thereby.

More of their children, the first-born generation, entered the charmed circle, but for the immigrants themselves, as Glazer and Moynihan write, "The point about the Melting Pot . . . is that it did not happen."

Measuring the contribution of immigrants to American life is like measuring the contribution of salt to ocean water: it is everywhere and difficult to separate out. Certainly the English language has been altered and enriched. Italian spaghetti, Mexican tacos, Polish sausage, Chinese egg rolls, Jewish knishes, and Danish pastries symbolize the flavor and piquancy foreign nationalities have added to America. New styles of recreation such as the Sunday picnic took firm hold. The Irish and the Chinese, among others—sometimes almost literally—moved mountains as they constructed the nation's canals, railroads, and gas and electric works. The foreign-born in factories, mills, and mines made possible the industrial growth that turned America into a world power.

The New Religious Balance

A new Protestant theology

Protestantism was deeply rooted in rural and small-town America. Most rural Americans at the turn of the century were Protestant and over half of those Americans who had a religious affiliation in 1890 belonged to the mainstream denominations: Methodist, Baptist, Presbyterian, Disciples of Christ, and Congregationalist. By 1900 Protestant attitudes had become, in the words of one church historian, "the creature of American culture." Most churchmen accepted the economics of laissez-faire, the cult of success, the idea of progress, and the belief in the United States as a nation chosen by God for a great humane mission. Protestant leaders defended the status quo and enjoyed a huge following. Still, rapid social change was undermining their footing. They were begin-

> *In the history of the world, the man who is ahead has always been called a heretic.*
>
> ROBERT J. INGERSOLL (1833–1899)

ning to wonder how to cope with big cities, class conflict, urban poverty, and large-scale European immigration, which included millions of Catholics and Jews.

Charles Darwin's theory of evolution exploded like a time bomb under America's Protestant pulpits. At first some Protestants considered it a new form of atheism. Darwin's *Origin of Species* (1859) and *The Descent of Man* (1871) threatened many basic Christian beliefs, especially the story of the creation of man and woman in Genesis. The Bible taught that God created Adam and then Eve from his rib, whereas evolutionists announced that people had evolved from lower forms of animal life over millions of years. But most Protestant theologians finally came to terms with the theory of evolution. President James McCosh of Princeton, a Presbyterian minister, saw a general similarity between Genesis and evolution, where everything proceeded from the simple to the most complex. The religious writer John Fiske thought evolution proved that God sought the perfection and preeminence of human beings. The most popular preacher of the Gilded Age, Henry Ward Beecher, declared himself "a cordial Christian evolutionist." He saw a divine design in nature and "an ascending scale" in the animal world. He abandoned the Calvinist notion of original sin and the fall of man and stressed love and joy. Beecher's *Evolution and Religion* (1885) became a standard work for Protestants who broadened their beliefs to encompass Darwin. In the 1890s this set of liberal Christian ideas was named the "New Theology," or "Modernism."

Believers in the New Theology held that God was not a stern and demanding despot but a kindly and forgiving diety. Doctrine was not important to them. A good disposi-

tion and good conduct were enough to win a person entry into a church and perhaps into heaven. The main purpose of religion was to save individual souls, not to improve society generally. Beecher went even further with evolutionary theory by accepting Social Darwinism as his guide to industrial society. He would have no truck with workers who joined unions and caused strikes. If people worked hard, they would be rewarded. If not, they would fall by the wayside as they deserved.

In keeping with the liberalizing trend in religion, even freethinkers—those who rejected religious authority and dogma completely in favor of reason and scientific thought—could attract an audience. The most famous freethinker of his time was Robert G. Ingersoll (1833–1899), who hoped to take God out of religion altogether and put an end to what he called supernaturalism. "Robert Godless Injuresoul," as his enemies called him, considered himself an agnostic. "The religion of the future is humanity," Ingersoll stated in 1881. He was a celebrated orator and an influential Republican who, at the GOP convention in 1876, nominated his friend James G. Blaine for president.

Bible criticism and comparative religion were two additional trends in American thought that reflected a liberalized religion. According to many scholars the Bible was not the Divine Word but a human creation that consisted of sixty-six books of poetry, history, folklore, and moral teachings—a collective work put together over a period of a thousand years. Most of the Bible scholars who pursued this line of inquiry were in no sense atheists or agnostics. Yet they were roasted as such by Fundamentalists who reviewed their work.

Religion was not held in the highest esteem by intellectuals. Most American philosophers were lay people, not clergy as in earlier periods of American history. They were interested in religious experience rather than in theology per se. Few intellectuals considered the churches inspiring or spiritually satisfying.

Revivals and social action in the cities

On the other hand church membership was definitely on the increase, and organized religion had never been stronger in the United States than in the post-Civil War era. Revivals were the main means by which Protestants brought the unchurched into the fold. Since the 1830s the most astute revivalists saw that the cities needed to be won over to Christ. In 1873 the evangelist Dwight L. Moody devised the techniques of urban revivals. With ushers, choirs, and assistant ministers coordinating details in a businesslike manner, revival meetings rolled on schedule. Moody was an impassioned speaker, though his sermons did not build toward an outburst of religious frenzy, as had been the fashion of the early backwoods revivalists. Even more colorful was the evangelist William A. (Billy) Sunday, an ex-baseball player who started a revival crusade in 1896 that continued for decades and made him world famous. However much these men hoped to appeal to the poor, they drew mainly middle-class audiences.

To supplement revivals in building church memberships, Protestants counted increasingly on religious education. Moody originated the Baptist Sunday School movement, an extremely influential form of Christian education. He also founded the Moody Bible Institute in 1889. This organization recruited and trained religious educators. Thus some of the revivalists acquired a new look in the cities.

In its own way Protestantism was develop-

Evangeline Booth, daughter of the founder of the Salvation Army, began her evangelistic preaching at the age of seventeen. Virtually every member of the Booth family took an active role in the Army's "warfare against evil." Evangeline was commander of the Salvation Army in the United States from 1904 to 1934.

ing new strategies for the times. The Young Men's and Young Women's Christian Associations offered a haven for unattached young people in the city. The Y's tried to provide a home away from home. The Salvation Army, transplanted from England, served the downtrodden of the urban slums. It collected cast-off clothing for derelicts, fed the hungry, cared for the sick, conducted schools, and preached morality and sobriety. The traditional Protestant missionary work had been directed mainly at the western frontier. Now Baptists, Congregationalists, Presbyterians, and Methodists began trying to convert immigrants in the cities from Catholicism or Eastern Orthodoxy. The missionaries learned foreign languages so they could visit the homes of immigrants. By and large these efforts failed, however.

Though personal salvation remained the focus of nineteenth-century Protestants some clergy believed that modern social conditions were corrupting to individuals, and that social evils must be tackled if souls were to be saved. This belief came to be known as the Social Gospel. One of its spokesmen, Washington Gladden, rejected the theory that labor was a commodity and that wealth was accumulated by the "natural law" of "greed and strife." Not profits but Christian love should guide the relations between worker and employer. The Social Gospel ministers were the radical fringe of many denominations. Walter Rauschenbusch, another leader of the Social Gospel movement, considered himself a Christian Socialist. They prodded church members to develop a social conscience by taking a greater interest in working people. During the Progressive era, many middle-class Protestants supported better wages and hours for workers, improved conditions for women and children in industry, and housing reform.

With the growth of immigrant populations many downtown Protestant churches in Boston and New York followed their parishioners to the suburbs. A few remained behind. In the spirit of the Social Gospel those who stayed established "institutional churches" in the ghettos. These were settlement houses with a religious affiliation. They tried to combat crime, poverty, drunkenness, prostitution, and other social ills. They offered everything from medical care to spiritual guidance, from English-language instruction to athletics, from vocational guidance to day nurseries.

Christian Science was an important new religion in the later nineteenth century. Its founder, Mary Baker Eddy (1820–1910) came to her belief in healing-through-faith after suffering ailments which were not cured by medicine. Her lectures, published in *Science and Health* (1875), eventually found a large audience. She organized the Christian Scientists' Association in 1876 which established the First Church of Christ, Scientist, in Boston in 1879. Her ideas had a special appeal for well-to-do urban women, who were particularly aware of their health.

Black Protestants

Negro churches were a focal point for the black community at the end of the nineteenth century. In fact, during Reconstruction they were the single most important form of community organization for the newly freed slaves. Southern blacks formed independent Methodist and Baptist churches to help foster civil rights and education for themselves. After Reconstruction the churches adopted a more conservative social stance, in tune with the idea that blacks must now accommodate themselves to white prejudice instead of bucking the trend.

Whether in country or city the black Protestant church continued to be the center of community life. By 1900 some 2.7 million of the 8.3 million blacks in the U.S. were affiliated with churches. The African Methodist Episcopal church alone, which dated back to the early nineteenth century, claimed over 450,000 members. In cities like Atlanta and Philadelphia, black churches performed welfare services similar to those of the white institutional churches. They offered evening schools for adults and recreation for children.

In terms of theology the black Methodist and Baptist churches had their conservative and liberal wings. But evangelical Protestantism was extremely important to blacks and was practiced in the thousands of one-room rural churches of the South. Sometimes blacks defected to other Protestant denominations or to the Catholic church. But whatever the denomination, the ministers remained the leaders of the black community. United States Senator Hiram R. Revels, for example, was a minister in the African Methodist Episcopal church. As W. E. B. Du Bois once declared: "The Preacher is the most unique personality developed by the Negro on American soil. A leader, a politician, a 'boss,' an intriguer, and idealist—all of these he is. . . ."

The Catholic church and lay trusteeism

The Catholic church loomed large in America in part because of the size of its membership. By 1906 Catholics made up approximately 17 percent of the U.S. population. The church was most influential among the ethnic groups with the highest birthrates— Irish, Poles, Italians, French Canadians, and Mexicans.

The church insisted on retaining control over the education of Catholic children. It considered the public schools a form of Protestant education. At the very least it sought the use of the Catholic version of the Bible in the public schools. Around 1870 the church opened a political campaign for public funds for parochial schools in New York State. When the courts blocked this move, the bishops went ahead anyway to build a number of parochial schools with church money. That Catholics should reject the major American institution favoring democracy and national unity—the public schools—caused ripples in the nativist pond.

To Protestants the Catholic church appeared strong and unified, yet internally it was fractured along ethnic lines. Most priests and bishops were Irish. But the Irish clergy were deeply resented by Poles, Italians, French Canadians, and Germans, who much preferred priests of their own background who spoke their own languages. The ap-

Secularism is a religion of its kind, and usually a very loud-spoken and intolerant religion.

JOHN IRELAND (1838–1918)
Archbishop of St. Paul

pointment of priests and the control of church property were the main issues. Theology seldom entered the discussions. In Germany a prominent Catholic layman named Peter Paul Cahensly urged the Vatican to establish American parishes on the basis of nationality, since the United States was not genuinely a unified nation. The Vatican rejected "Cahenslyism" in 1890, but the idea continued to thrive. Cahensly's analysis of American nationality distressed many Protestants.

In 1897 disaffected Polish Catholics formed the Polish National Catholic church, the only permanent schism of Roman Catholicism in the United States. (In 1960 it counted 280,000 communicants.) Italian and Lithuanian Catholics came close to breaking away from the mother church but in the end remained in the fold. Finally the church worked out a truce whereby parish affairs were controlled by local nationalities, but the appointment of clergy remained in the hands of the bishops, among whom the Irish were the dominant group.

Catholics coping with city problems

In the big cities, where it had a loyal following among the immigrant working class, the Catholic church responded actively to industrial problems. Though conservative in most matters, the church took a relatively liberal position on labor unions. In 1887 when the pope was seriously considering criticizing the Knights of Labor, James Cardinal Gibbons, archbishop of Baltimore, wrote the Vatican a memo strongly praising the organi-

zation. He pointed out that "labor is now so organized that without belonging to the organization it is almost impossible to earn one's living." Archbishop John Ireland of St. Paul declared: "I hate that view of labor which makes it a mechanical force, like the rotation of a railroad engine or a turbine, purchaseable at mere market value. . . . I must keep well in mind the dignity and rights of man." In 1891 Pope Leo XIII issued an unusual encyclical on labor, *De Rerum Novarum*. Leo rejected both pure laissez-faire capitalism and pure socialism. Within the framework of free enterprise, Leo approved justice and action on behalf of labor.

Catholic social action surfaced in a variety of voluntary associations of laymen, guided by the Catholic clergy. The Knights of Co-

lumbus started in 1882 as a fraternal organization which offered insurance to Catholics. Soon it branched out into charity and social services for city Catholics. The Society of Saint Vincent de Paul, originally a French association, was introduced into the U.S. in 1845. Twenty years later its seventy-five chapters and conferences provided boarding houses and industrial schools for poor children and moral guidance for young men. The Young Men's Union, founded in 1875, also offered recreation, night-school education, and vocational training. The Sisters of Charity and other religious orders made similar services available to girls and women. Priests inspired by *De Rerum Novarum* organized the Catholic Action Movement to bring about laws to help the working class. It re-

ceived official church sanction and became in effect a counterpart of the Protestants' Social Gospel movement. Father John A. Ryan, an economist who pioneered in the field of minimum wage legislation, led this movement. His idea of "a living wage" was used as a basis for gauging the extent of poverty.

An influx of East European Jews

In Abraham Cahan's novel *The Rise of David Levinsky* (1917) a pious young Jew leaves Russia and makes his way to America, the Promised Land. Lonely and dejected, he is at first comforted by the enveloping warmth of the Orthodox synagogue. But slowly he deserts the practice of ancient laws and adapts to big-city life. The author, himself an immigrant, arrived in this country in 1882, following a bloody pogrom. He was trained in Orthodoxy but was strongly drawn to rationalism and socialism. Cahan founded the *Jewish Daily Forward*, which became the largest and most influential Yiddish-language newspaper in the United States. His novel and his career reflect much of the history of Jewish life in America in the nineteenth and early twentieth centuries.

In 1880 the 250,000 American Jews were still largely of German origin. They lived as business and professional people, usually in small towns of the South and Midwest. Few settled in the Northeast. They were known for supporting numerous charities and hospitals. Of the 270 temples in America in 1880, the majority followed the Reform tradition.

In the 1880s America witnessed a huge wave of Jewish immigrants.* They arrived as refugees from persecution and economic hardship in czarist Russia and the Hapsburg empire. These immigrants, largely Orthodox and numbering about three million, drastically altered the profile of American Judaism. Most of them settled in New York, Boston, Philadelphia, and other large cities in the Northeast, where they filled the most wretched ghettos. Many found a niche in the garment trades and other light industries. Jews, who never comprised more than 3.5 percent of the population, began to have

*This was the third wave of Jewish immigration. The first was Sephardic (see Chapter 5) and the second was German (see Chapter 13).

an influence on the economic, social, and cultural life of the cities that was far out of proportion to their numbers in the country as a whole.

American Jews of German background tried to steer clear of the strange new East European immigrants. Class and culture divided them. In a moment of panic, a Jewish newspaper even suggested that the government should curtail the Jewish influx by using the new federal law designed to stop Chinese "undesirables." In time, however, the older Jewish community helped out their less fortunate brethren.

The recent arrivals and their children rose swiftly on the social ladder, so swiftly in fact that theirs was called "the greatest collective Horatio Alger story in American immigration history." The startling improvement in the Jews' occupational status has been attributed to the cultural values they brought from Europe and adapted to good advantage in the U.S. The tradition of Talmudic learning—the study of ancient religious writing— instilled in school-age youngsters disciplined study habits and an appreciation for learning. Children were encouraged, if possible, to get an advanced degree. Also, European Jews were used to being self-employed as they had been forcibly restricted to certain trades and crafts since medieval times. This custom was translated in America into a high evaluation for independence, thrift, sobriety, and work—much on the order of the Protestant Ethic that had motivated Christian Americans since colonial times. Even while the parents worked at menial and low-paying jobs, the younger generation was moving forward to better education and careers.

The flood of poor though ambitious Jewish immigrants created strong resentments on the part of native-born Americans. A wave of anti-Semitism occurred in the 1880s. Curiously it affected the upper-class Jews more than the newcomers. The wealthy banker Joseph Seligman was refused admittance to the Grand Union Hotel in Saratoga, New York, in 1887. Private schools and clubs that had once been open to Jews now closed their doors to them.

The fact that the new Jewish immigrants were mainly Orthodox while the established Jews were of the Reform tradition caused a dramatic clash. Members of Reform congregations rejected the Bible as divinely inspired, refused to think of Jewish law as having been handed down from Moses, and set aside all Mosaic laws which were "not adapted to the views and habits of modern civilization." Nor did Reform Jews regard themselves as a separate or chosen nation. "We consider ourselves no longer a nation," a Reform spokesman said, "but a religious community, and therefore expect neither a return to Palestine . . . nor the restoration of any of the laws concerning the Jewish state." By contrast the Orthodox held fiercely to Talmudic law.

The clash between the Orthodox and Reform was complicated by the rise of Conservative Judaism, an offshoot of the Reform movement. Conservative Jews felt that the Reform Jews had rejected too many traditions and rituals. They tried to maintain a middle position between the Orthodox and the Reform. The three-way split of Judaism— four-way if one adds secularized Jews—remained a permanent feature of the American Jewish community.

Review

Today's "white ethnics" are descended from European immigrants of the late nineteenth and early twentieth centuries. The poor of southern and eastern Europe arrived in vast numbers in this period and after about 1890 settled mainly in the industrial cities of the Northeast and Midwest. Many naturalized immigrants became part of the political machines by exchanging their votes for a variety of services. As their children became Americanized, rifts opened between the generations. With the reemergence of nativism there began a drive for antiimmigration laws which resulted in the passage of a literacy test for immigrants. The individual and collective contributions of immigrants have played a major role in America's progress.

Between 1865 and 1918 Protestantism in America had to make many adjustments—to industrialism, urbanism, and Darwinism and to the mass immigration of non-Protestants. Some sects made peace with Darwin through a body of liberal Christian ideas called the New Theology. Evangelists organized urban revivals to help save lost souls in the city. Social Gospel ministers prodded the churches to develop a social conscience. "Institutional churches" were established in the cities to combat social ills. In the cities as in rural areas, the church remained the focal point for the black community. Christian Science meanwhile became an important new sect of the post-Civil War era.

The Roman Catholic population grew rapidly, especially in the cities. The church was very influential among ethnic groups and aroused nativist anger by insisting on the control of Catholic children's education. Although the church appeared unified to Protestants, it was actually split along several lines, mainly ethnic. While the church was basically conservative, it took a relatively liberal attitude toward unions. Voluntary associations were created to serve the needs of urban Catholics.

Before the 1880s most American Jews were of German extraction. They practiced the Reform tradition and lived comfortably in small towns in the South and Midwest. In the 1880s a wave of Jewish immigrants, mainly from eastern Europe and of Orthodox belief, arrived in America. Most of these three million people settled in the poorest ghettos of the Northeastern industrial cities, but through hard work and a reverence for learning they and their children rose swiftly on the social ladder. Ironically, the established American Jews were the most direct target of a wave of anti-Semitism in the 1880s. The religious differences which arose in those years between Orthodox and Reform traditions would become a permanent aspect of life in the American Jewish community.

Questions

1. What caused the white ethnics to emigrate from Europe at the end of the nineteenth century, and why did so many choose America as their destination?
2. How did the churches adjust to meet the conditions of the urban industrial scene?
3. Trace the reemergence of nativism between 1865 and 1918. Why do you think nativism has surfaced during times of social and economic stress? Do you see any signs of it now?
4. How did Protestant thought change in the years after the Civil War? Include a consideration of Darwinism, the New Theology, the Social Gospel, Bible criticism, and comparative religion.
5. Describe the religious differences within both the Catholic and the Jewish faiths.

Women celebrate the opening of the National Woman's Party headquarters in Washington, D.C., 1920.

We are no longer petitioners, we are not wards of the nation, but free and equal citizens.
CARRIE CHAPMAN CATT (1859–1947)

22

22
In the Victorian Age

When Elizabeth Cady Stanton declared at the first woman's conference at Seneca Falls, New York, in 1848 that women should demand the vote, she shocked even the most militant feminists. In the coming years feminists spent more time on securing property rights for women, improving educational opportunities, and gaining acceptance in the professions than they did on securing the franchise. Not until after the Civil War did suffrage become a major goal of the movement. The determination of the suffragists was nothing short of amazing. For over forty years they conducted hundreds of separate campaigns in the state capitals and in Congress until they finally achieved their goal in 1920.

The increasing demands by feminists for greater freedom and greater equality with men reflected strong undercurrents of social change. As the role of the family changed, so too did the role of women in the family. More of them were working outside the home, achieving greater economic independence, and breaking into the professions. Many of these events were beyond the control of any feminist leaders or organizations, and this must be taken into account when studying the organized feminist efforts.

"Hello Girls" work at a telephone exchange.

The Family in the Gilded Age

The Victorian family and pressures of society

Many Victorian males blamed the feminist movement for filling their wives' heads with "dangerous" ideas about divorce, career, or financial independence. Feminist writers and speakers did influence people, but social change that had little to do with organized feminism was more immediately responsible for altering the quality of life in the American home. For one thing, the family was becoming less home-centered. Many of its old functions were being taken over by society. Teachers were caring for the children's education while doctors were healing the sick. Clothes and food did not have to be prepared exclusively at home, but were available outside. Heavy immigration supplied the household with cheap domestic labor, thus reducing the middle-class housewife's work load. New appliances like sewing machines also reduced the time and effort required for house chores. In cities and towns working-class women sought factory jobs to supplement their husbands' meager salaries. On farms, new machinery was easing the need for child labor, and therefore was reducing family size. In the cities family members often went in separate directions to work or play.

In 1870, 15 percent of American women worked outside the home. By 1920 the figure had risen to 21 percent. Of the more than 300,000 women who held factory jobs in 1870, most were employed in the textile, garment, and shoe manufacturing industries. The largest single field of employment for women was domestic service. By 1900, 1.8 million women and girls laundered, cooked, and cleaned in homes other than their own. Other growing fields for women included teaching, sales, and secretarial work. As the clerical staffs in industry increased with the invention of the typewriter and other business machines, office work attracted more and more women.

Far more black married women worked outside the home than white, and they worked at more menial jobs and for less pay. Because the earning power of the black male was exceedingly low, his wife's work might be essential to survival. Since blacks lived for the most part in rural places, they worked mainly at farm labor. In the cities the women commonly did laundry or domestic work. They seldom got factory jobs if white workers were available for hire. In short, black women were among the most readily exploited in the job market.

In immigrant families women also worked to help the family survive. But the cultural pattern brought from Europe to the urban ghetto of America dictated that the mothers stay home if possible. Those who held jobs generally did not work alongside their husbands. Most often single or divorced or widowed immigrant women worked in factories, while married immigrant women stayed home and did piece work. They tended the children, cooked, and cleaned while assembling clothing, shelling nuts, making paper flowers, or performing other unskilled, low-paying work at home.

Women were also getting more education. At the turn of the century 5000 women graduated from accredited schools, as compared with 22,000 men. The old saying that woman's place is in the home could not, and did not, apply in more and more households.

To a greater degree the old maxim still applied on the family farm. The farm wife was a major force in taming the West. She worked alongside her husband, helping out with field work and tending livestock. The family

Modern conveniences—like the stove being demonstrated here by a "Yankee peddler"— made rural life less harsh. Such visits were a welcome diversion for rural families and kept them in touch with life "back East."

vegetable plot usually grew under her personal care. In addition she had to feed the entire family, nurture the young and sick— and endure the loneliness. At harvest time she might have to cook steadily for days to feed the added number of field hands. And many days were spent preparing and storing foods that would last through the cold winter months.

The pioneer woman has been successfully portrayed in literature, often as an immigrant or as a child of immigrants. Homesick for her native Norway, Beret, in O. E. Rölvaag's *Giants in the Earth* (1927), never adjusts to the hardship and solitude of the South Dakota plains. Her bitterness and alienation poison the lives of those around her. Willa Cather wrote several novels about life on the Nebraska frontier where she grew up. The hero-

ines of such books as *O Pioneers!* (1913) and *My Ántonia* (1918) are strong, patient, and enduring—the very symbol of the farm woman as pioneer.

By the century's end most rural families lived a more settled and less isolated life. The farm woman's chores were comparatively lighter, and she had a bit more leisure and comfort. Nor was she as lonely since fewer farms were totally isolated, and village and town life was more active.

Whether on the farm or in the small town or city, the American family was basically nuclear, consisting mostly of parents and children, and on occasion a few live-in relatives. Most couples had to make it on their own or not at all. The emotional strain on the marriage partners was one of the factors that led to a growing divorce rate. In 1867 about one marriage in every thirty ended in divorce. By 1920 the figure was one in seven. Some observers suggested the need to educate young people for marriage or to forbid remarriage after divorce.

The Victorian woman was expected to marry, have children, and take care of the home in a graceful manner and without complaint. Mothers were in charge of their children's moral and religious instruction. They were especially attentive to their sons' upbringing, since the boys might eventually grow up to become community leaders. According to the "cult of true womanhood" (see p. 299), women were gentler, more moral, and more humane than their husbands. Ironically, the same qualities that made women better suited for such humane activities as club work, collecting for charities, and organizing church functions, also prepared them for the suffrage drive.

The Victorian father was expected to rule the family with a firm hand, while his wife was supposed to be a dignified but submissive helpmate. Ideally she should be innocent, helpless enough to need her husband's guidance, and a good and dutiful servant to the needs of others. That she should be passive sexually was taken for granted. Pregnancy and birth, so often fatal in those days, were feared by many women. Since their main responsibility was to produce the next generation, they were supposed to accept the pain and hardship of childbearing with good grace.

During the Victorian Age* prudery was probably at an all-time high. The mere mention of sex or reproduction in polite company was a social offense. Under the prodding of vice-fighter Anthony Comstock of Boston, Congress in 1873 passed a law banning all "obscene" material from the mail. This included information on contraception and anything with "amorous, exciting" language or ideas. Stephen Crane's *Maggie, A Girl of the Streets* (1893) had to be privately issued under a pen name, at the author's expense. Theodore Dreiser's *Sister Carrie* (1900), which described the corruption of a young girl, was suppressed for twelve years.

Prostitution increased rapidly in the cities. In some places attempts were made to license rather than eliminate it. Supposedly this would allow the police to contain it in a "red-light district." In practice, licensed prostitution corrupted the police, menaced public health, and provided a cover for criminal activities. The "white slave traffic" (the practice of luring young girls into brothels and forcing them to remain there) resulted in passage of the Mann Act of 1911, which forbade taking women across state lines for immoral purposes. Gradually, around 1917, the red-light districts were closed down, and prostitution took more covert forms.

The shifts in childhood

In America, as in other advanced nations, the birthrate declined throughout the nineteenth century as industrialism increased. From an economic standpoint, large families became unnecessary. On the farm, tractors and other machines reduced the need for human labor. In fact, in an industrial society large numbers of children hampered a comfortable life style.

All the fruitfulness of the present generation, tasked to its utmost, can hardly fill the gaps in our population . . . made by disease and the sword. . . . Shall they be filled by our own children or by those of aliens? This is a question that our own women must answer; upon their loins depends the future destiny of the nation.

HORATIO STORER
Why Not? A Book For Every Woman, 1868

*Queen Victoria, who ruled England from 1837 to 1901, came to symbolize middle-class respectability and prudishness in the English-speaking world.

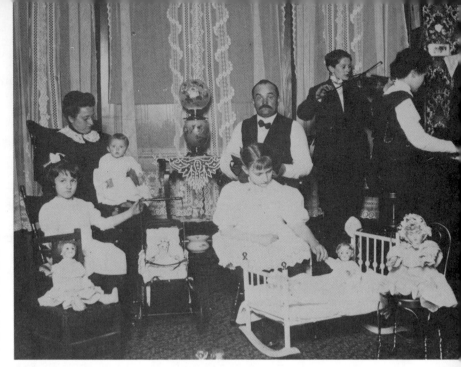

A "typical" Victorian family — Mr. and Mrs. E. E. Schlieske and their children. Freed from the drudgery of housework, but unable to seek work outside the home because of social expectations, the Victorian wife practiced "entire, perfect dominion over the unformed character of [her] infant."

The average age of marriage rose a few years between 1860 and 1890, which also contributed to the falling birthrate. Families of three or four children had become usual by the end of the century.

Although the birthrate declined on a national level, immigrants continued to have large families. The fertility of the Europeans, most of whom were "non-Nordic," seemed a threat to many middle-class Americans. In Theodore Roosevelt's annual message of 1905, he declared that Germany had risen to the level of a world power because it had won "the warfare of the cradle." He urged native-born Americans to have more children if they wanted their country to aspire to world leadership.

Childhood patterns changed in the late nineteenth century. A great many youngsters worked for pay, though the rising curve of child labor peaked in the early twentieth century and began to fall off afterward. In 1900 about 1.7 million children under the age of sixteen were working full time. More specifically, at the turn of the century one quarter of all boys between the ages of ten and fifteen

had jobs, as did one tenth of all girls. But child labor laws were passed, and enforcement improved. By 1920 those figures were cut in half. More public schools were established, along with compulsory attendance laws. School attendance more than doubled between 1870 and 1900. In the early 1900s public education in the South made remarkable strides. Children spent more time at school and with their friends. Boy Scouts, Girl Scouts, and other groups created new interests outside the home. (Organizations like the Kiwanis Club and the Daughters of the American Revolution did the same for adults.) Farm children also had less work.

Though children living in a rural setting normally worked as hard, or harder, than city-bred youngsters, American literature at the end of the century tended to idealize rural and small-town childhood. Writers of fiction stressed the relative freedom from adult pressures. In Mark Twain's *Tom Sawyer* (1876) and *Huckleberry Finn* (1884), the young male of the rural town seemed to have only casual guidance. Tom and Huck rarely did any serious work and had time to enjoy the outdoors before settling down. The most popular and enduring picture of small-town girlhood was Louisa May Alcott's *Little Women* (1868). In some ways the opposite of the Twain stories, Alcott's book paid tribute to the warmth, sentiment, and togetherness of a closely knit and loving family.

More and more the complaint was heard that America was a child-centered society. Writers on child rearing and travelers from abroad chided American parents for their lax discipline. In the words of an Englishwoman in 1871, the country's youngsters were "spoilt, capricious, precocious little men and women." Child-rearing books dwelt on the disorderliness of children, their lack of purpose, and lack of respect for others. They were considered too "childish" compared to previous generations.

America's first recognition of adolescence as a separate state of growing up came in the Gilded Age. The teen-age years, or the period from the onset of puberty to maturity, were previously not isolated in popular or scientific writing, but became a subject of concern on the part of moralists, clergy, and psychologists. Adolescence initially came into view as a problem of urban living. Moralists viewed the city as a trap for innocent young people. City life was weakening the relationship between children and adults and was strengthening peer relationships. Gangs and juvenile delinquency threatened the social order. Young people had to choose from a bewildering variety of careers, and could not just become farmers or artisans, the two main jobs open to them in earlier times. Psychologist G. Stanley Hall of Johns Hopkins University wrote of teen-age years as a time of extreme emotions and "violent impulses." His book, *Adolescence* (1904), was the first full-length study of the subject.

The Struggle for Suffrage

Disappointment after the Civil War

The years from the end of the Civil War to 1890 were years of disappointment and disorganization for those who believed in woman's suffrage. Before the war many feminists had worked hard for black emancipation, thinking that it would certainly bring women the vote. The freed black men would be enfranchised, and in the process so would women. They got a rude awakening in the summer of 1866 when the Fourteenth Amendment was presented to Congress. For the first time it introduced the word *male* into the Constitution. It defined voting rights as belonging to men only. Pioneer suffragists Elizabeth Cady Stanton and Susan B. Anthony were furious. They predicted that unless women were granted the vote along with Negroes, time would pass them by. It outraged them that black men should get the vote before white women. They spoke angrily about giving the vote to "Africans, Chinese, and all the ignorant foreigners the moment they touch our shores." Black abolitionist Frederick Douglass, a supporter of female suffrage since 1848, tried to persuade women of the overriding importance of the franchise for black males, but with no success. The black abolitionist matriarch Sojourner Truth sided with the women: "There is a great stir about colored men getting their rights, but not a word about the colored women theirs, you see the colored men will be masters over the women, and it will be just as bad as it was before. . . ."

Stanton and Anthony threw themselves into a petition campaign to defeat the Fourteenth Amendment. They met with opposition from other feminists, led by Lucy Stone of Massachusetts, who had always subordinated women's rights to Negro rights. The Fourteenth Amendment carried, and so did the Fifteenth, which assured the right of suffrage to black men but not to women.

Controversy over tactics and theory

These amendments split the suffrage movement. The Stanton-Anthony forces formed the National Woman's Suffrage Association to get the vote through a national constitutional amendment. Lucy Stone's followers, who were content to proceed one state at a time, formed the American Woman Suffrage Association to bring about state referendums on the suffrage question. Lucy Stone and her husband Henry Blackwell set out in the spring of 1867 to enlist support for a Kansas referendum on woman suffrage. They rode by wagon all over the state, only to suffer defeat. This was the first of scores of state referendum campaigns between 1867 and 1918.

The suffrage campaign crept along for years. Hoping her action would lead to a test case, Susan B. Anthony voted in the 1872 election. She was tried and convicted of a civil offense, but her case was never heard by the Supreme Court. In the meantime, in *Minor* v. *Happersett* the high court ruled that

the Constitution did not convey the voting privilege to all citizens. In 1878 Anthony designed a suffrage amendment and presented it to Congress. It was rejected.

The split in the women's movement ended in 1890 when the two suffragist organizations merged as the National American Woman's Suffrage Association (NAWSA). Elizabeth Cady Stanton and Susan B. Anthony headed the new group. The two of them edited the suffragist journal *The Revolution* and lectured and wrote tirelessly on feminism. A woman of wide-ranging interests, Stanton believed that suffrage was too limited a goal for the women's movement. But by the time of Anthony's death in 1906, no one doubted any longer that women's suffrage would eventually come to pass. The only question was when.

The most original feminist intellectual was Charlotte Perkins Gilman, author of *Women and Economics* (1898). She expressed the new theories of the women's movement. Producing goods, educating children, and nursing the sick were social necessities now performed outside the home. Society had taken over many of the important functions of the family, Mrs. Gilman reasoned, except the drudgery. This it left to the woman of the house. She argued that communal laundries, kitchens, and nurseries staffed by trained professionals should take over the remaining functions of the home. This would at least liberate women for more useful functions than cooking and cleaning. While most American feminists rejected these cooperative schemes, British and Scandinavian feminists were more receptive.

It is not that women are really smaller-minded, weaker-minded, more timid and vacillating; but that whosoever . . . lives always in a small dark place, is always guarded, protected, directed and restrained, will become inevitably narrowed and weakened by it.
The woman is narrowed by the home and the man is narrowed by the woman.

CHARLOTTE PERKINS GILMAN (1860–1935)

I cannot sympathize fully with an anti-man movement.
I have had too much kindness, aid, and just recognition from men
to make such attitude[s] of women otherwise than painful. . . .

ELIZABETH BLACKWELL (1821–1910)
First American woman to receive a medical degree

Conservative views of many suffragists

In the nineteenth century, the public often found it hard to distinguish between women's liberation and sexual license. The confusion was understandable in light of the publicity given to people like the Claflin sisters. In the 1870s Tennessee Claflin and Victoria Claflin Woodhull edited a scandal-mongering newspaper, *Woodhull & Claflin's Weekly,* which advocated a "higher" sexual morality—that is, free love—as well as spiritualism, quack healing, and women's legal rights. In November 1872 they reported that the Reverend Henry Ward Beecher was having an affair with a married woman friend of theirs. They said they admired both lovers but criticized them for keeping their romance secret. The woman's angry husband sued Beecher, and the trial provided the nation with weeks of titillating news. Eventually the courts vindicated Beecher. In the aftermath *Woodhull & Claflin's Weekly* was suppressed. In fact, all publications that dared discuss free love or other unconventional subjects were censored by the post office. Feminist leaders turned their backs on Victoria Woodhull and Tennessee Claflin, who fled the country for a time.

This episode ended all public discussion by feminists of unconventional sexual relations. From then on women reformers discussed far more conventional topics: How could mothers better exercise moral influence over their children? How could women eliminate intemperance, godlessness, poverty, disease, and war? How could feminists end the exploitation of children and working mothers by factory owners?

Most feminists took a conventional Victorian view of sex roles. Few objected to marriage or motherhood. Nor did they equate matrimony with slavery. They felt suffrage would make women better mothers and better citizens. Generally, they believed that the home was women's proper sphere. When Anthony Comstock of Boston or Josiah W. Leeds of Philadelphia undertook crusades against obscenity, feminists applauded. They strongly approved the formation in 1895 of the American Puritan Alliance, whose mission was to suppress prostitution and obscenity. When Judge Ben Lindsey proposed "companionate marriage" or Mrs. Havelock Ellis suggested trial marriage or separate homes for spouses, most feminists turned thumbs down. When a Swedish woman proposed motherhood without marriage, her ideas were received coldly in the American women's movement. Anarchistic or communistic experiments which smacked of free love got the same response.

As a whole, the feminists of this period were moderate reformers, not radicals. Despite some alliances with immigrants, blacks, and the working class, the leaders were white and middle class. Few had a firsthand knowledge of poverty and most were college educated. In brief, they were an elite and a minority within that elite. A few were unmarried. A study of twenty-six of the most important suffragists at the turn of the century shows seventeen were married, and three had been divorced. Those who were married had children.

The antis

When asked why they became suffragists some women would reply, as the novelist Mary Austin recalled, "'Well, it was seeing what my mother had to go through that started me'; or, 'It was being sacrificed to the boys in the family that set me going'; or, 'My father was one of the old-fashioned kind.'" She remembered how women became angry relating accounts of how the dominant males had prospered at the expense of the females. Even the men who backed suffrage and publicly supported their wives' political activities privately confessed that they resented having to keep house on numerous occasions. By the turn of the century feminist speakers were no longer bombarded with rotten eggs and catcalls as they once had been. But the opposition was sometimes quite strong.

If the nineteenth century is to be governed by the opinions of the eighteenth, and the twentieth by the nineteenth, the world will always be governed by dead men.

ELIZABETH CADY STANTON (1815–1902)

The antifeminists, or "antis" as they were sometimes called, charged the movement with subverting all of Christian society. They accused feminists of violating biblical teachings. Had not God subordinated Eve to Adam? Had not Saint Paul decreed that women must remain silent in church? Feminists who favored sexual equality and careers for women threatened the family and encouraged juvenile crime and rape. If women had the vote, political arguments between husbands and wives would "make every home a hell on earth." Voting for women would lead to women serving on juries and running for public office. And women, said the antis, were unsuited for "the turmoil and

battle of public life." Furthermore, they were already protected by men and so had no need to vote.

The antis were impressively organized. They got much support from liquor interests, who feared the feminists would bring about Prohibition. The wives of prominent men, like the wife of General Sherman, lent their voices to the antifeminist cause. Both the Protestant and the Catholic clergy also supported the antis. Industrialists, who saw their authority challenged by the feminist pressure for factory legislation, supported them, too. Southerners, hoping to lure more industry with the offer of plenty of cheap female labor, opposed both women's suffrage and factory legislation.

In the 1890s the antifeminists formed a national organization called Associations Opposed to the Extension of Suffrage for Women, which had the support of former President Cleveland. Much of the contents of *The Remonstrance*, the major "anti" publication, expressed simple male chauvinism. Some of it, however, asked valid questions. If women were going to vote as progressively as the suffragists claimed, why had their vote made no visible difference in Colorado, where they were enfranchised in 1893? Why, for example, had Colorado not raised the minimum wage for women workers? Was it logical for women to seek *equality* in politics but *preferential treatment* in industry? If women were naturally inclined toward pacifism, as feminists claimed, why had the women of the North and the South been so militantly in favor of the Civil War?

Women's groups for reform

Feminism, which had been allied with abolitionism, was linked with other social movements as well. It formed a strong bond with the temperance movement. Male drunkenness was often tied to wife beating, child neglect, gambling, and prostitution—all evils that affected women especially. The Woman's Christian Temperance Union (WCTU) was founded in 1874 to press for state and local laws forbidding the sale and consumption of liquor. Its members favored a constitutional amendment which would outlaw liquor everywhere in the country. Carry Nation of the WCTU was best known for her hatchet-swinging, bottle-smashing forays into saloons and liquor stores. Despite her eccentricities, she was a brilliant organizer.

Late in the 1890s, under the leadership of Frances E. Willard, the temperance movement reached its peak and moved closer to feminism. The organization could call on more than 200,000 adult members and nearly as many juveniles in 10,000 local chapters spread through every state and territory. Suffrage interested the WCTU because with the vote women could more effectively attack the sale and consumption of liquor. The WCTU also worked for a host of other reforms: industrial legislation, reform schools for delinquent girls, adult education for working women, and world peace through international arbitration. In many communities the WCTU was a constant thorn in the side of corrupt politicians, liquor interests, and brothel keepers. The movement gave women a valuable political education. But it stirred the liquor lobby into making indiscriminate attacks on women's groups including suffragists. In self-defense the latter sometimes tried to dissociate themselves from the temperance workers. Suffragist Abigail Scott Duniway once threatened to have a prominent temperance leader arrested if she crossed into Oregon during a suffrage campaign.

A high point in the woman's movement was reached in 1893 when 150,000 women from twenty-seven countries attended the Chicago World's Fair. Special lectures and discussions were organized that covered every conceivable topic from "Cholera in Hamburg" to "Assyrian Mythology," from "Financial Independence of Woman" to "Complete Freedom for Women." A permanent organization, called the General Federation of Women's Clubs, emerged from these meetings. The GFWC enabled its one million or more members and hundreds of local associations to back moderately progressive causes and to discuss cultural topics. Soon the organization turned away from culture. "Dante is dead," declared Mrs. Sarah Platt Decker, GFWC president in 1904. "He has been dead for several centuries, and I think it is time we dropped the study of his *Inferno* and turned our attention to our own." The GFWC shifted to lobbying for the fifty-four-hour workweek for working women in Rhode Island, the Pure Food and Drug Act, the National Child Labor Bill, and various other reforms.

A variety of other women's organizations met particular needs. The Association of Collegiate Alumnae helped girls go to college and find professional jobs when they graduated. The National Federation of Settlements was the largest organization of settlement-house workers, most of whom were women. The Daughters of the American Revolution, founded in 1890, took up the cause of patriotism. The Parent-Teacher Association worked to improve the public schools.

In the past, suffragists had often looked down on immigrants. They had ignored, or not been aware of, the plight of working women. Immigrant women were equally scornful of suffragists. The problems they had to face were entirely different. Many factory women were underpaid and worked a twelve-hour day at dangerous jobs. Male union leaders gave lip service to the idea of equal pay for equal work but scoffed at women's efforts to organize. The Women's Trade Union League, organized in 1903 by Mary Kenney and others, had little support from the parent organization, the AFL. Nor did feminist organizations give it much backing.

Elizabeth Gurley Flynn, a Wobbly organizer, addresses striking textile workers in Massachusetts (1912). Influenced by her mother, an early suffragist, and her father, a Socialist laborer, Flynn became involved in union activities at an early age. "We hated the rich, the trusts they owned, the violence they caused, the oppression they represented."

Starting in the early twentieth century, however, feminism linked up with elements of the labor movement. This alliance began in 1909, when the shirtwaist makers, mostly women, went out on strike in New York. The strike lasted thirteen weeks, all through a bitterly cold winter. The wealthy feminist Mrs. Oliver H. P. Belmont hired a great hall in New York to rally support for the strikers. NAWSA president Anna Howard Shaw sat on the dais next to Mary Dreier, the strike leader. The women's movement took up the cause of working women even more wholeheartedly after New York City's Triangle Fire on March 25, 1911, in which 146 women garment workers died (see p. 372). Feminists sought safety laws and regulations to ease the conditions of women and children in industry. They also fought for equal pay for equal work.

One small group of well-educated women formed the National Consumer's League to improve the life of industrial workers. Its leader, Florence Kelly (1859–1932), was a vice-president of NAWSA. As a lawyer and government labor inspector, she knew the facts about the exploitation of women and children better than others. Kelly organized a brilliant defense of the Oregon Ten-Hour Law when it was challenged in the Supreme Court. By amassing overwhelming sociological evidence to show how overworking women undermined the social order, she paved the way for attorney Louis D. Brandeis to make a distinguished legal defense. This was the first use of sociological evidence before the high court, which upheld the Oregon law.

Until the 1890s feminism made little headway in the Old South. Not only had the movement begun with close ties to abolition, but its stand on sex equality found little sympathy among southerners, male or female. But in the 1890s the suffrage movement began to attract followers in the South, too. It did so when southern feminists decided to fight for the rights of *white* women, to the exclusion of their black sisters. This appealed to Jim Crow and offended the older northern feminists who remembered their abolitionist beginnings. But the new strategy was consistent with the overall plan of feminism, which was to make as broad an appeal as possible.

Black women formed their own organizations to help overcome both race and sex discrimination. Ida B. Wells, a southern black newspaper editor, formed the New Era Club for black women. Mrs. Josephine St. Pierre Ruffin, a Massachusetts suffrage leader, issued the call in 1895 for the Boston convention that led to the formation of the National Association of Colored Women. Organizations of white women sympathized with the efforts of organized black women but did not join forces with them.

A renewed drive for the vote

None of the suffrage campaigns before 1890 succeeded. But Wyoming, which had had universal suffrage as a territory since 1869, entered the Union in 1890 with voting rights for women. Wyoming men supported the suffrage provision as a way of attracting females to the sparsely populated state. The victory for suffragists in Colorado in 1893 was even more impressive, for there was no such ulterior motive involved. This triumph owed much to the organizational gifts of Carrie Chapman Catt. Utah and Idaho came around in 1896. Utah's vote for equal suffrage was something of a fluke. Mormon patriarchs had no desire to encourage the independence of women, but they hoped that by giving women the vote they could maintain their political advantage over non-Mormons in Utah.

Suffragist organizers traveled from Kansas to the West Coast and back again, in blazing summer heat and in freezing winter cold. Although losing far more often than they

Suffragists post notices in Cincinnati, Ohio (1912). Women had been granted the right to vote in western states, but eastern states continued to defeat woman suffrage referendums by decisive margins. By 1915, grassroots efforts began to pay off; referendums that year were narrowly defeated. "It was the beginning of the end," one suffragist said.

Personally, I believe in woman suffrage, but I am not an enthusiastic advocate of it because I do not regard it as a very important matter.

THEODORE ROOSEVELT (1858–1919)

won, they were becoming expert at precinct work and lobbying. In 1911 they convinced Californians that women should be allowed to vote. Oregon, Kansas, and Arizona followed suit in 1912. But the large industrialized eastern states, particularly New York, Pennsylvania, and Massachusetts, long held firm against equal suffrage. The big breakthrough came when New York voted for woman suffrage in 1917.

The suffragists' persistence gradually gained them influence, if not power. The remarks of a senator justifying a controversial vote to his constituents were fairly typical. His wife had been impressed by what a feminist speaker had to say about a particular piece of legislation. "Then she telegraphed me to get busy supporting it, and all her friends did the same. For the sake of domestic harmony I'll have to do it."

Even though Congress did not yet feel pressured by the campaign for a federal suffrage amendment, by around 1900 many of the reforms championed by activist women since the early part of the nineteenth century had made considerable progress. However powerful the resistance, women had forced open the doors to various professions, even in medicine and law. By 1890, 36 percent of all professionals (including teachers, nurses, and librarians) were female, a figure which would remain relatively stable for the next seven decades. Colleges were slowly becoming co-ed. Divorce and property laws had improved on a piecemeal basis, state by state. Even temperance, suffrage, and wage-and-hour laws had been realized in some states.

The suffragists tried not to line up with any one political party, hoping that all parties would eventually support them. But in 1912 they abandoned nonpartisanship to back Theodore Roosevelt's Progressive party. TR was no crusader for equal suffrage, but he did not object to letting women vote. More important, the party needed every vote it could get, so an endorsement for suffrage made political sense. The suffragist leadership believed that even if the Progressives lost in 1912, they might get enough votes to force the winning party to embrace equal suffrage four to eight years later. This was precisely what happened.

In England the militant suffragists were chaining themselves to mailboxes, getting themselves arrested, and conducting well-publicized hunger strikes in jail. Upon her return from a visit to England, the young American feminist Alice Paul was determined to employ equally dramatic tactics in America. She organized the first suffragist parades and outdoor rallies in this country. In 1913 she held an outdoor rally in Washington that stole the limelight from Wilson's swearing-in ceremony. The rally drew a large, hostile crowd. The police lost control, and festive Washington was the scene of a riot. Alice Paul and others soon founded a splinter suffragist group, the Congressional Union for Woman Suffrage (CU), later converted into a political party known as the Woman's party (WP). Its purpose was to organize a campaign in the nation's capital to revive the federal suffrage amendment, which had lain dormant since 1893. In a few months they had gathered 200,000 signatures favoring an amendment and presented them to the new president. He was somewhat astonished by the event, since the petitions were in reply to his statement that the matter of suffrage had never been brought to his attention.

In 1914 the large and moderate GFWC endorsed suffrage, signifying that the cause had at last won over the mass of middle-class women. Under the direction of Alice Paul and Carrie Chapman Catt, millions of dollars were collected and a massive lobbying machine was tuned up for the final push to secure a federal suffrage amendment. The tone of the campaign was conservative; in 1916 placards carried by suffragists read: "To women give the vote,/For the hand that rocks the cradle,/Will never rock the boat."

World War I, the last step toward the vote

Soon afterward the country became embroiled in the First World War. One feminist described it as "an expedition of masculinity run amuck." Like many feminists, the distinguished social worker Jane Addams was a pacifist. A member of the Woman's Peace party, she became the leading voice of the feminist antiwar groups. In 1915 these women arranged an international meeting where they called upon the world's neutral nations to limit armaments, nationalize munitions, replace rival armies with international police patrols, eliminate the diplomatic alliances that apparently had caused the war, grant universal woman suffrage, and establish world government "to substitute Law for war." The only flaw in this effort was an unfounded conviction that they could deter the warring powers from further aggression. The more radical women pacifists who demonstrated during Wilson's preparedness program in 1916 were physically attacked, verbally abused, and arrested. This provided a taste of the hostility that antiwar dissenters of both sexes would later encounter during World War I.

America's declaration of war in April 1917

caused women pacifists to reappraise their stand. A few continued to oppose America's participation in the war, but the main body of pacifists supported the fighting. The idealistic goals expounded by President Wilson appealed to their humanitarian instincts. Besides, Mrs. Catt and others could see that by joining in the war effort women would get the vote sooner. Their English sisters, who were vigorously supporting the war, had been promised suffrage at the end of the fighting and were already being admitted into new occupations. Parliament was also granting such benefits as motherhood allowances for families of servicemen. American feminists therefore pressed the government to allow them greater participation in the war effort.

Like the Civil War, the First World War was a great awakening for women. Wilson stopped short of giving them new powers or rights, but he used feminist organizations to bolster morale and stem antiwar sentiment. Women were channeled into useful activities like selling war bonds and staffing the Red Cross, the YWCA, and other volunteer organizations. Thousands of women (whites only) were hired as office workers by the federal government. The Suffrage Association raised $200,000 to maintain an overseas hospital in France and conducted an Americanization program for immigrants. Some women found their way into new industrial jobs. The iron-and-steel industry employed forty thousand women in 1918, a threefold increase over prewar years. But these jobs were considered temporary, and most women factory hands were quietly fired after the armistice.

Much to their credit, the prowar feminists did not take part in any purges against their pacifist sisters. When Woman's party pickets were assaulted and arrested at the White House, Mrs. Catt, who disagreed with their tactics, used all her influence to help them get the lightest possible sentences. Similarly,

Suffrage for women is a part of the
complete democracy so aptly named by
Mr. Wilson as the object of this war. . . .
The government . . . must start about
setting the world right for democracy
by giving American women the franchise. . . .

From *Women Citizen,* 1919

most of the women who specialized in giving pep talks in theaters, schools, and churches flatly refused to use the inflammatory patriotic prose suggested by the Committee on Public Information.

The suffragists' strategy paid off. President Wilson, in a special address to the Senate in 1918, said it was inconsistent for the country to wage a war for democracy overseas but to bar American women from voting at home. He took note of the patriotic work performed by women during the war, and urged passage of the Anthony Amendment. "I tell you plainly that this measure which I urge upon you is vital to the winning of the war and to the energies alike of preparation and of battle." Congress dragged its feet for a while longer but finally approved the equal suffrage amendment on June 4, 1919. The states made it legal and binding a few months before the election of 1920. Seventy-two years had passed since Elizabeth Cady Stanton first proposed the idea at the Seneca Falls conference.

Review

The family was becoming less home-centered, and this led to changes in the quality of family life. More women worked outside the home, children spent more time at school, while clothing, food, and medical care were provided more by outside sources and less by the household itself. Domestic service, the largest field of employment for working-class women, eased the middle-class housewife's work load. Survival for black families often depended on the labor of black married women, who were readily exploited on the job market. Because of their cultural patterns, married immigrant women more often supplemented their husband's income by doing piecework at home rather than taking outside jobs. The pioneer farm wife continued to be a major force in taming the West, and she was symbolized in literature by her strength, patience, and endurance. But by century's end most rural families were enduring less isolation and loneliness than before. Whether rural or urban, however, most Victorian couples had to make it on their own, and the emotional stresses led to a growing number of divorces. The role of Victorian husband required him to be absolute ruler of the roost, while the Victorian wife was expected to be innocent, submissive, and a civilizing influence on the more aggressive men.

Compulsory school attendance for youngsters became the rule, and by the turn of the century the number of children laboring in factories and mills was shrinking. With the increase in industrialism, the birth rate and size of families declined throughout the nineteenth century. Adolescence was regarded as a separate stage of development for the first time. New organizations for adults and children drew them away from each other. Child-parent relationships weakened, and young people looked more to peers for their values. Observers were beginning to refer to the nation as too child-oriented. The youth culture was under way.

A dispute over the vote for blacks split the suffragist movement in the 1860s, and the break was not healed until 1890 when the National American Woman's Suffrage Association was formed. Contrary to myth, most suffragist reformers were socially conservative, holding to conventional views of marriage and sex. Antifeminists, well-organized at the turn of the century, sometimes raised important questions about the validity of suffragist arguments. Feminist groups moved closer both to the temperance and labor movements. When feminism gained ground in the South, black women were forced to form their own organizations. Women had won the vote in several states by 1917, and suffragism reached its culmination during the First World War. Suffragists who were moved by Wilson's idealism also hoped that by supporting the war they would achieve the vote sooner. They were right.

Due in part to the role they played on the home front, American women were finally granted the vote in 1920, seventy-two years after it had been demanded at the Seneca Falls convention.

Questions

1. How did family structure and childhood patterns change in the Gilded Age? What factors contributed to change?
2. Why did the vote for blacks split the women's movement? Which organizations resulted from this rift, and who headed them?
3. What arguments did the "antis" raise in opposition to the feminists?
4. What did the feminist movement achieve by about 1920? What did it fail to accomplish?
5. Identify and give the significance of: (a) *Adolescence,* (b) the Claflin sisters, (c) Florence Kelly, (d) *Minor* v. *Happersett,* (e) Carrie Chapman Catt, (f) the cult of true womanhood, and (g) Charlotte Perkins Gilman.

community

Labor Day crowd on Main Street in Buffalo, New York, 1900.

The splendor, picturesqueness, and oceanic amplitude and rush of these great cities . . . completely satisfy my senses of power, fulness, motion, &c., and give me . . . a continued exaltation and absolute fulfilment.

WALT WHITMAN   (1819–1892)

23

23
A Century of Cities

Many Americans in the Gilded Age found it hard to maintain a sense of community. The tooth-and-claw business competition and the rage for personal success pitted one individual against another. The social distance between rich and poor, labor and capital, immigrant and native-born, black and white, was never greater. Sometimes the divisions erupted into bloody violence. Americans were a mobile people and their physical movements tended to increase the feeling that life was unstable. Immigration was the most unsettling experience of all, leaving most immigrants with a sense of rootlessness. And life in the big cities was notoriously impersonal compared with that of the peasant or farm villages from which so many Americans had sprung. Thus the search for community went through a difficult phase in the latter part of the nineteenth and first part of the twentieth centuries.

An aspect of community life that must be featured prominently in a history of the Gilded Age is the growth of cities. This phenomenon was worldwide. Yet nowhere were people more conscious of the growth of cities than in the United States. A novelist of the time labeled the nineteenth century the "century of cities." Cities, he added, "have given their own twist to the progress of the age—and the farmer is as far out of it as if he lived in Alaska. Perhaps there was a time when a man could live in what the poet calls daily communication with nature and not starve his mind or dwarf his soul, but this isn't the century."

*Let us cherish no utopian schemes of turning people back to the rural districts.
Every new good road, every new canal, every new railway, every new invention,
every economic improvement, in short, nearly all
industrial progress centralizes the population in cities.*

RICHARD T. ELY   (1854–1943)
American economist

The City, Center of Action

A spurt of urban growth

In the Gilded Age cities covered more land, reached higher into the sky, and absorbed far more people than ever before. New towns multiplied on the prairies and plains of the West and along the Pacific coast. Between 1860 and 1910 the number of residents in towns of 2500 or more rose from about 20 percent of the total population to nearly 46 percent. By 1920 the halfway mark was passed: 51 percent of Americans lived in urban areas. During these five decades the United States became a nation of urban dwellers.

Several trends of the Industrial Revolution dovetailed with city growth. The armies of unskilled and semiskilled laborers that were needed by factory and farm owners could best be found in cities and towns of the East, where the immigrants debarked from Europe. Immigration from overseas was the greatest single source of industrial labor. Either the factory was brought to the labor supply, or the labor supply to the factory; in any case a city or town would result from this combination. One fifth of all city dwellers in 1890 were of foreign birth.

The railroads that spread across the country in the late nineteenth century, another trend of the Industrial Revolution, converged in cities and towns. The spreading railroad network also created new cities and towns on the frontier. Practically every modern American city was founded before the rail system was completed at the end of the nineteenth century. Some cities rose for no reason other than the presence of the railroad. Abilene and other western cowtowns were such communities, constructed to take cattle to slaughterhouses further east. In other cases rails gave existing villages a new lease on life. At the outset of the Civil War nine cities had a population of 100,000 or more. By the turn of the century the number had risen to thirty-eight.

Finally, the new technology of the Industrial Revolution had immediate applications in city transportation, architecture, and public utilities. The technology of steam, steel, and electricity was essential to big-city life. Until about 1890, the use of steam made for a compact city. The bulky coal-fired steam boilers were often built or assembled at the site of a factory. Also their fuel was best delivered by train. Thus commercial, industrial, and residential activity was crowded near the railroad depot. But the arrival of electricity and, early in the twentieth century, of the gasoline-driven truck changed the formula of growth. Electric trolley cars and interurban railways encouraged suburban growth.

The face of the modern city

By combining the wonders of the iron or steel skeleton and the electric elevator, architects devised a new type of building—the "skyscraper." The first such structures rose in Chicago in the 1880s. Credit for this inno-

While the railroads often created new cities and towns, they also aided the growth of existing settlements. Founded in 1864, Helena, Montana (pictured above), was already a boom town by the time the Northern Pacific Railroad was completed in 1883. But the railroad and rich silver strikes nearby helped Helena maintain its advantage over rival Anaconda, becoming state capital in 1889.

vation belongs to designer William Le Baron Jenney who in 1884 replaced the masonry-bearing wall with iron and steel in constructing the new Home Insurance Building in Chicago. Even a seven- or ten-story office building, hotel, or store could hold hundreds or thousands of people on a small piece of real estate. A typically American form of architecture in its first years, the skyscraper proved both functional and profitable. It symbolized the dynamism and excitement of American society.

While ten-story skyscrapers were being built, streetcars drawn by horses still carried passengers in the brick-paved streets below. In 1887 inventor Frank Julian Sprague intro-

duced his clanking electric streetcar in Richmond, Virginia. It enabled people to live on the fringes of town and still get to work cheaply and swiftly. By the turn of the century over 800 streetcar lines and 10,000 miles of track were in operation throughout the country. Sprague soon electrified an entire railroad train. Around the turn of the century, New York electrified its elevated steam railways and built an elaborate elevated-and-subway system running the length of Manhattan Island and into Brooklyn. It carried hundreds of thousands of passengers daily, unhindered by the tangle of street traffic. Soon there would be additional elevated lines in Boston, Chicago, Philadelphia, and Kansas City. The old walking city with its small radius gave way to the larger streetcar city. Soon this, too, was replaced by the automobile city, which pushed out urban boundaries even further.

Iron and steel bridges boosted the influence and wealth of many cities. A railroad bridge like the one built across the Missouri River at Kansas City in 1869 could bring more trade to a river town. Bridgeless rivals lagged behind in the race for commercial traffic. One of the greatest innovations in bridge construction was the wire rope or steel cable, which allowed engineers to span waterways of imposing width. The cable was first perfected in the construction of Brooklyn Bridge by designer John A. Roebling and his son Washington. After his father's death the younger Roebling, crippled in a construction accident, directed building operations from his sick bed. He watched the construction of the Brooklyn Bridge with field glasses, sending orders to the work crews with his wife's help. Completed amid great fanfare in 1883, Brooklyn Bridge joined two independent cities: New York City on Manhattan Island and Brooklyn on Long Island. It encouraged their eventual merger.

Other technological improvements also stimulated urban growth. Telephone companies had 48,000 subscribers in 85 cities in 1880, 800,000 subscribers two decades later. Urbanites now had instant communication. In 1892, New York and Chicago were connected by phone. With asphalt paving, streets became smoother and quieter and were passable even in rainy weather. Blacktop also made bicycles and cars practical forms of transportation. Electric bulbs glowed late into the night in theater and business districts and encouraged more offices, stores, and factories to stay open after dark. Electricity set the tempo for the new rhythm and excitement of city life.

The regional spread of cities

The Northeast remained the most highly urbanized region in the United States. New York City, with its active seaport and financial district, led the way. It was world famous for its size, its impressive architecture, and its glittering entertainments. New York was the first American city to reach a million in population (1870). It ensured its preeminence by merging with neighboring Brooklyn in 1898, which until then had been the second largest city in the country.

Midwestern cities started later but grew even faster than their eastern rivals. Minneapolis, St. Paul, Detroit, Milwaukee, Columbus, and Cleveland expanded rapidly in the 1880s and 1890s. Chicago's rise was nothing less than phenomenal. With fewer than 5000 people in 1840, the city had nearly 300,000 in 1870 and 1,700,000 at the turn of the century. It was not only a railroad center but the hub of a vast commercial-industrial-financial empire. Even the devastating fire of 1871 failed to diminish its energy.

In the Far West, the growth of San Francisco, Los Angeles, Portland, and other cities was also spurred by the railroads. (San Francisco recovered from its 1906 earthquake as fast as Chicago had from its fire.) Los Angeles had a tiny population in 1865. But in

Chicago . . . seethed with a peculiarly human or realistic atmosphere. It is given to some cities, as to some lands, to suggest romance, and to me Chicago did that hourly. It sang. . . .

THEODORE DREISER (1871–1945)
In *Newspaper Days*, recollecting 1890

1900, shortly after it became part of the nationwide rail system, its population jumped to 100,000.

The rate of urbanization in the South trailed that of the rest of the nation by about fifty years. In 1900 the South's urban population stood at about 15 percent—the national urban population had reached that mark in 1850. Not until after World War I would the South's urban status change markedly.

The three zones of a metropolis

As observers studied the largest cities of the late nineteenth century they began to notice repeated patterns of land use. Whether the metropolis in question was Chicago, Cincinnati, New York, Pittsburgh, or Boston, there were typically three separate zones in each case. The first was downtown. Here, where the streets, trolleys, and rail lines converged, were located the largest stores, office buildings, and hotels. The clustering of stores, a relatively new development in urban land use, was the main attraction of the downtown area. In addition, this central city included concert halls, ballparks, museums, zoos, and theaters. Also located downtown, but set apart from the shopping centers, were the slum neighborhoods, which housed the immigrant poor and the most recently arrived native-born as well. Here the city's working classes lived in tenements and in converted homes abandoned by the rich. The slums, as these neighborhoods were called, were often situated near factories or the railroad yard in the downtown section.

The second zone, some distance from downtown, was the suburbs where the rich or upper-middle classes could escape the crush, live on open or wooded estates, and enjoy the country while still being able to ride to town to work, shop, or play. In the third zone, located between the core of the city and the most remote suburbs, lived the lower-middle classes and the immigrants who had begun to adjust to American life. This the sociologists called the "zone of emergence." In this zone a couple could afford at the very least a row house or cottage. The housing was not elegant, but it was much better than the slums. And the children could attend better schools while the breadwinners could get to work by trolley, elevated, or subway line.

Tenement life

The lightning speed of city growth, which caused the supply of basic services to fall behind human needs, created many problems. One such problem was the lack of housing for the newest immigrants from overseas or from rural places in the United States. In the crowded slums of large cities people were jammed into low rental apartments or boarding homes especially designed to meet the very minimum of housing standards. These were the tenements.

The very best tenement building afforded a bare minimum of light, air, and space, and a maximum of noise, stench, and inconvenience. In *How the Other Half Lives* (1890) Jacob Riis described the main hallway of a tenement:

The hole is dark, and you might stumble over the children pitching pennies back there. Not that it would hurt them; kicks and cuffs are their daily diet. . . . All the fresh air that ever enters these stairs comes from the hall-door that is forever slamming, and from the windows of dark bedrooms that in turn receive from the stairs their sole supply of the elements God meant to be free. The sinks are in the hallway, that all the tenants

Opposite page: The rear of a tenement on Baxter Street in New York (late 1880s), photographed by Jacob A. Riis. Above: A bedroom in a rear tenement building on New York's East Side (1910), photographed by Lewis W. Hine. In How the Other Half Lives *(1890) Riis asked, "What sort of an answer, think you, would come from these tenements to the question 'Is life worth living?'"*

may have access—and all [be] poisoned alike by their summer stenches.

In 1894, the New York Tenement House Commission found that while tenement life had improved somewhat over the past half century, conditions were still very ugly.

At the turn of the century more than half of New York's population lived in tenements. One slum ward in lower Manhattan with about 1000 people per acre was the most crowded spot on the face of the earth, including Bombay, India. One investigator counted 26 occupants in a room measuring 12 by 12 feet. Of the 250,000 people covered by another inspection, only 300 had access to bathrooms in their residences.

Here [in the city] are to be found the greatest wealth and the deepest poverty. And it is here that popular government has most clearly broken down.

HENRY GEORGE (1839–1897)
Progress and Poverty, 1879

The very worst living accommodations in the city were the rear tenements, small ramshackle buildings surrounded by larger structures and almost totally lacking in human comfort, convenience, or sanitation. In 1894 the infant mortality rate was 110 per 1000 births in ordinary tenements and 205 in rear tenements, which the housing commission of 1894 labeled "veritable slaughter houses." On one block on Mulberry Street, 155 children had died in a single year (1882). As a result of the Commission's exposé, rear tenements were outlawed, but little else was done to improve the deplorable housing conditions.

From time to time housing reformers exposed the worst conditions and pressed for reforms. They managed to get the rear tenements outlawed and to place certain restrictions on new construction. For example, in 1879 the housing reformers unveiled an improved apartment plan known as the dumbbell tenement, which called for an indentation in the side wall of each building that allowed a narrow shaft of light to penetrate into most apartments during some part of the day. But the tenement remained a firetrap and breeding ground for vermin, crime, and disease.

The problem for the housing reformers was how to satisfy the tenants' need for decent housing and the owners' demand for adequate income from their property. Some reformers tried to introduce solutions involving what is now known as urban renewal, while others pressed for public housing modeled after projects already built in Eu-rope. But these ideas were rejected as socialistic. Building codes and zoning laws became the two main tools for controlling city growth. Zoning was first established in San Francisco's Chinatown to restrict the location of Chinese laundries. Afterward, other uses were found for it, for example, the limitation of the height of skyscrapers in some districts where they might overpower other, smaller structures.

Building codes found some early applications in New York City. Following the suggestion of Lawrence Veiller, the country's leading housing expert, the New York Tenement House Law of 1901 listed requirements for all *new* buildings. Every apartment had to have a toilet, and windows were required in all bedrooms. Each room had to have at least seventy square feet of living space. Buildings had to have better fire escapes, and stairwells had to be fireproof. The building could occupy only 70 percent of the site; the remaining 30 percent was to be reserved for courts and walks. Because the law ignored older buildings, it did not immediately improve slum housing very much. Many old-law tenements erected before 1901 survived into the 1960s.

Faltering urban services

Housing was not the only urban problem. As newcomers continued to crowd in, the need for gas, electricity, water, sewers, streetcars, and other public utilities multiplied. Roads had to be paved. Fire and police protection, garbage collection and mail delivery, food inspection and schooling—all required new expenditures. But property owners resented higher taxes to pay for these services. In order to make the necessary improvements, the city fathers often had to run hat in hand to the state capitol for money. Here they were up against rural interests, which were cool to the needs of the city. The lack of home rule for American cities contrasted glaringly with

As the demand for services outstripped the city's ability to provide them, even a mild snowstorm often resulted in scenes like the traffic congestion shown in this photograph by Edwin Levick. Even when the cities tried to deal with their problems, the "cures" sometimes created new ones; the introduction of electric streetcars and subways prompted some city dwellers to quip (inspired by Andrew Carnegie), "The public be jammed."

the situation in Britain, where municipalities were gaining much greater power to cope with local issues.

American cities built newer and more efficient public utilities than European cities, but they often paid high construction prices. There was big money in the building of utilities. Waterworks were usually publicly owned, but other utilities were prizes for private investors. A "traction combine" (streetcar corporation) that built a new and modern transportation system might get a long-term monopoly (sometimes for a thousand years). Often there were no limits on the rates utility companies could charge, but they were protected from taxes.

In the eighteenth century most American cities had been small, well-managed, and pleasant places to live. But by 1850 city services had fallen behind in supplying fresh water, carrying off sewage, cleaning the streets, collecting household trash, clearing away snow, and generally maintaining a level of decency. The air smelled worse after factories and railroads moved in. The control of communicable diseases was poor (the germ theory was not widely accepted until the early twentieth century). Fire control became more difficult, and the loss from major fires increased. Even mail delivery fell apart. It could take a week for a letter to move from one side of New York City to the other.

New York City fleeced by the Tweed Ring

In every major city political machines, controlled by bosses, ran the government. The fact that so much new urban construction was needed provided splendid opportunities for graft. The classic example of the corrupt urban political machine was the Tweed Ring of New York City. That the city functioned at all was not the result of its formal government but of an informal political machine organized by a three-hundred-pound carpenter-turned-alderman, William Marcy Tweed (1823–1878). Tweed headed the Tammany Hall organization, which in turn ran New York's Democratic party. In fact, in 1868 a Tweed cohort was elected governor of New York, giving the Ring considerable clout in Albany as well as New York City. At the peak of its power (from 1868 to 1871) the Ring constructed extensive new public works in New York City. It administered contracts through an intricate system of patronage, kickbacks, "boodling" (bribery), and padding bills. As much as 85 percent of the padding went to the Ring.

Under-the-table deals often brought Tweed huge returns. A private contractor who received $279,000 to collect city garbage had to kick back $40,000. Some transactions were incredibly brazen. At one point Tweed's men sold the city hall to pay off a municipal debt and then bought it back at a loss. The Tweed Ring stole somewhere between $30 million and $200 million from the New York City treasury.

Tweed's downfall began in 1871. The New York *Times* used inside information to expose his treasury raid. Cartoonist Thomas Nast roasted him in *Harper's Weekly*—so effectively, in fact, that Tweed offered Nast half a million dollars to go abroad and take art lessons. When the thieves had a falling out, some turned against the others, giving the authorities enough hard evidence on which to prosecute. To his amazement, Tweed was convicted on 104 criminal counts of fraud and bribery and sentenced to twelve years in jail.

Bossism of the Tweed variety was crooked and costly. In its less ugly forms it had benefits which were widely understood and accepted. The bosses accomplished much of the necessary physical construction of cities. They helped the immigrant poor find jobs, receive charity, and cope with the complexities of the law. Judges and police protected favored interests of ghetto communities. In return the bosses could count on naturalized voters throwing the vote to candidates placed in office by the machine. Building and printing contractors got choice contracts. Real estate interests got advance notice of the new location of city improvements. Workers for city utilities knew that their jobs were secure. Where the rake-off to politicians was of modest proportions, it was known as "honest graft."

Turning out the crooks

In succeeding decades the boss system of urban politics was not destroyed but it was cleaned up and the city governments were made more effective. One of the most efficient and secure machines was that of Republican George B. Cox of Cincinnati, Ohio, who ruled there from 1894 to 1911. Cox's secret was that he dealt successfully both with the ghetto and with the zone of emergence. To a city wracked by labor violence, street crime, and business stagnation, he brought order and material progress which even reformers could respect. But in many other cities, especially during the Progressive era, the reformers mounted a campaign against urban corruption and machine politics.

Crusading journalists and editors uncovered a great deal of corruption. The most famous exposé of municipal wrongdoing was Lincoln Steffens' *The Shame of the Cities*, serialized in *McClure's Magazine* in 1902 and 1903. Steffens described crime and corruption in St. Louis, Minneapolis, Philadelphia, Chicago, and New York. He told in detail how the boodle was spread among political cliques. A $250,000 bribe bought utility franchises in St. Louis, for example. The step beyond exposure was prosecution. Some courageous district attorneys like St. Louis' Joseph Folk and San Francisco's Francis Heney vigorously prosecuted criminal cases despite heavy risks. Heney was shot in court during the San Francisco graft prosecution of 1907. The most prominent reform bosses were successful businessmen with social consciences. Hazen S. Pingree was elected mayor of Detroit after defeating the streetcar and gas company monopolies. Once in office, Pingree shifted the utilities from private to city ownership. Samuel ("Golden Rule") Jones of Toledo also backed "municipal socialism" but broadened it to include such projects as free kindergartens and park concerts. Cleveland's Mayor Tom L. Johnson developed similar programs. Cleveland was sometimes spoken of as the best-governed city in the country from 1901 to 1909.

In addition to municipal socialism, reform-

This famous anti-Tweed cartoon by Thomas Nast is captioned, "A group of vultures waiting for the storm to blow over — 'Let us prey.'" George Washington Plunkitt, an outspoken district boss in the Tammany Hall organization, once told a reporter, "If there is some stealin' in politics, it don't mean that the politicians of 1905 are, as a class, worse than them of 1835. It just means that the old-timers had nothin' to steal. . . ."

Make no little plans; they have no magic to stir men's blood.

DANIEL H. BURNHAM (1845–1912)

ers tried out various other remedies after 1900. *Initiative, referendum, and recall* made officials more responsive to public needs. *Legislative reapportionment* increased the number of city representatives in the state legislature and diluted the strength of rural voters, who seldom cared about the city's problems. Under the *city-manager system* the city government was run by a full-time, trained professional instead of by political partisans. Some reformers tried to have the party labels dropped in municipal elections, arguing that national parties had no relevance to local politics. In many cities candidates began to compete in such *nonpartisan elections.* By World War I most cities had adopted one or more of these reforms, and city government was generally cleaner than it had been for some time.

Planning land use in the cities

The contemporary cities were growing helter-skelter. Even though the slums, zone of emergence, and suburbs had started sorting themselves out, everyone complained of congestion in the cities. Even on the fastest transit lines patrons needed physical stamina to buck the crowds getting in and out of downtown. The downtown streets were narrow, crowded, and dirty, for they had not been designed to carry the volume of horse, trolley, and foot traffic. Open spaces, parkways, and parks, if they had once existed, were eaten up by new transportation systems and building construction, so that outdoor recreation facilities were often extremely limited. Railroad and factory smoke and cinders dirtied the air and sometimes the drinking water. Little attention was given to basic design elements—the ancient art of city

planning was a lost one in America. Few people realized, for example, that the grid pattern of city streets, though useful for merchants and shoppers, created dangerous, crowded, and noisy conditions for residents.

To remedy these problems, the art of city planning was revived. The two men most responsible were Frederick Law Olmsted and Daniel H. Burnham. Olmsted was a successful farmer on Staten Island. He believed in the need for city parks to restore the health and spirits of the city dweller. His masterpiece was Central Park, a large oasis in the middle of Manhattan. Here people could stroll, picnic, nap, paddle a rowboat, or ride a horse. He separated foot and vehicle traffic and brought in water to flow into brooks and ponds. Many scoffed that only the rich would use such a park, but it proved an instant success with all New Yorkers. Olmsted believed that all cities should be interlaced from end to end with tree-lined streets and landscaped parkways. Altogether he designed some twenty parks and sixteen communities across the country, plus numerous cemeteries and college campuses.

In 1893 Olmsted joined a team of architects, sculptors, and landscape designers to create a world's fair on the shore of Chicago's Lake Michigan. Under the direction of architect Daniel H. Burnham, a glistening "White City" was built for the World's Columbian Exposition. It was a showcase of huge buildings, open space, serene reflecting pools, broad strips of greenery, and vistas of lake and sky. Utility wires went underground and streets were blacktopped. The most astounding feature of the fair was electricity. Farmers fresh from the prairies could scarcely believe the after-dark panorama of lights. Colonnades, arches, and sculpture were all

Over 27 million people visited the "White City" built for the 1893 World's Columbian Exposition in Chicago. While the City Beautiful ideal sparked great interest in city planning and land use reform, it also stimulated a classical revival in urban design and architecture, which emphasized ornamentation over functionalism.

mirrored in the many lagoons. The Fair, seeming to reaffirm the nation's grandeur, was a tonic to a depression-ridden America.

Some visitors to the Fair went home as missionaries for city planning. The City Beautiful movement spread throughout the country, promoting new concepts of urban design and reconstruction. Most major cities soon appointed planning commissions. Congress voted a federal commission to revamp Washington, D.C., according to the ideas of Burnham and Olmsted. The Fair's architectural style was copied in many railroad stations, libraries, banks, and public buildings.

Chicago hired Burnham to design a master

plan for metropolitan growth. After years of study and consultation with the downtown business community he came up with an overall scheme to integrate downtown Chicago with the suburbs, preserve the city's lake front, redirect the flow of downtown street traffic, relocate the railroad yards, and develop museums and other public institutions which would promote civic unity. Burnham's 1908 plan was partially adopted.

The urban middle class sought its own utopia in the suburbs. According to Justice Louis Brandeis, wealthy Bostonians used to tell their sons: "Boston holds nothing for you except heavy taxes and political misrule. When you marry, pick out a suburb to build your house in, join the Country Club, and make your life center about your Club, your home and your children." In the 1880s and 1890s streetcars made it feasible for the middle class to buy single-family houses reasonably near where they worked. Even the most monotonous looking suburban tract offered comfortable living in contrast to the sooty chaos of the city. Once settled in the suburbs, few families would move back downtown.

This rural civilization, whose making engaged mankind since the dawn of history, is passing away. The city has erased the landmarks of an earlier society. Man has entered on an urban age.

FREDERIC C. HOWE   (1867–1940)
Municipal reformer

Paradises Lost and Found

The small towns that stayed behind

The tremors of city growth were felt in the hinterlands. In 1890 about 41 million persons lived on farms or in country towns. The small town was long a sentimental favorite of Americans. "The country town is one of the great American institutions," wrote sociologist Thorstein Veblen, born in Cato Township on the Wisconsin frontier, "perhaps the greatest, in the sense that it has had and continues to have a greater part than any other in shaping public sentiment and giving character to American culture." Those who had once lived in a nineteenth-century country town would have agreed, especially if their town was beginning to decline, as so many of them were in the twentieth century.

Towns were in the grips of forces beyond their control. Their lives often depended on where the ribbon of railroad track lay. It came to the towns that offered the best cash subsidies or real estate grants. Towns that bid too low were left without access to markets. The railroad brought excitement and prosperity to some communities, but it undercut others, for freight rates could be murderously high when a town was served by only one railroad. Local economies were also strongly influenced by industries in nearby big cities. The great flour mills of Minneapolis grew at the expense of many smaller milling operations in the farm country. Chicago's industrial growth forced out small factories within a radius of a hundred miles. Local merchants who had to compete with big-city chain stores or mail-order houses often lost their shirts.

The lure of new careers, higher wages, and excitement drew the young from farms and small towns to the big city. "It is a striking characteristic," wrote Henry J. Fletcher, a prominent midwestern lawyer in 1895, "that . . . large masses of people, apparently against their own interests, leave the country where homes are cheap, the air pure, all men are equal, and extreme poverty unknown, and crowd into cities where all these conditions are reversed." The effect was, in his eyes, a net loss to society. "The constant depletion of the smaller towns of the country, steadily draining away the best, producing absenteeism and local stagnation, must be regarded as an evil of great magnitude."

A study of an Indiana town showed that between 1877 and 1910 about 90 percent of the high-school graduates left the community for good. As a result of migrations like this one, many of the residents of small towns were beyond their most productive years. Towns filled with old-timers often could not raise the taxes needed to maintain local government services at a respectable level.

Many speeches delivered to graduating high-school classes urged young people to stay on the farm or in the country town. Such pleas did little good. Between 1800 and 1890 the population in more than half of the townships of Illinois and Ohio declined. In New York State populations in 600 out of 900 townships dwindled. The exodus included adults as well as youngsters.

Communes less active

Before the Civil War one way to escape the ills of society had been to form a commune — a utopian colony. But after the war the communal movement weakened. Commune members grew older, and their schisms deepened. Sometimes the death of a strong leader left an unfillable void. Fewer people chose them as an alternative to city or suburban life. The values of self-reliance and personal success may have counteracted the desire for community.

Relatively few new communes were established. Temperance advocates from the Midwest, trying to escape the "whiskey-sodden" Irish and Germans, formed a dozen or more "dry" colonies in the West. The most famous was Greeley, Colorado. Blacks who wanted to escape Jim Crow laws in the South settled several towns in Oklahoma. Socialists occasionally still banded together to form cooperative colonies. But these communities rarely succeeded financially or lasted more than a few years.

Socialists formed the Llano del Rio colony in California's Mojave Desert in 1914. Most of its members were farmers and small businessmen, and property was jointly owned. By cooperatively cultivating two thousand acres of desert land, they were soon able to supply about 90 percent of their food needs. Their school had 125 children in 1917 and included one of the first Montessori kindergartens in the state. Eventually legal problems relating to water rights destroyed the colony.

Several successful religious communes were formed in California, the most notable of which was the Theosophist Colony established in 1897 at Point Loma, San Diego. Its five hundred members regulated their lives by the teachings of occult and Eastern religions. Point Loma became famous for its musical and theatrical programs before it was torn apart by internal dissension in the 1920s.

The city and community

Since colonial times, many American intellectuals have viewed cities with a scornful eye. In the late nineteenth century such critics recognized the city's advantages but believed them outweighed by the drawbacks. Many leading thinkers attacked the cities of the Gilded Age. The Reverend Josiah Strong argued that "the city has become a serious menace to our civilization." The radical Henry George held that the city was the place of "the greatest wealth and the deepest poverty." Its corruption, George said, rivaled that of ancient Rome. Unless something were done to tame the cities, they would produce "brute force and wild frenzy." Novelist Henry James loved pre-Civil War New York. He celebrated quiet, graceful, tree-lined Washington Square in his early work. But he found the New York of the 1880s overgrown with oppressively tall buildings. At the beginning of the skyscraper age he could foresee the future New York as "a huge, continuous fifty-floored conspiracy against the very idea of the ancient graces." Critic and novelist William Dean Howells considered cities so vice-ridden and inhumane that he wanted them destroyed every twenty years or so. In his utopian novel *Looking Backward*, Edward Bellamy pictured a renewed Boston in the year 2000 A.D. All urban problems had been solved through state socialism and technology, and the city was once more adorned with trees and green parks.

But as the cities grew, commentators on urban life found it impossible to ignore the needs of those who made their homes in the city. Intellectuals concerned themselves with finding or establishing the sense of community in the urban environment. Improving community life within the city was the chal-

We were to live in the neighborhood, . . . identify ourselves with it socially, and, in brief, contribute to it our citizenship.

LILLIAN WALD (1867–1940)
Founder of New York's
Henry Street Settlement House

lenging goal of the settlement house, an English invention brought to America in the 1880s. The settlement houses established by Jane Addams and others were exciting places. Most famous was Chicago's Hull House, founded in 1889 by Jane Addams. A large mansion in the midst of the immigrant slums, Hull House provided day-care nurseries, medical care, savings programs, and courses in citizenship, public health, cooking, sewing, art appreciation, politics, and literature. It was intended to serve as an enlarged family center. By 1895 at least fifty settlement houses were scattered throughout the country. They were staffed by young residents, mostly women, fresh out of college. The successful settlement house was one that increasingly turned over its functions to city government and private individuals. In their own way, though, some of the immigrant poor were developing the organization skills to create parks and services and, in general, to improve their own communities.

The leading educator and philosopher of his time approved heartily of the settlement-house idea. As the founder of progressive education, John Dewey (1859–1952) worked for student-centered education and school-centered communities. He hoped to train young citizens to cope with science and the complexities of modern living. At his Laboratory School, started in 1896 in Chicago, he tried to put his theories into practice. Dewey's theories were widely accepted (and wildly distorted) by other educators. The cities of Quincy, Massachusetts, and Gary, Indiana, organized experimental programs where each school was intended to be "a model home, a complete community and embryonic democracy."

By the end of World War I almost half of the American people were urbanites. Even people who lived on farms and in small towns were affected by the new life style of the city. America was now, some said, an urban civilization.

Review

Cities grew with the continued spread of the Industrial Revolution. By 1920 more than half the nation's citizens were urbanites. Skyscrapers symbolized the excitement and aspiration of city life. New transportation forms expanded the city's limits and great iron bridges eased commercial traffic. The use of electricity stepped up the urban tempo. Only in the South did a rural tradition persist without marked change.

By the end of the nineteenth century the typical American city was segmented into three zones. The downtown zone was primarily a cluster of shopping areas and businesses; the slums were also part of the downtown zone but set apart in different neighborhoods from the stores and offices. The suburban zone was located at some distance from the central city and served as a residential area for the upper-middle classes. Between the downtown area and the suburbs was the "zone of emergence," where the lower-middle classes lived in row houses or cottages. Meanwhile the lower classes were jammed into tenements in the downtown slum neighborhoods.

Turn-of-the-century housing conditions for the cities' poor and for working-class families generally were crowded, unsanitary, and unsafe. New tenement laws in New York City had no effect on the many old buildings. Cities found themselves unable to finance all the services demanded by the rapid growth of their populations. Local political machines kept the cities' wheels turning even as they engaged in all manner of corruption. Many instances of this corruption were exposed by journalists of the Progressive era. The disastrous effects of haphazard city growth revived the art of city planning, and the Chicago World's Fair helped launch a City Beautiful movement that spread through the nation.

Rapid urban growth threatened the small towns. Their future could depend on whether or not the railroad came their way. Expanding cities and their factories could also strangle towns as much as a hundred miles away. And more and more young people deserted the towns for the opportunities of the city. Not all Americans were attracted by urbanism. Intellectuals tended to deplore its coldness, ugliness, and cruelty. And the dying commune movement seemed to offer little in the way of alternatives. Reformers set out to improve community life within the city. Settlement houses were a center for urban social action. John Dewey sought to create school-centered communities that could develop citizens capable of coping with modern life.

Questions

1. In what ways did the Industrial Revolution affect city growth? Include the changes taking place in the labor force and the new technology of steel, steam, and electricity.
2. Describe the life of the urban poor in the Gilded Age. Compare life in the urban ghettos then and now. What differences do you see?
3. What efforts were made to improve urban housing in the Progressive era? How successful were the housing reformers? What contributions did city planners make to urban life?
4. Discuss forces controlling the life and death of small towns.
5. Why were communes dying out? Do you believe that the kind of nonutopian community envisioned by John Dewey would be desirable today? Why?

Lumbering in Washington state, early 1900s; photograph by Darius Kinsey.

The destruction of the forests
of this country will be the
murder of its future
prosperity and progress.

CARL SCHURZ   (1829–1906)

24

24

The Great Barbecue

The nineteenth-century Industrial Revolution is a turning point in history if only because of its impact on the environment. At no previous time had society changed the natural world as much as it would—first with steel and steam, later with electricity. The cost of this technology to the American environment is measured in this chapter.

The idea that there is a cost to consider is a relatively new one for Americans. For centuries they had regarded the earth's bounties as free, or very nearly so. The soil, rivers, mines, wells, and forests seemed inexhaustible—and some yields were increasing. Farmers, using new machinery, were raising more food with each passing year. Such bounty made a mockery of Malthus' gloomy prediction that there would come a day when there would be too many mouths to feed and too little food to eat. The ample physical boundaries of the country and the existence of a frontier reinforced a general sense of well-being.

But the frontier finally disappeared. In its 1890 report, the Census Bureau marked an official end to it. The cities were growing much bigger. The remaining wilderness and natural resources, the mineral reserves, range, farm, and timber lands seemed suddenly scarcer and more valuable. Some Americans began examining who owned these treasures and how they were being used. They demanded government protection for the public lands. By the century's end the conservation movement had begun.

A Feast Under Way

The Industrial Revolution on the loose

Gouging the earth for ores and coal, drilling for oil, cutting trees for railroad ties, fouling the air with chemicals and nerve-shattering noise—these were some of the typical and accepted results of the new technology in the years between the Civil War and the First World War. Professor Howard Mumford Jones has aptly named those decades the "age of energy." People first confronted with the disadvantages of the new technology could dismiss and even romanticize them. Technology was making life easier. It meant progress.

Railroad tracks went where they pleased. In some instances they went right through the center of town. The locomotives announced their presence long before they came into sight. They belched out smoke, steam, and sometimes live cinders. Steam engines often turned peaceful farmland or beautiful riverfront scenery into a freight yard. Chicago's freight yards and terminals sprawled all over the city. The Pennsylvania Railroad roared into Washington, D.C., only a short distance from the Capitol. All of this was tolerated because the iron horse was considered the key element of a growing economy.

Factories had the same license to do as they pleased, and with important consequences to the environment. One iron or steel mill standing alone did not matter much, but fourteen or forty of them spewing smoke, their furnaces aflame, could totally alter a town's condition of life. William Glazier described Pittsburgh in 1886:

By all means make your first approach to Pittsburgh in the night time and you will behold a spectacle which has not a parallel on this continent. Darkness gives the city and its surroundings a picturesqueness which they wholly lack by day-light. . . . the scene is so strange and weird that it will live in the memory forever. . . . In truth, Pittsburgh is a smoky, dismal city, at best. . . . But her inhabitants do not seem to mind it; and the doctors hold that the smoke, from the carbon, sulphur and iodine contained in it, is highly favorable to lung and cutaneous diseases.

Steam engines wasted 20 percent of the coal they used for fuels, which rose into the sky as smoke. Toward the end of the century the shift from steam to electrical energy, especially hydroelectric power, resulted in a cleaner and more efficient use of resources. The techniques used in mining and milling of ores laid waste the environment. Giant steam shovels ripped up the earth to create open-pit mines. A prominent feature of most mining or mill towns from Pennsylvania to Idaho was their mountains of slag or ore. Miners' shacks were located on top of or next to these man-made heaps, and the children played on them.

Industries gave no thought to protecting the environment. Deadly fumes from a Tennessee copper mill created a desert in the midst of a lush forest. Factories dumped industrial wastes into rivers and lakes without any regard to the damage they caused. Sewage and poisonous chemicals destroyed fish and made drinking water hazardous. Custom and law condoned this fouling of water resources. By and large a company could legally use river water any way it wished, and it was not held responsible for the condition of the water affected downstream.

In the beginning no one believed that automobiles could hurt the environment. In 1909, in the balmy days of the horseless carriage, the editor of *The Automobile* predicted that when cars became popular, they would *relieve* the congestion caused by horse-and-

buggy traffic. Another writer was convinced that cars would produce fewer accidents than horse-drawn vehicles. Auto manufacturers promised also that use of their products would result in cleaner streets by eliminating horse manure. Bicyclists, who foresaw little danger from autos, lobbied actively for paved roads, only to be pushed off those roads later by high-speed cars.

Exploiting the Great Plains

Mark Twain, who was co-author of a novel called *The Gilded Age*, probably also invented the term "great barbecue" to describe the way Americans misused the public domain after the Civil War. As a product of the frontier, Twain had seen the greed with which people had plundered public property and thoughtlessly stripped away its natural riches in the name of progress. An empire of forests, mines, farms, and grazing land was gobbled up in a short time. Perhaps the most dramatic ecological change in American history occurred in the two decades after the Civil War on the Great Plains, the valley and plateau lands that stretched west from about the 100th meridian to the eastern slope of the Rocky Mountains (see map, p. 160).

The pioneers who pushed onto the grass-

A view of Pittsburgh steel mills (which were controlled by Andrew Carnegie) in the early 1900s. Supplied by the ample ore mines of Allegheny County, Pittsburgh was "the center of steel."

All hail, King Steel, and success to the republic . . . where he is to sit enthroned and work his wonders upon the earth.

ANDREW CARNEGIE   (1835–1919)

game, particularly buffalo or bison, was killed off or pushed out. In the entire history of encounters between humans and four-legged animals, few ended as decisively as the buffalo hunt in the American West in the late nineteenth century. Before white settlement, 60 million of the humpbacked beasts trampled the grasslands. Their herds were, according to one naturalist, "almost certainly the greatest animal congregations that ever existed on earth." (See maps, p. 504.)

The buffalo supplied the Indians with clothing (robes), shelter (tepees), fuel (dried chips), and food. Whites used buffalo mainly for robes, leather goods, food and sport. The chance to farm the prairies and Great Plains made the removal of the buffalo inevitable. While protecting railroad construction crews, General Phil Sheridan ordered his men to wipe out the Indians' source of supplies in order to starve the tribes into submission. William F. ("Buffalo Bill") Cody killed 4280 buffalo in eighteen months while working as a hunter to supply food for construction workers on the Kansas Pacific Railroad. The sport hunters also took a toll of the buffalo, although shooting these animals was usually

land and deserts of the Plains found themselves in a new kind of terrain. Here less than twenty inches of rain fell each year. This meant that they must either irrigate or practice dry farming, that is, tilling the soil to prevent natural moisture from evaporating. Fewer trees were available for fuel and fencing. The topsoil was shallower here, and the ground cover (mostly bunch grass) was thinner. By comparison with the land east of the 100th meridian, this was an arid landscape with limited possibilities for normal farming.

The arrival of the railroad led to an era of intensive settlement in this region. The big

WHERE THE BUFFALO ROAMED

At one time the buffalo, or bison, ranged freely over two thirds of North America from the Appalachians to Nevada, and from the Great Slave Lake to the Gulf of Mexico. Over the nineteenth century their numbers were steadily cut as white settlers from the East relentlessly moved into the Great Plains.

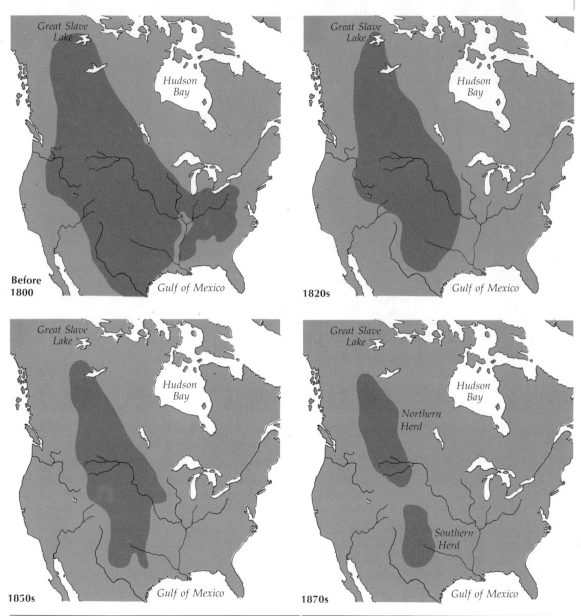

SOURCE: Adapted from J. A. Allen, "The American Bison, Living and Extinct," *Memoirs, Museum of Comparative Zoology,* Vol. 4, No. 10, Harvard University Press, 1876.

VIRGIN FORESTS OF THE UNITED STATES

According to Ridgley and Ekblaw, virgin forests are natural forests untouched by human activities. When virgin forests are cut for lumber, the forests that replace them are called second-growth forests. If these, in turn, are cut, their replacements are third-growth forests. If virgin forests are cut and no effort is made to renew them, the regions left are called cut-over land; if swept by forest fires, they are known as burned-over land.

When the Pilgrims landed, about a half the area of the present United States was covered by virgin forests, the other half by prairies, steppes, and deserts. By 1850, when the U.S. population was about 23 million, the virgin forests had been cut for lumber or cleared for agriculture from New England westward to Illinois as well as along parts of the Atlantic Coast. Forests still remained in the Appalachian Highlands and the Far West. By 1926, with a population of about 110 million, our virgin forests had disappeared from the East and many other parts of the country, and commercial interests were trying to make use of the forests of the West. Today large areas of second- and third-growth forests, cut-over land, and burned-over land have replaced the extensive forests of 1620.

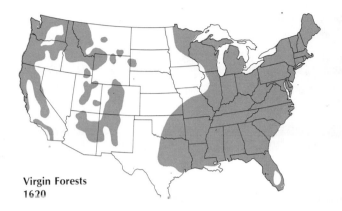

**Virgin Forests
1620**

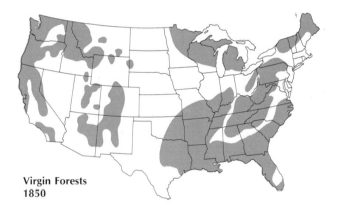

**Virgin Forests
1850**

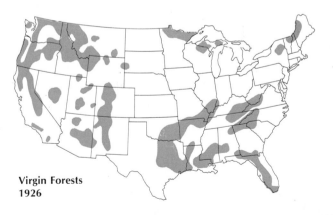

**Virgin Forests
1926**

SOURCE: Adapted from Douglas C. Ridgley, and Sidney E. Ekblaw, *Influence of Geography on Our Economic Life*, 1938, pp. 528–29.

The aftermath of a buffalo slaughter. "Apart from man, the buffalo had but few natural enemies," wrote naturalist George Bird Grinnell in 1892; but that one natural enemy was sufficient to decimate the great herds.

about as "sporting" as shooting cows in a pasture. Trains would stop to allow passengers to bring down buffalo or pronghorn antelope, another favorite target. Crew members cut and mounted the heads, as mementos of western travel. They left the carcasses to rot.

In the 1870s a new tanning process made shoes and saddles of buffalo leather commercially profitable. When a serious depression put people out of work in the East, many of the unemployed men went west to kill buffalo, causing mass carnage on the Plains. In 1873 seven million of the animals were killed. The last major organized buffalo hunt was in 1882. Four years later the bison had edged so near extinction that scientists from the Smithsonian Institution had trouble bagging good specimens to stuff for posterity. In 1893 only about one thousand buffalo survived in Yellowstone National Park. A year later poachers had cut the number to twenty. Not a moment too soon, Congress imposed heavy fines on poachers in the national park, the first federal law protecting the bison.

While the bison were being destroyed and

the Indians removed, railroads kept pushing west. Cowboys drove great herds of Texas cattle to the Kansas railheads or farther north to fatten on the open range (unfenced public lands) of the central and northern Plains. By 1888, just after the long cattle drives had ended, a grand total of 10 million cattle had been moved. Sheepmen, much despised by cowboys because their "woolies" nibbled the grass down to the roots, followed the cattlemen.

At the same time, wheat farmers ("nesters," in cowboy lingo) also staked out claims in the Plains. By using ingenious techniques like dry farming and by applying new inventions, the farmers of the Plains eked out a living from the arid, treeless environment. Rifles helped them battle Indians. After 1874 Joseph Glidden's barbed wire was used by cattlemen to fence off land they owned or claimed. It also helped farmers protect their crops from grazing cattle and sheep. Barbed wire ended the era of the open range. The windmill attached to a water pump was a handy invention, though on windless days it might have to be cranked by hand.

Yet the soil of the western plains was too thin and fragile for the numbers of farms and ranches it supported by the 1880s. Cattle and wheat growers gave little thought to the natural limits of the land. A terrible example of this occurred during World War I, when farmers started using Ford tractors to plow up the western plains. They produced bumper harvests of wheat for the Allies but overworked the soil. Soon afterward, erosion became an unexpected problem. The dust storms in Oklahoma and elsewhere on the western plains in the 1930s were a direct consequence of this earlier abuse of the land.

Planned and unplanned destruction of the forests

Vast ecological changes were occurring in the forests as well. Now that much of the eastern

woodland had given way to farms, the main lumbering activity shifted to the Midwest, to the Rocky Mountains, and finally to California and the Northwest. Immense quantities of lumber were consumed by railroads, the export trade, and the home construction industry. Frame homes built with two-by-fours used up huge amounts. Consumption of newsprint made from wood pulp also skyrocketed when high-speed presses came into use in the 1880s. By the end of the century about three-and-one-half times as many trees were cut each year as were sprouting to replace them.

Much of the land suitable for timber cutting, grazing, or farming was publicly owned when the Civil War ended. The rationale for transferring the public domain into private hands was that the land and its resources were useless as long as they remained untapped. Once exploited, they would bring material progress. And only in private hands could they be taxed. Theoretically, when the land was transferred to private hands it was with few exceptions supposed to go to ordinary citizens, not to railroads or other big business combinations. But the laws concerning the public lands were usually loosely drawn and poorly enforced, so that in the end the big railroad, coal, timber, and cattle interests took possession of great portions of those lands.

The Timber Culture Act of 1873 granted 160 acres of public land to anyone who agreed to plant 40 acres of it in trees. Five

The forests of America, however slighted by man, must have been a great delight to God; for they were the best He ever planted.

JOHN MUIR   (1838–1914)

years later Congress reduced the 40-acres minimum to 10 acres and allowed settlers and miners to cut timber on public lands free of charge for their own use. By the Timber and Stone Act of 1878 the government sold off lands and forests in California, Oregon, Nevada, and Washington that were supposedly "unfit for cultivation." Customers paid $2.50 per acre, with a limit of 160 acres. These laws invited fraud by lumber companies. The firms hired front men to make personal claims and later transfer their holdings to the corporation. Private corporations and speculators eventually acquired over 13 million acres of forest land.

Similarly, the Desert Land Act of 1877 resulted in a giveaway for ranchers. The law granted up to 640 acres at $1.25 an acre to anyone who promised to irrigate the land in three years. The cost of irrigating was so high that very few individuals had the capital to undertake it. Cattle ranchers bought up acreage for grazing but never got around to irrigating the soil.

Like the legendary Paul Bunyan, lumbermen liked to tackle the tallest and fattest trees. They proudly toppled California's giant redwood trees, many of which were seedlings when the Egyptians built their pyramids. Although extremely durable, the wood of this species is brittle. When a big tree fell it shattered, so that only about half of the lumber could be salvaged.

Lumbermen caused accidental fires in the dry "slash" (sawed-off limbs, chips, leaves, needles, and bark). To avoid such dangers they applied the "cut-out-and-get-out" approach to forestry. They chopped out only the most readily available timber and moved on before the sun created a tinderbox. This was a highly destructive and inefficient method of lumbering.

Forests were also at the mercy of fires purposely set by farmers. Pioneers often started fires to clear new land quickly. (According to folk tradition, the smoke of a forest fire was a health tonic.) Historian Stuart Holbrook writes: "These thousands upon thousands of clearing fires . . . these little fires creeping sleepily along the fences, 'making pasture land,' clearing the back forty, these friendly little blazes were burning an empire."

In the fall of 1871, the Midwest was gripped by intense drought. A roaring inferno erupted on both sides of Green Bay, creating a pall of smoke that blotted out the sun for two hundred miles, charred 1.3 million acres of woodland, destroyed untold numbers of birds and animals, and claimed the lives of 1152 people near the lumber town of Peshtigo, Wisconsin. This was the highest toll ever recorded in a North American fire, five times higher than the Chicago blaze that same year. In that same dry year of 1871 2.5 million acres of forest land were ravaged by fire in northern Michigan.

Some of the Great Lakes forest areas burned twice within fifty years and needed intensive reseeding to grow back again. In 1894 fire put much of Wisconsin out of the timber business for a generation. Near the turn of the century, on a yearly average, deliberate or accidental fires (many caused by lightning) killed fifty people and destroyed 50 million acres of woodland at a cost of $50 million.

Commercial killing of wildlife

American wildlife fell to its lowest ebb in the decade between 1880 and 1890. It was not only timber cutting, farming, and the general disruption of grassland and forest that caused the decline but also vigorous commercial hunting. Until early in the twentieth century, almost any furred or feathered creature was fair game for the hunters. State game laws were weak and poorly enforced, and federal laws were nonexistent. As a result, some types of deer ceased to roam in vast areas east of the Rockies, and the elk confined itself to the western mountains.

Some hunters made fortunes supplying feathers to makers of women's hats. Their favorite hunting ground was the Florida Keys, where some of the most spectacular birds on the continent nested. They shot the most birds during the nesting season, when feathers were most colorful and fledglings most numerous. One hunter is said to have slaughtered over 130,000 birds.

Like the buffalo, the passenger pigeon became a victim of mass killing. Once, some 2 billion passenger pigeons inhabited North America. During colonial times, migrating pigeons darkened the sky at midday. These birds nested in enormous flocks. Late in the nineteenth century organized hunting parties preyed on the passenger pigeons. When 136 million fluttered into the trees at Petosky, Michigan, in 1878, an army of hunters wielding guns, nets, and firebrands attacked them. A railroad carried away carloads of bird carcasses at prices ranging from ten to twenty-five cents a dozen.

This was the final mass hunt of the passenger pigeon; the species never fully restored its losses. When a mateless female named Martha died in her cage at the Cincinnati Zoo in 1914, the passenger pigeon became extinct. That year William T. Hornaday, a leading wildlife conservationist, told the Yale University School of Forestry, "The same low order of intelligence that denuded China of her forests, and turned her hillsides into gullied barrenness has swept away fully 95 percent of the birds and mammals of America that were most useful to man."

Slowing the Damage

The early conservation movement

Anyone who opposed the vandalism of the public domain went against the popular grain — as well as against organized lobbies. Still, by the end of the nineteenth century some people began demanding protection for natural resources. Among them were natural scientists, sport hunters, nature enthusiasts, and government officials. Even some lumber corporations were using trained foresters. Together they helped found the conservation movement.

The first attempt to preserve a wilderness area came in 1872. A year earlier a government exploration team had viewed the magnificent geysers, breathtaking craters, and stately mountains in Wyoming territory. They reported that the Yellowstone-area was probably worthless to mineral hunters. The winters were too severe for cattle and the land unfit for farming. Even the Indians avoided it. From a commercial standpoint the Yellowstone region appeared to have little value. Congress then felt free to designate it as a "pleasuring ground." It drew generous boundaries around Yellowstone National Park and guaranteed "all timber, mineral deposits, natural curiosities or wonders within the park and their retention in their natural condition." This was the beginning of the system of national parks.

Carl Schurz, secretary of the interior in the Hayes administration, was the first cabinet-

ELLEN SWALLOW RICHARDS (1842-1911)

MOTHER OF ECOLOGY

"And now I ask you here tonight to stand sponsors of the christening of a new science. . . ." With these words Ellen Swallow Richards, the nation's most prominent woman scientist, introduced "oekology" to a fashionable Boston audience in 1892. Oekology—now known as ecology—joined together the main disciplines she had been working in for twenty years, including chemistry, biology, nutrition, and oceanography, in order to study the environment as a whole. As she faced her listeners, Ellen Richards expressed her alarm at the country's rapidly changing environment. Describing the home as the basic environmental unit affecting people's health, growth, and attitudes, she carefully explained her firmly held belief that environmental education had to begin there.

Her speech was well received. But the times were not ripe for ecology. Rather than coming together, the branches of science were going their separate ways, developing independently of each other. Nor was Richards' cause helped by the fact that many of her advocates were women, most of whom were not scientists.

Born Ellen Swallow in Massachusetts, she graduated from Vassar and became the first woman to enter, graduate from, and teach at the Massachusetts Institute of Technology. Through her work as a chemist Richards participated in studies of air and water that made her one of the world's experts in water analysis and pollution. She conducted major water surveys that were models of their kind and that led to the development of modern municipal sewage methods and the establishment of water quality standards. She also carried on basic studies in air pollution and added new science courses to MIT's curriculum. In their own home, Richards and her husband devised revolutionary new methods of heating, air circulation, and waste disposal that would later become standard features in home and industry. She also applied her considerable scientific and organizational gifts to promoting and guiding early movements that sought to benefit consumers and improve nutrition.

In 1908 Ellen Richards launched her second science, euthenics. If ecology was the study of the total environment and its interrelationships, euthenics was the method by which that environment was to be stabilized, protected, and controlled. In the last years of her life this prolific scientist wrote fourteen books and delivered hundreds of speeches espousing her beliefs. Disturbed by the growing production and consumption that produced so much waste, she intended her books as a series to help people better understand their own relationship to their surroundings. Her writings dealt with consumerism, the economics of production, the effects of air, water, and food on human health, environmental education, euthenics (including a plan for a model city), and an analysis of sanitation systems.

The young Ellen Swallow once wrote: "I have an almost Napoleonic faith in my star." It seems inconceivable that the memory of this woman could have almost vanished from her country's mind. Her ideas were far ahead of her time. But her visions were often brilliant, largely accurate, and, if anything, more timely now than they were in her own day.

level officer to challenge wholesale destruction of natural resources. Incensed that the timber barons were "not merely stealing trees, but whole forests," he delivered a landmark report to Congress in 1877. In it he proposed a network of government preserves and reforestation projects comparable to those of European nations. Congressional opponents charged that his "Prussian" proposal (Schurz was a German immigrant) was undemocratic. Congress ignored the Schurz Report and instead passed the ambiguous Timber and Stone Act of 1878 (see p. 508) which, because of several loopholes in the law, failed to halt the destruction of forests by big lumber companies. In 1885 the U.S. Land Commissioner, reacting to evidence of large-scale land frauds, stopped issuing land titles where swindling was suspected and set aside 2.7 million acres for bona fide settlers only. Two years later he was fired and his reforms revoked.

In the absence of reliable information about water supply, soil fertility, or climate, unfounded beliefs flourished with regard to the Great Plains, Rocky Mountains, and southwestern desert. The myth of the "Great American Desert" (see p. 329) still hung on. Another prevalent myth was that the arid West was really an extension of the "Garden of the World," a tremendously fertile land temporarily lacking in water, which should be developed very much like the eastern part of the country.

The earliest clarification of myths about the Great American Desert came from Major John Wesley Powell's *Report on the Lands of the Arid Region of the United States*, delivered to Congress in 1879. The one-armed Civil War veteran gathered his information personally as head of a U.S. Geological Survey expedition. He braved the white waters of the Colorado River, inspected the irrigation works of Indians, Spaniards, Mexicans, and Mormons, and studied data from botanists, geologists, and other specialists. Major

Powell concluded that while most of the arid region had no commercial use, small parts of it could be sorted out for selected timber cutting, pasturage, farming, and mining. About 5 percent of the overall total could be recovered for farmland by dams and irrigation channels.

Powell blasted that sacred cow of American land policy—the 160-acre (quarter section) farm. In the arid West, he believed, 800 acres should be the minimum for an irrigated family farm, and for unirrigated ranch land four square miles (2560 acres) should be the minimum. The Powell Report marked the beginning of scientific understanding and the end of myth concerning the West. But for Congress to act on Powell's ideas required an effort on a scale that was then considered impractical. The report was shelved for some years.

John Muir, prophet of the wilderness

While Carl Schurz, Major Powell, and others were striving to keep business from destroying the environment, the naturalist John Muir took a different tack. The Scottish-born Muir (1838–1914) grew up on a Wisconsin pioneer farm and had lived close to nature from an early age. Later he discovered the writings of Emerson and Thoreau and became a Transcendentalist. Wilderness, he felt, should be preserved for its own sake, for its purely spiritual and aesthetic values. While in college he blinded himself temporarily with a woodworking tool and vowed that, should he ever recover his eyesight, he would devote his life to nature. This he did by moving to California, where he herded sheep, wrote poetry, and studied the wilderness. Muir wandered through the loneliest and most fearsome wilds of the West, including the Sierra Nevada Mountains. As an avid disciple of Emerson, Muir was understandably disappointed when the philosopher visited him at Yosemite and boarded at a

posh hotel instead of camping out with him under the stars.

Yosemite Valley, then under California's control, was poorly protected from commercial users. Sheep, which Muir called "hooved locusts," were damaging the valley. Muir pressed for federal laws to protect the wilderness in magazine articles, while magazine editor Robert Underwood Johnson lobbied in Congress for a preservation bill. The first major conservation act since Yellowstone was passed by Congress with the support of the Southern Pacific Railroad, which hoped for a flourishing tourist trade to Yosemite. By then the lumbermen agreed that the giant redwood trees were too brittle for commercial use. In 1890 President Benjamin Harrison signed the law establishing Yosemite and Sequoia National Parks in California.

After another year's prodding from Muir and others, Congress passed the Forest Reserve Act. It repealed the Timber Culture Act and authorized the president to limit commercial cutting in certain portions of public land. Harrison set aside 13 million acres as national forests. Congress also repealed the Preemption Act. This law had been set up to allow squatters to purchase land at low prices, but it had been abused by land speculators, and had encouraged a free-for-all development of public land. The Carey Act (1894) permitted the president to give each state up to one million acres of the public domain for irrigation and reclamation.

creatures was also fostered by museums like the Smithsonian Institution.

With the closing of the frontier in 1890 and steady increase of urbanization, Americans in many walks of life began to yearn for the wilderness. A back-to-nature movement began to sweep the country. Readers devoured novels such as Jack London's *The Call of the Wild* (1903) and *White Fang* (1905), which depict dogs struggling for survival in the Alaskan wilds. Another favorite was Edgar Rice Burroughs' *Tarzan of the Apes* (1914) which concerns a young English boy who is mothered by a great ape and grows to manhood in the jungle.

Some writers went to great extremes to gather their information about wild nature. In 1912 the wildlife painter Joseph Knolles called a press conference in Maine to announce that he was going to survive on his own in the woods for sixty days. He smoked his last cigarette, stripped naked, and disappeared into the wilderness. Right on schedule "Nature Man" Knolles returned hale and hearty—clad in a bearskin—praising the virtues of self-reliance. He was an overnight sensation but had to pay a fine for killing a bear in violation of state law. He soon published a work entitled *Alone in the Wilderness*.

Scouting was a popular phase of the back-to-nature movement. The artist and nature writer Ernest Thompson Seton organized scouting activities in this country based on the model of the British scouting movement. An early scouting pamphlet set forth the movement's purpose: the boys of today who

These new laws resulted partly from organized pressure from volunteer groups. Conservationism at that time was the concern chiefly of a tiny minority of intellectuals and wealthy persons. Muir founded the Sierra Club in 1892 to encourage camping and climbing in the wilds, so as to increase public awareness of the desirability of wilderness preservation. The exclusive Boone and Crockett Club founded in 1885 by Teddy Roosevelt and ninety-nine other sportsmen (membership was limited to one hundred) sought a national park system and laws protecting big game. The American Ornithologists Union tried to protect birds. Eventually many endangered species of wildlife had separate organized lobbies. Interest in wild

Members of the Sierra Club gather for an elaborate picnic in a sequoia grove during their annual camping trip in 1903. Among the stated purposes of the Sierra Club was "to explore, enjoy, and render accessible the mountain regions of the Pacific Coast."

live "in our cities and villages, do not have the chance, as did the boys of the past . . . to become strong, self-reliant, resourceful, and helpful, and to get acquainted with nature and outdoor life. . . ." The Boy Scouts of America, incorporated in 1910, had clubs in forty-four states and claimed over 100,000 members within three years. The *Scout Handbook* began to climb the best-seller lists. Several scouting groups for girls began with similar objectives and organization.

Gifford Pinchot and organized conservation

As president, Theodore Roosevelt was attracted to the ideas of a young government forester, Gifford Pinchot (1865–1948), the founding father of organized conservation.

Pinchot conceived of a forest not as a mine to be exhausted as quickly as possible but as a farm whose crop could be grown again and again. Although he loved the wilderness, he was more concerned with the efficient use of resources than with the preservation of nature. Pinchot wanted a federal program that would protect not only forests but also hydroelectric power sites, mineral reserves, soil, and wildlife. These resources were threatened by corporate greed, government complicity, and public ignorance. Made head of the forestry division of the Agriculture Department in 1905, he coordinated all the government's conservation programs. Pinchot also rallied a small band of government technicians and volunteer groups to plan a long-range program of managed resources. TR encouraged Pinchot to transfer control of the public forests from the Interior Department, with its giveaway philosophy, to the less political Department of Agriculture.

Roosevelt, the effective conservationist

The organized conservation movement came into its own during Theodore Roosevelt's presidency. It wove itself into the fabric of the Progressive movement, which hoped to elevate trained specialists above politicians in government and to moderate the power of the monopolies. The president was himself a life-long naturalist, sportsman, and believer in the strenuous life. To some people he seemed to personify the back-to-nature movement. Action to conserve natural resources also fitted Roosevelt's concept of an expanded executive branch.

When TR came to office in 1901, cattle and timber interests, railroads, and power companies were still feasting off the public domain. That bonanza ended in 1905, when his attorney general indicted some of the West's richest lumber barons on charges of defrauding the government in the national forests. The president reserved 125 million acres as national forests and suspended activities in all publicly owned coal fields. He temporarily withdrew 2500 power-dam locations from development by private utilities companies, giving them the flimsy excuse that the sites were needed for ranger stations. Through these actions Roosevelt (assisted by Pinchot) hoped to create a more orderly development of resources on public land.

Roosevelt enthusiastically supported the National Reclamation Act of 1902, known also as the Newlands Act. This bill established the Bureau of Reclamation and channeled money from the sale of public land into flood control and hydroelectric power in the arid region of the West. Oddly enough, some of the West's most devout believers in rugged individualism supported the Reclamation Act. They realized that private financiers could never raise enough capital for the

The time has fully arrived for recognizing in the law the responsibility to the community, the state, and the nation which rests upon the private owners of private lands.
The ownership of forest land is a public trust.

THEODORE ROOSEVELT (1858–1919)
Special message to Congress, 1909

reclamation projects that they needed to compete with the farming states in the East.

Volunteer groups like the American Game Protection and Propagation Association, the Sierra Club, and the National Audubon Society pressed for wildlife protection. Numerous laws were passed to protect endangered species. Roosevelt effectively promoted five national parks, four big-game refuges, and fifty-one bird sanctuaries. The first federal wildlife statute, the Lacey Act of 1901, prohibited crossing state lines with dead animals or birds killed in violation of state laws. Other federal laws protected duck, brown bear, elk, antelope, and sea otter. International treaties limited the hunting of seals and migratory birds.

Roosevelt convened a special White House conference on conservation in 1908. Some 550 governors, industrialists, conservationists, and federal officials met in the White House under Pinchot's chairmanship. The meeting led to the creation of conservation commissions in forty-one states, as well as the National Conservation Commission, the Inland Waterways Commission, and the Country Life Commission.

The Conservation Commission, headed by Pinchot, inventoried the nation's resources for the first time. It carefully distinguished exhaustible resources from renewable resources. Although generally optimistic, the Commission unearthed some disheartening findings. The yearly waste of minerals through poor mining and treatment methods exceeded $300 million. Oil pro-

Dam Hetch Hetchy! As well dam for water-tanks the peoples' cathedrals and churches, for no holier temple has ever been consecrated by the heart of man.

JOHN MUIR (1838–1914)

ducers wasted about 400 billion cubic feet of natural gas, "the most perfect known fuel," in 1907 alone. Rivers were washing away 783 million tons of American soil each year. Between 1901 and 1908 the yearly flood damage increased from $45 million to $238 million. All of the waste came from "ignorance, indifference, or false notions of economy." Strict government measures were needed at once to avoid future scarcities.

Gifford Pinchot lost his job during President Taft's administration when he clashed with Secretary of the Interior Richard A. Ballinger over opening the Alaskan coal fields. The Pinchot-Ballinger rift made headlines as a titanic conservation struggle, although it had far more to do with personalities and politics than with conservation. Pinchot's tactlessness helped bring about his removal, but he had already earned a lasting place in history. Pinchot's ideas on the "wise use" of resources still prevail today in some government circles.

The Hetch Hetchy fight

From the outset there have been two kinds of conservationists. The practical ones seek a wise use of the wilderness, and the aesthetic ones want to preserve wilderness for its own sake. The first kind was represented by Pinchot and the second by Muir. They had been good friends but parted company when Pinchot, against Muir's advice, allowed sheep to graze in Yosemite National Park. They clashed again in an even more fundamental argument over whether or not Hetch Hetchy River in Yosemite National Park should be dammed to supply drinking water for San Francisco. Muir could not imagine a worse assault on nature than to drown Hetch

Hetchy Valley, which he considered as beautiful as Yosemite Valley. San Francisco Progressives argued that a city-operated dam in the Sierra Mountains would undercut the greedy Pacific Gas and Electric Company, a private monopoly that hoped to supply the city's water and power. When the issue came to a head, Pinchot gave his blessings to the building of the Hetch Hetchy Dam in Yosemite National Park.

Muir, the Sierra Club, and other wilderness defenders were outraged. They pointed out other sources of water and proclaimed Hetch Hetchy an invaluable treasure. "These temple destroyers," Muir intoned, "devotees of ravaging commercialism, seemed to have a perfect contempt for Nature, and instead of lifting their eyes to the God of the Mountains, lifted them to the Almighty Dollar." When President Wilson signed the Hetch Hetchy measure in 1913, both Pinchot and Roosevelt supported him. Aesthetic conservationism had lost out to practical conservationism. Muir died brokenhearted one year later.

However, the drowning of Hetch Hetchy Valley rallied the faithful. Wilderness advocates promoted conferences on the national parks in 1911, 1912, and 1913, out of which came the National Park Service Act of 1916. This law established for the first time comprehensive rules governing the national park lands, which by then consisted of 25 million acres of land, including twelve national parks, plus several smaller preserves and military parks (Civil War battlegrounds). Among the parks already established were Yellowstone, Crater Lake in Oregon, Glacier in Montana, Hawaii National Park, Lassen Volcanic in California, Mesa Verde in Colorado, Mount Ranier in Washington,

Wind Cave in South Dakota, and Rocky Mountain in Colorado. In setting up most of these parks Congress used the measuring stick first applied to Yellowstone: it established a national park only on land it considered worthless for commercial exploitation. The head of the newly formed National Park Service (1916) was successful businessman and nature enthusiast Stephen T. Mather, who occasionally tapped his own fortune to stretch the meager official budget. In addition, certain federal lands important for historical preservation or scientific investigation had been protected by Congress under the Antiquities Act of 1906.

By 1918 the conservationists had made the point that the great barbecue was not a free meal. There was a price to pay, and it had to be paid by the public in the form of wasted natural resources, including wilderness. The conservationists also stressed the need to save, or at least not to waste needlessly, some of nature's gifts. They had started what has proven to be an endless struggle to maintain a balance between exploitation and preservation of wild nature in America.

Review

The American environment underwent enormous change as a result of the Industrial Revolution, though most people ignored the damage the new technology caused or considered it a minor price to pay for progress. Machines gouged the earth, smoke and fumes dirtied the air, and sewage polluted waterways. The Great Plains probably underwent the greatest alteration as farmers and livestock men sought to adapt this arid region to their needs. Eastern forests had in large measure been cleared for farmlands and the trend continued all the way west. Soon many more trees were felled than were being replaced. They were also destroyed by fires. Public lands, sold to private owners, usually fell into the hands of cattle, lumber, and railroad interests. The habitats of wildlife were destroyed, and species of birds and animals were annihilated by hunters' guns.

By the century's end, people who demanded protection of the nation's natural resources were laying the groundwork for the conservation movement. The protection of Yellowstone began a system of national parks that later included Sequoia and Yosemite. Pressure from newly organized groups helped force passage of conservation laws. Actually there were two schools of conservation: the practical and the aesthetic. Gifford Pinchot, father of the conservation movement, represented the first group. John Muir of California spoke for the second. The fight over Hetch Hetchy highlighted the differences between them. After the loss of Hetch Hetchy Valley, the wilderness conservationists rallied to put forth stronger efforts. But their victories still left nature largely at the mercy of greedy and ignorant people. The effects of the assault on nature were not yet fully understood.

Questions

1. In what ways did the Industrial Revolution affect the environment?
2. Describe the steps that led to the steady exploitation of the Great Plains.
3. Identify (a) the Great Barbecue, (b) William F. Cody, (c) Joseph Glidden, (d) the passenger pigeon, (e) *Report on the Lands in the Arid Region of the United States,* and (f) Carl Schurz.
4. Describe the origins of the conservation movement. Give special consideration to Theodore Roosevelt's administration.
5. Trace the origins and expansion of the national park movement.

Selected Readings

OVERVIEW

A mine of information on practically any subject in any period of American history is Frank Freidel and Richard K. Showman, eds., *Harvard Guide to American History* (Harvard U. Press, 1974). Those interested in a general history of the Gilded Age might start with H. Wayne Morgan, *Unity and Culture: The United States, 1877–1900* (Viking Press, 1971).* See also Vincent P. De Santis, *The Shaping of Modern America: 1877–1916* (Allyn & Bacon, 1972);* and Vincent P. De Santis, ed., *The Gilded Age: 1877–1896* (AHM Pub., 1973..*

WEALTH

An excellent overview of economic history is Thomas C. Cochran and William Miller, *The Age of Enterprise: A Social History of Industrial America* (Harper & Row, 1968).* A "new economic history" is Douglass C. North, *Growth and Welfare in the American Past* (Prentice-Hall, 1966).* The captains of industry receive lively treatment in Matthew Josephson, *The Robber Barons* (Harcourt Brace, 1962);* Frederick Lewis Allen, *The Great Pierpont Morgan* (Harper & Row, 1949);* and Allan Nevins, *John D. Rockefeller* (Kraus Reprint, 1940). A shocking and influential work is Robert Hunter, *Poverty* (MSS Information, 1972). Stephen Thernstrom has written a path-breaking work: *Poverty and Progress: Social Mobility in a Nineteenth-Century City* (Atheneum, 1969).* The city is Newburyport, Massachusetts.

A taste of the labor turmoil of the times will be found in three informative works: Milton Meltzer's brief and readable *Bread and Roses: The Struggle of American Labor, 1865–1915* (Random House, 1967);* Almont Lindsey, *The Pullman Strike* (U. of Chicago, 1943);* and David Brody's *Steelworkers in America: The Non-Union Era* (Harper & Row, 1970).*

POWER

The stormy politics of the years after the Civil War are covered in E. Merton Coulter, *The South During Reconstruction* (Louisiana State U. Press, 1947), a traditional interpretation, and Kenneth M. Stampp, *The Era of Reconstruction, 1865–1877* (Random House, 1965),* a revisionist interpretation.

Gilded Age politics has many historians. Written with an acid pen is Matthew Josephson, *The Politicos* (Harcourt Brace, 1963).* Much more sympathetic is H. Wayne Morgan, *From Hayes to McKinley* (Syracuse U. Press, 1969). Richard Hofstadter's sweeping and exciting *The Age of Reform: From Bryan to F.D.R.* (Knopf, 1955) is basic. An influential older work—John D. Hicks, *The Populist Revolt* (U. of Nebraska Press, 1960)*—is still

*Available in paperback.

worth reading. Paul W. Glad, *McKinley, Bryan, and the People* (Lippincott, 1964)* deals with the election of 1896. Gabriel Kolko, *The Triumph of Conservatism* (Quadrangle, 1967)* holds that progressivism was less liberal than many people thought.

There are numerous biographies of leading politicians. See Allan Nevins, *Grover Cleveland* (Dodd, Mead, 1932) and Henry F. Pringle, *Theodore Roosevelt* (Harcourt Brace, 1956),* which is still the most lively and readable work on TR. See also TR's *Autobiography* (Octagon, 1973). John A. Garraty, *Woodrow Wilson* (Harper & Row, 1970)* is a brief treatment of a complex and important figure.

WAR

Frank Freidel, *The Splendid Little War* (Little, Brown, 1958) is a pictorial history with lively commentary on the Spanish-American War. Theodore P. Greene, ed., *American Imperialism in 1898* (Heath, 1955)* brings together varying interpretations of an important episode in foreign policy. See also Howard K. Beale, *Theodore Roosevelt and the Rise of America to World Power* (Macmillan, 1966).* Robert E. Quirk, *An Affair of Honor* (Norton, 1967)* deals with Wilson's misadventure in Mexico.

There is no scarcity of books on World War I. Barbara Tuchman, *The Guns of August* (Dell, 1971)* is a graphic account of the outbreak of the conflict. Arthur S. Link, *Wilson the Diplomatist* (Watts, 1965)* is written by the leading Wilson scholar. Hanson Baldwin, *World War I* (Harper & Row, 1962) is a general account. The revisionist histories of the twenties and thirties are "must" reading. See, for example, Harry E. Barnes, *Genesis of the World War* (Fertig, 1970). Social history is treated by Preston W. Slosson, *The Great Crusade and After: 1914–1928* (Watts, 1971). An unforgettable novel of life in the trenches is Erich M. Remarque, *All Quiet on the Western Front* (available in a number of editions).*

RACE

Scientific racism is covered by John S. Haller, Jr., *Outcasts from Evolution* (U. of Illinois Press, 1971).

William T. Hagan, *American Indians* (U. of Chicago Press, 1961)* and William Brandon, *The American Heritage Book of Indians* (Dell, 1961)* are useful general accounts. Dee Brown, *Bury My Heart at Wounded Knee: An Indian History of the American West* (Bantam, 1972)* deals with the era 1860–1890. John G. Neihardt, *Black Elk Speaks* (Pocket Books, 1972)* is a poetic account of the Plains tribes. Alvin M. Josephy, Jr., *The Nez Percé Indians and the Opening of the Northwest* (Yale U. Press, 1971)* and S. M. Barrett, ed., *Geronimo, His Own Story* (Ballantine, 1974)* are both valuable. Theodora Droeber, *Ishi in Two Worlds: A Biography of the Last Wild Indian in North America* (U. of California Press, 1961)* deals with a remarkable figure who was "captured" in 1911.

Rayford W. Logan, *The Betrayal of the Negro: from Rutherford B. Hayes to Woodrow Wilson* (Macmillan, 1965)* deals with newspaper opinion. Two dominant blacks are described by Elliott M. Rudwick, *W. E. B. Du Bois: Propagandist of the Negro Protest* (U. of Pennsylvania Press, 1969) and Louis R. Harlan, *Booker T. Washington: The Making of a Black Leader, 1865–1901* (Oxford U. Press, 1972). A basic work on segregation is C. Vann Woodward, *The Strange Career of Jim Crow* (Oxford U. Press, 1974).*

Two important books on the Chinese are Gunther P. Barth, *Bitter Strength: A History of the Chinese in the United States, 1850–1870* (Harvard U. Press, 1964) and Alexander Saxton, *The Indispensible Enemy: Labor and the Anti-Chinese Movement in California* (U. of California Press, 1971).

NATIONALITY AND RELIGION

A rich literature awaits the students of the "new immigration." A good overall introduction is Maldwyn A. Jones, *American Immigration* (U. of Chicago Press, 1960).* On particular groups, see Humbert S. Nelli, *The Italians in Chicago, 1880–1930: A Study in Ethnic Mobility* (Oxford U. Press, 1973);* Theodore Saloutos, *The Greeks in the United States* (Harvard U. Press, 1964); Moses Rischen, *The Promised City: New York's Jews, 1870–1914* (Harper & Row, 1970);* and Oscar Handlin's *The Uprooted* (Little, Brown, 1973).* A valuable intellecutal history is John Higham, *Strangers in the Land* (Atheneum, 1963).* William Preston, Jr., *Aliens and Dissenters* (Harper & Row, 1963) deals with the "Americanization" campaign during World War I. Two classic novels on immigrant life are Ole E. Rölvaag, *Giants in the Earth* (Harper & Row, 1965) and Willa Cather, *My Ántonia* (Houghton Mifflin: 1961).* A warm and human story is Ann Novotny, *Strangers at the Door* (Bantam, 1973).*

Two comprehensive and balanced works on religion are Winthrop S. Hudson, *Religion in America* (Scribner, 1973)* and Sydney E. Ahlstrom, *A Religious History of the American People* (Yale U. Press, 1974).* A basic work for this period is Henry F. May, *The Protestant Churches and Industrial America* (Octagon, 1963). See also John T. Ellis, *American Catholicism* (U. of Chicago Press, 1969).* A valuable description of Jewish life is Jacob R. Marcus, ed., *Critical Studies in American Jewish History* (Ktav, 1971).

WOMEN AND THE FAMILY

A well-written and scholarly book—perhaps the best of its kind—is Lois W. Banner, *Women in Modern America* (Harcourt Brace, 1974).* Dee Brown, *The Gentle Tamers: Women of the Old Wild West* (Bantam, 1974)* is rich in detail. The more advanced student may want to consult Ross E. Paulson, *Women's Suffrage and Prohibition* (Scott, Foresman, 1973).* Aileen S. Kraditor, *The Ideas of the Woman Suffrage Movement, 1890–1920* (Doubleday, 1971)* and William L. O'Neill, *Divorce in the Progressive Era* (Watts, 1973)* are valuable. A famous autobiography of a leading feminist is Jane Addams, *Twenty Years at Hull House* (New American Library, 1910).* For an interesting sidelight, see Scott, *The Southern Lady*, cited on p. 337.

COMMUNITY

The book that started modern American historians thinking and writing about cities is Arthur M. Schlesinger, *The Rise of the City: 1878–1898* (Watts, 1971).* Two brief overviews are Constance M. Green, *The Rise of Urban America* (Harper & Row, 1965)* and Charles N. Glaab and A. Theodore Brown, *A History of Urban America* (Macmillan, 1967).*

On urban politics a delightful work is William L. Riordan, ed., *Plunkitt of Tammany Hall* (Dutton, 1963),* in which the machine politician tells all. See also the classic work on corruption, Lincoln Steffens, *The Shame of the Cities* (Farrar, Straus, 1904).* An influential interpretation is Harold Zink, *City Bosses in the United States* (AMS Press, 1930). On a reform boss see Melvin G. Holli, *Reform in Detroit: Hazen S. Pingree and Urban Politics* (Oxford U. Press, 1973).*

Concerning immigrant life in a late nineteenth-century city, an indispensible work is Jacob Riis, *How the Other Half Lives: Studies among the Tenements of New York* (Dover, 1971).*

Those interested in architecture and city planning will find these works rewarding: Christopher Tunnard and Henry H. Reed, *American Skyline* (New American Library, 1953);* Stanley Buder, *Pullman: An Experiment in Industrial Order and Community Planning, 1880–1930* (Oxford U. Press, 1967);* Clarence S. Stein, *Toward New Towns for America* (MIT Press, 1957);* and S. B. Sutton, ed., *Civilizing American Cities: A Selection of Frederick Law Olmsted's Writings on City Landscapes* (MIT Press, 1971).

ENVIRONMENT

A well-written and informative introduction to the subject is Udall, *The Quiet Crisis*. See also Nash, *The American Environment*, which has a valuable bibliography for the beginner. An insightful, intellectual history by the same author is *Wilderness and the American Mind*. (Publishing details for these three books are on p. 167.)

On national conservation activities see U.S. Department of the Interior, *Highlights in the History of Forest and Related Natural Resource Conservation*, Bulletin 41, revised. A moving biography of John Wesley Powell is Wallace Stegner, *Beyond the Hundredth Meridian* (Houghton Mifflin, 1954).

Movie still from *Our Modern Maidens,* 1929.

IV

Chronology

1918
World War I ends.

1920
U.S. Senate rejects Versailles Peace Treaty. Women's suffrage amendment is ratified.

1921
Marcus Garvey taps deep feelings of black nationalism.

1924
Harding administration scandals exposed by Congress.

1927
Charles A. Lindbergh flies alone, New York to Paris.

1928
Election of Herbert Hoover.

1929
Stock market crash, start of Great Depression.

1933–1938
New Deal era. Franklin D. Roosevelt is president until 1945.

1939
Germany invades Poland; World War II begins.

1941–1945
U.S. in World War II.

The acceleration of life for us has been so great that into the last few years
have been crowded the experiences and the ideas of a normal lifetime. . . .
We have been forced to become realists overnight, instead of idealists,
as was our birthright. . . . We have been forced to live in an atmosphere of
'tomorrow we die,' and so, naturally, we drank and were merry.

JOHN FRANKLIN CARTER (1897–1967)
Member of the "lost generation," writing in 1920

overview
Prosperity, Depression, and War

Two decades after the war that ended what Woodrow Wilson had hoped would be the "culminating and final war for human liberty," the world was plunged into an even more devastating conflict. So short a time had elapsed between the defeat of "the Kaiser and his Huns" and the march of conquest of the Axis powers that many persons alive today remember both wars. Much of the Army brass in the Second World War had first seen combat in World War I.

During the interwar years Europe and the United States experienced yet another catastrophe, the Great Depression of the 1930s. In America it occasioned a remarkable burst of social legislation called the New Deal. The twenty-seven years covered in Part 4 of this book fall into three chronological segments: the twenties, the depression and the New Deal, and finally the Second World War.

Peace without victory

The United States never ratified the Versailles Treaty ending the First World War and it never joined the League of Nations, which had been Wilson's hope for preserving the peace. Probably most Americans would have favored membership in the international organization, but many senators believed that signing the League Covenant—a part of the Treaty—would commit the United

States to the kind of "entangling alliances" it had been avoiding all through its history. Senator Henry Cabot Lodge of Massachusetts led the fight for a "reservation" that would let Congress decide when the United States would go to the aid of another League member. President Wilson took his case to the country, but in the midst of the speaking tour he suffered a collapse. A week later he had a stroke from which he never fully recovered.

Because Wilson refused to let the Democrats vote for the Treaty as amended by its opponents, it was rejected by the Senate and, with it, membership in the League of Nations. Wilson dreamed that the presidential election of 1920 might be a "solemn referendum" on the League, with a vote for the Democratic candidate representing a vote for League membership. The voters chose to return to normalcy with the Republican candidate, Warren G. Harding. The successive Republican presidents, Harding, Coolidge, and Hoover, and even the Democratic president Franklin D. Roosevelt in his early years in office, embraced "isolationism." That is, the United States in the 1920s and most of the '30s avoided alliances with European powers — such as mutual defense pacts — that would commit America to any joint action abroad.

Pleasure and profits

"Jazz Age," "Age of the Flapper," "Lawless Decade" are some of the labels pasted on the twenties. The "hot" jazz from the black ghettos, the short skirts and bobbed hair of the New Woman, and the methodical violation of prohibition by criminals and ordinary citizens alike — these seemed to typify the spirit of the times. This postwar spirit was in sharp contrast to the spirit of idealism and self-sacrifice that marked the Progressive Era and the war years. The smashing election victory in 1920 of Harding and Calvin Coolidge, his running mate, over the Democratic ticket of James M. Cox and Franklin D. Roosevelt seemed to signal a longing for the good old days of peace, prosperity, and private pursuits.

In the twenties the pursuit of pleasure, excitement, and novelty became big business. Advertising took on greater importance than ever before. The public played new games, danced new dances, crowded into movie theaters and sports arenas. The heroes of the age were movie stars like Rudolph Valentino, athletes like Babe Ruth and Jack Dempsey. Towering over them all was the hero of heroes, Charles A. Lindbergh, who flew alone across the Atlantic in 1927. Newspapers, newsreels, and radio reports made all America familiar with "celebrities" — from multimillionaires like Henry Ford to hoodlums like Al Capone.

Enterprising Americans applauded President Coolidge's opinion that "the business of America is business," and Herbert Hoover's philosophy: "The sole function of the government is to bring about a condition of affairs favorable to the beneficial development of private enterprise." Corporate heads had established their credentials as national leaders during the war, and for the most part the country was content to give them free rein in the twenties. By

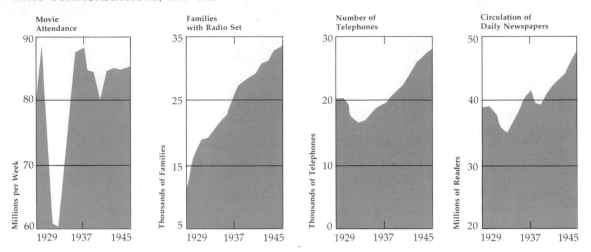

Americans became increasingly influenced by mass media of communications in the twenties. Despite the depression, interest in the media increased rapidly in the thirties and forties.

SOURCES: American Telephone and Telegraph Company. *Editor and Publisher.* Federal Communications Commission. *The Film Daily.* National Broadcasting Company.

the same token, many citizens believed that unions were un-American. The overall rise in the standard of living suggested that poverty and want would soon be eliminated, that there would be, as the Republicans said, a chicken in every pot and two cars in every garage.

Industry poured out goods for consumers. Radios, pianos, vacuum cleaners, refrigerators, telephones, and washing machines appeared in more and more homes. Ford's Model-T "flivvers," selling for a few hundred dollars each, could put even poor families on wheels. And the installment plan helped. With the growth of consumerism and the advertising that encouraged it, avoiding debt became one more puritanical attitude that was going out of style. If the dynamic industrial expansion of earlier decades was no longer taking place, no one seemed worried by that. Nor did many Americans ask what would happen when demand for the household appliances and other consumer products was satisfied. Then as now economics was a mystery to most people.

Social conflict

Not everyone drank bathtub gin or went to the movies every night during the twenties. Despite the frivolous overtones of the decade, different segments of society were in collision. During the summer of 1919, race riots occurred in various cities; thirty-eight persons—both whites and blacks—were killed in Chicago alone. In that same year a "Red Scare" erupted. With the triumph of Bolshevism in Russia, there had been increasing talk of world revolution. A rash of strikes in the U.S. after the armistice aroused fears of domestic subversion, and anarchist bombs increased the tension. In 1920 Attorney General A. Mitchell Palmer ordered thousands of arrests and had over five hundred "dangerous aliens" deported. Renewed hostility toward foreigners brought on the immigration quota laws of 1921, 1924, and 1929. This legislation drastically reduced the annual flow of immigrants from millions to thousands. It was directed especially at cutting down the entrance of newcomers from southern and eastern Europe.

The rise of the big cities had placed rural and small-town America on the defensive. The trial of John Scopes for teaching Darwin's theory of evolution in a Tennessee high school represented this clash as well as the confrontation between religious fundamentalism and scientific rationalism. The Ku Klux Klan was revived, this time as a nationwide organization that made a fortune for its promoters. A sort of self-proclaimed knighthood of WASP America, the hooded fraternity was particularly strong in small towns but had a following in cities as well, both in the South and in the Midwest. The KKK hounded Catholics, Jews, foreigners in general, labor leaders, radicals, people whose conduct it considered immoral, and, of course, blacks.

Still another conflict was between "wets" and "drys." When Prohibition stimulated gangsterism and wholesale violation of the law, the "wets" were finally able to kill the "noble experiment" by a new amendment in 1933.

Culture in the Jazz Age

Artists in various fields gave expression to the new values and attitudes abroad in the land. In *The Sun Also Rises* (1926) and *A Farewell to Arms* (1929), Ernest Hemingway dealt with the wartime and postwar disillusionment of the younger, "lost" generation. Sinclair Lewis' *Main Street* (1920) and *Babbitt* (1922) were brutal satires of the small-town attitudes and commercial values of Middle America. Dramatist Eugene O'Neill, in such plays as *Desire Under the Elms* (1924) and *Strange Interlude* (1928), made use of the psychological insights of Sigmund Freud, whose theories were very much in vogue in the twenties. The poetry of Ezra Pound, the novels of John Dos Passos, and the architecture of Frank Lloyd Wright are representative of the innovations in artistic expression that characterized the decade.

Negro Americans contributed to the outpouring of artistic talent in the twenties. The great migration of blacks from the South to the urban North continued after the war, and in the twenties white intellectuals suddenly became aware of the gifted poets, novelists, and essayists in New York's Harlem. Jazz, created by black Americans, exerted a powerful influence on American popular music. In all its forms it won dedicated white fans, and performers, at home and abroad. But whether America was "home" for blacks was strongly questioned by the flamboyant Marcus Garvey and the thousands who supported his short-lived back-to-Africa movement.

A GOP decade

Most Americans in the twenties had faith in the Republican party and its presidential candidates. The scandalous misconduct of some of Harding's cabinet members and other appointees was not fully revealed until after the president's death in 1923. Calvin Coolidge, who had been vice-president, helped clean up the mess and was handily elected to the presidency in 1924. That the corruption of the Harding administration did not rub off on Coolidge is a tribute to his "image" as personification of old-fashioned American small-town virtues. In 1928 the Republican Herbert Hoover defeated the Democrat Alfred E. Smith by 6 million votes and an electoral vote advantage of five to one. A highly successful engineer, government administrator, and secretary of commerce before reaching the White House, Hoover made "rugged individualism" a household term.

The Great Depression

In 1929 the stock market crashed. Then began the collapse of the economy and, with it, the Hoover administration and the Republican party. Stock prices started to plummet on October 24, wiping out hundreds of speculators. In the months that followed, bank loans were not repaid and banks failed. Industries that had produced more goods than they could sell laid off workers. As the number of jobless increased, demand weakened further and more businesses closed. The jobless could not meet mortgage payments and lost their homes. Bank failures meant the loss of millions of dollars in savings. Agriculture, which had not shared in the general prosperity of the twenties, now faced disaster as farm prices slipped lower and lower. During 1931 unemployment climbed above 20 percent of the work force.

The destruction of morale was one of the consequences of the depression. It shattered the faith of many citizens in the American Dream. They waited as Hoover sought to deal with the growing disaster within the framework of self-help, voluntary cooperation, and decentralized government. And the depression became worse. Men who had always held steady jobs were forced to line up for free soup in order to stay alive. Families that had lost their homes sometimes had to take refuge in shantytowns built of junk. Begging for nickels and dimes—formerly a monopoly of professional panhandlers and hoboes—became a common occupation on the streets of America's cities. "Brother, Can You Spare a Dime" was a popular song of the day.

CHRONICLE: A HARD LIFE TO SWALLOW

. . . a record of the depression exodus by Dorothea Lange

The photographs in this chronicle are the work of
Dorothea Lange, one of a team of photographers employed by the Farm Security Administration from 1935
to 1942. The administrator of the FSA, Rexford Guy
Tugwell, later recalled that the agency's purpose was
"not only to bring the resources of government to the
assistance of those who were distressed or starved out
but to make certain that never again should Americans
be exposed to such cruelties. . . . It seemed important
to record the incredible events of those years; and the
best way was to photograph them." Lange and her
husband, Paul S. Taylor, collected her photographs, re-
inforcing them with words spoken by the subjects of
the photographs, in *An American Exodus: A Record of
Human Erosion*. Their book traced in poignant, timeless
images the migration of impoverished workers from the
dust bowls of the Southwest to the farms of California.

"Yessir, we're starved, stalled and stranded."
migrant refugee

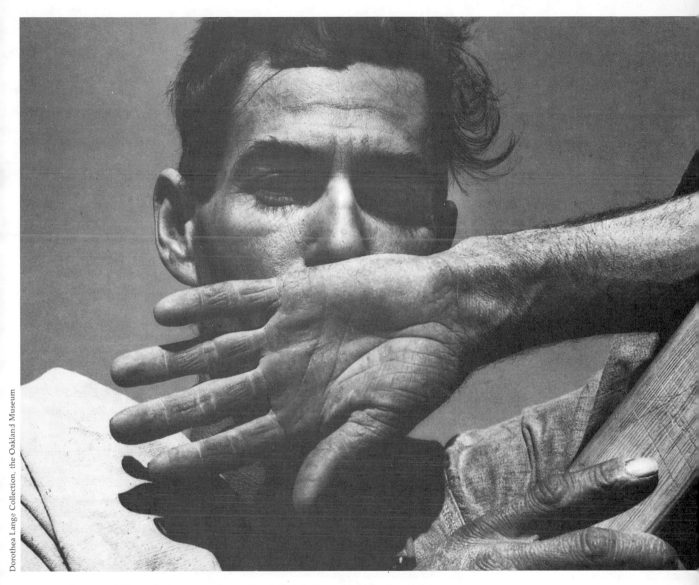

"People just can't make it back there, with drought,
hailstorms, windstorms, duststorms, insects. People exist
here and they can't do that there. You can make it here
if you sleep lots and eat little, but it's pretty tough,
there are so many people. They chase them out of one camp
because they say it isn't sanitary—there's no running water—
so people live out here in the brush like a den o' dogs or pigs."

tenant farmer from Cook County, Texas

*"What bothers us
travellin' people most
is we cain't get no place
to stay still."*

Photographs: Dorothea Lange Collection, The Oakland Museum

Roosevelt's three R's
— the New Deal

Governor Franklin Delano Roosevelt of New York defeated Hoover in 1932 by a margin even greater than Hoover's over Smith four years earlier. Roosevelt's inaugural message—"The only thing we have to fear is fear itself"—and his promise of a "New Deal" had a solid ring. The New Deal began with a succession of major legislative acts in the first hundred days after the inauguration and included a renewed burst of legislation in 1935. It was intended to bring *relief* (immediate aid to those in greatest need), *recovery* (loans, subsidies, or other assistance to big business in order to get the wheels of industry turning again), and *reform* (long-range projects and institutional changes to prevent future depressions).

Some of the most important innovations to provide relief were the Civilian Conservation Corps (CCC); the Federal Emergency Relief Administration (FERA), which gave funds to state relief agencies; and the Works Progress Administration (WPA), an agency that spent $11 billion and eventually found work for millions.

The National Industrial Recovery Act (NIRA) sought to encourage recovery by suspending the antitrust laws and granting industrial and trade associations the right to draw up codes of fair competition. A new federal agency, known as the National Recovery Administration (NRA) was established to administer the provisions of this law. Similarly, Congress established the Agricultural Adjustment Administration (AAA), which had the power to enforce reduction of crop acreage and restore farm price "parity"—that is, provide subsidies that would re-create the balance that had existed between farm prices and industrial prices.

Under the heading of reform came the Tennessee Valley Authority (TVA), a giant federal agency that constructed dams and power plants and provided electricity in seven states; the Social Security Act, which furnished some financial security to the aged and the unemployed; and the Security and Exchange Commission (SEC), to regulate stock exchanges and the securities they traded so as to prevent a recurrence of the wild speculation that led to the crash of 1929.

The New Deal embodied elements of the Populist movement (farm supports) and of Progressivism. Although by no means a consistent, unified program, it included some of the most important legislation in American history. Federal intervention to combat the depression improved public morale, brought about a mixed economy involving government and business as major partners, and marked the first steps toward the so-called welfare state. The one thing it did not do was lick the depression. The unemployment rate remained above 10 percent until 1941.

FDR must be considered one of the most extraordinary of American politicians. He was reelected three times, in 1936, 1940, and 1944, the last time only five months before his death. One of his lasting legacies was greatly expanded presidential power.

While pursuing his domestic recovery program, FDR "kept the world at bay." In other words, he continued the isolationist policies of his GOP predecessors toward Europe and the Far East. In Latin America he followed Hoover's lead and, as part of a "Good Neighbor" policy, renounced the right of the United States to intervene in the affairs of Latin American countries.

Isolationist and antimilitarist sentiment was extremely strong during the 1930s. In 1935 and 1937, as war clouds formed overseas, Congress passed Neutrality Acts intended to prevent the nation from being drawn into a European war. But the aggressions of Nazi Germany on the European continent and of imperial Japan in China had apparently unavoidable consequences for the U.S., and after 1937 the Roosevelt administration became increasingly involved in international affairs.

The Second World War

After Germany's invasion of Poland in 1939 and the resulting declarations of war against Germany by Great Britain and France, the chances of America remaining neutral faded rapidly. In a matter of months only Britain stood between the U.S. and the conquering Nazi armies in the West. FDR took steps to see that Britain did not fall. Under the Lend-Lease Act of 1941 the U.S. agreed to act as Britain's arsenal and food supplier. In November of that year, after Germany had turned on Russia, its former ally, Lend-Lease was extended to the Soviet Union.

Japan's attack on Pearl Harbor, Hawaii, on December 7, 1941, smashed American ships and planes, killed 2300 American servicemen, and unified the nation behind a war against the Axis—Germany, Italy, and Japan. Antiwar and isolationist sentiment practically vanished. As in World War I, the president took charge of mobilization, and the federal government became the focus of centralized planning. By 1945 over 15 million Americans were in uniform.

The Allies, led by the United States, Great Britain, and the Soviet Union, concentrated first on liberating Europe. Russia initially bore the brunt of Hitler's armies and came close to collapse. But the Battle of Stalingrad, the major land engagement of the war, turned the tables. In 1943 Allied bombers attacked cities in Germany, and Allied tanks drove the Germans from North Africa. Then British and American forces invaded Italy. In the Allied invasion of Normandy, France, beginning on June 6, 1944, a million troops landed on the beaches within weeks. This enormous operation was under the overall command of General Dwight D. Eisenhower. Paris was liberated in August 1944, and after one last, violent counterattack, Germany surrendered in May 1945.

Until the spring of 1942, Japanese forces carried the emblem of the Rising Sun to far-flung areas of the Pacific. But in May and June of that year the naval battles of the Coral Sea and Midway successfully blocked a Japanese invasion of Australia and constituted a turning point. From 1943 to 1945 the U.S. carried on a costly island-hopping campaign that rooted Japanese forces out of the Solomon, Gilbert, and Marshall Islands and finally from Iwo Jima and Okinawa. On August 6, 1945, an atomic bomb was dropped on the Japanese city of Hiroshima. A second bomb hit Nagasaki on August 9, and Japan gave up on August 14. On September 2, 1945, General Douglas MacArthur formally accepted Japan's surrender on board the battleship *Missouri*.

Roosevelt, Prime Minister Winston Churchill of Great Britain, and Marshal Joseph Stalin of the Soviet Union held a number of meetings during the war to hammer out strategy and make postwar political arrangements. Despite the serious ideological differences between the capitalist powers and the Communist state, the three men were able to work together to crush the Axis. But at their last meeting, at the Crimean resort town of Yalta in February 1945, with the end in sight, national interests were rapidly taking precedence over common goals. Still, there was agreement to go ahead with a United Nations organization so set up that the U.S. Senate need have no fears about a loss of sovereignty.

The war ended "on a note of triumph and tragedy." While tyrannical foes had been defeated, the awesome destruction caused by the atomic bombs dropped on Japan foretold even greater horror in any future world conflict. About 30 million people died in World War II—half of them civilians. Total casualties for the United States (dead and wounded) were over one million. And even before the celebration of V-J Day, the day of Japan's surrender, had subsided, the first chill of the Cold War between the U.S. and U.S.S.R. could be felt. America turned to the postwar period with some apprehension.

Bewildered investors mill about on the planked surface of Wall Street outside the New York Stock Exchange following the drastic decline of October 24, 1929. Although President Hoover assured the nation that "the fundamental business of the country is on a sound and prosperous basis," worse was yet to come. On Tuesday, October 29, stock prices fell so quickly that many stockholders could not find buyers at any price.

25

25
The Roller Coaster Years

For today's college students the twenties, thirties, and forties are ancient history. Most of what they know of these decades comes from old movies. But their parents and grandparents have vivid memories of the Jazz Age, the Great Depression, and World War II. Those eras left their mark on people. For better or worse, many social attitudes— including attitudes toward wealth and poverty—were formed then. So it makes sense for young people to learn more about their source.

The First World War was a dividing line in American economic history. First, the United States became a creditor nation—it was owed money by many other nations. This improved its standing in world affairs and quickened the pace of overseas trade and investment. Second, the already great capacity of America's factories to create wealth increased. The problem of how to consume that wealth was more acute than ever. Third, the type of wealth being produced underwent change: the economy produced more and more services compared to goods. By the time of the Great Depression yet a fourth major trend made itself felt: the tremendous involvement of the federal government in the activities of a market economy, in which traditionally only the buyers and sellers were supposed to control matters.

For a decade after World War I the American economy was the most vigorous in the world. Then in 1929 a depression brought the country to its knees. No other domestic crisis (except perhaps the Civil War) ever sapped the nation's self-confidence as badly as the Great Depression. But self-confidence—if not prosperity—was partially restored by the New Deal (1933–1938). This remarkable program of government intervention profoundly affected every segment of society, including business, organized labor, and the farmers.

The Prosperous Twenties and the Great Depression

Living high in the '20s

Considering the period between 1870 and 1929 as a whole—and ignoring the very real hardship that came from depressions—the U.S. enjoyed a period of strong economic progress. The yearly growth rate in those six decades averaged a healthy 3.5 percent. Worker productivity rose more than twice as rapidly as the size of the work force. Even though population expanded from 76 million in 1900 to 123 million in 1930, there were plenty of jobs available. The normal unemployment rate was unbelievably low—3.2 percent. Per capita income rose at around 1.6 percent per year. This means that at constant prices per capita income more than doubled between 1870 and 1920, rising from $700 to $1500. Medical improvements increased the life span. The average work week fell from 60 hours in the 1870s to 44 hours in the 1920s. In the three decades after 1900 the country created $75 billion worth of new homes, $9 billion in farm buildings, and over $30 billion in industrial equipment. Nowhere in the world was there anything to equal it.

Following the war, there was a brief period of economic fumbling. The government withdrew from centralized management and offered almost no planning or direction to peacetime conversions. Shortages appeared in many areas, driving consumer prices up. Farm surpluses began to hurt farm income, as the prices for agricultural commodities dived. Unemployment rose sharply. A rash of postwar strikes, linked in the public mind with Bolshevism, was followed in 1920–1922 by a drop of 28 percent in union membership.

In the 1920s economic emphasis shifted from capital goods to consumer goods. Prior to the war most money had been invested in the development of capital goods (those materials necessary to the manufacture of consumer goods), such as coal, oil, timber, factories, and iron or steel rails. The consumer economy, which still flourishes in the United States, first came into its own in the twenties. Consumer goods—automobiles, refrigerators, radios, gas stoves, and other appliances—began to attract more investment capital. The automobile industry, with its appetite for steel, glass, rubber, and gasoline, led the way. Nearly 2 million passenger cars were sold in 1917. By 1929 there was one automobile on the road for every six Americans.

Pressure to consume was everywhere. Ad agencies ballyhooed products as never before, erasing the differences between necessities and frills. Manufacturers produced goods that would wear out or become outdated swiftly, a pattern called "planned obsolescence." Once Benjamin Franklin had taught that thrift was a prime virtue. Now it seemed that spending was becoming a greater virtue. In this way the consumer economy changed basic social values.

In 1921 there was a deep but quick business recession, with a drop in prices and employment, but afterward the free enterprise system seemed to have a limitless future. Business was never in more sure command of the marketplace. The voices of Progressive critics calling for the breakup of business combinations became muted. Responsible public figures predicted that poverty would soon disappear. They noted the steady rise in the stock market. Here was a sure ladder to success. No one should miss the opportunity to invest in stocks. As of September 1929, to amateur investors the Wall Street picture seemed rosy indeed. Anyone who had bought $1000 of representative stocks each year, starting in

1920, would have been worth $9000 in 1926; $20,000 invested in 1928 would possibly have yielded twice that amount by September of 1929. In the summer months of 1929 Westinghouse stock doubled, and AT&T went up by a third, but the high stock prices did not mirror high corporate earnings. Ten million people of low and moderate income played the stock market game in the late 1920s. The rules of the Stock Exchange permitted them to buy stocks "on margin" with cash payment of only a fraction of the price, in the hope that they could sell it at a higher price, pay off their debt, and still pocket a profit. In other words, they were speculating on credit.

The crash

When the stock market crashed in 1929, it scattered debris over the entire economy. On October 29, over 16 million shares were traded and the prices of stock plummeted downward. One gilt-edged investment trust (Goldman, Sachs and Company) lost half its value in one day. The value that most stocks

had piled up over a year's time vanished in a single 24-hour period. Within weeks $30 billion in paper values were wiped out. At first people watched Wall Street in amused silence, for its antics seemed not to affect the economy generally. A temporary rise in stock prices gave investors new hope. However, the other indicators of economic health were on their way down: manufacturing, farming, banking, and commerce felt the pinch. In the spring of 1930 the nation went into a state of profound shock and panic, from which it did not fully recover for ten or twelve years. The 1929 crash was part of a worldwide economic collapse known in this country as the Great Depression.

What caused the depression? Economists and historians are still groping for answers. The most reasonable explanation has to do with a slump in investment. A healthy market economy depends on a steady growth in the level of investment in basic goods and services. When such investment remains constant or declines slightly, the whole economy can go into a slump. Sluggishness may

BUSINESS FAILURES, 1920–1941

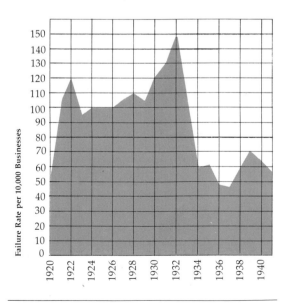

BANK FAILURES, 1920–1941

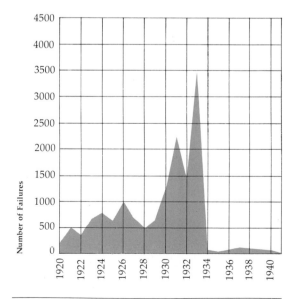

Every man has a right to life; and this means that he has also a right to make a comfortable living.

FRANKLIN D. ROOSEVELT (1882–1945)

occur for various reasons: lack of business confidence, lack of new technology in which to invest, scarcity of bank money, high interest rates on bank loans, or declining population growth. When investing stops, the bad effects may begin to multiply and the slump may begin to feed on itself. A slight reduction in growth may soon produce a 50 percent drop in investment and may in turn cut personal income by 10 or 20 percent. This "multiplier effect" was at work in the two years following the crash of 1929.

Actually, as early as 1925 the rate of capital formation (the rate at which savings become investments) began to decline in most basic industries. Even autos ceased for a time to attract new investment. With hindsight it is clear that speculative stocks were absorbing more than their share of savings, as the economy began to stagnate after 1926.

Another major factor in the depression was the low buying power of American workers. Despite *overall* improvements in the standard of living, the nation's wealth, including personal income, was poorly distributed in the first quarter of the century. This created a practical difficulty. In 1929 the average factory worker earned less than $1500 (equivalent to about $3000 after World War II), and members of certain groups, like southern tenant farmers, made far less than that. Farm income generally was low, and wages lagged far behind factory profits. In some industries machines replaced men, leading to technological unemployment. As a result millions of Americans could not afford the vast quantities of goods that were for sale. Advertising campaigns and buying on time were at best temporary solutions. The economy of the prosperous twenties was suffering from overproduction and underconsumption.

There were other reasons, too, for the depression. Wartime allies owed the United States billions of dollars in war loans, and in addition Germany owed the Allies billions more in reparations. Few countries were able to pay off their war debts, and U.S. investors and banks were stuck with defaulting foreign bonds. American tariffs, the highest ever in the 1920s, made it difficult for foreign nations to sell goods to the U.S. and thus earn dollars to repay their debts.

Meanwhile the relative income of the rich increased. Tax laws contributed to this rise. During the war Congress had clamped a special tax on excess profits. In 1922 Secretary of the Treasury Andrew W. Mellon secured a law eliminating this tax altogether, at the same time reducing the maximum surtax on personal income from 65 to 50 percent. Within four years this maximum was reduced to 20 percent. Thus wealthy Americans had relatively more money to spend. Yet there were too few of them to make much of a dent in the consumption of basic consumer goods. In short, prosperity in the '20s was onesided.

Start of the Great Depression

After the crash came the depression. Manufacturing, farming, banking, and commerce began to feel the pinch. Factories closed, farms and city homes were repossessed by banks, and the banks in turn were unable to repay depositors. Workers lost their jobs, farmers their land, and the middle class its savings. Families that had been comfortably well off tasted poverty. A railroad worker reported a typical experience to a member of the president's cabinet: "We go to market once in a while to look at the nice vegetables, then go home and eat macaroni and oatmeal." By 1933 there were about 1000 bank foreclosures on urban homes each day; many families were evicted on short notice. In the big cities the homeless built "Hoover-villes"—shantytowns made of packing crates and tar paper where they could at least come in out of the rain. Able-bodied workers were fired and could find no jobs. There was as yet no such thing as unemployment compensation. By 1933 20 percent of the entire work force was out of work. Among racial minorities the figure was much higher. The government soon stopped counting the number of jobless for fear of further undermining morale. As a stop-gap some turned to selling apples on the street corners of the bigger cities; others took to panhandling. Millions of Americans hummed the popular tune, "Brother, Can You Spare a Dime." In the winter hungry and demoralized people lined up daily at soup kitchens set up by private charities. The more footloose hopped freight cars and went west or south "to starve in a warmer climate."

Among the hardest hit by the Great Depression were poor farmers. Many had had a foretaste of the depression throughout the twenties when farm income slipped. Thousands of small farms were repossessed by the banks. The tenants and sharecroppers of the South, who had worked marginal land owned by others, lacked sufficient credit with which to buy seeds or tools. In Oklahoma and Arkansas the problem was compounded by serious drought and dust storms. Droves of "Okies" and "Arkies" loaded their furniture on Model-T Fords and headed for the Promised Land of California, where they wound up in farm labor camps. These migrants are symbolized by the unforgettable Joad family in John Steinbeck's novel, *The Grapes of Wrath* (1939).* "'We got

*Other novels which depicted life during the depression were James T. Farrell's *Studs Lonigan* (1932–1935), a trilogy concerning the Irish Catholics of Chicago, and Erskine Caldwell's *Tobacco Road* (1932) and *God's Little Acre* (1933).

nothin', now,' Pa [Joad] said. 'Comin' a long time—no work, no crops. What we gonna do then? How we gonna git stuff to eat? . . . Git so I hate to think . . . seems like our life's over an' done.' "

One of the most alarming aspects of the depression was the banking crisis. Banks had gotten careless with other people's money, investing in questionable projects. When depositors began demanding their savings in cash, many banks had to close their doors. They were overextended on loans and could not foreclose fast enough or produce enough cash to satisfy their depositors.

Hoover and the crisis

In 1932 an army of jobless World War I veterans descended on Washington to demand government bonuses. While most left after being turned down, a remnant of the "Bonus Expeditionary Force" camped with wives and children on Anacostia Flats near the Capitol. Its representatives lobbied in Congress for immediate payment of the bonuses that vets were slated to receive later on. President Hoover considered the bonuses inflationary and refused to bargain with the vets. Instead he ordered the army to evict them from Washington. Amid clouds of tear gas, rumbling tanks, and the smoke of burning huts, the demonstrators left the city.

Herbert Hoover had had a brilliant record in World War I as food administrator and director of European relief. The tall, round-faced man was perhaps best known for his humanitarian efforts in saving war victims from starvation. When he entered the White House, he enjoyed the vigorous support and full confidence of the great majority of voters. By the end of 1932 his stock with the public had plummeted.

Hoover neither caused the depression nor "fiddled while Rome burned," as some critics charged. But he was a firm believer in

Herbert Hoover (1874-1964)

AN ALGER HERO—WITHOUT THE LUCK

At ten he was a poor orphan. At forty he had amassed more money than he would ever need. At forty-five he was world-famous and hailed as a great humanitarian. At fifty-four he was elected president in a smashing victory. At fifty-eight he was dealt a crushing defeat in his bid for a second term. For the next decade and more, he was reviled and ridiculed by his fellow citizens. Then the tide of public opinion—not the man—changed once more. The scapegoat of the thirties died a Grand Old Man of the Republic.

Herbert Clark Hoover came from a Quaker community in Iowa. His father, a black-smith, died when Herbert was six; his mother died three years later. The boy was brought up by Quaker uncles, first in Iowa, then in Oregon. He had worked from early childhood and continued work-ing as he attended Stanford University. His ambition was to become a mining engi-neer. He achieved his goal, building a career that took him all over the globe. By the time World War I began, Herbert Hoover was one of the best and most successful mining engineers in the world.

In London when the war came, he was pressed into service helping stranded Ameri-cans return home. He was then given the seemingly hopeless task of—somehow—feeding the Belgian people, who were living under German military occupation. As soon as the United States entered the war, Hoover was made responsible for seeing that all the Allied populations—military and civilian—were adequately fed. After the Armistice he was charged with the even more awesome job of fighting off the threat of starvation on the war-ravaged continent.

Then came the presidency, the crash, and the depression. Hoover did not cause the economic collapse, and he tried hard to cure it. Principle and experience led him to rely chiefly on the methods of voluntary cooperation that had served him so brilliantly in his relief work. But the situation was now different and the earlier methods were not sufficient.

Hoover returned to government service in 1946 when President Truman put him in charge of a Famine Emergency Commission to investigate and report world food needs. In 1948 and again in 1953 he headed commissions that recommended organi-zational reforms in the executive branch of the government. Finally, in 1955, the old man retired—to write more books, and to speak out as he thought necessary. When he died, he had survived his presidency longer than any other chief executive. And he had found the hearts of his countrymen.

In June of 1932 the "Bonus Army" of World War I veterans converged on Washington to demand immediate payment of bonuses scheduled for 1945. Here veterans occupy the Pennsylvania Railroad yards after officials refused to provide a train to take them to the capitol. Congress defeated the bonus, and President Hoover had to call out the regular army to disperse thousands of veterans.

voluntary cooperation among citizens. He detested government coercion, especially coercion by the federal government, and advocated local initiative. As he saw it, the basic cause of the depression was the inability of European nations to pay off the war debts. With a little patience, the free enterprise system would work itself out of the doldrums. "Prosperity," he confidently predicted, "is just around the corner."

In the end, though, necessity forced Hoover to try to stop the depression through large-scale federal aid. Under the Reconstruction Finance Corporation (RFC), which he signed into law in 1932, troubled private industries could receive government subsidies. The idea was to help revive banks, railroads, and other big enterprises threatened with bankruptcy, so that they would restore production and buying power and raise employment levels. This "trickledown" effort to cope with the crisis failed. The RFC increased neither capital formation, economic growth, nor employment. Hoover also tried to control credits and to expand public works, but these efforts were equally unsuccessful. Human suffering existed on a vast scale. Business confidence continued to sink.

Roosevelt's first hundred days

Hoover's efforts to cope with the crisis lacked gusto and political savvy. Worse yet, they simply failed to prevent the depression from worsening. This cost him the 1932 election. He was replaced by Franklin Delano Roosevelt (1882–1945), who in fact incorporated some of Hoover's ideas into his own schemes for combatting the depression.

FDR had no master plan for dealing with the crisis, nor even any special knowledge of economics. (At college, economics had been one of his weaker subjects.) But he bore the legendary Roosevelt name and possessed considerable political savvy. He followed in the footsteps of his illustrious cousin Theodore, serving in New York's state legislature, then in the Navy Department, and later as governor of New York. His wife, Eleanor, a distant cousin, was an important influence in his political career and became a public figure in her own right. Perhaps his most invaluable asset was his amiable personality, which invited confidence and loyalty. Stricken by polio in 1921 and confined to a wheel chair, Roosevelt still pursued an active career. He sensed the nation's despair and pledged himself to a "new deal for the American people."

FDR was convinced that the era of rugged individualism was over, and that strong federal action was necessary. Several courses were open to him. He could set up long-term government planning and public spending. He could regulate the trusts more vigorously and help small businessmen and farmers compete in the open market. Or he could rely on big business to restore prosperity. The last resembled Wilson's wartime mobilization, which FDR knew from first-hand experience as wartime Undersecretary of the Navy. A doer and an experimenter at heart, he shifted from one plan to another. The attitude in the White House was one that the country appreciated: try something, try anything—if it doesn't work, try something else.

The New Deal began right after inauguration day. On March 5 FDR ordered a four-day bank holiday to deal with the banking crisis. He convened a special session of Congress starting on March 9, which lasted until June 16. During this "first hundred days" of the new administration, Roosevelt rushed fifteen major bills through Congress to bring about relief, reform, and recovery. The package included laws to reopen solvent banks and to protect the bank savings of small depositors. The Emergency Banking Act gave the president emergency powers to regulate credit, currency, and foreign exchange. The boosting of farm income got a high priority rating under the New Deal. The Agricultural Adjustment Act (AAA) restricted and subsidized farm production to raise prices and income (see pp. 353–354). The Emergency Relief Act provided relief funds to help bail out bankrupt cities and states. Speculation on the Stock Exchange was sharply curtailed. Never before had Congress so quickly passed such a welter of laws with such far-reaching implications.

Notable among long-term New Deal re-

forms was the Tennessee Valley Authority (TVA), a giant government corporation created by Congress in 1933. TVA had authority to build dams, manufacture and sell hydroelectric power and fertilizers, control flooding and prevent soil erosion, and promote conservation in a huge, chronically depressed area of the South. The TVA cast its net into seven southern states, covering an area of over 40,000 square miles. (See also Chapter 32.)

FDR's pet New Deal program, also established in 1933, was the National Recovery Administration (NRA). Its main goal, as established under the National Industrial Recovery Act (NIRA), was to cut excess production so as to stabilize the market for big producers. To accomplish this, the NRA relied mainly on the trade associations of big businesses (associations of auto manufacturers or steel companies, for example). Representatives of business, labor, and consumers gathered in Washington to regulate themselves. They were asked to establish production levels and prices and to limit wages and hours so that more workers could hold jobs. Meantime, the government suspended the antitrust laws. The NRA, led by General Hugh Johnson, a former military officer, was modeled after World War I production policies. It drafted some eight hundred production codes. The NRA was able to stimulate employment, causing a slight economic upturn. The NRA's Blue Eagle emblem became the symbol of the early New Deal.

But the ambitious plans of the NRA soon began to fall apart. Consumers were outraged by rising prices. Labor complained that management was ignoring the requirement to bargain collectively. To union leaders the NRA was the "National Run Around." Some small businesses refused to accept production codes that had been drafted without their participation. The Schecter Poultry Company of Brooklyn sued the government for interfering with its operation. In its 1935 decision the Supreme Court declared the NRA unconstitutional on the basis that Congress had given away too much authority and was meddling improperly in *intra*state commerce. The "sick chicken case" completely destroyed the NRA.

Keynes' theories of spending

Forced to consider new policy alternatives, FDR turned to public spending. Partly this course was urged on him by his "Brain Trust," his informal cabinet of college professors. They were impressed by the theories of the British economist John Maynard Keynes. Keynes argued that during depressions a nation should stimulate the economy by spending more than it took in. When prosperity returned, it should balance the scale by increasing taxes and cutting back spending. He blamed the Great Depression on poor distribution of income. Those with the highest incomes saved too much money, and those with the lowest incomes could not buy what they needed. Therefore neither class encouraged economic growth. Spending, according to Keynes, was the way to save capitalism.

While Keynes' theories mystified FDR, the president spent enough to increase the national debt from $23 billion in 1933 to $37 billion in 1938. By 1936 a slight business upturn was in the works, and new jobs were being created. Then inflation suddenly loomed as a

UNEMPLOYMENT, 1929–1945

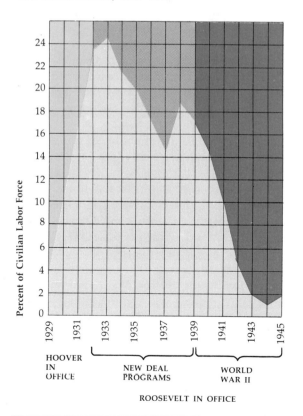

GOVERNMENT EXPENDITURES, 1929–1945

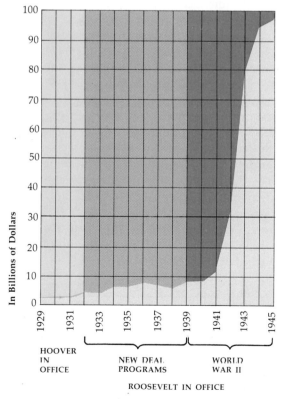

danger. The administration promptly ordered cuts in spending. This caused a new recession. Although FDR was forever damned by conservatives as a "big spender," his biggest spending programs occurred not during the depression but during World War II.

Remedies for one third of a nation

In a burst of optimism Herbert Hoover declared in 1928: "We in America today are nearer to the final triumph over poverty than ever before in the history of any land. The poorhouse is vanishing from among us. We have not yet reached the goal, but, given a chance . . . we shall soon with the help of God be in sight of the day when poverty will be vanquished from this nation." A few short years later in 1937, Franklin Roosevelt reported, using a memorable turn of phrase, that "I see millions of families trying to live on incomes so meager that the pall of family disaster hangs over them day by day. . . . I see one third of a nation ill-housed, ill-clad, ill-nourished."

As of 1929 the poor laws of the United States bore a striking resemblance to those of Elizabethan England and colonial America. Relief should be made as disagreeable as possible so that the poor would prefer to find work. Those on relief should forfeit certain rights; in fourteen states in 1934 they forfeited the right to vote. Relief was mostly in the hands of local law enforcement agencies or politicians. Very few trained social workers focused on relief cases. During the depression wealthy people donated money to churches and charitable organizations. The last place a jobless worker sought relief was in Washington. Before 1933 Republicans and Democrats alike believed in Grover Cleveland's theory: "While the people should cheerfully and patriotically support their government, its functions do not include the support of the people."

Hoover and many others believed that massive federal relief would raise the public debt, causing further economic woes, not to mention exerting a weakening effect on rugged individualism. Hoover, who had been extremely sensitive to the suffering after World War I, felt certain that charities and local agencies could cope with the distress. When he approved modest federal loans to state relief agencies in 1932, he was not tampering with the traditional handling of poverty. But when the federal loans gave out and private help was not enough, millions of hungry people were still pounding on the doors of local relief agencies.

Franklin Delano Roosevelt, whose father had been a wealthy New York gentleman farmer and financier, never had any personal contact with poverty. Nevertheless, as governor of New York he organized the first state-wide system of poor relief, one that was run by professionals. His top staff in Washington included several men and women experienced in dealing with the working poor. Head relief administrator Harry Hopkins was a trained social worker. Secretary of Labor Frances Perkins (the first woman cabinet member) had experience in the field. In his wife, Eleanor, FDR had an alert troubleshooter and adviser who was in frequent contact with blacks, poor whites, and other segments of society where privation was a way of life.

Like other aspects of the New Deal, the approach to poverty was a mixed bag. It consisted of various reforms advocated for over forty years by Progressives, social workers, Socialists, feminists, and labor leaders. For social policy FDR depended most on Harry Hopkins. The Iowa-born social worker had once studied Applied Christianity, an early form of sociology, and had his first brush with poverty while working in New York City's immigrant slums before World War I. While governor, FDR had made him a top social-service administrator in New York

Especially during the early years of the depression—before the advent of Social Security, unemployment compensation, or welfare—feeding hungry, jobless Americans was left largely to private charity. The men in this line are waiting for a five-cent meal in New York City, while the sign solicits contributions from luckier citizens.

during the early years of the depression. Hopkins and Roosevelt rejected a policy of direct relief—handouts of money, food, or clothing. Instead they preferred work relief as a way of reducing immediate suffering. Roosevelt also tackled the problem of chronic poverty through social security and minimum wage laws. In the end, it was work relief that had the more dramatic effect.

The first batch of work-relief measures included the Civilian Conservation Corps, which recruited unemployed young men from families on relief to work on conservation projects. The National Youth Administration subsidized part-time jobs for students who needed money for their education. The Federal Emergency Relief Administration gave outright grants to states and cities to continue existing relief programs. The Civil Works Administration in the winter of 1933–1934 provided temporary jobs on public works to about 4 million workers.

But none of these programs turned the economy around. Millions still suffered from poverty and deprivation. And pressure mounted for more drastic economic reforms.

Dr. Francis Townsend, a California physician, had organized an effective old people's lobby. On behalf of hundreds of thousands of elderly people, Townsend called on the government to pay every citizen over sixty $200 a month, to be spent within that month. Senator Huey Long of Louisiana ("The Kingfish") stirred up political dust with his "Share-Our-Wealth" program of radical income redistribution. A brilliant and popular leader, Long threatened to run for president on a third-party ticket in 1936. Roosevelt considered him a threat to his future, until Long was assassinated in 1935.

Roosevelt next took a step to the left. His "Second New Deal" focused on direct aid to workers and farmers (rather than on recovery programs for business). The Works Progress Administration (WPA) became an employer of jobless workers. Three million persons went on the payroll in the first year and over 8 million by 1943. The WPA built highways (664,000 miles), bridges (77,000), airports (285), reservoirs, parks, and playgrounds. Programs that supported jobless artists, writers, and stage performers were also included. Before it expired in 1943, the WPA had spent over $11 billion. The WPA was attacked as "boondoggling," but it added considerably to purchasing power and the preservation of skills, morale, and personal dignity for millions of Americans.

The same law that established the WPA created the Resettlement Administration (RA). It was intended to help the tenant farmers, sharecroppers, and migratory laborers who were the long-time victims of big landlords. For many of these people poverty, ignorance, disease, and (if they were blacks) racism were a way of life. The RA bought farm land and became a landlord to tenants, offering them long-term leases with credit rates that they could handle. It also built cooperative farm villages. Blacks as well as poor whites benefited. The RA was the brainchild of the New Deal's most persistent advocate of long-term social planning, Rexford Guy Tugwell. In the words of historian Paul Conkin, the RA "was not only one of the most honest but probably the most class-conscious of the New Deal agencies. Soon it antagonized practically every vested interest, a good mark of its relative effectiveness." Congress voted grudgingly for the RA budget. After 1937 support dwindled altogether, as conservatives gained strength in Congress. It became a shoestring operation that was quietly phased out during World War II.

Social Security and tax reform

Two weeks after recommending the WPA the president submitted a social insurance bill to Congress. It offered a measure of economic security to the aged, to those who lost their jobs, and to the chronically infirm. As finally approved, the Social Security Act of 1935 had three basic features. *Old-age insurance*, supported by a tax levied on wage earners and employers, gave retired persons a pension of about $75 a month at age sixty-five. *Unemployment insurance* made payments to jobless persons for a limited number of weeks. *Public assistance* gave help to disabled persons and dependent children who could prove their need. Most unemployment benefits and public assistance were administered by the states. Some New Dealers suggested adding a prepaid health plan to the package, but since the idea was politically controversial it was not forwarded to Congress.

Critics pounced on Social Security from both sides. It was too paternalistic and would destroy the American spirit of individual-

When the Works Project Administration was created in 1935, Roosevelt declared that "preference should be given to those projects which will be self-liquidating in the sense that there is a reasonable expectation that the government will get its money back at some future time." Many economists considered WPA a good investment even if the money were not returned, but the attitude of businessmen was often closer to the one illustrated in this cartoon.

ism. It covered too few people with unemployment insurance. It placed too many costs on the workers least able to pay and it gave too many benefits to those who needed them least. Welfare would be too dependent on the states, the poorest of which would provide the worst services and make a mockery of the law. In spite of these complaints, the bill sailed through Congress. The public gave its hearty approval for Social Security, which in time offered greater coverage and benefits.

In 1935 the administration tried to push tax reforms through Congress. It proposed a progressive income tax, an inheritance tax, gift taxes, and taxes on big corporations. New Dealers claimed that existing tax laws had loopholes and benefits for the wealthy, who were suffering less during the depression than were the poor. A "soak-the-rich" tax failed in Congress in 1935 but passed in 1937 in a much watered-down form.

The Fair Labor Standards Act of 1938 was the final New Deal social reform that in any way dealt with poverty. It set a minimum wage of 25¢ an hour and maximum hours for workers in interstate commerce, and it abolished child labor. This law had only a slight effect in raising worker income.

Legacies of the depression

The greatest benefit offered by Roosevelt and the New Deal was hope. Programs like Social Security, WPA, and RA gave back to many Americans a sense of personal dignity and a belief in their country, which they had lost around 1931. They helped millions survive the worst of the depression. In Roosevelt, people felt they had a president who cared, who understood. They showed their appreciation by electing him to an unprecedented four terms. Certainly no administration ever tried harder than Roosevelt's to force economic growth or to erase poverty. It did succeed in creating one boomlet in 1933 and another in 1936. Yet after the drastic slump that began in mid-1937 nearly a fifth of the labor force and over one quarter of the nation's factories stood idle. "Dr. New Deal" had not been able to cure the depression. The most sobering fact about FDR's administration is that it failed to bring about substantial economic growth or reduction of poverty.

Although often accused by conservatives of ruining the free-enterprise system and paving the way for socialism, FDR never intended to destroy the market economy. Rather, he hoped to restore it to good health and turn it toward socially acceptable goals. The New Deal did greatly increase the level of federal management over the economy in its attempts to end the depression. Had Roosevelt really wanted socialism, he could have started by nationalizing the banks in 1933. Congress would have readily consented, because the bankers were in thorough disrepute. A more pertinent issue, perhaps, is whether a managed economy can sustain

high employment, prevent depression, or eliminate poverty. FDR's experience with the New Deal casts doubt on this.

The president acted vigorously, and the people appreciated his vigor. Yet it is true that the administration lurched from one strategy to another. First, under the NRA, it promoted collusion among big businesses; later it tried to punish monopolies. First it spent money to stimulate the economy; then it cut spending to balance the budget; finally it went back to spending again. Sometimes it took excursions into long-term planning, but often it drew back from permanent commitments. What finally ended the depression was not the New Deal but the Second World War (see Chapter 27).

On many Americans over forty-five, the depression left, in the words of Caroline Bird, an "invisible scar." Fear of poverty marked indelibly the childhood memories of many parents of the 1950s, 1960s, and 1970s. These memories help create the "generation gap" between parents and their children, most of whom have never known comparable economic insecurity.

Workers Winning Their Rights

Fighting for power

In the 1920s and 1930s organized labor suffered some of its worst agonies. Under the New Deal it emerged for the first time as a recognized interest group.

Many bitter strikes occurred after World War I. Unions struck to maintain the benefits and bargaining powers that they had built up during the war in the face of sudden inflation. Clothing and textile workers, dockers, longshoremen, telephone operators, and railroad workers all held successful strikes. In 1920 union membership reached a new high of 5 million.

Labor's most serious organizing setback was the collapse of the 1919 steel strike. It involved an attempt to gain union recognition in the most basic of all American industries, which employed 250,000 workers. The steel union, broken in the Homestead Strike of 1892, had never regained its footing. Most steel workers were satisfied with their wages, which averaged over $6 a day, but they found the hours and conditions nearly unbearable. Their work day was twelve hours long. As a steel worker wrote: "Power, beauty, poetry, what? Give the mill time. It

> *I'll never recognize any union.*
> HENRY FORD (1863–1947)

will blind your eyes and wilt your legs like all the rest. Soon like all the rest you will plod in and plod out; stripped to bare muscle sensation; a numbered human machine that eats, sleeps and works." Union organizers pointed out that workers had no say in plant operations or any useful grievance machinery. They called the company unions "pet dogs in a kennel." At U.S. Steel, the largest of the steel companies, management refused to talk to organized labor. It smeared the union organizers as "bolsheviks" and "anarchists." Throughout the industry ethnic divisions remained strong. WASP strikers cursed the "hunkies" who replaced them. Organizers were not allowed to make speeches or to organize peaceful picketing. They were also subjected to physical abuse. And in the end the union lost the strike.

American workers could have been paid higher wages than they received in the 1920s. Worker productivity rose 49 percent during those years, and profits rose accordingly. Wages, however, never went up at the same rate. The fact that workers could not buy as much as they produced may have contributed to the depression of the 1930s. Furthermore, in industries like automobile manufacture, mining, and transportation, workers were being replaced by machines. Here the price of progress was unemployment.

Management generally resisted unions with all its might. Nor was it shy about using violence when necessary. Management considered both the union shop (where all employees have to join the union) and the closed shop (where only union members are hired) as "un-American." The biggest employers resolved to tolerate only the open shop (where hiring is done without regard to the union), or the nonunion shop.

Some employers who strongly opposed national unions sponsored company unions and provided bonuses and profit sharing for their employees. They also put up modern factories and granted wage increases from time to time. Henry Ford's $5-a-day wage in 1914 had shocked the American business community. Yet like many big employers Ford used professional strikebreakers, private police, paid spies, tear gas, and bullets in dealing with unions. Labor organizers were beaten so mercilessly at Ford's plant that the overpass to the entrance was known as "the doorway to HELL." According to information unearthed by Senator La Follette's investigating committee, American industry spent about $80 million on antilabor agents in 1926.

The widespread poverty in the depression made the public more sympathetic to union goals. Even before the New Deal, Congress passed the Norris-LaGuardia Act (1932). It outlawed yellow-dog contracts (which forced a worker to agree not to belong to a union while employed by the company) and curtailed the use of injunctions in peaceful strikes. More hopeful still, the National Industrial Recovery Act (NIRA) in 1933 gave workers the right "to organize and bargain collectively through representatives of their own choosing . . . free from the interference, restraint or coercion of employers."

Most important for labor was the National Labor Relations Act, or Wagner Act, of 1935. When the NIRA was voided by the Supreme Court, Senator Robert Wagner redrafted the section on labor and pushed it through Congress. Management was required to permit unions to be organized, to deal collectively with unions, and to allow the closed shop. The Wagner Act created a federal labor board to hear claims of unfair labor practices. Roosevelt signed the Wagner Act somewhat reluctantly. Conservatives denounced it as fascism, a reference to the government-sanctioned unions of Mussolini's regime in Italy.

Formation of the CIO

When the Wagner Act was passed, only 3.5 million out of 39 million workers belonged to unions. It seemed like a godsend to the organized. So when Daniel Tobin of the AFL called the Wagner Act "rubbish," he angered many other union people. But craft-union leaders like Tobin had never cared much for the mass of unskilled immigrant workers or white-collar workers. Nor did they have any intention of organizing them. This sparked the old feud within the Federation between the craft unions and the industrial unions (see pp. 369–370).

The United Mine Workers, having expanded from 150,000 to 500,000 under the NIRA, were the strongest industrial union in the AFL. Its president, the beetle-browed, Shakespeare-quoting John L. Lewis, intended to use the Wagner Act to its fullest advantage. David Dubinsky and Sidney Hillman of the needle trades, along with leaders of the auto, rubber, and steel workers, also favored industrial unions. In 1935 they formed the Committee for Industrial Organization within the AFL. This first CIO embraced skilled and unskilled workers, immigrants and natives, blacks and whites. At a national AFL convention, the conflict between the industrial unionists and the craft unionists was so sharp that Lewis landed a fist on the jaw of William Hutchinson of the carpenters' union. President William Green of the AFL ordered the CIO to disband and a year later expelled the new group for "dual unionism." Efforts to heal the breach in labor's ranks did not succeed until the 1950s.

The CIO further broke with tradition by identifying closely with one political party, in this case the Democrats. Lewis' mine workers contributed heavily to FDR's reelection campaign in 1936 and slyly used the president's name in drives for new members. One poster declared, "The President wants you to join the union." FDR was slightly embarrassed by labor's warm embrace.

1937, a year of strikes

Big companies shrugged off the Wagner Act as unconstitutional until the Supreme Court gave it the stamp of approval late in 1937. The CIO then used the new law as a battering ram to gain recognition, wage increases, and members. It also used the old-fashioned strike. In 1937, the worst year ever for strikes, over 28 million work days were lost.

Led by Walter Reuther, the auto workers struck at the Chevrolet plant in Flint, Michigan. In a particularly fierce struggle, the workers invented an illegal but highly effective weapon, the sit-down strike. They barricaded the doors and squatted on car seats at Chevrolet Plant No. 4, the key factory in General Motors' empire. They refused to leave until management met their demands for recognition and higher pay. Meantime, the strikers' wives barricaded the factory gates and sneaked food inside. The police refused to attack the women. To prevent a bloody confrontation, the Michigan governor kept up a steady round of negotiations. The sit-down strike was a blatantly illegal invasion of private property, but it won recognition from GM in January 1937.

Chrysler Corporation followed suit shortly, leaving Ford as the only holdout among auto manufacturers. The rubber industry and U.S. Steel settled with the CIO without strike. Smaller steel companies held out. On Memorial Day in 1937 police killed four strikers at the Republic Steel Corporation in Chicago in the culmination of a four-month labor-management battle. The strike was broken.

The rights and interests of the laboring man will be protected . . . not by labor agitators but by the Christian gentlemen to whom God in His infinite wisdom has given control of the property interests of this country.

TOM M. GRIDLER (1877–   )
Republic Steel executive

Union victories

Labor's long struggle for recognition in the basic industries was nearly over. The Wagner Act and the organizing strikes of the 1930s were shaping a new future. Management soon accepted collective bargaining as standard practice. Union membership more than tripled between 1933 and 1941. Labor violence subsided. The courts recognized labor's right to picket peacefully and to hold meetings. The Supreme Court upheld a minimum-wage law and a wages-and-hours law for women and minors, two long-term goals of the labor movement.

By the end of the 1930s editorial writers commonly spoke of the struggle between Big Labor and Big Business. But labor had far less power than management, as became clearer during World War II. After the fighting had begun, labor secured a government pledge of high wages and price controls. In exchange they gave a no-strike promise for the duration. Yet the unions took no part in the policy decisions on manpower or production. When the war and navy departments awarded billions of dollars in contracts to companies that violated the Wagner Act, the AFL and CIO (renamed the Congress of Industrial Organizations) could do nothing about the antiunion policies of the military branches. Labor unrest increased as the war went on. Unions failed to build on the power they had won in 1937, except in one respect: their membership rose from 9 million in 1940 to nearly 15 million in 1945.

In Chicago on May 30, 1937, four workers were killed and eighty-four wounded as police used guns, tear gas, and clubs to break up a march of strikers at the Republic Steel works. This was one dramatic incident among many in the continued bitter struggle between management and laborers who sought collective bargaining rights.

Farmers Join "the System"

Early depression for the farmers

America's "golden age of farming" ended about 1920, when European crops returned to the world market. For the time being the world market was crammed with food, and farm prices began a long decline. By 1932 wheat, which had been over $2 a bushel in 1920, reached an all-time low of 32¢ a bushel. Continued overproduction made matters worse.

As their prices dropped and their costs increased, American farmers defaulted on their mortgages and lost their farms. Farmers who managed to hang onto their farms realized that no matter how hard they worked, they could probably never own them free and clear of debt. In the 1930s dust storms in the Southwest swept away or buried thousands of acres of wheat, grass, and corn.

The number of tenant farmers rose from about 35 percent in 1890 to 40 percent in 1930. In the South, where some 68 percent of the people still lived in rural areas in 1930, about half of all farmers were tenants. And in the Black Belt of Georgia, Alabama, and Mississippi as many as eight out of ten were tenants or sharecroppers. There a farm family was lucky to clear over $200 a year. Since the end of Reconstruction, illiteracy, malnutrition and disease, soil erosion, and a sense of hopelessness had been the sharecroppers' constant lot. In a novel written in the 1920s a white tenant expresses a prevalent mood: "If I was to start to hell with a load of ice, there'd be a freeze before I got there."

The organized farmers of the Middle West devised a scheme by which the government would support farm income. The McNary-Haugen bill called for government purchases of corn, wheat, cotton, and other commodities to be sold overseas at world prices. The bill was proposed in five congressional sessions from 1924 to 1928 and was passed twice, only to encounter Coolidge's presidential veto. Finally Hoover approved a similar scheme in 1929, but it was not much help to the farmers. The country had committed itself to industrial growth and high tariffs, which made it difficult to sell farm surpluses overseas. Few farmers shared in the general prosperity of the country during the 1920s. When the Great Depression hit, many had been going downhill for at least a decade.

Not that farmers lacked influence on Capitol Hill. One of the most vocal congressional lobbies was the American Farm Bureau Federation, a voluntary group formed in 1920 by Seaman A. Knapp. It was linked with a network of county agents, farm specialists from the state agricultural colleges. The Farm Bureau drew much strength from the corn-hog country of the Middle West. Its president once said, "I stand as a rock against radicalism." While the Farm Bureau denounced Populism, some of its ideas came out of the old radical farmers' movement: cooperative marketing; readjustment of freight rates, tariffs, and taxes; and improved personal credits. The Farm Bureau was the force behind the farm block, a group of twenty-two senators from major agricultural states of the Midwest and South, who held the balance of power in the Senate in the early 1920s. They passed many minor laws but had trouble with their pet project, the McNary-Haugen bill.

AAA support for farm prices

The major breakthrough in farm policy was Roosevelt's Agricultural Adjustment Act of 1933. Its basic idea was to raise farm prices by paying farmers to reduce production. By subsidizing the staples that were grown, the prewar balance—or parity—between farm

Destruction of farm products to raise prices became a controversial issue during the 1930s. Secretary of Agriculture Henry A. Wallace argued that this practice would keep farmers from bankruptcy and prevent shortages and still higher prices later. But the sight of wasted food—like the milk being poured onto a street in Harvard, Illinois—angered many people.

and industrial prices could be restored. A tax on food processors would provide the money for the payments to farmers. The AAA program was administered by the Agriculture Adjustment Administration, under Secretary of Agriculture Henry A. Wallace, a prominent Iowa corn farmer.

In the first year of the AAA, Wallace ordered the destruction of "excess" farm goods. Growers killed 6 million piglets, emptied milk cans on the ground, left oranges to rot, and plowed under every fourth row of cotton. In 1934 and 1935 the government paid over $1 billion in farm supports to take 30 million acres out of cultivation in those two years. The system paid off almost immediately in higher prices and farm income. Wheat rose from 38¢ per bushel in 1932 to $1.02 in 1936. The price for cotton doubled, and the price for hogs tripled. Henry Wallace went on to become vice-president.

Other elements of the New Deal for farmers included the Resettlement Administration and the Emergency Farm Mortgage Act of 1933, which lent farmers money to save their farms. But the AAA farm supports were the heart of the program—and a rousing success story. By 1939 higher farm prices, rising family income, and increased overall efficiency were pointed to with pride by New Deal administrators and by farm leaders. Throughout the heartland, silos were beginning to bulge again with surpluses kept off the market by government orders. Abundance once more threatened to drive prices down, but that problem was ended by the outbreak of World War II.

During the war the farm program went so well that farmers realized 110 percent of parity. Essentially the same government-support program exists to this day. Like organized labor, organized farmers had "joined the system" as a successful interest group. The farmers, traditionally the most independent producers in American life, had found a place in the welfare state.

Review

Prior to 1928 the U.S. had enjoyed fifty years of productivity and prosperity. Led by the auto industry, the country had become a consumer economy after World War I. Until the crash everything seemed rosy, but the nation went into shock when Wall Street crumbled on October 29, 1929. Farmers lost their land, workers lost their jobs, and a banking crisis loomed. President Hoover opposed government interference in the economy. But when he did compromise by approving the Reconstruction Finance Corporation (RFC), it did not help. Franklin D. Roosevelt, Hoover's successor, had personality, a caring and confident air, and a pragmatic approach. During his first hundred days in office Congress passed reform, relief, and recovery legislation. TVA was the most notable long-term reform, although FDR's favored program was NRA. The administration adopted a program of government spending when an inflation threat caused cutbacks and a new recession. The New Deal faced antiquated poor laws. Its most effective approach to poverty was work relief, but unemployment remained high all the same. Mounting pressure led to the Second New Deal, which focused on direct aid to farmers and workers, as well as a social-security program. Despite FDR's personal popularity and the promise of hope he offered, it was World War II, rather than the New Deal, which ended the Great Depression.

The loss of the 1919 steel strike was a serious setback for labor. Wages for workers in the 1920s had not kept up with productivity or profits. Management often opposed unionism with violence. But the depression and the spread of poverty softened the public toward unions, and in 1935 organized labor made strategic gains with passage of the Wagner Act. The old differences between craft and industrial unions split the AFL and produced the CIO. Following a series of strikes, labor's fight for recognition was drawing to a close. Many of the working conditions which it had long demanded were being met. By World War II Big Labor was as common a term as Big Business, although the experiences of those years proved that labor was not nearly as powerful as management.

Farmers did not share the general prosperity of the 1920s. The close of World War I ended their "golden age." They were again competing on a world market and by 1932 prices had fallen to disastrously low levels. Farms were heavily mortgaged and many indebted farmers lost their land. In the southern Black Belt eight out of ten farmers were tenants or sharecroppers. The Farm Bureau was a major link to Washington. Although the Bureau shunned Populism, it adopted some of the ideas of that movement. FDR's major agricultural breakthrough came with the AAA, a program which forced a rise in farm prices, income, and efficiency. The same basic system still exists today. Farmers, too, benefited from the welfare state.

Questions

1. Compare and contrast the social and economic philosphies of Herbert Hoover and Franklin D. Roosevelt.
2. Identify and give the function of the following "alphabet" groups: (a) RFC, (b) AAA, (c) TVA, (d) NRA, (e) CCC, (f) WPA, and (g) RA.
3. What was the Second New Deal and how did it differ from the first?
4. Trace the gains made by labor from the end of World War I through World War II.
5. Talk to someone you know who lived through the Great Depression and find out what he or she considered the best and worst aspects of the New Deal administration.

FDR shakes hands with a miner in Wheeling, West Virginia, during the 1932 campaign.

In the event that the
Congress shall fail . . .
and . . . the national
emergency is still critical,
I shall not evade the clear
course of duty that will
then confront me. I shall
ask the Congress for the one
remaining instrument to
meet the crisis—broad
executive power to wage a
war against the
emergency. . . .

FRANKLIN DELANO ROOSEVELT
(1882–1945)

26

26
Rise of the Welfare State

Around the time that Franklin Roosevelt took office as president, Adolf Hitler assumed power as Nazi dictator of Germany. Could it happen here? Would the despair of the depression bring on some sort of American dictatorship? Or perhaps a revolution? At the time of the Bonus March in 1932 social upheaval seemed possible. Some leftists believed that socialism was just around the corner. Many on the right thought it might be necessary to use force to "put down the Communists." The situation in some ways resembled Germany just before the rise of Hitler.

Still, it did *not* happen here. The depression produced neither a revolution nor a dictatorship. The political system remained intact. What did happen was that Roosevelt managed to preserve orderly government, and this may be one of the most important accomplishments of his administration. The secret of his success, as this chapter will show, lay in his ability to establish a moderate welfare state.

The Power Elite

Shifting classes

Power is a controversial subject. Some people believe that it is widely distributed in America, shared by many groups more or less the way the Founding Fathers intended. Others say that it is concentrated within an elite. There is a disagreement about its exact make-up, but in general the power elite is said to include individuals and families of great wealth, the top executives of major industries and financial institutions, high-ranking politicians and presidential advisers, and, more recently, the top officers in the military.

Rows of clerical workers, part of the new white-collar middle class. They had no particular political identity, wrote British historian James Bryce in Modern Democracies *(1921); in fact, Bryce could only identify one division in American political thought — that between the rich and the poor. "Among the rest there are no sharp and permanent oppositions of political tenets or of social sympathies."*

No one questions that to some extent power in America has been associated with social class. A person from Park Avenue or the Gold Coast has more chance of gaining power than a citizen of Shanty Town or Tobacco Road. Whether the main factor is having money, bearing the right family name, attending the right prep school, driving the right car, sponsoring the right charity, or visiting the right resorts, the importance of class is not arguable.

Americans have always tolerated great differences of wealth in their society. But those at the bottom of the ladder have wanted to feel that they could move up. During the twenties Americans felt that they could rise with relative ease. Having money was certainly the quickest way up. Going to a prestigious college, getting a good job, or marrying into a well-connected family could be useful too.

The first half of the twentieth century saw an important switch within the middle class. The number of farmers declined while the number of white-collar workers multiplied. Prosperous farmers represented the old middle class. Their income came from land. They invested their own money, took their own risks, and upheld the Protestant Ethic. But with advancing farm technology the total number of farmers dropped from 30 percent of the labor force in 1920 to about 5 percent in 1940. At the same time, the number of white-collar workers—professionals, salespeople, clerks, managers, office employees in general—increased. Though the members of this new middle class no longer lived off the land, they still shared many of the values of the old middle class.

You will never make a good merchant of yourself by reversing the order in which the Lord decreed that we should proceed—learning the spending before the earning end of business. . . .

GEORGE HORACE LORIMER (1867–1937)
Letters from a Self-Made Merchant to His Son

The shifting class structure had an effect on the distribution of political power. The new middle class as a whole was so huge and varied that it had no political clout unless and until its particular smaller elements banded together to form associations. There was, and is, no such thing as a "white-collar lobby" in Congress, though medical associations, consumer groups, etc., voice particular needs. One segment of the middle class that increased its ability to influence legislation was the farmers. As their numbers declined, the remaining ones became better organized in Washington, thus creating a major change in the politics of agriculture. Most of them now organized according to their market specialties. Thus the corn growers, the cattle industry, the dairy farmers each spoke with separate voices. Meanwhile, the well-financed Farm Bureau was better able to stand up for the farmers' overall needs. The mem-

bers of the farm bloc in the Senate enjoyed power out of proportion to their numbers. The U.S. Constitution provides for two senators from each state, regardless of population. Seven hundred thousand North Dakotans, most of whom lived in rural areas, elected two senators, just as did seven million New Yorkers, most of whom were urbanites.

Unchecked corporate power

While big firms never totally dominated American life, they controlled a vast segment of its economy. In 1929 the two hundred largest corporations were worth nearly as much as all other nonbanking firms combined. In the board rooms of a small number of American corporations, decisions were made that deeply affected the life of the nation—determining what consumers could and could not buy, how many jobs would be available, and which raw materials and technology would be developed. The overseas investments of such corporations even helped determine America's foreign policy.

Sometimes the same men sat on more than one board of directors. Through such "interlocking directorates" the corporate elite magnified its overall strength. In this way the House of Morgan, the single most powerful financial firm, controlled hundreds of companies in railroading, shipping, finance, electricity and manufacturing.

Still, corporate power was no burning issue in the 1920s. Under Wilson's wartime leadership, even the most dyed-in-the-wool Progressives had learned to live with big business. Business leaders rarely had to justify their power, and their image was much better than it had been before the war. Trust-busting was a dead issue for several reasons. For one thing, Americans liked what the big corporations produced. For another, the government condoned or even encouraged business combinations. Under the Webb-Pomerene Act, signed by Wilson in 1918, businesses that engaged in foreign trade could not be prosecuted for violating the Clayton Antitrust Act. In 1920 the U.S. Supreme Court ruled that the government could not attack a corporation simply because it was big. The Commerce Department under Herbert Hoover encouraged competing firms to form trade associations, share market data, standardize their technology, and reduce competition. These activities were approved by the Supreme Court in 1925. The Court ruled that trade associations could encourage competitors to compare prices, so long as they did not raise prices as a result.

In the 1920s the Justice Department stopped trust-busting. Regulatory agencies became inactive. One close investigator said that the Federal Trade Commission seemed to be trying to commit hara-kiri.

Cooperation between businesses usually stopped short of monopoly. Generally a few big firms divided up a market between themselves but resisted the temptation to crush one another in the process. Thus, in autos, while many smaller firms went under during the depression, General Motors, Ford, and Chrysler continued to share the market without one company totally dominating the rest.

The courts had long ago decided that the holding company was a legal form of business combination. This type of business organization was used for extreme types of stock manipulation during the 1920s. By bold action one person could gain control of great corporate assets. A Chicago financial wizard, Samuel Insull, did this, perfecting the pyramiding of holding companies. He piled one holding company on top of another in the electric power field until a single board of directors controlled an empire of public-utility holding companies. He was not in the business of producing electricity but rather of owning companies that owned others that did so. One dollar invested in the top-level holding company controlled over $2000 worth of assets in actual electric power companies. Similarly, the Van Sweringen syndicate, backed by Morgan, erected a pyramid of railroad holding companies that controlled a vast network of trunk lines. The absence of government regulations and the money of thousands of small-time investors encouraged the growth of these paper monsters. They contributed little or nothing to real economic growth.

The business of America is business. . . . The man who builds a factory builds a temple. The man who works there worships there.

CALVIN COOLIDGE (1872–1933)

By the 1920s, corporations were changing structurally. Salaried officers were taking over control of most giant businesses, replacing the founders and their heirs. Some of the newcomers clashed on policy matters with the old-time business heads. Andrew Carnegie (who died in 1919) symbolized a dying breed when he said to a group of college students, "I do not believe that even the presidents of these [new] corporations, being only salaried men, are to be . . . classed as strictly businessmen at all." He urged young men entering big corporations to seize the initiative: "Boss your boss just as soon as you can." The transfer of power to the new corporate executives has been called the "managerial revolution." After this shift it was much harder to know exactly in whose hands corporate power lay.

Despite its own acclaim of rugged individualism and free enterprise, industry lobbied for and received both direct and indirect support from the government. At public expense Congress built a nationwide system of roads that guaranteed the success of the trucking and auto industries. Both the airlines and the companies that made planes

Holiday travelers line up at the New York entrance to the Holland Tunnel. While government-funded roads, bridges, and tunnels certainly benefited the public, they also formed indirect subsidies for the auto industry, which experienced phenomenal growth during the 1920s. By 1929, over 26 million motor vehicles were registered in the U.S.

benefited from the airports, radio guidance systems, and light beacons that were built, owned, and operated with tax dollars. They also profited from government airmail contracts. The vast federal funds spent on highways, bridges, and tunnels assured the profits of the heavy construction firms. Tariff regulations that placed a duty on imports helped domestic manufacturers compete with foreign ones. These duties were generally higher in the 1920s than before the war. In short, during the flush twenties the U.S. government was subsidizing entire industries.

Power and the New Deal

The New Deal was inconsistent in its approach to business combinations. Initially it was not hostile to them. The NRA, with its program of self-regulating trade associations and its suspension of the antitrust laws, was an effort to give special help to the biggest and most efficient businesses (see p. 543). Only after the collapse of the NRA did the attack on the power of the "economic royalists" begin.

Following in the footsteps of the Progressive movement the New Deal did use regulatory agencies as watchdogs over business. In 1934 Congress created the Security Exchange Commission (SEC) to supervise the stock exchanges, which had been in turmoil since October 1929. A year later the SEC took steps to supervise public-utility holding companies. The Federal Reserve Board was granted new authority under the Glass-Steagall Banking Act (actually signed by Hoover) to control the banking industry's lending policies. In practice this helped loosen tight money. In 1935 the Federal Power Commission got broad new powers over electricity that was transmitted across state lines. The expanding telegraph, cable, and radio industries came under the federal eye when Congress established the Federal Communications Commission (FCC) in 1934. A law (1938) requiring certain manufacturers to list the ingredients of their product on the wrapper gave more power to the Food and Drug Administration. The FDA also began to look into false advertising.

The regulatory agencies never quite lived up to liberals' expectations. In practice they often served the industries they were supposed to supervise. Their rules helped big firms at the expense of little ones. The SEC law, for example, was drafted by the Wall Street law firm of Sullivan and Cromwell, which represented some of the biggest stock brokerage firms of all. Also, the officials appointed to regulatory agencies usually came from the very businesses they were asked to control.

Just as the New Deal was running out of steam in 1938, FDR appointed a genuine trustbuster to head the antitrust division of the Justice Department. Thurmond Arnold, a Yale law professor, investigated and prosecuted big combinations more vigorously than any predecessor in that office. In the next five years he took on General Electric, the Aluminum Company of America, and other giant corporations, demanding fairness in the marketplace from them. An implied threat to big business was that unless it complied with the Justice Department, the administration would press for laws directly controlling private business. Eventually Arnold was accused of interfering with the war effort, so he had to back off.

Many who study the sources and uses of power in modern times consider the Roosevelt years a watershed in the rise of government bureaucracy and the military. Although the federal bureaucracy had grown in earlier years, it mushroomed more or less suddenly during the time of the New Deal and the Sec-

While political cartoonists saw Uncle Sam getting "all tangled up" by the ballooning federal "alphabetocracy," FDR's political opponents viewed the growth of the federal government with serious alarm. As each new agency brought the government into a new sector of private life, many felt, as Wendell Willkie said during the 1940 campaign, that "today it is not big business that we have to fear. It is big government."

ond World War. The giant federal bureaucracies became new power centers, angering those who recalled Jefferson's maxim, "That government governs best which governs least." The alphabet soup of government agencies multiplied readily in response to the depression. Farmers, business people, and private citizens who had dealings with federal officials complained of the growing complexity and rigidity of government regulations. Bureaucrats—the very term became a dirty word—seemed to be wallowing in red tape, incapable of making decisions.

While hostile critics considered the growth of bureaucracy a conspiracy on Roosevelt's part, it had relatively little to do with partisan politics. It was actually a worldwide trend in the twentieth century. It was linked to the centralization of government and the growth of business and population. Modern communications technology made it possible for Washington-based agencies to stay in daily touch with numerous offices scattered in the field. Naturally many bureaucrats resented the accusation that they were indifferent to human needs; they felt themselves to be public servants performing a valuable service for their country.

Another segment of federal government that underwent growth during the Roosevelt years was the military. In the twenties Harding, Coolidge, and Hoover had paid little attention to the generals and admirals. During his first term even FDR let the civilians in his administration make the important decisions affecting the military establishment.

But as World War II drew close, Roosevelt turned for advice to the Chiefs of Staff. During the war he consulted them directly rather than through the civilian secretaries of War and the Navy. After Pearl Harbor the Joint Chiefs advised him on diplomatic matters. Thus out of the necessities created by global war, the military assumed new power.

Some called Roosevelt a dictator, but a better term would be "power broker." Although he was one of the strongest presidents in American history, part of his power lay in knowing how to gain the cooperation of different segments of society by giving them something of what they wanted. Labor and management, the farm bloc and city bosses, southern Bourbons and northern blacks, civilians and the military—all found themselves dependent on him or beholden to him in one way or another. This was a secret of his success as a four-term president. But how did FDR come to power in the first place? Let's go back to the early twenties and trace the political developments that eventually brought Roosevelt to the White House.

From Country Boy to Gentleman Farmer

Normalcy and the Teapot Dome scandals

In the election of 1920, Senator Warren G. Harding, the Republican presidential candidate, suggested that the country was tired of Wilsonian idealism and wanted "a return to normalcy." The fact that he won over 60 percent of the popular vote—the greatest landslide since James Monroe in 1820—indicates that he was right. The election also showed how strong tradition was in American politics. Harding represented, says Andrew Sinclair, the old-time traits of "the Country Boy, of the Self-Made Man . . . of the Political Innocent . . . of America First, of the Reluctant Candidate, of the Dark Horse, of the Smoke-Filled Room, of the Best Minds. With the help of these and other fictions, a most ordinary man reached the White House." An ailing Woodrow Wilson, bundled up against the weather, was wheeled slowly out of the White House in March 1921. His going marked the end not only of Democratic rule and liberal reform but also of a strong presidency. Harding returned the power to Congress.

Harding's administration was tainted by the worst corruption since the Grant administration. Interior Secretary Albert B. Fall conspired to turn over federal oil reserves at Teapot Dome, Wyoming, and Elk Hills, California, to private oil firms. In return he received a $100,000 "loan." He was later sentenced for bribery. Other Harding appointees were also involved in shady deals. Attorney General Harry M. Daugherty took bribes from liquor interests during Prohibition. The head of the Veterans Bureau cheated the government out of millions of dollars appropriated for new hospitals.

Harding, a much beloved president before the scandals became public, had nothing directly to do with the criminal conduct of his cronies. Just before he died he cursed his "damn friends" for betraying him. The Teapot Dome scandals may have contributed to his early death from heart trouble in August 1923. The country learned of the details shortly afterward. Only the Watergate scandals of the Nixon era left a worse smear on the pages of presidential history.

Harding was replaced by his vice-president, the stolid Calvin Coolidge. He was sworn in at home by his father, a local judge in Plymouth, Vermont, in the glow of an old-fashioned kerosene lamp. Coolidge, who has been called a "Puritan in Babylon," embodied the old-time virtues of small-town rural America. To let Congress have its way whenever possible, to do little with executive authority other than trim the budget, to respect the wishes of the business community, especially the conservative U.S. Chamber of Commerce — these were some of Coolidge's basic aims as president.

A new coalition of voters

In the 1920s both parties were still run mostly by small-town lawyers, businessmen, and newspaper editors. Often favoring Prohibition, they were always suspicious of city bosses, immigrants, and labor unions. In the South many were staunch fundamentalists.

Since McKinley's day the GOP had boasted a majority of the registered voters. Yet profound changes were in the making. Among the factors altering national politics were the shift of voters from country to city, the impact of the depression, and the coming of age of a new generation of ethnic voters.

The most visible and long-lasting change was the gradual formation between 1924 and 1936 of the new Democratic coalition. The changing order in politics was first seen at the Democratic national convention of 1924, when Governor Alfred E. Smith of New York made a bid for the presidency. Smith was a Tammany Hall politician of Irish Catholic parentage. He battled the candidate of rural Democrats, William G. McAdoo, for 103 ballots. Both of them finally lost to a dark horse, John W. Davis, who was soundly defeated by Coolidge in November.

Smith won the Democratic nomination in 1928, but in the election his Catholicism, his opposition to Prohibition, and his urban-immigrant ties were all against him. In the end, the WASP, rural, and dry votes for Herbert Hoover far outnumbered those of ethnic, urban, and wet America.

Ever since the days of Jefferson and Jackson, political alliances in America have been continually forming and breaking down. In the course of his first term FDR created one of the largest and most durable political combinations in American history. By 1936 his coalition consisted of organized labor and the elderly, big-city ethnic groups and farmers, midwestern Bull Moosers and eastern Jews, blacks and southern Bourbons, a smattering of liberal Republican newspaper editors and a host of intellectuals. No more motley combination had been seen since the days of Jackson.

Of course, FDR had implacable enemies. By 1936 conservatives deeply resented his leftward drift, and the business community grew cold to him. He was denounced as a "traitor to his class." Meanwhile, he began

AL SMITH (1873-1944)

FROM THE SIDEWALKS OF NEW YORK

He sported a brown derby cocked over one eye, smoked big cigars, drank beer, and referred to opposing political arguments as "baloney." Alfred Emmanuel Smith was born on New York's Lower East Side, and he had worked in the Fulton Fish Market in his youth. For years and years he had been a part of New York City's Democratic organization, a big-city political "machine," the infamous Tammany Hall. In addition, Smith was of Irish descent, and he was a Roman Catholic.

Yet, in the 1920s Al Smith dared to dream of being president of the United States. He was forgetting, it seemed, that America's presidents were Protestant gentlemen who came from rural places or middle-sized cities in respectable states like Ohio. Forgetting that decent people did not speak out publicly against prohibition. Forgetting, for that matter, that presidential aspirants should be careful of their language, mind their manners, and, above all, preserve their dignity. Al Smith said, "Baloney!" He also said, "Let's look at the record." And quite a record it was. Just eight years of schooling, but a lifetime of experience. Term after term as a state assemblyman, rising to speaker of the Assembly. Sheriff of New York County. President of the city's board of aldermen. And then, in 1918, election as governor. Organizer of a commission to restructure the state government, he was ousted in 1920 but bounced back in 1922 and stayed until 1928.

He left behind him an efficiently organized state government; new state hospitals, improved housing, safer factories, child welfare laws, state beaches, parks and parkways; a remarkable record of administrative skill, of honesty and fairness, of concern for the working class, the poor, the "rabble." ("I'm the rabble," Al said once.)

In 1924, at the Democratic National Convention, Franklin D. Roosevelt nominated him for the presidency and called him "the Happy Warrior." He didn't get the nomination. As 1928 approached it seemed certain that he'd be chosen. But from high places and low there came a roar of protest. The Ku Klux Klan screamed hateful charges, and Protestant clergymen joined in solemnly regretting the unfitness of a Catholic for the position of chief executive.

Smith fought back, defending both his faith and his fitness, but, despite receiving the Democratic nomination, he never had a chance against Herbert Hoover in that year of Republican prosperity. Outside the South he won only two states, and in the South he lost seven. But among those who voted for him were millions of big-city people—immigrants and the children and grandchildren of immigrants, many of them Catholics—who heard for the first time a candidate who spoke for them and who cared for them. The shift of the big cities to the Democratic party was under way.

attacking the "economic royalists" as the major cause of the depression. Yet it is wrong to see him as a doctrinaire politician. On the contrary, the president acted as a political broker, balancing off the demands of different interest groups. Big business got the NRA, organized labor the Wagner Act, farmers the AAA, major Wall Street brokerage houses the SEC. International fur traders gained a special reciprocal tariff, conservationists basked in the TVA, and senior citizens and the working class enjoyed Social Security.

Even relatively unorganized interests had their day in the sun—nonunion workers, small farmers, the poor, the blacks, all had a shadow place in the Roosevelt coalition. In fact, it was they who assured him his big pluralities. What was soon called the "Roosevelt coalition" remained more or less intact from about 1936 until the administration of Lyndon B. Johnson.

ELECTION OF 1928: ELECTORAL VOTE

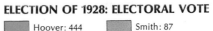

Hoover: 444   Smith: 87

ELECTION OF 1932: ELECTORAL VOTE

Roosevelt: 472   Hoover: 59

FDR's P.R.

No president ever used the media more skillfully than Roosevelt. He was the first to fully exploit radio. Nineteen million homes had wireless sets in 1932 and 33 million by 1944. "I want to talk for a few minutes with the people of the United States about banking," he said in his first famous "fireside chat" over radio. In a warm and resonant voice, with an aristocratic accent, he broadcast a series of messages about the burning issues of the day. His air of fatherly strength in the midst of despair heartened his listeners. They were immensely impressed that the president's main concern seemed to be how to relieve their sufferings. His formal speeches before large audiences were also broadcast. These, too, he handled superbly. He continued to make maximum use of radio during the most agonized periods of the Second World War.

FDR tried to hold a press conference almost every week. When he did so, he invited all White House reporters directly into his office, where he bantered with them on a first-name basis. With his instinctive talent for public relations, he made news even when none existed. Through the press he sent up trial balloons, attacked his enemies, lectured Congress, gave off-the-record background information, and otherwise made his presence felt. The press was the main link between the government and the people. After 1935 over 80 percent of newspaper publishers in America opposed FDR editorially, though they gave him wide coverage and big headlines.

The Democratic party under FDR

Roosevelt had far greater pulling power than the Democratic party as a whole. In fact, from 1933 to 1935 he tried to soft-pedal his party affiliation, carefully referring to himself as "president of all the people." Even when he flew his Democratic colors in 1936, he went out of his way to help friendly Republican candidates at election time and to snub unfriendly Democratic ones. Roosevelt's political successes were in many ways solo performances. "There's one issue in this campaign," he told a close associate in 1936. "It's myself, and people must be either for me or against me."

FDR won reelection in 1936 with a majority greater even than Harding's. The Democratic party swept through the big and near-big cities, many of which had been Republican strongholds practically since Lincoln's day. Even more important, a majority of registered voters were Democrats for the first time. Evidently the new laws, including Social Security, had turned the trick. As a result of their support at the polls, Jews and Catholics got more appointments to high government posts after FDR's reelection. Among the minority representatives were Harvard law professor Felix Frankfurter and his students Benjamin V. Cohen and Thomas G. Corcoran, who were enrolled in Roosevelt's Brain Trust. FDR named Frankfurter to the Supreme Court in 1939.

Oddly enough, as city voters became more important in national politics, the old city bosses began to lose their authority. The slowing down of immigration decreased the supply of naturalized voters. Also the end of Prohibition dried up a stream of cash that had flowed into politics from the underworld. The depression bankrupted cities and sent their officials to Washington begging for money. Federal agencies took over the welfare functions formerly handled by city machines. This left local political bosses with fewer favors and patronage jobs to dole out.

There were still city bosses, of course—Frank Hague of Jersey City, Ed Crump of Memphis, Tom Pendergast of Kansas City—and FDR worked with all of them. But with rare exceptions, their days were numbered.

Third parties in losing battles

Third parties continued to have only marginal success. The best third party showing occurred in 1924, when the Conference for Progressive Political Action (CPPA), a coalition of farm groups, labor unions, Socialists, Progressives, and independents ran Robert M. LaFollette for president. He amassed nearly 5 million votes out of about 29 million cast. The CPPA platform attacked monopoly and supported nationalizing hydroelectric power and railroads, collective bargaining, the abolition of war, and lower tariffs. It elected a dozen governors and three dozen senators and congressmen in 1922, but fell apart after 1924.

The Socialist movement never fully recovered from wartime repression. The formation of the American Communist party in 1920 split the country's far left. During the depression years the Communists made some headway in the labor movement and among intellectuals, but as an electoral force they got nowhere. The Communists ran presidential candidates from 1924 to 1940 but never won more than a sprinkling of votes. Their stature rose slightly during the war years, when Soviet-American friendship was official government policy, though politically they remained inconsequential. Socialist candidate Norman Thomas ran every four years from 1928 to 1948. Although an appealing representative of the left, he did poorly at the polls.

The right-wing Union Party nominated North Dakota congressman William Lemke in 1936. With the backing of various right-wing groups, he was expected to threaten

Roosevelt's bid for reelection. But FDR had sufficiently undermined both the right and the left with his New Deal program to keep Lemke's popular vote well under one million. (Roosevelt defeated Alfred M. Landon, the Republican candidate, by 11 million votes and carried all but two states.)

Failing to pack the Supreme Court

FDR never forgave the Supreme Court for rejecting the NIRA, which he believed would cure the depression. With a huge popular vote under his belt in 1936, he tried to force the Court into submission by "packing" it with new judges who might favor his policies. When he asked Congress to let him appoint one new justice for each one who failed to resign after reaching the age of 70, Congress, after months of debate, gave him a resounding "No!" FDR justified his bombshell proposal with vague talk of "judicial efficiency," but no one believed it. The plan to pack the Court was FDR's greatest political blunder. He had gone against the advice of his best counsellors. The country resented FDR's attempt to alter the balance of power.

Not since Wilson had tried to ram the League of Nations through the Senate had any president put more on the line. Unless he could do something to counter the arch-conservative Court, the president feared the entire New Deal would be wrecked. But the Court-packing went poorly. Senator Joseph Robinson, who was supposed to engineer the passage of a bill changing the Court's composition, died of a heart attack in the midst of battle. Not only did Congress refuse to budge; it threw back in FDR's face measures he considered important to the nation's prosperity. Southern Democrats and conservative Republicans blocked reform at every turn. In the spring of 1938, with the stock market again dropping and unemployment again rising, the New Deal had come to a roaring halt.

While Roosevelt failed to pack the Court, he achieved part of what he wanted. The Court began to consider New Deal laws acceptable under the commerce clause or the general welfare clause of the Constitution, and before long vacancies made possible a more liberal membership. Nevertheless, the Court-packing plan strengthened his congressional enemies and caused FDR irreparable political harm.

In the Democratic primaries in 1938 the president attempted to purge the party of a number of his conservative opponents in Congress. He took special pains to attack his archenemy in the Senate, Georgia's Walter George. But George won an overwhelming victory at the polls, and FDR retreated. The New Deal, less than five years old and supported by an overwhelming majority in the 1936 presidential election, was dead. FDR was the victim of what a political scientist has called "the deadlock of democracy." Presidential liberalism was neutralized by congressional conservatism. A president may have strong ideas, but Congress, however loosely organized and internally divided, is able at least to say "No!" and thereby assert its will.

In 1940 Roosevelt went on to win an unprecedented third term, and in 1944 an even more astonishing fourth term. In the 1940 campaign Roosevelt ran against Wendell Willkie, an appealing GOP lawyer, who had represented the electrical power industry in its struggle against the TVA. Willkie, a Republican liberal, did not oppose the New Deal but insisted that the GOP could handle reform better. He stressed foreign policy and warned that FDR was scheming to involve the country in the war. Willkie did poorly in the November balloting. Four years later FDR easily defeated New York's Governor Thomas E. Dewey, declaring that in the midst of war it was wrong for the country to "change horses in midstream."

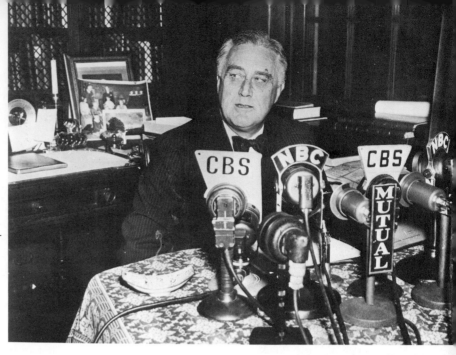

FDR's unique rapport with the American people led to an unprecedented (and unequalled) four terms in office. It was perhaps best illustrated by his fireside chats, in which he "talked plainly" about the nation's problems—and about his own proposed solutions. After his death, Eleanor Roosevelt summed up the source of the Roosevelt "magic". "There was a real dialogue between Franklin and the people."

Roosevelt evaluated

So far, economic collapse by itself has not caused any revolutions in America. The economy collapsed in 1837, 1873, and 1893 without altering the basic system. It did so again in 1929. Roosevelt's relief and reform measures helped preserve the system by restoring popular faith in government. If a proletarian revolution ever posed a threat, the Social Security Act, the WPA, and the Wagner Act averted it. These reforms satisfied, at least in part, the country's yearning for security within the market economy. Neither Communists nor Socialists had much influence. FDR usually managed to undermine his most extreme political enemies, sometimes even persuading them to join him. He worked masterfully within the existing party system.

From this perspective the "Roosevelt revolution" was no revolution at all. Rather it was a series of pragmatic reforms and compromises that saved capitalism from its enemies. Perhaps the most revolutionary and enduring aspect of the New Deal was the welfare state, that is, those reform laws and policies

based on the proposition that government is to a large degree responsible for the social and economic well-being of its citizens. The initial intent of the welfare-state measures was to supply temporary answers to a particular crisis—specifically, to provide relief and hope for the vast numbers of homeless and helpless Americans. It has since become permanent. And, as it has now come to be understood, it often means support, too, for groups that are already comfortably well off.

Had Roosevelt survived the Second World War, he might have tried to realign the two parties. FDR had come up against the inertia in Congress and been forced to watch his liberal reforms blocked. In June 1944, he told a close friend, "Well, I think the time has come for the Democratic party to get rid of its reactionary elements in the South, and to attract to it the liberals in the Republican party. . . . We ought to have two real parties—one liberal and one conservative." He hoped to link arms with Willkie and form "a new, really liberal party in America" by 1948. But Willkie died in October 1944 and Roosevelt a half a year later, and the dream never materialized.

Review

As long as social mobility is possible, Americans have tolerated the fact that power is often a function of social class. During the 1920s people felt optimistic about their ability to climb the social ladder. The declining number of farmers and increasing number of white-collar workers was changing the face of the middle class, and this affected power distribution. Farmers had a strong lobby in Washington and were overrepresented in Congress. But the wide-ranging white-collar middle class had little political clout. Big business, though, had enormous power: the largest 200 firms possessed nearly as much worth as all others combined. Their actions affected huge areas both at home and abroad. In the 1920s they faced little opposition. Corporation managers, unlike the older robber barons, concentrated on moderate, steady profits and stressed teamwork.

In the depression big business received even more help from the government than it had in the 1920s, although the administration set up watchdog regulating agencies. Under the New Deal the federal government itself gained more power than ever before. The new bureaucracies became power centers, and local government and big business grew more dependent on Washington. The military also gained more power and, particularly during World War II, had direct access to the president, advising him on diplomatic as well as military matters. Franklin Roosevelt acquired vast power by giving different vested interest groups something of what they wanted and by making them beholden to him in a variety of ways.

When the ailing Woodrow Wilson left the White House in 1921 he was replaced by Warren G. Harding, "the country boy." The Harding administration was tainted by the graft and corruption of his political cronies. Calvin Coolidge embodied the virtues of small-town rural America, whose elite still ran party politics in the 1920s. But the election of 1924 indicated a shift in coalitions as the population moved from country to city and the impact of a new generation of ethnic voters emerged. One of the most powerful political coalitions in American history formed under Roosevelt, and it held fast for some thirty years. Roosevelt was a master of the media, and used the press and radio to gain support for himself and his programs. His reelection in 1936 was evidence of his popularity. Third parties won only marginal success. Both the right-wing and left-wing parties ran presidential candidates and both fared badly. After Roosevelt's 1936 election triumph, he made an attempt to control the Supreme Court by "packing" it. This unsuccessful maneuver was his worst political blunder. In 1938 the stock market fell again, unemployment rose, and the New Deal died an early death. In spite of this the president was elected to third and fourth terms. Roosevelt had undermined the position of critics and extremist political groups by initiating reforms and restoring the citizen's faith in government.

Questions

1. In what way were the 1920s favorable to big business?
2. How did the New Deal encourage big business? What forms of regulation did it employ to supervise corporate power?
3. Trace the growth of power in the federal government under FDR.
4. FDR felt a need for party realignment and the topic is raised regularly by various politicians. Do you think the idea is a good one and, if so, along what lines do you think parties should be realigned?

Adolf Hitler reviews "soldiers" of the German labor service, each shouldering a shovel;
Zeppelin Meadow, near Nuremberg, September 8, 1937.

"Government of the people, by the people, for the people" —if Hitler wins, this will be the discarded ideal of a decayed civilization.

Committee to Defend America by Aiding the Allies, June 10, 1940

27

27
Twice in a Lifetime

In 1918 none of the great statesmen could put Humpty Dumpty together again. The Great War had made a mess of the world, and the damage was not repaired. War certainly had not made the world safe for democracy, nor put an end to war, as Wilson had hoped. Instead, hard on the heels of the armistice, Europe was struck by famine, revolution, and civil war. The huge war debts that the Allies had piled up, and the huge reparations Germany was assessed in the peace settlement, helped bring on a worldwide depression in 1929. Internal disorder and despair laid Germany open for the dictatorship of Adolf Hitler. Militarism also won out in Italy and Japan. Twenty-one years after the armistice of 1918 a second and even more destructive world war broke out. And again the United States was drawn into the conflict.

This tragic series of events raises questions that are hard to answer even now. Why, with the memory of the suffering of World War I still so fresh, was it not possible for statesmen to prevent World War II? Should the U.S. have intervened earlier to stop Hitler's aggression? Did America's isolationism in the 1920s encourage the militarists abroad? Did this country provoke Japan unnecessarily?

The Second World War was a major turning point in American history. Today, more than three decades after V-J Day, its effects are still felt. America's status as a superpower, the role of anticommunism in American policies, the growth of the military-industrial complex, and the extraordinary expansion of the powers of the executive branch of government are some of the legacies of World War II.

Threats Between Two World Wars

Rejecting the League of Nations

At the Versailles Conference in 1919 Woodrow Wilson fought doggedly for his Fourteen Points (see pp. 412–413). But the assembled leaders of Britain, France, and Italy—the other major Allied nations—rarely saw eye-to-eye with the American president on the provisions of the treaty ending the Great War. Neither Britain nor France nor Italy could put aside bitter resentment against Germany, as Wilson had hoped.

Germany was forced to admit its war guilt and pay reparations to the Allies. It had to return Alsace-Lorraine to France and accept occupation of its Saar Basin and its Rhineland. All of Germany's holdings abroad were taken over by Allied powers under a mandate system. More in keeping with Wilson's liberalism, Yugoslavia, Czechoslovakia, and Poland were among the new nations created out of the shattered Russian, Austro-Hungarian, and Ottoman empires. Most significantly, the Versailles Conference agreed to establish a League of Nations to keep the peace. Wilson considered this an enormous triumph. The members of the League would swear to respect each other's boundaries and use collective sanctions against aggressors.

Much to Wilson's dismay, the U.S. Senate refused to accept the idea of a League. A group of "reservationists" led by Republican Senator Henry Cabot Lodge of Massachusetts hoped to modify the Versailles Treaty, and a group of "irreconcilables" led by Idaho Senator William E. Borah and California Senator Hiram W. Johnson would not accept the League under any terms. Opponents feared that the League, which provided for collective action against aggressors, would pull America into unwanted wars and undermine Congress' power to decide when American troops should or should not be committed in a war.

In September 1919, while on a strenuous speaking tour in support of the League, Wilson suffered a disabling stroke from which he never fully recovered. In November 1919 and again in March 1920, with the president refusing to compromise, the Senate rejected the Versailles Treaty. So completely did American officials reject the League in the 1920s that for some years they refused even to respond to letters sent from League headquarters in Geneva, Switzerland. The United States had entered another isolationist phase.

The term "isolationist" can be misleading. It is true that Presidents Harding, Coolidge, Hoover, and Roosevelt in his first term avoided any sort of "entangling alliance" or cooperative military pact. On the other hand, no one objected to America's continuing search for world markets and economic influence. Before World War I, the main flow of investment capital ran from Europe to America. But during the war the movement of capital had reversed itself, and America had become the world's leading creditor nation. This gave it new authority in world affairs. Thus in 1924, when the European economy was on the verge of collapse because of Germany's inability to pay its reparations to France, Britain, and Italy, it was a Wall Street financier who came to the rescue. He was Charles G. Dawes, who, acting on President Coolidge's authority, worked out a scheme whereby the U.S. lent Germany over $100 million, which Germany used to make its war reparation payments to the Allies. The United States also continued to intervene in Latin American affairs. And even the most hidebound isolationists favored pacts with other nations to limit arms and discourage aggression—if those pacts would not commit them to anything they might not want to do.

Antiwar moves during the 1920s

As the machinery of World War I was dismantled, a surge of intense antimilitarism occurred. It lasted for nearly two decades. Ernest Hemingway's *The Sun Also Rises* (1926) and *A Farewell to Arms* (1929) spoke for a generation that had been deeply disillusioned by the war. These young people saw it as a tragic waste of lives, thrown away for meaningless slogans and phony ideals. Antiwar organizations were formed in colleges and universities on both sides of the Atlantic and gained strength with the passing years. The old pacifist movement, whittled down in size and radicalized by persecutions during the war, began to blame war on economics. Pacifists lamented America's refusal to join the League and supported disarmament and arbitration of international disputes.

President Harding called the Washington Conference on disarmament and Pacific affairs in 1921. To it came representatives of Great Britain, France, Italy, Belgium, Portugal, the Netherlands, China, and Japan. On the first day of the meeting chairman Charles Evans Hughes, the U.S. Secretary of State, startled the assembled dignitaries by proposing that the world naval powers scrap some of their battleships and that the Pacific nations promise to protect China's boundaries and observe the Open Door policy. Three separate treaties were signed. In accordance with the naval treaty, which established a ratio for capital ships, more than 1.8 million tons of battleships were destroyed. In the other two treaties the signers agreed to respect the status quo in the Pacific.

For the first time in modern history, the major powers had consented to disarm. The agreements avoided an arms race, which might have forced the U.S. to build and maintain a larger and more costly two-ocean navy to protect its Pacific bases. Businessmen hailed this as a sound economy. But the naval treaty applied only to battleships (many of them obsolete), not to cruisers, destroyers, or submarines. Nor did it set up a policing agency. As a result, a build-up of the naval force proceeded steadily in some nations (Japan primarily), although on a lower level.

In 1928 the U.S. and France signed the Kellogg-Briand Peace Pact (Pact of Paris), which renounced war "as an instrument of national policy." This treaty was ultimately signed by sixty-two nations. Partly the result of intensive pressure by the peace movement, the Pact was ratified by the U.S. Senate by a vote of eighty-five to one. Because the Paris Pact did not outlaw *defensive* war, critics belittled it as "a mere pompous gesture," an "international kiss." It did not define aggression or suggest machinery for avoiding war during crises. Still, it placed a moral burden on the aggressor. Some interpreted it as a step toward American membership in the World Court, an agency of the League of Nations.

The good neighbor

Dollar Diplomacy continued in Latin America until the late 1920s. Americans invested heavily in Latin American oil, tropical fruit, sugar, and minerals. The U.S., by landing

We are in the midst of all of the affairs of Europe. . . . We are sitting there dabbling . . . and intermeddling in their concerns. In other words . . . we have forfeited and surrendered, once and for all, the great policy of "no entangling alliances" upon which the strength of this Republic has been founded for 150 years.

WILLIAM E. BORAH (1865–1940)
Senator from Idaho, Senate speech, 1919

marines several times in Nicaragua, Haiti, Santo Domingo, and Cuba, punished Latin American governments that defaulted on debts or otherwise threatened American holdings. When the revolution in Mexico erupted again in 1925, Mexican President Calles demanded that foreign oil operations be curtailed in his country. Four U.S. oil firms denounced the "Bolshevik" and "anti-Catholic" tendencies of the new regime and beseeched Coolidge to send in troops. The Senate turned thumbs down on military intervention in Mexico, however, and called for arbitration. In 1927 the American ambassador, Dwight Morrow, conducted long and tedious negotiations with the Mexican government, finally winning a peaceful settlement.

President Hoover felt that, despite the Roosevelt Corollary of 1904 (see p. 408), repeated meddling in Latin America contradicted the spirit of the Monroe Doctrine and was not in the best interests of the United States. He called this new hands-off approach to Latin America the "Good Neighbor Policy." FDR followed in Hoover's footsteps. In 1933, at a Pan-American Conference, the United States denied the right of any state to intervene in the affairs of another state, and in 1934 it specifically renounced its right to intervene in Cuba, thereby abrogating the Platt Amendment (see p. 409). Roosevelt also took American troops out of Haiti. This marked the first time in many years that no U.S. forces were stationed in Latin America.

Hostility toward communism in Russia

One of the more difficult challenges to American statesmanship after 1917 was Russia. In setting up the Soviet Union, the Bolsheviks—Marxian revolutionaries under V. I. Lenin—established a regime that American leaders considered basically hostile to their political and economic system. Similar revolts seemed to threaten Spain, Germany, Hungary, China, Mexico, and—so it seemed to many Americans—the United States. When the Soviet Communists repudiated czarist debts, claimed state ownership over national resources, and threw out foreign investors, American leaders grew alarmed. Wilson saw the Bolsheviks as opposed to everything he stood for—law and order, constitutional democracy, and civil liberties.

With the less-than-candid explanation that the U.S. would not meddle in domestic Russian politics, Wilson sent troops into Russia. They landed in two places, Murmansk and Archangel in northwestern Russia, where they helped an Allied force protect huge Allied munitions stores. Near Vladivostok in Siberia the Americans helped the Japanese prevent Red soldiers from gaining complete control over the Trans-Siberian railway. The American troops fought mostly a defensive action and accomplished very little in "the frozen war." Mistrusting British and French motives in Russia, Wilson withdrew the U.S. forces in 1919.

Wilson, Harding, Coolidge, and Hoover refused to recognize the U.S.S.R. or allow

American public opinion had been initially sympathetic to the Lenin-Trotsky Bolshevik regime. But when that regime sued for a separate peace with Germany in March 1918, there was hope in America and western Europe that anti-Bolshevik Russians would be able to reinstate the "legitimate" government of the country. To this end American troops were sent to join Allied forces already in Russia. Above: U.S. troops in Vladivostok, 1919.

trade with the Soviets. Harding excluded them from the Washington Conference. Finally, in 1933, FDR recognized the Soviet government, hoping to improve American trade during the depression. A bloody political purge by Communist party chairman Joseph Stalin in the 1930s alienated many of the American liberals who had originally applauded the Russian Revolution. In a sense the Cold War between the U.S. and U.S.S.R. originated in 1917 and was only temporarily suspended between 1941 and 1945.

Maintaining U.S. isolation

During his first term FDR was as isolationist as any of his GOP predecessors. He resisted entering into agreements or any alliances that might interfere with solving the nation's domestic crisis. For this reason he helped undermine an international monetary conference in 1933 which might have stabilized world currency—at the expense of the domestic economy. He considered America's entry into the League a dead issue, although he did not oppose the world forum in principle. Improved overseas trade he saw as vital to economic recovery. With this in mind FDR lobbied actively for the Reciprocal Trade Agreements Act of 1934. Within ten years he had signed reciprocal trade pacts with twenty-nine countries, reversing the high-tariff policies of his Republican predecessors.

Through 1936 the Roosevelt administration scarcely raised an eyebrow to signs of a deteriorating world. Japan's military strength in Asia continued to grow after its attack on Manchuria in 1931. After 1933 Germany rearmed under Adolf Hitler. Britain and other sea powers built up their navies. Italy invaded Ethiopia in 1935. In open violation of the Versailles Treaty, Hitler reoccupied the Rhineland in 1936. In the same year civil war broke out in Spain (and soon Germany, Italy, and Russia took a hand in the fighting). Roosevelt detested dictatorship and saw the dangers of rearmament but felt it would be imprudent to involve the U.S., even if Congress and the public would permit such action.

The country was much impressed by Senator Gerald P. Nye's investigation (1934–1936) into the munitions industry in 1914–1917. The Senate Munitions Investigating Committee, headed by the isolationist Nye, probed for a possible alliance between the munitions industry, Wall Street banking houses, and the military. It found no criminal conspiracy, but it did expose war profiteering and suggested that the weapons industry had helped draw America into the war on the side of the Allies. To prevent recurrence, the committee proposed that the government should take over all the war-related industries.

The Nye hearings strengthened the country's antiwar mood. They fueled the argument that "the merchants of death," businessmen who profited from the miseries of war, were responsible for America's entry into World War I. Highly respected historians in the 1930s charged that the country's

involvement in the Great War had been a tragic mistake. Not only munitions makers but greedy international bankers, clever British propagandists, and pro-British sentimentalists in the Wilson administration had caused the error. It must never happen again.

So once again, as it had in the fateful years from 1914 to 1918, the U.S. tried to walk a tightrope of neutrality. But this time the situation was even more complex. Could the United States protect its freedom of the seas without running afoul of Japanese naval power? Could "the home of the free" totally ignore the oppression and aggression practiced by the fascist dictatorships? In the age of the airplane was any country safe from attack by bombers? How could the U.S. defend the Philippine Islands and the Open Door in China without new ships for the navy? But with increased naval armament, how could it avoid becoming embroiled in war? How should the U.S. treat nations which wanted to buy war matériel or to borrow money or to transport arms in American ships?

To keep the nation out of war the isolationist Congress passed three neutrality laws. The Neutrality Act of 1935 rigidly authorized the president to ban the export of arms to warring nations and to stop U.S. citizens from traveling on ships of such nations except at their own risk. The Act failed to include basic resources like oil and steel, which could be used in warfare. FDR signed it most

If there is anything in American tradition and practices to guide us, it is that a wider spread of economic calamity will culminate in a foreign war, rather than in a drastic reorganization of domestic economy.

CHARLES A. BEARD (1874–1948)
American historian, writing in 1935

reluctantly. The 1936 Neutrality Act widened the coverage to include loans and credits to belligerent nations. A year later FDR got Congress to pass a neutrality law applying not only to wars between nations but to civil wars as well. It covered other basic resources of war in addition to arms and loans, and it made travel on belligerent ships by Americans unlawful. Although this last law, the Neutrality Act of 1937, gave the president more options in carrying out its provisions, in practice it was just as ineffective as the first two. Technically all buyers of war goods were equal in the eyes of the law. However, the neutrality acts on the whole favored the wealthier and stronger buyers—Japan rather than China, Italy over Ethiopia, and the Spanish fascists over the Spanish republicans. These acts were not a permanent solution to anything.

Shifting toward intervention

When Japanese forces invaded China in 1937, Roosevelt began to turn from isolation to intervention. During Japan's take-over in Manchuria in 1931, the U.S. had done little more than express outrage. But this time the Japanese seized Peking, bombed Shanghai, and sacked Nanking. In a memorable address FDR urged the world to "quarantine" aggressors, a clear call for collective security. The speech aroused the isolationist senators, who raised a new hue and cry against foreign entanglements. Nevertheless, the internationalist in Roosevelt came more and more to the fore. He backed naval rearmament and authorized the sale of some $86 million in munitions to China, a belated—and futile—attempt to preserve the Open Door in Asia. For the next four years, while the U.S. and the Axis powers moved on a collision course, isolationists and internationalists were locked in a great debate over foreign affairs.

Germany, Japan, and Italy formed the Axis partnership in 1936 as a "bulwark against Communism" and proceeded to flex their muscles. Hitler and Mussolini helped General Francisco Franco overthrow the leftist government of the Spanish Republic. The Soviet Union supported the Spanish Loyalists. Meanwhile black-shirted storm troopers abused German Jews, who were made the scapegoats for Germany's ills since 1918.

At the Munich Conference of 1938 British Prime Minister Neville Chamberlain and French Premier Édouard Daladier agreed to let Hitler take part of Czechoslovakia if he promised to end his aggression. Hitler had already rearmed Germany, reoccupied the Ruhr, and invaded Austria. He now proceeded to dismember Czechoslovakia. Munich whetted his appetite for still further aggression.

Some Americans admired the European dictators. Hadn't Mussolini made the trains run on time? Wasn't Franco defending the church against anarchy and atheism? Who could resist Communist Russia better than Adolf Hitler? Even if they hated democracy, the dictators would certainly never challenge the United States. But if Britain and France pitted their feeble forces against the Axis war machine, they were doomed. Prominent Americans (like Charles Lindbergh) who thought along these lines formed the "America First Committee" to insure the country's isolation and nonintervention. On the other hand, liberals who had formerly backed isolation were beginning to think that American intervention might be necessary to stop the march of aggression.

When Hitler's troops crashed into Poland in September 1939, Britain and France declared war on Germany. World War II had begun. A nonaggression pact between Germany and the Soviet Union had made Hitler's attack possible. In the following year Nazi armies used blitzkrieg ("lightning war") tactics to conquer Norway, Denmark, the Netherlands, Belgium, and

France. Meanwhile, German planes bombed Britain in preparation for invasion. Technically, the U.S. remained neutral through these events, but Roosevelt and an ever growing number of Americans were clearly rooting for Britain and France and against the Axis.

In the climax of the great debate over foreign policy, the crucial turning point from isolation to collective security was the Lend-Lease Act of 1941. This law was prompted by Prime Minister Winston Churchill's alarming report that Britain was running out of both cash and credit. At FDR's insistence, Congress voted to make munitions and supplies available to European nations fighting Hitler.

At that point the country was traveling a far more dangerous path than it had a few years earlier. Neutrality acts had given way to the Lend-Lease policy. That policy helped save Britain, and later Russia, but an accompanying increase in naval aid cost American lives. In October 1941 a German submarine torpedoed the American destroyer *Reuben James,* killing over a hundred seamen.

> *We are now in this war. We are all in it — all the way.*
> *Every single man, woman, and child is a partner*
> *in the most tremendous undertaking of our American history.*
>
> FRANKLIN DELANO ROOSEVELT   (1882–1945)

World War II

Pearl Harbor

War came to the U.S. unexpectedly. On the morning of December 7, 1941, Japanese planes streaked out of the sky to bomb and strafe the U.S. naval base at Pearl Harbor in Hawaii. This carefully planned attack killed more than two thousand U.S. servicemen and sank or disabled nineteen ships. It dealt a terrible blow both to the nation's naval power and to its pride. Congress declared war on Japan one day later, and Germany and Italy then declared war on the United States.

Although America had fumed and fussed since 1931 over Japan's aggressions in Asia, it had not attempted to join with other nations in slowing down Japan's activities. It had also refused to mediate Japan's differences with other nations. Japan's full-scale war against China had slowly but surely closed the Open Door to commerce. The U.S. retaliated by imposing modest restrictions (some of which were voluntary on the part of American business firms) on the sale of airplanes and aviation gasoline, scrap metals, and machine tools to Japan. Japan, however, not only refused to get out of China, as the U.S. demanded, but in 1941 its soldiers occupied French Indochina and were poised for a leap at the British Empire. The U.S. froze Japanese assets in this country. It also joined in an embargo to end all oil shipments to Japan. This posed a serious threat to Japanese industry and spurred Japan on to seize new oil fields in the western Pacific. It also strengthened the power of the military in Japan, and when the U.S. continued to call for their withdrawal from both China and Indochina, the Japanese proceeded with plans for conquest.

In spite of the fact that U.S. intelligence

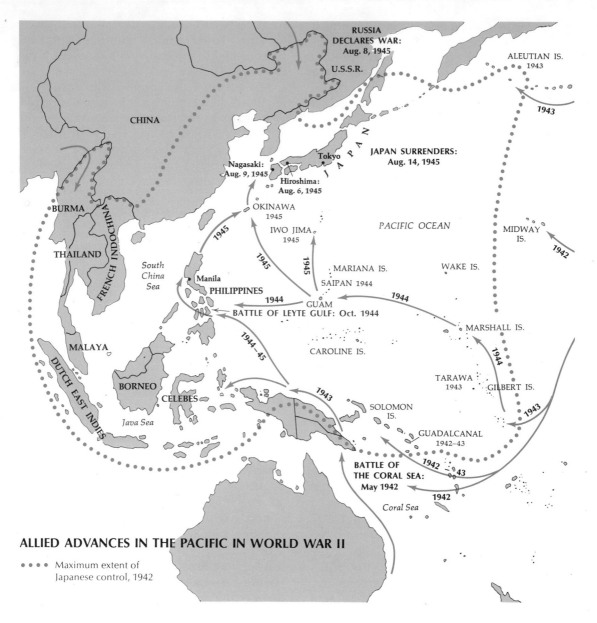

ALLIED ADVANCES IN THE PACIFIC IN WORLD WAR II

● ● ● ● Maximum extent of
Japanese control, 1942

had broken the Japanese military code, it was unable to piece together the exact contents of the Japanese war plan. Japanese planes were airborne over the northern Pacific while the special Japanese envoys were still negotiating in Washington. Later, FDR's enemies blamed him for provoking the attack on Pearl Harbor, much as Lincoln was blamed for provoking the attack on Fort Sumter. Critics claimed that the president deliberately pushed Japan too far and took inadequate precautions because he secretly hoped for an excuse to enter the war against the Axis and for an incident that would rally public support behind the move. This portrait of Roosevelt as a monster who invited the destruc-

ALLIED ADVANCES IN EUROPE
IN WORLD WAR II

●●●● Maximum extent of
Axis control, 1942

UNITED
KINGDOM

Leningrad

Moscow

•Hamburg
GERMANY
Berlin

Warsaw

USSR

Stalingrad

D-DAY:
June 6, 1944
Brest

GERMANY SURRENDERS:
May 7, 1945

Paris•

FRANCE

Neutral

Vienna•
Budapest

ITALY

Rome

Naples•

GREECE

ALLIED INVASION OF
NORTH AFRICA: Nov. 8, 1942

Algiers

Oran

Casablanca

Bizerte

SICILY

INVASION
OF ITALY:
Sept. 3, 1943

MOROCCO

INVASION
OF SICILY:
July 10, 1943

TUNISIA

Tripoli

ALGERIA

El Alamein

BRITISH DRIVE:
Oct. 1942

LIBYA

EGYPT

tion of America's Pacific fleet merits little
consideration. His policies may have provoked Japan. But the Japanese attack on
Pearl Harbor succeeded because of that
country's incredible daring and strategic
brilliance. As a gamble it was a smashing
success — with ultimately horrifying consequences for the gamblers.

Allied war objectives

The U.S., "the arsenal of democracy," was
the major power among the Allied nations.
Britain, already badly battered and with its
global empire crumbling, was America's
closest partner. Russia, distrusted in the
West for its Communist ideology, became

the third big power in the alliance after Germany turned on the Soviet Union. For the war effort to succeed, cooperation among these three was essential. In August 1941, before Pearl Harbor brought the U.S. into the war, FDR and Britain's Prime Minister Winston Churchill met secretly on a warship off the coast of Newfoundland to discuss America's increased involvement. They issued a joint communique, known as the Atlantic Charter, which stated their postwar objectives. "Freedom from fear and want" would be the goal of all peoples after the "final destruction of the Nazi tyranny." They agreed that, as victors, they would not seek any new territory but respect the right of self-determination of all nations. Equal access to raw materials and freedom of the seas must also be available to all. Aggressor nations would meanwhile be disarmed. The charter also alluded vaguely to a league of nations. Later, as the Declaration of the United Nations, the document was approved by twenty-four other countries, including the Soviet Union, and was regarded as a major statement of war aims.

Achieving victory

Until 1942 the Axis powers made stunning progress against the Allies. In Europe Hitler's forces conquered France in 1940 and then, in 1941, invaded Russia despite a non-aggression pact between the Nazis and the Soviets. Italy had already joined forces with Germany. Now Russia joined the Allies as Nazi armies advanced on Moscow. In North Africa, German tanks drove into Egypt and threatened the Suez Canal. Only Germany's air war against Britain, which was supposed to precede an invasion, failed dismally. In the Pacific, Japan's navy ruled as far east as

On June 6, 1944, the proper combination of tide, weather, and moonlight made possible the successful launching of the greatest amphibious assault in history. The Allied force of five thousand ships, ten thousand aircraft, and 4 million assault and supporting troops mounted the massive D-Day invasion of a sixty-mile beach area on the north coast of Normandy. But some of the landings ran into difficulties. The premature discharge of troops in three to five feet of water led to heavy casualties (far left), and the Germans raked the beach with destructive fire. One third of the initial tanks were lost by launching them hopelessly far out at sea, but once the Nazis had been routed from trenches cut in the hillside (foreground, near left), landing of supplies and reinforcements went smoothly.

mans at Stalingrad and started the slow push toward Berlin.

The long-awaited second front in Europe came on June 6, 1944, when over 175,000 Allied assault troops, under the command of General Dwight D. Eisenhower, landed on the shores of Normandy in France in the greatest amphibious operation of all time. Germany's last violent effort to turn the tide came in December 1944 in the Battle of the Bulge in Belgium. Despite this costly setback, both the Western Allies and the Russians were rapidly closing in on the German heartland by March 1945.

Shaping the postwar world

The most crucial diplomatic meeting since Versailles was held at Yalta, a spa in the Russian Crimea, in February 1945. It was here that the map of the postwar world took shape. Roosevelt, Churchill, and Stalin agreed that Germany was to be divided into four occupation zones and pay heavy reparations for war damage, especially to Russia. (A working figure of $20 billion was mentioned.) Russia gained Polish territory, and Poland received parts of Germany, with final boundaries to be established at a future conference. In exchange for agreeing to join

Wake Island. Its armies captured the Philippines and the East Indies and ranged across Southeast Asia to the Indian border.

Toward the end of 1942 the Allies began a rollback on several fronts which continued almost without letup for two years. Earlier, the naval battles of the Coral Sea and Midway so damaged the Japanese fleet that Australia was no longer in serious danger. In the spring of 1943 German forces in North Africa were crushed between Allied armies advancing from west and east. The western Allies then crossed the Mediterranean and invaded Italy. In the most decisive land battle of the war, the Russians repulsed the Ger-

The last meeting of the "Big Three" Allied leaders—Churchill, Roosevelt, and Stalin—took place at Yalta, the summer palace of Czar Nicholas II in the Russian Crimea, an area that had only recently been liberated from the Nazis. Roosevelt and Churchill came to the conference firmly convinced that Russian cooperation was essential for the future success of the United Nations. The Yalta agreement was signed on February 11, 1945.

the war against Japan after the defeat of Germany, an important consideration in early 1945, the Russians were to regain the territory they had lost in the Russo-Japanese War of 1904–1905. This included parts of Sakhalin Island along with important concessions in the Chinese province of Manchuria. Russia was also to receive the Kurile Islands, which it had never before owned. In Poland and Yugoslavia the Russians promised to establish coalition governments that would include at least some non-Communists. Aside from the Far East-

ern settlements, the Yalta agreement left most major questions deliberately vague, a sign of growing tensions between the victors. Nevertheless, they did agree to the formation of a permanent United Nations organization. Russia accepted the voting procedure demanded by the United States— granting a veto to the big powers—which would avoid the stumbling block that had prevented the U.S. Senate from accepting the League of Nations.

Two months later, in April 1945, Roosevelt was dead of cerebral hemorrhage. Not long after that, critics began to charge him with having "sold out to Stalin." Some alleged that declining health had dulled his mind, others that he had been naive to accept "Uncle Joe" Stalin's promise to permit free elections in eastern Europe. But the more extreme came to see another sinister conspiracy afoot: always "soft on communism," FDR had probably given Manchuria to Russia with the knowledge that it would wind up in the hands of the Red Chinese. In the 1950s Senator Joseph McCarthy of Wisconsin would charge that Yalta was a second Munich and a prime example of the Democrats' "twenty years of treason."

Roosevelt's defenders replied that his mental powers never flagged during the Conference, that at the time winning a Russian commitment to help finish the war in the Pacific had seemed extremely important, and that—given the fact that Russian forces were in full control of eastern Europe—there was not much the U.S. could do but accept Stalin's promises of good intentions in that area.

In June 1945, four months after Yalta and seven weeks after the surrender of Germany, representatives of fifty Allied nations met in San Francisco to sign the United Nations charter. Since veto power in the Security Council guaranteed the U.S. freedom of action, the Senate approved the charter by a vote of eighty-nine to two, after only six days of debate. By acting as host nation, America dramatized its support of the new organization. Japan had not yet surrendered, but the future looked bright.

Despite the accord displayed at the UN meeting, suspicions were increasing on all sides between Russia, the United States, and Britain. A final wartime summit meeting took place at Potsdam, Germany, in July 1945. It involved a settlement for Germany (then occupied by all of the major Allies) and also a settlement for Rumania, Bulgaria, and Hungary (completely occupied by the Soviets). The look of the Big Three had changed. FDR had been replaced by Truman, while Churchill's seat was taken by the newly elected British prime minister, Clement Attlee. Truman resented the Soviets' stubborn insistence that Russia have an exclusive sphere of influence in eastern Europe. Stalin, for his part, was angered by Truman's efforts to achieve American influence in eastern European settlements, nor did he appreciate Britain's and America's refusal to permit Russia to acquire desperately needed reparations from Germany. The Soviet Union ended up getting German capital goods, but no cash reparations with which to repair its badly battered nation. In a year or two the mutual suspicions already apparent in Potsdam would be described as "the Cold War."

Gearing up the war machine

Knowing about the strong antiwar sentiment of the 1960s and 1970s, today's students may find it hard to understand why Americans backed the war effort so strongly in the 1940s. For many, victory for the Nazi regime meant the destruction of everything they believed in—democracy, freedom, and human decency. The thought of living in a world dominated by such power was too terrible to bear. For others, Pearl Harbor and the death of two thousand Americans on American soil made the difference. The "day of infamy" washed away all doubts. With few exceptions, Roosevelt's political enemies put aside their criticisms of him as the country rallied behind its elected leader. No event in U.S. history was more unifying than the attack on Pearl Harbor. For most Americans, the sense of national purpose lasted until 1945.

The war mobilization plan was an updated and streamlined version of the one used during World War I. One task was to assemble a fighting force. In 1940 there were only 500,000 men in service. With the country still opposed to peacetime conscription, an extension of the draft act cleared Congress three months before Pearl Harbor with only one vote to spare. After the Japanese attack young men jammed the recruitment centers to enlist, although in time voluntary enlistments were suspended in favor of conscription. By 1945, 15 million Americans had served on active military duty.

The other main task of war mobilization was to coordinate production activities. A special agency, the War Production Board (WPB) was given tremendous authority in 1942 and 1943 to direct the home front effort. It put into operation plans left over from the last war and modified more recently by military and industrial planners. Donald Nelson headed the WPB for much of the time. The major policymakers in war production were the biggest war contractors. As in World War I antitrust laws were suspended for the duration.

Separate agencies under WPB (and its successor, the Office of War Mobilization) came into being to deal with a host of specific functions. These included labor control and civilian defense, rationing and price control, fair employment practices and housing, scientific research and the care of alien property, transportation and shipping, rubber, petroleum, and fuel production, war information and censorship. For each function there was a government agency. The new wartime agencies multiplied the size of the Washington bureaucracy far beyond what it had been under the New Deal. While organized along New Deal lines, they were often staffed by conservatives. Inbound trains to Washington brought a host of new faces, many of them Republicans and business leaders previously hostile to FDR's administration. Some were dollar-a-year men (wealthy people who served for little pay). Many of the old New Dealers remained in Washington redirecting themselves to the war effort.

No other administration, not Wilson's during World War I nor Roosevelt's during the New Deal, had ever taken such an active role in the economy. Private businesses were not nationalized. But through centralized planning, allocating resources and capital, and government purchasing, the economy moved toward regimentation. The WPB and its subordinate agencies set all priorities for production and allocated all raw materials to factories. Tax money was spent to build new factories, which were then leased to private firms. The government bought over half of all the goods produced. Because Washington assigned contracts on a "cost plus" basis, not on competitive bids, employers tended to hire more workers and requisition more supplies than they needed. This system was wasteful—but it worked.

The administration fixed prices on practically all commodities. It also rationed gasoline, tires, sugar, meat, and numerous other scarce goods. Rent was controlled in communities with crowded housing. In short, the government's authority in the marketplace was all but supreme for the duration.

The Second World War ended serious unemployment. By 1940 the relief lines, so common in the previous decade, began to disappear. Within a year or two every ablebodied civilian, including farmers, scientists, and both skilled and unskilled workers, found a job. Washington officials controlled wages and even "froze" labor in certain occupations. It did not prohibit strikes, but during the coal walkout of 1943 Congress gave the president stern powers to deal with wartime labor disputes.

Former foes of federal spending fell silent after Pearl Harbor. In 1944 alone the government spent $100 billion without arousing more than a murmur of dissent. By the end of the war the national debt exceeded $250 billion. The increase of productivity (the Gross National Product rose from $91 billion to $166 billion in four years) made it all seem worthwhile. Price control and taxes helped hold the line against inflation. At Roosevelt's

The unemployment that had not yet been eliminated during the depression by one New Deal agency or another disappeared entirely as the nation mobilized for war. Defense plants frequently hired women to fill labor shortages on the assembly line as well as in the office. Rosie-the-Riveter was a familiar sight until the war's end, when returning veterans forced her to return to domestic tasks.

insistence the war was mostly financed by taxes.

American factories turned out planes, ships, and guns in unbelievable quantities. The defense industries also produced mountainous confusion and waste. But in the end the war effort was a great triumph of American industry. The U.S. put to use its great talent and experience with mass production, making good on its promise to become "the arsenal of democracy."

Getting the job done

For most civilians wartime regimentation was relatively painless. Jobs were plentiful, wages were high. The disagreeable aspects of the civilian war effort seemed minor compared to what soldiers at the front were experiencing. To sacrifice some luxuries for the duration—"to use it up, wear it out, make it do, or do without"—became a way of life. Civilians accepted price control and rationing with minor grumbling. Hanging blackout curtains and taking part in air raid drills were petty discomforts compared to those

endured by civilians in other countries. Except for some random shells fired from Japanese submarines at the coast of southern California in 1942, and some incendiary balloons which started forest fires in the Pacific Northwest, mainland America was spared the ravages of war.

The wartime regimentation was in some respects less extreme than in 1917 and 1918. There was less vigilante action against pacifists and dissenters and fewer trials for sedition and treason. On the other hand, there was considerable mind-bending official propaganda. In addition, 1500 conscientious objectors were jailed (a greater number than in World War I) because draft boards defined pacifism narrowly. And 110,000 persons of Japanese ancestry, most of them U.S. citizens, were forced into "relocation centers" for the duration (see pp. 608–609).

Late in the war the government hinted darkly of a plan to draft civilians for war work. It never materialized, but as military historian Walter Millis has written, the modern centralized state had developed an "almost unbelievable power . . . to drain the whole physical, intellectual, economic, emotional and moral resources of its citizens to the single end of military victory."

What was fighting all about? In the First World War the war aims were idealistic and were clearly set forth in the Fourteen Points. There were ideals now as well. Roosevelt enumerated them in his Four Freedoms speech of January 6, 1941: freedom of speech, freedom of religion, freedom from want, and freedom from fear. These were repeated often during the war years. But the president was aware of the disillusionment created by Wilsonian idealism, and he gave even more play to the practical goal of defeating the enemy as quickly as possible. The country's major objective after December 7, 1941, was to destroy the Axis so that people could go back to their normal lives.

The poet Archibald MacLeish observed that in World War II many soldiers were willing to die "who are nevertheless unable to understand clearly, or to imagine precisely, what our victory in this war will be." Civilians and soldiers seemed grimly sober rather than intensely idealistic. The state of mind of the American GI was personified by Bill Mauldin's cartoon characters Joe and Willie, two bone-weary, stubble-faced soldiers who, totally lacking in military élan, were willing to finish the job, however miserable.

Birth of the atomic age

Adolf Hitler committed suicide on April 30, 1945, in his bunker in Berlin. The Nazi Reich that he hoped would last one thousand years surrendered on May 7. Japan refused to surrender. From all reports, and from the evidence of the costly progress of America's island-by-island advance, the Japanese military government was prepared for a suicidal last-ditch defense of the homeland. Then, on the morning of August 6, 1945, a lone U.S. bomber flew over Hiroshima and dropped a single atomic bomb. It inflicted 180,000 cas-

ualties. Days later a second bomb vaporized the city of Nagasaki. The government of imperial Japan surrendered on August 14.

During the war only a few Americans had questioned the morality of obliteration bombings. Prior to Hiroshima and Nagasaki, Allied planes had inflicted terrible casualties by fire bombing Tokyo in Japan and Dresden in German and many other civilian centers in both Nazi Europe and Japan. A few American dissenters asked why so many innocent noncombatants had to die along with soldiers. The official response was that the incineration bombing of civilian targets was essential to the victory over bestial and desperate foes.

The dropping of the atom bomb came after an intense, secret debate among scientists, politicians, and military leaders. A few of the nuclear scientists who developed the weapon urged that its awesome power be demonstrated on an empty Japanese island, not on densely populated cities. Otherwise, they argued, the United States would be establishing a precedent that could mean its own devastation when other nations developed nuclear weapons. As the country that first produced the bomb, the U.S. should be most careful to use it in a humane way in order to insure its moral leadership in the postwar world. The military, however, feared that demonstration explosions might fail, that the only two existing bombs might be duds. President Truman believed that the use of the bomb was justified. "We have used it [the atom bomb] in order to shorten the agony of the war," he explained at the time, "in order to save the lives of thousands and thousands of young Americans." Truman was later accused of playing atomic politics. Critics charged that he had dropped the bomb mostly to end the fighting before Russia could declare war on Japan and muscle in on the Asian peace settlement. (The Soviet Union declared war after the bombing of Hiroshima.) He never replied to these

Albert Einstein (1879-1955)

$E = MC^2$

In 1905 a Bavarian-born patent office clerk published the first of a series of articles on the interrelationship between time, space, and matter. The twenty-six-year-old's Theory of Relativity demonstrated, among other things, the theoretical possibility of atomic energy. His work quickly turned the scientific world upside down and gained him enormous fame.

Albert Einstein's early hatred of militarism and war had led to his belief in pacifism. He openly opposed Germany's role in World War I and was saved from persecution only because he had become one of that nation's most famous citizens.

After World War I the scientist became an international celebrity. His strong social conscience made him speak out against the injustices he saw around him. A Jew, a pacifist, a democrat, and an activist, he became a target for the growing Nazi movement in Germany. His works were burned, his classroom attacked, and his life increasingly endangered. In November 1933, he fled Germany with his family and was offered asylum in many countries. The Institute of Advanced Studies at Princeton, New Jersey, had a long-standing invitation to Einstein to join its staff. He accepted, and upon his arrival undoubtedly became one of the most famous immigrants ever to seek refuge in America.

Einstein became an immediate favorite of the students. His humor, availability, and modesty eased some of the awe they felt for the great man. They grew used to seeing him stroll on campus, with his long unruly hair and old sweaters, unencumbered by socks, suspenders, collars, or ties.

Shortly after settling at Princeton, Einstein renounced pacifism, stating, "As long as fascism rules in Europe, there will be no peace." In 1939, when he learned that Nazi Germany was conducting experiments in nuclear fission, he sent a letter to President Franklin Delano Roosevelt. Along with subsequent messages from Einstein, this letter helped lay the groundwork for government backing of the Manhattan Project that produced the atomic bomb.

Einstein, who had become a U.S. citizen in 1940, fully supported his new land's entry into World War II. But he was opposed to dropping the atom bomb on a city, and was deeply saddened by the destructive raids on Hiroshima and Nagasaki. Even before the war ended, he predicted a postwar arms race and urged "an internationalization of military power." In his last years he stated his belief in the need for a world government and international security force.

It was perhaps one of the great ironies that the genius of this gentle, quiet man led directly to the manufacture of the atomic bomb. Yet he himself may have summed up the situation best: "The discovery of nuclear chain reaction need not bring about the destruction of mankind any more than did the discovery of matches. . . . To have security against atomic bombs . . . we have to prevent war."

After the bomb fell, one of the first American observers to enter the city commented: "There's no doubt when you look at it that Hiroshima is the greatest man-made disaster in the history of the world. You can stand at its center and for four square miles around there is nothing left but total destruction. The only things left standing are a few concrete-reinforced buildings, with their insides charred and ruined, an occasional bare chimney, and trees with every limb and every leaf torn off." The human toll: more than 135,000 killed or injured.

charges and never doubted the correctness of his decision. The atomic bombs had, in fact, led swiftly to Japan's surrender.

The Allied nations had triumphed over tyranny, but the cost in human lives had been staggering. The exact number of civilian and military deaths from all countries, Allied and Axis, has been estimated at anywhere between 35 to 60 million. The figure included 6 million Jews who were deliberately and brutally exterminated by the Nazis. An additional 6 million political prisoners

and POWs may also have died in concentration camps of starvation, disease, and ill treatment. Twelve to 15 million Russians died in the war. Poland lost more than one fifth of its population, the highest percentage of dead in any one country. For its part, the U.S. lost 290,000 in combat. The total number of the world's wounded and homeless was, of course, many times greater than its dead. But in spite of everything, the war was over. The peoples of the world entered the atomic age with a mixture of hope and anxiety.

Review

Woodrow Wilson was bitterly disappointed when, after months of debate, the U.S. Senate refused to accept the League of Nations.

With antiwar sentiment strong, the country entered an isolationist period. But isolation did not end America's overseas credit and investments nor its Dollar Diplomacy in Latin America. Herbert Hoover disapproved of Dollar Diplomacy and introduced the "Good Neighbor Policy." FDR later followed his example. Russia posed a knottier diplomatic problem. Fearing Bolshevik expansion, the U.S. joined other Allied forces in an unsuccessful invasion attempt to oust the Russian Communists. The U.S. did not recognize the Soviets until 1933. Roosevelt continued the U.S. isolation policy in his first term even as he pushed for foreign trade agreements. His administration made no attempt to involve itself in the threatening world events of 1936. The Nye hearings solidified America's anti-war attitudes.

In 1937 FDR began to shift from a position of isolation. For four years the nation moved closer to direct conflict with Germany and Japan as the Axis powers became more aggressive. World War II broke out in 1939 when Nazi troops invaded Poland, and Britain and France declared war on Germany. In his 1940 election Roosevelt promised to keep the country out of war even as the Lend-Lease Act of a year later turned the nation from isolation. The Act helped save Britain, and later Russia, but provoked German attacks on U.S. seamen.

On December 7, 1941, Japan attacked Pearl Harbor and the U.S. was at war. It was the most powerful ally in the struggle against the Axis powers. FDR and Churchill had already met and hammered out the Atlantic Charter. Toward the end of 1942 the Allies began to block the enormous advances made by the Axis powers. U.S. and British forces defeated the Italians and Germans in Africa and, after Stalingrad, the Russians began an advance on Berlin. The second front opened in June 1944, and in 1945 the Allies closed in on Germany. Yalta became the most controversial and crucial Allied conference. Growing tensions between the powers left many postwar issues vague. In June 1945, representatives from fifty nations met to draw up the United Nations charter. The Senate approved U.S. membership.

Pearl Harbor unified the nation behind the war effort. The WPB was granted wide authority over the home front war effort. Wartime agencies supplanted New Deal agencies. The bureaucracy mushroomed further as the government regimented the economy to aid the war effort. Unemployment ended and war production was high. The worst abridgments of civil liberties were suffered by Japanese Americans. Civilian life, spared the destruction suffered by so many countries, was relatively painless and most citizens shunned luxuries and accepted rationing.

Germany conceded defeat on May 7, 1945. In August the U.S. dropped an atomic bomb first on Hiroshima and then on Nagasaki, after secret high-level debates on whether to bomb a densely populated area. Japan surrendered officially on September 9. The war had ended but the cost in lives and suffering and destruction was almost beyond belief. An exhausted world entered the atomic age.

Questions

1. Why did the U.S. Senate reject the League of Nations but agree to membership in the United Nations?
2. Describe the efforts of the U.S. to isolate itself after World War I.
3. Identify and define: (a) Versailles Treaty, (b) 1921 Washington Conference on disarmament, (c) Good Neighbor Policy, (d) Munich, (e) Lend-Lease, (f) Neutrality Act, and (g) the Big Three.
4. What was the significance of the Atlantic Charter and the meetings at Yalta and Potsdam?
5. How did the home front change as New Deal agencies gave way to wartime mobilization?

Japanese Americans awaiting relocation; Hayward, California, 1942. Photo by Dorothea Lange.

Whenever and wherever the constitutional guarantees are violated in the treatment of a minority . . . the whole fabric of American government is weakened. . . . The test of America is the security of its minority groups.

RAY LYMAN WILBUR   (1875–1945)
Chancellor, Stanford University

28

28

The Ugly Abyss

When the archaeologist Henry Fairfield Osborn wrote in 1926 that "racial discrimination is inherent in biological fact and human nature," many intellectuals agreed with him. Racism had strong backing in the scientific community. Scientists frequently argued for tighter laws to limit immigration and to prevent marriage between people of different races. Yet by then "scientific racism" had been challenged from within the academic world and was beginning to lose ground.

The first important rebuttal to scientific racism came from anthropologist Franz Boas, a German immigrant to the United States. In an epochal work, *The Mind of Primitive Man* (1911), Boas rejected the theory that linked intelligence with race. After studying people of different racial and ethnic backgrounds, he concluded that there was no connection between physical traits like skin color on the one hand and mental capacity or creativity on the other. It followed then that no race was biologically superior or inferior.

Others soon agreed with Boas. Psychologist Otto Klineberg, examining the results of intelligence testing done in World War I, showed that while whites generally had higher IQs than blacks, the average IQ of blacks from four northern urban states exceeded that of whites from four southern rural states. If that was the case, then intelligence might be explained by poor schooling and other social lacks. In effect, newer studies were reviving the eighteenth-century scientific belief that the main differences among people were environmental, not hereditary.

By the Second World War racial theory had changed enormously. The drastic reduction of immigration relieved nativists of the fear of race suicide. More important, Hitler's "master race" theories and his efforts to exterminate the Jews caused a violent revulsion against racist doctrines. By the 1940s most scientists had concluded from existing evidence that racism was not a valid scientific doctrine but a dangerous myth. When America joined the fight against Hitler, racial discrimination at home seemed all the more unjust. Optimists predicted a dramatic improvement for nonwhites in the future. A widely praised study of blacks, Gunnar Myrdal's *An American Dilemma* (1944), suggested that after World War II racism would rapidly diminish.

Return of the "Vanishing" Redman

The calamities of the Dawes Act

A generation after the Wounded Knee massacre in 1890 Indians were still fighting for survival. In the 1920s, the death rate for Indians still exceeded the birthrate. The prospects looked so grim that in 1911 Franz Boas, using the past tense, declared that the Indians had "vanished comparatively rapidly." The Indians survived because of their own will, as well as new public policies. By the 1940s trained observers were hailing the return of the "vanishing" Indian.

The Dawes Severalty Act of 1887 (see p. 428) had proved a disaster for native Americans. The law provided for individual Indians and families to receive land allotments and citizenship rights. Also, huge chunks of reservation land were sold to whites, reducing the overall Indian holdings from 138 million acres to 48 million. The allotment and sale of reservation land effectively destroyed many reservations, and this too satisfied the intent of the law. Through the normal process of inheritance, allotments to individual Indians were sliced up into smaller and smaller pieces until many were too small to support individual owners. By the 1920s, great-grandfather's allotment of 160 acres, distributed to twenty or thirty descendants, could be a checkerboard of tiny parcels, worthless for farming or any other economic use. Coal operators, railroad developers, cattle ranchers, timbermen, and farmers leased the allotted Indian land through the Bureau of Indian Affairs, usually for a nominal payment. These whites got far more use from Indian properties than did Indians, who sometimes received less than a dollar a year for the household. The BIA grew in size and became increasingly bogged down in bookkeeping and paper work as the reservations deteriorated.

The Dawes Act turned few Indians into Christian farmers, as it had been intended to do. Instead it deprived many of a sense of personal worth that could best be achieved by retaining their tribal identity. It also contributed to chronic poverty and ill health. Field studies indicated that, among Americans, reservation Indians suffered the most from communicable diseases, illiteracy, infant mortality and malnutrition. Those who left the reservation usually had trouble finding jobs. Typically they hired on as circus roustabouts, Wild West show performers, or day laborers on construction gangs. As a group the most successful Indians in the regular work force were the Iroquois, who specialized in skyscraper construction work. When work was scarce, many Indians returned to the reservation—a familiar, if bleak, environment. Despair was widespread and often took the form of alcoholism. Still, the 1930 census counted 332,000 Indians in the country, a significant increase from 244,000 in 1920.

The government made some reforms. The BIA was reorganized, schools were upgraded, and better medical services were offered

An Apache family poses in front of their home near Coolidge Dam, Arizona. The harsh, squalid conditions of reservation life were rarely seen by tourists; glowing accounts of "nature's fortunate children" were based on an hour's entertainment when Indians, dressed in traditional clothes, would reenact traditional ceremonial dances.

on the reservations. President Hoover, however, supported the idea that the reservations should be shut down within twenty-five years and the Indians completely integrated into American life.

A New Deal for Indians

In the 1920s a reform group known as the Indian Defense Association (IDA) sought a new approach for the reservation Indians. They influenced Hoover's Commissioner of Indian Affairs but he could not influence

Congress. The IDA had far better success when its secretary, John Collier, was appointed to the post of Commissioner of Indian Affairs by FDR. Collier had an unusual background as a social worker, teacher, and life-long student of Indian culture. He helped draft the Indian Reorganization Act of 1934, which is sometimes known as the Collier Act. It had four basic goals for those tribes that wished to participate. First, it aimed to end allotment and, where possible, to buy back allotted land for tribal use. This would enlarge some reservations to more productive size. Second, the Act encouraged Indian self-government by making the tribes into corporations and economic cooperatives. Training Indian civil servants and hiring them into the BIA was a third goal. The final goal was to make long-term, low-interest loans for basic development of the reservations.

Under the Indian Reorganization Act the government spent about $70 million for Indian reform in three years. The New Deal also sponsored ecological research, reclamation, and irrigation in Indian country. Numerous reservation roads, bridges, hospitals, and community facilities were constructed. Indian crafts were revived. Schooling improved.

The "Indian New Deal" had its limitations, though, in that the Reorganization Law did not include the Five Civilized Tribes of Oklahoma, and the Navajo Indians refused to participate in the reforms. Disputes between the BIA and Indian tribal organizations went on endlessly, and a great many participating tribes remained on land that was next to worthless.

Effects of the Second World War

For Indians, World War II was a time of confusion, hope, and rapid change. Ongoing efforts to rebuild the reservations came to a halt, while roads, clinics, and schools once again deteriorated. But fifty thousand Indians entered defense work and greatly increased their incomes. They also got railroad and factory jobs, work that had previously been denied them. The Navajos, for example—most of whom scratched out livings as sheepherders—suddenly found themselves drawing factory wages.

Some 25,000 Indians served in the armed forces. Many, especially those from tribes with a strong warrior tradition, volunteered. The Indian GI was admired as a combat soldier. As a Sioux newspaper put it, the Indian soldier "still feels like an Indian, [but] he is the envy of all the others who want to, but cannot be, Indians." Four hundred Navajos from reservations in New Mexico, Arizona, and Utah were recruited into the marines as radiomen. Codes based on the Navajo language were among the few never broken by the enemy. Marine Ira Hayes, a Pima Indian who in 1945 helped plant the Stars and Stripes atop Mount Surabachi on the Japanese stronghold of Iwo Jima, was the most famous Indian GI of World War II.

Athough no one could prophesy what opportunities would be available to Indians in peacetime, in the 1940s it was apparent that the Indian was no longer vanishing. While some Indian tribes had perished altogether, others, like the Pueblo, had survived poverty, famine, and disease by nurturing their religion and tribal customs.

Blacks: From Plantation to Ghetto

Moving north

After three hundred years on southern plantations, many American blacks packed their few belongings and began moving off the land. Some went to southern cities. Most headed north. The great migration from south to north, which numbered half a million during the First World War, continued after as well. The blacks were trying to escape the poverty of sharecropping, the ravages of the boll weevil, and the humiliations of Jim

Crow. Northern factory jobs looked promising and gave them a feeling of hope. Blacks sought the same American Dream as did other groups: decent jobs, better homes, and an education for their children.

Blacks arriving in the northern cities gravitated to friends and relatives in the ghettos. Even though the Supreme Court had declared in 1917 that cities could not formally segregate neighborhoods, the practice continued. City governments and private landlords tried to enforce racial and ethnic boundaries with the help of restrictive covenants, which until the 1950s permitted property owners to refuse to sell to certain groups, especially to blacks. There seemed to be no escaping Jim Crow. Blacks had to send their children to segregated schools, drink in segregated bars, and keep out of many public places. The ghettos became more and more crowded.

The mass movement of blacks into the North touched off bloody race riots. In 1919, twenty-five such riots flared up across the country. The worst occurred in Chicago. The outward provocation for the riot was the death, probably accidental, of a Negro child at a lakefront beach where blacks were unwelcome. Angry black protest met with violent retaliation. For thirteen days in July anarchy reigned in Chicago. Fifteen whites and twenty-three blacks were killed, 537 people were injured, and a thousand families were left homeless. According to a careful survey, rivalry over jobs and friction over housing underlay the outbreak. A new element in the Chicago riot was that blacks

fought back and sometimes took the offensive.

In the South seventy blacks were lynched in the first year after World War I. Between 1918 and 1921 twenty-eight were publicly hanged and then burned at the stake, usually charged with the murder or rape of a white. Hooded Klan members were responsible for many of these brutal crimes. They belonged to a brand-new Ku Klux Klan, the older organization having died after Reconstruction. The new Klan was a nationwide organization claiming a membership of 5 million by 1923, whose purpose was to unite "native-born white Christians for concerted action in the preservation of American institutions and the supremacy of the white race." They made blacks a major target, but they also took out after labor leaders, Asians, Jews, Roman Catholics, and "foreigners" generally. Local authorities did practically nothing to stop the lynchings. Policemen and sheriffs, who often belonged to the Klan, looked the other way during racial disturbances. Federal authorities, including those in the White House, ignored the problem.

Garvey's back-to-Africa plan

The mixture of hope and resentment among northern blacks during the 1920s produced the noteworthy social movement led by Marcus Garvey. Jamaican-born Garvey arrived in Harlem in 1916. There he set up the headquarters of his Universal Negro Improvement Association, which sought to liberate blacks by first segregating them from whites and organizing self-help efforts, and then by sending them to a new African homeland. Black-white integration he dismissed as unthinkable, for it would ruin the purity of both races. True liberation, he asserted, could come about through linking up with the 400 million other blacks of the world, especially those of Africa. Garvey's slogan was "Africa for the Africans, at home and abroad." Flamboyantly clothed in a purple

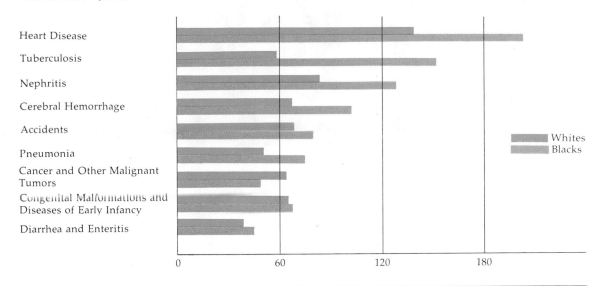

DEATH RATES FOR WHITES AND BLACKS IN THE SOUTHEAST, 1930

(Rates Per 100,000 Population)

Heart Disease

Tuberculosis

Nephritis

Cerebral Hemorrhage

Accidents

Pneumonia

Cancer and Other Malignant
Tumors

Congenital Malformations and
Diseases of Early Infancy

Diarrhea and Enteritis

Whites
Blacks

0   60   120   180

SOURCE: Adapted from Bureau of the Census, *Vital Statistics—Special Reports, 1930*.

uniform with gold braid, topped off by a feathered helmet, he preached a version of racial pride. "Black is beautiful" was Garvey's phrase.

Whites could not fathom Garvey's charisma, but blacks who were suffering from riots, job discrimination, crowded living conditions, and the Klan revival, made him their hero. Many backed him who hadn't the slightest intention of going to Africa. Yet they got from him a sense of pride and self-confidence, if nothing else. He greatly admired Booker T. Washington who, before his death in 1915, endorsed Garvey's plans. He detested black leaders who wanted to stay in America and fight for full equality. For the NAACP and W. E. B. Du Bois, Garvey had nothing but contempt. Du Bois in turn considered him a demagogue.

Garvey named himself the head of the "Provisional African Government-in-Exile" in 1919 and collected funds for a Black Star steamship line. He promised to deliver his

followers to Africa where they would establish a new nation. But the waters never parted for this black Moses; he never led a single colonist to Africa. Some of his partners made off with the money collected from his 2 million followers. Garvey, whose own hands were probably clean, was convicted of mail fraud and sent to prison. He was released and deported by President Coolidge in 1927, and died in London in 1940 without ever having set foot in Africa. Garvey's advocacy of black pride and black nationalism touched a deep chord among blacks and would be echoed in some militant movements of the 1960s and 1970s.

The Harlem Renaissance

A great flowering of black artistry occurred in the 1920s among Harlem blacks. In those years Harlem was one of New York's important business districts and the liveliest black

Ma Rainey and her Georgia Band, one of the many black bands to come out of the South and take Harlem by storm during the Renaissance. Many condemned jazz—an article in The Etude, *a classical music magazine, described it as "saturnalian," "wanton," "musical epilepsy," and "sinister"—yet thousands would flock each night to the famous black nightclubs of Harlem.*

ghetto in the country. It attracted many aspiring black writers, musicians, and intellectuals who would achieve national and international recognition in fiction, poetry, essays, theater, jazz, and classical music. Here was the Harlem Renaissance. Its fame began with the publication of Claude McKay's book of poetry, *Harlem Shadows* (1922), which included "If We Must Die," a bitter commentary on white violence. Essays by young Negro authors appeared in *Crisis* and *Opportunity* magazines, among others. In 1925 a leading New York Journal, *Survey Graphic*, published a special issue devoted to the Renaissance. Edited by a young black philosophy professor, Alain Locke, this issue gave national recognition to the literary movement.

Blacks had begun to disappear from the New York theater about 1910. But in 1921 the first of a series of Negro revues, *Shuffle Along*, made its appearance. The dancers Josephine Baker and Bill Robinson appeared in a succession of hits that made them famous across the country. As the black poet Langston Hughes put it, "Harlem was in vogue" in the 1920s. In the 1930s whites continued to draw upon the outpouring of black talent in plays, concerts, and musical comedy.

Jazz in its original forms was a distinctive black idiom. It wailed out of the Dixie brothels where it was born and swept over the country. The twenties emerged as the Jazz Age. The melancholy tones of blues singers like Bessie Smith were captured on phonograph records and broadcast on radio. Virtuoso performers like Louis Armstrong and composer-band leaders like Duke Ellington began to attract enthusiastic fans, both black and white. White musicians, beginning with Paul Whiteman, Benny Goodman, and George Gershwin, made further innovations. Blues and jazz began as deeply personal expressions of the black experience in America. Eventually the white culture in America adapted them, as did many other parts of the world.

The medium that least reflected the talent of the Harlem renaissance was the movies. Hollywood still portrayed blacks in stereotyped form. Black men often appeared as childish, slow-witted, and shuffling comics. Black women usually played maids who were either passive and loyal or giggling and stupid.

Black hardships in the 1930s

The depression speeded the exodus of southern black sharecroppers, tenants, and farm laborers from the deep South. Since the main path of movement was to the northern cities, this migration complicated life in urban ghettos, where many blacks—"the last hired and the first fired"—were already out of work.

Throughout the depression, Franklin Roosevelt said nothing about black-white relations—but he managed to win black support, anyway. So as not to anger southern white politicians, the president refused even to condemn lynching. But his wife, Eleanor Roosevelt, kept channels open between the black community and official Washington. She was on especially close terms with educator Mary McLeod Bethune, who was made Director of Negro Affairs in the National Youth Administration.

Because FDR had no fixed policies about improving the social and economic conditions of blacks, the matter rested with the individual heads of the New Deal agencies. Much depended on their personal beliefs and on the degree to which black organizations could make their desires known. Secretary of Interior Harold Ickes (a former officer of the Chicago NAACP) and Harry Hopkins, the New Deal relief administrator, had a clear notion of the need for racial justice. Many others did not. Black organizations demanded that Negro advisers be appointed in all agencies and that black farmers and workers be given fair treatment under the NRA and AAA. But Negroes were poorly organized for economic action, and could do very little to affect the policies of these two agencies. Several dozen government bodies hired black administrators. Ickes appointed as his adviser the economist Robert C. Weaver (destined to become Lyndon B. Johnson's secretary of housing and urban development, the first black appointed to a presidential cabinet).

By the late 1930s Negro rights organizations had concluded that Negroes were badly organized and, despite certain gains, were basically lacking in power. As W. E. B. Du Bois said in 1934, "The campaign of appeal for social justice has reached its limits . . . power is now needed to reinforce appeal."

Some blacks began looking for power in the labor movement. At least, the newly emerging CIO unions were attempting to make basic improvements in race relations. The United Mine Workers, the United Auto Workers, and the International Ladies Garment Workers Union recruited black workers and protected them against discrimination. Thus, in a new departure, the majority of southern black miners in the coal industry were organized and covered by contracts. The older AFL unions made far fewer accommodations to blacks, however.

Regardless of the spotty record of FDR in the New Deal on racial matters, the majority of black voters were converted from the party of Lincoln to the party of Roosevelt. Black voters had long felt isolated from the GOP. In 1928 Hoover set out to attract the southern white vote, and deliberately snubbed blacks. By contrast, thousands of Negroes received benefits from various New Deal programs. After 1936 blacks generally registered and voted Democratic.

A new Negro will return from the war —a bitter Negro if he is disappointed again. He will have been taught to kill, to suffer, to die for something he believes in, and he will live by those rules to gain his personal rights.

Letter from a black soldier, 1944

New roles during World War II

One million blacks served in America's armed forces during the Second World War. In 1941 the army and navy had ironclad Jim

Crow policies. Protests from black organizations led to token appointments of high-ranking black officers. Benjamin O. Davis became the first Negro advanced to brigadier general. Usually blacks were kept in all-Negro units under white officers and assigned to truck transport or the loading and unloading of ships. The army remained Jim Crow, and morale in these units was low. Segregation eased somewhat as the war progressed. For the final push against Germany the army was integrated on the platoon level. Eighty black pilots of Davis' 332nd Fighter Group won the Distinguished Flying Cross. Luckily, there were fewer racial incidents involving GIs than in the First World War.

There was significant racial tension on the homefront, though. The flow of blacks into jobs and housing previously considered for whites only led to frequent violence. In June 1943 rioting in Detroit left twenty-five Negroes and nine whites dead. It took six thousand soldiers to restore order.

Organized pressure won blacks the best job opportunities they had ever had. When defense plants first hired blacks, almost all of the jobs were unskilled and paid poorly—jobs vacated by whites who were moving up. Since the administration had no plans to desegregate the job market, black labor leader A. Philip Randolph of the Brotherhood of Sleeping Car Porters began organizing 100,000 Negroes for a protest march on Washington to show their determination to attain job equality. Impressed by the seriousness of the threat, Roosevelt signed an executive order in 1941 which provided that "there shall be no discrimination in the employment of workers in defense industry or government. . . ." All government contractors would have to comply or be called up before a Fair Employment Practices Committee (FEPC). FDR had taken his first important public stand on racial questions. Randolph called off the demonstration.

War industries were not totally free of prejudice in hiring, but the FEPC did help black wage earners improve their job ratings and raise their incomes. The steel industry, for example, employed 100,000 blacks during the war, many of them at skilled jobs. It is an interesting footnote that Martin Luther King's March on Washington in 1963 was organized along the same lines as Randolph's threatened demonstration.

Mexican Americans: Forgotten Americans

The wetbacks

After World War I a great wave of Mexicans hit the country. The migration of Mexicans and of blacks shared a common cause. When Congress cut off European immigration in 1921 and 1924, a shortage of labor in the U.S. created job opportunities for both groups. The influx from south of the border was spurred by two forces: the push of the Mexican revolution between 1910 and 1920 and the pull of U.S. labor needs, mainly in the Southwest. The flow of migrants peaked in 1924, but slowed significantly after 1929, and remained low throughout the depression. In the four and a half decades from 1900 to 1944 an estimated 730,000 Mexican immigrants entered the country, half of them arriving during the twenties. By the 1940s the Mexicans had become the second largest racial or ethnic minority, second only to blacks. In many respects they were the least-known minority, the forgotten Americans.

Most Mexican immigrants were "wet-backs"—migrant workers who swam or waded across the broad, shallow Rio Grande River instead of entering the country legally. There were no immigration quotas for Mexicans, but those who planned to stay in the United States had to present a visa, pay a head tax, and pass a literacy test at a border-crossing station—all of which took time and money. Most of the newcomers were peasants or poor city people. They settled in the southwestern states, where the need for cheap manual labor was greatest. They worked as copper miners, farm hands, and railroad section hands. Many farm irrigation systems and railroad lines were built or maintained by Mexican workers.

Sometimes entire families migrated; more often it was single men. After the wetbacks had jumped the border, labor contractors, called "coyotes" or man snatchers, transported them at night by truck to their jobs. These contractors arranged with fruit growers and others to deliver a certain number of workers at a given time for a given rate. The migrants paid the contractor for his service. In this way the Mexicans avoided dealing with border guards.

Many employers preferred Mexican labor. They worked for little pay, arrived in large numbers, and seemed passive. Illegal immigrants were not likely to risk their jobs by complaining or by joining unions. They often spent their paychecks in the U.S., carrying finished goods home to Mexico. One grower wrote to the California governor in 1919: "I will say that if the white farmer, or white men in the State of California, could get an ample supply of Mexican labor, they could do all the truck gardening, raising of sugar beets, cantaloupes, vegetables, and other products which the Japanese and Hindus and Mohammedans are now doing. . . ."

In spite of what the whites thought, the Mexicans were not always so docile. In the 1920s and 1930s dozens of small Mexican unions emerged in farming, coal and copper mining, canning and packing, and even sheepshearing in New Mexico. The unions frequently struck in the 1930s, especially in agriculture. In California farm wages sometimes dropped as low as nine cents an hour during the depression. AFL unions would have nothing to do with the Mexicans. Radicals, including Communists, tried to organize them. During strikes, California farm employers and local law officers pulled out all the stops to destroy the unions. Indiscriminate arrests, excessive bail, deportations, and beatings by vigilante groups were used to intimidate the strikers. So Mexican workers who tried to gain control over their own lives by forming unions had little success.

Some of the older Spanish-speaking families drew away from the new Mexican immigrants. They felt threatened by the job competition and falling wages near the border. They were citizens. Yet whites lumped them together with the new wetbacks and treated them like greenhorns. Some of the old-timers in the Southwest, especially those who spoke English, began drifting farther north in search of better jobs. They followed the crops in the Pacific Northwest or got work in the mills and factories and on the railroads in the upper Midwest. By the time World War II began, there were sizable colonies of Mexicans in and around Chicago, St. Louis, and other major cities.

Inching toward the mainstream

Compared to other immigrant groups, Mexicans were slow to adopt American ways. Many expected to return to Mexico. Of those who stayed, the "illegals" suffered the most.

They lived in constant threat of exposure. They feared not only the immigration authorities but *all* authorities — teachers, social workers, census takers, and police. Anyone who might learn the truth and have them deported was a threat. This fear rubbed off on their children, many of whom were U.S. citizens by birth. Migrant laborers rarely stayed long enough in one place to buy land, pay taxes, or acquire a stake in society. Often they lived in isolated places in housing provided by railroads, mining companies, or growers, so they seemed "invisible" to most Americans.

Because they moved frequently or lived in isolation, Mexican Americans never built the political base which had brought social and economic advancement to many groups of European immigrants. With few exceptions, Mexican American voters had no power. They were given few patronage jobs and had little or no representation in state or local government. Self-help groups were traditionally weak.

The number of Mexican-born people in the U.S. actually declined in the thirties, from about 640,000 in 1930 to 377,000 in 1940. The depression sharply reduced migration from Mexico. Also, to lighten the welfare rolls and reduce the labor surplus in the U.S., federal and state officials sent a half million people back to Mexico. A great many were native-born American citizens. It cost Los Angeles County $425,000 to pay public assistance to six thousand Mexicans but only about $77,000 to deport them. In short, the local governments saved money by paying the train fare of Mexicans and Mexican Americans to "go home." Some left voluntarily, some had to be coaxed, and a few were physically removed. For several years a monthly train, filled with *repatriados*, traveled from southern California to Mexico City. About 200,000 left the country in 1931 and 1932 alone. Not all who went back to Mexico lived in the Southwest. Half of those

of Mexican descent in Illinois, Michigan, and Indiana were among those who left the country in the thirties.

The zoot suit riots

Mexican Americans who remained in the States faced discrimination in jobs, housing, schools, and public places throughout the country. At restaurants, swimming pools, theaters, and hotels in the Southwest the "White Only" sign applied to the Spanish-speaking as well as to blacks. Racial incidents were not uncommon.

The first such episodes to receive nationwide coverage were the "zoot suit riots," or "pachuco riots," in Los Angeles during the summer of 1943. After the internment of the Japanese a year earlier (see pp. 608–609), the Los Angeles press methodically attacked a segment of the Mexican community. These were the "pachucos"—youths who spoke a patois of Spanish and English and who were accused of "shirking war duties" and of "gangsterism." Newspapers ridiculed the "zoot suits" worn by the young males— wide, baggy, high-waisted pants with narrow cuffs, long-tailed jackets, and broad-brimmed hats. In June 1943, incidents flared on street corners between servicemen and young Mexican Americans. Groups of sailors cruised the downtown area in taxis, searching for "zoot suiters." They stripped and beat their victims. The police made wholesale arrests of the zoot suiters. The servicemen, who were later shown to have provoked the incidents, were not arrested. For a time the rioting brought the normal business of downtown Los Angeles to a complete halt. The Germans broadcast news of these incidents throughout Latin America, labeling the Americans as racial hypocrites.

Other Mexican Americans did their share of the fighting and dying in the war. Because a hitch in the service brought economic security—and to Mexican nationals it also

In June, 1943, these pachucos —dressed in typical "zoot suit" style—drove through Los Angeles waving American flags and white flags of truce to signal their willingness to end the hostilities between Mexican Americans and Anglo servicemen.

brought U.S. citizenship—young men of Mexican background crowded the recruitment centers. About 750,000 Mexican Americans served as GIs in the war, probably the highest proportion of any ethnic or racial group in the armed forces. They encountered little racial discrimination. Unlike blacks, they were assigned to combat duty in all parts of the globe. Many died or were captured in the Philippines in 1942. On the island of Saipan, Guy Gabaldon, a GI raised by a Japanese family in Los Angeles, persuaded about a thousand Japanese soldiers to surrender. This won him the Silver Star. Seventeen other Mexican Americans earned the Congressional Medal of Honor.

Braceros imported by agreement

The war created a labor shortage in southwestern agriculture. The whites who might have worked in the fields found higher paying jobs elsewhere. The Japanese (who normally did not work for whites as field hands) were detained behind barbed wire. And immigration from overseas had stopped. To relieve the shortage, the U.S. in 1942 agreed with Mexico to import *braceros* (field hands) on a regular basis. Wages and working conditions were set by negotiation. There were abuses in the program, but it significantly helped solve the farm labor shortage and improved the earnings of the Mexicans who came.

The Internment of "An Enemy Race"

Asian exclusion laws

Throughout the years 1918 to 1945 racial bigotry toward persons of Asian background continued actively, particularly on the West Coast. It expressed itself most fully in immigration and naturalization policies. The Chinese were already excluded by law from entering the country or becoming citizens. The National Origins Quota Law of 1924 imposed the same restrictions on the Japanese. In Tokyo July 1, 1924, was designated "Humiliation Day" and was commemorated by hate-America rallies.

In one respect the Filipinos were a special case: as residents of an American colony they were exempt from the Asian exclusion laws. The majority of those who arrived between 1920 and 1934 mainly worked on the West Coast as agricultural workers. When the Philippine Independence Act was passed in 1934, it ended the special treatment of Filipinos and cut their immigration to a trickle. In 1930, of the 35,000 in the U.S., most lived in California. Stockton, California, was known as "the Manila of the United States."

Japanese detention during the war

The most unprecedented racial incident in American history was the "relocation" of Japanese Americans during World War II. In one great sweep practically an entire minority—citizens and aliens alike—was stamped "an enemy race" and placed behind barbed wire. It represented the culmination of a long history of anti-Asian bigotry—as well as a severe case of war hysteria.

In the early months of the war Japanese forces were not only advancing in Southwest Asia and in the South Pacific but even gained a foothold in the Aleutian Islands, a U.S. possession off the Alaskan coast. In February 1942, a Japanese submarine surfaced

Hollywood supported the war effort with movies like "The Purple Heart." A gloating, cunning Japanese general (Richard Loo) ticks off Japan's conquests. The defiant, courageous American (Dana Andrews) responds, "This is your war. . . . You started it! And now you're going to get it, and it won't be finished until your dirty little empire is wiped off the face of the earth!"

This is a race war . . . and we might as well understand it. . . . I am for catching every Japanese in America . . . and putting them in concentration camps. . . . Damn them! Let us get rid of them now!

JOHN RANKIN, 1942
Congressman from Mississippi

off Santa Barbara, California, and fired several shells at an oil installation, causing little damage but great anxiety.

The commander of the Sixth Army in California advised Washington that in his judgment as a military man all persons of Japanese background had to be removed from the Coast and, if necessary, locked up in special camps. Otherwise they might help the enemy in the event of a Japanese attack. Demanding such action were the press and patriotic organizations, as well as public officials. The governor of California and his attorney general, Earl Warren, were among those who advised relocating the Japanese. (Years later Warren, who became Chief Justice of the Supreme Court, expressed deep regret for his advocacy of the internment policy.) President Roosevelt ignored the advice of Attorney General Francis Biddle, who argued against relocation on legal grounds. On March 2, 1942, acting in the interest of "military necessity," Roosevelt signed the executive order which authorized the move. No hearings were held and no indictments handed down. In short, the rights promised in the Bill of Rights were ignored. The American Civil Liberties Union, one of the few organizations to protest the move, called the wholesale roundup the greatest single assault on the Constitution in the nation's history.

The evacuation proceeded rapidly and smoothly. Some 112,000 persons of Japanese ancestry, more than half of whom were Nisei (born in America of Japanese immigrant parents — and thus citizens of the United States), were taken into custody. The army descended on a community and gave the Japanese five days to dispose of their property and settle their personal affairs. Businesses were shut down, farms left abandoned, homes hastily boarded up, furnishings sold at a fraction of their dollar value. An estimated $400 million was sacrificed in the frantic sell-offs. Soldiers first took the evacuees to fairgrounds, racetracks, and large pavilions. Soon they removed them in auto and truck caravans to ten relocation centers. Located on the barren western deserts, these camps consisted of rows of wooden barracks, covered with tarpaper and surrounded by barbed wire. The entire evacuation, "a bloodless pogrom," was completed in 137 days.

The civilian agency that ran the camps, the War Relocation Agency, wanted to let the inmates govern themselves. But the army, which was in charge of security, did not agree and imposed prison discipline. At Tule Lake, California, some young internees resisted, especially when told to take an oath of allegiance. Guards dealt with them sternly. Resentful of their treatment, six thousand internees later renounced their American citizenship. After the war about 4700 of them sailed for Japan.

In Hawaii where they were a much larger proportion of the total population than on the West Coast, all 130,000 persons of Japanese ancestry remained at large throughout the war. There the U.S. military argued that these people were too involved in war work on the islands to be locked up. Their freedom was a military necessity.

Japanese loyalty during World War II

Not one Japanese or Nisei was cited for sabotage or spying in the territory of Hawaii or on the United States mainland. (In California some officials saw the total absence of sabotage or spying before the internment as an ominous sign of an enemy ready to pounce. They used it as an argument to justify internment.) Even when Japan's threat to the U.S. mainland receded completely in 1943, the Japanese in the U.S. were kept out of sight and out of mind.

Thousands of Nisei youth from the mainland and Hawaii volunteered for military duty and served with great distinction. The Nisei GI had a burning desire to erase the stigma of "traitor" that hounded him and his family. In the Pacific Nisei soldiers volunteered for dangerous missions, facing possible death if captured by Japanese soldiers. The 100th Infantry Battalion, made up entirely of Nisei soldiers, fought in Italy, winning the most decorations of any unit of its size. One Nisei who served with distinction was Daniel Inouye, later elected senator from Hawaii.

The relocation had grave constitutional implications for all Americans. The U.S. Supreme Court ruled in 1943 and 1944 that in wartime the courts must not question military wisdom. In *Korematsu* v. *United States* (1944) it ruled that, owing to the wartime emergency, the relocation of citizens without due process of law was constitutional. The decision is a reminder of how fragile the Bill of Rights may become in times of crisis. Dissenting Justice Frank Murphy said the decision plunged the Court "into the ugly abyss of racism." Justice Robert H. Jackson said, also in dissent, the detention of the Japanese will be "like a loaded weapon ready for the hand of any authority that can bring forward a plausible claim of an urgent need."

Review

U.S. policy had decimated Indian land holdings, and the reservations deteriorated as the Bureau of Indian Affairs grew larger. Reservation Indians endured the lowest living standard of any Americans, and some people believed the Indians would "vanish" completely. Under the New Deal money spent on necessary improvements offered tribes and individuals new hope. The Indian New Deal ended during World War II, but many Indians increased their income by entering defense work. Indian men who served in the armed forces were admired as combat soldiers, and the Navaho codes were among the few not broken by the enemy. Notwithstanding their suffering, the U.S. census in the 1930s indicated Indians might be making a numerical comeback, and by the 1940s it was clear they were not about to "vanish."

The black migration north was unable to escape Jim Crow and segregation. The mass movement crowded the ghettos and ignited northern race riots. In the South the KKK inspired terror. Marcus Garvey's short-lived Back-to-Africa movement filled many black people with a sense of pride and self-confidence. The movement north also produced a flowering of black culture in the 1920s, particularly in Harlem. It expressed the dreams of the new Negro. The '30s sent more dispossessed southern farm people to already over-crowded slums. Even though FDR had not commented on race relations, blacks came to support him and became part of his coalition. Black soldiers in World War II entered Jim Crow armed services and morale was low in segregated units. Restrictions eased as the war lengthened, and the military experienced few racial incidents, though racial violence did occur on the home front. Impressed by demands for job equality, Roosevelt signed an executive order to end job discrimination in defense industries and government agencies.

After World War I a large wave of Mexicans came to the U.S. Most were migrant workers who had entered illegally. They settled mainly in the Southwest where the labor demand was greatest. Employer opposition destroyed their attempts to organize unions. Mexican Americans were slower to assimilate than most other immigrant groups and they had no political base from which to assert themselves. Mexican nationals living in the U.S. declined in numbers during the depression. Mexican Americans faced social and economic discrimination, as well as racial and cultural conflict. The most famous incidents were the zoot suit riots of 1943. They were ironic because Mexican Americans probably had the highest proportion of any ethnic or racial group in the armed services. Within the service they did not face the same discrimination as black men. On the civilian front, in order to ease a growing labor shortage, the U.S. and Mexico agreed to a program of importing *braceros* in 1942.

Discrimination against Asian Americans in the U.S. climaxed with the relocation of Japanese Americans in World War II. Because of fear that they might otherwise aid the enemy, FDR signed the relocation order in 1942. The interned Japanese Americans suffered financial loss as their properties were hastily sold off. Relocation camps, ringed by barbed wire, were run under strict discipline. Hawaiians of Japanese descent remained at large throughout the war and were involved in crucial war work. Not a single person of Japanese background was ever cited for spying in the U.S., and thousands volunteered for active duty, serving with distinction. The treatment of the Japanese is a harsh reminder of how the Bill of Rights can be trampled in times of crisis or hysteria.

Questions

1. Describe the goals of the Indian Reorganization Act of 1934.
2. How did the lives of black people change during the depression and World War II? Why did they become part of FDR's coalition?
3. Why did many agricultural employers prefer Mexican workers?
4. The internment of the Japanese was necessary in the interest of military necessity for no one could know ahead of time whether their presence would inspire subversive activities. Do you agree or disagree? Why?
5. Identify and define: (a) *The Mind of Primitive Man*, (b) John Collier, (c) Ira Hayes, (d) *Harlem Shadows*, (e) E. Philip Randolph, (f) War Relocation Agency, and (g) the Korematsu case.

nationality and religion

Prohibition: destruction of beer on New Jersey docks, 1923.

This generation's deepest need is . . . a fresh sense of personal and social sin.

HARRY E. FOSDICK
(1878–1969)

American clergyman, writing in 1922

29

613

29

The Old Order and the New

In the 1920s the nation appeared to some to be going through a moral and social breakdown. Scantily dressed young women drank and smoked like men. Instead of having wholesome good times in groups, couples paired off to dance cheek-to-cheek, watch sexy movies, and neck in parked cars. Sunday was becoming a day for recreation rather than religious observance. More emphasis was placed on having fun than on doing honest work. And foreigners seemed to be everywhere. The newcomers often had strange ways, engaged in radical politics, and gave birth to far too many babies. Many old-stock Protestant Americans worried about the renewed surge of immigration at the end of World War I—particularly about the influx of more southern and eastern Europeans, who crowded into the cities. The reaction has been called the Revolt of the Old Order. It included the rise of the Ku Klux Klan, the Red Scare, the opposition to Al Smith as a presidential candidate, and the Scopes "monkey trial" in Tennessee. The finale of the rebellion was a law cutting off the free flow of European immigration.

Closing the Door

Pressure for cutting off immigration
In the early 1920s Henry Ford staged a colorful pageant near his auto plant. Workers wearing their native costumes danced their native dances and sang in their native tongues. With the music playing tarantellas, polkas, jigs, and horas, they whirled their way into a large replica of a "melting pot." Soon they emerged from the other end—all dressed alike in ordinary street clothes and singing "The Star-Spangled Banner." Ford assumed that conforming Americans could be turned out as neatly as Model-Ts.

IMMIGRATION TO THE UNITED STATES, 1900–1930

Year	All Countries	Europe	Asia
1900	448,572	424,700	17,946
1905	1,026,499	974,273	23,925
1910	1,041,570	926,291	23,533
1915	326,700	197,919	15,211
1920	430,001	246,295	17,505
1925	294,314	148,366	3,578
1930	241,700	147,438	4,535

SOURCE: *Historical Statistics of the United States: Colonial Times to 1957.*

IMMIGRATION QUOTAS TO THE UNITED STATES, 1924–1930

Country	Per 1924 National Origins Act*	Per Law of 1929**
Germany	51,227	25,957
Great Britain	34,007	65,721
Ireland	28,567	17,853
Sweden	9,561	3,314
Norway	6,453	2,377
Poland	5,982	6,524
Italy	3,845	5,802
Russia	2,248	2,784
Greece	100	307
Asia	1,300	1,323
Africa	1,200	1,200
All Others	621	600
Total	**164,667**	**153,714**

*Annual quota was 2 percent of foreign-born residents of the United States per 1890 census.

**Annual quota was one sixth of 1 percent of the number of white residents of the continental United States in 1920.

SOURCE: *Historical Statistics of the United States: Colonial Times to 1957.*

Other native-born Americans were less certain than Ford. They began a nationwide crusade to shut the doors on the eastern and southern Europeans. The wartime Congress had already passed a literacy test to reduce the flow. But this had little effect on postwar immigration, which boomed again as soon as the fighting stopped. Labor leaders and nativists informed Congress that the country was "full." The economy no longer needed cheap labor, because machines were replacing unskilled workers. The frontier was closed, and the best farmland was already settled. Reams of statistics "proved" that insanity, epilepsy, venereal disease, and tuberculosis, as well as inborn tendencies to criminal activity, were rampant among "foreigners." Nativists implied that closing down immigration would put an end to radicalism, political corruption, poverty, and slums. They suggested that, without the "foreigners," America could reach a state of near perfection. Labor hinted that unemployment would disappear almost immediately. A congressman blurted out that all the "wops," "dagoes," "Hebrews," and "hunkies" should be kept out of the country.

Responding to the barrage, Congress in 1921 passed a quota law which limited the number of newcomers allowed to enter the U.S. annually from each nation to 3 percent of residents from that nation living here in 1910. When the law failed to quiet the antiimmigrant forces, Congress in 1924 passed the National Origins Act, which dropped the quota to 2 percent of the residents from any foreign country living in the U.S. in 1890. Shifting the base year to 1890 penalized the eastern and southern Europeans most heavily. The nationalities quota law expressly excluded the Japanese, as they were "aliens ineligible for citizenship." In 1929 a law was enacted that limited annual total immigration from outside the Hemisphere to 150,000. Because the largest quotas went to countries that no longer provided large numbers of immigrants—Great Britain and Germany, for example—the actual annual immigration was kept below that figure. The same basic system remained in effect until 1952 (see p. 764).

The lack of an immigration quota for Mexicans created a favorable situation for migrants from south of the border. When the farm labor shortage became acute after the start of World War II, the U.S. set up a program with Mexico to import braceros *(field hands). Here* braceros *line up at the entrance of a migratory center in Mexico for a bureaucratic stopover on the trip to the United States.*

The nativists' claim of "standing room only" had little basis in fact. Throughout America's history immigrants had flocked to this country when work or land was available and had stayed away, or even returned home, when times were hard. From 1931 to 1936 240,000 more aliens left the country than were admitted. Some economists claimed that the reduction of European immigration made the depression worse, because it reduced the market for finished goods at a time of declining births. The fact that the depression came after immigration slowed suggests that in the past immigrants had been unfairly tagged as a cause of business downturns. Some industries, particularly corporate farming, faced labor shortages as early as the mid-1920s. They looked for cheap labor in Mexico, the Philippines, and the West Indies. The Mexican *bracero* program which began in the 1940s was a direct result of this search.

Leaving the old ways behind

As fewer newcomers passed through Ellis Island, the identity problems of the children and grandchildren of immigrants attracted more attention. They were citizens by birth and could speak English, but society considered them hyphenates—Italian-Americans, Polish-Americans, Russian-Jewish-Americans. Living in a transition zone between the Old and New Worlds was often hard. Other children teased them about their peculiar accents, different eating habits, and odd religious practices. As they matured, many of the second generation abandoned the ethnic social clubs and foreign-language newspapers that interested their parents. Anxious to become full fledged Americans, they dropped their mother tongue and Anglicized their names. They kept their ties to their church, but often quit going regularly to services, much to the dismay of their parents and grandparents.

It was natural enough for the second and third generation to lose touch with Old World customs. Some became Americans with all the passion of the newly converted. As soon as possible they fled from the ghettos to middle-class suburbia. The move from slum to suburb usually required a move from working class to middle class. The elderly often remained behind in the immigrant ghettos as the neighborhoods' ethnic identity changed. Blacks or Puerto Ricans filled the gaps left by those who had moved out of the ghettos.

Ethnic and religious differences played a part in marriage customs. Some families maintained taboos about the intermarriage of their offspring across national boundaries; for instance, some Irish families opposed marriage of their children to Italians or Poles. Yet these ethnic boundaries blurred in a generation or so. The more enduring marriage barriers, those between religious affiliations, remained well-defined into the second and third generations. In a study of intermarriage and church membership in New Haven, Connecticut, from 1870 to 1940, Ruby Jo Kennedy reported that "cultural [that is, ethnic] lines may fade but religious barriers are holding fast. . . ." The boundaries dividing the three major religious affiliations, in short, were firmly fixed. Kennedy's conclusion was that a "triple melting pot" existed. Marriage was rare between Jews and Gentiles, as well as between Catholics and Protestants.

The ethnic bigotry and discrimination of the twenties showed itself in admissions into higher education and voluntary associations. Colleges and universities set quotas on the number of Jewish entrants. Fraternities and sororities "rushed" only the "right" people. Jews and Catholics often had to set up their own college associations. In the suburbs property owners signed restrictive covenants to keep the neighborhoods "pure." Membership in private country clubs was also highly selective with members of certain racial, religious, and ethnic groups firmly excluded. Resort hotels also excluded blacks and Jews. The courts upheld these restrictions until after World War II.

Protestants, Catholics, and Jews

Protestant trends in the twenties

Most American Protestants in the twenties would probably have identified themselves as liberal, or Modernist. They believed in human goodness and moral progress, and they accepted the Darwinian theory of evolution. They did not necessarily believe in Christ's return to earth. Most Protestant leaders were not political in orientation, but they did not necessarily object to ministers who preached the Social Gospel—those who favored correcting the sins of runaway private enterprise.

A deeply resentful minority of conservative Protestants battled against these liberal attitudes. These Fundamentalists, found chiefly in small towns and rural areas, particularly in the South, took the Bible as gospel and believed in Christ's return. Salvation had great meaning to them: those who were not saved were bound for hell. Fundamentalism in the southern Bible Belt conducted its struggle both inside and outside the churches. Fundamentalists fought doggedly to outlaw the teaching of Darwin's theories in the public

Clarence Darrow, chief counsel for the defendant, addresses the jury during the Scopes "monkey trial." Darrow framed the point at issue broadly: "Scopes isn't on trial, civilization is on trial. The prosecution is opening the doors for a reign of bigotry equal to anything in the Middle Ages. No man's belief will be safe if they win." John T. Scopes was convicted, however, and fined $100—but the penalty was later set aside.

schools and to enforce the prohibition of alcoholic drinks.

One of the most unifying and exhilarating victories ever won by Protestants was Prohibition, but the Prohibition Amendment ratified in 1919 turned out to be only a temporary victory for the "dry" crusade. From then until 1933 Protestants had to fight a rearguard action against the "wets." But while they fought to preserve Prohibition, the crime and corruption that accompanied it were arousing public support for repeal.

Local and state governments also wanted repeal so that they could collect badly needed revenue from liquor taxes. When repeal came in 1933, Protestantism suffered a terrible blow.

The most famous contest between theology and secularism in American history took place in a heat-drenched courtroom in Dayton, Tennessee, in 1925. Tennessee had passed a new law—a result of Fundamentalist pressure—that banned the teaching of "any theory that denies . . . Divine Creation," in other words, the teaching of evolution. Other states—Oklahoma, Florida, Mississippi, Arkansas—had similar laws. A first-year high-school science teacher, John T. Scopes, deliberately violated the law, and the state of Tennessee brought him to trial. The prosecution's chief lawyer was William Jennings Bryan, the perennial Democratic presidential candidate and an ardent Fundamentalist. The most famous trial lawyer of the day, Clarence Darrow, headed the defense. Darrow was a civil libertarian, a wit, and an agnostic. The two attorneys met head on. Bryan agreed to take the stand as an expert witness on the Bible, whereupon Darrow forced him to defend the most extreme antiscientific positions. Bryan did so with much gusto, to the delight of the townspeople in the courtroom.

Called the "monkey trial," the proceedings made headlines for weeks. Reporters sent 2 million words of copy from the court house in July. The acid-tongued journalist H. L. Mencken wrote daily on-the-scene columns. Most of them belittled fundamentalism and Bryan. "Heave an egg out of a Pullman and you will hit a Fundamentalist almost everywhere in the United States," Mencken observed. While much of the country cheered Darrow for his defense of reason and free speech, the other part championed Bryan for his defense of tradition and the Scriptures. In the end the court found Scopes guilty and ordered him to pay a fine. Bryan's death a week later, which some people attributed to the stress of the trial and the abuse he had suffered, was a severe blow to fundamentalism.

In Los Angeles Aimee Semple McPherson, the first major woman revivalist, adapted Hollywood theatrics to fundamentalism. She opened her stadium-sized Angelus Temple in 1923 to preach the Foursquare Gospel (the Savior, Baptism, Healing, and the Second Coming). "I bring spiritual consolation to the middle class, leaving those above to themselves and those below to the Salvation Army." An evening in Angelus Temple was like watching a musical revue: lights flashed, an orchestra blared, a chorus sang, and costumed players dramatized scenes of good and evil. Sometimes Sister Aimee roared down the main aisle on her motorcycle to a throne adorned with thousands of carnations. "Who cares about old Hell, friends?" she would ask in her sermon. "Let's forget

Although one critic described Aimee Semple McPherson's services as "supernatural whoopee," she kept the five thousand seats of her Angelus Temple filled by demonstrating that worship was fun. In addition to a huge choir, a brass band, and a pipe organ, the Temple featured a "Miracle Room," where stacks of crutches and wheel chairs from faith cures were displayed. "I am not a healer," McPherson once said. "Jesus is the healer. I am only the little office girl who opens the door and says 'Come in.'"

about Hell. Lift up your hearts. What *we* are interested in, yes, Lord, is *Heaven,* and how to get there." Her own radio station beamed these colorful services to a wide audience. Strikingly handsome in her furs, capes, and jewels, she was as much a celebrity as any Hollywood movie star. Widowed once and divorced twice, she mysteriously "disappeared" into the ocean in 1926, reappearing after a month-long love affair. Her "resurrection" in Mexico annoyed many of her followers.

As it affected ordinary people, the religion of the twenties often concerned matters of personal health, happiness, and success. How to succeed in business was the theme of the most popular book about Jesus in the twenties, Bruce Barton's best seller, *The Man Nobody Knows* (1925). Barton was a Sunday School student, a preacher's son, and a man of deep religious faith. He was also an advertising executive with the firm of Batten, Barton, Durstine, and Osborn. His book about Christ used the jargon of the adman. Jesus was portrayed as "the most popular dinner guest in Jerusalem," a muscular, sun-tanned businessman who "led the most successful life on this planet." Christ chose to remain poor and to seek love. His parables were "the most powerful advertisements of all time." Corporation executives and traveling salesmen, clerks and waitresses, all devoured the book.

Protestantism during the depression

Protestant clergymen expected that the hardship and the uncertainty of the depression would bring on a religious revival. Actually, church attendance fell off somewhat between 1930 and 1940. People still believed in God and the hereafter, but they had doubts about organized religion. Still, the thirties was a time of intense self-examination in religious circles for several reasons. First, the end of Prohibition delivered a blow to organized

Protestantism. Then, too, the failure of capitalism to satisfy basic human wants and the obvious suffering of millions suggested that the optimism of liberal Protestantism was false and superficial. Finally, the rise of European dictators and the outbreak of war in 1939 caused further questioning. Theologians reexamined the bases of their beliefs.

The American theologian who made the most penetrating new analysis of the human condition was Reinhold Niebuhr (1892–1971). After witnessing the failure of the social system and what he felt was the basic inadequacy of liberal religion, Niebuhr evolved a blend of fundamentalism and Marxism called "Neo-orthodoxy." Liberal theology was too complacent for him. It did not give enough recognition to God's omnipotence, to the importance of original sin, or to Christ's redemption. Nor did it fully understand the injustice and misery caused by capitalism. His work *Moral Man and Immoral Society* (1932) was a milestone in American theology, and it eventually made Niebuhr the outstanding Protestant theologian of his time. It criticized the Social Gospel as well-meaning but naive, and it went on to examine other aspects of political behavior and social ethics. Niebuhr came from a Bible-Belt evangelical background in Missouri. He held a ministry in a poor working-class district of Detroit in the 1920s and was permanently affected by the terrible poverty he saw around him. In 1928 Niebuhr joined the faculty of Union Theological Seminary in New York. His book *The Children of Light and the Children of Darkness* (1934) explored the contest between democracy and totalitarianism. It also championed the world leadership of the U.S. Because of his unusual mixture of beliefs—religion (Fundamentalist), social science (Marxist), activism (anti-Russian), pessimism, and a feeling of irony and paradox—Niebuhr had an appeal for many intellectuals who had turned away from theology and organized religion in the 1920s.

Social Reconstruction among the Catholics

Throughout the twenties the Catholic church remained suspect in Protestant America. Two indications of this were the rise of the new anti-Catholic Ku Klux Klan and the campaign against Al Smith in 1928. The hatred of Catholics had several dimensions. Some Protestants claimed that the Catholics' allegiance to Rome conflicted with their allegiance to the U.S. They also associated Catholicism with liquor, because many American Catholics of German, Italian, Irish, and Polish descent were "wets" who opposed Prohibition, and with political corruption, because many belonged to the big-city political machines. Some Protestants felt that the Catholic parochial schools were a danger to public-school education. In Oregon anti-Catholic forces lobbied successfully for a law compelling all youngsters to attend public schools. The U.S. Supreme Court overturned it in 1925.

In 1919 the Catholic bishops in the United States announced a program called Social Reconstruction. Basically, it called for continuation of some wartime regulations with a blending-in of new ones, such as the eight-hour day, a family living wage, a national employment service, reclamation of public land, public housing, labor's right to organize and bargain collectively, regulation of monopoly, and support for producers' cooperative societies. The program was intended to win greater social justice for the working class, a group with which the Catholic church had strong ties. To muster support for Social Reconstruction, the bishops formed the National Catholic Welfare Conference (NCWC) in 1922. Monsignor John C. Ryan, the principal author of Social Reconstruction, was an active force in the NCWC. Known to his enemies as "the red priest," Ryan had long championed the trade union movement and progressive social causes. Conservative Catholics joined conservative Protestants in

Changes in our economic and political systems will have only partial and feeble efficiency if they be not reinforced by the Christian view of work and wealth.

Bishops' Program of Social Reconstruction, 1919

condemning the Welfare Conference for its liberal tendencies. Nativists pointed accusingly at Social Reconstruction as an example of the way the "alien" Catholic church was undermining the American way of life, and of why Congress had to pass a more stringent immigration law.

In the twenties the Catholic church in New England was embroiled in an internal struggle involving a conflict of nationalities and in an external one concerning the parochial schools. The controversy over Social Reconstruction also managed to get dragged in. The church was trying to speed up the process of assimilation among immigrants; it strongly urged Catholic immigrant parents to send their children to parochial schools to achieve this goal as quickly as possible. This separatism irritated some Protestants. It was denounced at KKK rallies, where cries were heard for laws forcing all children to attend public schools. Meanwhile French Canadian Catholics who had migrated to New England resented the efforts of the Irish hierarchy to suppress local (French) control over church property. They found it convenient to brand the Welfare Conference an "Irish" conspiracy. Pressure against Social Reconstruction and the NCWC grew so strong that the bishops finally relented. They all but abandoned both the organization and the program in the 1920s.

While Social Reconstruction had seemed very radical in the 1920s, it found greater acceptance in the 1930s. The American bishops revived Social Reconstruction during the New Deal. Catholic welfare workers, clergy, and volunteers tried to stimulate interest in

Father Coughlin, known in the 1930s as the "radio priest," received more mail each week than President Roosevelt. His inflammatory attacks on liberals and labor unions proved as stirring in person as on the airways. Here Coughlin addresses a Cleveland crowd, some 10,000 strong, in 1936. Eventually he had the whole group parading around the hall in his honor for an hour.

the cause. In 1931 Pope Pius XI had helped their cause by calling for social justice and better wages for labor. In America this was translated into advocacy of the welfare state.

In the thirties the most famous American Catholic was Father Charles E. Coughlin, the "radio priest" from Royal Oak, Michigan. A spell-binding preacher, Coughlin had a weekly broadcast that reached ten million listeners. His doctrine was a mixture of Italian fascism, Midwest Populism, and even a smattering of Social Reconstruction. He told his audiences that an international conspiracy of Jewish financiers was behind the depression and that FDR might be a part of the conspiracy. Coughlin published a weekly journal, *Social Justice,* and formed a political party, the National Union for Social Justice. He called for the nationalization of the banks, power, oil, and other industries that controlled "our God-given natural resources." Many working-class and middle-class German and Irish Catholics who had been hard hit by the depression were ardent followers of Father Coughlin. He was attacked by other Catholic priests. A member of a coalition of right-wing radicals who tried to topple FDR in 1936, Coughlin had the wind taken out of his sails by Roosevelt's Second New Deal.

FDR was the first president to court Roman Catholics. He appointed more than a token number as judges and cabinet members. Only four Catholics had ever sat in the cabinet before 1933; fourteen would serve in the next two decades. The president's most highly publicized move was to send a personal envoy, Myron C. Taylor, on a diplomatic mission to the Vatican. This first official contact between the U.S. and the pope in Rome agitated many Protestants, but it pleased Catholic voters enormously. Catholics became more and more a part of the Roosevelt coalition.

Roosevelt's hands-off policy in the Spanish Civil War reflected, in part, his deference to Catholic attitudes. The pope considered communism, not fascism, the greatest danger in the world, and bestowed his blessings on General Franco as a defender of the faith. Officially the American bishops shared this view. They changed their minds about fascism after 1941, however, and vigorously supported America's war effort.

Shifting traditions among the Jews

In 1920 there were four million Jews in America, half of them living in New York City. Most had come from czarist Russia and Poland and a lesser number from the Austro-Hungarian empire. They far outnumbered the older German Jewish families. To a greater extent than other immigrant groups, the Jews represented the complete social and political spectrum: aristocrats and proletarians; wealthy and impoverished; highly educated and illiterate; Socialists and political conservatives. More than a few were Zionists—believers in the return of the Jews to a homeland in Palestine.

In the Jewish community from eastern Europe a renaissance reached its high point in the 1920s. Its unifying force was Yiddish, the language spoken by most European Jews; derived from German with some borrowings from the Slavic languages, it is written in Hebrew characters. Yiddish novelists, playwrights, poets, journalists, and essayists blossomed. The Yiddish theater, centered on Second Avenue in New York, attracted enthusiastic audiences. At one time nine Yiddish theaters were operating in Manhattan. They presented an endless selection of melodramas, musicals, variety acts, and high drama, sometimes in translation. Many of the performers, directors, and producers later became famous in Hollywood and on Broadway.

Each of the five Yiddish dailies published in Manhattan catered to a different political view. The ten-story building occupied by the *Jewish Daily Forward* dominated the skyline of Manhattan's East Side, just as the newspaper itself dominated Jewish journalism. The editor, Abraham Cahan, was considered one of the most influential people in the Jewish community.

Secularism became a major current among Jews in the 1920s and 1930s. According to one estimate, there were 50,000 Reform, 75,000 Conservative, and 200,000 Orthodox Jews in America in the late thirties. Since these numbers add up to only a fraction of the total number of Jews, the majority of American Jews did not belong to any of the congregations. As immigrant families deserted the ghetto for neighborhoods with better schools and housing, they generally deserted the Orthodox ritual. Mainly, the older Jews who stayed behind in the ghettos nurtured the eastern European religious tradition. In the new neighborhoods the Jewish community established Hebrew schools in conjunction with synagogues. Some secular schools were established for the study of Jewish history and culture. Zionist and Socialist clubs and Yiddish cultural associations also arose in Jewish neighborhoods. Normally the synagogues formed the nucleus of community life, but in the twenties and thirties a network of Jewish community centers developed in the larger Jewish centers of population. These provided lectures, concerts, athletic events, social clubs, summer camps, and after-school activities for children.

Orthodox rabbis denounced the secularism and bemoaned the break with ancient tradition. Conservative and Reform Jewry was more tolerant. In a major work, *Judaism as a Civilization* (1934), Rabbi Mordecai Kaplan, perhaps the leading Conservative rabbi, warmly embraced secular Jews. He founded a movement called Reconstructionism that welcomed all Jews.

Reform synagogues changed, too. Once dominated by prominent German Jews, they gradually were taken over by Jews of eastern European origin who were abandoning orthodoxy. These synagogues began to revert to some of the older religious practices, such as Friday night prayer over wine (Kiddush). The older Reform rabbis had once insisted that the Jews were a religion, not a people. The younger rabbis veered toward Zionism, which insists that the Jews are a nation.

Anti-Semitism is an ancient form of bigotry. In the 1920s and 1930s it became more overt and organized than it had been in the past, and took the form of an obsessive fear of Jewish political and economic power. Jew-hating propagandists created elaborate myths which asserted that Jews were part of a world conspiracy plotting to control government, industry, banking, and the media. From 1920 to 1927 the *Dearborn Independent*, a newspaper owned by Henry Ford, published a series of documents known as *The Protocols of the Elders of Zion*, which outlined a secret plot by Jews and Communists to conquer the world.

We will so wear out and exhaust the Gentiles . . . that they will be compelled to offer us an international authority, which by its position will enable us to absorb without disturbance all the governmental forces of the world and thus form a super-government.

"The Protocols of the Elders of Zion"

Supposedly written by Jewish conspirators, the *Protocols* had actually been fabricated by the czar's secret police in 1905. For years Ford's friends, including ex-President Taft, begged him to stop spreading lies. He finally admitted his mistake and publicly apologized to the Jewish community. American Nazis and other right-wing groups continued to use the *Protocols* in the 1930s — and do so to this day.

The spread of anti-Semitism in Europe in the interwar years threatened the Jews in this country as well. A study entitled *Organized Anti-Semitism* by Donald S. Strong cited 121 separate anti-Semitic organizations in the United States between 1933 and 1940. Two of them, the German-American Bund and the Christian Front, were paramilitary groups that followed the lead of Germany's Nazis and bullied and harassed Jewish storekeepers in New Jersey and New York. Many newspapers carried anti-Semitic propaganda. Congressman Burton K. Wheeler, a leading isolationist, charged in a radio address that Lend-Lease aid to Britain was financed by an international conspiracy of Jewish bankers. The most influential anti-Semitic remarks were delivered by Charles A. Lindbergh, the aviation hero, in September 1941. Lindbergh warned that "the three most important groups which have been pressing this country towards the war are the British, the Jewish, and the Roosevelt administration. . . ." He considered the Jews "the most dangerous" because of their influence in the media and the government.

Hitler's attempt to exterminate the Jews in Germany profoundly disturbed American Jews and made them more conscious of their Jewishness. Many had close relatives in Europe but could do little to save them from the Nazis. Attempts by Jewish leaders to have Roosevelt intervene with Hitler and steer intended victims to the U.S. met with little success. Immigration policy had frozen in 1924, and no one, not even the president, seemed willing or able to thaw it out in 1942. The victimization of European Jews converted many American Jews to Zionism. A Jewish state in Palestine seemed like the best place to harbor the refugees and perhaps preserve Judaic culture generally. In 1944 militant Zionists came from Palestine to raise funds and win political backing in the U.S. for a new state of Israel. Many prominent non Jews in America also favored the cause. But as Britain, our war-time ally, bitterly opposed it, the matter was deferred until after the war.

Review

Many people in the 1920s thought the country riddled with moral decay, partly because of the presence of many-tongued, radical foreigners. In spite of an immigration restriction they continued to flow into a country that no longer had use for cheap labor. Nativists believed that without the "foreigners" the nation's problems would disappear. Sensitive to the pressure, Congress passed new antiimmigration laws which greatly limited the entry of Europeans and Asians. As immigration lessened, attention focused on the children and grandchildren of immigrants who tended to move away from the older cultures, thus leaving the elderly and more recent arrivals behind in the ghettos. Even as some of the ethnic divisions blurred with time, religious differences held fast.

While most Protestants considered themselves liberal, a dedicated minority of Fundamentalists battled against liberal Protestant attitudes. The most unifying element for Protestants was the fight for Prohibition. When Prohibition was repealed, organized Protestantism suffered a severe setback. One of the most famous courtroom cases in American history involved a clash between Fundamentalist belief and secular scientific teaching. The 1925 Scopes monkey trial attracted the public's attention. The depression and the war that followed gave rise to a reexamination of religious beliefs. Reinhold Niebuhr's "Neo-orthodox" analysis made him the most famous theologian of his day.

The propaganda of the Ku Klux Klan and the campaign against Al Smith indicated continuing distrust and fear of Catholics. The leftist bent of the National Catholic Welfare Conference as well as the conflict over parochial schools stirred up some Catholics as well as Protestants. FDR wooed the Catholics. He appointed them to high positions and made the first official contact between the U.S. and the Vatican.

By 1920 half the Jews in the U.S. lived in New York City, and most of these were from eastern Europe. The Jews represented a complete social and political spread. Like the blacks they, too, experienced a cultural renaissance in the 1920s, especially in New York City. With the Yiddish language as a cultural adhesive, they expressed themselves most fully in literature and the theater. Most American Jews were not tied formally to any of the religious divisions. In new Jewish communities secular centers and cultural events dominated. Older Jews who remained in the ghetto embraced traditional religion. Anti-Semitism took the form of a fear of Jewish political and economic power, much of it initiated by *The Protocols of the Elders of Zion* published by Henry Ford. When Nazism flooded Europe with anti-Semitism, the ripples spread to America. The new rise of anti-Semitism raised Jewish self-awareness. But their attempts to bring European victims to the U.S. met with little success. The horror of what was happening to their European relatives turned many American Jews to a belief in Zionism.

Questions

1. What were some of the nativist arguments against immigration? Do you believe any of their points were (or still are) valid?
2. What were the basic differences between liberal and Fundamentalist Protestants? How were they expressed in the Scopes trial?
3. Explain the Social Reconstruction program.
4. What form did anti-Semitism take between the two world wars? How did it affect American Jews?

Flappers being arrested for wearing "abbreviated bathing suits" (1922).

In effect, the woman of the Post-war Decade said to man, "You are tired and disillusioned, you do not want the cares of a family or the companionship of mature wisdom, you want exciting play, you want the thrills of sex without their fruition, and I will give them to you." And to herself she added, "But I will be free."

FREDERICK LEWIS ALLEN
(1890–1954)
Only Yesterday, 1931

30

30

From Flapper to Rosie-the-Riveter

Each decade between the two world wars featured women in a different role. The roaring twenties were a time of personal rebellion against established Victorian prudery. The New Woman—the flapper—viewed herself as a liberated being. Unimpressed by the feminist cause, she did not express her rebellion or her independence politically. Indeed, the feminist movement practically ceased to exist after 1920 when women voted in a national election for the first time. The depression ushered in a more sober and reflective woman. She was now less interested in proving her independence than in making a living. She later had to rise to meet a wartime emergency, where she was then burdened with many demands but rewarded with new job opportunities.

"THE GIRL HE LEFT BEHIND" IS STILL BEHIND HIM
She's a WOW WOMAN ORDNANCE WORKER

Women in Normalcy, Depression, and War

The sexual revolution

In the 1920s all outward signs indicated the presence of a sexual revolution. The relaxed morals of the war years continued on into the postwar period. The restless mood of young women was matched by the disillusioned veterans who returned from the battlefields of France, cynical about traditional values. Together these young people challenged the Victorian standards of their parents.

A popular symbol of this rebellion was the flapper, a young woman with bobbed hair, flattened bosom, shortened skirt, and a flair for unconventional fun. In many homes parents stood bewildered as their young daughter donned skimpy dresses and applied makeup for a night on the town. As a final gesture of defiance she placed a long cigarette holder between her teeth, for she intended to smoke in public along with men. She and her date might visit a speakeasy and drink bootleg whiskey. Or perhaps they would go to a dancehall and move to the nervous beat of the Charleston. Before returning home they might "neck" in the back seat of his auto. In this way the new woman felt she was demonstrating her independence both as an adult and as a woman.

Social scientists declared that the rise of premarital sex was most pronounced among middle-class women with college backgrounds. The same pattern held true for contraception. Although public discussion of birth control was still taboo in the 1920s, its private practice was gaining strong acceptance. In 1922 sociologist Katherine B. Davis interviewed a thousand married women, most of whom were college trained and middle class. She found that 75 percent used contraceptives to limit family size and insure a higher standard of living for themselves. Less educated women in lower income brackets were far slower to accept this practice.

The popular culture of the Jazz Age reflected new erotic themes. Radios and phonographs played songs with titles like "I Need Lovin'," "Hot Mama," "I Gotta Have You," and "Hot Lips." Movie houses featured such films as "Blind Husbands," "Kiss Me Again," "Forbidden Paradise," "Why Be Good?" and "Flaming Youth." Many contained scenes showing sexual passion and illicit love. Movies were not the only form of technology affecting the new morality. The automobile, so convenient for family outings, also gave youngsters an easy chance to slip away from parental control. "Necking" in the back seat of a sedan became an American dating ritual.

But if a sexual revolution did occur in the twenties, it had strict limitations. Sex-role conditioning for children remained the same as before. And, as historian Lois Banner has pointed out, the daughters and granddaughters of the "flaming youth" would still have to carry on the struggle for sexual equality. Many of the changes that had started before the First World War did continue a bit further in the twenties but then slowed considerably after a few years. In spite of all the sophisticated talk and flaunting of convention, most young college women observed traditional moral customs. Studies showed that only 25 percent of college women had had sexual intercourse before marriage in the thirties. Most admitted afterward that they had led conventional private lives. Those that had an affair expected it to lead to love and wedding bells. College was still a place to "catch a man" and settle down with him in conventional marriage and parenthood.

In the meantime, the majority of working-class, immigrant, and rural households remained relatively untouched by changes in sexual morality. So, what appeared to be a revolution was really a gradual and partial change.

Athough magazines, newspapers, and the radio often proclaimed that women were fully liberated, antifeminism was still strong. Editorialists, psychologists, and politicians warned middle-class women to pay greater attention to their husbands' and children's needs and less to their own careers. Self-styled former feminists wrote confessionals for women's magazines, telling how miserable they had been while doing organizational work and how happy they became once they decided to remain home and mind the family.

Psychologists, most of whom were male, were practically unanimous in their opposition to the liberation of women. The source of some of this opposition was Sigmund Freud (1856–1939), the Austrian physician who founded psychoanalysis and became one of the intellectual giants of the twentieth century. In one sense Freud had a liberating effect. He asserted that, for both men and women, sex was a natural and agreeable aspect of the human condition. On a popular level some interpreted this to mean that women had as much reason as men to seek compatible sex partners. But he also theorized that women's psychology was basically warped by their envy of the male sex organ and that their sense of inferiority could be overcome only by having children. This led to the conclusion that women were biologically destined only for motherhood and domesticity. Freud's statement, "Anatomy is destiny," was often quoted. Thus, Freudian psychology also had a strong, antifeminist bias.

Marriage patterns

Despite the radical talk of free love, most young people eventually married and settled down. Anarchist Emma Goldman advocated "voluntary motherhood." Novelist Fanny Hurst announced that she and her husband would remain married but live in separate apartments, a form of wedlock advocated by psychologist Havelock Ellis. But for the great majority, the traditional family prevailed.

In a work entitled *Our Changing Morality* (1924) feminist writer Florence Guy Seabury bemoaned the fact that the Victorian images of women died hard. So far as she could tell, modern literature portrayed woman as a role player but rarely as an individual in her own right. Judging from the writings of H. L. Mencken, D. H. Lawrence, and others, she could not really tell who the new woman was. "A changed morality cannot successfully emerge when half of those who participate are regarded not as people but functions. As long as women are pictured chiefly as wife, mother, courtesan — or what not — defining merely a relationship to men — nothing new or strange or interesting is likely to happen. The old order is safe," she concluded.

What was different in the 1920s as opposed to the nineteenth century was that young women expected to have more equal partnerships with their husbands. Marriage, one expert advised, must provide an "entrance into a fuller and richer life; an opportunity for sharing joys and sorrows with a mate who will be not merely a protector or provider but an all-round companion. . . ." But the area of housework and cooking remained solely with the woman. According to theory, the new refrigerators, vacuum cleaners, and other appliances eased the housewife's burden and allowed her more time to express her domestic talents creatively. Yet a close analysis of the daily routine for the average wife-mother produced a disturbing picture.

In most instances where "hostility reactions" were intense for months immediately after unemployment first hit the family, the relations of individuals within the home more or less adjusted themselves; very gradually and very painfully, of course; and the family stuck together in a loose, desperate way, fighting the battle against inimical economical forces.

LOUIS ADAMIC (1899–1951)
Author and journalist

With the rapid disappearance of servants from the middle-class household, she had relatively more cooking and cleaning to do than before. In 1929 the U.S. Department of Agriculture reported that the average housewife put in fifty-one hours a week at routine domestic chores like cleaning and cooking. She was not far behind her farm sister, who worked sixty-two hours a week.

The depression ended the era of the flapper. Hemlines fell as the nation's mood sobered. Pleasure seeking gave way to job seeking. Women who earlier had sought personal independence were now engrossed in trying to earn a living.

The depression touched family life by lowering the rate of births and divorces. With family income falling, couples decided to economize by having fewer children. This probably reflected the greater role of women in family decision making in the depression. As for divorce, couples planning a break-up simply could not afford the costs involved, and stayed together out of necessity.

With relatively little money to spend on entertainment, urban families were forced to spend more time together. Families ate dinner at home and then turned on the phonograph or radio in the evening. Listening to "Amos 'n' Andy" or "The Lone Ranger" was cheap family entertainment. Once a week they went to a movie, where for a few hours Hollywood dreams replaced Main Street realities. The talking pictures (first invented in 1929) catered to family audiences with musicals, full-length animated films, and dramas.

As the depression worsened, the stress on families became more apparent. Unemployment figures for men were staggering. In a culture that evaluated men by their wage-earning capacity, the depression was not only economically destructive to males; it also hurt them socially and psychologically. As the men became more demoralized, the power of women within the family tended to increase. Women often became the stable element that held the family together. The figure of the matriarch became more familiar. She was perhaps most sympathetically symbolized by Ma Joad in *The Grapes of Wrath*. This new pattern for middle-class white America resembled that of low-income immigrant and black families, most of whom had spent their entire lives in a state of economic depression.

Women in the job market

How much progress women made in the outside working world in the twenties is open to discussion. Certainly new careers were becoming available to them. The 1920 census showed women working as truck drivers, miners, steeplejacks, aviators, and sheriffs. Amelia Earhart, the pilot who flew the Atlantic alone in 1932, was an example of a liberated woman with a fabulous career. Still, the *overall proportion* of women in the work force remained nearly constant for a decade: about 20 percent in 1920, 22 percent in 1930. Pay discrimination for women wage workers was rampant—they were paid ap-

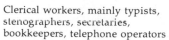

Clerical workers, mainly typists, stenographers, secretaries, bookkeepers, telephone operators

Factory workers and laborers

Household workers, mainly maids, housekeepers, cooks, laundresses

Professional workers, mainly teachers, nurses, social workers, librarians

Service workers (nonhousehold), waitresses, beauticians, hospital attendants, cleaning women, practical nurses

Farm workers

Salespersons, mainly retail trade

Managers, officials, and proprietors, including postmasters, store owners, buyers, executives

Craftspersons and forewomen, including carpenters, mechanics, electricians

Types of Jobs

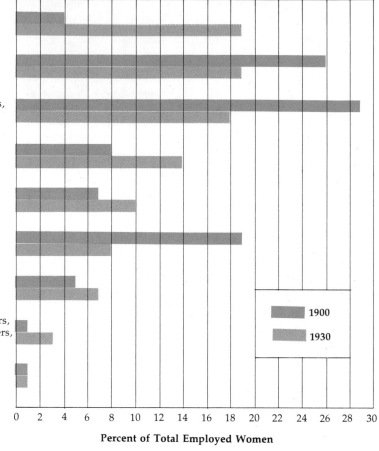

1900

1930

0 2 4 6 8 10 12 14 16 18 20 22 24 26 28 30

Percent of Total Employed Women

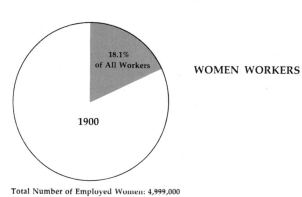

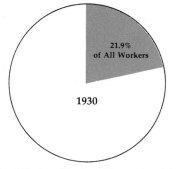

18.1% of All Workers

WOMEN WORKERS

21.9% of All Workers

1900

1930

Total Number of Employed Women: 4,999,000

Total Number of Employed Women: 10,396,000

SOURCE: *Historical Statistics of the United States: Colonial Times to 1957.*

proximately ten cents less an hour for unskilled work than were men. Gradually as the work force increased in the service and trade areas, women wage earners were attracted more and more to clerical jobs in stores and office work. These were low-paying occupations where women gradually displaced men. Domestic employment for women declined. Still, the twenties were not a prosperous time for unskilled workers, which is what most women in the job market were. Day-care centers were practically nonexistent. Unions were too weak to help overcome job discrimination, even if they had wanted to.

The percentage of women working outside the home remained essentially the same in the thirties as it had in the twenties. Professional women continued to have special difficulties getting and holding jobs. A National Educational Association study in 1930–1931 indicated that 77 percent of 1500 city school systems refused to hire married women as teachers. In spite of this, the percentage of *married* working women actually increased from 12 percent in 1930 to 15 percent in 1940.

A very few women became highly successful in businesses that catered to their own sex. Helena Rubinstein and Elizabeth Arden became wealthy and famous in the cosmetics field. But Rubinstein, who called herself "Madame" and wore expensive jewelry for "added courage," said, "It was not easy being a hard-working woman in a man's world."

As the movies became increasingly popular, stereotypes emerged that expressed society's views of women: the sweetheart, the flapper, the vamp, the femme fatale, the wife, and the working girl (who almost always became the nonworking wife as the picture ended). Mary Pickford, who starred in many films as the pure and wholesome girl-next-door, was called America's Sweetheart. Theda Bara was the seductive and exotic vamp. This character later evolved into the femme fatale typified by Greta Garbo and

Jean Harlow, the "Blonde Bombshell," at her slinkiest in a scene from "Dinner at Eight." The movies of the thirties capitalized on the revolution in morals, but sometimes they promised more than they could deliver; producers of one picture advertised "brilliant men, beautiful jazz babies, champagne baths, midnight revels, petting parties in the purple dawn, all ending in one terrific smashing climax."

Marlene Dietrich. Sex American-style was personified in the twenties by the flapper, Clara Bow, and in the thirties by Jean Harlow, a vamp with a sense of humor and a heart of gold. Mae West was one of a kind. She strutted through the thirties purring out racy dialogue and flaunting the conventions of sex and marriage with humorous good nature.

In most films the power of women was the power of sex, as defined by men in their own terms and fantasies. But in the 1930s and 1940s Bette Davis, Rosalind Russell, and Katharine Hepburn evolved a new type: the independent, strong-minded, and witty woman who could hold her own with the most charming and intelligent men. Even though male dominance usually prevailed in the last scene, the overall image was that of woman as a self-reliant, self-respecting individual.

World War II's effect on women

The Second World War pulled so many millions of men out of the job market that women's participation in the labor force became crucial. The government urged women to fill the gaps in the assembly line as well as the empty desk chairs in the offices. Millions responded. Rosie-the-Riveter was welcomed into every plant. Thousands of women joined the WACs and the WAVEs, the newly created women's divisions of the army and navy, to replace servicemen in noncombat jobs. Thousands of other women did volunteer work with the Red Cross and the USO. In many other areas, including local political organizations, women had a larger role than ever before.

To help recruit working mothers, the government opened day-care centers that accommodated 100,000 children by 1945. More school-age boys and girls were on their own during the war years. As juvenile delinquency increased, some editorial writers urged Rosie-the-Riveter to go home and take better care of her children.

Few men expected that women would keep their jobs after the war. Supposedly women were simply doing their patriotic best to keep the nation moving until the men returned from the war. But at the peak of the war effort, the Woman's Bureau took a survey and found that of those working women who had been housewives at the time of Pearl Harbor, more than half wanted to keep their jobs indefinitely. They faced disappointment. As soon as the war ended, women were fired in large numbers and replaced by returning servicemen. Feminist organizations were too weak to lobby against the forced exodus. Peace was about to usher in a whole new era of domesticity for women.

The Decline of Organized Feminism

Freedom through birth control

Organized feminists had achieved a great deal over the years. The efforts of women like Angelina Grimké, Elizabeth Cady Stanton, and Susan B. Anthony had not only won the vote for women but also helped abolish slavery and reduce drunkenness; improved educational and professional opportunities for women; and corrected many inequalities in divorce law. In addition, feminist agitation had bettered the conditions of women and children employed in industry.

Once organized feminism had achieved the vote, though, it entered a period of disunity. Most suffrage organizations had no further reason to continue, so they disbanded. Individual feminists and feminist organizations tried to regroup and fight for other goals important to women, although they found it impossible to find an issue as unifying as suffrage. "I am sorry for you young women who have to carry on the work for the next ten years," the veteran suffragist Anna Howard Shaw told a young feminist, "for suffrage was a symbol, and now you have lost your symbol."

Crystal Eastman, a militant Socialist, believed that in order to obtain the vote, women had masked their true feelings. "Now [1920] they can say what they are really after; and what they are after, in common with all the rest of the struggling world, is *freedom*." Equal pay for equal work was high on the agenda. Boys and men needed to help in the house, and girls and women should forego their economic dependence on men. Public child care was a necessity for some working mothers. Birth control could give women a degree of power over their own lives. The Nineteenth Amendment was just the beginning of the road to liberation.

The term "birth control" was invented by Margaret Sanger (1883–1966). She came from a Catholic family of eleven children. As a trained nurse working in the immigrant slums of New York, she knew that table-top abortions were common among poor women, and she had seen some of the tragic results. Sanger had studied contraception in France, whose stable population was then one of the world's marvels. A philosophical anarchist, a romantic Socialist, and a sometime Greenwich Village rebel, she defied tradition and devoted her entire career to the cause of birth control.

Sanger once wrote, "No woman can call herself free unless she can choose consciously whether she will or will not be a mother." Her husband was arrested because of his involvement with her pamphlet *Family Limitation*. The arresting officer was Anthony Comstock of the Society for the Suppression of Vice and a pioneer in the antipornography movement. Inspector Comstock called Margaret Sanger "a heinous criminal who sought

During the 1930s Margaret Sanger worked to change federal laws so that doctors could provide their patients with contraceptive information. Soon, favorable court decisions made federal legislation unnecessary.

to turn every home into a brothel."

In spite of such attacks, many people joined Sanger's organization, the American Birth Control League, later renamed the Planned Parenthood Foundation. Founded in 1921, it offered information on venereal disease, feminine hygiene, and contraception. Although often an abrasive and difficult person, Sanger became a world leader in family planning. By the time she died in 1966, most legal barriers against birth control in this country had fallen. Her death was noted the world over. In terms of practical accomplishments, few women reformers ever surpassed Margaret Sanger.

Those who hoped that women would vote as a bloc and overthrow bossism and corruption were disappointed. Starting in the 1920 election it was discovered that local issues, class status, and ethnic bias influenced women's votes much more than the fact that they were female. Except when a male candidate was accused of moral or sexual wrongs or when prohibition was at stake, women voters cast ballots the same way as their husbands. And a great many simply failed to vote.

Most women who tried to run for public office found themselves locked out of the smoke-filled rooms where party chiefs made the important decisions. Jeanette Rankin (1880–1973), suffragist and pacifist, did not let this stop her. She had worked as a field secretary for the National American Woman Suffrage Association (NAWSA) and had helped to secure the vote for women both in California and in her home state of Montana. In 1917 Rankin became the first woman elected to Congress. There she introduced the Nineteenth Amendment. Her vote of conscience against U.S. participation in World War I cost her her seat in Congress. Twenty-four years later Jeanette Rankin returned to Congress and cast the only No vote on America's entry into World War II.

However rebellious against the Victorian prudery of their elders, most of the younger women were not greatly attracted to organized feminism. They turned to more exciting pastimes than attending the meetings, rallies, and socials sponsored by women's groups. Before the Nineteenth Amendment was ratified, suffragist leader Carrie Chapman Catt had organized the League of Women Voters to help mobilize the women's vote when it materialized. The League did an excellent job of sorting out political issues but was very slow moving and conservative. As a result, it had almost no appeal for younger

women and was deprived of energy and ideas. The fact that organized feminism was not attracting the new generation loomed as one of its most serious failures.

In 1921 Alice Paul formed the National Woman's Party for only one purpose: to obtain a constitutional amendment giving women complete legal equality with men. As introduced in Congress in 1923 the Equal Rights Amendment (ERA) read: "Men and women shall have equal rights throughout the United States and every place subject to its jurisdiction." For the next ten or fifteen years the ERA ran into stonewall opposition both from the labor movement and from feminists who feared that equality would undermine the laws that protected women workers. ERA supporters agreed that such laws had once served a vital purpose. But, they insisted, the laws had outlived their usefulness. Now they actually hindered women who wished to climb higher in their jobs or careers. Members of the Woman's Party viewed the special industrial laws as old-time paternalism. (Indeed the courts had justified these laws on paternalistic grounds. In 1908, in *Muller* v. *Oregon*, the Supreme Court upheld a state maximum hour law for women, ruling that "woman has always been dependent upon man" and needed man's "protection." Also, "her physical structure and a proper discharge of her maternal functions" justified laws protecting her from "the greed as well as the passion of man.") ERA backers won the support of Judge Ben Lindsey of Denver, a pioneer in family law, who declared that "what is known as special legislation for women is in fact not for women at all, but for children."

Some of the most bitter attacks against the ERA amendment came from feminist organizations. The General Federation of Women's Clubs and the National Consumers' League, headed by feminist leader Florence Kelly, attacked ERA head-on. Kelly, a long-time fighter for protective legislation for women and children, termed the proposed amendment "insane." It would take several more decades for the ERA to gain the full acceptance of feminist organizations.

The Woman's Party tried to support for public office only candidates who would endorse the ERA. When presidential hopeful Al Smith took a swipe at the party, saying, "I believe in equality, but I cannot nurse a baby," the Woman's Party threw its support to Herbert Hoover. Hoover didn't support the ERA, but at least he was vague on the subject.

An erosion of feminist causes

Those feminists who had fought for social reform over the years were dealt several heavy blows by the Supreme Court in the 1920s. In the Adkins Case (1923) the Supreme Court wiped out all federal minimum wage laws for women as a violation of the right to free contract. The Court also overthrew all federal child labor laws. Organized feminists tried to make an end run around the Court by pushing for a constitutional amendment outlawing child labor. However, many groups, from the powerful National Association of Manufacturers and the Catholic church to the innocuous Playground and Recreation Association, opposed it as a Socialist plot to destroy the family. The amendment passed Congress in 1924, but it was ratified by only six states. Thus child-labor laws, next to suffrage and Prohibition the reforms most important to the feminists, came to a halt.

The Red Scare produced more pressure against organized feminism. The "antis" linked the women's movement with Bolshevism and the Soviet Union. The Daughters of the American Revolution smeared the Woman's Party as an arm of the American Communist party and therefore of the Russian Communists. The General Federation of Women's Clubs, the largest and most conser-

The Daughters of the American Revolution was open to women with one or more ancestors who had aided the Patriots. Their "blue-blooded" patriotism and conservative views were the subject of a speech by FDR at their annual meeting in 1938; he later recalled, "I said . . . Keep in the front of your heads all of the time, dear ladies, first, that you are the descendants of immigrants [and] secondly, that you are the descendants of revolutionists. They did not know whether to applaud that or not."

vative feminist group, lost many affiliated clubs during the Red Scare. Even the more liberal clubs lost members.

The settlement-house movement, made up mostly of women who were concerned with the welfare of immigrant families, had always been a source of ideas and strength for feminism. It too was losing steam. In Jane Addams' day women social workers had lived among the immigrant poor, sharing their hardships. As immigration fell off, the need for such services was less immediate. Besides, as social work became a profession, the duties grew more routine and less personal.

Prohibition was another lost ideal. Anyone who really wanted liquor could get it at the local speakeasy, which was as simple to locate as the neighborhood church. Worst of all, the "noble experiment" helped create organized crime, which thrived on bootleg whiskey and prostitution. Many speakeasies had brothels attached.

Feminist activities in the labor movement, never very successful to begin with, lost effectiveness. Fewer than 3 percent of all working women were unionized by 1924. The percentage of women in the skilled trades was static or declining, in spite of the organizational efforts of the National Women's Trade Union League. Fearing that women would steal men's jobs, the AFL leadership refused to subsidize the women's union beyond the barest minimum. Still small and struggling, the NWTUL disappeared at the end of the Second World War.

Feminism and the New Deal

By the time of the depression the organized women's movement was dead. Still, individual feminist leaders and remnant groups found the New Deal extremely receptive to their ideas. Such pressure groups as the League of Women Voters, the NWTUL, and the Consumers' League helped develop some of the most important social welfare laws of the thirties. The Consumers' League, for example, helped draft a number of the NRA codes for labor and promoted both the Social Security Act of 1935 and the Food, Drug, and Cosmetic Act of 1936. Old-time feminists, including Roosevelt's secretary of labor, Frances Perkins, the first woman cabinet member, took part in government affairs.

The most prominent woman during the New Deal period was the president's wife, Eleanor Roosevelt (1884–1962), a confirmed feminist. A humanist, she served as advocate for many groups whose lack of power often made them invisible—women, minority groups, the poor. It was largely due to Mrs. Roosevelt's urging that so many women came to work for the federal government during FDR's administrations. She was roasted daily by the press for her activism. Her high-pitched voice and plain looks made her the object of endless ridicule from Roosevelt haters. But her warmth and sincerity won her public approval.

The president did not interfere with his wife's activities, which were often helpful to him. For example, when she entertained the girls of a Washington reformatory at the White House, most of whom were black, the southern press was outraged. FDR remained silent. While he himself avoided offending any southern congressional leaders, his wife was helping win the black vote.

Eleanor Roosevelt's advocacy of the rights of women and minorities was constant. Her advice was not always taken; her suggestions were often shelved. She was a defender and publicizer of causes, rather than an initiator. But throughout the Roosevelt period, the president's wife was the conscience that would not let the nation forget that, for many Americans, freedom and equality had yet to be achieved.

Review

The rebellion against Victorian prudery was symbolized by the flaming-youth generation and the high-spirited, short-skirted flapper of the 1920s. Jazz age music, Hollywood movies, and the automobile all contributed to or reflected changing mores. But antifeminism continued strong, and writers and psychologists warned women that their destinies were tied to their families and homes. In the end most young people married and settled down to traditional family life. The image of the domestic woman was strengthened, but now there were expectations of closer marital partnerships. The depression brought a sobering effect. Unemployment forced families closer together in the home, and recreation largely became a family affair. But as the depression wore on, family stress deepened, and this in turn brought the image of the matriarchal woman to the fore. Although women forged into new fields in the twenties and thirties, the proportion of women in the work force remained the same as before, and pay discrimination was the rule. World War II made women a crucial part of the labor force. Although many wanted to keep their jobs after the war, they were frequently fired to make way for returning servicemen.

Organized feminism fell apart after it achieved the vote. The fight for other goals, such as equal pay and birth control, was carried on both by organizations and individual women. Women did not vote as a bloc, as some suffragists had hoped they would, and they still had little political power. Organized feminism was especially unsuccessful at recruiting the new generation. The National Woman's Party was formed to obtain complete legal equality with men. The Equal Rights Amendment, introduced into Congress in 1923, was opposed overwhelmingly by both labor and women, including many feminist organizations. Social feminists were also dealt several setbacks by the Supreme Court, the failure of prohibition, and the Red Scare. The settlement-house movement and the National Women's Trade Union League also lost steam. The women's movement had almost died by the time of the depression. Remnant groups and individual feminists found an ally in the New Deal, which drafted some of the social welfare laws they championed. Eleanor Roosevelt was the most prominent woman in the New Deal era. She served many powerless groups by functioning as a direct link to the White House. Her support of women and minorities was constant, and she did not let the nation forget that they were not yet equal.

Questions

1. Identify and define: (a) *Our Changing Morality*, (b) Crystal Eastman, (c) *Family Limitation*, (d) Jeanette Rankin, (e) Alice Paul, (f) Mae West, and (g) Frances Perkins.
2. What causes led to the "death" of the women's movement?
3. What changes did the family of the 1920s have to face in the 1930s?
4. The movies of the period fostered stereotypes of the way society saw women. What current movies do you think typify today's view of women?
5. What were the arguments for and against the ERA?

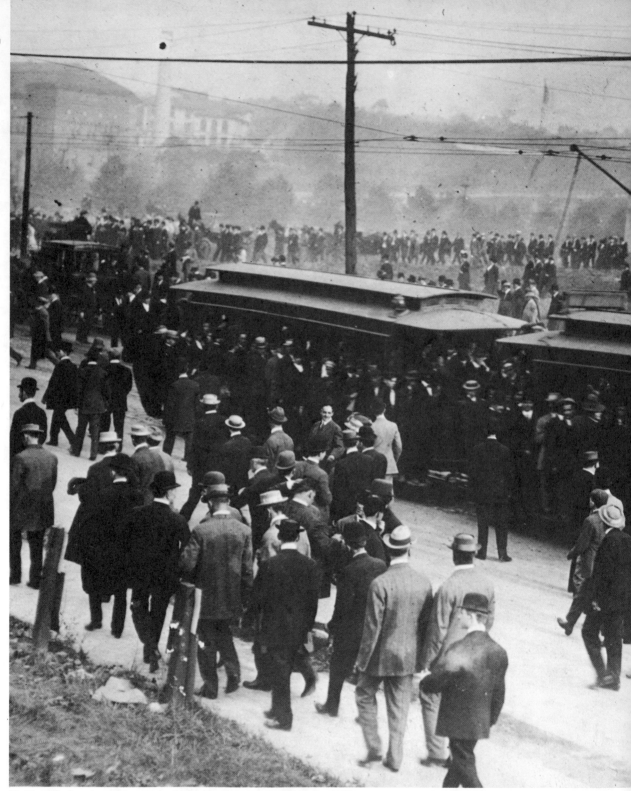

Unidentified metropolitan area after a sporting event during the 1920s.

In the United States there is more space where nobody is than where anybody is. This is what makes America what it is.

GERTRUDE STEIN (1874–1946)
American writer

31

31
An Urban Nation

Organizing an ideal community takes patience, self-denial, faith in the future, and a willingness to cooperate with others. Few attempts have been successful. During the interwar years utopian communities, such as Brook Farm and Oneida had been, were now no longer part of the American Dream. Most of the experimental colonies that survived the Civil War had failed by the end of the century. Americans were now defining the good life in terms of personal property and individualism, not community.

Ideas about community life have been singled out for special treatment in each of the five chapters on community. The first part of this chapter focuses on community life as seen by American intellectuals from the end of World War I to the end of World War II. In the period from 1918 to 1945 new utopian communities were in short supply, but the era had many commentators who wrote on the good—and the bad—life in America. Novelists and essayists, sociologists, architects, and city planners made a searching analysis of their society. The ideas that they aired about big cities, suburbs, and small towns helped shape new public attitudes. Mostly they were critical of community life.

The second focus, on the city, covers the period when the cities officially "came of age." In 1920 the census announced that a majority of Americans for the first time resided in cities. The 1920s were years of relative peace and quiet in urban America, though the depression years grew more tumultuous. A major innovation in urban affairs occurred in the 1930s—the direct and massive involvement of the federal government in city administration and finance. The New Deal approach to cities, as to other areas, produced both hope and disappointment.

The Search for Community:
An Intellectual Pursuit

Main Street under attack

Intellectuals in the first half of the twentieth century generally did not paint a rosy picture of community life in America. They had hopes and dreams, but these were muted; what most impressed them was the reality of alienation.

American literary tradition has expressed so much negativism about big cities that one might have expected it to look more favorably upon small towns. Yet in the early part of the century small towns also came under sharp attack. The "revolt from the village," a literary bombardment against rural and small-town America, began after the war and lasted well into the thirties. Often the sharpest critics were the small towns' renegade sons and daughters. Some belonged to the "lost generation" of writers who sat in cafés on Paris' Left Bank, writing of their own home towns with mingled longing and hate.

To many of the new American writers, every aspect of small-town life merited criticism. *Winesburg, Ohio* (1919), a short story collection by Sherwood Anderson, dealt with characters trapped and tormented in their midwestern village. Poet and critic Van Wyck Brooks found American small towns "frostbitten, palsied, full of morbid, bloodless death-in-life." Sinclair Lewis' *Main Street* (1920) painted a devastating portrait of the provincials, bigots, and philistines of "Gopher Prairie" (Sauk Center, Minnesota).

Lewis' satiric novel *Babbitt* (1922) dealt with a larger community, the new, shiny middle-class city of Zenith. Its hero, realtor-booster George F. Babbitt, leads a drab home life. He attempts to change by flirting with liberalism and having an affair but soon returns to the fold. *Babbitt* was a major best seller, and the hero's name came to symbolize the narrow-minded and complacent American of middle-class background. But Nazism and America's entry into the war in 1941 changed Sinclair Lewis' mind about Middle America. For all their faults, the Babbitts in the end seemed to him the last hope of civilization, and he apologized to them publicly.

The community under the microscope

For the first time university scholars began to study community life in a systematic way. Sociologists at the University of Chicago started an in-depth study of Chicago which led in time to the study of other cities and to the founding of urban sociology as a subspecialty. The leading scholars at Chicago were Ernest W. Burgess and Robert E. Park. Burgess became famous for developing a theory that cities grew outward in concentric rings that surrounded the central core. Park's work was aimed at helping all city dwellers achieve a new order — "a social control [similar] to that which grew up naturally in the family, the clan, and the tribe." For the next twenty years he and the faculty and graduate students at Chicago dissected various urban zones, districts, areas, neighborhoods, and subcommunities. They looked at the city in its ecological setting and treated it as an organic unit. They produced distinguished works that analyzed immigrant ghettos, boy's gangs, hobo life, wealthy areas, small towns, and new suburbs.

One of the classic community studies was *Middletown*, published by Robert S. and Helen M. Lynd in 1929. Here, and in a follow-up study issued eight years later, the Lynds put

The main street of Ripon, Wisconsin, was typical of many in midwestern small towns. In 1929 Ripon celebrated the seventy-fifth birthday of the Republican party, which was allegedly born there in a little white schoolhouse. During the '20s literary figures deplored American materialism, prosperity, Puritanism, and conformity—characteristics which, in distilled form, they perceived in small-town life.

Muncie, Indiana, under a microscope. Their team of investigators pried into every corner of the town of 35,000 people. They studied the transition to industrialism and social mobility in the small, ethnically homogeneous town. They found the people often sharply divided along class or occupational lines. In some ways the workers and those in business lived widely separate lives. Yet they were united by the enthusiastic spirit of the business community. Middletowners were chronic joiners and town boosters. This

was reflected in the scores of organizations— men's fraternal groups, noon luncheon clubs, women's service clubs—which met regularly in the Chamber of Commerce building. Business people asserted that Middletown could outdo any rival community. Boosterism appealed even to the youth, and the high-school basketball game was as much a show of town spirit as it was an athletic event. Middletowners admired the slogan "United We Stick, Divided We're Stuck./ United We Boast, Divided We Bust."

Another classic community study was the Yankee City series published from 1941 to 1947 by anthropologist W. Lloyd Warner and his associates. The subject this time was industrial Newburyport, Massachusetts. The town was closely examined in five volumes based on "millions of social facts" collected by thirty research assistants during the 1930s. Warner dissected the town when it was undergoing heavy stress. Founded in the colonial era, Newburyport had become a major shoe-manufacturing center. In the midst of the depression a strike broke out at the largest shoe factory. Amazingly, immigrants and natives, Jews and Gentiles, descendants of old Yankee families, and ethnics, all united in support of the strike. Warner's study uncovered two reasons for this rare display of solidarity. First, local factory owners had recently sold out to a bigger firm headquartered in Boston and New York, and, second, craft work was declining in the factory and new assembly-line methods devalued the workers' sense of importance. They resented the disappearance of old face-to-face relationships with management and felt like cogs in a machine. A small, weak, unaffiliated union mobilized community sentiment and won a victory which would have been impossible a generation earlier.

From this study Warner formulated his famous (and controversial) theory about social status in America. There were, he asserted, six classes worth considering: upper-upper, lower-upper, upper-middle, lower-middle, upper-lower, and lower-lower. Warner and most other social scientists were accused of oversimplifying and distorting community life to make it conform to their own biases. Yet through their efforts the study of community life had reached new sophistication.

Regional planning and garden cities

The profession of city planning had emerged in the U.S. around the time of the Chicago World's Fair of 1893. By the 1920s it had established a reputation for competence in regulating the flow of city traffic and water, in designing parks and parkways, in constructing playgrounds and bridges, and in laying out streets and housing projects. Some planners believed in improving the city on a piecemeal basis. Others were profoundly critical of city life and urged a drastic overhaul on a grand scale—that is, a regional approach. They formed the Regional Planning Association of America (RPAA) to foster urban decentralization. Its members included architects, city planners, and intellectuals interested in community reform. An eloquent advocate was Lewis Mumford, writer and critic of city planning and architecture. He was concerned with the way some communities were growing "cancerously" large while others were shriveling, no attempt being made in the meantime to achieve a balance. In *The Culture of Cities* (1938), a classic work that traces the roots of urban life, Mumford appeared extremely optimistic about the future of cities. Thirty years more of urban crisis and decay soured him considerably.

The most impressive outgrowth of the regional planning movement was the New York Regional Plan, a ten-volume survey based on years of research about the New York metropolitan area. Funded privately by the Russell Sage Foundation, the plan made comprehensive recommendations for future development. Basically it approved of the automobile as the main mode of transport—an idea challenged in other quarters. Some civic leaders in and around New York accepted the plan on principle and it was implemented partially and on a piecemeal basis. Other metropolitan centers came under similar scrutiny, but with less success. After publication of the New York Regional Plan in 1931, however, the value of regional planning was no longer in dispute.

Another result of the regional planning

We began the experiment with three assets, courage—foolhardiness our city friends called it; a vision of what modern methods and modern domestic machinery might be made to do in the way of eliminating drudgery; and the fact that my wife had been born and had lived up to her twelfth year on a ranch in the West.

RALPH BORSODI (fl. 1920–1933)

movement was the attempt to adapt the English concept of the "garden city" to American conditions. Since the turn of the century planners and builders in England had been creating small, self-contained experimental towns entirely surrounded by "greenbelts." The belts of wild or cultivated land provided the towns with income from farming and parkland for recreation; most important of all, they restricted the maximum size of the community. About thirty thousand people were the limit for a garden city. Factories were essential to provide jobs, but they had to restrict themselves in location and number in order not to destroy the human values of the community. Real estate was to be cooperatively owned by the residents and profits limited.

The garden city idea was first tried here by suburban developers during the 1920s. Architect Clarence Stein, a leading member of the RPAA, sold the notion to some real estate men who were opening land in the outlying areas of New York City. Stein's ideas took shape first in the new suburb of Sunnyside, in the borough of Queens, and, to a greater extent, in Radburn, New Jersey. Radburn was situated on a 1600-acre site some sixteen miles from Manhattan. Stein abandoned the customary grid of straight city streets in favor of super blocks and gently curving streets. In the center of each super block was a park for recreation. Stein called it a "common" or "village green," after the familiar feature of Old New England towns. Pedestrians crossed roads on bridges and overpasses, while special service roads were designed for garbage collection and deliveries. Each single-family house and each unit in a duplex had a livingroom window that looked out on a private garden. In Stein's mind Radburn was the first attempt to learn "how to live with the auto" or "how to live in spite of it." The Radburn community was not designed for low-income families and it suffered financially during the depression, but it still won international acclaim for its experimental design.

Another garden city planner, Clarence Perry, stressed the belief that through proper planning suburban Americans could revive the neighborhood, a dying form of community. City people were too crowded together and yet too isolated from one another to participate in neighborhood activities. He concentrated on creating community centers where family life could flourish. A typical center included an elementary school, a shopping complex, a recreation hall. Here children could play safely and adults gather in a friendly atmosphere. Instead of feeling alone and alienated, families could join their neighbors in wholesome activities. In modified form Perry's ideas found their way into many suburban developments.

Back to the land

Some city dwellers decided to drop out of urban life altogether and take up subsistence farming. They hoped to demonstrate that it was possible to live off the land on a small, self-sufficient homestead, and make or grow all of their own goods. In 1920, long before the crash, Ralph Borsodi and his family fled New York City, which he considered "one of the most fantastic creations in the history of man." The Borsodis started a family farm. They cultivated and processed their own food, and even made their own clothing. The family was the center of this farm utopia. In his book, *This Ugly Civilization* (1929), Borsodi championed what today would be called "family ecology." He wrote:

To be able to abandon the buying of the product of our non-essential and undesirable factories, and still be comfortable, the home must be reorganized—it must be made into an economically creative institution. It must cease being a mere consumption unit. It must become a production unit as well. It must be as nearly as possible an organic home—house, land, machine, materials and a group of individuals organized not for mere consumption but for creative and productive living.

Another Borsodi book, *Flight from the City: The Story of a New Way to Family Security* (1933), influenced thousands of middle-class urbanites who had decided to flee the cities during the depression. Certainly Borsodi had no impact on the mass of subsistence farmers during the depression who were beating a heavy path in the other direction—fleeing the countryside for the cities.

America's most distinguished architect, Frank Lloyd Wright, echoed the revival of agrarian sentiment. In 1935 he dreamed up an imaginary rural utopia called Broadacre City. Here he speculated that city people could escape from unemployment, exploitation, crime, and all the other ills of modern city life. Broadacre City, an agricultural community of four square miles with 1400 families and a ratio of about one person per acre, would stress the human dimension. It would have "*little* farms, *little* homes for industry, *little* factories, *little* schools, and a *little* university . . . and the farm itself, notwithstanding its animals, becomes the most attractive unit of the city." This ideal city, or town, would use all modern conveniences and be run democratically.

Wright's basic principle, which he applied in his own work, was "organic architecture" —buildings created to harmonize with the natural landscape. Inner and outer spaces were to melt together and flow naturally into one another. Wright detested New York City as it then existed. He suggested that five skyscrapers, each a mile high, be placed in the middle of Central Park. These would provide shelter and work space for everyone. The rest of the city could then be dismantled, brick by brick, and converted into an enormous park and playground.

The Exploding Metropolis

The magnetic appeal of the cities

Say the worst about American cities—that they are ugly, overcrowded, ungovernable, and violent—they still had a magic pulling power. Like magnets scattered across the map, they attracted outsiders by the millions, from all quarters of the globe, during war and peace, during depression and prosperity. Cities offered jobs and the thousand-and-one amenities of civilization: schools and stores, parks and museums, theaters and libraries, ballparks and zoos, cathedrals and concert halls, stock exchanges and banks. With a complete range of such attractions, American cities like New York, Chicago, and San Francisco were among the world's leading metropolitan centers.

In the nineteenth century the millions of American farmers and European peasants

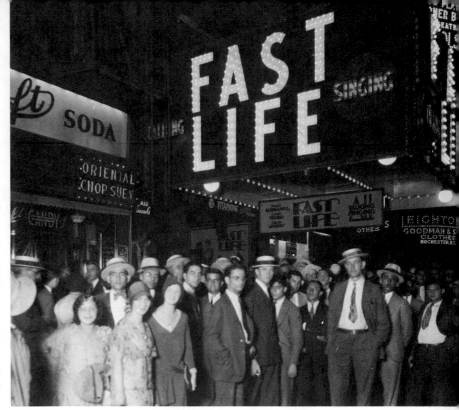

Commenting on the virtues of the American city as well as its problems, the Urban Committee of the National Resources Committee concluded in 1937 that "there is liberty of development in isolation and wide spaces, but there is also freedom in the many-sided life of the city where each may find his own kind. There is democracy in the scattered few, but there is also democracy in the thick crowd with its vital impulse and its insistent demand for a just participation in the gains of our civilization."

who had piled up in the cities often came there for compelling reasons. Their economic survival depended on it. But, given a free choice, how many urbanites would return to the land? Probably very few. The Chicago saloon keeper Mr. Dooley, in Finley Peter Dunne's popular newspaper column, expressed this thought to his companion, Hogan. "'We ought to live where al th' good things iv life comes fr'm,' says Hogan. 'No,' says I. 'Th' place to live in is where all th' good things iv life goes to. Iverything that's worth havin' goes to th' city an' is iced. . . .'"

By 1920 America's population was already 51 percent urban, and the proportion would grow even more in the next decade.* This had much to do with the shifting foundations of the economy. Retail trade and services were increasing, while farm income was falling. The rural population decreased by almost one million in the decade of the twenties. The Midwest and South were most seriously affected by the exodus of white

and black farm families, most of whom ended up in cities like Detroit, Pittsburgh, Los Angeles, New York, and Chicago. The pace of urbanization slowed down during the depression, but the census of 1940 recorded 57 percent of Americans living in cities. By the end of the Second World War the figure had risen even higher.

Large metropolitan centers dominated the urban scene. Established industrial cities matured still further in size, especially those associated with autos, oil, and steel (Detroit,

*The census definition, like many statistical definitions, was arbitrary and misleading. It held that a place with 2500 people was a city. Still it was symbolically important and widely accepted. Today, the U.S. Census rarely discusses "the city" as such, but instead refers to a Standard Metropolitan Statistical Area (SMSA). This is defined as a county "or group of contiguous counties which contain at least one city of 50,000 inhabitants or more or 'twin cities' with a combined population of at least 50,000," plus the adjacent counties which are "essentially metropolitan" and are socially and economically integrated with the central city. The major SMSAs have 100,000 people or more. There were 82 of them in 1900, 147 in 1950, and 247 in 1970.

GROWTH OF URBAN POPULATION, 1900–1940

	1900	1910	1920	1930	1940
Urban Dwellers	30 million	42 million	54 million	69 million	74 million
Rural Dwellers	46 million	50 million	51 million	54 million	57 million

SOURCE: Bureau of the Census.

AMERICA'S BIGGEST CITIES, 1900–1940

1900		1920		1940	
New York	3,437,000	New York	5,620,000	New York	7,455,000
Chicago	1,699,000	Chicago	2,702,000	Chicago	3,397,000
Philadelphia	1,294,000	Philadelphia	1,824,000	Philadelphia	1,931,000
St. Louis	575,000	Detroit	994,000	Detroit	1,623,000
Boston	561,000	Cleveland	797,000	Los Angeles	1,504,000
Baltimore	509,000	St. Louis	773,000	Cleveland	878,000
Pittsburgh	452,000	Boston	748,000	Baltimore	859,000
Cleveland	382,000	Baltimore	734,000	St. Louis	816,000
Buffalo	352,000	Pittsburgh	588,000	Boston	771,000
San Francisco	343,000	Los Angeles	577,000	Pittsburgh	672,000

SOURCE: Bureau of the Census.

Pittsburgh, Cleveland, Akron, Birmingham, Tulsa, Los Angeles). Resort cities enjoyed the most spectacular development of all; Miami, Florida zoomed from 30,000 in 1920 to 110,000 in 1930. The number of metropolitan areas increased, as did the number of people living in them. They cast their webs over surrounding territories through a network of transportation, communication media, and economics. The largest city newspapers were delivered daily far into the hinterlands. The big city advertisers addressed their messages to the same broad horizons. The major chain stores sold their standardized products throughout metropolitan areas all over the country.

Skyscrapers seemed to match in height the dollar value of downtown real estate. As land values went up, so did the steel spires. The value of urban land (a fraction of one percent of all U.S. land) doubled from an estimated $25 billion in 1920 to $50 billion in 1926. (Meanwhile the value of farm land fell from $55 billion to $35 billion.) The Gothic-spired 58-story Woolworth Building in New York City, completed in 1913, was the benchmark for many years. It was imitated in Kansas City, San Francisco, Cleveland, and elsewhere. Skyscrapers gave American cities a particularly romantic aura—that of a "gigantic, compact, and brilliant world," in the words of a French historian. The spires and crowns jaggedly silhouetted against the sky symbolized American dynamism. The Empire State Building, a 102-story office tower, was begun in 1929 and opened in the midst of the depression, to become for a while a financial white elephant to its owners.

A boom in the suburbs

Between 1920 and 1940 big city populations, businesses, and industries began to move out into industrial and residential suburbs. The suburban trend was an old one, but it became far more rapid and widespread than before. While metropolitan centers kept expanding, their greatest growth occurred on the outer edges rather than in the middle.

Technology had always influenced the size of cities, and it did so more than ever after World War I, when automobiles came into their own. During the nineteenth century reliance on railroads to deliver raw materials and take away finished products and stationary steam boilers to provide power kept factories in a relatively compact district, and workers were forced to live within walking distance of their jobs. Later, the electric trolley allowed people to live away from the heart of the city. Streetcar suburbs popped up along the trolley lines. Cars, which increased from eight thousand in 1900 to 32 million by 1940, further spread residential areas. People in the job market had new options on where to live or work. "Automobile suburbs" filled in the spaces left open by "streetcar suburbs."

Similarly, electrical power delivered by wire replaced steam power in industry, and trucks freed factories from dependence on railroad lines. These developments encouraged industry to move out of rundown, highly taxed properties in the crowded city to a suburb where space was far less expensive and taxes much lower. The rapid shift of industry and homes to the suburbs gave rise to the expression "exploding metropolis." The city was bursting open and scattering its contents on the adjoining countryside in one of the sharpest transformations in the thousands of years of its history.

The exploded metropolis required new and better highways to speed commuters and goods between downtown and the suburbs. Under the National Highway Act of 1916 federal money was earmarked for roads to connect cities and to develop virgin areas for real estate development.

Suburban growth on the fringes of a great metropolis did not necessarily ease the problems that came from urban crowding, however. No sooner was construction of the George Washington Bridge announced in the 1920s than a land boom erupted in Bergen County, New Jersey, across the Hudson River from New York City. Anticipating the new traffic to and from Manhattan, civic leaders on both sides of the Hudson River agreed to place all bridges, tunnels, wharves, ferries, terminals, expressways, and airports that served metropolitan New York under one management. The giant interstate and interurban agency, the New York Port Authority, worked too well. It smoothed the way for a record number of trains, cars, taxis, buses, and trucks to pour into and out of lower Manhattan each day. All these vehicles, plus millions of pedestrians, competed doggedly for every inch of available space. Some planners proposed banning private cars from Manhattan to ease the crush. The Port Authority, which received much of its revenue from tolls on cars and trucks, rejected the ban.

The rush to the suburbs, accompanied by the metropolitan immigration of blacks from the South, helped alter the racial composition of cities. The central city housed more blacks and fewer whites; in the suburbs the reverse was true. Between 1930 and 1940 Chicago's black population increased by 18 percent. The changing racial picture sharpened the extremes in income in the metropolitan areas. The lowest income, highest crime rate, and worst housing and schooling were found in a city's inner core.

Crime in the twenties

More frightening than the crush of traffic was the spurt of organized crime in the twenties.

Local police in most cities found themselves unable to cope with the growing gangsterism. Chicago's was the most notorious. Over seventy-five protection rackets flourished there in the 1920s. Small businesses paid gangsters an estimated $136 million yearly in protection money to avoid violence against themselves. In 1927 the Al Capone gang grossed over $100 million from bootleg liquor and beer, gambling, and prostitution. Over five hundred gangland slayings occurred in Chicago between 1920 and 1930. In the fifteen months from October 1927 to January 1929, a total of 157 bombs exploded there, but not one of the bombers was ever brought to justice. The gangsterism was so intimidating and the bribery and corruption of public officials so widespread that few criminals were prosecuted. Federal revenue agents and the FBI stepped in—they put Capone in jail in 1933—but it was the depression and the end of Prohibition, rather than the gangbusters, that halted this era of urban violence.

The new federal partnership

After the stock market crash in 1929 the symbol of urban life was no longer the speakeasy but the grim Hooverville down by the railroad yard, where the homeless unemployed huddled together for warmth. City and state treasuries went bankrupt. Public and private relief agencies were unable to deal with all the people who crowded their offices. Welfare workers threw up their hands in despair. The city reflected the hard times. Landlords stopped making repairs, builders halted projects in mid-construction, neighborhoods declined, sewers backed up, utilities were poorly maintained, and trolley and bus service deteriorated. The depression exposed the chronic ills of urban life that had seemed unimportant during the prosperous twenties: overtaxation, traffic congestion, racial and ethnic ghettos, inadequate parks and playgrounds, and insufficient fire and police protection. Above all, the housing shortage that had troubled American cities from the beginning of the Industrial Revolution became even more serious.

During the New Deal the federal government entered municipal affairs for the first time in history, and the cities welcomed it with open arms. Federal planners, welfare workers, budget experts, and engineers swarmed into the city halls of the nation to recommend new policies. City mayors looked to Washington for money and for new ideas. The United States Conference of Mayors was formed in 1933 with Mayor Fiorello La Guardia of New York City as chairman. The Conference became a vigorous force in shaping New Deal urban policies.

The New Deal advanced many community programs. To city planners, slum clearance, new towns, public housing, and regional planning were old ideas that dated back to the Progressive era. But few of them had ever left the drawing board. Now they were dusted off and put to work.

The administration focused on the thousands of middle-class families whose homes had been repossessed by banks for nonpayment of mortgages. Following a model developed by Hoover, the New Deal set up the Home Owners Loan Corporation in 1933, which helped people with endangered home mortgages. These were given long-term refinancing at low interest rates. By 1937 the HOLC had saved millions of homes by providing direct loans (but not subsidies).

Another agency, the Federal Housing Authority (FHA), insured loans made by private lenders for repairing old homes and for purchasing new ones. The FHA set higher building standards than had previously existed. By lengthening the term of mortgages, cutting out second mortgages, and consolidating payments of principal and interest, the FHA gave middle-income Americans a

"Home..."

PROPERTY IMPROVEMENT
CREDIT NOW AVAILABLE THROUGH
LOCAL FINANCIAL INSTITUTIONS
APPROVED BY THE
FEDERAL HOUSING ADMINISTRATION

BETTER HOUSING PROGRAM

"for those who live in houses, those who repair and construct houses, and those who invest in houses"..FRANKLIN D.ROOSEVELT

In spite of increasingly liberal FHA mortgages, private building construction lagged until 1939. The boom of the '20s had oversupplied the cities with apartments, hotels, and office buildings. But loans to middle-income families permitted them to keep houses they might otherwise have lost through foreclosure. The FHA was so popular with the middle class that it was one of the few alphabetical agencies to outlast the Age of Roosevelt.

chance to keep their own houses. For middle-income families the FHA was one of the most successful New Deal agencies. Yet it did little to ease the problems of the poor in the central city, who rarely owned their own homes to begin with. In fact, by encouraging the white flight to the suburbs, it aggravated racial and social patterns.

Public housing

The Public Works Administration (PWA), established in 1933, undertook major community projects that the cities could not afford to handle. It built or repaired an amazing assortment of schools, roads, parks, sewage treatment plants, and bridges. This put people to work, stimulated the economy, and helped the cities.

Congress had hoped that the PWA would tackle slum clearance and substantially ease the housing shortage. The PWA had begun some fifty housing projects in more than a score of cities and had constructed 25,000 dwelling units for 90,000 people when it ran into trouble. While slum dwellers, city politicians, and builders clamored for more federal housing, opposition to the program grew. The real estate lobby, suburban politicians, and southern members of Congress feared racial integration in public housing. They realized that much of Roosevelt's New Deal legislation rested on a shaky interpretation of the general welfare clause of the Constitution. Opponents of federal housing filed suits to keep the government from buying more land for housing projects. In the Louisville Lands Case of 1935 a U.S. court ruled that the government had gone beyond its constitutional powers in condemning private property for public housing. Government lawyers, fearful that unfavorable decisions might wreck not only the housing program but the entire New Deal, decided not to appeal. In fact, the administration backed away from the direct approach to housing.

A new formula was worked out by congressional supporters of public housing rather than by the administration. Under the National Housing Act of 1937, backed by Senator Wagner of New York among others, the federal government would earmark land for urban renewal and make the funds available to cities as long-term loans. The actual buying of the land and building and managing of the housing projects were turned over to the cities. The program was to be administered by the United States Housing Authority, which replaced the PWA in the housing field. Although opposed by conservatives, the new law was upheld by the courts, and the program produced more low-rent public housing than the PWA. As far as blacks were concerned, it was a key program of the New Deal.

Greenbelt towns

FDR himself believed that people were "better off in the country" and that cities were "rather hopeless," according to one of his brain trust, Rexford Guy Tugwell. The gentleman farmer always lurked just beneath the surface in FDR. Thus he was quite enthusiastic when Tugwell, as head of the Resettlement Administration, proposed that green-belt towns be built on the edge of all major cities and that city dwellers be enticed to resettle there. "The green belts linked together would form continuous, permanent open spaces around the city, protecting it and each suburb from overcrowding and sprawling, haphazard suburban development and encroaching industries." The communities were to be of various sizes and shapes, but all would fit the landscape.

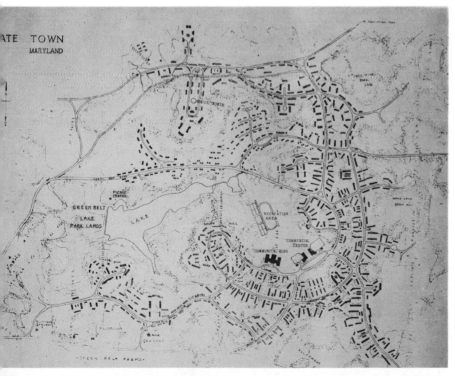

Plan for the layout of Greenbelt, Maryland, the "ultimate town." It was one of only three greenbelt towns actually constructed by the Resettlement Administration. Rexford G. Tugwell, head of the RA, described one of the agency's goals in 1935: "My idea is to go just outside centers of population, pick up cheap land, build a whole community and entice people into it. Then go back into the cities and tear down whole slums and make parks of them." RA was phased out in 1937.

Much influenced by the garden city concept and by the actual layout of Radburn, New Jersey, Tugwell hoped to construct three thousand greenbelt towns. He only built three: Green Hills, Ohio (near Cincinnati), Greendale, Wisconsin (near Milwaukee), and Greenbelt, Maryland (in the suburbs of Washington, D.C.). These New Deal utopias—denounced as "Communist towns"—proved expensive to build and had their appropriations slashed by Congress. Eventually, they provided homes for fewer than 2300 families. The government unloaded them at a loss after World War II. Nevertheless, the greenbelt towns have received high marks from those familiar with the story of housing reform. Historian Paul Conkin writes, "They represented, and still do represent, the most daring, original, and ambitious experiments in public housing in the history of the United States."

The New Deal's urban policy broke sharply with the past. Except for Washington, D.C., the federal government had never before played any role in the physical aspect of cities. Still, its final accomplishments were far less radical than its enemies feared and far less effective than its advocates hoped. Neither those who wanted to improve the city from within, nor those who dreamed of escaping to the country felt satisfied. The nation had not worked out an acceptable method of urban renewal. It had not provided enough decent housing, public or private, for the poor. Worst of all, perhaps, it had not accepted slum clearance as a step toward racial equality. The political deadlock that ended the New Deal in 1938, as well as the shift to defense production, canceled any further expansion of federal authority in urban affairs. What the New Deal did was to make the federal government a deciding partner in the future of cities.

Uncle Sam retained the power of the purse, even if he did not know what to do with it. After the war the partnership between the cities and the federal government would be renewed on a different plane, with the introduction of urban renewal, poverty programs, and revenue sharing.

Review

A literary bombardment of the small town began after World War I. Many of the critics were writers who were turning in anger on their own birthplaces. After the attack on Pearl Harbor small-town America was reexamined in a more favorable light. Universities also used their resources to focus on the community, both town and city. *Middletown* and the Yankee City series were important research studies. City planners, applying different bodies of knowledge to community life, could advise on traffic patterns, recreation areas, congestion, and other problems of modern living. Regional planning, an especially important field for community reform, included larger areas than narrow municipal limits. Some planners wanted to start fresh by creating new communities. Several garden cities were actually built. Agrarianism still had a strong emotional pull for many Americans. Their sentiment was echoed in Frank Lloyd Wright's plans for Broadacre City.

In spite of all the flaws, cities continued to attract people from all over the nation and the world. By 1920 51 percent of all Americans were urbanites, and the figure kept rising. Downtown areas became more densely populated as skyscrapers soared. But urban decentralization caused the greatest growth on the outer edges of metropolitan areas. This movement resulted in a change in the racial and economic makeup of cities. The advancing technology which continued to enable people and businesses to move farther and farther away from the central core of cities and led to the "exploding metropolis," also created more needs, such as for improved traffic lanes. Organized crime was another growing urban problem. Chicago became notorious for its gangsterism. The depression and end of prohibition caused a lowering of violent crime.

During the New Deal the federal government involved itself in municipal affairs for the first time. The New Deal presented many community programs, some of which had been conceived in the Progressive era, and cities welcomed the government aid. Housing was one of the most crucial areas for reform, but the public housing projects met stiff opposition. The greenbelt concept was put into effect, although on a far smaller scale than originally planned. The political deadlock in 1938 ended urban reform, and left many major differences unsettled. Still, the New Deal had given the federal government an important new role in the future of cities.

Questions

1. What was the garden city concept? How was it applied during the New Deal?
2. If you were planning a new community, what ingredients would you consider most important? What place would there be, if any, for the ideas of people like Clarence Arthur Perry and Frank Lloyd Wright?
3. Describe some of the major changes caused by the decentralization of cities.
4. What steps did the New Deal take to ease the housing shortage?
5. Identify and define: (a) *Babbitt,* (b) *Middletown*, (c) Radburn, N.J., (d) New York Port Authority, (e) Fiorello La Guardia, (f) National Housing Act of 1937, and (g) Rexford Guy Tugwell.

One of the greatest monuments of the extensive water-control projects undertaken in the 1930s, Hoover Dam created Lake Mead, the world's largest man-made body of water, and today helps to irrigate over one million acres in New Mexico, Arizona, and California. The power it makes available for turning electric generators is vividly displayed as torrents of water shoot from its canyon outlets during a test of valves.

32

32
CCC, TVA, and DDT

"Somewhere west of Laramie" was the caption for an automobile ad in 1926. The ad showed a pretty girl driving an open car, with her hair and scarf flying in the wind. Behind her rode a cowboy on a galloping horse. The ad combined several romantic symbols: young love, the West, and the freedom and excitement of speed. There was no conflict here between technology and environment. The car was not yet considered a polluter. It was a convenient way of approaching nature—and perhaps romance, as well.

Americans have had a long love affair with machines. In the years between the wars they generally assumed that science and technology could solve all problems. Physicists, chemists, and engineers knew better, of course. But it was not until the start of the atomic era in 1945 that a large segment of the public began to learn that science and technology could pose threats in addition to solving problems.

"Conservation" had become well established by the time of Theodore Roosevelt, although its precise meaning was often clouded. After World War I conservationists renewed their efforts to secure lost reserve forests, wildlife, and mineral resources, and to reclaim unused land for agriculture. But they had to deal with serious dilemmas. Assuming that conservation was a positive good, how much responsibility should the government rightfully take and how much should be left to private interests? If the government assumed major responsibility, should it do so at the state or at the federal level?

In practice, conservation policy generally reflected the philosophy of presidential leadership. From 1920 to 1932 laissez-faire dominated. Then, in Franklin Roosevelt's administration, the trend toward government control became stronger. As in urban affairs and community life, the New Deal experimented boldly in the field of conservation.

Nostalgia for the Wilderness

The pull toward nature

The more that Americans crowded into cities, the more they dreamed of wide open spaces. The wealthy suburban commuter made a living in the city but found rest and relaxation in a country home. The golf course, the stables, the inviting woods, and the rolling lawns offered the well-to-do family refuge from the city's turmoil. Even middle-class urban families were beginning to vacation in the country or at least to make it possible for their children to do so. "A little roughing-it for the kids" was considered essential. In the 1920s a million children took

their summer vacations at 7000 camps. Hundreds of thousands attended relatively primitive camps, including those run by the Boy Scouts, Girls Scouts, and Campfire Girls. Thousands of families vacationed on farms. The farmers, scratching for extra income in bad times, boarded the city slickers.

Wealthy, adventurous easterners visited dude ranches out West. A pioneer dude rancher, the wealthy Howard Eaton of Pittsburgh, took notables to his South Dakota ranch and then on horseback caravans as far away as Canada. One of his guests, famed

Many Americans felt they could best preserve their frontier heritage by experiencing the out-of-doors on camping expeditions. The popularity of camping was demonstrated by sales of the Boy Scout Handbook: in 30 years it sold nearly 7 million copies—second only to the Bible.

mystery writer Mary Roberts Rinehart, considered the trip one of the great experiences of her life. Over three hundred such dude ranches existed in 1930. There were also some 7 million sport hunters and probably an even larger number of fishing enthusiasts. Hoover once explained that "the spiritual uplift, the good will, cheerfulness, and optimism that accompanies every expedition to the outdoors is [what] our people need in troublous times of suspicion and doubt."

Books and movies mirrored the search for nature. Nature magazines and scouting publications like *Boy's Life* had millions of subscribers. The few novels that sold over 1.5 million copies between 1900 and 1930 all dealt with outdoor themes: Gene Stratton Porter's *Freckles* (1904) and *The Girl of the Limberlost* (1909), Owen Wister's *The Virginian* (1902), and Jack London's *Call of the Wild* (1904). Porter was a professional nature photographer as well as a novelist. Angered by a bad review, she once thundered at her critics that her stories "are straight, living pictures from the lives of men and women of morals, honor, and loving kindness . . . copied from life where it touches religion, chastity, love, home, and hope of heaven ultimately." Sensing that audiences clamored for natural scenery, a Hollywood studio filmed two outdoor epics on location. *The Alaskan* in 1924 and *The Canadian* two years later started a new trend in movies.

Conservation during normalcy

A student of conservation history, Donald D. Swain, has written, "Contrary to widely held opinion, the national conservation program did not deteriorate in the 1920s. It expanded and matured." Those years produced reforestation and expanded area for the National Forests, along with a nationwide system for fighting forest fires. A network of bird sanctuaries was laid out. Also bidding for mining rights on government land was made more competitive. Yet the rate of expansion and maturation was slower than in the days of Theodore Roosevelt and Gifford Pinchot. And it is also true that conservationists fought and lost major struggles in Congress.

Presidents Harding and Coolidge knew little about conservation and cared even less. Harding, in a reaction against strong government regulations during wartime, decentralized the conservation agencies. In some cases, enforcement of rules became voluntary. As the Teapot Dome scandals showed (see p. 564–565), some of Harding's colleagues interpreted the relaxation in conservation as an open invitation to steal. The dishonesty of Secretary of the Interior Albert B. Fall and certain oil speculators was reminiscent of the corruption in the Grant administration. In order to cut federal budgets and trim the size of government, Coolidge let the states enforce conservation laws.

But many old-line conservationists still held jobs in federal agencies, and several sat in Congress. A vocal minority of old-time Progressive senators fought a rear-guard action for conservation. They won a minor victory in 1920 when the president signed into law a bill authorizing the Federal Power Commission to license, and thus to control, hydroelectric power on public lands. The passive FPC did little with this law. More important was the struggle waged by Senator George W. Norris of Nebraska for the federal government to retain and develop a hydroelectric power plant at Muscle Shoals, Alabama. The government-owned Tennessee River facility had been constructed during World War I and, though it now stood idle, Norris saw its potential for manufacturing cheap fertilizer and electricity for the farmers of the Tennessee Valley. Henry Ford wanted to buy it as a business venture for $5 million. But Norris offered instead a bill for more electricity, flood control, and conservation on the Tennessee River. Coolidge vetoed it, as did Hoover, who explained that the Norris bill would "break down the initiative and enterprise of the American people. . . ." Norris forced the government at least to retain ownership of Muscle Shoals, thereby paving the way for what later would become the Tennessee Valley Authority.

As a former mining engineer with worldwide experience, President Hoover was concerned about conservation. No one in government had a more thorough background in resource planning management. He was a member of the National Academy of Sciences, and his duties as commerce secretary under Coolidge had included supervising federal agencies concerned with science and technology. But Hoover was firmly convinced that conservation had to be accepted by the people voluntarily, without government coercion. He also believed that it had to be decentralized, that is, administered by the states rather than by the federal bureaucracy. He clung to these beliefs even when he knew, for example, that the public mineral and grazing lands were being seriously mismanaged. When he invited the states to take greater control of the public domain, they declined for political and financial reasons. The mismanagement continued.

As president, Hoover supported research to improve the management of soil, mining, forests, and fisheries. He asked for larger appropriations for this work, and Congress provided them. His proudest achievement was Hoover Dam on the Colorado River. It produced electricity for southern California, controlled flooding, and made irrigation possible in a fertile but dry inland region. Herbert Hoover represented a transition between the conservation policies of Theodore Roosevelt and those of Franklin Roosevelt.

Aldo Leopold's search for wilderness

It took the wilderness movement about a decade to recover from the Hetch Hetchy disaster (see p. 516). In the 1920s it persuaded the Forest Service to set aside areas within the National Forests to serve as permanent tracts both for scientific study and for the enjoyment of those who wanted to witness nature as nearly wild as possible. A key wilderness leader was Aldo Leopold, who had entered the Forest Service back in the days of Gifford Pinchot. After graduating from Yale Forestry School in 1909, he served mainly in Arizona and New Mexico as an expert in game conservation. Leopold defined wilderness areas as "wild regions big enough to absorb the average man's two-week vacation without getting him tangled up in his own backtrack . . . free from motor roads, summer cottages, launches, or other manifestations of gasoline." Such areas, he believed, should be open to lawful hunting and fishing but should have no roads, fixed trails, or other permanent improvements.

Like Thoreau, Leopold tried to strike a balance between civilization and wilderness. "While the reduction of wilderness has been a good thing," he told the National Conference on Outdoor Recreation, "its extermination would be a very bad one." Along with historian Frederick Jackson Turner he believed that America owed much of its democracy and liberty to the frontier. How could these be preserved, he asked, if the frontier disappeared? Owing largely to his efforts, the Forest Service set aside the Gila Wilderness Area in 1924 as a special preserve within the Gila National Park. This was the first installment of what is today a nationwide system of wilderness areas.

Leopold's careful observations of wildlife convinced him that game preservation policies were sometimes so successful that certain species were threatened by an inadequate supply of food. To restore a natural balance a number of deer had to be shot, and to maintain it certain natural predators had to be protected. That proposal cheered the deer hunters but frightened the cattle ranchers who used the public domain for grazing.

Leopold's life became a search for harmony with nature. He hoped humanity could develop an ecological conscience before it was too late. In the 1930s his search drew him further into ecology, philosophy, and theology, including Eastern religions. In Oriental civilizations there seemed to be a superior relationship between wildlife and humans. From his ecological study he concluded that "A thing is right when it tends to preserve the integrity, stability, and beauty of the biotic community. It is wrong when it tends otherwise." Eventually he became president of the Ecological Society of America. Leopold's devotion to the environment places him in the company of George Perkins Marsh, John Muir, and Gifford Pinchot. He died in 1948 while fighting a brush fire on the banks of the Wisconsin River.

The wilderness ideal had important applications for Leopold's friend, Benton MacKaye, a regional planner who hoped to integrate nature into the lives of city people.

MacKaye proposed creating a scenic parkway in the southern Appalachian mountains. This region was comprised mostly of wild land and small farms, many of which had recently been abandoned. MacKaye's plan would permit campfires, rural lanes, and places for motorists to view the scenery, but no food stands or motels. The government eventually created the Appalachian Trail along the lines suggested by MacKaye.

Environmental reform is usually the result of persistent prodding by volunteer groups. In 1935 Robert Marshall, Leopold, MacKaye, and others formed the Wilderness Society. In their eyes commercial exploitation was ruining Yellowstone, Yosemite, and other national parks. Roads, camp grounds, and hotels for vacationers were encroaching on the scenery, and destroying natural habitats. The Society wanted select areas within the national parks and forests to be set aside for hikers who wished to experience real wilderness. As a result of steady pressure, the Forest Service in 1939 did set off new wilderness areas.

Today the government no longer has vast tracts of rich land to give away and we have discovered that we must spend large sums to conserve our land from further erosion and our forests from further depletion.

FRANKLIN D. ROOSEVELT (1882–1945)

Conserving the Earth's Resources

The CCC

FDR was no trained naturalist, but he was a life-long nature enthusiast. On his estate in Dutchess County, New York, he grew trees commercially according to the most scientific methods of forestry. He once listed himself in *Who's Who* as "a tree grower." He had headed the state's Forest, Fish, and Game

Commission. As New York's governor he had encouraged reforestation and doggedly opposed private interests that wanted to construct a power project on the St. Lawrence River. Roosevelt had none of Hoover's hesitancy about federal leadership in the conservation field. He favored a broad program of conservation that would interfere as little as possible with private business and attract popular support. During the depression conservation went arm-in-arm with economic recovery, but it was also intended to go well beyond it. The president did not shy away from large, multipurpose projects. "We seek to use our natural resources," he declared, "not as a thing apart but as something that is interwoven with industry, labor, finance, taxation, agriculture, homes, recreation, good citizenship. The results of this interweaving will have a greater influence on the future American standard of living than the rest of our economics put together."

Catastrophic floods, droughts, and dust storms helped him get his program through Congress. During rainy seasons, the Mississippi River and its tributaries went on the rampage several times in the thirties. Meanwhile the Southwest suffered from a lack of rainfall and from destructive wind storms. These natural disasters dramatized the need for flood control and soil reclamation.

The Civilian Conservation Corps (CCC) of 1933 combined job relief with conservation. Under the program, thousands of camps were opened for young men from families on relief. Over 3 million khaki-clad volunteers built small dams and footbridges, restored wildlife, planted 2 billion seedling trees, sprayed against insect pests, improved range conditions, and constructed public facilities in underdeveloped national parks. A lasting monument of the CCC is the belt of trees it planted in a north-south direction in the Great Plains. To this day it protects the soil from wind erosion.

Elsewhere the government purchased 11 million acres of cutover forest land and sent in the CCC to plant trees. The CCC was administered by personnel from the Army, the Department of Labor, and the Department of Forestry. The promoters of the CCC emphasized its moral and spiritual values, but they were also fully aware of the boost that the program gave to the economy. The young volunteers had to send some pay home each month, and in this way they helped their families acquire spending money. The Corps closed down in 1942 after the draft started. Probably no New Deal agency was better received. The CCC was the inspiration for John F. Kennedy's Peace Corps, Lyndon B. Johnson's Vista program, and Richard M. Nixon's Action program.

TVA: *Conservation on a grand scale*

The most ambitious effort in conservation went into the Tennessee Valley Authority (TVA). As the Tennessee River swept toward the Ohio, it coursed through seven states. It was the scene of generations of exploitation—lumbering, farming, and extensive drilling for natural gas and mining for copper among other things. Many of the people in the valley were abjectly poor.

Set up as a public corporation in 1933, the TVA devised a regional plan to build and operate power plants along the Tennessee River. Muscle Shoals Dam was fully integrated into the plan. Nine main-channel dams and numerous smaller ones employed hundreds of thousands of workers to produce low-cost electricity for the people of the region. The TVA also provided for flood control, navigation, reforestation, soil conservation, and outdoor recreation. It also manufactured fertilizer. The goal was, in the words of Arthur Morgan, TVA's first chairman, to take "the wreckage of rugged individualism"

A river has no politics.
DAVID E. LILIENTHAL (1899–   )
TVA Director

and return it to health. It was the most daring, far-reaching, and successful New Deal project in conservation, as well as in long-term social reconstruction. It was "almost pure socialism" in the heart of Dixie.

Congress considered six new regional valley projects, including those for the Missouri, Arkansas, and Columbia river basins. However, the resistance of the private power industry, the endless squabbling of the directors of TVA, and the conservative drift of Congress in the late thirties prevented any similar projects. Only previously authorized projects such as the Central Valley Project of California and the Grand Coulee Dam in the Northwest were allowed to proceed.

Today's conservationists attack the TVA, the Bureau of Reclamation, and the Army Corps of Engineers for destroying as much of the environment as they save. No such criticisms were voiced in the 1930s, when "a dam was A Good Thing." The clatter and roar of jack hammers, steam shovels, and trucks on such projects was music to the ears of thousands of jobless construction workers. Dams tamed unruly waters while providing electricity for isolated farms and growing cities. The glistening concrete walls and crack-

ling high tension wires of Grand Coulee, Bonneville, Norris, and Hoover dams were monuments to American ingenuity.

Soil conservation

No natural resource in the U.S. has been more neglected than the soil. According to Hugh Bennett's classic work on the subject, *Soil Erosion: A National Menace* (1928), each year "enough soil [is] being washed out of American fields and pastures to load a train of freight cars that would encircle the earth 18 times at the equator." A few years later he estimated that 3 *billion* tons of soil were being washed out of American fields and pastures *each year*. Since 1903 Bennett had worked quietly in the understaffed Bureau of Soils. As the son of a North Carolina farm family, he recognized the scope of the problem but was unable to move the policy makers. By the 1930s many places in the southern Piedmont and the Rio Grande Valley were so badly eroded that they were useless for farm-

TENNESSEE VALLEY AUTHORITY

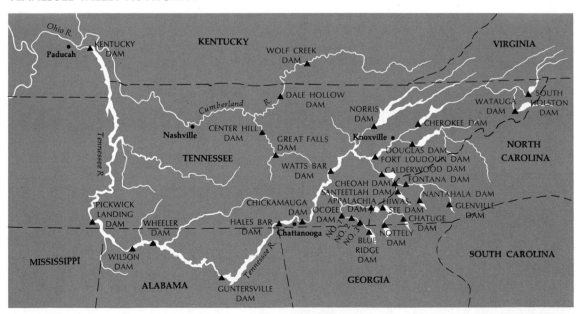

ing. Huge fertile areas had been brought to such a state by overcutting of trees, overgrazing of cattle, overplanting of crops, or a disregard for the natural contours of the land.

In the 1930s the dust storms on the Great Plains brought the problem home in a visible form. The western grasslands had been disrupted from the late nineteenth century, when white pioneers killed off or drove out the big game and the Indians to make way for cattle and sheep, and plowed up the wild grasses to plant wheat. The layer of soil was extremely thin, dry, and fragile. In World War I the wheat boom attracted farmer-speculators who used Ford tractors to rip up vast stretches of virgin prairie. Without the protective ground cover, tiny rills widened into gullies during rainstorms, and gullies expanded into gigantic canyons which snaked across entire counties. During the drought years of the Dirty Thirties, stiff winds drove the fine dust from Oklahoma and West Texas farms eastward, darkening the skies as far away as New York and Washington. In some cities street lights had to be turned on at noon.

By coincidence Hugh Bennett was testifying before a congressional committee on soil erosion when a dust storm blew in from the West. This underscored the testimony of the "Messiah of the Soil." The result was the Taylor Grazing Act of 1934, which prohibited cattle growers from overgrazing public land in the Plains states. It established grazing districts and provided for orderly procedures by which livestock raisers would help decide local policies for using public lands. The bill virtually closed the public domain to homesteading.

The following year the Soil Conservation Service was opened with Bennett as its head. It offered government aid to private landowners. In order to protect the soil from wind and water the Service suggested techniques such as contour plowing, strip cropping, grass planting, and crop rotation. It

During the decades leading up to the 1930s, farmers exploited the prairies west of the Mississippi with little thought of soil conservation. After a summer of drought in 1933, winds began stripping off the topsoil, creating dust storms like this one that hit Clayton, New Mexico, in 1937. Many died of suffocation and many more were forced from their homes to look for work in California and elsewhere.

also encouraged the use of legumes, fertilizers, and lime, along with the creation of ponds and woodlands, as part of an overall respect for the limits of the land. The government paid farmers to grow soil-building crops like clover and soybeans.

Stumbling into the atomic age

Several conservation measures cleared Congress in the waning days of the New Deal. Guns and ammunition were taxed for the support of wildlife research in 1937. That same year the U.S. signed a wildlife treaty with Mexico and a whaling treaty. The merger of various agencies in 1940 produced the Fish and Wildlife Service. The government

Crop dusting was just one of many ways in which the airplane and other gasoline-powered machines extended the ability of men and women to influence their environment. Newly-developed insecticides could be spread rapidly over large areas. The immediate effects were good; the hazards of DDT and similar products would not become apparent until well after World War II.

protected the bald eagle, the national emblem, whose numbers were dwindling. The New Deal's last major fling at conservation was the National Resources Planning Board. This group produced the first systematic inventory of the nation's resources since 1908. When it looked as if the Planning Board might evolve into a superplanning agency, conservative members of Congress quietly did away with it. Its findings were ignored.

The calamities predicted by conservationists have often been avoided thanks to new discoveries and inventions. No sooner had Pinchot's Conservation Commission warned that the U.S. was running out of mineral resources than fabulous new oil fields were uncovered in Texas and elsewhere. And even if some natural resources were giving out in the U.S., American companies were tapping

rich sources of tin, copper, manganese, rubber, and oil all over the globe. Most important of all, technology was producing substitutes for scarce materials. The chemical industry, which seemed able "to make anything out of anything," created plastics that in some cases could be substituted for wood and metal. Chemical fertilizers replenished tired soil and made marginal farms fertile. Nylon, cellophane, synthetic rubber, leaded gasoline, canned beer and other inventions came into common use. There was no thought that these same goods could become harmful to the environment. Nor did it seem possible that imported natural resources could also run short. Americans became even more addicted to the Myth of Superabundance.

The Second World War put heavy claims on the nation's human and natural resources, and while it lasted such matters as wilderness preservation were forgotten. The war also gave rise to scientific discoveries with vast ecological implications.

One of these discoveries was the insecticide DDT, first compounded in 1939. It was used during the war in a New Jersey military hospital to control swarms of flies. It worked, but when the chemical eventually made its way into the ocean, it killed batches of fish which then washed up shore. In tropical nations DDT was hailed as a miracle in the fight against malaria. It killed the germ-carrying anopheles mosquito. People doused themselves with the powder. Its potential as an insecticide for agriculture also became clear very soon. The positive features of DDT seemed at the time to overshadow its destructive powers.

In Chicago, in 1941, scientists created the first sustained nuclear reaction. Like a two-headed monster, nuclear energy promised both life and progress, and death and destruction. It first took the form of a nuclear bomb to be dropped on Japan. Curiously, the brilliant Franck Report, which examined the strategic uses of the weapon for President Truman, failed to mention the hazards of radiation or explore the dangers of atomic fallout. With hindsight it is clear that physicists, chemists, and engineers were developing and creating substances whose biological effects were as powerful as they were poorly understood. The environmental impact of these substances would be staggering.

Review

Urban Americans longed for the open spaces of the country as living conditions became more crowded in the cities. The wealthy owned country homes, and the middle class, or their children, vacationed on farms and at summer camps. Outdoor sports increased in popularity, and novels, magazines, and movies all reflected the naturalist trend. The laissez-faire administrations of Harding and Coolidge were not concerned with conservation laws, and even dismantled some existing agencies. Nevertheless, old-time Progressives and conservationists continued to fight the administrations' positions. Hoover's background made him sympathetic to conservation, but he believed in voluntary rather than government control. Some progress was made in the 1920s. Aldo Leopold, a leader of the wilderness movement, tried to achieve harmony and balance between wilderness and civilization, both in land and wildlife. His work involved him in an eventual study of ecology, and his example and beliefs were carried on by other individuals and groups.

FDR was a nature enthusiast and believer in conservation. Natural disasters helped him convince Congress of the need for a broad conservation program. The CCC program combined job relief with conservation and was a great success with the public. The TVA program, now under attack by some conservationists, was the New Deal's most extensive and successful conservation project, but proposals for other such programs did not materialize. Hugh Bennett was one of the first people to study the problem of soil conservation. The dust storms of the 1930s dramatized the problem. In 1935 Bennett became head of the Soil Conservation Service. Congress passed some more conservation measures toward the end of the New Deal, but shelved the findings of the National Resources Planning Board. World War II made conservation a secondary concern, even as new scientific wonders of far-reaching ecological concern were discovered. DDT seemed a blessing in spite of its dangers, while the impact of the atomic bomb and the possibilities of nuclear energy were so staggering that at first the hazards of atomic fallout were barely considered.

Questions

1. How did Hoover's ideas about conservation differ from those of Harding and Coolidge?
2. Describe the background and beliefs of Aldo Leopold and Hugh Bennett.
3. What was the CCC program? Do you think such a program could still be successful?
4. What caused the dust storms of the 1930s, and what steps were taken to try to avoid any more such disasters?
5. Why did Americans remain unconcerned when conservationists warned that natural resources were limited?

Selected Readings

OVERVIEW

Describing the era between the ends of the two World Wars, William E. Leuchtenburg and six other scholars have each written about their own area of specialization in *The Unfinished Century, America Since 1900* (Little, Brown, 1973).* Paul K. Conkin and David Burner often reveal their own opinions in *A History of Recent America* (Crowell, 1974).* Other studies which focus directly on this eventful time are David A. Shannon, *The Twenties and Thirties* (Rand McNally, 1974),* which is the third volume of *Twentieth Century America;* and Thomas C. Cochran, *The Great Depression and World War II* (Scott, Foresman, 1968).*

WEALTH

Frederick Lewis Allen, *Only Yesterday* (Harper & Row, 1957)* is a delightful popular history of the twenties. John Kenneth Galbraith, *The Great Crash* (Houghton Mifflin, 1955) is a brief and readable history of what happened in 1929. Studs Terkel, *Hard Times: An Oral History of the Great Depression* (Avon, 1971)* is a rich collection of autobiographical accounts by people who lived through the depression and by their offspring who heard the stories. See also Caroline Bird, *The Invisible Scar* (McKay, 1965).* David Conrad, *The Forgotten Farmer: The Story of Sharecroppers in the New Deal* (U. of Illinois Press, 1965) gives some insight into the plight of marginal farmers. Roger Daniels, *The Bonus March* (Greenwood, 1971) is engrossing. Melvin Dubofsky has edited a collection of readings entitled *American Labor Since the New Deal* (Watts, 1971).*

POWER

Political power is the subject, either directly or otherwise, of many books. A useful anthology is Frank O. Gatell, Paul Goodman, and Allen Weinstein, eds., *The Growth of American Politics*, vol. 2, *Since the Civil War* (Oxford U. Press, 1972).*

On the twenties see Oscar Handlin, *Al Smith and His America* (Little, Brown, 1958); *Herbert Hoover's Memoirs: The Cabinet and the Presidency, 1920–1933* (Macmillan, 1952); and Albert U. Romasco, *The Poverty of Abundance* (Oxford U. Press, 1968),* which deals with Hoover in the depression. *The Crisis of the Old Order: 1919–1933* by Arthur M. Schlesinger, Jr., (Houghton Mifflin, 1957) is the first volume of a trilogy, *The Age of Roosevelt* (Houghton Mifflin, 1959–1960).

*Available in paperback.

The literature on the thirties is rich and varied. Readable and sympathetic accounts are volumes 2 and 3 of *The Age of Roosevelt* (cited above), entitled *The Coming of the New Deal* and *The Politics of Upheaval*. More of FDR's administration is Paul K. Conkin's brief study, *The New Deal* (T. Y. Crowell, 1967).* Even more critical of FDR is Edgar E. Robinson, *The Roosevelt Leadership, 1933–1945* (Da Capo, 1972). FDR emerges as a power broker from James M. Burns' illuminating political biography *Roosevelt: The Lion and the Fox* (Harcourt Brace, 1963).* A fascinating dual biography is Joseph P. Lash, *Eleanor and Franklin* (New American Library, 1973).*

WAR

On the period before America's formal entry into the war, see William L. Langer and S. Everett Gleason, *The Challenge to Isolation, . . . 1937–1940* (Peter Smith, 1952) and by the same authors, *The Undeclared War 1940–1941* (Peter Smith, 1953). In addition see Richard Triana, *American Diplomacy and the Spanish Civil War* (Indiana U. Press, 1968) and George M. Waller, ed., *Pearl Harbor: Roosevelt and the Coming of the War* (Heath, 1965),* which is a collection of readings on why the U.S. was caught napping on December 7, 1941.

On the war itself see Louis L. Snyder, *The War: A Concise History, 1939–1945* (Simon & Schuster, 1960); Dwight D. Eisenhower, *Crusade in Europe* (Doubleday, 1948); and John R. Hersey, *Hiroshima* (Bantam, 1946). An interesting sidelight is told in Robert J. Donovan, *PT-109* (Fawcett World, 1973),* describing John F. Kennedy's career in World War II. The homefront is dealt with in the general survey by Richard Polenberg, *War and Society: The United States, 1941–1945* (Lippincott, 1972).* See also the more inclusive work, an anthology edited by Keith L. Nelson, *The Impact of War on American Life: The Twentieth Century Experience* (Holt, Rinehart, 1971).*

On diplomacy two valuable introductory works are Gaddis Smith, *American Diplomacy during the Second World War: 1941–1945* (Wiley, 1965)* and Athan Theoharis *The Yalta Myths: An Issue in U.S. Politics, 1945–1955* (U. of Missouri Press, 1970).

RACE

John Collier, the New Deal Indian commissioner, has described the native American culture in an eloquent, brief work, *Indians of the Americas* (New American Library, 1952).*

An introduction to black culture in the twenties is Nathan I. Huggins, *Harlem Renaissance* (Oxford U. Press, 1973).* The demands of the organized black community for better jobs and the responses of the New Deal are discussed by Raymond Wolters, *Negroes and the Great Depression* (Greenwood, 1971).*

Carey McWilliams, *North from Mexico: The Spanish-Speaking People of the United States* (Greenwood, 1949) remains the most informative brief treatment of the history of the Mexican Americans. Matthew S. Meier and Feliciano Rivera, *The Chicanos: A History of Mexican Americans* (Hill & Wang, 1972)* is lucid and up to date. Manuel Gamio, *The Life Story of the Mexican Immigrant* (Dover, 1972)* is a series of autobiographical sketches. See also an anthology of Mexican American literature, edited by Philip Ortego, *We Are Chicanos* (Washington Square Press, 1973).*

An excellent survey of the internment of the Japanese, focusing on the civil liberties issue, is Jacobus TenBroek et al., *Prejudice, War, and the Constitution* (U. of California Press, 1954).* The anti-Japanese movement prior to 1942 is covered by Roger Daniels, *The Politics of Prejudice* (U. of California Press, 1954).*

NATIONALITY AND RELIGION

Leonard Dinnerstein and David M. Reimers, *Ethnic Americans: A History of Immigration and Assimilation* (Dodd, Mead, 1975)* is the best brief analysis of the subject and covers a wide variety of ethnic groups. On the religious history between the world wars, see the works by Ahlstrom and Hudson, cited on p. 519.

WOMEN AND THE FAMILY

Information on the history of women in the twenties and thirties can be found in Bird's *The Invisible Scar* and Terkel's *Hard Times* (both cited above), as well as Robert S. and Helen M. Lynd's *Middletown* (Harcourt Brace, 1959).* On women's political behavior see Tamara K. Hareven, *Eleanor Roosevelt: An American Conscience* (Quadrangle, 1968), as well as Lash's *Eleanor and Franklin* (cited above). Robert C. Angell, *The Family Encounters the Depression* (Peter Smith, 1936) is also useful.

COMMUNITY

The Lynd's *Middletown* (cited above) and *Middletown in Transition* (Harcourt Brace, 1963)* are pioneering works on small-town America. Accounts of the most fascinating mayor of America's largest city are Arthur Mann's *LaGuardia: A Fighter Against His Times, 1882–1933* and *LaGuardia Comes to Power, 1933* (both published by the U. of Chicago Press, 1969).* Facets of architecture and urban planning are dealt with in Roy Lubove, *Community Planning in the 1920's* (U. of Pittsburgh Press, 1964).* The greenbelt towns are the subject of Paul K. Conkin's *Tomorrow a New World: The New Deal Community Program* (Cornell U. Press, 1959).

ENVIRONMENT

Valuable for its wide coverage of the subject and for its bibliographical essay is Richard Highsmith, et al., *Conservation in the United States* (Rand McNally, 1969).* This is a basic textbook on resource management. Conservation before the New Deal is the subject of Donald Swain's *Federal Conservation Policy 1921–1933* (U. of California Press, 1963). The famous scandal of the twenties is dealt with by Morris R. Werner and John Starr, *Teapot Dome* (Kelley, 1959). Richard Lowitt, *George W. Norris: The Making of a Progressive, 1861–1912* (Syracuse U. Press, 1963) is a biography of the father of the TVA. See also John H. Kyle, *The Building of T.V.A.* (Louisiana State U. Press, 1958). The most famous conservation institution of all finds a biographer in John A. Salmond. See his *Civilian Conservation Corps, 1933–1942* (Duke, 1967). Hugh Hammond Bennett, the "soil Messiah," is the subject of Wellington Brink's biography, *Big Hugh: The Father of Soil Conservation* (Macmillan, 1951). Marion Clawson and R. Burnell Held, *Federal Lands: Their Use and Management* (Johns Hopkins, 1957) touches on many aspects of environment and conservation.

Rush hour on the subway: a view from inside.

V

Chronology

1945
Roosevelt dies, succeeded by Harry S. Truman. World War II ends. Cold War starts.

1947
Marshall Plan aid to Europe.

1950–1953
Korean War.

1952
Dwight D. Eisenhower elected president.

1956
Montgomery, Alabama, bus boycott.

1960
John F. Kennedy elected president.

1960–1973
Indochina War.

1963
Kennedy assassinated, succeeded by Lyndon B. Johnson.

1968
Richard M. Nixon elected president.

1969
First U.S. moon landing.

1970
Equal Rights Amendment passes Congress.

1972
Nixon visits China and the Soviet Union, wins reelection in landslide.

1973–1975
Economic recession.

1974
Nixon resigns presidency, succeeded by Gerald R. Ford.

Americans are still engaged in inventing what it is to be an American.
That is at once an exhilarating and a painful occupation.

THORNTON WILDER   (1897–1975)
Author and playwright

overview
Our Times

The blinding flash and mushrooming cloud formation over Hiroshima in August of 1945 signaled the start of an age of anxiety concerning the very survival of the human race. Every generation sees itself as "charged with remaking the world," the French existentialist Albert Camus wrote, but the task of the postwar generation was "perhaps even greater, for it consists in keeping the world from destroying itself." Several times the leading nuclear powers seemed to approach the very brink of nuclear destruction, particularly in the confrontation over Cuba in 1962.

The man from Missouri

President Harry S. Truman acted as midwife to the age of anxiety. He was aware of the magnitude of his responsibilities when he assumed office in April 1945. He told reporters, "Boys, if you ever pray, pray for me now. I don't know whether . . . you ever had a load of hay fall on you, but when they told me what had happened [Roosevelt's death], I felt like the moon, the stars, and all the planets had fallen on me. I've got the most terribly responsible job a man ever had."

To the public, he was best known as a hard-working Missouri senator who had directed a competent investigation of waste and corruption in war industries. A compromise candidate for vice-president, he had been told next to nothing about presidential policies. Plain and unsophisticated by comparison with FDR, Truman suddenly found himself president of the most powerful nation on earth, in a world in total disarray. The international political scene was almost too complicated to comprehend: Russia solidifying its military and political power in eastern Europe, communism gaining in China, Germany dismembered, Japan shattered, Britain, France, and Italy physically and economically exhausted, Europe's overseas empires in the process of liquidation, Israel struggling to be born. At home, the public demanded immediate demobilization, while inflation, labor unrest, a congressional backlash against presidential power, and the potential of serious economic depression loomed in the background.

Truman lost ground in the 1946 election when the GOP won control of both houses of Congress for the first time since 1928. Congress proceeded to block his "Fair Deal," a continuation of the New Deal. But Truman had always advanced through "pluck, tenacity, enthusiasm and luck," and he did so again. In 1948 the "Dixiecrats" bolted the Democratic party in opposition to his liberal stance on civil rights, while former Vice-President Henry Wallace, who resisted Truman's hard-line anti-Communist foreign policy, drained away some liberal Democratic votes by running as a Progressive. Truman's GOP opponent, Governor Thomas E. Dewey of New York, felt certain of victory. But Truman ran a "give-'em-hell" campaign and won reelection in the biggest upset in American political history.

The Cold War and Korea

The last months of the Second World War set the stage for the Cold War, an era of hostility and tension between the U.S. and its "free world" allies and the Soviet Union and its Communist bloc—the "Iron Curtain" countries. Truman refused to accept a Russian sphere of influence in eastern Europe or to make available American finances to reconstruct a war-torn Soviet Union. Stalin saw these acts as a betrayal of trust by a wartime ally and a future threat. Within months of the war's end, mutual fear and suspicion had destroyed the Grand Alliance. In an effort to "contain communism" President Truman offered large-scale aid for countries prepared to resist Communist aggression or subversion. In March 1947, Greece and Turkey became the first beneficiaries of this "Truman Doctrine." The same year saw the launching of the Marshall Plan, named for Secretary of State George C. Marshall, which by 1950 had made available more than $12 billion dollars to war-torn western Europe. This European recovery program produced astonishing results in reviving such countries as Italy and France.

The major emphasis of U.S. aid shifted from economic assistance to armaments in 1949 when the U.S. and eleven other nations (plus an additional four later on) formed the North Atlantic Treaty Organization (NATO). This one-for-all-and-all-for-one military pact relied ultimately on the protection of the American nuclear umbrella. The Soviet bloc countered this alliance by creating the Warsaw Pact. In the next several decades the U.S. spent some $3 trillion bolstering the defenses and economies of anti-Communist nations throughout the world. But this enormous expenditure never purchased a sense of genuine security.

The scene of hostilities soon shifted from Europe to Asia, where in 1949 the Communists, under Mao Tse-tung, won control of mainland China. Next year North Korean Communist troops invaded South Korea, which the U.S. had helped create. Truman rushed the case to the U.N., where, in Russia's absence, North Korea was branded the aggressor and ordered to withdraw. When the fighting continued, the U.N. established a Korean command under General Douglas MacArthur. Nearly half the troops were American. After a seesaw conflict during which an advance to the border of China brought a flood of Chinese soldiers to the aid of the North Koreans, the war finally reached a stalemate. Peace negotiations opened in July 1951 and dragged on for two years. The armistice finally signed in 1953 restored the boundary line to its approximate prewar position. Communism had been "contained," but most Americans were either embittered or bored by what Truman's critics called a no-win war.

Eisenhower and the McCarthy era

After being out in the cold for twenty years, the Republican party reentered the White House in 1953 with Dwight D. Eisenhower, the immensely popular World War II commander. The GOP also won control of both houses of Congress for the next two years. The unpopular Korean War, inflation, some instances of corruption within the Truman administration, and the outrageous charge of "twenty years of treason" leveled by the Communist-hunting Republican senator, Joseph McCarthy, all helped defeat the Democrats. Eisenhower's moderation surprised some New Deal liberals and embittered conservative Republicans. Although a weak chief executive in domestic affairs (he turned economic policy over to his conservative treasury secretary and preferred to let Congress or the states or cities take action on social problems like racial discrimination and urban blight), in foreign affairs he supported the aggressive stance of Secretary of State John Foster Dulles, who threatened the U.S.S.R. with "massive retaliation" and called for "liberation" of the "enslaved" peoples of eastern Europe.

A severe heart attack did not prevent Eisenhower's easy reelection in 1956. During his second term a spirit of accord with the U.S.S.R. began to emerge, but the chance for a formal détente was shattered when an American spy plane was downed in Russian territory. In his Farewell Address to the nation Eisenhower warned the public of the growing power of America's "military-industrial complex."

From soon after World War II until 1945, as the U.S. pursued its worldwide mission of halting the spread of Red power, an often hysterical fear of subversion, disloyalty, and spying gripped the nation. Investigations and trials — of the leaders of the American Communist party, of Julius and Ethel Rosenberg, of former State Department official Alger Hiss, and of top physicist J. Robert Oppenheimer — combined with revelations of disloyalty and defections in Canada and Great Britain and gave credence to the view that the country was in danger of destruction from within. Truman initiated a loyalty check on government employees. The House Un-American Activities Committee, various Senate committees, state agencies, and the FBI conducted active investigations. Senator McCarthy made the headlines repeatedly by attacking "subversion in government" through innuendo, unsupported accusations, and ever shifting targets. The State Department was effectively paralyzed by McCarthy's melodramatic charges, and even prominent politicians found it difficult to confront him directly. Eisenhower made no strong public remonstrance when McCarthy attacked his lifelong associate, General George C. Marshall. Finally, after his tactics had received television exposure, McCarthy was himself reprimanded by the Senate and went into total eclipse. Subsequently the Supreme Court handed down various rulings limiting the scope of government inquiry into private beliefs and associations.

JFK and LBJ

The election of John F. Kennedy, the youngest man ever to be elected president and the first born in the twentieth century, promised a renewal of vigor in Washington after a period of drift. Although he had served in the Senate without distinction and, as a Roman Catholic, had a handicap no earlier presidential candidate had been able to overcome, Kennedy had an excellent war record, an appealing personality, a vast family fortune, and a sparkling life style. Even so, his margin of victory over Richard M. Nixon in 1960 was only 100,000 votes. JFK established the Peace Corps and the Alliance for Progress in Latin America and gave stronger support to the fight against racial discrimination than had any of his predecessors. But most of his "New Frontier" legislation was blocked by Congress. His record was badly marred by the abortive Bay of Pigs invasion of Cuba, though the country generally approved his leadership in the fearful Cuban missile crisis of 1962. A nuclear test ban treaty with the U.S.S.R. was perhaps his most solid achievement.

Kennedy's assassination while in a motorcade in Dallas, Texas, on November 22, 1963, stunned the nation. A presidential commission headed by Supreme Court Justice Earl Warren investigated the killing and concluded that there had been a single assassin, Lee Harvey Oswald (who was also murdered). But a sizeable segment of the public continued to believe in the existence of a larger conspiracy. (In 1968 the president's younger brother and heir apparent, Senator Robert F. Kennedy, was killed by a gunman while campaigning for the Democratic presidential nomination.)

Lyndon Baines Johnson took the oath of office on the same plane that bore John F. Kennedy's body from Dallas to Washington. Although he lacked Kennedy's charisma, his experience as Senate majority leader stood him in good stead. Capitalizing on a national—and congressional—mood of grief and remorse, he began a drive to win enactment of the Kennedy legislative program. LBJ was reelected a year later, defeating Arizona Senator Barry Goldwater by the largest margin in any presidential election up to that time. Goldwater's outspoken conservatism, including his proposal that the Social Security system be dismantled, frightened moderate voters. Goldwater's call for an aggressive "win" policy in Vietnam contrasted sharply with Johnson's apparent moderation. After the election LBJ pressed forward his "Great Society" programs—the "war on poverty," civil rights, urban renewal, pollution control, the upgrading of education, medical care for the aged—the greatest expansion of social legislation since the 1930s. But he confounded those who had voted for him as a peace candidate in 1964 by sending ever larger numbers of American servicemen into the war in Vietnam, turning that conflict into an American war. Johnson told the public that the U.S. could afford both guns and butter, but enormous military expenditures not only siphoned off funds that might have furthered domestic reforms but set the economy on a course that would result in a major recession in the 1970s.

The Middle East and the moon

During the years of America's full involvement in the Vietnam War, other foreign affairs received short shrift. But before and after that period, the Middle East demanded U.S. attention. President Truman recognized the new state of Israel in 1948, an action that incensed Arab nations. During the Eisenhower administration the U.S. withdrew a promise of economic aid to Egypt when the Egyptian government negotiated an arms deal with the U.S.S.R. Immediately afterward Egypt took control of the Suez Canal. When Israel attacked Egypt in October 1956 and British and French forces occupied the canal zone, both the U.S. and the U.S.S.R. applied heavy pressure to force the withdrawal of all foreign troops.

In 1957 the Eisenhower Doctrine was announced: the U.S. would supply arms and men if necessary to uphold anti-Communist regimes in the Middle East. As this country continued to supply financial and military aid to Israel, becoming the chief guarantor of its independence, the Soviet Union increased its own involvement with Arab nations. But during the repeated clashes between Arabs and Israelis, the two major powers took no direct part in the fighting, and between wars the U.S. in particular sought to work out a settlement.

The Cold War competition between the U.S.S.R. and the U.S. spurred a vigorous and costly space program in each country. Russia put Sputnik I into orbit in 1957 and sent a manned spacecraft around the earth in 1961. In the same year a U.S. rocket shot Alan B. Shepard, Jr., 115 miles above the earth's surface, and in 1962 John Glenn orbited the earth. Even more ambitious flights followed until, in 1969, the U.S. achieved the first successful moon landing. Both powers also launched unmanned spacecraft to investigate the distant planets.

The years of rage

There were many facets of American life after midcentury that invited celebration or at least satisfaction. As the Gross National Product exceeded $1 trillion, the great majority of Americans enjoyed one of the highest standards of living of any people on earth. Although battered by McCarthyism, the Bill of Rights survived and continued to guarantee individual liberties such as could be found in few other countries. Industry went on turning out a seemingly endless variety of consumer goods; medical science, labor-saving devices, and an abundance of reasonably priced foods combined to increase longevity; and shorter workweeks offered new opportunities for leisure and recreation. Science and technology promised still more physical comfort and convenience.

These promises may have helped heighten the discontent that brought on the violence of the 1960s. It was a decade of urban riots, campus uprisings, and public demonstrations from one end of the country to the other. The riots in the black ghettos reflected impatience with unkept promises and bitter resentment at having too small a share of affluence. This same impatience and resentment was expressed on Indian reservations and in the *barrios* of Spanish-speaking Americans. Campus unrest was partly the affluent generation's rebellion against the amassing of more and more possessions as a worthy or adequate goal. A vocal minority of young people were questioning the values on which the American "system" seemed to be based: the work ethic, money making, endless consumption, material success, and conformism. They pointed to the injustice and hypocrisy that went along with affluence. In the colleges and universities in the mid-1960s many students also complained that impersonal, unseen forces were running their lives on campus. Many young men felt that they were being controlled against their will when the government began drafting them for service in Vietnam.

Organized feminism sprang back to life in the sixties. Encouraged by the Civil Rights Act of 1964, which outlawed discrimination on the grounds of sex as well as of race, women began to move into new areas of employment. The National Organization for Women (NOW) was formed in 1966. In 1970 Congress finally approved the Equal Rights Amendment. It still remained for the states to decide whether or not the amendment would become part of the Constitution of the United States.

The quality of the environment and consumer rights also became major focal points for reform. From small beginnings, they had grown into major movements by the 1970s. Visions of the future notwithstanding, the quality of life seemed to be declining measurably as a consequence of the pollution of earth, air, and water. Rachel Carson's *Silent Spring*, chronicling the disastrous implications of pesticides, brought the problem of environment into public focus. Public advocate Ralph Nader supplied the same impetus to the swelling consumer movement.

The "Negro Revolution" earned headlines from the late 1950s to about 1970. In 1954 the Supreme Court decided in *Brown* v. *Board of Education of Topeka* that "separate but equal" schools were unconstitutional. Civil rights advocates believed that the same logic applied to public accommodations. In 1956 a bus boycott led by Martin Luther King, Jr., in Montgomery, Alabama, challenged the tradition of Jim Crow in public transportation. In 1960 black college students in Greensboro, North Carolina, used the "sit-in" technique in attempts to integrate public lunch counters. King's nonviolent noncompliance with laws he considered immoral or unjust became an accepted strategy on many fronts. With the song "We Shall Overcome" ringing in its ears, Congress passed the Civil Rights Act of 1964, outlawing discrimination in public accommodations, and the Civil Rights Act of 1965, eliminating literacy tests and other barriers to voting.

But there were many blacks for whom such gradualism was unacceptable. The Black Muslims and other militant groups called for racial pride, resistance to white violence, and separatism rather than integration. "Black power" became a slogan of leaders who scorned King's tactics as too slow and his goals as too conservative. Looting and arson in the ghettos called attention to the desperation of the inner-city blacks, but it also raised fear and resentment among whites. With King's assassination, the movement for black freedom and equality lost the leader most admired and respected by white America. Congress listened to complaints that the blacks were moving too far, too fast, and the "Negro Revolution" ground to a virtual standstill.

Vietnam

In 1960 the United States sent two thousand military advisers into Vietnam, and from then on the conflict cast an ever lengthening shadow over the country. Basically arguing that the loss of South Vietnam would mean the fall of all Southeast Asia to communism (the "domino theory"), "peace candidate" Lyndon Johnson committed 500,000 ground troops in the ground-and-air war against the Vietcong guerrillas and North Vietnamese regulars. The war alienated a considerable portion of the younger generation and seriously divided the nation. By 1968 Johnson was faced with apparently irrepressible domestic dissent. Optimistic predictions by the U.S. military and the administration were contradicted by a successful major Vietcong offensive, whereupon the military called for still more Americans to be sent overseas. In the New Hampshire presidential primary Senator Eugene McCarthy, a pronounced dove, challenged Johnson and scored 42 percent of the vote. He was himself challenged by Robert F. Kennedy, who was assassinated while celebrating his victory in the California Democratic primary. LBJ announced to the nation that he was ending bombing raids on North Vietnam's cities—and would not stand for reelection. The ensuing Democratic convention in Chicago ended with a "police riot" (so designated by the official Walker Report) against youthful antiwar demonstrators. Hubert Humphrey, LBJ's vice-president, was finally nominated. The GOP convention chose Richard M. Nixon. Nixon narrowly defeated Humphrey, while Alabama Governor George Wallace won a healthy 9 million votes as the candidate of the American Independent party.

Nixon, who described his political career as a series of crises, had made an amazing political comeback after losing the 1962 California gubernatorial election. Elected in part on the promise that he had a secret plan for ending the war, he withdrew some American troops and stepped up the training of Vietnamese to take over the fighting. But in 1970 and 1971 his decision to invade Cambodia and Laos sparked heated demonstrations on the home front. Meanwhile, Nixon and his special emissary, Dr. Henry Kissinger, were working toward détente with China and Russia, a diplomatic policy in ironic contrast to Nixon's long-time reputation as a hard-line anti-Communist opposed to détente. His visit to China in 1972 was an important, if inconclusive, step toward peaceful coexistence with the world's most populous nation. In November of that year, having "wound down" the war by removing U.S. ground forces, he was reelected president in an overwhelming victory over the liberal Democratic dove, George McGovern.

Negotiations with the Vietcong and North Vietnamese, initiated by President Johnson, dragged on throughout 1972. In December, Nixon ordered the heaviest bombing raids of North Vietnam ever undertaken. In January 1973 a cease-fire was finally signed. American prisoners of war were returned, and all remaining American forces were withdrawn. The fighting in Vietnam never really stopped, however, and in 1975, after Congress had announced an end to U.S. military aid, South Vietnamese resistance collapsed.

Watergate and after

Conceivably, Richard M. Nixon's reelection victory might have been even greater had not burglars been caught in Democratic National Headquarters in Washington's Watergate building in June of 1972. But their connection with the Committee for the Reelection of the President was not immediately disclosed, and after it was, the president disclaimed any administration connection with the crime. Persistent news media investigations kept the case alive, and a year after the break-in televised hearings of a select Senate committee exposed criminal activities originating in the White House. In July 1974, as the number of indictments, convictions, and confessions continued to mount, the House Judiciary Committee recommended impeachment of the president for obstructing justice, misusing federal agencies, and interfering with the powers of Congress. On August 9, Richard M. Nixon resigned the presidency.

He was succeeded by Gerald R. Ford, a long-time congressman from Michigan whom Nixon had appointed to the vice-presidency in 1973, after his running-mate in the 1972 election, Spiro Agnew, had himself resigned, accused of accepting bribes and evading taxes. Ford soon pardoned Nixon for whatever crimes he might have committed. As his own vice-president, he chose Nelson Rockefeller, the former governor of New York. Henry Kissinger continued as secretary of state and, with the president, fought hard for additional aid to South Vietnam until the collapse of military resistance there. More consistently conservative than Nixon, Ford reluctantly accepted deficit spending to combat serious recession and unemployment but sought to compensate by vetoing congressional measures he considered too costly. Although the post-Watergate Congress was lopsidedly Democratic, many of the vetoes stuck.

On the eve of its two hundredth birthday, the United States had weathered its most divisive foreign war and, in the complex of corruption called Watergate, perhaps the most serious constitutional crisis in its history. How much damage had been done to the spirit of the nation and to the confidence of the people in their elected officials only future historians would be able to say.

wealth

Patriotism and abundance have been closely allied in America's self-image, and never more so than in the 1960s. During this period the flag became the symbol of the prosperous "silent majority" which angrily rejected the reforms demanded by students and minority groups. Here a Fourth of July block party brings together affluent suburbanites along with the ping-pong tables, spyder bicycles, charcoal grills, and lawn furniture made available by the consumer economy.

33

33

Dawn of the Postindustrial Era

Predicting the country's economic future is a risky business. Until the recession of 1973–1975 many optimists said that despite temporary setbacks, the United States had reached a stage where all good things were possible and economic growth could be almost limitless. They noted that while the U.S. took two hundred years to become a trillionaire nation (producing one trillion dollars worth of goods and services each year), it might need only ten more years to *double* that annual production. Technology produces goods at an ever increasing rate. Computers and highly efficient automation techniques continue to replace human labor—both mental and physical—and thereby sustain a high level of economic growth. New sources of energy wait to be tapped.

The pessimists have been more in evidence since the recent recession. They counter that, since the world is running out of almost everything except people, we must now begin to face "the limits of economic growth." The rate of technological change must slow down or civilization as we know it will end in a series of wars, famines, and ecological disasters. Even in the powerful and wealthy United States, economic growth must slacken as vital resources run out. Science and technology are compounding social problems rather than solving them.

No final answers about America's future are possible now, and none will be found in this fifth and final chapter on economic trends in American history (see Chapters 1, 9, 17, and 25). Still, a review of the extraordinary "era of affluence" that followed the Second World War may make possible a better understanding of future trends. The first section of this chapter concerns economic growth and welfare, particularly the way wealth is distributed in postwar America. The second and third sections deal with the status of workers and of farmers in the postindustrial era.

The term "postindustrial era" has come

into use recently to describe a society in which the largest segment of the work force is no longer engaged in manufacturing. Instead it supplies specialized services. Highly automated machines do most of the important physical work. This change has touched the entire society, profoundly affecting not only industrial workers but all of the people.

The Trillionaire Nation

Record growth after 1945

Though World War II brought record employment, most Americans remembered the hard times of the 1930s, when millions lost their jobs, homes, farms, savings, and—most shattering, perhaps—their sense of dignity and personal worth. According to expert estimates, it would take 60 million jobs to keep everyone employed after the return of peace—and where were all those jobs to come from? Once the guns stopped shooting, people braced themselves for a return of large-scale unemployment. Anticipating the worst, Congress passed the historic Employment Act of 1946, by which the federal government promised "to promote maximum employment, production and purchasing power."

The gloomy predictions proved false. More than 60 million jobs were created. As soon as the war ended, a heavy demand for consumer goods created a major boom in manufacturing. Consumers took out their wartime savings and went on a buying spree to acquire cars, major appliances, and other goods that had been denied them during the depression and war years. The Cold War emphasis on containing communism everywhere contributed to spectacular economic growth. The Marshall Plan and the numerous military assistance programs accounted for an enormous amount of industrial activity. During the Korean War (1950–1953) national defense outlays reached $53.5 billion, the same level as in 1945. Strong unions in the basic industries kept wages at a high level.

Private companies invested heavily in research and development. The country was entering what one economic historian called the "longest and steadiest period of capital accumulation in American history."

Continuing after the Korean War, the good times came to be known as "Eisenhower prosperity." But cutbacks in defense spending soon afterward led to a recession in 1957–1958. After a brief upswing another slowdown occurred in 1960–1961, and the jobless rate reached 6.7 percent. With a recession at hand President Kennedy suggested increased government spending to stimulate growth and cut unemployment.

The Cold War drove the U.S. to efforts to outdo Russia in everything. When the Soviets launched their first Sputnik satellite into orbit in 1957, the U.S. went into a frenzy of activity not only in aerospace engineering but also in education. Soviet Premier Nikita S. Khrushchev's boast that the U.S.S.R. would "catch up with and surpass" capitalist America was taken seriously in many quarters. The yearly rate of economic growth in Russia was then about 7 percent compared to America's 2 or 3 percent. Therefore, achieving a faster rate of growth received high priority in government.

Theoretically the American economy was a market economy, dependent on the decisions of private buyers and sellers. But by the middle of the twentieth century its state of health was determined to a considerable extent by the federal government through tax-

RICH NATIONS, POOR NATIONS

The chart shows the close relationship between a country's wealth and the conditions of life of its citizens.

COUNTRY	PER CAPITA INCOME[1]	OVER-ALL BALANCE OF PAYMENTS[2]		AGE LIMITS FOR COMPULSORY EDUCATION	INFANT MORTALITY RATE[3]	LIFE EXPECTANCY[1]	
		SURPLUS	DEFICIT			MALE	FEMALE
Sweden	$5596		− 184	7–16	9.6	72.0	77.4
United States	$5523		−8375	6–16	17.6	67.4	75.0
Japan	$3292	1241		6–15	11.7	70.5	75.9
Italy	$2298		−4611	6–14	25.7	67.9	73.4
Brazil	$ 425		−1037	7–14	170.0	60.7	60.7
Mexico	$ 684	31		7–13	46.0	49.9	49.9
Egypt	$ 210		− 117.6	6–12	114.0	51.6	53.8
Burma	$ 73		− 34.4	No law	200.0	40.8	43.8
Ethiopia	$ 79	Not Avail.		7–15	216.0	26.0	28.0
Zaire	$ 118		− 106.5	6–14	104.0	37.6	40.0

[1]Latest available figures
[2]Latest available annual figures, in millions of U.S. dollars
[3]Number of deaths per 1000, one year old or less
SOURCE: *The New York Times*, September 28, 1975.

es, bank credits, direct spending, and subsidies. As a consequence of depression, war, and the Cold War, the president and Congress had developed tools to influence employment, inflation, the gold supply, the balance of payments, prices, wages, and the rate of economic growth. They rarely adopted consistent or long-term programs of control—and those that were attempted were always resented in some quarters. But by law the government could engage in nearly every form of economic management except long-term planning and nationalization of private properties.

Ever since the New Deal, government policy—consciously or otherwise—had been directed toward guaranteeing the income of various segments of society. A classic but by no means isolated case was that of farmers and farm supports. Thus the American economic system was sometimes known as "welfare capitalism."

Computer-age technology

In the postwar era, technology greatly contributed to economic growth. Television, tape recorders, calculators, air conditioners, "miracle fabrics," insecticides, plastics, xerography, and, of course, computers, were mass produced. Most of these items were based on scientific discoveries or inventions that had been produced before the Second World War. Sometimes giant new corporations were formed to develop them into marketable form. Some commentators talked of a "perpetual industrial revolution" in America.

Futurists claim we have reached the dawn of the "postindustrial era," when super machines will take over work and thought from humans. Technologists will soon equip us with robots, laser-beam communications, "plasma" for limitless supplies of cheap energy, and societal planning on a scale as yet unimaginable. One may like or despise this "brave new world," but, they say, it is upon us.

At the center of the postindustrial era stood the high-speed computer. Just as in the nineteenth century machines had replaced human and animal labor, in the second half of the twentieth century a machine was taking over some forms of decision making. Electronic computers were routinely used for inventory control, market projections, and payroll deductions. More important, manufacturers were interlocking the computers with production machines. This combination, named "cybernation," was already widely applied in industries like food processing and chemical refining. In automobile manufacturing cybernation could conceivably design, manufacture, and assemble cars with a minimum of human help. After the initial stages of programming, the machine could do the "thinking." This would include making repairs and inventing new parts and processes to suit particular needs.

Scholars are astonished by the increasing rate of technological change over the centuries. Hunting with clubs and stones lasted for fifty thousand years, farming was invented a mere ten thousand years ago, the invention of writing is four or five thousand years old, printing on a mass scale began around five hundred years ago, and accurate time-keeping has been with us only 250 years. Steam engines were invented about 170 years ago, electric dynamos have been perfected for less than a century, and nuclear energy belongs to this generation. Economist Kenneth Boulding observed that "the date that divides human history into two equal parts is well within living memory. . . . The world of today . . . is as different from the world in which I was born [in the 1920s] as that world was from Julius Caesar's. I was born in the middle of human history. . . . Almost as much has happened since I was born as happened before."

Greater production is the key to prosperity and peace. And the key to greater production is a wider and more vigorous application of modern scientific and technical knowledge.

HARRY S. TRUMAN (1884–1972)

American technology accomplished great triumphs, but its application was often uneven.* While astronauts Neil Armstrong and Edwin Aldrin walked on the moon in July 1969, many New Yorkers were finding it hard to complete a ten-cent telephone call because of overloaded circuits. The spaceship worked beautifully, but the country's fishing fleet was obsolete. Automobile manufacturers denied Ralph Nader's charge that cars were "unsafe at any speed," but in 1972 they recalled more defective cars than they manufactured new ones.

Historically, business efficiency, like technology, had been a major factor in America's amazing capacity to produce wealth. In the post-Civil War period, the concentration of business ownership and management, although it violated democratic ideals, often resulted in an increase in business efficiency. The titans of industry, and the large corporations founded by them, made large-scale investments, purchases, and sales that reduced the unit price of the goods they sold. Consumers benefitted accordingly. As corporate concentration reached an all-time high (in 1969 the top two hundred manufacturing corporations, according to testimony before a Senate subcommittee, controlled two thirds of all manufacturing assets), it intensified the question as to whether this was the most efficient system for the production of wealth. Some observers, however, pointed to the savings in unit cost, to inventions, and to technological progress in big firms. (The power wielded by big corporations is dealt with in the next chapter.)

*The ecological impact of new scientific discoveries and technology is discussed in Chapter 40.

The computer's importance in the laboratory or office becomes especially apparent when it breaks down. Despite the inconvenience, many workers feel inwardly pleased when electronics fail; it reassures them, as John F. Kennedy expressed it, "that however extraordinary computers may be, we are still ahead of them, and that man is still the most extraordinary computer of all."

The affluent society

Because of its extraordinary postwar boom America came to be known as "the affluent society," after the title of a book published by economist John Kenneth Galbraith in 1958. In some respects the label was misleading (as the author himself acknowledged). Certainly property ownership was no more evenly distributed than before. A tiny number of Americans—4 or 5 percent—owned most corporate stocks and bonds, federal, foreign, and municipal bonds, personal cash, and real estate. Those with over $60,000 net worth could be called "rich, " if not "super rich." The size of this elite had remained stable for some time. In 1922 one percent of Americans owned about 61 percent of all corporate stock; in 1953 one percent owned 76 percent. In 1922 the richest 2 percent of

all families held 33 percent of the private wealth in the country; in 1958 their share stood at 32 percent. The rich stayed rich or got richer partly because of favorable tax laws. Tax laws favored the upper-income brackets on the theory that this group should be encouraged to invest and thereby stimulate economic growth. By using loopholes hundreds of millionaires paid little or no taxes. Roughly $60 billion in taxes were "lost" this way each year. Talk of tax reform to close the loopholes and make the rich feel the pinch was common at election time, but, on Capitol Hill, it rarely got beyond the stage of cloakroom gossip.

The middle class was also participating in the affluent society. If "middle class" meant all families with incomes between $10,000 and $25,000 yearly, then a majority of the population became middle class in the last quarter of the twentieth century. This segment aspired to send its children to college, to own homes and cars, and to enjoy long weekends and vacation travel. Through advertising and television, the middle-class life style became a nationwide norm. But by the seventies, the middle class was in a squeeze. Skyrocketing prices were making it harder for middle Americans to maintain the way of life they had achieved. Mounting taxes and the cost of homes, cars, appliances, recreation, and college education for their children made it necessary for both parents to work and often required an extra "moonlighting" job or overtime for the breadwinners.

The rediscovery of poverty

The boom years of the 1940s and 1950s sparked a theory that "welfare capitalism" could entirely eliminate poverty. By the standards of 1935–1936, poor families had increased their income by as much as 120 percent in 1962. This was an extremely favorable sign. It meant that affluent America would soon eliminate want. A few "pockets of poverty" might remain in Appalachia and elsewhere for a time but, according to the new utopians, welfare could handle the situation on a temporary basis.

Then, in the 1960s, affluent America rediscovered poverty. Michael Harrington's book, *The Other America* (1962), deeply impressed John F. Kennedy. It showed that poverty, although often invisible to the middle class, was still very much alive. The poor were surviving in tenements, boardinghouses, flophouses, sanitariums, retirement homes, and rural labor camps. Unlike the old immigrant poor of the cities, today's slum dwellers were living lives without hope. The "other America," Harrington noted, was "populated by the failures, by those driven from the land and bewildered by the city, by old people suddenly confronted with the torments of loneliness and poverty, and by minorities

BUSINESS ACTIVITY, 1941–1971

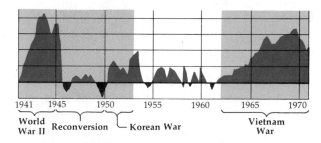

The thirty years from 1941 to 1971 were a period of great prosperity. Recessions were relatively short and mild. Yet the mechanization of agriculture and the automation of industry placed new demands on the skills of persons looking for jobs. In the sixties, as America became involved in the Vietnam War, there was a sharp impact on industrial production. A serious recession followed the end of the war.

facing a wall of prejudice."

According to the government, in 1962 a family of four with an income of $3195 or less was living in poverty (by 1970 this threshold amount was $3968). At the time of the rediscovery of poverty, between 17 and 23 percent of all American families—some 30 million people, or one fifth of the nation—was ill housed, ill clad, and ill nourished. For a decade after 1959 the number of persons officially designated as poor decreased by 5 percent of their total each year. Then in 1970 the number of poor suddenly shot upward by 5 percent, to a total of 25.5 million persons. Poverty was now associated with a growing number of people in several categories: children in fatherless homes, older people, and the chronically unemployed of minority groups. In 1969, 4.8 million people aged sixty-five or older lived in poverty, and the trend was upward. About half the poor lived in rural areas.

The children of low-income parents attended inferior schools and dropped out sooner than the majority of youngsters. They ate less protein and were in poorer health than the national average. In the slums life expectancy was lower and infant mortality higher than in the country as a whole.

The war on poverty

Theoretically the nation could ignore the poor, because the nation's poor were already covered by the system of public assistance created in the 1930s. Yet this was a hopelessly inadequate program which, some observers felt, was helping make poverty a permanent status for millions of people. Another solution seemed to be to redistribute income through income tax reform. But such a strategy might require cuts in defense spending and necessitate higher taxes for the middle class, and these steps would meet with stiff political resistance.

The civil rights movement and the ghetto riots of the 1960s were not specifically aimed at eradicating poverty, but they created a sense of urgency about the desperate straits of many black Americans. In January 1964 President Johnson called for a "war on poverty." In response, Congress passed the Economic Opportunity Act that year. It authorized a program that included job training and work-study grants for youngsters from families with the lowest incomes, especially nonwhites. The new law established the Office of Economic Opportunity (OEO) which administered smaller agencies and programs. One of its agencies, the Job Corps, enrolled ghetto youth for schooling and on-the-job training. A second, Volunteers in Service to America (VISTA), known as "the domestic Peace Corps," was intended to train community workers and organize self-help projects in the slums. An OEO project that showed special imagination was Head Start, a program for preschool children.

Many white middle-class Americans had little enthusiasm for the war on poverty, since they believed they were footing the bill for troublemakers and freeloaders. Mean-while, some of the poor complained that antipoverty funds were being sidetracked to pay high-salaried administrators. Soon the OEO was competing for funds with the war in Vietnam, and while Johnson promised to deliver both guns and butter, guns took top priority. By the end of his term, budget cuts had terminated the war on poverty before a "victory" was even in sight.

Johnson used other devices to reduce widespread economic problems. One was an increase in Social Security retirement benefits. Another was a comprehensive prepaid medical insurance plan. The U.S. was then the only major industrial nation without a comprehensive plan, even though its outlays for medical care were the highest in the world. But ever since Truman had proposed a federal medical aid program, the American Medical Association had fought it tooth-and-nail as "socialized medicine." In 1965 Congress passed the Medicare Act, a program of limited medical assistance to the elderly. Though marred by waste and inefficiency, Medicare stimulated new interest in a plan with wider coverage.

By the late 1960s the welfare system was in the doghouse. Practically everyone agreed that it was wasteful and unfair both to those who paid for it and to those who received its benefits. It humiliated the recipients by prying into their personal affairs. In some states benefits were barely at the subsistence level. In others they were high enough to discourage some of those who could work from accepting low-paying jobs when they could go on receiving payments. Accounts of welfare cheating, usually greatly exaggerated, infuriated taxpayers. Congress began to give serious attention to the most revolutionary welfare proposal since Social Security: a guaranteed annual income. It was based on a theory that a shift of only 5 percent of the national income could give all American families a minimum income of $5000. A measure designed by Daniel P. Moynihan, Nixon's assistant for urban affairs, was introduced in Congress in 1971 and passed by the House. It proposed a minimum annual income of $2400 for a family of four. But liberals objected that the amount was inadequate and conservatives fought it on principle. So the measure died, at least for the time being.

The limits of growth

Because the United States had thrived on rapid growth, few Americans were prepared for the news that, in the future, growth might well be limited by the dwindling supplies of world resources. But some were already expressing doubts that more was always better. The Gross National Product, Robert F. Kennedy pointed out, "includes the destruction of the redwoods and the death of Lake Superior. It grows with the production of napalm and missiles and nuclear warheads and [chemical warfare]." More attention had to be paid to the *quality* of life. Doomsayers became more numerous and vocal in the seventies, lending new urgency to the question of growth. In 1972 the Massachusetts Institute of Technology issued a report entitled *The Limits of Growth*, which suggested that at the existing rates of world population growth and use of resources the "physical limits to growth are likely to be encountered in the lifetime of our children." The time would come when simply keeping the old system in running order would require all available resources; no new machines could be developed. The only way to avoid catastrophe was to establish a global balance between births and deaths and put a halt to new technology.

Few people could accept the no-growth doctrine at face value. Yet most could not deny that continuing growth of population and productivity posed many long-term problems. The U.S. and other developed nations seemed to be dependent on a dwindling oil supply. How rapidly alternate energy sources could be developed and at what cost to the environment remained to be seen.

In addition, the "Ghosts of Depression Past and Depression Future" still haunted the country. Weren't cycles of prosperity and recession built into our economic system? Could there be—would there be—another great depression like that of the thirties? Six recessions occurred in the thirty years following World War II, the deepest and most threatening in 1973–1975. Even in the years between 1953 and 1963 American manufacturing failed to create enough new jobs to keep up with population growth. President Kennedy was advised to accept the notion of 4 percent unemployment as normal; by the mid-1970s 6 percent was considered normal by some economists. Higher unemployment seemed to be chronic. Unskilled jobs became scarcer as new agricultural machines replaced farm laborers in the South and Southwest. Cutbacks in aerospace during the 1960s led to further reduction of the work force. A tax cut and stepped-up war spending in 1964 helped stimulate the economy. But by 1970–1971 the drain of goods to the Vietnam War was having serious negative effects on the economy. Money for investment became scarce and interest rates rose. This was a major cause of inflation. Meanwhile, with 5.6 percent of the work force unemployed, millions of wage earners were idle.

At each economic downturn, some experts argued that a major catastrophe was next to impossible because the government now played too big a role in the economy. Uncle Sam already guaranteed bank deposits and extended unemployment insurance amounting to almost half what a wage earner would normally receive. He could, in an emergency, hire the unemployed directly. Others said that falling investments by investors and sagging income among the public could feed upon each other and thereby start the country, and perhaps the world, on a deep depression. Not only did the predictions of experts differ; there was also no consensus about what, if anything, to do to prevent a depression. To combat inflation in 1971 President Nixon turned unexpectedly to wage and price controls. These had limited effects, as they were enforced for only a short time.

The recession of 1973–1975 included for the first time in history the dual conditions of high unemployment and high inflation. It became the most serious economic crisis since the thirties. Higher prices for food and fuel affected most households. In the midst of the trouble, the Arab oil-producing nations reduced the supply and raised the prices of crude oil. Meanwhile, with over 8 percent of the work force unemployed early in 1975, more people were applying for unemployment compensation than at any time

since Social Security was founded in 1935. By June unemployment topped 9 percent.

How to deal with this "stagflation" (a stagnant economy and inflation)? Liberals, remembering the FDR years, asked for government spending and price controls. Conservatives called for reducing government constraints on private business, the size of the government bureaucracy, and domestic spending programs in order to bring the budget into balance. Some senators thought that strict limitations on oil imports were needed to save the country from the stranglehold of the Arab oil producers. In 1975 Congress passed a tax cut of $25 billion to stimulate spending and investment, which President Ford signed into law.

Unions Join "the Establishment"

Unions in peacetime

When World War II ended, labor unions felt threatened by inflation, depression, and loss of membership. They called major strikes to win pay raises and solidify recent gains in the automobile, steel, shipping, coal, and railroad industries. With 4.7 million workers involved in labor disputes, 1946 was the biggest strike year in American history. For the first time big employers made no concerted effort to deny union demands. It was simpler to grant raises and pass the costs on to the consumer.

Management had resigned itself to working with the unions. But it resented the Wagner Act as too restrictive; it also feared the liberal policies of the CIO and the influence of Communists in the labor movement. Enraged by the work stoppages of 1946, conservatives in the Republican-controlled Congress decided to push through reforms. Congress passed the Taft-Hartley Labor-Management Relations Act of 1947 over

President Truman's veto. Taft-Hartley outlawed the closed shop (where an employer must employ union members only). In addition, it authorized the states to pass "right-to-work" ordinances. These laws would outlaw not only the closed shop but the union shop as well (where an employer is required to employ workers who will agree to join a union after being hired). In the nonindustrial states, especially in the South, this would seriously restrict union organizing drives. Taft-Hartley also required union leaders to swear an oath each year that they were not Communists and did not believe in violent revolution. In disputes affecting the national interest, unions would now have to observe an eighty-day cooling-off period before striking. They were required to reveal their financial records and were forbidden to spend dues money on federal elections. Overall, Taft-Hartley sought to end "unfair" labor practices and restrict the power of the big unions.

Labor publicists termed it a "slave labor law." The metaphor was overdrawn, but unions were clearly entering a more defensive period. Looming on the horizon were other serious challenges to the labor movement: inflation, automation, unemployment, racketeering, McCarthyism, and racial unrest.

Practically everybody had complaints against organized labor. The general public fumed at the gangster domination of some unions. Anti-Communists inside and outside the ranks of labor believed that the CIO was riddled with subversives. Liberals charged that labor bosses had lost their taste for social change and that the labor movement was no longer the cutting edge of progressive reform. Management accused labor's top leaders of trying to whittle away at the power of management. Government economists said that union-negotiated raises were inflationary. Republicans resented labor's tendency to vote Democratic, while Democrats bristled at those labor leaders who strayed into the Republican camp. Racial minorities called labor unions racist. Meantime, rank-and-file unionists feared that the "fat-cat union bureaucrat" knew nothing about life on the assembly line and was selling them out.

During the McCarthy era of the 1950s conservatives exerted tremendous pressure on the CIO to purge itself of Communists and Communist sympathizers. Eleven CIO unions that refused to do so lost their charters, while the CIO generally lost both membership and power as a consequence. Since the house of labor seemed incapable of kicking out the racketeers who had taken over some unions, Congress undertook the job. A special Senate subcommittee headed by Estes Kefauver and John McClellan helped expose gangsters in a number of AFL unions. Committee counsel Robert F. Kennedy made his mark by attacking the Teamsters Union. Although two presidents of the Teamsters Union, Dave Beck and James Hoffa, went to jail, and the union was expelled from the AFL-CIO, the Teamsters went on to become the biggest and strongest union of all. The Landrum-Griffin Labor-Management Act of 1959 was a consequence of the Senate hearings. It created new machinery to make unions more democratic and to protect them from gangsters and corruption.

Organizing the unorganized

Despite the fact that union membership rose to a high-water mark of some 17 million in the late 1950s, only 36 percent of nonfarm workers were organized in the U.S. in 1956 as compared with 50 percent in Britain and 90 percent in Sweden. Labor, then, still had plenty of workers to organize. But since the proportion of blue-collar workers was declining (from 40 percent of the total labor force at the end of the war to 30 percent by 1970), labor's future lay with white-collar workers, whose numbers were increasing. To meet its potential the labor movement had to overcome certain structural defects.

For one thing, the split between the AFL and CIO that dated back to the 1930s was hampering efforts of union solidarity. The AFL had nearly 11 million members and the CIO around 5 million in 1955. By then the fight to "expel the Reds and hoods" had ended. The deaths of AFL leader William Greene and CIO leader Philip Murray, who remembered the bitter split in the thirties, opened the way to a merger. The AFL-CIO was formed in 1955, with George Meany as president and Walter Reuther of the auto workers as first vice-president.

One of the most promising fields of recruitment for the labor movement was that of public employees. Squeezed by inflation, wage controls, and tight government bud-

> *There is one thing that the worker doesn't do like the middle class: he works like a worker.*
> HARVEY SWADOS (1920-   )
> Author

gets, they became more militant and better organized. Starting in the 1960s there were periodic work stoppages by subway engineers, bus drivers, garbage collectors, teachers, policemen, bridge tenders, and sewage maintenance operators. After failing to win wage increases, the postal workers went on strike in 1970, in violation of the law. They won their demands without having to pay any penalties. By the mid-seventies approximately 5.2 million white-collar workers in private and public work were represented by unions. The American Federation of Government Employees had 300,000 members.

Traditionally AFL unions had not gone out of their way to recruit racial minorities, and members of these minorities bitterly resented union discrimination. Tensions reached a peak in the 1960s when the NAACP locked horns with the AFL. The black civil rights organization charged outright discrimination, especially in the building and needle trades. A target for racial militants was the apprentice training programs controlled by unions. Some headway was made, but the progress was slow.

Those who wanted labor to press for large-scale social reforms were often disappointed. Lobbying activity along these lines was minimal. The anti-Communist campaign left labor disorganized politically. Also, affluence and a taste for power greatly reduced the appetite of labor leaders for welfare crusades. Besides, big labor was winning important benefits for its own members at the bargaining table. These included supplemental unemployment insurance, enlarged pension plans, and medical care. Having achieved these successes through bargaining, labor was less inclined to engage in lobbying efforts for public laws to help all workers.

Blue collar goes middle class

In the 1950s many blue-collar workers were not only earning as much as white-collar workers but were also adopting their life styles—from homes in the suburbs to vacations in Florida. Even George Meany agreed that labor "to some extent has become middle class." Whether a person did hand labor was still an important dividing line, however. To maintain the middle-class standard of life often required jobs for both husband and wife, overtime work, and part-time jobs for older children. And the industrial workers often lived with the nagging fear of being replaced by a machine. A work injury could force early retirement—a problem the white-collar worker rarely had to face.

American workers may have been the best-paid workers in the world (as management claimed)—but were they the happiest at their work? In the 1970s "blue-collar blues" hit many assembly lines. It manifested itself in a high rate of turnover among younger workers. Other symptoms were large-scale absenteeism and petty sabotage, alcoholism and drug abuse. Workers at the most modern and efficient industrial plant in the world, the Chevy Vega plant at Lordstown, Ohio, went on strike in 1972 complaining of unbearable conditions on the assembly line. Management disputed the claims of worker discontent, but a government survey found that the more efficient the assembly line, the more unhappy the worker. Work that was oversimplified and fragmented caused serious mental and physical strain. Taking a cue from industrial plants in Japan and Scandinavia, some American employers began to experiment with new work schemes to make the worker feel like more than just a cog in a machine. An electronics manufacturer allowed the individual worker to assemble television sets in their entirety. The final product was slightly more expensive but of higher quality.

Management tended to minimize the ill effects of automation, saying that while new machines caused short-term dislocation, in the long run they created new jobs and a better life for all. But labor often saw automation as a decided threat. One labor expert estimated in 1963 that automation was eliminating four thousand jobs (net) *each week.* Unions demanded either a share of the higher profits that came with automation and increased productivity or special benefits for the workers replaced by machines. Or they wanted both. A creative compromise was found in West Coast longshoring. When cargo-container ships revolutionized the industry and reduced the need for workers, labor and management signed contracts which guaranteed incomes and pensions to those

workers replaced by the new technology. The long-range alternatives for workers in automated industry were a lighter work load at forty hours a week, a work week shortened to thirty or thirty-five hours without a reduction in pay, or a smaller work force. Each solution had its disadvantages. For the problems created by automation there was no simple cure.

A new problem loomed on the horizon—the runaway corporation. As American business opened factories in foreign countries in order to hire cheaper labor and realize tax advantages, many jobs were being lost at home each year. Some labor analysts identified it as the most serious problem of this generation. Thus, while labor had an enlarged political and economic significance, its future was not unclouded.

Labor was part of America's Cold War consensus, vigorously supporting America's anti-Communist foreign policy in Korea, in Vietnam, and, for that matter, in every corner

On the assembly line, workers have had little cause for pride in their products. An angry auto worker, after crawling to work through crowded traffic, asked why "we've got to turn out more every minute . . . and there isn't even any room for them on the highways." Imagine the reaction of the woman shown here when she returns home and relaxes in front of the television set to be told that using antiseptic mouthwash will keep others from whispering about her breath.

of the globe. In 1967 "hard hat" construction workers in New York demonstrated in favor of America's involvement in Vietnam and wielded clubs against antiwar demonstra-tors. Observers who recalled the days when labor was on the receiving end of violence took the episode as typifying labor's changed status in American society.

The Overflowing Horn of Plenty

Space-age farming

Futurologists can already visualize the farm of the twenty-first century. Giant harvester-planter machines glide on hundred-foot-wide tracks across huge fields, taking in one crop and setting out the next in a single sweep. Cattle feed in high-rise barns. Grain is shipped to market in pneumatic tubes. Overhead, a helicopter darts about, reading temperatures and spraying chemicals. High in a bubble-domed control tower sits a "farmer" in a lab coat, monitoring a TV screen and a computer which automatically signals the order to plant, harvest, water, or feed. It is a scene more appropriate to Flash Gordon than to Thomas Jefferson or even to César Chávez.

This fantasy farm merely projects those changes brought about in agriculture by new developments in science, technology, and management in the decades following World War II. Enormous increases in the use of chemical fertilizers led to a vast expansion of farm output. Through the use of hormones calves were fattened in five months instead of the two and a half years previously required. New grain species were producing three and four times as much yield in two thirds the growing time—a miracle known as the "Green Revolution." By 1970 American farmers were seven times as productive as they had been fifty years earlier, and the grocer was marketing ten times as many food varieties. Growers could also boast that for all the griping that went on at the supermarket checkout stand, American consumers spent a smaller portion of their incomes on food than any other people on earth.

Farm surpluses and subsidies

"I have seen today how the slaves of capitalism live," Soviet Premier Nikita Khrushchev joked on a visit to Coon Rapids, Iowa, in 1959, "and they live pretty well." His host for the day was Rosswell Garst, a farmer, banker, and seed merchant, who grew about one hundred bushels of wheat per acre, far more than his Russian counterpart. The U.S. was then among the ten or so major food-exporting nations of the world. In 1967 American growers comfortably fed 200 million in their own nation, and had surpluses that could feed 160 million people in other lands. While in other parts of the globe one billion people went to sleep hungry each night and thousands died of malnutrition or starvation before the morning (perhaps one person every ten seconds in 1970), Americans jogged and dieted to work off unwanted fat.

Agriculture was heavily subsidized. Until Europe recovered from World War II, demands for U.S. farm goods remained strong. But soon afterward American farmers' granaries began to bulge with unsold wheat and corn, the result of increased production and limited demand. To prevent overproduction from undermining farm income, the government updated the New Deal farm program. Farm support was three-pronged. First, the government bought excess farm commodities to stabilize prices at a high level. Second, by acreage allotments and soil-bank restrictions (buying up marginal land and converting it to forests or recreational uses), it restricted production. Third, Washington sold farm surpluses overseas or donated them to friendly hungry nations.

Since the New Deal era Washington has spent well over $50 billion on farm supports. It paid out about $300 million in 1948, $7.6 billion in 1964, and $3 or $4 billion yearly in the early 1970s. The big and medium farmers got the largest benefits. One member of Congress estimated that in 1972 40 percent of all subsidies went to only 5 percent of the nation's nearly 3 million farmers. Conservatives wanted to get the government out of the farm business but seemed unable to find a way of doing so without undermining farm income and the entire agricultural economy. Georgia's Senator Herman Talmadge, a staunch conservative, said he would be a "traitor" to the people of his state if he voted to undo the farm supports. About half the farms of his state were marginal and would probably go under without help from the government.

The corporate farm and farm laborer

Rising farm productivity had for some decades gone hand in hand with a dwindling number of farms and farmers. In 1920 one out of three Americans was engaged in farming; in 1970 only one in twenty-two followed that vocation. Between 1969 and 1974 the size of the farm population remained relatively steady. But even if 2 million more American subsistence farmers left agriculture, the food supply on the dinner table would remain about the same.

"Do we get bigger, or do we give up?" was a question frequently asked in farm households in the postwar years. Many farmers found ways to increase the size and efficiency of their operations. But land and equipment were expensive, so the younger generation often chose to give up farming and head for the city. The older folks usually stayed on the farm until they retired or died, at which time the family holdings were sometimes swallowed by giant farm corporations. Many observers of the farm scene announced that the days of the family farm were numbered.

Though that claim was somewhat exaggerated, corporate farms were responsible for an ever increasing share of the farm output. Among their numbers were million-dollar operations, owned by, or financially linked with, packinghouses or industrial conglomerates. In California some farmers surveyed their "factories in the fields" by airplane. Corporate farms hoped to achieve higher profits by driving out inefficient growers and acquiring a maximum part of the market. They claimed they were producing superior products at the lowest possible price. According to consumer groups, though, the reduction of the number of growers in certain areas of agriculture—cattle raising, for example—and the rise of corporate farming helped explain the rise of food prices in 1973–1974.

Thus, improved technology and management, a reduction in the number of farmers, plus billions of dollars in government price supports seemed to have done the farmers—and the American people as a whole—a world of good. Yet not all farmers had a share in all this progress. Those who benefitted least were the farm laborers. Most agricultural workers—white and black, Chicano and Puerto Rican, native and foreign—lacked elementary rights and privileges that other workers took for granted: collective bargaining, minimum wages, unemployment insurance, and old-age pensions. Their lives were plagued by chronic unemployment, low wages, poor housing, ill health, high infant mortality, bad schooling, and sometimes even hunger. Ironically, the growers with the biggest subsidies were often the first to op-

Commercial fertilizers, stronger hybrid plants, and improved distribution helped to double and triple the yield of farmland, make crop rotation unnecessary, and encourage the growth of huge, one-crop farms. Such crops proved particularly susceptible to pests and required massive applications of modern insecticides.

pose welfare benefits for the rural poor. A government study showed that in Madera County, California, where subsidies guaranteed annual incomes as high as $133,000, the growers adamantly opposed a guaranteed annual income for farm workers. César Chávez' United Farm Workers Union (UFWU) fought to end "the harvest of shame." It won contracts with grape and lettuce growers around 1970, but the progress of agricultural unionism was painfully slow. However, in 1975 the California governor signed into law a historic bill that provided the right of collective bargaining for farm workers. Similar moves were expected in other agricultural states as well.

Review

Spurred by consumer spending and by Cold War competition with the Russians, postwar America entered what came to be known as the "age of affluence." Advances in science and technology were adding considerably to national wealth. The key to technological advance was the computer, the "thinking machine" of the mid-twentieth century.

Contrary to expectation, the age of affluence did not eliminate poverty, nor was wealth redistributed. The middle class carried the largest proportional tax burden. Although the middle class did enjoy relatively prosperous times in the 1950s and early 1960s, it later felt the growing squeeze of inflation, rising taxes, and rising unemployment.

During the Kennedy-Johnson years, when the economy began to sputter, the nation rediscovered poverty. The major governmental response, President Johnson's war-on-poverty program, lost out to the economic demands of the Vietnam War. Welfare reform was long overdue. A guaranteed minimum income for all Americans was briefly considered by Congress, and then abandoned.

In the 1970s, an increasing number of people began to question the prevailing belief in unlimited economic growth. Was it possible always to have more, when world resources were limited? Weren't developed nations dangerously dependent on dwindling supplies? A serious recession from 1973 to 1975 posed additional questions relating to economic stability. Was the U.S. heading for another great depression? If so, what could be done to prevent it? Experts offered different answers as unemployment and inflation took their toll in affluent America.

After World War II big labor enjoyed considerable power through collective bargaining. But the labor movement had mellowed. The Taft-Hartley Act of 1947 modified the Wagner Act of 1935. Organized labor survived the campaign to sweep out criminal and Communist influences, and in 1955 the AFL and CIO merged. Meanwhile, blue-collar workers struggled to achieve and sustain a middle-class life style. White-collar workers, faced with an escalation in the cost of living, joined unions in increasing numbers. Hard-hat support for the Vietnam War symbolized labor's political conservatism in the 1960s.

Affluent America enjoyed abundant farm productivity. New machines, new chemicals, and new management techniques brought about ever larger operations and ever increasing yields. By 1967 the U.S. was feeding over 350 million people at home and abroad. Farming remained heavily subsidized by the government, with the larger, more efficient operators receiving most of the benefits. Corporate farming increased its share of the total market and family farming decreased. Many farmers who had neither the land nor the equipment to benefit from modern techniques held a marginal position in the economy. Agricultural laborers remained most economically depressed of all, even in the years of record farm productivity.

Questions

1. How did the Cold War affect the U.S. economy?
2. Identify: (a) United Farm Workers Union, (b) Taft-Hartley Act, (c) Office of Economic Opportunity, (d) "welfare capitalism," (e) *The Other America,* and (f) the "postindustrial era."
3. Should the welfare program be expanded, improved, or replaced by something different? Explain.
4. Describe the major problems that faced organized labor in the years after World War II.
5. Do you believe the nation would suffer from the disappearance of the family farm? How so?

power

John Dean III testifies before the Watergate Committee.

The investigation of this Select Committee was born of crisis, unabated as of this very time — the crisis of a mounting loss of confidence by American citizens in the integrity of our electoral process which is the bedrock of our democracy.

SENATOR SAM. J. ERVIN, JR.
Opening session of the Senate Select Committee on Presidential Campaign Activities, May 17, 1973

34

34
The Nightmare of Watergate

In 1876 the United States celebrated its centennial happily. The Philadelphia Fair was a joyous hymn to America's past and to its future greatness. A century later the nation approached its bicentennial in a more sober mood. Watergate, the defeat in Vietnam, inflation, unemployment, and the energy crisis had put a damper on the celebration.

There was at least one concern that the citizens of bicentennial America shared with the Revolutionary generation—a concern over political power—its abuse by the executive authority and its excessive concentration in the hands of a few. Having fought a bloody rebellion against a domineering king and his ministers in parliament, they took special pains under the new framework of government to prevent the recurrence of abuses by the nation's presidents. Because of the threat to liberty posed by concentrated power, they attempted to create a government whose branches would check and balance one another, and whose ultimate authority would rest with the governed. In this way no one faction, rich or poor, North or South, agrarian or commercial, might reign supreme. Two hundred years later a generation of Americans were again pondering the nature of power. Who had too much power, who had too little, and how the balance between the two could be adjusted—these matters preoccupied Americans of the 1960s and 1970s as they had the generation of the Founding Fathers.

Even before Watergate a great many Americans—minorities and college students, hard hats and bureaucrats, housewives and office workers—were distressed by their own sense of powerlessness. The theme of powerlessness was featured in many political speeches on all sides during the 1968 presidential campaign. Not only the voices of the New Left, but Richard M. Nixon himself also gave eloquent expression to the theme when he said: "The power to control decisions immediately affecting one's life is vanishing. . . . That unique, precious, indescribable thing—the *individual* human mind, heart and spirit—is being injured, or neglected, or slighted. . . . What we need is not one leader, but many leaders; not one center of power, but many centers of power."

After Watergate a few critics called into question the very framework of government itself. Was the Constitution, framed in the era of the powdered wig, still applicable in the space age? How could the slow-moving federal system deal swiftly and decisively with racial injustice, urban rot, and environmental pollution? Could the government cleanse itself of corruption and greed? Could the Bill of Rights survive in an age of electronic snooping by government agents?

In the period of Watergate two centers of power attracted the most attention. These were, first, the presidency, including the executive departments and agencies. The FBI and CIA were said to be virtually unchecked and unbalanced. The second, giant corporations, were accused of wielding too much economic power and political influence.

Big Government and Big Business

The powerless and the powerful

In the 1950s sociologists identified a sense of powerlessness as a root cause of "alienation," which, with apathy and conformity, was seen as a growing trend in American society. Perhaps this postwar mood was caused by the threat of nuclear extinction, or by the fear created during the McCarthy era. Some attributed it in part to the consumer economy that encouraged people to indulge themselves in material goods—cars, TV sets, clothes, split-level homes, and other creature comforts—and to ignore the well-being of the community as a whole. Professors complained that a "silent generation" of college students had totally divorced itself from any interest in public issues, either social or political. For many young men, the goal was a secure position in a big, paternal corporation, marriage, a family, and a home in the suburbs.

The white middle class was "voiceless, powerless and frustrated." So wrote sociologist C. Wright Mills in *White Collar* (1951). Mills analyzed the implications of millions of people becoming locked into bureaucratic structures in government and private industry. David Riesman in *The Lonely Crowd* (1950) believed Americans were becoming "other directed." Instead of obeying their own individual values, or the Protestant Ethic, or the doctrine of rugged individualism, people now adjusted to whatever standards of behavior they thought their neighbors and co-workers embraced. This, Riesman said, was inevitable in an age of status seeking. William II. Whyte, Jr., in *The Organization Man* (1956) described one segment of white-collar society—the male, middle-level, corporation executive. He lived comfortably in a split-level suburban house and gave the most productive years of his life to a large business concern. At work he was part of a team effort, his personal initiative and responsibility diluted by the committee approach to problem solving. Although well-adjusted and secure, he too felt powerless and dependent.

If so many people felt powerless and voiceless, who had power? Some critics believed that the country was in the hands of an elite. Mills, in *The Power Elite* (1956), assigned power to a coalition of military brass, corporation heads, and the executive branch of government. Since 1945, he asserted, the military had held the upper hand. Others agreed that the country was run by an elite but placed corporate and financial leaders at the top of the heap. A second major group of analysts insisted that, while power elites existed, the influence of any one of them was tempered by equally strong opposing forces. Thus "veto groups" modified one another's power and prevented any single power structure from gaining domination. This was the balancing of power that James Madison had believed would develop in America, and this, according to some scholars, was the way American society now operated.

The imperial presidency

For the most part Americans have, at least in retrospect, preferred strong presidents. Jackson, Lincoln, Wilson, and both Roosevelts are among the popular favorites who ruled with a strong hand. The more passive leaders faded from memory or, like Calvin Coolidge, became the butt of national jokes. For most liberals the ideal situation was a president and a Congress of the same party (preferably Democratic) working together for a program of moderate reform. Fondly they recalled FDR's achievements in his first hundred days in office. Conservative critics, particularly after Roosevelt ran for a third term, warned of the possible abuse of power by a strong president. But for the most part both conservatives and liberals in the 1940s and the 1950s accepted the ever expanding power of the presidency. A startling change of opinion occurred in the 1970s in the wake of Vietnam and Watergate.

Starting with Franklin D. Roosevelt, the presidents gradually took power, and the Congress gradually gave it away, until the balance clearly favored the chief executive. Once the balance had shifted, it was difficult to readjust. By the seventies the country had

what Arthur M. Schlesinger, Jr., has called the "imperial presidency."

In 1940 Franklin D. Roosevelt gave Britain fifty old American destroyers in exchange for naval bases in the Atlantic and the Caribbean, a deal criticized at the time as usurping the Senate's treaty-making power and inviting war with Germany. FDR's authority as commander in chief grew steadily through the Second World War, although in most important instances he did call upon Congress for approval of his decisions. From the beginning of the Cold War the new military technology, and especially the threat of nuclear attack, seemed to require a chief executive with almost absolute power in foreign affairs. Truman had the country's support when he showed his determination to "stand up to Stalin." Few people objected when he sent troops into Korea in 1950 without asking Congress for a declaration of war. Although Ohio Republican Senator Robert Taft complained that "the president simply usurped authority, in violation of the laws and Constitution," many of his Senate colleagues shrugged indifferently. Had Congress been consulted, it probably would have agreed with the president.

Eisenhower made some effort to restore the balance by calling for congressional support for intervention in the Middle East in 1957. Generous (though vague) authority was given him by Congress before U.S. troops landed in Lebanon the following year. Also, when trouble arose with China over Formosa (Taiwan), he requested a joint resolution from Congress to back military intervention. Since the Second World War presidents had been making executive agreements, even secret and far-reaching ones, with foreign countries without consulting the Congress. Isolationist Senator John W. Bricker of Ohio offered a constitutional amendment in 1953 to halt this extension of presidential power. He feared a repeat of "disastrous" executive agreements such as Yalta and Potsdam entered into by Roosevelt and Truman. Nevertheless, the Senate felt comfortable with the Republican Eisenhower in the White House and defeated the Bricker amendment.

Presidents Kennedy and Johnson took extraordinary executive action without consulting Congress. In the Cuban missile crisis of October 1962, an event that has been called the greatest crisis of the postwar era, Kennedy kept congressional leaders in the dark until two hours before he publicly ordered the navy to turn back Russian ships delivering missiles to Castro. Johnson's military intervention in the Dominican Republic in April 1965 was a warlike act committed strictly on presidential initiative.

It is hard to quantify the power of the presidency, but one measure may be the increase of White House aides. While Jefferson ran the executive branch with a secretary and a clerk, today as many as 5400 White House staff members are used to conduct the business of the presidency. In the words of George Reedy, a former presidential press secretary, these aides have become "faceless agents of power." Special legislation is also a measure of executive authority. A congressional committee has observed that there are 470 major provisions of the law that empower the president to govern the economy, assign military forces, restrict the travel of private citizens, allocate manpower, and seize the means of production—all in the interest of "national security."

By 1968, when Richard M. Nixon was inaugurated, the office of president was already becoming that of a sort of elected monarch. Nixon accelerated the trend. He felt that the presidency gave him a four-year mandate to exert strong executive leadership in domestic as well as in foreign affairs. The will of Congress to oversee presidential authority or to act on its own prerogative was minimal in Nixon's eyes. Thus he impounded (refused to spend) billions of dollars scheduled for health, education, and welfare that Congress had voted over his veto. When asked by Congress to provide information for congressional investigation of wrongdoing in the executive department, Nixon used "executive privilege" and "national security," as well as the constitutional separation of powers, as reasons for refusing to provide it. His attorney general claimed that executive privilege gave the president the right to order 2.5 million federal workers not to testify. This conception of the president and his subordinates as above the law led finally to the Watergate disaster.

A corporate society

In the years after World War II the enormous power wielded by giant corporations also became a matter of growing concern. Big business tended to see its interests and the national interest as synonymous. Charles E. Wilson, Eisenhower's secretary of defense, announced that what was good for General Motors (the company he had headed) was good for the U.S. In 1957 William T. Gossett of the Ford Motor Company declared: "The modern corporation is a social and economic institution that touches every aspect of our lives; in many ways it is an institutional expression of our way of life. . . . Indeed it is not inaccurate to say that we live in a corporate society."

The sheer size of big businesses had become staggering. General Motors' yearly income topped the combined revenues of New York, New Jersey, Pennsylvania, Ohio, Delaware, and the six New England states. The $17 billion assets of Standard Oil of New Jersey approached the combined assets of Chicago and Los Angeles. At the end of World War II the one hundred largest manufacturing firms accounted for 23 percent of the total value added to American products in manufacturing; by 1975 they accounted for 33 percent. The relative position of these few firms in the economy was secure. Their presidents,

"I'd like to teach the world to sing in perfect harmony,/I'd like to buy the world a Coke and keep it company." That song, created in 1971 to convey Coca-Cola's image as "the real thing," proved immensely popular; and the company has proved so successful at selling the world a Coke that it does well over half its business overseas. Cokes sold in foreign countries are usually produced locally, but the image is distinctly American.

who could fit into a college lecture hall, represented as much wealth and economic clout as the heads of the next largest 300,000 industrial firms, a group that would overflow four Yankee Stadiums.

The overall trend in business was not toward monopoly but toward oligopoly (a Greek word meaning "few sellers"). In many fields of manufacturing, for example, the three biggest companies accounted for at least two thirds of all the business. This held true in autos, trucks, farm machinery, tires, cigarettes, aluminum, liquor, meat packing, copper, tin cans, office machinery, and heavy electrical equipment. By their command of a large share of the market, oligopolies possessed an immunity from normal price competition. If they did compete with one another because the law demanded it, their competition was far stronger in product design, advertising, and consumer services than in prices. Such companies acquired the ability to control wages, to expand or contract the job market, to speed up or reduce inflation, and to influence the economy in other ways. Generally, one large firm set prices. General Motors' policy, according to a congressional hearing, was to set car prices that would bring an annual profit, after taxes, of 15 to 20 percent. The other car manufacturers would then follow GM's lead, a practice called "managing prices." Expert congressional witnesses testified that GM and Ford could easily destroy the few remaining domestic competitors in the automobile field, but deliberately chose not to do so to avoid antitrust suits.

In the postwar years two types of business combinations attracted much attention — conglomerates and multinational corporations. The conglomerates, many of which were formed in the 1950s, were "smorgasbord corporations" in which companies producing unrelated products were clustered together under one ownership. Thus the Coca Cola Company that had marketed only "the pause that refreshes" now had additional subsidiaries that made instant coffee, cattle feed, and concentrated orange juice. Litton Industries had well over a dozen subsidiaries, ranging all the way from a restaurant chain to a shipbuilding operation and from a manufacturer of typewriters to a manufacturer of medical supplies. Encouraging these sprawling economic empires was a stock market in which investors no longer looked for good annual dividends but instead demanded surging growth, both in the companies they invested in and in the prices of their stocks.

The multinational corporation has been defined by economist Robert L. Heilbroner as "a corporation with producing branches or subsidiaries in more than one nation." He called it a "revolutionary development in international economics." Of the top one hundred American industrial firms, sixty-two have production subsidiaries in six or more nations. Pepsi Cola is produced in 114 countries. Ford Motor Company has forty overseas subsidiaries. The activity of multinationals is especially great in Europe and Canada. The American multinationals annually sell $200 billion worth of goods overseas. Five sixths of those goods are produced *outside* the boundaries of the U.S. This means, among other things, a substantial loss of wages and taxes within the corporations' home country. One multinational, Standard Oil of New Jersey, actually does more business overseas than at home. Some companies are both conglomerates and multinationals — the International Telephone and Telegraph Company (ITT) is one example.

In their normal operations, multinationals deal not with foreign governments, but with bankers, corporate heads, and labor unions of many countries. Existing government agencies find it difficult to check or balance their power. Thus one observer defines a multinational corporation as a company that operates in several countries and is con-

Multinational firms are an irresistible force. Many firms are larger, stronger, in economic terms, than some nations.
ROY L. ASH (1918–   )
Director of Litton Industries

trolled by none. They cannot help but affect American foreign policy. Import-export agreements for oil and other vital resources have usually been arranged by the multinationals and then submitted to the executive branch for approval. Multinationals have also intruded often into the domestic politics of other nations. ITT's president claims the company is "a good citizen" in every country where it operates. But ITT memos released by newspaper columnist Jack Anderson showed that in 1970 ITT was deeply implicated (along with the CIA) in trying to prevent the election of Marxist Salvador Allende as president of Chile. After his election Allende nationalized the holdings of ITT.

Like the manufacturing companies, banks also accumulated wealth and influence over government affairs at home and abroad. Six New York City banks held $64 billion in assets in 1967, with their holdings spread out worldwide. Forty-nine banks controlled 150 of the largest American corporations. The "House of Rockefeller," a loose term referring to Chase Manhattan Bank of New York and other financial institutions controlled by the descendants of oil baron John D. Rockefeller, was one of the giants of world banking. The quiet and unassuming David Rockefeller, brother of the vice-president and head of Chase Manhattan, was considered by some to be the most influential private citizen in the land. His bank had over $23 billion in assets in 1970. He was, in the words of *Time* magazine, "one of that little group of men who sit at the financial hub of the world's wealthiest nation and by their nods give the stop or go sign to enterprise from

Bonn to Bangkok." The people associated with the Rockefellers have long held influential posts in government. In recent years Secretaries of State John Foster Dulles, Dean Rusk, and Henry Kissinger have had some association with them, and Nelson Rockefeller was appointed vice-president in 1974.

Modern corporations often resemble private governments that rule without the consent of the governed. They have assumed the power to "tax" consumers, to affect public health and safety, and to influence the quality of life. The auto industry is a case in point. By switching from functional car bumpers to ornamental bumpers, automobile manufacturers took a course of action that resulted in "taxes" of about $1 billion a year in auto repairs for drivers in the 1960s. Similarly, when they decided *not* to use the impact-absorbing steering wheels invented in the 1920s, their decision contributed to the deaths of an estimated thirteen thousand automobile drivers yearly. And when the industry converted to high-compression engines after World War II, it greatly increased air pollution from lead and other dangerous substances. None of these decisions was made with malicious intent, but neither were they made with public participation.

The critics: Kefauver and Nader

Corporations, like all interest groups seek favorable legislation. Owing to their considerable financial resources, their ability to influence public policy and the political process is undeniably great. Capitol Hill has long been a vast beehive of corporate lobbying activities. Some corporations hired several full-time lobbyists to represent their interests there. These lobbyists were often former government lawyers or congressmen who, upon their retirement from government, entered private law practices in Washington. Federal law prohibited corporate po-

litical contributions for national elections. Yet some firms have considered it essential to contribute money to both parties, even in violation of the law. In 1972 major corporations contributed about $500,000 to the Committee to Reelect the President. Seventy-six members of the Seventy-ninth Congress were associated with law firms, including firms that represented large corporate interests. Some representatives continued to receive money from their law firms and have frequently voted on issues in which they had a personal financial stake. Ninety-five representatives of the Seventy-ninth Congress were officeholders or stockholders of banks. They too were involved in a conflict of interest. Nor have corporate lobbying practices been limited to influencing Congress. Lobbyists and officials of big firms have monitored the actions of regulatory agencies. And they have sought appointments and other favors from the executive branch as well. Retired executives and lawyers are well represented in the councils of government, even in the regulatory agencies that are created to control business. They contribute to political campaigns (sometimes in violation of the law) and conduct well-coordinated lobbying efforts to secure favorable legislation.

The antimonopoly spirit goes back a long way in American history—some would say as far back as the Boston Tea Party, which destroyed the tea of the East India Company, a trade "monopoly." Today's opponents of big business usually call for stronger regulatory laws. Some want to abolish special quotas, tariffs, and even patent privileges that give giant corporations an unfair advantage over genuine competitors. A Senate committee estimated that oil import quotas cost the public about $7 billion yearly, or about 5 cents on each gallon of gasoline. Populist critics want stronger and more independent regulatory agencies to act in the public's behalf, and also stronger regulation of lobbying and campaign practices. Only as a last resort do some critics demand a breakup of the biggest corporations.

Democratic Senator Estes Kefauver of Tennessee and consumer advocate Ralph Nader were the two most outspoken critics of big business in the postwar decades. As chairman of the Senate Subcommittee on Antitrust and Monopoly from 1957 to 1963, Senator Kefauver concluded that the largest corporations in such fields as drugs, automobiles, and steel had developed an immunity to competition and had to be controlled. His investigation of price fixing resulted in jail sentences for minor officials of General Electric, Westinghouse, and twenty-seven other manufacturers of heavy electrical equipment. A suit against the companies was settled for $500 million. Picking up after Kefauver's untimely death was Senator Philip A. Hart of Michigan who proposed a law that would give smaller firms a chance to catch up with the giants. Many big industrial producers, Hart asserted, charged artificially high prices that cost the consumer from $50 to $60 billion annually. Hart wanted to compel these manufacturers to share their technical information with competitors or be split into smaller companies.

One of the sharpest thorns in the side of American business was consumer advocate Ralph Nader. While serving as a government traffic safety consultant, Nader learned much about the auto industry as well as about federal regulatory agencies. In a well-documented study, *Unsafe at Any Speed* (1965), he attacked the American automobile as a potential death trap. Many people considered him a meddling zealot, but when he won a $425,000 award and a public apology from General Motors for harassing him and spying on him, his credibility increased immensely. Nader and his associates ("Nader's Raiders") investigated not only manufacturers but also those government agencies most directly involved with consumers—the

Federal Trade Commission, the Food and Drug Administration, and the Interstate Commerce Commission. They filed suits to force compliance with the law and they lobbied successfully for major new laws to improve such things as auto safety and coal mine operations, meat standards and radiation control. In the 1970s Nader worked for the creation of a new regulatory agency, the Consumer Protection Agency.

In the sixties some liberals tried to reform corporate power from within. At the annual stockholders' meetings they questioned corporate policies at home and abroad. They tried to give those corporations a "social conscience." Thus the Polaroid Corporation was attacked for doing business with the white supremacist Republic of South Africa. Liberal stockholders in oil companies demanded that their directors institute policies that were "ecologically sound."

Few industries have ever been the target of so much public wrath as the oil industry was in the 1970s. Despite the Arab oil embargo many doubted the seriousness of the oil shortage. At a time of lengthening lines at the gas pumps in 1973, the oil industry announced soaring profits, an announcement which created suspicion in the public mind that the gasoline shortage was merely a pretext for squeezing the customer.

Early in the sixties "consumerism" had been dismissed as the work of "cranks" like Nader. But in the late sixties and early seventies consumer outrage spread, and the consumer movement was no longer casually dismissed. A growing number of consumers were insisting that the government protect their interests as it protected the interests of the producers of goods and services. Throughout the twentieth century sporadic efforts by organized consumers had tried to influence legislation. Of late, though, as consumers spent more and were more prone to credit buying "on easy terms," advertisers had become more aggressive. In television they had an extraordinarily persuasive tool. Their motto was "Sell the sizzle, not the steak," meaning that they advertised the psychological qualities of a product rather than the factual information. As advertising and products increased, no one consumer had the requisite skill, time, patience, or information, to solve all the dilemmas of shopping for goods and services.

Much consumer activity took the form of pressure to require the government to establish mandatory standards of production and better labeling by manufacturers or processors. In 1969 consumer groups pressured the United States Department of Agriculture to reduce the fat content of frankfurters: this they considered a major triumph. They also wrung from Congress a truth-in-packaging law. As the Federal Trade Commission was geared to bust trusts, not protect consumers, several senators introduced legislation to establish a consumer protection agency of one sort or another. Business lobbyists preferred not a new agency but a presidential assistant to help consumers. Also, almost all states and many cities created consumer protection boards. Consumer organizations asked for greater representation as "public" members on boards that made rules affecting the costs and quality of goods and services.

Defenders of big business

Big corporations under heavy attack for wielding excessive power were not without supporters. They had often claimed that corporate powers were extremely limited. They were irked by what they considered excessive governmental restraints, especially from regulatory agencies. These, they argued, limited their willingness to invest, and as a result the entire country suffered.

The benefits of free enterprise over socialism or other economic systems were much publicized during the Cold War. The National Association of Manufacturers and other groups stressed the virtues of private enterprise for national security and prosperity. During the energy crisis of the seventies, major oil producers claimed that they were leaders in the fight for conservation and ecology and that they were indispensible to the nation's future.

To charges of using money to influence government action, they replied that their behavior was no different from that of other interest groups, and that they were forced by circumstance to influence politicians or go out of business. A corporation head who confessed to giving money to the Nixon campaign in 1972 charged that the campaign fund raisers used implied threats against his firm. Corporations who admitted to bribing foreign government officials said that they could not exist otherwise in most countries of the world. For example, the United Fruit Company admitted paying a $1 million bribe in Honduras.

As for the "corporate conscience" argument, most officers of big firms asserted that, legally and morally, corporation directors were responsible solely to their stockholders—although hopefully in most cases there was no conflict between the interests of their stockholders and those of the public at large. The conservative economist Milton Friedman of the University of Chicago, in his *Capitalism and Freedom* (1962), argued that a corporation's only purpose was to earn a profit—"to use its resources and engage in activities designed to increase its profits so long as it stays within the rules of the game." Its obligation was to engage in "open and free competition without deception or fraud." In his view most American corporations were behaving properly, and in this way were serving the public interest well.

Some American businesses argued for *more*, not less, big business. In the 1960s Japanese and German cartels (giant business combinations set up—sometimes with government sanctions or capital—to discourage competition) were competing successfully with American companies throughout the world. American antitrust laws prohibited the formation of such cartels in the U.S. Also, it was asserted that big corporations were esssential to the security of the nation and of the free world. Thus when Lockheed Corpo-ration, at one time the country's biggest defense contractor, got into financial trouble it asked Congress to guarantee a private bank loan to the firm. This government aid was deemed necessary to save both thousands of jobs and a corporation that was militarily important.

Shifting Party Loyalties

Dropping out of politics

Few occupations are today held in lower esteem by Americans than that of politician. Mistrust of politicians goes hand-in-glove with rising voter apathy and an increase in independent voting habits. Both major parties have lost the faith of the electorate. With each passing decade fewer people have voted for president or contributed time and money to the major party organizations. The young, the poor, and the nonwhite have been especially disaffected. So, too, are a growing number of ordinary, middle-class, white citizens. In 1876 85 percent of those eligible to vote cast ballots; in 1972 the percentage was down to 56. In 1974 almost 80 percent of Americans between eighteen and twenty years of age failed to vote. In many off-year elections the majority of voters stayed home on election day. Those who did cast ballots increasingly tended to split their ticket.

In the sixties the Democratic coalition Franklin D. Roosevelt had forged in the thirties began to fall apart. Organized labor, racial minorities, white ethnics, and southern Democrats began to assert their independence. More voters still registered Democratic than Republican but they could not be counted on to put the Democratic party in power. In fact, Democrats managed to win only three of the seven presidential elections between 1948 and 1972. The states with the largest Democratic registration—New York, California, Illinois, Michigan, and Massachusetts—frequently elected Republican governors. In 1968 many northern blue-collar workers, an important segment of the Democratic coalition, wandered off the reservation to vote for George Wallace as president.

The city bosses, who had once helped to keep the parties working on a day-to-day basis, continued to lose their grip in the postwar decades. The decline in the number of patronage jobs and the increase in federal benefits and unemployment insurance helped undermine the strength of the bosses among the urban poor. Regular party labels seemed to lose their meaning in city politics. Mayor John Lindsay of New York eventually repudiated the Republican party and was forced out of politics. He had tried to act as power broker among the warring political factions of the city but had to admit that New York was becoming unmanageable. In Los Angeles Democratic Mayor Sam Yorty featured himself as a maverick, even to the extent of refusing to back John F. Kennedy for president. The Democrats later disowned Yorty. In many cities, as whites fled to the suburbs and blacks gained majority status, local party machines had to be rebuilt from scratch. The one major city boss to survive into the 1970s was Richard J. Daley of Chicago, a six-term mayor.

> *The attitude of this country toward anything can be changed overnight with television.*
>
> TONY SCHWARTZ
> Commercial artist and
> presidential campaign
> consultant

Politics in the television era

Television revolutionized political campaigning and the methods by which politicians sought and retained power. In 1946 only eight hundred families owned TV sets; by the 1960s TV reached into 46 million homes. The medium offered the voter a close-up of the candidates and raised new possibilities for image building. Political hucksters packaged and sold candidates like detergents. Much depended on a candidate's ability to *project* an image, whether or not the reality matched the image. In a radio speech explaining a controversial slush fund in 1952, Richard M. Nixon's references to his wife's cloth coat and to his little dog Checkers touched many listeners and thus helped him survive as Eisenhower's running mate. On the other hand, he failed to project a warm image in his TV debates with John F. Kennedy before the presidential election in 1960. The two contenders were in basic agreement on important issues but, as one expert said, Nixon came across like the "mean western railroad lawyer" and Kennedy as the "friendly western sheriff." This contributed to Nixon's defeat in the very close election.

In the television era the incumbent president had the immense advantage of prime-time exposure. He could always convene a press conference or beam a special message directly into the homes of millions of viewers. The Federal Communications Commission issued a ruling that, under some circumstances, the networks must give equal time to opposition candidates. But even this could not help the opposition overcome the advantage held by the incumbent.

During the television era the costs of campaigning mushroomed. Big money became a vital feature of national politics. This made it easier for fat-cat donors to "capture" candidates and influence their behavior after the election.

Presidential politics

Postwar presidential politics were shaped by many forces, among them the advent of prosperity, the expansion of executive power, and the challenge of the Cold War. Lacking Roosevelt's social breeding and polish and having very limited experience and background in international affairs, Harry S. Truman came to the Oval Office at a time when decisions of worldwide consequence had to be made. Fortunately, he had an appealing forthrightness that helped him overcome the handicap of following a powerful and widely popular president. After his election victory in 1948 he tried to promote a program he called the Fair Deal, modeled after the New Deal. It included public housing, federal aid to education, compulsory health insurance, and civil rights legislation. Truman had great trouble instituting his domestic policy. A reaction against liberal reform had set in, and except for a modest housing act, the Fair Deal went unfulfilled.

Many Republicans had been waiting since 1936 for a conservative leader who would roll back "creeping socialism." They wanted someone who would repeal the income tax and Social Security laws, as well as balance the budget and reduce the size of big government. In 1952 many conservatives pinned their hopes on Ohio's senator, Robert Taft, the son of President William Howard Taft. But the GOP convention bypassed him in favor of the popular hero of World War II, General Dwight D. Eisenhower, a man of unknown political views, who had once been considered for the Democratic nomination. Terming himself a "moderate Republican,"

Eisenhower favored turning over some governmental functions to the states and to private business. Yet in some ways he gave the New Deal a forward push. By extending Social Security coverage, broadening the 1949 housing act, expanding price supports for farm commodities, and creating a new Department of Health, Education, and Welfare, the first Republican president in thirty years seemed to make the New Deal permanent.

John F. Kennedy heralded the arrival of a "new generation of Americans" in the seats of power. He had made his way in the political world as congressman and senator, backed by a family fortune, a remarkable political organization, personal charm, and a decided intelligence and wit. This combination helped him overcome the serious liability of being a practicing Roman Catholic in a predominantly Protestant country. In his inaugural speech he declared, "Ask not what your country can do for you; ask what you can do for your country." Kennedy's New Frontier program called for tax revision, health care for the aged, and a department of urban affairs. Elected by a razor-thin majority in 1960 and facing a conservative coalition in the Congress, Kennedy was unable to get his reforms rolling. Congress rejected most of his proposals. But Kennedy's suggestion of a Peace Corps, an expanded housing program, and public financing of an area redevelopment program for depressed rural regions did become law.

The tragedy of President Kennedy's death from an assassin's bullet in 1963 elevated Vice-President Lyndon B. Johnson to the White House. A commission headed by Chief Justice Earl Warren found that Kennedy had been shot by a lone assassin, Lee Harvey Oswald. But the report of the Warren Commission failed to allay a widespread suspicion that the killing was the work of a conspiracy. Johnson had far greater success with Congress than Kennedy, especially after a smashing victory at the polls in 1964. The

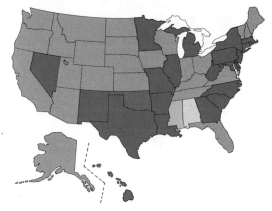

ELECTION OF 1960: ELECTORAL VOTE

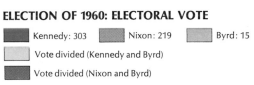

first phase of Johnson's "Great Society" program was modeled on the New Deal, and the Fair Deal, and Kennedy's New Frontier. The Economic Opportunity Act of 1964 created the Office of Economic Opportunity (OEO) to ride herd over various programs in a "war on poverty" (see p. 688). Johnson also produced a major education bill, the Higher Education Facilities Act of 1964.

In 1965 came the next phase of Johnson's reform: a billion-dollar program to fight poverty in Appalachia, an aid-to-education act, the Medicare Act, antipollution bills, and an act creating a new Department of Housing and Urban Development. Johnson also pushed through a liberal immigration act and two historic civil rights acts—one on public accommodations and employment and another on voting rights. Johnson accomplished a most extraordinary legislative record during a single congressional session. Soon afterward Congress balked at further legislative reform, and by 1967 the president's domestic program was being starved out of existence by the mounting cost of the Vietnam War.

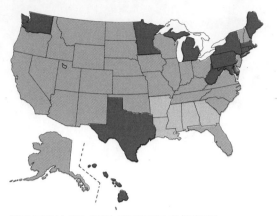

ELECTION OF 1968: ELECTORAL VOTE

Nixon: 302

Humphrey: 191   Wallace: 45

Winds of change

Grass-roots political activity was relatively weak in the sixties among the regular party organizations. It was stronger among non-partisan groups that were formed to bring about particular legislative reforms. Some of these achieved notable success. The Senior Citizens Lobby worked for Medicare, the Women's Caucus pushed the Equal Rights Amendment through Congress, and Ralph Nader's Private Citizen, a consumer-oriented group, and Common Cause, a nonpartisan "citizen's lobby" created by John Gardner (a Republican who had served in Johnson's cabinet) pushed for election reforms. At state capitals and in Washington, Common Cause pressed for laws to limit campaign donations and spending, and to force candidates and public officials to disclose their financial interests. It produced a pre-Watergate law forcing big political contributors to identify themselves. In a move toward public financing of elections, Common Cause influenced Congress to bring about a change in the income tax form that allowed private citizens to allocate one dollar of their taxes for the financing of political campaigns.

Many attempts have been made to change the political process through constitutional amendments. The electoral college has been a favorite target; since 1824 some five hundred proposals have come before Congress to change or kill that body. In 1972 the fear that George Wallace's candidacy might create a three-way tie and throw the presidential election into the House of Representatives created a new flurry of interest in reforming the electoral college. For a while its days seemed numbered. Yet when Wallace's vote proved smaller than expected, the idea was again pushed aside. Few people really believed in the electoral college, but it gave the voters of the most populous states a political advantage over the less populous ones that they were reluctant to give up.

The Twenty-fifth Amendment (1967) changed the line of presidential succession. Kennedy's assassination forced a realization that the constitutional provision was inadequate. Had Kennedy survived in a coma, it was not clear who would have exercised presidential authority; and had both Kennedy and Johnson died, the secretary of state, an appointed officer, would have become chief executive. The new amendment corrected these defects but created new ones, for in 1974 it gave the country both a president and vice-president who had not been elected to those offices.

The Twenty-sixth Amendment, which lowered the voting age to eighteen years in 1971, introduced a new element into the chemistry of American politics. It enfranchised 10 million new voters in 1972 and promised to add 16 million more in 1976. Young voters were slow to "drop into" politics after having "dropped out" in the early sixties. Nevertheless, politicians began to woo young constituents.

The winds of change reached hurricane force for the Democrats at their 1968 convention. The Vietnam War had already split the party into "hawks" and "doves" and sent the leading hawk, President Johnson, into retirement. During the meeting at Chicago, anti-war demonstrators clashed with police in the parks and streets along Lake Michigan. The convention's speeches and hoopla, which TV carried live to the nation, were interspersed with sights and sounds of violence. Chanting demonstrators were clubbed by helmeted police as sirens screamed. Tear gas drifted up into the delegates' hotel rooms. The debacle at Chicago helped assure a Nixon victory over the Democratic candidate, Hubert Humphrey, that fall.

During the next four years the Democratic party's convention rules underwent an overhaul. The new rules, pushed through by supporters of Senator George McGovern's presidential candidacy, called for a larger representation of women, blacks, Chicanos, Indians, and young people in state delegations. After refusing to comply with the new rules, Chicago's Mayor Richard J. Daley, head of the Illinois delegation and a prime mover of the 1968 convention, was barred from the gathering. The McGovern wing had improved minority representation in the Democratic party, but in so doing it lost the centrist position that FDR, Truman, and Kennedy had nurtured. The rejection of Daley (and AFL-CIO head George Meany) cost the party precious financial support and votes in the November balloting.

The Republican party remained the minority party in terms of voter registration after World War II. Even when the GOP finally picked a winner in Dwight D. Eisenhower, overall party strength did not improve. When the GOP sought to offer "a choice, not an echo," and named Barry Goldwater, a solid conservative, as its candidate for president in 1964, the whole party went down to shattering defeat.

How Number Two might become Number One had plagued GOP strategists since 1936. According to Kevin Phillips, a young Nixon aide in 1968, the GOP could turn the trick by courting Middle America—that is, by tap-

ELECTION OF 1972: ELECTORAL VOTE

Nixon: 521   McGovern: 17

ping the roots of discontent among white ethnics, hard-hat workers, and overtaxed property owners. Even the Jewish and black voters who opposed forced integration in the cities would be wooed. Phillips argued that the Democrats were evading the "gut issues" that mattered to these voters: street crime, college riots, the welfare mess, "permissiveness" among the young, forced integration through bussing. The FDR coalition was falling apart. Admittedly the GOP would have to live down its reputation as the party of "standpatters." It must, he felt, look neither to the left nor the right but to the progressive center, as in the days of Theodore Roosevelt. By so doing it could scoop up the cast-off pieces of the Democratic coalition and sweep to victory. This strategy to some extent guided the Nixon forces in 1968.

The ordeal of third parties

The American electoral process is unkind to minor parties. It works on a winner-take-all principle that gives no representation to the small, special-issue party. In presidential elections the winning candidate on the state level gets *all* the electoral votes of that state. In congressional elections there is but *one*

The delegates who met in 1972 to nominate George McGovern represented a true cross-section of America, but the party organization that set quotas and brought the delegates together during the primaries failed to unite the party during the ensuing campaign.

seat for an entire district. Thus the biggest parties can count on winning power at some time, while the minor ones must assume they will never win power, except in the rarest of cases. All the same, small special-interest parties—such as the Socialist Worker, Socialist Labor, Communist, Prohibitionist, and National States' Rights parties—have often run presidential candidates. The apparent weaknesses of the major parties contin-

ually invite parties to challenge them. In their bids for power, third parties try to replace one of the major parties, or at least compel it to adopt some pet reforms.

A big year for third parties was 1948. Two wings of the Democratic party broke away to form new parties. Former Vice-President Henry A. Wallace, after clashing with Harry S. Truman over foreign policy, ran as the presidential candidate of the new Progressive party. The liberal New Dealer favored closer relations with the U.S.S.R. rather than the get-tough policy supported by Truman. At the same time, Senator Strom Thurmond of South Carolina, a vigorous foe of Truman's civil rights policies, ran for president on the States' Rights (Dixiecrat) ticket. Despite the defections, Truman proceeded to defeat the GOP candidate, Thomas E. Dewey, in a victory called the greatest political upset of the century. The third-party efforts collapsed.

A far more impressive third-party showing was that of George C. Wallace, who received 10 million votes in 1968. Although strongly identified with the South, the Alabama governor attracted many northern supporters who fancied themselves the "silent majority," or "forgotten Americans." Angry about hard times and enforced school bussing, fearful of street criminals and black activists, and frustrated because the "liberal establishment" was doing nothing to cure these ills, white factory workers flocked to Wallace's American Independent party. Since most of his vote came from Democrats, he helped Nixon win the presidency, but both major parties were in awe of his popular appeal. Partially paralyzed by a would-be assassin's bullet in 1972, Wallace nevertheless continued to represent a significant bloc of voters.

For a brief moment the New Left made a bid to become a major political alternative. This loose coalition of anti-Establishment types, many from the civil rights and antiwar movements, was especially strong on the college campuses. It distinguished itself from the Old Left (Communists, Socialists, etc.) which had had a decidedly Marxian bent and sympathy for the U.S.S.R., and which had been decimated during the Red Scare of the 1950s. For a brief time in 1968 the presidential candidacy of Democratic Senator Eugene McCarthy stirred hopes for a New Left-liberal coalition. But McCarthy dropped out of the race, leaving a political vacuum.

The People's party, formed in 1972 by the New Left, ran the noted pediatrician Dr. Benjamin Spock for president. Nixon's peace initiatives undermined Spock's candidacy, and he made barely a ripple in the election. The New Left, apparently more of a mood than movement, had already begun to fade.

Watergate

The break-in at Democratic national headquarters in the Watergate building in Washington, D.C., occurred on June 17, 1972. At first the Nixon administration dismissed it as "a third-rate burglary attempt." But as the story unfolded — thanks almost entirely to the stubborn efforts of a few newspapers — the true extent of the dishonest and illegal acts committed by the president and his associates became public knowledge. Watergate brought about the most serious confrontations among the branches of government. In the end it brought down a president.

Many of the facts were brought out at the televised hearings of a special Senate committee chaired by Senator Sam J. Ervin, Jr., of North Carolina. The Committee to Reelect the President, some of whose employees had engaged in the break-in, had illegally amassed an immense slush fund from giant corporations and private donors. White House officials and aides had condoned the use of electronic espionage equipment against political opponents. A special White House investigative group, "the plumbers,"

had engaged in yet another burglary. The White House had drawn up an "enemies list" that it hoped the Internal Revenue Service would use to intimidate political opponents. All of this, and more, suggested a hunger for power and a police state mentality in high places that had no precedent in U.S. history.

Each time the president went before TV cameras to explain the strange happenings to the nation, he was caught up in new contradictions. A battle developed between the president and the special prosecutor appointed to investigate Watergate over the possession of tapes of conversations made in Nixon's own offices. Published transcripts of some of these recordings revealed the president in compromising conversations, urging his aides to prevent full disclosures. Nixon claimed, on ground of executive privilege and separation of powers, that the tapes need not be revealed to Congress or in the courts, but the Supreme Court ruled against him.

Throughout 1974 calls for the president's resignation or impeachment grew louder. In July the House Judiciary Committee, after historic debate, handed down three articles of impeachment. One cited Nixon for covering up the Watergate break-in: obstructing justice and withholding evidence, interfering with federal agencies, and condoning the payment of hush money to the convicted Watergate burglars. Other abuses of presidential power were the subject of a second charge by the committee: misusing the Internal Revenue Service to try to punish political enemies and establishing an illegal investigative agency ("the plumbers") for a break-in at a psychiatrist's office in the hopes of finding evidence that could be used against Daniel J. Ellsberg. (Ellsberg, an opponent of the Vietnam War, had incurred Nixon's anger because of his role in releasing to the press the Pentagon Papers — extensive background information about the war.) The "Houston plan" to harass other war dissenters was also cited in this charge. A third charge was that Nixon's failure to produce vital tapes and written documents for the congressional inquiry was "subversive of constitutional government." Efforts by some committee members to charge Nixon with bombing Cambodia illegally were set aside.

The Nixon administration displayed an extremist concept of executive power. This showed itself in Nixon's repeated use of Vice-President Agnew to intimidate the media, and in his secretive handling of the Vietnam War. Nixon's personal annoyance with criticism and dissent was so extreme that his aides once sought to eliminate every sign-carrying demonstrator from a public gathering where the president appeared. Testimony by top White House aide John Ehrlichman suggested that the President had surrounded himself with men who believed that the chief executive "in the interests of national security" could suspend the Fourth Amendment which protects citizens against unreasonable search and seizure. It is slight exaggeration to say, as some constitutional scholars have, that for five days in July 1970 when the Houston plan was in effect, the U.S. Constitution was suspended and the country was governed by authoritarian rule.

Seeing the erosion of support even among his strongest congressional backers, the president finally resigned on August 9, 1974—the first American chief executive ever to do so. Vice-President Spiro T. Agnew, elected with Nixon in 1968 and reelected in 1972, did not succeed Nixon. Agnew had come under fire from a Baltimore grand jury investigating charges of kickbacks and tax fraud in Maryland, where he had been governor. In October 1973 he had pleaded no contest to a charge of income tax evasion and stepped down from office. President Nixon had then announced the appointment of House Minority Leader Gerald R. Ford of Michigan to the vice-presidency. Now Ford succeeded Nixon, declaring minutes after being sworn

in that "our long national nightmare is over." Within weeks Ford pardoned Nixon and thereby protected the former president from all criminal prosecution in the Watergate matter. The pardon met with less than universal public approval. Jury trials of eighteen top Nixon aides continued to grind through the courts. Nixon's closest associates, former Attorney General John N. Mitchell and presidential aides John D. Ehrlichman and H. R. (Bob) Haldeman, were convicted in the cover-up trial.

The outcome of Watergate exposed the weakness of the Twenty-fifth Amendment. Under its provision an appointed vice-president (Ford) became president and, in turn, he appointed a new vice-president (Nelson Rockefeller), who took office at the end of 1974. For the first time in U.S. history neither the vice-president nor the president had been elected to their respective offices. The difficulty could have been avoided had the amendment provided for special elections.

Both the FBI and CIA were implicated in the Watergate cover-up. Evidence unearthed at the time suggested wrongdoing by these agencies, including illegal searches by the FBI and domestic spying by the CIA. A larger implication of the controversy was whether the two powerful intelligence agencies could be better checked and balanced by other branches of the government to prevent further serious abuses of power.

Despite all the tacky, frightening, and bizarre aspects of Watergate, the transfer of power from Nixon to Ford occurred swiftly and smoothly, providing a measure of national relief. But when the furor died down, the question remained as to whether there was any way to prevent future misuse of power in the highest offices of the land. Could legislative reforms be instituted to reduce political corruption and to restore the balance between the president and the Congress? Many of the issues raised by Watergate have yet to be faced.

Review

Long before Watergate, a growing number of Americans felt estranged from their government and questioned the way its power was exercised. Presidential power had expanded steadily since FDR. Modern military technology seemed to demand a chief executive who could act swiftly and vigorously, without the unwieldy procedures of Congress. By the time of the Nixon administration, the U.S. had developed what some observers called an "imperial presidency." In the seventies, presidential power became a matter of special concern.

Corporate power was another controversial issue. The biggest corporations represented enormous wealth and influence. Multinational corporations affected both domestic and foreign policy. Sometimes they intruded into the domestic affairs of other nations. And their influence on American politics was undeniable.

By the mid-1960s Americans distrusted politicians of both parties. Their distrust was reflected in a rising number of citizens who refused to give their allegiance to either party. City bossism declined. The importance of TV campaigning rose. A candidate's success or failure depended increasingly on the ability to project the right "image."

The hopes of many conservatives were dashed when Eisenhower failed to fight for the repeal of social legislation passed under Roosevelt and Truman. Both Republican and Democratic administrations continued most of the New Deal programs. Lyndon B. Johnson greatly expanded them.

By the 1960s major party organizations were weaker, and nonpartisan groups lobbying in the public interest began to influence important legislation. In 1968 the candidacy of Hubert Humphrey failed to sustain the Democratic coalition created by FDR. The Republicans, while also divided, achieved unity and success that year by courting the discontented elements of Middle America. In the same year, and again in 1972, these elements also responded strongly to the populist appeal of George Wallace of Alabama.

Watergate was the greatest crisis ever to involve the presidency. Televised hearings unfolded tales of corruption, intrigue, and illegal conduct in the Nixon administration. The testimony before the Senate committee also raised numerous questions about the exercise of power by the CIA and FBI. Each was implicated in illegal acts. Nixon lost almost all of his congressional supporters and faced certain impeachment. In 1974 he became the first U.S. president to resign from office. The preceding year his vice-president, Spiro T. Agnew, had also resigned, after pleading no contest to a charge of income tax evasion. Nixon was succeeded by Gerald R. Ford, whom he had appointed to succeed Agnew. Upon becoming president, Ford appointed his own vice-president, Nelson Rockefeller.

Questions

1. Do you believe that power in the U.S. (a) is held by one or more elite groups or (b) is spread out and balanced among many groups? What recent events can you cite that will support your view?
2. What circumstances led to the shifts in the power balance between Congress and the president?
3. Large corporations wield ever increasing power in national and world affairs. What are some of the good results of large-scale corporate enterprise? What are some harmful results?
4. What are the "lessons of Watergate"? What questions have the scandals raised in your mind? Have they influenced your own feelings about government?

war

U.S. missile warheads stockpiled in West Germany.

Today, every inhabitant of
this planet must contemplate
the day when this planet may
no longer be habitable. . . .
The weapons of war must
be abolished before they
abolish us.

JOHN F. KENNEDY (1917–1963)

35

35

Two Scorpions Locked in a Bottle

For a god nobody admits worshiping anymore, Mars has done quite well. The god of war has claimed millions of lives since 1945. More than fifty wars have been fought, for an average of about one war every five months. The stated reasons for these contests have varied from struggles for national liberation, stopping communism, defense of homeland, to counter insurgency. Hovering like a dark cloud has been the specter of World War III.

For much of the time since 1945 the world has been preoccupied by the "Cold War," a recurrent military, political, and diplomatic struggle between the United States and the Soviet Union, together with their respective allies. Owing principally to the Cold War, the nations of the world have spent about $125 billion on armaments each year since 1945. Nor has all this armament brought much security: the stockpile of nuclear bombs is sufficient to destroy humanity several times over.

Had the United States followed the script it used in the days after World War I, it would have turned isolationist in 1945. Instead it remained internationalist. In Korea between 1950 and 1953 it fought a full-scale conflict; in Vietnam from 1960 to 1973 it did so again, and with disastrous consequences.

The fall of South Vietnam and neighboring Cambodia to Communist-led forces in the spring of 1975 brought the curtain down on a tragic American adventure in foreign policy. Over fifty thousand American dead, five times that many wounded, and billions of dollars in American aid could not prevent the fall of South Vietnam to rebel forces. What went wrong? Should we have done more to "save" Southeast Asia? Russia and the U.S. had switched to a policy of "détente." Did this mean the Cold War was ending or had already ended? Was a new and hopeful era over the horizon? Or would there be new Vietnams to cope with? It seems an appropriate time to review the thirty years of Cold War.

Wars Cold and Hot

One world or two — or three

During the Second World War the major powers had worked out a "Grand Alliance" which many people hoped would continue afterward. The former Republican presidential hopeful Wendell Willkie looked forward optimistically to "One World," a continuation of big-power cooperation into the future. The results were strikingly different: between 1945 and 1947 two worlds emerged, with yet a third in the offing.

The world in 1945 was greatly altered from what it had been when Hitler invaded Poland in 1939 and touched off the conflict. All of Europe lay in shambles. Germany was literally dismembered by the occupying allied nations. Britain, although one of the victors, had lost its grip on a world empire. France and Italy, suffering from physical destruction, remained politically and economically demoralized.

The U.S. was now the most powerful nation militarily and economically. Its navy, army, and air force were spread out over the world and it retained a monopoly on nuclear power. Spared the terrible destruction suffered by its allies, it also boasted the strongest economy in the world. The U.S., together with Canada and western Europe, would soon form a political bloc, known much too loosely as the "free world." But the Russians had more men in uniform than the U.S., and they still occupied the countries they had entered in the drive against Germany. The U.S.S.R. would form a second bloc of nations, known variously as Communist, Socialist, or "Iron Curtain" countries, after a memorable phrase of Winston Churchill's.

Meanwhile, in the "underdeveloped" part of the world, the former colonies and dependencies of European nations were emerging into nationhood. Eventually they would be called the Third World. In Asia, Africa, and Latin America, revolutionaries and nationalists, who were often influenced by Marxism to some degree, assumed a principal role. In some countries they saw themselves as having to form new nations on the heels of departing foreign colonial powers. Elsewhere (in Latin America) they saw the problem as wresting control from native military officers, landlords, and corrupt politicians. In either case, guerrilla warfare usually erupted to bring about "liberation." China, Cuba, and the U.S.S.R. would provide revolutionary models, or even weapons. The U.S. supported the general idea of helping the Third World to make needed social reform, but often found itself on the side of the status quo, especially where the rebels were tinged with Marxism. The internal strife in the Third World produced as many bloody conflicts — including the Vietnam War — as did external conflicts fought across geographical boundaries. Thus the three worlds found themselves in a volatile state.

Hostility between Russia and the U.S.

In 1945 the Soviet Union and the United States renewed the mutual hostility that had started in 1917. Each perceived the other as having gone back on promises and posing a threat. Russia's need for a buffer zone in eastern Europe to uphold Soviet Communism clashed head-on with America's traditional belief in freedom and independence. It clashed also with the view held by some prominent Americans that the U.S. should have free access to the world's markets and raw materials and exert dynamic leadership over world trade. As Henry Luce, the publisher of *Time, Life,* and *Fortune,* said in 1941, the postwar period must be an "American Century."

Totalitarian regimes imposed on free peoples, by direct or indirect aggression, undermine . . . the security of the United States. . . . It must be the policy of the United States to support free peoples who are resisting attempted subjugation by armed minorities or by outside pressures.

HARRY S. TRUMAN (1884–1972)

America's get-tough policy toward Russia came in the first fifteen months of Truman's presidency, following the death of FDR in April 1945. In Truman's eyes Stalin had reneged on a promise to allow freedom of political choice in Poland. But it was Winston Churchill, in an address at Fulton, Missouri (March 1947), who warned that Russia was lowering an "Iron Curtain" across eastern Europe. This aggression, Churchill advised, must be strongly opposed by the United States. His much-heralded speech gave the public their first full awareness that the Cold War was already well under way.

At first America's major Cold War weapon was economic. In order to revive western Europe and halt the westward spread of communism—and, indirectly, to prevent a renewal of depression in the U.S.—Truman initiated an ambitious program of economic aid. The Economic Recovery Program, or "Marshall Plan" (named after Secretary of State George Marshall), represented an outlay of $15 billion which Congress allocated between 1948 and 1951. With amazing speed the Marshall Plan brought Germany, France, Italy, and other western nations back to their feet, at the same time undermining Communist parties that were threatening to achieve parliamentary majorities. It probably also helped prevent a threatened postwar depression in the U.S. In every way the Marshall Plan proved a remarkable success.

Soon, though, the U.S. was giving more military than economic aid to its allies. In the spring of 1947 Greece was wracked by a Communist uprising and Turkey was feeling intense Soviet diplomatic pressure. Britain was too weak to exert its traditional force in this corner of the globe. At Truman's request Congress voted $400 million in military and economic aid to Greece and Turkey. Under this "Truman Doctrine" the U.S. proposed to aid all countries asking for help in their fight against Communist aggression or subversion. The theory of containment, as developed by the State Department's George F. Kennan, was to exert pressure all along the edges of the Russian sphere, not only to stop the spread of communism but also to produce, Kennan hoped, "either the break-up or the gradual mellowing of Soviet power." As elaborated within the Truman administration, containment assumed that communism was a monolithic force centered in Moscow, where Dictator Stalin pulled the strings that moved his puppets throughout the world. It also held that Stalin wanted to engulf not only eastern Europe but also western Europe and possibly the entire world. Communism was spreading in China. The only way to protect the "free world" from the "Communist world" was to encircle the Soviet Union and its satellites with troops and weapons for an indefinite period.

Containment achieved notable successes in western Europe. In June 1948 the Russians, reacting angrily to a dispute involving German currency, cut off all ground transportation between West Germany and Berlin, a city completely surrounded by Russian-held territory. Rather than let Berlin starve, the U.S. and Britain airlifted up to 4500 tons of supplies daily into the city. The Russians finally backed down from the "Berlin blockade" and reopened normal commerce with the beleagured city. Give-'em-hell-Harry S. Truman had scored a signal victory by "standing up to Joe Stalin."

To enforce the policies of containment the U.S. developed a series of far-flung military alliances. The most important pact was the

North Atlantic Treaty Organization (NATO). It was the first long-term U.S. alliance and one that George Washington might have condemned as "entangling." Fifteen nations signed this pact, agreeing that an attack on one would be an attack on all. Each country came under the cover of America's nuclear umbrella. Would the U.S. risk all-out war simply to protect, say, the NATO ally Luxembourg? For the time being the answer seemed to be yes.

The policy of containment, and the way it was being carried out, had critics from the outset. When Senator Robert Taft, basically a supporter of the get-tough line, heard about one of Truman's early Cold War speeches he objected that it threatened a war with Russia. Journalist Walter Lippmann insisted that the Soviet Union had no intention of dominating western Europe and that as applied to areas outside Europe, containment depended on unreliable governments and would surely fail. Instead, Lippmann urged a recognition of Soviet interests and a neutralization of central Europe. In 1947 former Vice-President Henry Wallace, then serving as secretary of commerce in the Truman administration, urged East-West cooperation and a restoration of wartime détente.

But the vast majority of Americans supported Truman's reaction to Russia. The "average man" from Missouri was standing up tall to Stalin, who was now classified with Hitler as a tyrant and enemy of freedom. Containment was the "brave and essential response of free men to Communist aggression." Many liberals who had previously championed the One World ideal now supported Truman's hard line. The containment of communism became the basis of a political consensus that lasted until the 1960s.

Revisionist historians now say that the Cold War was at least as much the fault of the United States as of Russia. Truman, they observe, engaged in diplomacy with an atomic bomb strapped on his hip. While Russia was determined to have satellite states to safeguard its western frontier, their argument follows, there is no reason to think that Stalin intended a military attack on western Europe. Russia desperately needed western capital in 1945–1947. By canceling Lend-Lease payments to Russia four days after the defeat of Germany, the U.S. signalled its unwillingness to give the Soviets such help. The Russians would have to rebuild their ravaged country on their own. As for the Communist rebellion in Greece, Stalin clearly disapproved of it and let it die on the vine. Nor did he have much enthusiasm for the Communist uprising in China, although he did give it assistance. Thus Truman was probably overreacting to the Soviet threat. So goes the revisionist view of the origins of the Cold War.

An unstable element in the Cold War contest was the underdeveloped nations that were throwing off political or economic imperialism. For the United States the dilemma was how to maintain its political influence and commercial interests and prevent Communist takeovers without appearing to be the enemy of social reform and defender of the status quo. This often proved impossible.

Much hinged on the future of China, the largest and most important Asian nation. After World War II the United States tried to shore up the Nationalist government of Chiang Kai-shek and then sought to work out a settlement between the Nationalists and their Communist foes. But in 1947 the civil war exploded, and in 1949 the People's Republic of China was established with Chairman Mao Tse-tung as its head. Chiang's government fled to Formosa (Taiwan), where it continued to be recognized as the government of China by the U.S.

The Korean War

In 1950 containment met a stiffer test in Asia than any it had encountered in Europe. Ko-

THE KOREAN WAR

— — — Armistice Line: June 26, 1953

▼ ▼ ▼ ▼ ▼ Pusan perimeter: Farthest advance of North Korean forces, Sept. 1950

•••••••••• Farthest advance of United Nations forces: Nov. 1950

rea, a long-time Japanese colony on the Asian mainland, had been split in two at the 38th parallel by Soviet and American occupation forces at the end of World War II, and separate governments were established. Early in 1950 Secretary of State Dean Acheson omitted South Korea from a list of Asian countries the United States would automatically defend. In June of that year North Korean soldiers invaded South Korea. Despite Acheson's pronouncement, President Truman quickly decided that the invasion must be opposed. With the Soviet delegation absent and therefore unable to exercise its veto, the UN Security Council condemned the North Korean aggression and called on its members to come to the aid of South Korea. U.S. General Douglas MacArthur was named commander of UN forces, and on June 30

U.S. troops reached Korea. Although other countries sent soldiers, the great majority of the UN forces remained American.

The problem in Korea was how to conduct the "police action," as Truman called it, and beat back the Communist North Koreans without involving the Soviet Union. Russia had already acquired the atom bomb, and an armed clash could set off World War III. At first the UN forces retreated southward. American military strategists had always warned against a land war in Asia, and total defeat seemed imminent until General MacArthur directed a daring amphibious landing that drove the enemy northward across the 38th parallel. MacArthur continued to press northward until the fighting approached the Chinese border. Chinese soldiers entered the war and pushed the UN battle line far south again.

General MacArthur hoped to bomb China but was blocked by Truman. In an extraordinary move intended to go around the president and appeal directly to the public, the general wrote to a congressman that "here in Asia is where the Communist conspirators have elected to make their play for global conquest . . . if we lose the war to Communism in Asia the fall of Europe is inevitable. . . ." This action nettled Truman. He believed that the general was trying to make foreign policy and thereby undermine presidential leadership. Truman also saw disastrous consequences in expanding the war. "Against the dubious advantages of spreading the war in an initially limited manner to the mainland of China," the president noted, "there must be measured the risk of a general war with China, the risk of Soviet intervention, and of World War III, as well as the probable effect upon the solidarity of the free world coalition." In April 1951, Truman relieved MacArthur of his command on grounds of insubordination. The general came home to a hero's welcome and addressed Congress but gradually faded from public view.

Truce talks began in 1951, but fighting continued even after Eisenhower went to Korea following his election in 1952. The armistice negotiations finally concluded in July 1953 left Korea divided much as it had been when the war began. Total American casualties in Korea exceeded 157,000, and the cost of the war for the U.S. was $53 billion. The North and South Koreans and the Chinese together suffered over 3 million killed and wounded. Though the war ended in a deadlock most Americans felt that they had stopped an unprovoked aggression which otherwise might have led to a complete Communist takeover of Southeast Asia.

Dulles brinkmanship

The fiercest American cold warrior was John Foster Dulles, Eisenhower's secretary of state. A dogged anti-Communist, Dulles decided that under Truman containment had been "negative, futile, and immoral." He flatly declared that it was time to "liberate" the "captive people" behind the Iron Curtain and "unleash" Chiang Kai-shek's Nationalist forces. Communist aggression anywhere should be met, Dulles declared in 1954, by "massive retaliation" with nuclear weapons. The U.S. should be able to "retaliate, instantly, by means and at places of our choosing." "If you are scared to go to the brink [of nuclear war], you are lost."

This policy of brinkmanship coincided with a search for economy in the Eisenhower administration. Nuclear bombs, it was hoped, would cost less and work faster than the conventional weapons needed in a war like the Korean conflict. Dulles' strategy of massive retaliation was never put to the test, for in 1949 the Soviets exploded their first nuclear weapon, and in 1953 they matched the U.S. development of a hydrogen bomb. When the Russians perfected an intercontinental ballistic missile (ICBM) in 1957, the

Dulles policy was abandoned. But the fantastically expensive nuclear arms race speeded up. No one could foresee where it would end. An American nuclear physicist likened the U.S. and U.S.S.R. to "two scorpions locked in a bottle," poised to kill each other in deadly conflict.

After France was forced out of Indochina by rebellious Vietnamese in 1954, Dulles put together the Southeast Asia Treaty Organization (SEATO), an alliance which lacked the guarantee of united action that gave NATO its muscle. Besides, three major Asian nations—India, Indonesia, and Burma—refused to sign the SEATO pact, choosing instead to remain neutral. Dulles condemned them bitterly. The U.S. signed other treaties with Japan, Nationalist China, the Philippines, South Vietnam, Turkey, Iran, and Pakistan. By the mid-fifties the Soviet Union and China were practically ringed by regimes receiving military aid from the U.S.

The Caribbean and the Cold War

No continent was completely free of the great ideological and military contest of the superpowers. In the 1930s the U.S. had renounced military intervention in Latin America as part of the "Good Neighbor" policy. Yet the U.S. had long considered the Caribbean an American sphere of influence and it continued to do so. Right-wing military regimes took over in most Latin American countries in the 1950s, and many were recognized by the U.S. Their repressive rule made social revolutionaries out of reformers, and the resultant rising influence of Marxists alarmed the U.S. Political rebellions in Cuba, Guatemala, and Panama were perceived as a threat to vital interests of the United States, especially since Communists were active in the area. In 1954 the Central Intelligence Agency (CIA) backed a force of Guatemalan exiles in Honduras in a successful attempt to overthrow a pro-Communist regime in Guatemala. In 1958 when Vice-President Nixon faced angry crowds in Peru and Venezuela, the U.S. rushed forces into the Caribbean and placed them briefly on alert.

In 1959 the rebel forces of Fidel Castro overthrew the Cuban dictator Fulgencio Batista, who had enjoyed many years of cordial relations with American business interests. Castro proceeded to condemn the U.S., seize American property, and develop a close friendship with the Soviet Union. The U.S. retaliated by ending all trade with Cuba and in 1961 sponsored an ill-fated attempt by Cuban exiles to overthrow the Castro regime. Eighteen months after the failure of the Bay of Pigs invasion, the United States discovered that Soviet missiles were being installed on Cuban soil.

The Cuban missile crisis of October 1962 produced the most frightening moment of the Cold War. President Kennedy confronted Soviet Premier Nikita S. Khrushchev, demanding immediate removal of the weapons in Cuba and asserting his determination to block any attempt to ship more missiles to the island. While the world held its breath, a Soviet freighter loaded with missiles approached the American naval blockade. At the eleventh hour Khrushchev agreed to recall the missile-carrying vessel and to withdraw the missiles already landed in Cuba, in exchange for Kennedy's promise not to attack Castro. In retrospect it is clear that the world came closer to nuclear holocaust in 1962 than at any other time before or after.

When violence flared in the Dominican Republic in 1965, President Johnson sent in the marines to "prevent a Communist takeover." The marines never found the Communists but remained for a year to "keep order." During the Nixon administration the CIA is believed to have worked to "destabilize" the Marxist regime of Salvador Allende in Chile, which was finally replaced by a military dictatorship.

The United Nations—hope deferred

Throughout their wartime alliance the Big Three—the U.S., Britain, and the U.S.S.R.—were agreed in principle on the creation of an international organization to safeguard the peace in the postwar world. With American involvement in the organization assured, the world could hope to avoid a repetition of the "lost peace" of 1918–1920, when the U.S. refused to join the League of Nations. At the United Nations Conference at San Francisco in 1945, the Charter of the new organization was signed by representatives of fifty countries. Almost immediately, however, the UN became a battleground for the Cold War rather than an instrument for world peace.

The 1946 session of the UN was the scene of two heated debates. First, Iran charged Soviet interference in its internal affairs, whereupon the Soviets countercharged that Britain was interfering improperly in Greece and in the East Indies. The second wrangle involved the atom bomb. The big powers had agreed the year before to let the UN control atomic energy, but were unable to work out an acceptable plan. At that time the U.S. had a monopoly on atomic weapons, and the Soviets were working desperately to break it. In the UN they demanded that the U.S. destroy all of its atom bombs. The U.S. representative insisted on worldwide inspection of nuclear production before his nation would give up its nuclear superiority. This deadlock allowed the nuclear arms race to continue almost without letup for the next three decades.

For the most part the UN was incapable of forcing its will on either of the big powers. Important breaches of the peace have not been taken to the UN Security Council. The UN action in Korea was an exception, explained by the fact that the Soviet delegate was boycotting the Security Council when the vote was taken to send in UN troops. But the Soviet invasion of Hungary and its inter-

Eleanor Roosevelt (1884-1964)

FIRST LADY OF THE WORLD

"The story is over." So said Eleanor Roosevelt to reporters when she returned to New York after her husband's death in April 1945. She did not envision any public future for herself and expected to live out her life quietly. Eight months later she reluctantly accepted President Truman's request that she join the American delegation to the first session of the General Assembly of the United Nations, which was to be held in London in January 1946. This launched an association which would dominate many of her remaining years, carry her to all parts of the world, and earn her the unofficial title "First Lady of the World."

Although she considered herself unqualified to be a delegate, she emerged as the most effective American voice in the General Assembly. She was proudest of her role, as head of the Commission on Human Rights, in forging the UN's Declaration of Human Rights. The document emerged slowly over a two-year period of political maneuvering and dissent arising from the different political, religious, social, and national aspirations of the delegates. It was largely through her patience, tact, skill, and fortitude that the final draft was presented to the General Assembly for passage on December 10, 1948.

When the Eisenhower administration did not reappoint Mrs. Roosevelt to America's UN delegation in 1953, she became an unflagging supporter of the American Association for the United Nations (AAUN), convinced it was imperative that the UN have the support of the peoples of the nations it represented. In 1952 and 1956, when she was in her seventies, Eleanor Roosevelt campaigned vigorously for Adlai E. Stevenson. While she was unable to obtain a third nomination for him in 1960, all Democrats with presidential ambitions continued to seek her endorsement. In 1961 she was a leading spirit behind the Democratic reform movement in New York City that defeated the forces of Tammany Hall. At seventy-five she became a visiting lecturer at Brandeis University and still carried on a full-time writing career, turning out a daily newspaper column, magazine articles, and books.

Critics, and they were many, called Mrs. Roosevelt shallow; they claimed that she oversimplified both problems and solutions, that she contradicted herself constantly, and that she was basically an amateurish meddler. She remained calm through the barrage, having learned to view herself with a humor and detachment that had been absent in her earlier years. She was a pragmatist, influenced by changing circumstances, her own growth, and an abiding belief in democracy. Her greatest gift, and one that touched so many millions, was her ability to communicate her own humanity and concern for others.

vention in Czechoslovakia, and the American presence in Vietnam were never placed on the Security Council agenda for debate. In the General Assembly, meanwhile, the U.S. for many years could count on a majority for any resolution it introduced into that body. But the increasing number of member Third World nations caused it to lose this dominance.

Quite plainly though, there was a role for a world organization. The UN has served well as a clearinghouse of information and a relief agency for its 126 member nations, including many poor countries, a numerical majority of the membership. Difficult global problems have demanded global solutions— for example, airplane hijacking, the arms race, disease control, famine, air and water pollution, weather control, the uses of outer space, and the exploitation of ocean resources.

The UN has been an imperfect instrument of world order, although in its defense it must be said that it was never intended to settle a struggle like the Cold War. "The UN is a mirror of the world we live in," Britain's Lord Gladwin once explained, "and if the reflection is ugly, it is not the mirror which is to blame."

The Domestic Side of the Cold War

McCarthyism

In 1947 Senator Arthur Vandenberg, a conservative Republican who had become a convert to internationalism, remarked to President Truman that in order to win public support for a proper foreign policy, it might be necessary to "scare hell out of the American people." Fear did indeed play a role in American political affairs in the Cold War era, but it was by no means limited to external threats to U.S. security.

A second great Red Scare began in the United States in the late 1940s and lasted well into the next decade. Eventually it came to be called "McCarthyism," after the junior senator from Wisconsin who used it most irresponsibly. But in truth Truman himself initiated it in 1947 when he established the federal Loyalty Review Board, the first such agency ever established in peacetime. Its job was to purge the government of "disloyal and subversive" employees. The Board held secret hearings in which wild rumors and gossip were given the same attention as facts. The accused did not have the right to face their accusers. Standards of proof were often so vague that a "potential" subversive was considered as dangerous as an "actual" one. Of the 6 million federal workers checked, 7000 were fired as security risks, including many alleged homosexuals. No spies were found. The federal program inspired numerous state and local screening programs of a similar nature. Labor unions, school boards, universities, and the movie industry also sought to uncover and drive out "subversives." Even moderate liberals were in danger of being labeled "commies," "pinkos," or "fellow travelers." Often careers were destroyed by smear tactics alone.

The second Red Scare fed upon the seeming decline of America's world prestige. In the fight to contain communism, an open-ended battle of worldwide proportions, China had fallen to the Reds, the war in Korea was going poorly, and America's atomic supremacy was threatened. The House Un-American Activities Committee (HUAC) investigated the political associations of thousands of private citizens. The most celebrated of them were Hollywood writers and producers—the "Hollywood ten" who refused to cooperate and were jailed for con-

During the Army hearings in 1954, Senator Joseph McCarthy (right) constantly interrupted others with cries of "Point of order, Mr. Chairman, point of order," and continued flinging wild verbal assaults and unsupported accusations. Finally chief Army counsel Joseph Welch (left) had had enough; wracked by emotion, he challenged McCarthy: "Have you no sense of decency, sir, at long last? Have you left no sense of decency?" McCarthy never recovered the public's support, which alone had made him such a powerful figure in Washington.

tempt of Congress. Many actors, directors, and writers were blacklisted. The top eleven leaders of the Communist party were convicted of advocating the violent overthrow of the government in violation of the Smith Act of 1940. In 1948 Alger Hiss, a former high State Department officer, was denounced before HUAC as having been a Communist spy ten years earlier. Largely through the efforts of Congressman Richard M. Nixon, he was convicted of perjury in 1950. Cases of spying for Russia were uncovered in Canada and England as early as 1946 and created a great scare in the U.S. as well. In 1953 two Americans, Ethel and Julius Rosenberg, were ac-

cused of passing nuclear plans to the Russians and were executed. J. Robert Oppenheimer, the nation's leading physicist and the "father of the A-bomb," was questioned in 1953 on his alleged Communist associations and stripped of his top-secret clearance.

In February 1950, in a sensational address in Wheeling, West Virginia, Senator Joseph R. McCarthy of Wisconsin declared that he had uncovered fifty-seven Communists (later increased to 205) in the State Department. Though never substantiated, this accusation launched him on a meteoric career. He made repeated use of what one critic called the "multiple untruth," a complicated, vague, and daring accusation that was so overblown it was often impossible to refute. Truman called it "the big lie."

McCarthy first concentrated his fire on the State Department, particularly the Asian section, which was held responsible for the "loss" of China to the Communists. He attributed China's fall to treason in the department. Because former Secretary of State George C. Marshall, chief of staff of the U.S. Army in World War II, had tried to achieve a settlement in China in 1947, McCarthy dubbed him a member of a "conspiracy so immense and an infamy so black as to dwarf any previous venture in the history of man." McCarthy considered Truman "soft" on communism. As the 1952 presidential election drew near, he referred to the Democratic candidate Adlai Stevenson as "Adlai the appeaser" and made reference to the Democrats' "twenty years of treason."

In 1954 McCarthy took on the army for allegedly coddling subversives. Hoping to bring his campaign directly to the American public, he permitted the hearings of his Senate Committee on Government Operation to be televised. Before the live cameras he hurled charges and insinuations and appeared in the role of an irresponsible bully, badly damaging his public standing. These month-long hearings marked the high point—and the downfall—of McCarthy's career. The Senate officially "condemned" him in 1954. He was in political limbo at the time of his death in 1957.

The U.S. Supreme Court, under Chief Justice Earl Warren, repaired some of the damage done to the Bill of Rights in the name of anticommunism. In 1957 it ruled that congressional investigative committees must observe certain limits in questioning witnesses. The Warren Court also ruled that merely advocating the violent overthrow of the government, without taking further steps in that regard, was not a crime. Nor could the government fire employees under the loyal-

ty-security program just because of their political activities. McCarthy's career had collapsed, the Korean War had ended, Stalin had died, and American and Russian leaders were beginning to speak of "peaceful coexistence." These events helped put an end to the mood of fear and intimidation in American politics.

The military-industrial complex

In his Farewell Address in 1961 President Eisenhower drew attention to another domestic feature of the Cold War, when he cautioned the country about the dangers of the "military-industrial complex." Coming from a five-star general, this observation was impossible to dismiss lightly. It raised questions not only about the exercise of power but about the domestic impact of perpetual Cold War.

Normally the size of the military establishment and the importance of military priorities have shrunk dramatically after a major war. They did so again for a few years after 1945, but then expanded steadily throughout the late forties and fifties. Owing to the Cold War, the military acquired "automatic priority" over all national resources, so its needs largely determined the national budget. The military exercised considerable influence in the executive and legislative branches, though by and large military men kept a healthy distance from Capitol Hill and got their way indirectly. Major defense policies came from civilians in the Department of Defense. Congress had placed that department under civilian control in 1947, according to the provisions of the National Security Act. In fact, interest groups who depended on defense jobs often forced Congress to enlarge the military budget asked by the Pentagon or requested by the president. Also, the Pentagon developed a large, smoothly functioning public relations machine which continuously educated the public on matters close to its heart.

What some have called the "militarization of American life" was by no means a military conspiracy. The industrial half of the "military-industrial" complex also gained stature. And the ties between the Pentagon and big business were strengthened by the employment in defense industries of former military men. In 1969 ninety-five of the biggest contractors employed over two thousand retired officers. As defense spending soared to $50 billion and more, some private firms, as one assistant secretary of defense noted, "became in reality agents of the government."

Government contracts were most desirable because their cost-plus basis guaranteed the supplier a fixed profit no matter how high his costs. Some firms became so heavily dependent on government contracts that they seemed unable to survive without them. Lockheed sold 80 percent of its aircraft output to the Defense Department. The lion's share of military contracts went to a handful of big firms. At the request of the Department of Defense, the Justice Department obligingly curtailed some antitrust laws. Thus business concentration occurred in the name of national defense.

The Pentagon swelled in size and scope. In 1969 it employed 1.2 million soldiers and civilians, stationed throughout the globe (in comparison with about 320,000 that the Russians assigned to four East European countries). The Department of Defense owned 39 million acres of land, an area approximately the size of Hawaii. Its budget of some $80 billion about equalled Britain's Gross National Product.

When military budgets came under fire during the Vietnam conflict, evidence of widespread waste began to surface. Critics observed that a long-term rivalry between the major military branches had saddled the country with three times as many nuclear weapons as were needed for actual defense. Air Force bombers, Army ICBMs, and Navy submarines armed with nuclear weapons were poised to retaliate against any attack. Since only the subs were invulnerable, some experts argued that the missiles and bombers could be scrapped without any danger to national security. Also, they claimed that as of 1971, cost overruns (expenditures in excess of estimates, caused by blunders in planning or manufacture) totaled a whopping $24 billion. A Senate committee decried the fact that the Department of Defense spent about $40 million yearly in public funds trying to convince the public that the military budget should be increased. Liberal critics of the military-industrial complex argued that as much as 50 percent of the arms budget was fat. They asked for a reordering of national priorities that would redirect spending into domestic programs. Defenders of the military budget countered that regardless of waste and duplication, expensive modern military hardware must continue to have top priority until diplomats could find better solutions to world problems. For the U.S. there could be no such thing as a second-best military posture. So far, defense spenders have had the last word.

The Tragedy of Vietnam

Vague beginnings in Indochina

The debate over why the U.S. got involved in Vietnam and why it stayed so long will continue into the future. For years most Americans accepted at face value the official explanation that the U.S. was involved in Indochina merely to meet a moral obligation to an

Terrified South Vietnamese children flee from an accidental napalm attack near Trang Bang, South Vietnam. Photographs like this (which won a Pulitzer Prize and the Press Photo of the Year Award for photographer Huynh Cong Ut), as well as nightly on-the-spot news reports, brought home to the American people and to the world the true horror of modern war.

ally that was trying to resist Communist subversion. If South Vietnam fell to the Communists, the other countries of Southeast Asia would tumble "like a row of dominoes." Critics of the war charged that Vietnam represented no vital interest to the U.S. and that we persisted there only because of the "arrogance of power," or the pull of "welfare imperialism," or the ego needs of "the foreign policy elite." To historians it appears that, like the Civil War, Vietnam will be subject to intensive scrutiny and will come into clearer focus with time, as each generation provides new insights.

The seeds of U.S. involvement in Indochina were planted in 1945 and grew gradually. When it reverted back to French control at the end of the Second World War, Vietnam could look back at thousands of years of national history, much of it a struggle against outsiders. With massive outlays of American aid, France tried for eight years to hold on to its valuable colony. Its greatest enemy was the nationalist leader Ho Chi Minh, a Communist popularly recognized for his resistance to the Japanese occupation during World War II. In 1954 Ho's guerrillas forced the French army into a last-ditch stand at the fortress of Dien Bien Phu. The French defenders called desperately for an American air strike to bail them out, but President Eisenhower, shaking off the advice of Vice-President Nixon and Secretary of State Dulles, vetoed the idea of direct U.S. intervention. Dien Bien Phu was lost, and the French gave up Indochina.

At the Geneva Conference of 1954 France and the Communist-led rebels agreed that Vietnam would be temporarily divided into two zones, the northern one controlled by Ho (in Hanoi), and the southern one governed by the emperor (in Saigon). General elections and reunification were scheduled for 1956. France, Britain, the U.S.S.R., and China signed the Geneva Accords. While the U.S. did not do so, it pledged to honor the agreement. In fact the U.S. became the chief supporter of the southern sector.

President Eisenhower refused to allow the national elections to take place in 1956, for he feared a Communist victory. Kennedy greatly enlarged the U.S. involvement in Vietnam although he had no intention of fighting a major war there. He adopted a military theory quite the opposite of Dulles' massive retaliation. Kennedy proposed to deal with revolutionary insurgents by assigning highly skilled special forces like the "Green Berets" to help allies fight limited "brush-fire wars" with conventional (nonnuclear) weapons. Under this "counterinsurgency plan" the U.S. would in effect conduct preventive warfare against Moscow and Peking without inviting another Korea or a nuclear catastrophe. It was first tested in Vietnam when a small band of "military advisers" was sent in. Gradually, though, the handful of advisers became a large band of combat soldiers.

In 1960 South Vietnamese dissidents organized the National Liberation Front (NLF), a coalition of many political groups led by Communists. Its military branch, the Viet Cong, soon ruled much of South Vietnam's countryside. Meanwhile, the regime of Ngo Dinh Diem, who had replaced the emperor, controlled the towns and cities. Diem was followed by a series of generals. The most durable of these was Nguyen Van Thieu, who became president of the Republic of (South) Vietnam in 1967.

Under Lyndon B. Johnson the war was thoroughly "Americanized," although at no time did he ask Congress for a declaration of war. The deepening involvement in Vietnam, like American foreign policy generally, was never fully opened to public debate. Instead, it was engineered by a tiny handful of policy makers, sometimes called "the foreign policy elite." During the 1964 election, Johnson, the "peace candidate," told the nation, "We have tried very carefully to restrain ourselves and not to enlarge the war." But according to the secret Defense Department survey known as the Pentagon Papers, Johnson had already begun large-scale military operations against North Vietnam and, contrary to the advice of the intelligence community, was planning a concerted air war against the North. The South Vietnamese government was unpopular and its army ineffectual, while the Viet Cong showed no signs of weakening. The reported "attack" on a U.S. naval vessel in the Gulf of Tonkin in 1964 drew from Congress a resolution giving the president authority "to take all necessary measures . . . to prevent further aggression." In the Senate, only Wayne Morse and Ernest Gruening voted against granting the president this authority. Congress later re-

scinded the Gulf of Tonkin Resolution after it learned that the attack had been contrived. Johnson eventually sent 500,000 ground troops into Indochina and undertook saturation bombing of the North. This was intended first "to bring Hanoi to its knees"—and then to bring it to the conference table. But Hanoi refused to bend and showed how far it was from defeat in the savage Tet offensive of January-February 1968. The reaction of America's military leaders was to ask for still more ground troops. At this point Johnson said no and began a slow withdrawal of American forces.

One of the symbolic and tragic episodes of the brutal Vietnam conflict was the My Lai massacre. On March 16, 1968, a patrol of American soldiers under the command of Lieutenant William L. Calley, Jr., rounded up and executed between twenty and seventy civilians, mostly women, children, babies, and old men at the village of My Lai. A court martial convicted him of murder in April 1971. My Lai forced the public to look at the war's moral implications. International law and military law (including the U.S. Army Field Manual) clearly held commanders responsible for criminal acts of troops under their control. If Calley was following orders, who else was guilty? How could the U.S. justify saturation bombing of non-military targets or "free-fire zones" where pilots were free to fire rockets and cannons almost at will? Was killing civilians at close range more criminal than dropping napalm on them from the sky? None of these questions was fully answered.

Nixon and the end of the Cold War consensus

By 1968 events had conspired to undermine the American policy of containment. A basic assumption in Washington during the early Cold War years was the belief that communism was a unified, tightly organized,

Moscow-based movement. This seemed plausible at first. Yet the continuing feud between Peking and Moscow and the refusal of little Albania to follow the Soviet line contradicted this claim. Americans no longer accepted the Cold War in the terms stated twenty years earlier. At home the Vietnam conflict triggered an antiwar movement which came to be the largest in American history. War protesters conducted "teach-ins" on college campuses in 1964. Then came street demonstrations and sit-ins at draft boards. An antiwar rally in New York City in 1967 drew 300,000 people, while a prowar rally brought out fewer than 25,000.

The political debate surrounding Vietnam indicated that after twenty years the Cold War consensus in America was crumbling. People of varying points of view and all walks of life began to oppose the war. Some believed that Vietnam represented no vital interest of the U.S., others that the war was unwinnable. Even some retired military brass joined in dissent against prevailing government policy. Brigadier General Hugh B. Hester, Ret., declared: "The Vietnam war is not a war of self-defense or even of general self-interest. It is a war in the profit interest of only a very few." In a bitter congressional debate, the "hawks" urged stepped-up military activity, even the use of nuclear weapons, to break the impasse in Indochina. The "doves" demanded withdrawal. Though President Johnson initiated peace talks in Vietnam in 1968, he considered it cowardly to withdraw altogether in the face of armed force. Antiwar sentiment persuaded him not to run again in 1968.

In the 1968 election presidential candidate Richard M. Nixon hinted that he had "a secret plan" to end the war. Whatever the meaning of this statement, it took over four years for a peace to materialize. His main approach was to slowly "Vietnamize" the war by shifting responsibility for the fighting to the army of South Vietnam. This con-formed to the "Nixon doctrine," an overall policy in which the U.S. announced it would gradually withdraw ground troops from Asia, while continuing to supply anti-Communist allies with all possible weapons and air and naval support. The number of American soldiers in Vietnam fell to 27,000 early in 1973. Still, like Johnson, Nixon considered it a sign of cowardice and betrayal simply to pull up stakes and withdraw. Instead he pressed for "peace with honor."

Meanwhile Nixon ordered the bombing of neutral Cambodia, and in May 1970 an "incursion" into that nation, to "deprive the Vietnamese Communists of sanctuary." In 1972 he ordered the blockading of North Vietnamese ports and the mining of Haiphong Harbor. During the Christmas season he called for the most destructive air strikes in history against North Vietnam.

The Selective Service Act of 1948 had met little serious opposition during the Korean War, but as the Vietnam War dragged on, the draft became a major issue. In the 1960s many young men claimed conscientious objector status. Others evaded the draft in a variety of ways, an estimated seventy thousand fleeing to Canada. A presidential commission documented the many inequities of the system, affirming, for example, that it worked the greatest hardship on low-income families and racial minorities. Young men from black, Chicano, and poor white families lacked the money or skills to avoid being drafted by going to college, whereas affluent white youth could use college and graduate school as a means for gaining deferment. The commission's proposal for a volunteer army received the president's approval. By letting the draft law expire in 1972 Nixon deflated some antiwar sentiment.

After the complete withdrawal of American ground forces from Vietnam and the return of American prisoners of war in 1973, the matter of amnesty for draft evaders arose. Neither Nixon nor President Ford would grant a general amnesty as Truman had in 1952, though Ford offered a conditional amnesty. Only a fraction of those eligible accepted the offer before it was withdrawn.

Measuring the costs

Early in 1973, after many months of negotiations, Secretary of State Henry Kissinger and the North Vietnamese and NLF representatives worked out a cease-fire agreement under which American prisoners of war would be returned simultaneously with the withdrawal of American military forces from Vietnam. Nixon hailed this as "peace with honor." Over 50,000 Americans had been killed and hundreds of thousands wounded. Over 500,000 Vietnamese civilians were dead, a million wounded, and 10 million left homeless. The U.S. Air Force had dropped 7.4 million tons of bombs on four Indochinese nations, or three times as many bombs as had been used by all contestants in World War II. The final dollar cost of the war to the U.S. was difficult to estimate, but it probably ran to about $350 billion. Considering the casualties and political polarization, as well as its effect on the economy, Vietnam was the costliest conflict in American history.

ESTIMATES OF COSTS OF U.S. WARS
In millions of dollars

	Original War Cost	Estimated Ultimate Cost
World War II	288,000	664,000
Vietnam War	128,000	352,000
Korean War	54,000	164,000
World War I	26,000	112,000
Civil War		
(Union only)	3,200	12,952
Spanish-American War	400	6,460
American Revolution	100	190
War of 1812	93	158
Mexican War	73	147

SOURCE: Adapted from *Statistical Abstracts of the United States,* 1974.

The beginnings of détente

Two events in the life of Richard M. Nixon demonstrate the dramatic twists of American foreign policy in the last quarter century. In 1949 Nixon, a California congressman, pilloried anyone who suggested cooperation with Russia or China. In 1972 Nixon the president flew on an elaborate state visit to Peking, to normalize relations with Red China. A few months later he became the first American president to visit Moscow. Some observed that *only* a noted anti-Communist like Richard M. Nixon could have made the spectacular Peking-Moscow gambit. Ironically, the Indochina War that had started as another "containment" of communism continued as before. Over the rice paddies of Vietnam American B-52 bombers delivered a noisy counterpoint to Nixon's speeches in Peking and Moscow.

Relations between the two superpowers definitely began to thaw in the 1970s. The change was based on a realistic conclusion of both the U.S. and the U.S.S.R. that a heavy reliance on nuclear diplomacy was pointless. Although the fundamental ideological differences remained, the new word was "détente."

President Ford retained Henry Kissinger as head of the State Department and continued to advance the policy of détente. He visited Russian Premier Brezhnev at Vladivostok in 1974, and Secretary Kissinger flew to Peking for further talks with the top Chinese leaders. In July 1975 détente moved a step further when two manned spacecraft of the U.S. and the U.S.S.R. linked up in orbit. The three-year project involved extensive cooperation of engineers, managers, and pilots of the two superpowers which had engaged in thirty years of bitter and often dangerous rivalry. This Apollo-Soyuz mission opened the way for further joint space exploration. Though many people feared that détente was a trap for the U.S., a war-weary nation breathed a little easier as a result of

President Nixon and Premier Chou En-lai review Chinese troops in Hangchow during Nixon's historic visit to the Peoples' Republic of China in 1972. The trip officially ended the U.S. policy of ignoring Red China, and signalled a crucial turning point in world affairs.

this new policy.

Détente could not cool all the hot spots in the world. The Arab-Israeli conflict threatened repeatedly to get out of hand and bring about a confrontation between Russia and the U.S. The U.S. backed Israel while the Russians aided Egypt and some of the Arab states. Secretary of State Kissinger made a series of spectacular diplomatic attempts to defuse the Near East struggle.

Nixon's "peace with honor" in South Vietnam never brought peace to that country, and in the spring of 1975 there came a complete debacle. First South Vietnam and then Cambodia fell to Communist-led forces.

When Congress refused to authorize further shipments of military supplies to the South Vietnamese government, the president blamed it for the loss of Vietnam and expressed fear of a revival of isolationism. This fear seemed unfounded for a country with a military budget of around $90 billion and worldwide military commitments, but there appeared to be growing agreement that the United States had no business playing world policeman. Somewhere between the poles of extreme isolationism (as had existed between 1920 and 1934) and of perpetual intervention (1947–1965), the nation would have to find a new position in world affairs.

Review

The end of the Second World War led to a prolonged hostility between the U.S. and the U.S.S.R. called the Cold War. America viewed communism as a monolithic force directed solely from Moscow. In order to

stem the growth of Communist parties in western Europe and ward off Communist-supported revolutions—and to strengthen its own economy—the U.S. provided billions in economic and military aid. To buttress its policy of containing communism, the U.S. entered into a series of military alliances around the globe. Containment remained the foundation of political consensus in America until well into the 1960s.

The U.S. wanted to prevent Communist takeovers without seeming to oppose social reforms. As the U.S. was especially interested in stopping communism in Asia, the Red victory in China was a bitter disappointment. When North Korea attacked South Korea in 1950, Truman decided to make a stand there. The war ended inconclusively, although for a time the spread of communism seemed to have been stopped in Asia. The Korean action had been sponsored by the UN, but that organization had become more of a forum for the Cold War than a vehicle for achieving world harmony.

"Brinkmanship" was an avowed diplomatic technique of President Eisenhower's Secretary of State Dulles, but the most frightening incident of the Cold War was the Cuban missile crisis during the Kennedy administration. Johnson and Nixon also took a hard-line approach in this hemisphere.

An important internal byproduct of the Cold War was the Red Scare of the late 1940s and early 1950s. It was an attempt to cleanse the government of subversives and it spread to many areas of public and private life. Not until after the end of the Korean War and the censure of its most irresponsible advocate, Senator Joseph McCarthy, did the obsessive anti-Communist purge begin to subside.

The Cold War also contributed to the ever growing scope of the military-industrial complex. Civilian interest groups often demanded even larger defense budgets than those asked for by the Pentagon. Many industries depended heavily on government contracts, and the government often aided industry in the name of national defense.

American involvement in Vietnam began in 1945 and grew slowly. The U.S. aided the French; after their defeat, similiar aid was extended to anti-Communist South Vietnamese regimes. Under President Kennedy an increasing number of military advisers accompanied the flow of arms. In the Johnson administration America's armed forces went to war in Southeast Asia. Opposition to the war began to escalate by the mid-1960s and eventually produced the largest antiwar movement in U.S. history. The Cold War consensus broke down. Johnson withdrew as a presidential candidate in 1968 and was succeeded by Richard M. Nixon, whose approach was to "Vietnamize" the war. Finally, in 1973, after expanding the war into Cambodia and authorizing savage air strikes against North Vietnam, he concluded a settlement which he termed "peace with honor." Fighting continued after the withdrawal of U.S. forces, and in 1975 both South Vietnam and Cambodia fell to the Communists. Vietnam was the costliest war America ever waged.

By the 1970s "détente" was replacing the containment philosophy of previous decades. No real consensus had yet replaced the Cold War ideology, as the U.S. tried to find a new position for itself in world affairs.

Questions

1. Identify: (a) Iron Curtain, (b) Marshall Plan (c) Gulf of Tonkin Resolution, (d) NATO, (e) détente, (f) brinkmanship, and (g) Joseph McCarthy.
2. Trace the course of U.S. involvement in Southeast Asia since 1945.
3. How did the Cold War affect U.S. domestic affairs? How did domestic affairs affect U.S. foreign policy?
4. What was the theory of "containment" and how was it applied?
5. "The UN is a mirror of the world we live in. . . ." Discuss. Do you think the UN could become effective? Explain your opinion.

race

Young Lords occupying a church in East Harlem, 1970.

Those who live with us are our brothers; . . . they share with us the same short moment of life; . . . they seek—as we do—nothing but the chance to live out their lives in purpose and happiness, winning what satisfaction and fulfillment they can.

ROBERT F. KENNEDY   (1925–1968)

36

739

36

American as Apple Pie

"Racial injustice is as American as apple pie, but so is the struggle against it," says psychologist Kenneth Clark. "We've never been able to have our injustices in peace." Certainly this observation applied to the postwar generation, which was marked by extraordinary racial strife. What American racial minorities wanted and what their militancy accomplished are the questions to be examined in this chapter.

The United States has had no monopoly on bigotry. According to one estimate, ethnic and racial clashes throughout the world between 1945 and 1967 produced nearly 7.5 million fatalities during thirty-four major violent incidents and hundreds of lesser ones. In every quarter of the globe people have been abused because of their religion, ethnic background, or skin color. Though South Africa's blacks outnumber whites by four to one, they have suffered under a brutal system of segregation and discrimination called apartheid. A million Muslims, Sikhs, and Hindus died in religious warfare in India in the late 1940s. The Ainus of Japan have been considered social outcasts by the majority of the population. Australia treated its native aborigines like animals and for many years enforced a lily-white immigration policy. Tribalism has led to deadly conflicts in Africa, as between the Ibo and Hausa tribes in Nigeria. Since 1948 there has been no peace between the Arabs and Israelis in the Middle East. In the U.S.S.R. the freedom of Jews, as well as of Ukrainian and Latvian minorities, has been restricted. Many thousands of Arabs from North Africa live in France as second-class citizens. The Indians of Brazil have suffered genocide. The Catholics and Protestants fight on in Northern Ireland. But the fact that there were racial and ethnic troubles elsewhere in the world gave no comfort to those Americans who suffered daily from discrimination in the ghettos, reservations, and barrios.

The victory over Nazi Germany and its

Master Race theory in 1945 created a new potential for racial understanding: scientists and humanists alike were revolted by the doctrine of racial supremacy and its ghastly results. Still, racism remained firmly entrenched in the laws, institutions, and customs of a land where, purportedly, "all men are created equal." Hotels and buses, businesses and unions, government agencies and schools continued to discriminate against minorities much as they had for generations. By law many southern states effectively barred millions of blacks from voting. The entire country paid a price for discrimination, in violence, crime, disease, and the wasted resources of stunted bodies and minds. Only a few profited financially from discrimination, through price and rent gouging, substandard wages, and, in some areas, a system of peonage in which laborers were bound to their employers by debt and convicts were leased to private contractors.

Demands for racial reform in the postwar period were to some extent linked to the Cold War and to the emergence of the Third World. American leaders who wanted the support of African and Asian nations against the Soviet bloc were discomfitted by racial discrimination at home. Embarrassing incidents occurred when African delegates to the UN experienced racial discrimination in American hotels and restaurants. American UN delegates who attacked Soviet oppressions in eastern Europe were likely to be answered by withering denunciations of mistreatment of American blacks. Government leaders concluded that the country must rid itself of glaring racial injustice.

Meanwhile, racial minorities in the U.S. began to feel a kinship with Africans and Asians who were fighting against white imperialism. Martin Luther King, Jr., studied Mahatma Gandhi's strategy for overthrowing the British empire in India. Young militants also began to discover their own heritage of struggle in America.

While each racial minority developed its own agenda for reform and its own unique style of militancy, all the postwar activists shared the sense of urgency expressed in the slogan of the early civil rights movement, "Freedom now!" The younger generation repudiated the compromisers — "Uncle Tom," "Uncle Tomás," and "Uncle Tomahawk." They sought a new sense of pride in their own cultural roots.

Some militant leaders rejected middle-class values altogether, but most wanted a bigger share of middle-class benefits. That is, racial minorities responded to the same American Dream as whites. Hollywood's versions of middle-class suburban life, TV ads for consumer goods, and promises by liberal politicians of an approaching "end to poverty" offered minorities new hope for the immediate future. The age of affluence produced a "revolution of rising expectations" for those at the bottom of the heap. They were given reason to believe that their lives would improve markedly very soon.

The Second Reconstruction for Blacks

"We shall overcome"

Well into the 1950s, efforts to end Jim Crow moved along strictly legalistic and peaceful lines. Integration was the main objective and the NAACP the major protest organization. In 1948 President Truman proposed antilynching, antipoll tax, and antisegration laws, as well as a commission for fair employment practices. No previous president had tried harder to satisfy the demands of blacks for an end to discrimination. But Congress rejected his proposals. Truman ordered an end to segregation in the armed forces and an end to discrimination in federal hiring, but civil rights reform moved about as slowly as it had ever since the end of Reconstruction in 1877.

Change came in 1954 when the NAACP won a historic Supreme Court decree. In *Brown* v. *Board of Education of Topeka* the Court declared an end to school segregation. Reversing the "separate but equal" ruling of 1896, it held that pupils "required on the basis of race to attend separate schools were deprived of the equal protection of the laws guaranteed by the Fourteenth Amendment." Segregated schools must be integrated with "all deliberate speed." A stunned South stiffened to resist. In 1957 Congress established a Civil Rights Commission to monitor voting practices. That year President Eisenhower sent a thousand paratroopers to help integrate Central High School in Little Rock, Arkansas.

Hoping to speed the end of Jim Crow, Negro rights leaders developed more forceful techniques. The most important was nonviolent action that involved challenging laws by breaking them. It began with a seemingly minor incident in Montgomery, Alabama, the "Cradle of the Confederacy," in 1955. While returning home from work one day, Mrs. Rosa Parks, a black woman, boarded a bus and sat down in the first row of the "colored" section. As the bus filled with passengers, the bus driver asked her and three other passengers to give up their seats, as southern custom and law had long decreed. The other passengers moved back, but Mrs. Parks refused. She was tired out from a day's work, she had paid her fare, and she had a proper seat. Rather than stand in the back of the crowded bus while a white person took her place, she preferred to be arrested, and promptly was. In response, the Reverend Martin Luther King, Jr., led a boycott of Montgomery's buses. For a solid year blacks stayed off the city buses, until they won a favorable court decree. At Greensboro, North Carolina, in 1960, black college students staged a "sit-in" at a segregated Woolworth lunch counter. In the following months seventy thousand people "sat in " at various southern eating places. This was the start of the Negro revolt, or "civil rights revolution," or "second reconstruction."

By working for racial justice through nonviolent civil disobedience, King became the nation's most prominent black leader. Liberal whites as well as blacks found his strategy acceptable. As a third-generation clergyman, influenced by the writings of Henry David Thoreau as well as Gandhi, he was trying to apply Christian teachings to the problem of racism. He and his followers in the Southern Christian Leadership Conference (SCLC) were arrested many times for violating state laws. When police used dogs and fire hoses on his marchers, the publicity won them widespread sympathy and additional support. In a "Letter from Birmingham Jail" on April 16, 1963, King explained: "One has not only a legal but a moral responsibility to obey just laws. Conversely, one has a moral responsibility to disobey unjust laws. . . . All segregation statutes are unjust because segregation distorts the soul and damages the personality." His moving speech, "I Have a Dream," delivered to 250,000 civil rights marchers in Washington in August 1963, was perhaps the most dramatic moment of the civil rights movement.

Twenty-one bombings occurred in Birmingham in 1963, as civil rights workers attempted to integrate the school system. A bomb explosion at a Negro Sunday School killed four young black girls. As a direct consequence of the civil rights movement, Congress passed the Civil Rights Act of 1964,

MARTIN LUTHER KING, JR. (1929-1968)

THE PRICE OF FREEDOM

On December 1, 1955, a black seamstress named Rosa Parks felt too tired to give up her seat on a bus to a white passenger. For her refusal to do so, she was arrested. That incident catapulted a young black minister named Martin Luther King, Jr., into international fame. King, in turn, forced America to gaze into the mirror of its own conscience, an experience that shook the nation.

Only months away from graduate study at Booton University, King was a happy husband and the proud father of a new baby. The boycott was to change the course of his life. He found himself heading an organization formed to fight the bus company. Within weeks he was arrested, and a few days later his home was bombed.

Although he experienced fear and rage and doubt and despair, King's struggle intensified. If his faith in the power of reason lessened a bit, his faith in spiritual power—the power of love and suffering—grew stronger. And so, gradually, did his belief in a nonviolent crusade against racial injustice, in the name of human dignity. For a whole year the boycott continued, until at last, after a Supreme Court decision, the buses of Montgomery were integrated.

In 1957, as head of the new Southern Christian Leadership Conference, King sent out the call for cooperative action against segregation. The crusade carried him hundreds of thousands of miles, but the longest miles were his marches, where he and those he led were cursed, stoned, clubbed, kicked, bitten by police dogs, knocked down by jets from fire hoses, threatened by guns and bombs, arrested, and imprisoned.

Ignoring the hatred and scorn heaped on him by extreme segregationists, black nationalists, and J. Edgar Hoover, King had a dream. He described it to an immense audience of marchers gathered in Washington, D.C., in 1963. It was the American Dream—of a free people, of a unified nation of equal citizens—the dream that is so often dusted off each Fourth of July and returned to mothballs the next day. Although the speech disappointed many militants, it moved many others to tears.

King and his nonviolent movement gained international recognition, and he was awarded the Nobel Prize for Peace in 1964. "I accept this award," he said, "in behalf of a civil rights movement which is moving with determination and a majestic scorn for risk and danger to establish a reign of freedom and a rule of justice." But there were many failures along with the triumphs. In Memphis, Tennessee, in 1968, he saw one of his own marches turned into a wild riot. But he rallied, and on the night of April 3 he told a cheering crowd in that city, "It doesn't really matter with me now, because I've been to the mountaintop." He was shot to death by an assassin the next day. His epitaph begins, "Free at last. . . ."

Nonviolent civil rights demonstrators in Birmingham were met by fire hoses, snarling K-9 dogs, and electric cattle-prods. Their perserverance in the face of such resistance forced the entire nation to reexamine continued segregation and discrimination.

forbidding all racial discrimination in public accommodations. It also ordered a halt to all discrimination in employment—racial, sexual, ethnic, and religious. The same law provided that any adult with a sixth-grade education could not be barred from voting on the grounds of illiteracy.

In 1964, the year King won the Nobel Peace Prize, the civil rights movement turned its attention to voter registration. After a dramatic march by black civil rights workers and their supporters from Selma to Montgomery, Alabama, Congress enacted the Voting Rights Act of 1965, which provided for federal officials to register black voters in the South.

More militant leaders in the wings

Blacks had long debated whether the best path to liberation lay in gradualism or in immediacy, in accommodation or in militancy, in integration or in separation. The Negro revolt of the 1960s also had its conflicting strategies. Whereas King and his followers worked for integration, other black leaders countered with cultural nationalism.

King's sharpest critic was Malcolm X, a brilliant spokesman for the separatist Black Muslim movement. Malcolm (born Malcolm Little) lived with the memory of a father murdered by the Ku Klux Klan. While doing time in jail for a serious crime, he was converted to the Muslims. When paroled he became the outstanding advocate for this sect. Later he and Elijah Muhammad, the head of the Muslims, had a falling out, and Malcolm went his own way. He would not shy away from violence, which he thought was created by whites in the first place. Guns might be necessary for blacks to attain mastery over their own lives. But he had begun work on a new strategy, less violence-oriented and with a strong pan-African ideal, when he was killed by black gunmen in 1965. His autobiography is an eloquent statement of black aspirations for equality and dignity.

Black consciousness and nationalism grew stronger as the movement for integration stalled. Responding to the theme "black is beautiful," younger blacks began wearing "Afro" hairdos and the traditional African *dashiki*, and demanded high-school and college courses in black studies. Some black businesses posted signs which read "Be Black, Buy Black!" More important was the "Black Power" slogan used in the sixties by Stokeley Carmichael, leader of the Student Nonviolent Coordinating Committee (SNCC), for rallying Negroes to gain control over their own communities. Its major premise was that the ghettos were "internal colonies" of the U.S. These colonies, they reasoned, were as badly exploited by white outsiders as the European colonies in Africa. To free themselves from colonial rule, therefore, American blacks must work with their own, not with white, organizations to improve, rather than destroy, the ghettos. King's SCLC and the NAACP opposed black nationalism and black power as divisive, yet these ideas appealed to the Congress of Racial Equality, originally a moderate group. Black militants now turned against the white civil rights workers in their midst. On the far left wing of the Negro revolt was the new Black Panther party, an avowed revolutionary movement founded by Eldridge Cleaver and others in Oakland, California.

"Burn, baby, burn!"

The civil rights movement could not channel the rage and frustration in the black ghettos, which erupted into riots in the mid-sixties. By then half the country's black population lived in the North, mainly in the large, crowded metropolitan centers. While the "Negro problem" now belonged to the country as a whole, its most explosive side was in the northern ghettos.

Unlike the white immigrants who had made it out to the suburbs, blacks found that, for all but a few of them, the ghetto was the end of the line. The majority were too poor to move on, and wherever they turned for better schools, neighborhoods, and jobs, they seemed to encounter the color bar. Urban renewal had either further reduced the amount of housing they could afford or produced enormous public housing projects that quickly became new crime-ridden, segregated slums. In Jersey City and Chicago, Harlem and Philadelphia, housing for blacks was dilapidated, crowded, rat-infested, and rarely repaired by absentee landlords. The rate of joblessness was highest in the ghettos, and jobs with a future were almost impossible for black youth to come by. Schools, parks, and playgrounds were inadequate and often unsafe. The juvenile crime rate rose. The numbers racket, drug pushing, and prostitution flourished unchecked. By the early 1960s ghetto watchers were predicting big blow-ups. In an eloquent essay on the growing hatred of blacks for their white oppressors, James Baldwin flatly warned in *The Fire Next Time* (1963) of serious disturbances.

The "long hot summer" of 1964 brought upheaval to New York, Rochester, Jersey City, Chicago, and Philadelphia. In 1965 the major riot occurred in the Watts area of Los Angeles, amid cries of "Burn, baby, burn!" Chicago and Cleveland saw further disturbances the following year. In 1967, 41 major riots rumbled through the country from coast to coast. The most serious occurred in Detroit, where 63 people died. The murder of Martin Luther King, Jr., in 1968 triggered riots in 125 cities, including the nation's capital. Then the violence subsided.

Historically, the ghetto riots of the sixties were of a new type. The rioters were black and the spectators white. The drama often unfolded on TV. Blacks burned and looted neighborhood stores, shouting obscenities against white shopkeepers, and hurling rocks at police and firemen. Some observers saw the sinister hand of Communists or organized conspirators in the Watts holocaust, but the FBI discounted this theory. All evidence indicated that the riots were spontaneous outbursts. Except for a few white police officers, national guardsmen, and newsmen, the riot victims were almost always black. Black rage had turned inward upon itself.

A presidential commission headed by Governor Otto Kerner of Illinois was charged with assessing the causes and cures of the rioting. In a 1968 report the Kerner Commission attributed much of the trouble to white racism, a conclusion that did not sit well with many whites: "What white Americans had never fully understood—but what the Negro can never forget—is that white society is deeply implicated in the ghetto. White institutions created it, white institutions maintain it, and white society condones it." The report noted a variety of difficulties, including "the residue of the unfulfilled expectations aroused by the great judicial and legislative victories of the civil rights movement." It cited "the frustrations of powerlessness," and found "a new mood . . . among Negroes . . . in which self-esteem [is] . . . replacing apathy and submission to 'the system.'" "Police brutality" and the "double standard of justice" were long-standing complaints in the riot-torn areas.

Achievements and the road ahead

The rioters prodded the government into spending many tax dollars in the ghetto, although with few lasting results. The civil rights movement achieved far greater successes than the rioters. More legislative reforms were enacted in the 1960s than at any previous time except during the first reconstruction period, from 1865 to 1877. The Civil Rights Act of 1964 and the Voting Rights Act of 1965 (renewed ten years later) topped the list of permanent reforms. In 1968 Congress also passed a fair housing law. A black civil rights attorney, Thurgood Marshall of the NAACP, was appointed to the Supreme Court. Some gains had been made in education, although resistance to segregation, especially in the big-city school districts of the North, was by no means fully overcome. Not least of all, blacks were achieving a sense of identity and pride.

Government doors began opening to blacks. Two and a half million of them could now vote in the South, and the voters helped elect hundreds of black officials. Most were on the local level, but blacks also won seats in Congress and the stage legislatures. Massachusetts elected a black senator, Edward Brooke. By 1973 Cleveland, Gary, Newark, Washington, D.C., and Los Angeles had elected black mayors. By 1975 the eleven states of the old Confederacy had no fewer than seventy-six black mayors, which was nothing short of a minor political revolution.

Despite the many tangible gains, however, one third of all Negroes still lived below the poverty line. Black unemployment rates normally ran four and five times higher than for whites. In Chicago's Woodlawn district, 25 percent of the black residents were unemployed before the recession of 1974. Housing and school segregation were probably greater in northern cities than they had been twenty years earlier, because of the flight of white families to the suburbs. The violent eruptions in Boston in 1975 over the school bussing issue was a reminder that large segments of lower-middle-class and working-class whites of the North still actively opposed the liberal faith in integration. Also, the resurgence of violent crime in the black ghettos suggested to observers that conditions there might be as desperate in the mid-seventies as they were a decade earlier.

Politics was the new style of the civil rights movement. Many of the old leaders were dead or in exile. Malcolm X had been killed in 1965. King was murdered in 1968 while organizing an antipoverty movement in the South. Whitney Young of the Urban League had died. Stokeley Carmichael had exiled himself to Africa for a time, while Eldridge Cleaver became an expatriate in Algiers and later in France. But since 1969 when the Negro revolt subsided, new black political leaders were using more traditional lines to consolidate gains and make new advances.

Chicano Awakening

Profile of the Mexican American

In 1970 the census takers counted ten million Spanish-speaking persons in the United States (informal estimates went as high as 16 million). Of the 10 million, one sixth were Puerto Ricans, concentrated mainly in New York City. Cubans, most of whom were located in Florida, accounted for another large segment. (The Cubans and Puerto Ricans are discussed in Chapter 37.) But the majority of the Spanish-speaking population—around 5,073,000—were of Mexican background. Most lived in the Southwest, in Texas, New Mexico, Colorado, Arizona, and California.

In the postwar years most Mexican Americans moved to the cities, having been drawn there by higher wages and pushed out of agriculture by machines and imported Mexican labor. The majority gravitated to the barrios (Spanish-speaking communities or neighborhoods) where housing and schooling were segregated. Those who stayed behind in rural areas, especially in New Mexico and Texas, still constituted a majority in some towns and greatly dominated community life. But those areas were economic backwaters. Jobs were scarce, schools were inadequate, and much of the housing lacked such basics as indoor plumbing. In fact, living conditions for these Mexican Americans were often worse than for all other nonwhites, even Indians.

Between 1950 and 1960 the numbers of Mexican Americans in the five southwestern states doubled, mostly due to natural increase. Their average age was young (about twenty years in 1960), and their family size relatively large (nearly five persons). These figures exceeded those of all other groups in those states except Indians.

The move to the cities generally opened new job possibilities, although exploitation, poverty, and illiteracy were common in the barrios. For the most part Mexican Americans worked at unskilled and semiskilled jobs. On an average their income lagged behind that of Anglo-Americans by about 50 percent, and their jobless rate was about twice as high.

The plight of the Mexican Americans, or Chicanos as they came to be called by the 1960s, was complicated by job competition from cheap labor from Mexico in the southwestern border area. Under pressure from the southwestern growers, Congress continued the *bracero* program after the war. In addition, employers and labor contractors privately encouraged millions of "wetbacks" to swim or wade the Rio Grande River, to be smuggled onto farms and ranches and into factories on the U.S. side of the border. From time to time, as labor needs declined in the U.S., the wetbacks were rounded up and sent home to "dry out." But loose enforcement at the border helped keep the seasonal labor plentiful and cheap. Many Mexicans returned frequently throughout the year. When farm machinery gradually cut the need for farm labor in the 1950s, the Justice Department made frequent raids in the barrios of the Southwest looking for "illegals." The mass raids by immigration authorities, which often swept up Mexicans who had lived in the U.S. for thirty or forty years (as well as American-born Chicanos), created deep resentment in the Chicano community.

Educational handicaps were so severe in the barrios as to insure economic hardship among the residents for some time to come. The average Chicano youngster stayed in school three or four years less than the average Anglo. Much of this attitude toward schooling resulted from generations of widespread isolation and from school segregation. Some schools lacked Spanish-speaking teachers entirely. Occasionally normal Chicano youngsters were diagnosed as retarded, when they simply had no idea of what was being said to them.

Poverty, as measured by standards of housing, health, and community services, also created severe disadvantages for Mexican Americans. In 1960 Spanish-surnamed people were 23 percent of the poor in the Southwest; a third of the urban Chicanos lived in substandard housing. Acute illnesses also ran higher among Chicanos than in the rest of the population.

The Chicano movement

The postwar period was characterized by an increase in political organization and militancy among Mexican Americans attempting to overcome social and economic handicaps. During the late forties returning war veterans organized to resist discrimination in public facilities, jobs, and schools. They also hoped to improve the representation of Mexican Americans in government. The League of United Latin American Citizens (LULAC), the oldest Mexican-American organization, challenged school segregation in a case that reached the U.S. Supreme Court. The decision in *Méndez* v. *Westminister* (1945) broke the back of segregated schooling for Mexican-American youngsters. In California, the Community Service Organization (CSO) was formed by Chicanos to register Mexican-American voters and candidates. It helped elect a Los Angeles city councilman who later went on to Congress, Edward Roybal. One of CSO's organizers, César Chávez, would become famous later as an agricultural labor leader. The GI Forum, a veterans' group, confronted discrimination in Texas.

Both the Democratic and Republican parties had ignored Chicanos. It was the purpose of the Mexican American Political Association (MAPA) to attract the attention of party bigwigs to the Mexican vote. The resentment of Mexican Americans toward liberal Democrats climaxed in 1966. President Johnson called a meeting of the Equal Opportunities Commission at Albuquerque, New Mexico. Fifty community leaders came

César Chávez and members of the UFW march during la huelga, *"the great strike."*
Chávez spent eighteen hours a day — and more — organizing the UFW. "The business of
convincing a man," he maintained, "is the business of spending time with him."

to testify, most of them moderates. They were kept waiting while the commissioners slowly drifted in for the gathering. There were no Mexican Americans on the staff. Dissatisfaction with the Albuquerque meeting coincided with rumblings among more militant Mexican Americans.

The Chicano movement originated in the sixties in the colleges and high schools of southern California and quickly spread through all Mexican-American barrios. It was intended to win economic gains and social recognition for Mexican Americans and their culture. The word Chicano (a modification of *Mexicano*) soon acquired a specialized meaning: "young activist American of Mexican background." The new generation, drawing inspiration from the Mexican revolution of 1910 and other Latin American movements for social reconstruction, began to assert itself in schools and colleges. They were Americans who took pride in their Mexican heritage. At high-school "blow-outs" (walkouts) students demanded bilingual instruction. In the colleges they demanded that Chicano studies programs be instituted. Theater groups, newspapers, artists and poets, radio and television stations, became part of the Chicano movement.

Four prominent leaders illustrate the variety of interests and objectives of the Chicano movement. César Chávez, organizer of the United Farm Workers (UFW), caught the public eye during the long grape strike and boycott in California. Chávez prided himself on a strategy of nonviolent direct action against the powerful California growers. His union formed cooperative stores and became a way of life for some followers. A nationwide boycott, the first in labor history, finally brought a victory for the striking grape harvesters. Chávez then struck the lettuce fields, although he met powerful resistance from both the growers and the rival Teamsters Union.

In New Mexico the Alianza movement fought to regain the land taken from Mexican Americans since the beginning of Anglo rule. The founder of the movement, Reies Tijerina, dreamed of restoring the farmers' rights to land and water and establishing a network of city-states dominated by Mexican Americans. Its full name was *Alianza Federal de los Pueblos Libres* — or Federal Alliance of Free City-States. While trying to reoccupy what they said was stolen land in a national forest, members of the Alianza were arrested. Tijerina was jailed in 1967 for kidnapping a county sheriff.

In Denver, Colorado, Rudolfo "Corky" Gonzales founded the Crusade for Justice, a community service organization staffed mainly by young people. The ex-featherweight contender preached both nationalism and separatism. His "Plan of Aztlán" proposed that Chicanos work to reclaim the southwestern part of the United States for themselves, although the method for doing so was left deliberately vague. Gonzales' poem, *Yo Soy Joaquín* (I Am Joaquín), is considered by Chicanos a moving expression of the mood of the younger generation.

La Raza Unida, a Chicano political party formed in Texas in 1970, was an expression of political separatism. José Angel Gutiérrez, the moving force of this organization, believed the time had come for Chicanos to reject the major parties and form a new political movement. Gutiérrez and two other La Raza party candidates were elected to the Crystal City, Texas, school board. Here and in other small, rural communities dominated by Chicanos, *La Raza Unida* built up a head of steam. The party spread to other states but met with far less success in urban areas.

Although the Mexican Americans had potential political clout, their low registration and voter turnout held them back. When Congress renewed the Voting Rights Act in 1975 it added new provisions to assist Chicano voters (as well as Asian Americans and Indians). Bilingual printing of ballots and related materials was expected to have far-reaching political effects in states like California.

No one claimed that the Chicano movement was universally accepted and admired. On the contrary, it created bitter foes even among Mexican Americans. Senator Joseph Montoya of New Mexico labeled Tijerina "a damned liar; an enemy of the United States, an exploiter, discredited charlatan, imposter, racist, and creature of the darkness." Similarly, Congressman Henry Gonzales of Texas believed that the La Raza party was "racist and un-American." Other Mexican Americans shared this opinion. Still, any Mexican American would admit that the movement had awakened the consciousness of the present generation and was helping bring about worthwhile social change.

More and more Mexican Americans appeared to reject the melting-pot goal and embrace cultural pluralism as an ideal. They hoped to become assimilated but not to allow their Mexican heritage to be forgotten. Bilingual and bicultural education—fluency in Spanish and English and awareness of the culture of both Mexico and Anglo-America—had a high priority among Mexican-American educators. Only by implementing such an approach to education could teachers lower the high rate of school dropouts. These objectives in school programs, they believed, would give youngsters the favorable self-image so vital to successful education, as well as equip them with skills for succeeding in a predominantly Anglo-Saxon society.

Termination Versus Self-Determination for Indians

At the bottom of the heap

In the affluent society Indians were at the bottom of the heap. The nearly 800,000 of them counted in the 1970 census (informally estimated as high as 1.5 million) had an average family income of $1500. That was 50 percent below the official poverty line. The average Indian lifespan of forty-four years was twenty years below the national average, the infant mortality rate three times higher, and the suicide rate twice as high. Some 460,000 Indians lived on or near reservations, where three quarters of the housing was substandard. At Fort Hale Indian Reservation in Idaho, suicides of ten-year-old children were recorded. Nearly half the Indians lived in city slums—"cement prairies" they called them—where conditions were rarely much better.

According to some whites, Indians had begun "to find themselves" in American society during the Second World War. Their service in the foxholes and defense factories had helped acculturate and integrate them into the mainstream. Supposedly whites were beginning to accept these "New Indians." Marine corps hero Ira Hayes of the Pima Nation was the best-known "New Indian." He had appeared in the memorable photo of GIs raising the Stars and Stripes over Iwo Jima island in 1945. Returning home from the Pacific theater of war with a chest full of ribbons, he was hailed as a national hero. But after a brief period of being toasted as a celebrity, Hayes found himself quickly forgotten, and doors that had opened to him briefly were once more shut. Bitter and drinking heavily, Hayes returned to his reservation. One cold night in 1955 he fell into an irrigation ditch and died of exposure. He was thirty-two, a victim of despair.

In the 1960s the young Indians' despair turned to militancy. Activists began making militant demands on white society. In the state of Washington they organized "fish-ins" along several rivers, claiming them as their ancestral waters. Richard Oakes, a Mohawk from New York, led a party of Indians onto Alcatraz Island in San Francisco Bay. They claimed possession of the "The Rock" by "right of discovery," under an old statute that allowed Indians to occupy unused federal lands. Their plan was to convert it into an Indian cultural center. But the former prison was a cold and lonely place for an Indian colony. Before being forced to depart from Alcatraz, however, the little band managed to draw attention to the plight of the Indian in the cities. This was the first of many such confrontations. From Puget Sound to Wounded Knee, South Dakota, the era of "Red Power" had arrived.

The folly of termination

In 1953 the Eisenhower administration made an abrupt move to terminate the reservation system completely and transfer all federal services for Indians from the Bureau of Indian Affairs to other federal agencies or to the states. The idea of "termination" came from the Hoover Commission on Governmental Efficiency. This body, headed by former President Hoover, held that the Indians had shown by their participation in World War II that they could swim in the mainstream of American life. The reservations were too poor to support the rapidly growing Indian population. Besides, closing the reservations would trim some fat from the federal budget. As a result, Eisenhower started phasing out the reservations.

Congress agreed that the reservations should be terminated "as fast as possible." To encourage the process it applied pressure on the Indians. Congress had previously set up a claims commission that allowed Indian tribes to sue the government for violating old treaties and to receive payment for tribal lands seized in the nineteenth century. Congress now provided that no tribe could press a claim before the commission until it agreed to terminate its reservation.

Most tribal leaders saw termination as a form of "cultural homicide." To them it looked like a land grab by the timber, mining, real estate, and ranching interests, which would benefit whenever a tribe was terminated. The policy also seemed like an underhanded way for the government to evade its legal responsibilities, set down in numerous treaties, to provide schools, public health, and other services to the Indians. Termination, Indian leaders charged, would put them at the mercy of poor and hostile state governments. Even the most progressive states could not provide the health and education services—however meager—then supplied by the BIA.

As a first step, the federal government terminated reservations containing some ten thousand Indians. This included the Menominee Indian Reservation, which became Menominee County, Wisconsin. Tribal land and resources were divided up among the members of the Menominee tribe. Indian services were transferred to the state. Private lumber companies and real-estate developers moved in. A sawmill which had been the mainstay of the reservation's economy became a private corporation. It fell into the hands of whites. The new board of directors adopted work rules which displeased many Indian employees, and it made unwise investments which brought the firm to the edge of bankruptcy. The formerly self-sufficient Menominees suffered serious losses to their economy, health, and cultural unity. In 1958 Eisenhower admitted the failure of the policy and announced an end to termination.

Looking for alternatives

Although termination was discredited, the government floundered endlessly in search of a new Indian policy. Meanwhile, Indians were developing their own approach. A group of native Americans called to a conference on Indian problems at the University of Chicago in 1961 drew up a "Declaration of Indian Purpose" which may be considered the beginning of the new Indian rights movement. The document was drafted by 420 Indians representing sixty-seven tribes. It asked to have Indian reservation lands restored and enlarged; in addition, it requested improvements in health, welfare, housing, and education. The Declaration also called for an overhaul of the BIA in order to make it responsive to Indian needs. Finally it made a demand that Indians be given the "right to choose our own way of life." The fish-ins and other militant actions underscored the seriousness of these objectives.

Presidents Kennedy and Johnson hoped to avoid Eisenhower's mistakes and leaned toward a program of self-determination for Indians. Yet neither one could come up with a successful program. Kennedy tried to resettle reservation Indians in the cities, but the depressed job market and impersonality of city life was disturbing to them. Many soon drifted back to the reservations where they still had no jobs or income but could at least hunt, fish, and live close to friends and relatives. Many of those who remained in the concrete prairies sank into loneliness and hopelessness. Johnson brought the war on poverty to the reservations, where some of his Great Society programs were greatly heralded. But the program became hopelessly tangled in red tape, old-fashioned paternalism, and budgetary cutbacks. Within three years, the war on Indian poverty had come to an end without bringing significant change.

Johnson had also given Congress an Indian reform measure which proposed that Indian tribes create investment capital for their own uses by mortgaging their tribal lands. Leaders from some thirty tribes were invited to Washington to discuss this Omnibus Indian Bill of 1968. They rejected it out of hand, realizing that a tribe that defaulted on its mortgage would lose its land as surely as if it were terminated. As a counterproposal the leaders suggested that Washington lend the Indians $500 million in "foreign aid." Many poor nations were getting loans from the government, so why could it not give money to develop the "underdeveloped areas of our country, the Indian reservations"? The 1968 bill never passed Congress, and the counterproposal was never seriously considered.

A perennial problem for Indian reformers was the BIA, an old, hide-bound government bureaucracy. Most of its sixteen thousand employees were patronage appointees without special talent or training for their jobs. Few were Indians. The Bureau wielded great authority over the lives of hundreds of thousands of Indians, on and off the reservations, who often accused it of being unresponsive to their needs. Tribal leaders asked for a bureau that would serve the Indians rather than the congressional committee that controlled its budget. A presidential task force appointed by Johnson recommended a thorough shake-up of the agency.

In a major policy statement in July 1970, President Nixon gave his blessings to self-determination and "cultural pluralism" for Indians. The Indian, Nixon declared, "can assume control of his own life without being separated involuntarily from the tribal group." Nixon broke with tradition and appointed an Indian, Louis Bruce, to the post of Commissioner of Indian Affairs. He also ordered a shake-up of the BIA by cutting the number of patronage jobs and making its top bureaucrats responsive to the White House. The BIA was now expected to respond to Indian needs as defined by Indians.

Few changes actually occurred in the operation of the BIA, although Nixon's announced policies had a refreshing new tone. Congress authorized the return of 48,000 acres of U.S. forest land to the Taos Indians of New Mexico. The Taos hailed the return of their sacred forest as a major victory for Indians. In Alaska 53,000 Eskimos, Aleuts, and Indians claimed possession of 390 million acres and demanded government protection and compensation for oil rights or land seized from them. Nixon suggested $1 billion compensation to the native people of Alaska for the loss of ancestral lands, infringement on human rights, and loss of cultural heritage since 1867. A settlement of $925 million was officially made in 1972.

The major need in Indian policy was to find a substitute for the bankrupt termination program. In 1972 Indian militants presented a sophisticated proposal known as the Twenty Point Program. It was brought to Washington by a group of demonstrators calling themselves the "Trail of Broken Treaties Caravan." The Twenty Point Program proposed that Indians again be allowed to sign treaties and contracts with the government. Even the worst treaty at least recognized the Indian tribes as separate and sovereign entities. It also asked that the BIA be dismantled entirely. In its place the program proposed a new, three-way agency run jointly by the president, Congress, and the Indians. These serious proposals were drowned out by other events: the take-over of the Bureau headquarters by Indian dissidents and the biggest Indian-white shoot-out in modern times, which occurred a few months later.

The scene was the village of Wounded Knee, South Dakota, across the road from the cemetery where the Sioux victims of the 1886 massacre lay buried. In 1973 young Sioux militants associated with the American Indian Movement (AIM) holed themselves up in the village with guns and demanded the return of land and rights stolen from the Indians over the past centuries. The National Guard and FBI agents surrounded the area with heavy weapons. The rebels held out for seventy-one days. Later, AIM leaders Russell Means and Dennis Banks were put on trial for conspiracy, larceny, and assault. In an impassioned plea, the defense attorney claimed that the militants were merely drawing attention to injustices and had no other recourse than to force of arms. The judge ruled that the government case depended on illegal wire tapping and other "misconduct." The two were acquitted.

Banks and Means called the verdict a victory for the American judicial system, though the cause of Indian rights had as yet made little headway. Sixty-eight others involved in the Second Wounded Knee argued in court that they could not be tried in a regular court but had to be tried by their own tribe, as provided for in an 1868 treaty between the U.S. government and "the Great Sioux Nation." In 1975 a sympathetic judge, who agreed that federal treatment of Indians had an "ugly history," nevertheless rejected the claim on legal grounds. The Indian rights movement showed greater success in publicizing their problems than in solving them.

For Asian Americans—a Note of Hope

An influx of Chinese

During a San Francisco festival in 1969, observers were astonished to find the flag of Red China flying over historic Portsmouth Square. It had been raised by militant Chinese youth calling themselves "Red Guards," or "Yellow Panthers." FBI director J. Edgar Hoover warned Congress of the threat of subversion from Red China. But many San Franciscans thought that if they had a "Chinese problem," it resulted not from subversion, but from poverty, overcrowding, inferior education, and unemployment. As in other minority communities, the young people in America's Chinatowns were attracting attention to social ills by making dramatic gestures.

The postwar years witnessed a big change in immigration policy toward Asians, which greatly affected the Chinese. In 1943 Congress had repealed the Oriental Exclusion Act, a monument to bigotry. Chinese women could now enter the country for the first time in many years; nearly eleven thousand Chinese women and girls arrived between

1945 and 1953. A later law allowed Chinese men who were permanent U.S. residents to bring in brides from Hong Kong or Nationalist China. In 1950 Congress also gave relief to Chinese college students who had lost their family support when the Communists took over in China, and a provision of the McCarran-Walter Immigration Act of 1952 dropped the long-standing ban against Asian immigrants. Still more important was the repeal of the National Origins Quota Act in 1965 (see p. 765), which created a large ripple of Chinese immigration.

There were about 435,000 Chinese Americans in the U.S. in 1970, a rise from 230,000 ten years earlier. San Francisco was still the main port of entry for the Chinese entering the U.S. as it had been since the gold rush, and San Francisco's Chinatown continued to be the major place of settlement. The influx of immigrants brought new burdens to an already overcrowded community. The San Francisco *Chronicle* described Chinatown as a community "where poverty, oppression, disease, and fear exist which have been further aggravated by the influx of poor, uneducated and poorly nourished immigrants from Hong Kong. . . ."

Individual Chinese Americans have been successful in many areas, most notably in architecture, finance, and the sciences. But the vocational progress of the community has been slowed by educational problems. California, the home of most Chinese Americans, made no special provision for educating Chinese-speaking youngsters; as a result, many were burdened with illiteracy. The bussing issue compounded the problem of education, for Chinese parents refused to let their children be bussed to strange schools outside the community in order to integrate the school system. A new problem in California Chinatowns, furthermore, was juvenile delinquency. Some Chinese youth, traditionally a remarkably law-abiding group, were becoming members of violent gangs.

Great strides for the Japanese

But if the the story of the Chinese Americans was somber, the opposite was true of Japanese Americans. When the gates of the detention camps swung open in 1944 and 1945, Japanese Americans faced an uncertain future. Many had lost their property in the early days of the detention, and the government took no responsibility for such losses. Under California law, those born in Japan still could not own land in the States.

In the face of these injustices the Japanese Americans went on to become extraordinarily successful and well adjusted. Though some felt permanently shamed and embittered, the great majority set out to build new lives in America. Some families decided not to return to the Pacific Coast, but to go to the East; the Japanese-American population was now much more widely scattered. Those who did return to the West Coast found little or no overt hostility on the part of whites. The Japanese took up their affairs quietly. Without fanfare they lobbied for an end to legal discrimination. In 1948 Congress established machinery for Japanese Americans to recover property unjustly taken from them during the war. The 44,000 claims that were made resulted in settlements totaling $38 million. The Alien Land Law was revoked by a California Supreme Court decision in 1952. That same year a new immigration law ended an old provision that prevented persons born in Asia from becoming citizens. The granting of citizenship created a new and hopeful atmosphere for the foreign-born Japanese.

Members of this older generation were high achievers, and they passed along to their children a powerful work ethic. In a short time Japanese Americans were making great strides in education. In fact, in 1960 the Japanese in California surpassed all other groups, including whites, in the average numbers of years of schooling completed. A great number entered the professions, including the teaching profession, which had been closed to them by law before the war.

During the 1960s there were no bumper stickers calling for "Japanese Power." The stern treatment given student rebels by S. I. Hayakawa, Japanese-American president of San Francisco State College, made him a hero among conservatives.

The anti-Japanese stereotypes that had once poisoned American journalism, movies, and politics vanished after the war, though some of the old racial attitudes died hard. When white children in Georgia in the 1960s were asked for a one-word description of the Japanese, a number replied, "sneaky." Most had never met anyone Japanese, but they had watched old World War II movies on TV. In some places, housing for Japanese Americans remained segregated. They were still absent from the very highest levels of the professions and of the corporate structure. They could not readily join country clubs or other private associations where the color bar remained in effect. Nor did they yet have the same earning power as whites with comparable educational backgrounds. Yet intermarriage was increasing rapidly, a sure sign of acculturation.

The rise of the Japanese Americans was most swift in Hawaii. Here they had a near-majority status. They had not spent the war behind barbed wire, and after the conflict the younger Japanese began reaching for the highest and most important offices in poli-tics and business. Daniel Inouye, a Purple Heart veteran of the Second World War, became U.S. senator, and many of his contemporaries went to Congress and into the state government of Hawaii. Other Hawaiian Japanese Americans became powerful in the world of business and finance.

During the uprisings in the black ghettos in the 1960s, a southern congressman suggested jailing the rioters in the camps that had held wartime internees. Title II of the Emergency Detention Act of 1950 provided that persons who threatened "the internal security of the United States" could be forcibly detained. This frightening proposal prompted Japanese American leaders to press for immediate repeal of the law so that the hated camps would not be reopened. That objective was eventually achieved.

The postwar history of the Japanese Americans on the mainland and in Hawaii offers a valuable lesson in race relations. In 1942 no nonwhite group was more bitterly despised; a generation later none was more generally accepted. Was it possible by any stretch of the imagination that this same condition could be achieved by other racial groups? Perhaps the way to racial peace was the acceptance on the part of all Americans that theirs was a nation of many races and ethnic and cultural groups. Perhaps the racial pride of blacks, Chicanos, Indians, and Asian Americans could lead to a new form of pluralism.

Review

The postwar period witnessed great agitation for racial justice—and some progress. Racial discrimination had resulted in serious social, political, educational, and economic disadvantages for nonwhites. For about a decade after World War II, demands for reform proceeded along quiet, legalistic lines. Then came the nonviolent direct action of Martin Luther King, Jr. Black nationalism also gained strength in the ghettos, and in the mid-sixties the ghettos exploded in arson and rioting. A government commission laid much of the blame for the violence on white racism. The fifties and sixties saw important progress in race relations. The Supreme Court decreed public school segregation to be illegal. Congress passed major civil rights legislation, and new employment opportunities were opened to black people. Politically, they came to play an increasingly important role, winning greater representation on both national and local levels. Yet Martin Luther King's dream remains unrealized. Unemployment, poverty, and involuntary segregation continue to plague millions of black Americans.

Militancy among Mexican Americans was directed against equally serious problems of poverty, illiteracy, disease, and substandard housing. In the late forties returning war veterans of Mexican background spurred a new movement aimed at combatting discrimination. In the sixties the Chicano movement, which began in southern California and spread throughout the barrios, was basically an expression of the militancy of students. The Chicano movement emphasized pride of heritage. César Chávez and "Corky" Gonzales represented different approaches to improving the lot of the Mexican American. Each had followers and critics. Chicano educators believed that biculturalism would best equip Chicano youngsters with the self-esteem and educational success necessary to escape poverty.

Indians occupied the bottom of the ladder in affluent America. They had the lowest income and shortest life-span of any group. Social conditions deteriorated on the reservations. President Eisenhower briefly tried to terminate the reservations. Most Indian leaders viewed the program of termination skeptically, and it ended as a practical failure shortly after it started. Presidents Kennedy and Johnson favored self-determination for Indians but were unsuccessful at implementing long-term reforms. President Nixon also favored self-determination for Indians and ordered a shake-up of the Bureau of Indian Affairs. Indian militants arrived in Washington in 1972 with a major new program for policy reform. But their proposals were forgotten in an avalanche of violence that included the second siege of Wounded Knee, South Dakota.

Recent decades have ushered in a new era for Asian Americans. A softening of immigration laws permitted a major influx of Chinese, most of whom settled in California. In San Francisco's Chinatown, problems of overcrowding, disease, illiteracy, and juvenile delinquency worsened as the population swelled. Japanese Americans recovered from their wartime detention swiftly and quietly. Favorable legislation helped them recoup some of the losses they had suffered. Soon they surpassed all other groups in California in average years of schooling completed. The Japanese Americans of Hawaii attained positions of power in both business and politics. Even on the mainland the formerly despised racial group became thoroughly accepted in a few short years.

Questions

1. Identify and give the significance of the following: (a) Rosa Parks, (b) Civil Rights Act of 1964, (c) United Farm Workers, (d) *Brown* v. *Board of Education of Topeka*, (e) Black Power, (f) termination, and (g) biculturalism.

2. Describe the two major strategies adopted by black activists. How did these strategies compare to the ones used by blacks in the late nineteenth century?

3. Is America a racist country? Explain your answer, with special reference to the events of the past three decades.

4. List the most important gains made by racial minorities since the end of World War II. Which are the most important accomplishments? In your opinion, what still remains to be accomplished in order to bring about a solution to racial issues?

5. Do you believe biculturalism is a healthy approach to minority problems? Explain.

By 1975 the American "melting pot" had not yet produced a homogeneous country, and ethnic differences still corresponded to economic divisions. As Nathan Glazer and Daniel Moynihan observed in 1960, "In New York City, when one speaks of the Negroes and Puerto Ricans, one also means unorganized and unskilled workers, who hold poorly paying jobs in the laundries, hotels, restaurants, small factories or who are on relief. When one says Jews, one also means small shopkeepers, professionals, better-paid skilled workers in the garment industries. When one says Italians, one also means homeowners in Staten Island, the North Bronx, Brooklyn, and Queens." Whether ethnic distinctions would continue when economic differences are reduced was yet to be seen in the coming decades.

37

37
A Time for Pluralism

When Martin Luther King, Jr., led his open-housing crusade into Cicero, Illinois, in the 1960s, an angry crowd greeted him with the chant, "Two-four-six-eight, we don't want to integrate!" King's head was bloodied by a rock. He faced similar encounters in the heart of nearby Chicago. At first he attributed the violence to southern whites newly arrived in the North. Closer inspection showed that his opponents were mainly people with Lithuanian, Irish, Polish, and Italian backgrounds. They had formed neighborhood organizations to "preserve their homes and schools." Throughout the northeastern and central states the civil rights movement was producing a backlash. Part of it came from "white ethnics"—descendants of immigrants from southern and eastern Europe. They were stirred up by black militancy, costly government programs for blacks, and the prospect of black people moving into their neighborhoods. Was this a simple case of white racism? Or was there more to the story?

As late as the 1950s the melting pot seemed to have fused all of America's ethnic groups into "one nation, indivisible." In the sixties the idea of cultural pluralism gained new acceptance in America. One commentator wrote that "cultural pluralism now contends with the melting-pot ideal as the goal governing the relationship among the peoples of the United States." The term *pluralism* had wider application in the sixties, for it could be used to describe the religious situation as well as ethnic developments.

Rise of the White Ethnics

Assimilation continues

Examining long-term trends in assimilation from around the First World War to the seventies, historians Leonard Dinnerstein and David M. Reimers concluded that in the mid-seventies "we are on the threshold of the disappearance of the European ethnic minorities." They cited the disuse of foreign languages in immigrant homes and churches and the slow decline of foreign-language newspapers. The loss of members by immigrant organizations was another indicator of assimilation. So too was the trend toward interfaith marriage.

Marriages across religious boundaries were becoming more common in the younger generation and were better accepted by the general population. Marriage between Catholics and Protestants was approved by two thirds of those responding to a Gallup poll in the seventies. Those Americans who were better educated and more mobile and had higher incomes were the most likely to intermarry or to tolerate interfaith marriage. The spread of higher education contributed to the trend because at college young men and women were more apt to meet and learn about people with varying cultural backgrounds. The "triple melting-pot" pattern noted by some earlier students of assimilation (see p. 617) seemed to be weakening.

The white ethnics

It is too soon to sound the death knell of ethnic identity in America. Other groups besides white ethnics were becoming more self-conscious. The increased pride of Mexican Americans has already been cited. The Soviet repression of freedom fighters in Czechoslovakia, Poland, and Hungary angered many Americans with ancestors or relatives from those countries. The influx of Puerto Ricans into New York City aroused established ethnic groups. Jewish identity was heightened by the Arab-Israeli contest in the Middle East. Because many white ethnics came from the blue-collar and lower-middle class, they felt the pinch of inflation and higher taxes keenly, and this was a factor in stimulating ethnic consciousness. Northern Ireland's civil war between Catholics and Protestants led to rallies, fund raisings, and political speech making in Irish American communities.

There were 40 to 70 million white ethnics in the country in the 1960s, depending on which groups came under this heading. Most thought of themselves as neither rich nor poor, but as working people. A large majority earned from $10,000 to $15,000 yearly. Most had Catholic, Greek Orthodox, or Russian Orthodox religious affiliations. They were *not* WASPs.

Though third-generation Americans had usually lost their grandparents' Old World languages, they often retained their ethnic identity in food selection and religious practices. "What the son wishes to forget," immigration historian Marcus Hansen has observed, "the grandson wishes to remember." Whereas children born to immigrants often felt ashamed of the way their parents spoke English, dressed, and ate, the third generation felt no such pain. The grandchildren felt more secure about their nationality and often resented attempts by WASPs to homogenize them. So they returned to those customs of their grandparents that they could duplicate. Young families of Italian and Jewish background commuted weekly from the suburbs to New York City to stock up on pasta and bagels or to eat in ethnic restaurants. In the fifties younger Italians attended Catholic mass more regularly than before, while many young Jewish families affiliated with synagogues. The trend slowed in the sixties, but for the time being, institutional religion was especially important in the ethnic suburbs.

During the sixties some liberals had stereotyped the white ethnics as "flag-wavers and racist." Michael Novak, author of *The Rise of the Unmeltable Ethnics* (1972), tried to correct the image. He suggested that the ethnics were possibly more antiliberal than they were antiblack. To them it seemed that liberal WASPs who demanded integration for black people usually lived in lily-white suburbs and sent their own children to private schools. Also, the ethnics took the work ethic seriously and resented anyone—including "welfare cheaters" and affluent college youth—who seemed to mock hard work and thrift. If white ethnics showed fierce contempt for flag burners, draft dodgers, and other opponents of the Vietnam War, there were historic reasons for this. Traditionally, WASP Americans had questioned the ethnics' loyalty to the U.S. Since 1917 many immigrants' sons and grandsons had died "proving" their love of country.

All immigrant groups continued to show signs of social mobility, improving their status from one generation to the next. Yet some that started at the bottom had not progressed as quickly as others. The Poles, Hungarians, and Russians, for example, began as unskilled workers in the factory system at the end of the nineteenth century and were just reaching middle-income status. In schooling and educational attainments they lagged behind Jews and white Protestants. They charged, like other white ethnics, that they were the victims of discrimination. They pointed out that in Buffalo, New York, a city with a 40 percent Polish American population, the State University law school in 1970 had only twenty-three Polish American students in a total enrollment of seven hundred. In addition the Poles were almost totally excluded from bank management in that city.

Ethnic groups showed particular resentment against ethnic slurs. The Italian gangster was a favorite stereotype of television and motion pictures. Asserting that it totally distorted reality, Italian Americans tried to combat it. When the novel *The Godfather* was being made into a film, the Italian American Civil Rights League and the Italian-American Defamation League confronted Paramount Pictures, demanding that it delete from the film any direct references to the "Mafia." Since Paramount had never intended to use that term, it "compromised." For similar reasons Mexican Americans protested the use of the "Frito Bandido" in television commercials, and Polish Americans denounced the use of the "Polish joke" in the media.

Some ethnic leaders tended to play upon racial and ethnic fears, but many tried to encourage dialogue across racial and ethnic boundaries and to bring about genuine respect and understanding. Large umbrella organizations, funded by the Ford Foundation or the Catholic church, pressed for scholarly studies in the field of ethnic affairs. The National Center for Urban Ethnic Affairs, headed by Monsignor Geno C. Baroni, was a notable organization of this type.

The Calumet Community Congress founded in 1970 was said to be "the largest and most successful community organization in America." It united 150 diverse organizations centered in a white ethnic working-class area south of Chicago. Founded by followers of the late Saul Alinsky, a Chicago-based community organizer, it tackled a variety of specific issues that were neglected by unions, including environmental pollution. The Congress consisted mainly of Poles, Germans, Czechs, and Hungarians. The Catholic church was a major supporter.

Some organizations concentrated on preventing violent racial disputes at the

An Italian-American grand-mother proudly presides over a family gathering at mealtime. Mario Puzo observed: "Like the character in Sandburg's poem who had inscribed on his tomb-stone, 'He et what was set before him,' the American-Italian always accepted life with enormous appetite."

neighborhood level. The Black-Polish Conference in Detroit and the North Ward Cultural and Educational Center in Newark performed valuable services along these lines. The National Housing Conference, consisting of delegates from over two hundred organizations, came together to discuss government housing policy and the activity of real estate interests. Though white ethnics predominated, the meetings included black and Latino delegates. Participants in Chicago's Citizens Action Program (CAP), an alliance of one hundred community organizations representing diverse racial and ethnic backgrounds, shared an interest in preserving their homes in older, deteriorating neighborhoods. When the government refused to include them in urban renewal projects, and savings and loan institutions refused to lend them money for home improvements, they threatened to withdraw some $55 million in savings. In this way CAP began to compel the banking industry to help them save their property.

Ethnic politics

Although unrestricted immigration from Europe had ended in the 1920s, the ethnic vote became an increasingly important factor in politics. As ethnic groups moved into the middle class, they demanded, and usually got, leadership positions in political organizations. They also made greater demands on the government. While this was especially true in the northeastern and north central states, it was increasingly true also in Texas, Florida, and California, where the influx of

Spanish-speaking immigrants had a growing impact.

Ethnic politics affected both parties. In 1948 the Democrats created the "Nationalities Division" as a show of gratitude to white ethnics who supported Truman's Cold War foreign policy. The GOP followed suit by forming the "All American Origins Division." Ethnic representation in Congress rose steadily over the years. The Irish had long led the way as ethnics in the Democratic party, but the Italians, Poles, and Jews (as well as blacks) were beginning to catch up. The 1960 victory of John F. Kennedy, a third-generation American of Irish Catholic descent opened the door a bit wider to all ethnics. Kennedy was not unscarred by prejudice and discrimination. A friend recalled that when his brother Edward was denounced for cheating on a college exam, John Kennedy privately bristled at WASP Americans. "They go in more for stealing from stockholders and banks."

City politics had a strong ethnic bias. A common practice at City Hall in metropolitan areas was to maintain a racial and ethnic quota for public jobs. Political parties devised ethnically and racially balanced tickets. In some cities WASPs were, like every other group, a numerical minority. Occasionally they assumed the role of mediator among various ethnic and racial factions. Mayor John Lindsay of New York was a case in point. New York City's Jews, blacks, and Puerto Ricans trusted him more than they trusted his two Italian American opponents in 1969, and helped reelect him as mayor.

White ethnics accused both major political parties of making false promises and engaging in tokenism. In 1954 the GOP promised to help "liberate the captive peoples of eastern Europe." But when the Hungarians rebeled against Soviet domination in 1956 and Russian soldiers killed 25,000 Hungarian civilians, Eisenhower refused to intervene. His stand cost the GOP some support among ethnic voters.

The GOP worked especially hard to lure back ethnic voters in the elections of 1968 and 1972. In his first campaign Richard M. Nixon narrowed the choice of his vice-presidential running mate to Spiro T. Agnew, of Greek background, and John Volpe, of Italian ancestry. He selected Agnew, but appointed Volpe to his cabinet. Candidate Agnew (the name was shortened from Anagnotopoulus) appealed to the pride of the ethnics: "We are a melting-pot nation that has for over two centuries distilled something new and, I believe, sacred," said Agnew. Running on the Democratic ticket was Maine Senator Edmund Muskie, who was of Polish American background. According to most estimates the GOP did win away some ethnic voters from the Democrats, though not a majority.

Could Americans sharpen their ethnic self-awareness without destroying national unity? Some feared it was impossible to do both. And yet more and more prominent Americans were abandoning the melting-pot idea in favor of cultural pluralism. "The 'melting pot' . . . is no longer working," declared Senator Richard Schweiker of Pennsylvania, "and too many people in modern society have lost the important values of community, identity, traditions, and family solidarity." He sponsored an Ethnic Studies Bill to "help bring about better understanding" among diverse groups of Americans and "encourage ethnic pride and ethnic identity." President Nixon signed it into law. Under its provisions colleges and universities prepared school curriculums and teaching aids containing information about various ethnic groups.

A new immigration policy

Democrats had long promised to liberalize the country's immigration policy, but during the early Cold War years Congress had not obliged. In fact, in 1952 it passed a tougher law, the McCarran-Walter Immigration Act, over President Truman's veto. The new law gave the Justice Department a weapon for screening out and deporting "alien subversives." It retained the national origins formula developed in 1924 (see p. 615). "The times . . . are too perilous for us to tinker blindly with our basic institutions . . ." Senator McCarran proclaimed. "If we scrap the national origins formula we will, in the course of a generation or so, change the ethnic and cultural composition of this nation."

After steady pressure by Presidents Kennedy and Johnson, Congress enacted the Immigration Act of 1965, which finally ended the national origins quota system. It set immigration limits according to this country's occupational needs, giving top priority to immigrants with skills. It also favored political refugees. There was now a total yearly limit of 170,000 immigrants from all nations, except those in the Western Hemisphere. These received a total yearly quota of 120,000.

The new policy was particularly helpful to eastern, central, and southern Europeans and Asians. Between 1951 and 1969, three and a half million immigrants came to the U.S., reestablishing it as the major "immigrant nation" of the world. The newcomers included 650,000 from Germany, 375,000 from Italy, 317,000 from Britain, 750,000 from Mexico, 500,000 from Asia, and 500,000 from the West Indies, notably from Puerto Rico and Cuba. Between 1965 and 1974 the yearly immigration from Asia rose from 21,000 to 131,000. About one quarter of the yearly immigration in the mid-seventies was Asian.

Modern American institutions were in some ways less equipped to cope with immigrants than they had been half a century earlier. The settlement houses and immigrant aid societies that had once cushioned newcomers against culture shock were gone. Government welfare workers were already

The idea behind this discriminatory [quota] policy was, to put it baldly, that Americans with English or Irish names were better people and better citizens than Americans with Italian or Greek or Polish names.

HARRY S. TRUMAN (1884–1972)
On vetoing the McCarran-Walter
Immigration Act

overworked and unable to deal with the individual's total needs. Most schools failed to meet the special language needs of immigrants, and this tended to isolate and insulate some of them.

Puerto Rican, Cuban, and Vietnamese arrivals

Puerto Rico became a U.S. possession in 1898, and its residents U.S. citizens in 1917. This made them eligible to migrate to the mainland without any quota restrictions. During and after the Second World War they were drawn by the opening of job opportunities. Puerto Rico's soaring population (its density per square mile was 546 in 1940 and 645 in 1950), its labor surplus, and its grinding poverty for 90 percent of the people, gave young families strong incentives to seek their fortunes on the mainland.

New York City, accessible by air from San Juan, Puerto Rico, was their major port of entry. By 1960 some 600,000 *Borinqueños* (from the Indian word for Puerto Rico, *Borinquen*) lived there, a tenfold increase over 1940. Like the poorest European immigrant arrivals of the last century, they suffered greatly from crowded housing, joblessness, disease, illiteracy, and juvenile delinquency. Most were unskilled and they engaged in menial work. Some entered the needle trade. With one third of all Puerto Rican families on relief, the average family income in 1970 was $4900. They represented a racial mixture of African and Spanish peoples and found racial discrimination far more pronounced here than on the island. The Puerto Ricans' dependency on Spanish coupled with the schools' inability to provide bilingual education, proved a severe handicap to their social advancement.

Meanwhile, through a program of family planning, improved public medicine, reduction of illiteracy, and increased industrialization, the residents of Puerto Rico experienced dramatic improvements in the standard of living since the 1950s. This slowed the rate of migration to the mainland and even encouraged a reverse movement.

The present generation of Puerto Ricans attempted to confront poverty and discrimination in an organized way, and produced a few articulate voices such as Congressman Herman Badillo. Yet on the whole, the Puerto Rican community lacked the self-help organizations and leadership of the sort that had aided other immigrant groups to improve their status. The church has been relatively weak in Puerto Rican culture and therefore was not able to provide the direction it did with European immigrants.

Another Spanish-speaking group has left an indelible imprint on the East Coast: the Cubans of south Florida. The refugees from Fidel Castro's Cuba got off to a better start and made more rapid progress than the Puerto Ricans. As anti-Communist émigrés they received a warm welcome in Miami, their major entry port, as well as in other cities where they settled. By agreement with Castro the U.S. government airlifted some 230,000 Cubans between 1965 and 1971. The new arrivals faced immediate problems of housing, schooling, and jobs, but they had several important advantages. First, as measured by schooling, skills, and income, they were the elite of Cuba. In their native land, 80 percent of them had had above average yearly incomes. The Caucasian racial element was more dominant among them, and the color bar therefore less

of a factor. Moreover, Congress provided special welfare benefits and a full range of social services to assist the Cubans, more than for most native-born poor people.

In no time at all, the majority reached middle-class status; in fact, said one study, they did so "faster than any other ethnic group since the Huguenots of colonial times." Only 13 percent of those in the U.S. lived below the poverty line in 1973. That is, their poverty rate is comparable to that of the U.S. population as a whole, and only half as great as that for Chicanos or Puerto Ricans. Cuban children mastered English swiftly and did well in school. By 1975 Miami had a majority Cuban population and a decidedly Latin flavor. Cubans had achieved notable success in restaurants and construction, gas stations and banks, hotels and factories, as well as in a variety of the professions. The city's Cuban American newspaper had a daily circulation of 600,000. The swift rise and growing dominance of Cubans in Miami offended some native-born Anglo-Americans. Bitter words were exchanged publicly between Cubans who supported bilingual schooling and Anglos who opposed it.

About three hundred anti-Castro groups sprouted in south Florida in the early 1960s, although many dwindled away after the Bay of Pigs disaster. The émigrés' increasing sentiment for peaceful coexistence between the U.S. and Cuba stirred up anti-Castro terrorists, who may have set off as many as fifty bombings in 1974–1975.

Following the end of the Vietnam War in 1975, President Ford granted sanctuary to over 130,000 South Vietnamese refugees. The majority appeared to be well educated and from upper-income groups. Initially, their arrival caused a negative reaction from those who feared it would increase job competition in a time of high unemployment and swell the size of welfare rolls. The old irrational fear of "Asian diseases" was also expressed. The opposition subsided, though, and organizations and individuals volunteered sponsorship of the new immigrants. Congress allocated $405 million to pay for resettlement. How the Vietnamese would adjust to American life remained a matter for speculation.

It is not possible to predict with any certainty the future course of the ethnic factor in the U.S. Based on the recent past the prospect is for two contradictory trends to continue side by side. One is a strengthening of ethnic self-awareness and a belief in pluralism. Many people will continue to reject the melting pot as either an ideal or a reality. The other trend is assimilation and social mobility for ethnic groups. Through the influence of mass education and the media ethnic boundaries will continue to blur.

The Post-Protestant Era

A modern religious awakening

The religious history of the United States since World War II divides itself into two parts. The first, a time of revival, took place in the late forties and fifties. The second occurred in the late sixties and seventies and involved ferment and crisis. The Cold War and the threat of nuclear war helped stimulate a major religious awakening in America. Skeptics scoffed that regular church attendance was the latest suburban fad. Still, the revival compared in some ways to earlier awakenings and amazed even the most blasé observers of the American scene.

Many signs pointed the way to a revival of religion. In 1950 over half the population belonged to churches and synagogues, and eight years later membership climbed to nearly two thirds of the total population. (By comparison, in 1860 only about 20 percent of Americans belonged to any church.) There were increases in Sunday School enrollments, church and synagogue construction, the publication and sale of religious books, enrollment in college courses in religion, and attendance at revival meetings. Big audiences came to hear sophisticated theologians like Jacques Maritain, Paul Tillich, Reinhold Niebuhr, and Martin Buber. For the first time, a religious awakening touched all denominations, including Catholics and Jews.

Of course, nothing could deny the continuing long-term trend toward secularism in the United States, as in the rest of Western society. But opinion surveys of the 1950s showed that over 95 percent of Americans believed in God, about 90 percent believed in prayer, and 77 percent believed in an afterlife — although only 5 percent expressed any fear of hell.

Some who praised religious values deliberately avoided any denominational label, and put their "faith in faith." In President Eisenhower's words, "Our government makes no sense unless it is founded in a deeply felt religious faith — and I don't care what it is." "In God we trust" was made the official national motto. The words "under God" were added to the Pledge of Allegiance, in imitation of Lincoln's Gettysburg Address. The "faith in faith" and the affirmation of belief in a nondenominational God were an extension of the "civil religion" that emerged in the early days of the Republic (see pp. 115–116).

The popular preachers

Positive thinkers attracted a large following. Rabbi Joshua Liebman's *Peace of Mind* (1946) and Norman Vincent Peale's *The Power of*

Positive Thinking (1952) advised readers how to avoid personal paralysis. The first words of Peale's book told the reader: "Believe in yourself! Have faith in your abilities! Without a humble but reasonable confidence in your own powers you cannot succeed." These works were in the American tradition in looking to religion for an immediate practical purpose.

Evangelical Christians, those who emphasized spiritual salvation through revival, also prospered. At an eight-week revival in Los Angeles in 1949 three thousand people made "commitments to Christ" following the electrifying sermons of the young Dr. Billy Graham. The personable Baptist minister later took his crusade to stadiums, churches, and halls all over the world. TV made Graham a household figure. Some questioned whether his converts remained converted after his crusade left town. Others criticized him for evading the social issues of urban decay, war, racism, and poverty. But though detractors predicted his early decline, he seemed to become a permanent religious force.

By no means did all American believers accept the neutral "faith in faith." Some believed it would undermine Christianity, the "true religion" of America. It displeased some advocates of fundamentalism (the belief in the Bible as a factual record of past events and future prophesies). In the 1950s Fundamentalists joined forces with leaders of the radical right such as Robert Welch of the John Birch Society and Alabama's Governor George Wallace to propose an amendment to the Constitution making Christianity the official religion of the U.S. They also hoped to legalize prayer in the public schools. The proposed amendment and the school-prayer effort encountered fierce opposition and got nowhere. In the *Regents' Prayer Case* (1962) the Supreme Court held that prayer, even nonsectarian prayer, could not be offered in the public schools. Court critics argued that the justices were interfering with the free exercise of religion, but the High Court stayed with Jefferson and the First Amendment, adding another stone to the solid wall dividing church and state. The court's decision was felt as a severe blow to many Protestant Fundamentalists.

The highest level of church attendance was reached in 1955, when almost half of the country's adults went to church in a typical week. By 1959 the postwar revival began to fade. Attendance at Christian churches leveled off at about 40 percent in 1972. The drop was sharpest for Catholics: 72 percent attended church in 1955, only 57 percent in 1972.

Beyond the Puritan era

Sydney E. Ahlstrom, Yale professor of church history, has written that in the sixties "the age of the WASP [and] the age of the melting pot drew to a close." The election of the first Roman Catholic president in 1960 and the action of the Second Vatican Council of 1965 ended "a unified four-hundred-year period in the Anglo-American experience." Puritanism was no longer in the saddle, and the Catholic church had given up its age-old Counter-Reformation against Protestantism, in itself a revolutionary shift in doctrine.

A sign of the times was a turning away from Western religion by many young people. Under the sign of Aquarius, members of the counterculture from Berkeley to Boston searched for new and different religious experiences. Many drug users experimented with "psychedelic mysticism." The drug culture acquired a leader in Timothy Leary of the Harvard faculty. Astrology and the occult took hold; some ten thousand full-time astrologers practiced their craft in the U.S. in the 1970s. Eastern religions stressing love and peace appealed greatly to a generation turned off by the violence of the Vietnam War. Yoga, Zen Buddhism, and Transcendental Meditation (TM) had big followings in the colleges. "Life is here to enjoy—tell everyone—no one has to suffer anymore," announced Maharishi Mahesh Yogi, the leading spokesman for TM.

As the sixties unfolded, the movements for civil rights, black power, peace in Vietnam, and feminism had an unsettling effect on organized religion. The example of Martin Luther King, Jr., who went to jail for his convictions, impressed the liberal clergy, in particular the younger members. A few joined his civil rights demonstrations in the early sixties. Still, when Eugene Carson Blake, a prominent Presbyterian and Secretary General of the World Council of Churches, was arrested in a civil rights demonstration in 1966, many church leaders were horrified. Soon other members of the clergy became involved in welfare unions, tenant councils, rent strikes, school boycotts, civil rights marches, antiwar demonstrations, and a variety of other social causes. One theologian likened the new Christian radicals to the Social Gospelers at the turn of the century, or to European religious dissenters at the end of the Middle Ages. By the time Father Daniel Berrigan was arrested for antiwar activities, many religious denominations had been touched by social upheaval.

Black churches that did not somehow accommodate themselves to rising black consciousness suffered, while the ones that did acquired new status. The Nation of Islam (the Black Muslims) enjoyed a period of rapid growth. It appealed to the ghetto poor as a "therapy against the ravages of the white-dominated hell called America."

In the late sixties, just when youth seemed most turned off by Christianity, a strong revival touched many younger people. This was the Jesus movement that started in the Pentecostal churches (a twentieth-century religious movement of those who, loosely defined, "seek to be filled with the Holy Ghost") and spread to the older Christian denominations. The "Jesus people" or "Jesus

freaks," as advocates of this movement were known, often adopted the life style familiar to the counterculture, but in a more disciplined and puritanical way. They tried to follow Christ's life as an example, and worked for love, charity, peace, and social justice. In 1971 the movement found expression in a popular rock opera, *Jesus Christ, Superstar.*

Radical changes in the Catholic church

In 1970 there were about 48 million Catholics in the United States. Although outnumbered by the combined Protestant churches, they were the largest Christian denomination in the country. In fact, more of the world's Catholics lived here than in any other nation except Brazil and Italy. With a dozen senators and over one hundred representatives, Catholics boasted the largest congressional representation of any single church. The church operated more than ten thousand grade schools and high schools and owned $26 billion in assets. The days when it had been an embattled immigrant church in a Protestant country had long since passed.

Like the Roman Catholic church in all nations, the American church was greatly affected by the historic Vatican Council of 1962–1965 summoned by Pope John XXIII. The Council ushered in a new era in world religious history. In effect it ended the Counter-Reformation started by the church four centuries earlier in an effort to destroy Protestantism. It encouraged a new ecumenical spirit in Christianity and, indeed, in religion generally.

In America, church services were thereafter to be said in English instead of Latin. Thus more people could understand the ritual. The altar became a simple table, and the communion rail that divided the priest from the congregation was often removed. The clergy was directed to preach from the Bible and the faithful to join in singing hymns.

Catholics were no longer required not to eat meat on Friday. Many of them went less frequently to confession than in the past.

Many of the changes in American Catholicism were intended to make the church more relevant to modern life. But they also destroyed some of the drama and mystery of the church and produced in some American Catholics anger, apathy, or restlessness. The number of converts to Catholicism fell off. Attracting and keeping new clergy became difficult. Questions of birth control and racial integration split both clergy and laity. Priests and nuns took up radical causes. Some married. An increasing number of the laity ignored the church's condemnation of artificial methods of birth control. These were disturbing trends within Catholicism. There was a growing polarization between traditional Catholics, who clung to the old ways, and liberal Catholics, who saw in the recent changes the dawn of a new day for the church.

Pope John's pastoral letter *Pacem in Terris* ("Peace on Earth") issued in 1963 stimulated a worldwide religious dialogue. Shortly after his death, the Second Vatican Council issued an important statement, "The Declaration on Religious Freedom," which strengthened the ecumenical movement. It showed that the Roman Catholic church was ready to engage in peaceful discussion with the Protestant churches. The Council also addressed itself to the age-old question of hostility between Gentile and Jew, and asserted that Jews were not "Christ killers."

Mergers had already begun to take place among various Protestant churches. For example, the Congregational-Christian church had joined with the Evangelical and Reformed churches to form the United Church of Christ. While actual merger between Catholics and Protestants seemed only a remote possibility, old hatreds appeared to dissipate as church leaders sat down to talk about beliefs they shared rather than issues that divided them.

The next pope, Paul VI, was more conservative and more to the liking of the American hierarchy. Still, most of the reforms initiated after the Second Vatican Council remained in effect and continued to have unsettling consequences.

John F. Kennedy's religious affiliation may have cost him 1.5 million votes in 1960, but the remarkable fact is that he won. He did so partly by facing the religious issue directly. In 1960 he entered the lion's den to address a meeting of Protestant ministers in Houston. JFK opposed federal aid to parochial schools and made it clear that his personal religious faith would in no way interfere with the performance of his constitutional duties as president of the United States. This helped his cause. However narrow the victory, it was of historic moment.

Severe financial pressures caused the Catholic church to seek federal aid for its schools. Facing a budgetary pinch, some 800 of the 11,350 Catholic schools simply did not reopen in September 1971. An argument for state support for parochial education was that unless the church continued its educational program, 2.1 million Catholic children would deluge the public classrooms and cause further problems there. President Nixon seemed to favor some form of aid to Catholic schools. But decisions of the Supreme Court made increased public aid to parochial schools difficult.

A revival of Jewish identity

An opinion poll in 1947 showed that only 18 percent of those Jews interviewed attended services at least once a month, while 65 percent of Protestants and 85 percent of Catholics did so. Soon, though, many Jews joined Reform or Conservative temples and went to services more regularly. In 1955, 31 percent of Jews in a poll said they had attended services recently. Orthodox Jewish rabbis suspected the motives of the new revival, attributing the rise in worship to a quest for assimilation. Sociologist Nathan Glazer agreed. "Middle-class suburban Jews wanted their children accepted by Gentile neighbors," he wrote, "and since religion was the American Way, parents joined temples." But the religious revival was as much an event for Jews as it was for Gentiles. Even many who rejected worship engaged in a serious study of Judaism.

Undoubtedly, the revival of Judaism was sparked by memories of the Holocaust—Germany's attempt to wipe out the Jewish people during World War II. Over 150,000 European Jews migrated to America after the war. Many were survivors of Nazi concentration camps who had spent time in displaced persons camps after the fall of Germany. They became a living reminder of the Holocaust.

The founding of the state of Israel in 1948 and its recurrent struggle with the Arab world strengthened Jewish identity in America. The sheer physical survival of Israel became a matter of grave concern to American Jews. Relatively few American Jews went there to settle permanently, but many contributed morally and financially to the support of the new Jewish state. Within days of the outbreak of the Six-Day War in 1967, Jewish groups in the U.S. had raised more than $170 million in emergency aid. During the Yom Kippur War of 1973 some ten thousand American Jews volunteered for civilian service in Israel. In addition, $100 million in cash was raised for social services on the home front in Israel.

In recent years about 80 percent of all religious Jews in America belonged to Reform or Conservative congregations, but one Orthodox group attracted a great deal of attention. These were the Hasidim ("pious ones"), members of a mystical eastern European sect that dates back to the eighteenth century. They were among the postwar immigrants to the U.S., settling first in areas of

"Whatever else a Jew may be," asserted Meir Kahane, "he is first and foremost a Jew, and let him not forget it if he wishes to survive. . . ."

New York City that were being vacated by earlier generations of Jews. Much of their time was spent in religious study with emphasis on prayers and the Torah. Their unique dress and traditional religious customs marked them off from other Jews. The Hasidim were a communal people. They opened kindergarten and all-day schools. Gradually they spread to other cities. They made a special appeal to younger American Jews who were flirting with Christian or Eastern religions. Their message to the youth was: "Identify!"

Despite the Hasidim, the vast majority of easten European Jews continued to show, in the most recent generation, a continuing trend toward social mobility and cultural assimilation. Their greatest impact continued to be in the entertainment and clothing industries, and in the arts and professions. Many achieved fame and success as actors, artists, musicians, social scientists, film producers, directors, and novelists.

The traditional commitment of Jews to education was a means of social mobility. Nearly half of all Jewish families in the country enjoyed a solidly middle-class income. Their successes tended to overshadow the fact that nearly 800,000 Jews lived below the poverty line and were overlooked by society.

Jewish writers were particularly prominent in the postwar period. The noted critic Alfred Kazin wrote, "I don't think that there has been anywhere in the history of the Jewish people anything quite like the influence that Jewish intellectuals have exerted on American culture." Novels by Saul Bellow, Bernard Malamud, and Philip Roth were commentaries not only on Jewish life in America but also on our society as a whole.

Of the more than 6 million American Jews, two fifths lived in and around New York City. They contributed greatly to its political, cultural, and economic life. One quarter of the city's inhabitants and almost half of its teachers were Jewish. This sometimes placed them on a collision course with blacks and Puerto Ricans who were trying to gain more control of ghetto schools.

Like all faiths, Judaism in the 1960s was said to be passing through a time of extreme crisis. The increase in interfaith marriages worried many rabbis, who were deeply aware of their shrinking congregations. They voiced concern over the "vanishing Jew."

The Central Conference of American Rabbis (Reform) in 1973 voted against letting Reform rabbis officiate at mixed marriage ceremonies. The New York Board of Rabbis, representing one thousand Orthodox and Conservative rabbis of metropolitan New York, voted to expel any rabbis from their organization who performed mixed marriages. Not all rabbis accepted this extreme position, though they all worried about the survival of Judaism as a religion and of the Jews as a people.

Although the U.S. was comparatively free of overt anti-Semitism in recent decades, this form of bigotry did find public expression from time to time. In the late sixties black radicals who identified with the anti-Zionism of the Arab world tried to arouse blacks against American Jews. The Anti-Defamation League of the B'nai B'rith, devoted to monitoring anti-Semitic activities, concluded in 1970 that less than one percent of the black community was affected by these efforts. Anti-Semitism surfaced again during the Arab oil embargo in 1974. Arab nations stated that they were withholding oil in retaliation for U.S. support for Israel. The immediate response of some Americans was to blame Jews in general, including American Jews, for the fuel crisis.

In 1974 General George S. Brown, chairman of the Joint Chiefs of Staff, stirred old fears when, in discussing Middle East problems before a college audience, he stated that "Jewish influence" in Congress "is so strong, you wouldn't believe, now. . . . They own, you know, the banks in this country, the newspapers." That a high public official should voice this often disproved myth disquieted the entire Jewish community.

Review

A decline in the number of immigrant organizations and foreign-language newspapers coupled with an increase in interfaith mar-

riages characterized the long-term trend toward assimilation in the postwar years. But a countertrend occurred in the 1960s: the "rise of the white ethnics." They tended to be working-class, of the Catholic or Greek Orthodox or Russian Orthodox faiths, and conservative in outlook. Like the blacks who were becoming increasingly aware of their own cultural background, the white ethnics also asked, "Who are we?—Who am I?"

Ethnic politics remained a major factor on both local and national levels. The ethnics sought important leadership positions, and their representation rose in Congress. Many of them were wooed by the GOP in the 1968 and 1972 presidential elections.

A new law in 1965 ended the national origins quota system of immigration and increased the flow of new immigrants. Refugees from Castro's Cuba, many from the professional and middle classes, received special treatment that helped them to adapt successfully, as a group, to life in the U.S. For the most part, though, there were too few social services to help bewildered immigrants. Welfare workers now dealt on a less complete and personal level with the 3.5 million persons who arrived between 1951 and 1969. Groups like the Puerto Ricans, who came in hopes of improving their lives, often ended up unemployed and trapped in overcrowded urban ghettos. In 1975 South Vietnamese were the newest immigrants to the country.

A religious revival, marked by an increase in church attendance and new enthusiasm for revival meetings, followed World War II. It peaked in the mid-fifties and then suffered a slow relapse. Churches seemed to be losing their grip on the young. During the sixties social movements affected organized religion. Following the example of Martin Luther King, Jr., more and more members of the clergy involved themselves directly in social causes.

By 1970 the Catholics were the nation's largest Christian denomination. They had the biggest representation in Congress of any single church. JFK's election represented a historic culmination of the rise of Catholics in politics. The Second Vatican Council and the teachings of Pope John XXIII effected great changes in the church. While the church came closer to the people, it also opened itself up to controversy. Government support for parochial schools continued to be a subject of public debate, but Supreme Court decisions continued to reinforce the wall that separated church and state.

Jewish self-awareness was strengthened by the memory of Hitler's destruction of six million Jews and, subsequently, by the existence of the state of Israel. The traditional Jewish commitment to education had helped American Jews achieve middle-class status. They especially influenced the postwar literary scene. Some religious leaders were concerned by the rise in interfaith marriages. Most American Jews were grateful for the apparent decline in anti-Semitism. Still, any stirring of such prejudice was considered a danger by a people permanently scarred by the Holocaust.

Questions

1. What forces led to the rising self-awareness of white ethnics in the U.S.?
2. Identify and explain the significance of: (a) Calumet Community Council, (b) Hasidim, (c) *Regents' Prayer Case*, (d) Pope John XXIII, (e) *The Power of Positive Thinking*, (f) McCarran-Walter Immigration Act.
3. Describe how the ethnic factor has affected recent American politics.
4. How did the Immigration Act of 1965 change earlier immigration policy? Do you believe it is healthier for the nation to have a restrictive or a liberal immigration policy?
5. How did the postwar religious revival affect the major religious groups?
6. Do you think differences between ethnic and religious groups are decreasing or increasing? Which trend is preferable to you? Explain your reasons.

women and the family

The world has been split in half for much too long—between masculine and feminine. . . . Perhaps our most crucial task at this point of history—a task for women and men—is not to celebrate these so-called differences between our natures but to question boldly . . . whether they properly exist at all, or whether they do not violently distort us, whether they do not split our common humanity.

BARBARA DEMING
Feminist theorist, writer

38

38

The New Feminism

The "death of the family" is so old a prophecy—the ancient Greek philosopher Plato mentions it—that it must be taken with a grain of salt. Yet some people seem afraid that this calamity will happen tomorrow. They are unnerved by news of unwed couples living together, illegitimate births, abortion on demand, skyrocketing divorce rates, "open" marriage, group marriage and "swinging" couples. But the family as an institution has shown remarkable staying power. In America it has functioned well on the colonial frontier, in the immigrant ghettos, on isolated farms, and in middle-class suburbs. The nuclear family (defined as "mama, papa, and the kids") has long been, and remains, the most basic type. There are even social scientists who still regard it as a "biological fact," like an anthill or beehive. In any case, it will most probably outlast all of us living today.

This chapter starts with a brief description of modern family life. It continues with a consideration of the third wave of feminism that started in the sixties. (The first phase of the feminist movement in America spanned the period from the 1830s to the Civil War; the second lasted from about 1890 to 1920.) The current women's liberation movement differs from previous feminist movements in the greater variety of goals it has sought and in the impact it has had on the whole society. Certainly it has affected family life more directly and powerfully than had either of its predecessors. Although its forward motion is not yet spent, some estimate of its historic impact is already possible.

The Nuclear Family in the Nuclear Age

Postwar homemakers

The return home of the GIs after 1945 encouraged a new emphasis on family life. Men and women craved the stable relationships that had been denied them during the war years. Anxiety about the atomic bomb and the Cold War drew people closer together at home. The media and the advertising industry underscored the theme of families searching for warmth and security. A leading women's journal called itself "the magazine of togetherness." "The family that prays together stays together" was a popular billboard slogan. Large families became the fashion, as the postwar "baby boom" got under way. The birth rate, having fallen to 18 per 1000 people in the midst of the great depression, reached 27 per 1000 by 1947 and leveled off at 25 per 1000 for a decade afterward. At first, the baby boom stimulated the economy. Later it led to acute teacher and housing shortages, and it had much to do with an increase in crime and unemployment. But at first most people saw it as an unmixed blessing.

Women were urged to forego jobs and careers in favor of motherhood and domesticity. Magazine articles, sermons, editorials, advertisements, and books by leading social scientists trumpeted the messages: woman's real place was the home. Films and TV reinforced the image of the happy homemaker. Businessmen were well aware that women were the leading buyers of consumer goods. They spent millions of dollars on ads and commercials that pictured women as contented wives, mothers, and homemakers.

This ideal version of wife-mother-homemaker, which was later called "the feminine mystique," was reinforced by the writings of social scientists. Psychologists reinforced the image of women as nurturing rather than creative individuals, intuitive rather than intelligent, submissive rather than adventurous, and emotional rather than logical. Placing tremendous stress on early childhood training as a way of developing wholesome adults, they emphasized that only mothers could care for the young successfully. Women social scientists sometimes embraced these ideas as heartily as men. Anthropologist Margaret Mead, herself a mother as well as a brilliant career woman, suggested at the time that it was better if women stayed at home.

But domesticity was being undermined by important social factors. In 1947 women made up only 28 percent of the American work force. By 1951 the proportion of women reached 31 percent, where it stayed for about a decade. Then it climbed dramatically, reaching 42 percent in 1970. Women were going to work in record numbers, whether from necessity or choice, whether to gain independence, or supplement family income and maintain the middle-class life style.

Advances in medical science encouraged women to pattern their lives around jobs or careers outside the home. For one thing, the life expectancy of women had increased from fifty years in 1900 to sixty-five years in 1950. Also, the oral contraceptives perfected in the 1960s made it easier than ever before for a woman to limit pregnancy. The average woman, who now had her last child at age twenty-six, could, if she desired, spend many years doing something other than housework.

The nuclear family in recent times

Though divorce and broken families were on the increase, and though the number of marriages seemed to be dropping, the great majority of Americans still found marriage ap-

Middle-class suburban housewives gathered together regularly for a ritual of plastic consumerism known as the "Tupperware party." The pleased hostess of the party pictured here explained, "I enjoy giving a Tupperware party in my home. It gives me a chance to talk to my friends. But really, Tupperware is a homemaker's dream, you save time and money because your food keeps longer."

pealing. Most adults married early, and if their first effort failed, they married again. The average marrying age in 1970 was near twenty-three for men and about twenty-one for women. Perhaps marriage was popular because divorce was so easy. By 1970 one in three unions was breaking up—twice as many as in 1935. Whether this meant shakier marital relations to start with or a greater willingness for unhappy couples to part was hard to know.

Traditionally a man had to be self-supporting before taking on a wife, and many men had delayed the move or remained bachelors. Now it was common for a wife to help support the family. It was also increasingly common for parents to subsidize the marriages of their offspring. While taking money from in-laws and parents might lead to emotional tangles, it enabled couples to marry sooner. In addition, the government, through veterans' benefits, FHA loans, and unemployment compensation encouraged marriage.

Older people fared less well in modern urban society then they had formerly. With the lengthening age span there were more of them. But families seemed less willing or able to care for the aged at home. Social Security benefits alone did not pay enough for most senior citizens to live by themselves above the poverty line. Sometimes they were sent to live, and die, in dismal nursing homes—"junkyards for old people."

Despite the country's relative affluence, American children were less well cared for than in some other advanced nations. Twelve other nations had lower infant mortality rates in 1972. In a former era the young children of working mothers would have been cared for by grandparents, aunts, or other relatives. Now hundreds of thousands of latch-key children had to fend for themselves during day light hours or received only nominal supervision. Some 6 million children had working mothers, but there was room for fewer than 700,000 of them in licensed day-care centers. President Nixon vetoed a day-care program, attacking the bill for its "family weakening implications."

While the nuclear family was still the dominant form, the number of families headed by women was increasing noticeably. Owing to death, divorce, separation, and desertion, the number of female heads of family rose from 5.6 to 6.6 million between 1970 and 1974. Over one third of these families lived below the poverty line. Welfare rules encouraged the trend, for they automatically reduced the benefits for the single woman with children who remarried, regardless of the actual need of her family.

The family was touched and changed by the women's movement more directly than it ever had been in the past. By 1972 nationwide magazines like *Life* were reporting that the "ideas of women's liberation are convulsing families" everywhere. More than ever before, fathers were changing dirty diapers and doing other forms of "woman's work." Some couples revived the marriage contract used by nineteenth-century feminists, in which husbands and wives outlined their duties in writing. The number of middle-class women who walked out on their husbands and children ("runaway wives") was beginning to increase. Countless unwed couples were living together, sometimes with the approval of parents. Unmarried women who gave birth were beginning to keep their babies rather than putting them up for adoption. "Experimental marriages," "open marriages," "communal families," and other alternative family life styles were attempted and publicized. Perhaps most important, a growing number of husbands and wives in traditional families were for the first time consciously and critically examining the roles they played within the home.

The birth dearth

After major wars there is often a baby boom. Yet the newest boom in a sense defied the long-term logic of history. Large families are the rule in traditional agricultural societies, not in modern industrial societies. So it was natural that in the U.S. the average number of births per mother should decline from seven births in 1800 to about two in 1930. The rise to four in 1950 was a reversal of the long-term trend.

Family planning has been increasingly accepted among the middle class in the twentieth century, although a study in 1970 showed that 44 percent of all births among married women in the previous five years were unplanned. "The pill," an effective oral contraceptive, became readily obtainable around 1960. Despite opposition from the Catholic church to the new birth control technology, the popularity of the pill spread also to Catholic families.

In 1971 came an unexpected "birth dearth." Women began having fewer babies than predicted, and from a peak of 27 per 1000 in 1947, the birthrate dropped to 17.3 per 1000. Several explanations were offered: more women now worked, the average age for having the first child was rising, couples were deciding to have fewer children to protect their affluence, and there was concern about overpopulation. If the baby bust continued, the U.S. would reach zero population growth (ZPG) within seventy years or so. Meantime, it worried the baby food manufacturers and pleased most school boards. Those concerned about the quality of life in America and the overpopulation of the globe heartily approved of the trend.

The generation gap

While the rebellion of youth is part of the human condition everywhere and at all times, in the U.S. in the sixties its violence was unprecedented. Many young people seemed to reject the basic values of the older generation totally. In some households parents and their young adult offspring found themselves arguing bitterly over almost every topic of discussion: civil rights, war, work, spending, saving, education, the use of drugs, and the length of hair. Ironically, it was affluent middle-class youth that most strongly denied middle-class values.

Some intellectuals saw the youth rebellion of the sixties as having lasting cultural importance—far beyond affecting the length of hair or the styles of dress. They saw in it an alternative to an existing culture that glorified science, technology, and bureaucracy to excess. The "counterculture," as they called it, would bring about profound changes in the "straight" culture. It would affect music and cinema, education and politics, and above all values concerning work, love, courtship, family, and community. It could, they believed, humanize the existing culture. Thus Charles Reich referred to the youth rebellion as the "greening of America." For the most part, though, the older generation was more than a little frightened by the uprising of young people. Vice-President Agnew voiced a widespread resentment when he blamed it on misguided college professors and "permissive" parents. The worst shouting across the generation gap stopped with the end of ground fighting in Vietnam, but it had left wounds in many homes that were not easily healed.

The core of the problem for women today is . . . a problem of identity—
a stunting or evasion of growth that is perpetuated by the feminine mystique. . . .
Our culture does not permit women to accept or gratify their basic need
to grow and fulfill their potentialities as human beings.

BETTY FRIEDAN (1921–   )
The Feminine Mystique, 1963

The Third Wave of Feminism

The return to militancy

In the twenties organized feminism in America went into limbo and stayed there until the sixties. Through much of that time only isolated "cranks" and "neurotics" criticized the status of women. In the sixties came the rediscovery of poverty, the civil rights rebellion, the opposition to the Vietnam War, and the rebellion in the colleges. A new generation of younger women, influenced by these movements for reform was coming to maturity. Feminism again became a social movement. Betty Friedan's *The Feminine Mystique*, published in 1963, helped trigger a nationwide interest in the third wave of feminism. In it she attacked psychologists, advertising executives, and editors of women's magazines, for brainwashing an entire generation of women into accepting their lot as homemakers and consumers.

The book meshed with other events. In 1961 President Kennedy had named a Commission on the Status of Women to study women's roles in government, business, politics, and education. The Commission was headed by Eleanor Roosevelt. Among its findings: women averaged 40 percent less pay than men for the same work, women doctors and engineers were a declining breed, women college graduates in 1960 were relatively fewer than thirty years earlier, women who were black were the most likely to suffer job discrimination. Although not a feminist, Kennedy set up a committee to promote jobs for women in government and industry. Nearly all of the states did the same.

The state commissions on women met in Washington, D.C., in 1966. Many of the delegates became bitter when Dr. Kathryn Clarenbach of Wisconsin was refused permission to introduce a resolution against sex discrimination in newspaper ads. She, along with Betty Friedan and others, resolved that the time had come to organize a new feminist group. They launched the National Organization for Women (NOW), whose slogan was "Full equality for women in truly equal partnership with men." Its objective was to end all discrimination against women in government, jobs, law, and education. By 1970 it had a hundred chapters. NOW hoped to win enforcement of new laws and regulations ending sex discrimination in hiring. In 1968 a second nationwide organization, Women's Equality Action League (WEAL), was organized by academic and professional women trying to stop discrimination in jobs, education, and taxation. In 1970 *Sexual Politics* by Kate Millet became a national best seller. *Ms.*, the first feminist magazine to acquire a wide circulation, was founded in 1972.

The new movement was composed of divergent groups and points of view, and unlike the suffragists, who subordinated everything to the vote, it had a broad list of reforms to present to the nation. The members of the new movement included both liberal reformers and radicals. The reformers filed suits, lobbied for new laws, and circulated petitions. They hoped to end various forms of discrimination as well as establish childcare centers and achieve improvements in the welfare rights of women with dependent children. Among their major objectives were improved Social Security benefits, legalized abortion, and a greater influence for women in political parties. For those who worked for legislative reform, probably the most important objective of all was the Equal Rights Amendment (ERA). Some organizations began to draft plans for a big campaign to push the ERA through Congress and the state legislatures. One thing the reformers did not want to do was destroy the family unit, which they felt to be a viable institution.

The radical feminists wanted somewhat different changes and adopted much more dramatic tactics to get them. Their anger toward men was more apparent. Many were college women who had taken part in leftist causes and were fed up with the way radical males had treated them. They attacked the family as a male-dominated institution, and they compared women to abused racial minorities. They invented the term *sexism* to parallel the word *racism*. The movement embraced many life styles. Some women considered having children out of wedlock, being single, being lesbian, as superior alternatives to conventional middle-class married life. The radicals organized "consciousness

Consciousness raising groups enabled women to express their half-formed fears, angers, and frustrations—to develop their self-awareness—and to discover that these feelings were shared by others. The experience was usually an emotional one; as one woman wrote after her first meeting, "I found that I am not strange in having these feelings; I am not alone!"

raising" groups for women only and published underground newspapers. In colleges they began a push for women's studies programs, the first of which began at San Diego State College in the spring of 1970. Scholars were urged to be alert for sexist premises in their research and to treat women more fairly in textbooks. The sexist elements in the English language were marked for extinction.

Radical feminists used attention-getting devices that assured them a spot in the evening news. At the Miss America pageant in Atlantic City in 1968 they hurled "false eyelashes, padded bras, spiked-heeled shoes, and steno pads into a 'freedom trash can.'" They didn't burn any bras at the pageant, as the press reported, but they did ridicule some of the articles that they believed symbolized women as sex objects.

At first "women's lib" was treated as the emotional outburst of neurotic, man-hating, love-starved females or, at best, as an interesting topic for TV talk shows. But the fact that the moderate and radical feminists were coexisting was a sign of the movement's strength.

Pressing for legal abortion

High on the agenda for most feminists, reformers and radicals alike, was achieving legal status for abortions. According to the Kinsey Report of 1948, a survey of sexual conduct, one out of four American women had at some time aborted a pregnancy. In effect this meant committing a felony, since in most states neither a pregnant woman nor a doctor could legally end pregnancy except to save a mother's life. It also meant risking sterility, infection, or death, as many women were enduring dangerous "table-top abortions" performed by quacks.

Since the nineteenth century all states had passed laws regulating abortion. As a general rule they prohibited abortion except to save the *life* of the mother. The leading reform organization, the National Association for the Repeal of Abortion Laws, wanted abortion on demand. Current laws, its members claimed, prevented a woman from making moral choices based on her own personal values. She could not control her own fertility. She could not spare an overpopulated world from having one more unwanted child.

The proabortion campaign met a vigorous opponent in the Catholic church, which taught that human life begins at the moment of conception and that abortion was therefore a form of homicide. Antiabortionists argued for the moral and legal rights of the fetus.

But the proabortion campaign made headway. As a first step in reform several legislators decided to allow therapeutic abortion. This permitted a doctor to perform an abortion to save the physical or mental *health* of the mother. Starting with New York in 1970 a few states went even further, passing laws granting abortion on demand. The Supreme Court upheld the new abortion laws in 1973. Yet the ruling was not clear-cut. For example, it did not protect Dr. Kenneth Edelin who was convicted of manslaughter in Boston for performing an abortion. The prosecution argued that the special technique he used may have allowed the fetus to take one breath, and technically, to become subject to the state's manslaughter laws. Meanwhile, the antiabortion camp continued its activities, by shifting to a campaign for a constitutional amendment to make abortion illegal once again.

The quest for economic and social equality

Significant advances in the struggle for women's equality occurred in the job market. By "mistake" a section was added to the 1964 Civil Rights Act that outlawed sexual discrimination. A southern Congressman put it there, convinced that it would kill the bill entirely. His plan backfired, and the feminist movement had acquired a new tool. Sexist customs and job regulations now came under attack by women journalists, stewardesses, athletes, professors, and labor union officials. The Bell Telephone Company was forced to provide millions in back pay to women employees who had been denied promotions on the grounds of sex alone. The women's movement could not, however, guarantee an improvement in the job market. Even after the new regulations and publicity, unemployment among women continued to rise, and the wage differential between men and women had not lessened significantly.

Women won new recognition in sports. The top women athletes of an earlier time were few and earned very little compared to male athletes. In 1948, the first year of professional women's golfing, Babe Didrikson Zaharias made around $3000. Women golfers would later earn more than ten times that amount. Billie Jean King made history when she earned over $100,000 in a single year in professional tennis and then went on to beat male star Bobby Riggs in a much publicized match. As coach, player, and businesswoman, she insisted on equal opportunities and rewards for women in sports. Women jockeys broke into the big time, and ten-year-old girls helped integrate

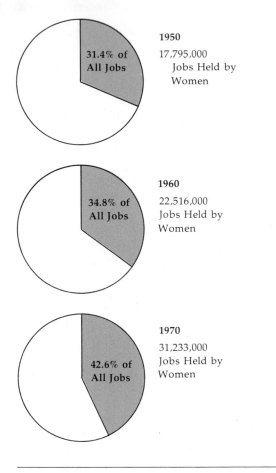

1950
17,795,000
Jobs Held by
Women

1960
22,516,000
Jobs Held by
Women

1970
31,233,000
Jobs Held by
Women

SOURCE: Bureau of the Census.

Little League baseball. Still, high schools and colleges continued to spend most of their athletic funds on sports programs for male students.

After years of effort women finally seemed to make a dent in the political system, although they had a long way to go before they would achieve equality with males. In 1970 only about one dozen of the 850 top office-holders in federal agencies were women. Only 13 out of 535 congressional seats were held by women. Among the most effective women on Capitol Hill were Senator Margaret Chase Smith of Maine and Representatives Shirley Chisholm and Elizabeth Holtzman of New York, Barbara Jordan of Texas, Edith Green of Oregon, and Martha Griffiths of Michigan. In an address to the House, Congresswoman Chisholm noted: "As a black person, I am no stranger to race prejudice. But the truth is that in the political world I have been far oftener discriminated against because I am a woman than because I am black."

At the 1972 Democratic convention half the delegate seats were assigned to women. Chisholm endorsed legal abortion there and announced her candidacy for president. In 1974 the Senate had no women members and the House only sixteen. But a record eight hundred Democratic and Republican women had been nominated for jobs ranging from city council to high positions in government. Ella Grasso, the daughter of Italian immigrants, was elected governor of Connecticut. She was the first woman ever elected governor who had not been preceded in that office by her husband. Though not a feminist she was unavoidably identified with feminism. As an opposition bumper sticker said: "CONNECTICUT CAN'T AFFORD A GOVERNESS."

Women began pushing open the doors to the ministry, which for most denominations was traditionally a male sanctuary. Sally Priesand and Sandra Sasso broke the "world's oldest bastion of male supremacy." They became ordained rabbis, finding acceptance in the Reconstructionist and Reform branches of Judaism, respectively. The Episcopal church was shaken to its foundation when eleven women were ordained as ministers in Philadelphia in 1974.

It would be premature to infer from this that religious institutions would undergo swift change. The Roman Catholic and Conservative and Orthodox Jewish denominations do not permit the ordination of women, and the Anglican church fought it vigorously. The ordination of the Episcopal women ministers was declared invalid by an emergency meeting of the two-hundred-member House of Bishops. About eighty Protestant denominations allowed women to become ministers, but in practice only 5 percent of them led congregations. The conservative Christians are probably the most actively organized opponents of feminism, reviving or preserving in many households the patriarchal attitudes of a century ago. The Christian conservatives seem to take the apostle Paul's teaching as their motto for women: "Be subject to your husbands."

In 1974 Marabel Morgan's *The Total Woman* topped the bestseller list of the National Religious Booksellers. Drawing on pamphlets first published in the 1920s, she advised women to look first to God, then to their husband, then finally to their profession or the public. Wrote Morgan, when a woman "surrenders her life to her husband, reveres and worships him, and is willing to serve him. . . she becomes really beautiful to him. She becomes a priceless jewel, the glory of femininity, his queen." Precisely how many households are affected by these beliefs is hard to estimate, but it is surely higher than some feminists would like to believe.

Fighting for ERA

The Equal Rights Amendment, first proposed in the 1920s and endorsed by Presidents Eisenhower, Kennedy, Johnson, Nixon, and Ford, was finally approved by Congress in 1970. Organized labor had opposed it for years. Even the League for Women Voters withheld endorsement until 1972. According to backers, ERA was needed to overturn discriminatory laws and court rulings. In some states women could be legally excluded from state universities, sentenced to longer prison terms than men for the same crimes, and excluded from certain jobs, like

bartending, simply because they were women. According to a government study by a panel appointed by President Nixon, many state laws on marriage, guardianship, dependency, and ownership of property and business "clearly discriminate against women." ERA would help equalize economic and educational opportunities. It would also make husbands and wives equally responsible for alimony and child support. ERA created controversy because it would make women eligible for a military draft, but backers pointed out that women in the military would be assigned only jobs for which they were physically suited.

Gradually even labor's opposition to ERA weakened. Union leaders had feared the result of destroying hard-earned laws which protected women against night work, overtime, and heavy lifting in factory jobs. But backers of ERA argued persuasively that technology had erased most of the jobs suited for men only; laws that had once protected women now prevented them from moving up the ladder. Also, the Civil Rights Act of 1964 had already removed the legal basis for sex discrimination in most hiring. So organized labor backed into its support of ERA.

After mulling it over for half a century, Congress approved this amendment which held that "equality of rights under the law shall not be denied or abridged by the United States or by a State on account of sex." Many senators privately opposed this potential twenty-sixth amendment but succumbed to the lobbying efforts of Women United, an umbrella organization of ninety-two feminist groups. Women United had Congress bombarded with 5 million messages in the weeks before the vote. New York's Senator Jacob Javits reported receiving ten thousand letters. The bill sailed through the Senate by a vote of eighty-four to eight. Congresswoman Griffiths shepherded it through the House, and it was sent to the states for approval.

Five years after Congress passed the proposed amendment, thirty-four out of a necessary thirty-eight states had approved it. But opposition mounted steadily. A "Stop ERA" Committee organized by antifeminist Phyllis Schafley hoped to kill the amendment, particularly in the southern states. Among the new "antis" were groups called Happiness of Women (HOW), American Women Are Richly Endowed (AWARE), and the Pussycat League. They opposed feminism on principle. In addition, they argued that ERA would clog the courts with test cases, and give more authority to an overgrown federal bureaucracy, which would have to enforce ERA. Feminists, by tradition a persistent lot, still predicted victory.

By comparison with other movements for social change, the third wave of feminism showed remarkable staying power. It accomplished major reforms and promised others yet to come. The movement, says historian Lois W. Banner, "At its very best . . . has counselled that men as well as women should be able to do and to be whatever they wish. . . . " This gave the movement a great deal of flexibility.

The future of the women's movement depended on its ability to overcome serious organizational weaknesses. Comprised mainly of middle-class women, it touched working-class white women very little and minority women almost not at all. (Some black women said that, unlike their liberated white sisters, they would like to be able to stay home and care for their families.) But small steps toward a mutual understanding among these groups indicated that the gulf between them might be bridged. Internal weakness in feminist organizations became most apparent following the 1973 U.S. Supreme Court decision liberalizing abortion. The victory made it harder to press for further legislative reforms. Organizations like NOW were unable to push ERA over the top in 1975, a year that the UN had declared International Women's Year.

Trying to advance women into better jobs and careers, the women's movement faced major obstacles that were largely out of their control. Law, college teaching, medicine, and skilled manual work were occupations with few openings compared to the number of applicants. In addition, while women had improved their job status, much of the economy seemed dependent on the availability of large numbers of unskilled, semiskilled, and part-time women workers. Their low wages and poor work conditions were not likely to improve rapidly. The job market was expanding too slowly, or not at all, to benefit most women workers.

Whether feminism would soon decline again also depended on unforeseeable circumstances. A major crisis like a war or depression might seriously undermine it. As had happened in the twenties, it could lose the support of the younger women. What if the sons and daughters of the new feminist mothers rebelled against feminism when they came of age? The upcoming generation held the secret.

Review

In the wake of World War II men and women sought refuge in family togetherness. Domesticity and larger families were looked upon as the only real fulfillment for women. Psychologists stressed that only mothers could meet the heavy demands of early childhood training. But women were soon entering the work field in record numbers.

The increasing divorce rate did not appear to diminish the popularity of the institution of marriage in America. First marriages occurred at a comparatively early age and it was not uncommon for wives to help supplement income. Older people were cared for less adequately than they had been in the past, and the children of working parents also suffered some neglect. Although the nuclear family was still overwhelmingly dominant, a growing number of families listed women as heads of households.

The postwar baby boom tapered off as new birth control methods made family planning easier. Families got smaller. The family was also affected by the feminist movement, which called for alternatives to domesticity for women.

The "generation gap" reached a high point in the sixties. An unprecedented number of young people rejected the values and goals of their parents. Anxious adults and angry youth viewed each other with hostility. The struggle lessened with U.S. withdrawal from Vietnam.

After dozing for many years, feminism reawakened in the tumultuous sixties. This third wave of the feminist movement encompassed many groups and views and focused on a wide range of goals. The movement included both reformers and radicals. Although their social outlook and tactics varied, the groups got along well enough for the movement as a whole to make substantial headway.

The feminists fought a number of battles. The fight over legalized abortion was the most controversial. It involved questions of personal liberty, morality, and religious belief. Entry into the clergy was another stormy matter. Women's attempts to increase their standing in sports and politics made some progress. The important goal of job equality, while enacted into law, was harder to achieve in practice. The movement gave high priority to passing the Equal Rights Amendment. But while ERA got through Congress in 1970, five years later it still had not been ratified by enough states.

The women's movement contained within it serious weaknesses as well as strengths. Its future depended largely on how it would be viewed by the new generation of young people.

Questions

1. Identify and give the significance of: (a) *The Feminine Mystique*, (b) Civil Rights Act of 1964, (c) Commission on the Status of Women, (d) ZPG, (e) Shirley Chisholm, (f) generation gap.
2. What changes has the family undergone since 1945? Do you think the changes have strengthened or weakened the family?
3. The women's movement was revived by a series of converging events. What were they?
4. How has the women's movement changed your own thinking? Has it affected the way you view the future? With which feminist goals do you agree? With which do you disagree?
5. NOW's slogan is, "Full equality for women in truly equal partnership with men." Do you believe that such equality would improve or worsen conditions for men? For women? Explain.
6. How do feminist reformers and feminist radicals differ? In what respects are they alike? Discuss the major strengths and weaknesses of the women's movement.

community

Elevated tracks and a concrete causeway slice through the "inner city."

To approach a city, or even a city neighborhood, as if it were a larger architectural problem, capable of being given order by converting it into a disciplined work of art is to make the mistake of attempting to substitute art for life.

JANE JACOBS (1916–   )
Sociologist

39

789

39

In and Out
of Supercity

"A community is a place where I feel wanted and secure." Perhaps this expresses what most Americans mean by the term "community." Unhappily, many of them feel neither wanted nor secure. In their neighborhoods they are troubled by street crime, high taxes, deteriorating schools, unemployment, pollution, and traffic congestion. Today these ills make the search for community harder than ever before.

It has been traditional to think of the nonurban as typically American. Our greatest heroes, from Daniel Boone to Dwight D. Eisenhower, hail from rural or small-town backgrounds. Few, if any, are identified with big cities. Yet cities have played a vital part in our history, and today they play a bigger role than ever. For better or for worse, it is in cities that most Americans now make their home. Cities received much attention from Washington during the sixties, the era of the "urban crisis." But federal cures for urban ills were less than successful, and while the urban crisis continued, Washington in the seventies no longer pretended to know how to solve it.

Many Americans feel that they must leave the metropolis to find a better life. Where shall they go? Small cities, towns, suburbs, farms, and communes provide alternatives. With the exception of farm life (a topic dealt with in Chapter 33), each receives some attention below.

Communes and Small Towns as Alternatives

Traditional communes

Here and there, in the late twentieth century, communes out of America's past survived, some in failing health but others doing remarkably well. In Canterbury, New Hampshire, and Sabbathday Lake, Maine, two Shaker communities barely clung to life in 1974, the two-hundredth anniversary of the founding of the Shaker sect. Once there were six thousand Shakers in communes at many locations. By 1974 only twelve "sisters" remained, ranging in age from forty-nine to eighty-nine years. The last "brother" had died in 1961. These survivors felt that their sect would be replaced by others. "It will continue," said one of them. "There will always be some people, although they may not be called Shakers, who want this feeling inside of joining with God."

The "feeling inside" was shared by the Hutterites, "the largest true communal group in the Western world." This religious sect, closely related to the Amish of Pennsylvania, was founded by Germans who settled in the Midwest in the 1870s. The Hutterites were persecuted during World War I when their young men resisted the military draft on religious grounds. The sect had then pulled up stakes and migrated to Canada. They returned after the Second World War, founding some seventy colonies in South Dakota and Montana. Each Hutterite commune contained about 130 members. There was a total of about twenty thousand Hutterites in the U.S. and Canada.

Hutterites encouraged strong family ties, religious piety, and the use of an Old German dialect. Cut off from the outside world, they thrived without seeking converts. Each colony was headed by a powerful male elder. Wealth was shared equally. Unlike their Amish cousins in Pennsylvania (also still thriving), who refused to use modern tractors or trucks, Hutterites used the latest farming equipment and were highly successful farmers. Television was prohibited in their communities, and social life was austere. Nearby towns were off limits to Hutterite young people. Those who strayed from the fold usually came back repentant. Members of communes who visited the Hutterites thinking they would be warmly welcomed were sadly mistaken. Hutterites especially detested the long haired, nonconformist youths who had set up retreat communes.

Retreat communes

A survey made at the University of California at Berkeley during the height of the student rebellion of 1964 showed that "many students feel alone in a community of strangers." Thus it is not surprising that disgruntled young rebels of the sixties were attracted to the idea of communal living. When high rents and police crackdowns on drug users drove hippies from the Haight-Ashbury district of San Francisco, some of them retreated to rural areas and formed communes. They were looking for a more primitive life, for a new way of self-expression, and, often, for a place to use mind-expanding drugs away from the pressures of straight society.

California and New Mexico were favored locations for new communes, and the years 1967 to 1969 the most active period of commune building. Among the better-known retreat communes formed in the 1960s were Paper Farm and Morningstar Ranch in California; Sunrise Hill, Massachusetts; Oz, Pennsylvania; and Tolstoy Farm, Washington. Some of the retreat communes were established by members of the "Jesus movement" who wanted to take up communal living in imitation of the early Christians.

Not all retreat communes were in the country; some were established in the cities. Groups of people got together and bought or rented large single-family residences in older neighborhoods. Here they adopted many of the same rules that might apply on a farm. These urban communes appealed especially to college students.

The occupants of most retreat communes came to the land trying to recapture the lost innocence of a world before factories and big cities. Their members took up vegetable gardening and handcrafts, ate organic foods, and had their children by natural childbirth. At counterculture communes the discipline was loose and the staying power weak. The trouble with everyone "doing their own thing" was that the more disagreeable and mundane tasks did not get done.

Service communes

Communes dedicated to a social purpose— the "service communes"—had greater staying power. Koinonia Farm, Georgia, founded in 1942, tried to bring both racial integration and farm technology to the rural southern poor. The Reba Place Fellowship, established in Indiana in 1957, was a Bible seminary whose members provided day care and other urban services to the surrounding community. Synergia Ranch in New Mexico devoted itself to ecology, while Cedar Grove, in the same state, was intended to propagate the Ba'hai religion.

The best-known service commune was Synanon, founded in 1958 to rehabilitate drug addicts and alcoholics. Established in numerous urban centers from California to New York and Puerto Rico, Synanon had hopes of reforming all of society. Its success owed much to the personal magnetism of its autocratic founder, Charles Dederich, a former alcoholic. Its financial success, resulting from ownership of gas stations, printing shops, and other thriving businesses (the foundation held assets worth $6 million in the 1970s), was remarkable in the history of American communes. Synanon members "played games" in which they evaluated and criticized each other on a highly personal level. This form of therapy was reminiscent of that practiced at John Humphrey Noyes' Oneida (see p. 310).

By 1970 the *New York Times* estimated that there were some two thousand communes, more than ever before in American history. Many seemed to have folded in the 1970s. Although numbers of people in "straight society" (that is, people not in communes) eyed them longingly, communes have yet to become a serious way of life for the majority of Americans.

Small towns reach bottom and make a comeback

A Gallup poll taken in 1966 indicated that 31 percent of all Americans would prefer to live in a small town. Oddly enough, at that time most small towns were in a slump. Growing metropolitan centers were gobbling them up and stealing away their most vigorous residents. High-school graduates who left Main Street to go to college or to find jobs often did not return. Towns in farming communities were slowly filling up with older people who were selling their farms and retiring on small, fixed incomes. The retirees were a stable lot, but lacked the vigor and the capital necessary to keep the towns economically and socially healthy.

As had been the trend ever since the twenties, many small-town institutions disappeared. Local newspapers folded or sold out to large metropolitan dailies. Local doctors who retired from practice could not find replacements among young medical school graduates, and their patients often had to travel many miles to get medical care. With the coming of TV many towns witnessed the closing of the last picture show. In 1956 Eric

The informal life of rural towns often appeared in the way businesses were run. "I tell my customers to pay their premiums when they can," remarked an insurance agent. "We look at each other every day; we have to trust each other." "I like the informality," added a furniture manufacturer. "But sometimes this closeness isn't good business. How could I fire a guy who was a good friend?"

Sevareid wrote that the towns were once "seed beds, ceaselessly renewing themselves, their seeds constantly renewing the nation." Now the seeds had lost the power of regeneration.

The more aggressive small-town businessmen of the South, Midwest, and Southwest, tried to lure industries by promising low taxes, cheap utilities, and an open-shop labor policy. Corporations were decentralizing. If a town landed one big branch office of a major company, it could usually reel in others. Not too many towns succeeded at this until the late sixties. Many small towns in the southern black belt were especially hard hit by the heavy northward migration of black people.

As the ghetto riots exploded in the big cities, though, small towns began to look more attractive. A small-town newspaper editor explained to a *Time* writer in 1970, "If we had our way, we'd build a fence around this town. We don't have your Mickey Mouse problems. We don't need them." By the seventies, many small towns had stopped sliding downhill and begun making a comeback. In the big cities pollution, crime, and especially declining employment were driving people away. In the metropolitan counties of the nation manufacturing jobs declined at a rate of 1.5 percent yearly from 1969 to 1974.

Meantime, in direct contrast, the number of such jobs in the nonmetropolitan counties increased by about 2.4 percent. Some federal agencies had a policy of helping small towns by building new roads or installing new offices in the underdeveloped counties at the expense of the overdeveloped ones. Southern Appalachia (particularly northern Alabama, and the middle part of the Cumberland Plateau) was hit by a drastic loss of population in the 1950s, but it showed a 13 percent increase in the late sixties.

Supercity, Warts and All

Urban sprawl

Two centuries ago 95 percent of all Americans lived in the country and 5 percent in the city. By about 1990 the proportions will probably have reversed themselves.

After World War II there was a rapid movement away from the core area of cities and toward the fringes, usually into the countryside beyond the city limits. Because of this process of urban sprawl American *cities* acquired only 2.4 million new residents between 1950 and 1955, but the population of *metropolitan areas*, which included the cities *and* the surrounding counties, rose by 12 million people.

Though urban sprawl occurred in many areas of the country, it was most noticeable along the borders of the continent in such states as Florida, Texas, Arizona, and California and on the northeastern seaboard. In the region from southern New Hampshire to northern Virginia it appeared that the cities of Boston, New York, Philadelphia, Balti-more, and Washington, D.C., were growing toward one another and would eventually merge. A geographer called this area "megalopolis" (Greek, meaning "great city"). Here were focused the nation's mass communications systems, its banks and government structure, and most of its corporate headquarters. Here also were the largest number of libraries, colleges, and museums in the country. Where there had been a "howling wilderness" three centuries earlier, there now stood a supercity, the largest concentration of wealth, power, and urban civilization anywhere on earth.

So far there was only one megalopolis, and it was limited to the northeastern seaboard. But a second one was building around the southern end of Lake Michigan, from Milwaukee to Chicago to Detroit, and a third in southern California with Los Angeles at its hub. Los Angeles, in fact, came to be the prototype of the sprawling metropolis, with its

METROPOLITAN, URBAN, AND RURAL POPULATION, 1960 AND 1970

	Metropolitan	% of Change	Urban	% of Change	Rural	% of Change	Total	% of Change
1960	119,595,000		125,269,000		54,054,000		179,975,000	
1970	139,419,000	16.6	149,325,000	19.2	53,887,000	0.3	203,212,000	13.3

SOURCE: Bureau of the Census. A metropolitan area is a central city with surrounding county or counties that are economically and socially integrated with the central city. An urban area is any area with 2500 or more inhabitants. In 1790 95 percent of Americans lived on farms. Today most Americans live in or near a big city. In 1970, for the first time, the Census showed that more Americans lived in the suburbs of big cities (74.2 million) than in the cities themselves (62.2 million).

endless webs of suburbs in search of a city. Here seemed to be the wave of the future.

Urban renaissance

Between 1945 and 1960 the major effort to cope with urban problems came from the cities, rather than from Washington. Nor was the federal government expected to take the lead in a period of full employment and sustained economic growth. Urban leadership was stronger and federal leadership weaker than before the war. The optimistic "new breed" of mayors, many of them college trained and relatively young, entered city hall full of energy and plans for improvement. Since the twilight of the New Deal mayors had learned not to look to Washington for initiative. Eisenhower was not dependent for his election on the support of city bosses and did not play the game of politics with them. In Pittsburgh, Mayor David Lawrence put together a coalition of businessmen, labor leaders, and civic-minded citizens to clean up the polluted air, revive the downtown business district, and provide housing for the poor. They used federal funds. In time they realized some of their goals. But in the recession of 1959–1960 the city leaders realized that they had reached the limits of their ability to improve the quality of life in their city. Throughout the country similar disappointments marked the end of a short-lived urban renaissance.

Urban crisis

The fact that Central City and Suburbia were going their separate ways was not in itself a fatal flaw. But because the division also involved a split between the white middle class and the black poor, it possessed the potential of a powder keg. The end of the renaissance and the start of an era of crisis came about because the ghettos were deteriorating as rapidly as the suburbs were expanding.

PERCENTAGE OF WHITES IN CENTRAL CITIES OF TWELVE LARGEST METROPOLITAN AREAS, 1940–1970

Areas	1940	1950	1960	1970
New York	93.6	90.2	85.3	73.2
Los Angeles-Long Beach	94.0	90.2	84.7	79.0
Chicago	91.7	85.9	76.4	65.4
Philadelphia	86.9	81.7	73.3	65.6
Detroit	90.7	83.6	70.8	55.7
San Francisco-Oakland	95.1	88.2	78.9	67.4
Boston	96.7	94.7	90.2	82.1
Pittsburgh	90.7	87.7	83.2	79.1
St. Louis	86.6	82.0	71.2	58.7
Washington, D.C.	71.5	64.6	45.2	27.7
Cleveland	90.3	82.7	71.1	60.9
Baltimore	80.6	76.2	65.0	52.9

SOURCE: Harry Sharp and Leo F. Schnore, "The Changing Color Composition of Metropolitan Areas," *Land Economics,* 38 (May 1962), 169–185, reproduced with permission; also *Census of Population and Housing, 1970,* U.S. Government Printing Office, 1972.

The first warnings of an impending explosion in the ghettos made no deep impression on most Americans. Those who lived in new suburban tract houses in the 1960s ignored the tensions in Central City. Magazine photographers toured the slums in 1964, documenting how the other half lived—in crowded, substandard housing, with schools wracked by turmoil, with expanding welfare rolls, with increasing dope addiction, delinquency, and crime. The Watts riot of 1965 was an eye-opener. It took place in the "nicest black ghetto in the country," an area of Los Angeles with grassy lawns and single-family homes. The violence there, in which thirty-four persons were killed, thousands injured, and six hundred buildings damaged or destroyed, was followed by similar upheavals in other cities around the nation. Attention focused on the state of the inner-city communities. "Sick cities," "urban blight," and "urban cancer" were now cover stories in *Life*, *Time*, and *Look*. The "urban crisis of the sixties" was primarily a racial

Huge project homes once promised hope for housing low-income families, but their large, impersonal hallways, courtyards, and stairways offered anonymity to criminals and little pleasure to residents. Some major complexes were deserted within years after they were finished. Architect Oscar Newman, who studied crime and building structures, concluded, "Ask the poor themselves what kind of housing they want. They'll describe what looks like middle-class row houses or suburban bungalows. To an architect, that's pure kitsch, but the poor are right in what they want."

matter, though it had larger dimensions involving pollution and congestion, and crime and violence that affected all urbanites. To study what went wrong it is necessary to deal with the components of the problem: housing and urban renewal, transportation, crime, and taxation.

Housing and urban renewal

One thing that went wrong was housing policy. The federal government spent some $10 billion on urban renewal without solving an acute housing shortage. In theory the Housing Act of 1949 promised to provide every citizen with a "decent, safe and sanitary place in which to live." But the policies of the Federal Housing Authority in underwriting home loans chiefly helped those who could afford new private homes, namely middle-class whites. Logically, urban renewal should also have provided more and better housing for all who were left behind, including blacks, whites, Chicanos, Puerto Ricans, and Indians. This it failed to do. The 500,000 public housing units in existence by 1962 simply did not begin to meet the needs of the urban poor or the lower middle class.

The slums were no longer a doorway to success, as they had been for European immigrants. To those who lived there now they seemed like, and usually were, the end of the line. One ghetto dweller described the slum as a "quagmire, a big quicksand. Just like you step in something, you just sink and can't get out of it. . . . I mean you can live here for millions and millions of years and you will see the same place, same time, and same situation. It's just like time stops here."

The theory of urban renewal after 1949 had been that the federal government would foot the bill for city governments to buy entire blocks of land and tear down blighted neighborhoods. Government-subsidized private contractors would then build new apartments, offices, and other structures. Around $10 billion was eventually appropriated. Some cities—San Francisco, New Haven, Philadelphia, and Washington, D.C. — used the federal money well. New corporate offices, high-rise luxury apartments, sports stadiums, and government buildings were constructed in the downtown business districts. In general, though, urban renewal did less than nothing for the lowest income groups. It removed over one million housing units without replacing any but the smallest fraction of them for the same income groups. Soon urban renewal came under attack from all sides. Civil rights groups called it "Negro removal," as it forced blacks out of decayed housing without supplying even temporary quarters. The dispossessed families had to double up in the already overcrowded slums. The relatively few public housing projects built under urban renewal were designed and operated on tight budgets. Some came off the drawing board looking like prison cell blocks. Even those with a less forbidding aspect somehow managed to deteriorate as soon as they were opened. Architectural critic Lewis Mumford called the new public housing "superslums." Elsewhere in Central City the federal bulldozers recklessly tore down neighborhoods which were old but otherwise quite livable. The story of mindless urban destruction was brilliantly described by Jane Jacobs in *The Death and Life of Great American Cities* (1961).

Transportation snarls

In l945 no one foresaw the postwar rush to the suburbs. Most planners assumed that city populations would level off and that cities would remain more or less within existing geographical limits. A federally subsidized road network in the fifties helped new suburbanite commuters get to and from work. But it did little for the poor and middle-class city dwellers still living in the city who were more dependent on mass transportation. And the highways created massive traffic snarls as the suburbanites drove into town and back each day.

So, another thing that went wrong in the postwar era was transportation policy. Federal policy onesidedly favored the automobile at the expense of mass transportation systems. Bumper-to-bumper traffic on surface streets, overloaded expressways, and lack of parking near work were common

PERCENTAGE OF NONWHITES IN SUBURBS OF TWELVE LARGEST METROPOLITAN AREAS*, 1940–1970

Areas	1940	1950	1960	1970
New York	4.6	4.5	4.8	13.1
Los Angeles-Long Beach	2.3	2.7	4.1	9.4
Chicago	2.2	2.9	3.1	4.0
Philadelphia	6.6	6.6	6.3	7.1
Detroit	2.9	5.0	3.8	3.9
San Francisco-Oakland	3.6	6.8	6.8	7.6
Boston	0.9	0.8	1.0	1.3
Pittsburgh	3.6	3.5	3.4	3.9
St. Louis	6.7	7.3	6.3	7.6
Washington, D.C.	13.7	8.7	6.4	8.7
Cleveland	0.9	0.8	0.8	3.5
Baltimore	11.9	10.2	6.9	6.5

*According to the Bureau of the Census, a Standard Metropolitan Area is a central city with its surrounding county or counties that are economically and socially integrated with the central city.

SOURCE: Harry Sharp and Leo F. Schnore, "The Changing Color Composition of Metropolitan Areas," *Land Economics*, 38 (May 1962), 169–185, reproduced with permission; also *Census of Population and Housing, 1970*, U.S. Government Printing Office, 1972.

complaints in and around every city.

Because the new suburbs were widely scattered, fixed-rail mass transit systems became less and less profitable. Many interurban train lines went bankrupt or barely broke even. In the twenty-five years following the war the use of mass transit declined by two thirds. Los Angeles' efficient interurban rail network, the Redcar Line, was dismantled in favor of cars, freeways, and buses. By the seventies an increase in smog, soaring gas prices, and a downtown parking squeeze were forcing even the citizens of Los Angeles to look into rapid transit.

The urban poor, elderly, and nonwhite had the worst transportation problems of all. A governors' commission investigating the Watts disturbances of 1965 found that if the residents in that area had had better access to mass transit, fewer of them would have been jobless; and therefore, it was presumed, fewer would have rioted.

Crime in the streets

Early one morning in March 1964 Katherine Genovese was returning from work when a man with a knife attacked her on a quiet residential street of Kew Gardens, a New York suburb. Behind closed doors or curtained windows thirty-eight people heard her terrified shrieks or saw her protracted death struggle. Not wanting to "get involved," they did nothing to help her, not even to call the police. This murder prompted fiery editorials and sermons throughout the land. What had happened to the good samaritans of America? Where was our sense of decency and community? Were we losing our nerve, our regard for our fellow human beings? The incident was extreme, of course, and cases could be cited where witnesses bravely intervened to stop serious crimes. But the Genovese murder exposed a painful side effect of urban living—paralyzing fear of street crime.

For a long time the experts could not even agree on the seriousness of urban crime. After weighing all the evidence for eighteen months a presidential crime commission reported in 1967 that it could not decide whether the rate of crime was actually on the rise or whether better techniques for recording crime statistics simply gave that impression. New data available that same year made it abundantly clear, however, that the rate of violent crime was increasing. To city dwellers, it was not news that their streets were unsafe. More and more people were buying guns, installing double and triple locks, window bars, and alarm systems. Guard dogs became common.

There were many theories about the reasons for the increase in crime. One key factor was demographic: the coming of age of the children of the postwar baby boom. Each passing year after 1961 brought another million youngsters over the age of fifteen, an age when delinquency was common. "Almost half the total increase in arrests in the first half of the 1960s," according to one expert, "was simply because there were more younger people around." Some critics thought the permissiveness of liberal judges in releasing offenders was to blame; others believed the miseries of poverty and the double standard of justice were at least as much the cause. Attempts were made to improve the administration of justice and the training of police officers. There were campaigns to stop the sale of hand guns and counter campaigns to preserve the right of all Americans to own guns. A major debate centered on the prison system: Did American prisons discourage crime or act as schools for criminals? Should the purpose of imprisonment be punishment or rehabilitation? In the 1970s crime remained a major problem in American cities.

Taxation and finance

Even in the good years of the 1950s and increasingly in the sixties and seventies cities faced severe financial strain. The flight of the middle class beyond the city boundaries and therefore beyond the reach of city tax collectors created a sharp drop in revenue. This came at the worst possible time since the social services needed by the poor were constantly growing. City expenditures often greatly exceeded revenues. In many cities public works were obsolete, the schools were overcrowded, the police and fire protection less than adequate.

American cities had limited tax sources, since they were creatures of the states and the states restricted their taxing powers. Some cities taxed income, but most had to rely on sales and property taxes, which hit low- and middle-income families the hardest. Since property taxes rose when buildings were improved, landlords often refused to make repairs. The tax system was one of the reasons that privately owned slum housing was as bad as it was.

Presidential leadership

Presidential leadership was not altogether absent from the field of urban affairs, but it produced less than spectacular results. Truman managed to wring a housing act out of a reluctant Congress in 1949, but accomplished little else. The strongest effort was made by Johnson. Yet the cities exploded at the very time they were getting the most attention from his administration.

Capitalizing on the mood of the country after John F. Kennedy's assassination, LBJ created a new Department of Housing and Urban Affairs in 1965 and a year later delivered to Congress the strongest message on the cities ever sent by any president. In it he noted the crisis proportion of problems of urban housing, finance, racial discrimination, welfare, crime, and unemployment. The ghetto streets, said he, were "streets of fear and sordid temptation, joblessness, and the gray anxiety of the ill-prepared." His basic Great Society programs for the poor, including VISTA, the Neighborhood Youth Corps, the Job Corps, and Operation Head Start were oriented to the cities. Johnson encouraged the active participation of the poor in neighborhood programs. In addition he urged the decentralization of urban populations under a New Town scheme. The plan included construction of seven villages of seven thousand people each, with factories, schools, and shopping centers, much on the order of successful New Towns in Scandinavia. Jonathan, Minnesota, was the first town to receive aid under this program. Owing to the priority of military budgets, the Kennedy-Johnson program for the cities suffered crippling cutbacks.

While the government floundered, private corporations were sponsoring New Towns that showed great promise at least for the middle class. Reston, Virginia, was a handsomely designed New Town financed by Gulf Oil. It aimed at a population of 75,000 by

The Federal Government carries on extensive research on the causes and cures of potato blight, but not of urban blight. It knows much of farmland use, little of urban land use; much of the economics of transporting hogs, but little of the economics of mass communication of people.

JOSEPH CLARK (1901–)

U.S. Senator from Pennsylvania

1980. Other planned communities created by private capital were Coral Springs, Florida (Westinghouse), Mission Viejo in southern California (Phillip Morris), and Irvine, California (Irvine Corporation), with a projected population of over 400,000.

In 1972, at President Nixon's urging, Congress authorized a revenue-sharing scheme by which the federal government returned to the states and cities $16 billion in tax receipts out of the federal treasury. Congress funded the scheme, but the funds ran out in a few years and were not renewed.

President Ford refused to bail out the cities that were hit hard by falling tax revenues during the recession year of 1975. His emergency relief program in 1975 included monies for the cities to use for hiring the jobless as temporary public employees. But beyond this he refused to go, fearing inflationary pressures on the federal budget. Detroit was forced to close municipal art galleries, cut back on park maintenance, stop fixing some alleyways, and fire police officers. New York City was in the worst shape of all. It had extraordinary bills to pay. It was the only city which had to pay welfare costs—and 900,000 people were on welfare. It was so deeply in the red that Wall Street bankers refused to buy municipal bonds unless the city froze the wages of municipal employees. Mayor

Abraham Beame begged President Ford for an emergency subsidy, which was refused. The city was finally helped out by the state at the cost of some of its economic independence.

Beyond the crisis

The urban crisis of the sixties trailed off into urban paralysis in the seventies. Some observers claimed that the modern city was already obsolete and destined for the junk heap of history. Whereas the city once provided military protection, and a safe place for worship and trade, this was no longer true. These observers pointed out that people can live, work, worship, and play in smaller, safer, and healthier communities. Therefore today's giant metropolis could be and should be abandoned.

But to abandon the city would be a political impossibility and a colossal waste of resources. Nor was it necessary in order to bring about more desirable conditions. Admittedly, racial segregation, poverty, joblessness, and the deterioration of physical facilities were gigantic problems to overcome. But it bore remembering that most people wanted basically the same thing—a decent community life—whether they lived in the city, in small towns, in communes, or in any other form of social organization.

Those who sought ways to improve their cities rather than abandon them received an abundance of advice. They were told by authorities or would-be authorities to pursue all or some of the following goals: save the central business district, clean up the air, build new transit lines, update the public schools, crack down on dope pushers and muggers, create more jobs, plant more trees, open day-care centers. These were a few of the commonly voiced objectives in and out of city hall.

The biggest problem was not how to decide what should be done about urban ills but rather on the means to do it. How to finance improvements, how to make decisions so that the average city dwellers as well as the professional planners became part of the process, and how to order the necessary priorities were among the more serious difficulties. In New York City, for example, billions of dollars were invested in unrented office space in the 1970s, yet there were not enough funds to pay the wages of garbage collectors or policemen.

One problem concerning the means of improving city life was the breakdown of urban democracy. The unwieldy structure of government made it hard to deal with complex issues. The two hundred or so metropolitan areas of the U.S. in 1960 were divided into no fewer than eighteen thousand local units of government. In some cases this helped preserve local initiative. But in many others it ruled out the possibility of attacking, on a regional basis, such troubles as crime, smog, water pollution, and traffic. Without a regional approach these issues often proved insoluble. A realization of this led to the formation of new and hopefully more efficient governments. In Miami, Nashville, and Indianapolis during recent decades various city, suburban, and county administrations have been consolidated into metropolitan governments. The results of these "metro governments," according to historian Howard P. Chudacoff, have been both "promising and frustrating." But some backers say they point the way for constructive regionalism.

Worst of all, in most cities there was too little citizen input into vital planning decisions. Major actions affecting the lives of thousands were still being made by an elite of professionals and bureaucrats who often had no stake in the matter except keeping their jobs. Local government was still a vital force in America; in recent years more taxpayers were involving themselves in particular local issues. But in general bureaucrats and politicians seemed fearful of neighborhood democracy. They often tried to circumvent it—as was the case in urban renewal.

Review

The search for community in America gave rise in the sixties to a renewed interest in communal living. Communes were more prevalent than ever. Some of them, particularly service communes, proved very successful. Others faltered and disappeared. For the most part, though, communes appealed only to a tiny minority of Americans.

Although in theory they represented the good life for many Americans, small towns in reality underwent a general decline in the 1950s and 1960s. Many were swallowed up by spreading metropolitan areas. Restless young people continued to migrate to the cities, depriving the towns of needed strength and vitality. But as urbanites became disillusioned with certain aspects of city life, small towns suddenly seemed to offer more opportunities and a more desirable life style. Many towns that had been wasting away began in the seventies to show signs of reviving.

During the years of general prosperity from 1945 to 1960, city leaders felt optimistic about dealing with urban problems. Some cities combined local initiative with federal funds to bring about civic improvements. Meantime, out in the suburbs, federal funds helped middle-class families buy and own homes and, by establishing new roads, helped them get to and from their city jobs. The recession of 1960 sobered those who were involved in the urban renaissance. The sixties were a time of urban crisis, which had decidedly racial overtones. This was made clear by the Watts riots of 1965 and the many urban disturbances that erupted across the nation in the following years.

Behind the crisis were several key factors. The Housing Act of 1949 failed to renew low-income neighborhoods. Urban-renewal proj-

Undoubtedly this would have to be corrected before the urban paralysis and defeatism of the seventies could be overcome.

ects sometimes caused increased congestion in such areas. Transportation difficulties and street crime were additional cause for concern among disgruntled city people. In addition, urban sources of revenue were dwindling at the very time that urban outlays were increasing. In the midst of the seventies some cities verged on bankruptcy.

Johnson's Great Society policies for the cities were starved by the growing costs of the Vietnam War. Nixon's support for a program of revenue sharing was well received in the cities, but the program was short-lived. The urban crisis of the sixties left many people feeling defeated and hopeless about their cities. Many would move out if they could. The great majority probably still preferred cities, but they wanted decent and safe neighborhoods. The goals were clearer than the means of achieving them.

Questions

1. Identify and give the significance of: (a) Synanon, (b) urban sprawl, (c) New Towns, (d) Katherine Genovese, (e) urban renewal, and (f) service communes.
2. Were you raised in a commune, small town, rural area, or city? In which of these would you like to spend your adult life? Why?
3. Do you have a "blueprint" for improving your own community? Which objectives do you think are shared by most other people there? What stands in the way of achieving those objectives?
4. Why have federal housing and urban renewal programs failed?
5. How are cities financed?

It is my own considered opinion, and I know it is shared by many colleagues, that the only sure technical solution for the urban air pollution problem is the outlawing of the internal combustion engine in cities.

DONALD E. CARR (1903–   )
Research chemist

40

40

We Have Met the Enemy and He Is Us

A great many people discovered the environment on April 22, 1970. The event was Earth Day, a nationwide ecological festivity in which hundreds of speeches were delivered on scores of college campuses to explain the ecological crisis. "Too many people," declared one leading biologist. "Affluence," said another ("The affluent society had become the effluent society"). If everyone were poor, theorized still another, the country would be healthier. The poor disagreed — at least one welfare rights spokesman warned against cutting back jobs and increasing unemployment simply for the sake of ecology. An electric power company director insisted that it was not industry but the public demand for goods and services that was creating pollution. A student activist pointed out that the educational system had failed to teach reverence for nature. A noted historian blamed Christianity for teaching that nature had no place in the human scheme, that natural things could be destroyed at will. A senator blamed "runaway technology." An environmentalist blamed politicians for being influenced by big business. One antiwar demonstrator warned that the ecology movement was drawing attention away from a more important issue, the war in Vietnam. Another thought that capitalism was to blame for ecological problems, as well as for the war. A spokesman for capitalism blamed the ecologists ("the disaster lobby," the "gloom mongers") for worrying everybody half to death without sound cause, while free enterprise was spending $3 billion yearly to clean up the environment. Pogo, the comic-strip possum of Okefenokee swamp, thought everyone deserved a share of the blame: "We have met the enemy," Pogo said, "and he is us."

Amid the confusion and scapegoating on Earth Day, some facts seemed irrefutable: in spite of efforts to ignore or prevent it, deterioration of the environment was increasingly evident. Pollution of earth, air, and water had been going on for decades, but in the quarter century following the end of World War II the results on every side could be seen and heard, tasted and smelled. Now a revolution of sentiment was under way.

Fouling the Nest

The global view

The level of strontium 90 in the atmosphere led some American physicists to yank their children off the streets and stop buying milk, which was easily contaminated by the deadly poison. In 1953 some people already had a painful awareness of "something gone drastically wrong" in the environment. It was a byproduct of atmospheric tests of U.S. nuclear weapons over the Pacific Ocean. Instead of filtering evenly over the globe as government scientists had confidently predicted, most of it was being dumped in the north temperate zone, where 80 percent of the world's population lived. Radioactive rain fell on half the globe, with the highest incidence occurring in Italy.

The radiation alarm highlighted the worldwide scope of many environmental issues and the need for international cooperation in seeking their solution. Soot that belched out of factory smoke stacks in the German Ruhr dirtied the snows of Norway. Crude oil that spilled from a ruptured tanker off the English coast fouled the beaches of France. Wheat grown, or not grown, in Kansas affected starving people in India. Small traces of strontium 90 lofted into the atmosphere over the Pacific Ocean in a bomb test might cause genetic damage or cancer to people living halfway around the globe.

In a sense, though, environmental problems had the greatest relevance for the U.S. Affluent people, population expert John Mayer wrote, "occupy more space, consume more of each natural resource, disturb the ecology more, and create more land, air, water, chemical, thermal, and radioactive pollution than poor people." The U.S., with only 6 percent of the world's population in the 1960s, consumed 30 percent of the world's annual output of natural resources.

"The air, the air is everywhere!"

Performers sang this lyric from the Broadway musical *Hair* while gagging and coughing into gas masks. Indeed, the air was a danger to life. On Thanksgiving Day in 1966, 168 elderly New Yorkers with respiratory difficulties died, probably from intense air pollution. This episode resembled the four-day siege of London fog in 1952, which killed four thousand people. An Egyptian stone monument in New York's Central Park had been more eroded by a century of New York air than by its previous three thousand years in Egypt.

Nor was New York's air the worst in the country. Los Angeles smog was notorious. This form of polluted air was first noted there in 1943. Gradually it became severe enough to destroy pine trees sixty miles away in the mountains and to endanger the lives of people with lung disorders. The main contributor to smog was the high-compression automobile engine, which burned its fuel imperfectly. The new Detroit models contributed to other forms of air pollution. Their exhausts spewed deadly fumes of lead, an element added to the gas to prevent engine knock. Tons of the poison blanketed

American cities daily. Brakes and tires also threw off dangerous particles of asbestos and plastic. In industrial cities stationary sources of pollution were especially offensive. The steel mills of Gary, Indiana, and Pittsburgh, Pennsylvania, made life miserable. Smoke from a Florida phosphate factory polluted the grass on which cows fed, infecting the animals with crippling bone disease.

Some scientists saw alarming long-range prospects in air pollution. One possible danger was the "green-house effect." Smoke and carbon dioxide in the earth's atmosphere might create enough of a permanent cloud cover to trap heat that was radiating from the earth's surface. This cloud layer would produce sufficient heat over a number of years to melt the polar ice cap, raising the level of the world's oceans enough to drown some coastal cities. Or the opposite might happen. The misty gunk in the sky could block out enough of the sun's rays to cool the atmosphere and expand the polar ice caps. This might usher in a new ice age, with disastrous consequences to agriculture and many other aspects of normal living. People would suffer either way.

Dying waters

To biologists water pollution was more alarming. Lakes and rivers were becoming too dirty for fishing, swimming, or drinking. Industrial wastes and sewage were a problem in all regions of the country. Many formerly clear, gurgling brooks now foamed with detergents. Many rivers stank. The sludge floating on the surface of the Cuyahoga River sometimes burst into flame as it passed through the city of Cleveland. Here was the "only body of water ever classified as a fire hazard."

Aside from the ugliness of it all, if the oxygen content of a river falls below a certain level, the natural filtration process stops, fish and other water creatures die, bacteria multi-

ply, and epidemic disease becomes a probability for those who use the water for drinking. With the ever increasing discharge of human and industrial wastes into America's river systems, the loss of oxygen in river water was a major threat to public health.

Lakes were suffering too. The Cuyahoga emptied into Lake Erie, one of the Great Lakes which was pronounced "dead" in 1969. Once a haven for fishing and other recreation, the lake had been "killed" by being used for half a century as a dumping ground for industrial and domestic waste. This, the world's twelfth largest lake, had aged fifteen thousand years in fifty years. Only sludge worms and poison-resistant carp still survived in it. In summertime a soup of algae two feet thick covered eight hundred square miles of its surface. According to biologist Barry Commoner in 1971, "Lake Erie represents the first large-scale warning that we are in danger of destroying the habitability of the earth. Mankind is in an environmental crisis, and Lake Erie constitutes the biggest warning." If wastes continued to be dumped into Lake Michigan at the existing rate, that great body of water had about a decade more of life. Happily, the warnings were heeded and the dumping soon slowed, saving the water from sure death.

Even the oceans, seemingly so vast as to be immune to human action, were showing signs of stress. A marine biologist noted in 1970 that "just in the past few years we are finding we can't sail anywhere in the Atlantic—even a thousand miles from land—without finding oil." The seams of tankers leaked oil all year round, quite apart from major spills. When the *Torry Canyon*, a 120,000-ton oil tanker tore itself open on a reef in the English Channel in March 1967, it spilled 36 million gallons of crude oil onto the Cornish coast and the shore of French Brittany, two hundred miles away. Thousands of birds died and tourism was interrupted. Tankers four times as large as the *Torry Canyon* were already on the drawing boards, and one million-ton vessels were in the talking stage.

The oil-well blowout off the coast of Santa Barbara, California, in 1969 had comparable results. Further blowouts from off-shore platform wells were considered likely as oil companies applied for new drilling leases. Though the oil industry afterward adopted new safety measures to curb future damage, the whole marine ecosystem of plants, birds, fishes, and animals appeared endangered from these episodes.

Along American sea coasts many estuaries that served as nurseries for marine life were being filled in to make new real estate. So much of San Francisco Bay had been filled in over the past few decades that that body of water no longer cooled the towns along its shores to the same degree as formerly. The summer temperature of the Bay cities was noticeably less comfortable.

Even more alarming changes occurred in those parts of the ocean that were used as dumping grounds for urban waste. Out in the Atlantic Ocean where New York dumped its waste were large fields of dead sea; all marine life apparently had expired.

Damage to the land and living things

The grizzly bear, blue whale, timber wolf, key deer, Florida panther, California bighorn, peregrine falcon, California condor, whooping crane, American bald eagle—all have become endangered species. To anyone familiar with American history it came as no shock to learn that mammals and birds were still endangered by such human activities as excessive hunting, spraying of chemicals, and disturbance of natural habitats. What was news in the seventies was the announcement by scientists that native American species of flowers, plants, and insects were also endangered by comparable causes. The Smithsonian Institution announced that two thousand species of plants were threatened.

Among them were many cacti of the southwestern deserts and Rocky Mountain wildflowers. Even many species of insects were imperiled (though not the mosquito or cockroach, which adapted very well to the human environment). Forty-one butterflies (like the Apache fritillary, with its three-inch flaming orange wings) were in peril. Environmentalists proposed that the butterflies be protected by the Department of the Interior.

Why be concerned about the disappearance of a few insects or plants when there are so many? Besides being beautiful and an integral and sometimes vital part of the local food chain, they often could be beneficial as sources of medicine, pest control, and even food. "Imagine the loss to mankind," said entomologist Paul Opler, ". . . if cinchona [the South American tree] had been destroyed before quinine was discovered as a cure for malaria."

One source of environmental pollution and damage to wild species and humans alike were new chemicals. Industry had long been notorious for befouling the air, land, and waters through the mindless dumping of chemical wastes. Now agriculture was equally to blame.

According to historian James Whorton, growers got themselves into the uncomfortable "dilemma of seemingly having to poison our food in order to protect it." In the 1950s they began routinely spraying large amounts of synthetic compounds (made by humans and not found in nature) to kill insects, weeds, and fungi. The insecticides chlordane, dieldrin, DDT, parathion, and malathion had dramatic effects in killing the bugs and microorganisms that preyed on grains, fruits, and vegetables. However, they were often also harmful to the birds, fishes, and animals, including people, who were exposed to them. Some farm workers who handled the poisonous sprays, powders, and liquids became ill or died. By soaking into

Surface mining in the United States is destroying 150,000 acres of land annually and has already defaced 3.2 million acres over the years. In 1970 about twenty thousand surface and stripmines were in operation; by 1980 an estimated additional 5 million acres will have been defaced by these operations or from their waste.

the soil and then trickling down into streams, these chemicals were carried far from their original sources. Some became even more concentrated as they passed through the food chain (for example, when birds ate contaminated fish). DDT destroyed the ability of some birds to produce strong eggshells, thereby threatening the survival of the species. For a time, the brown pelican hovered near extinction, an apparent victim of DDT poisoning.

Chemical fertilizers were an additional problem, for they were cheap, effective, and increasingly common. Unquestionably they permitted the farmer to grow more crops on less land. But the nitrates in chemical fertilizer, when absorbed by humans, turned into nitrites, a poisonous substance. The water supply of Decatur, Illinois, contaminated by chemical nitrates for farming, had an unacceptable level of nitrite. Most cattle were now grown on feed lots and their waste removed

rather than being allowed to return to the soil.

Road building, real estate development, and mining were also harming the environment. Wooded land was being cleared in the 1950s at the rate of one million acres yearly. If such loss of greenery continued, some biologists thought, it might seriously reduce the world's oxygen supply. In strip mining, mammoth steam shovels gouged away the top soil to uncover coal beds a hundred feet or so below the surface. The process was far cheaper than shaft mining but more damaging to the environment. About 150 acres in Kentucky were destroyed by strip miners daily during the early 1970s. Entire mountains had been torn down. Three billion tons of mining debris were being created annually by the U.S. mining industry.

Solid waste was also despoiling the land. Most people carried out the day's trash in soggy paper bags and forgot about it. But the disposal of 150 million tons of garbage and trash (over four pounds per person) each day was a nightmare. In the 1970s the nation discarded 7 million cars yearly, 100 million rubber tires, 4 million tons of plastic, and 20 billion bottles (100 for each person). Factories were dumping 10 million tons of steel and iron scrap. Much solid waste was simply dumped in an unsightly and unhealthy mess. Relatively little was being recycled, and finding a way to dispose of waste had become a great engineering puzzle.

Technology as culprit

A way of expressing the ecological crisis was to say that wealth was being produced in ways that were harmful to the ecosphere, that thin layer of land, water, and air which supported life on planet Earth. Age-old natural processes, some of them poorly understood, were being disturbed and ignored. People had forgotten, or had failed to learn,

that their species was biologically related to all surrounding life. Humans had broken out of the "circle of life," said Barry Commoner, and would have to find a way to "close the circle."

A major culprit, if not *the* major culprit, was the new technology. Many of today's pollution problems had simply not existed before the Second World War. Atomic energy, DDT, plastics, detergents, and chemical pesticides were either created during the war or developed because of wartime needs. Many of the newer industries used enormous amounts of energy. Aluminum and chemical plants, for example, accounted for about one quarter of the total industrial use of electric power in the U.S. Modern industry also used up nonreplaceable minerals like oil at an ever increasing rate. The new technology was based on brilliant theories in physics and chemistry—but not in biology. The scientific revolution of the past generation has been likened to a two-footed stool.

Cleaning the Nest

The quiet crisis

From the late forties to the early sixties the environmental problem was "a quiet crisis," in Stewart Udall's words. Only a handful of citizens were aware of the issue. Small groups of "nature freaks" like the Sierra Club and Audubon Society clashed repeatedly with commercial interests and usually went down to defeat. Gradually, however, their activity and publicity produced public awareness as well as some legislation.

Environmentalists won a memorable victory in the 1950s when they defeated the Bureau of Reclamation's plans for Echo Park Dam near the Colorado-Utah border. The giant new structure on the Green River was slated to drown out Dinosaur National Mon-

ument, a 320-square mile preserve of prehistoric fossils. Under federal law all such parks and monuments were to be preserved forever. Now one of them was to be sacrificed for water and power interests in the western states. If this could happen, asked the environmentalists, would any national park be safe? Wilderness advocates had no quarrel with water development in the West, only with such development as would destroy a protected wild area. Three hundred conservation groups combined in an effort to "Save Dinosaur!" They molded public opinion skillfully. Through a book of vivid photographs they reminded readers of the devastation caused by a dam in the beautiful Hetch

> *I look forward to an America not afraid of grace and beauty, which will protect the beauty of our national environment.*
>
> JOHN F. KENNEDY (1917–1963)

Hetchy Valley of California. Congressional mail ran eighty to one in favor of keeping Dinosaur wild. In April 1956, Congress killed the Echo Park Dam project.

Do books change history? If so, then Rachel Carson's *Silent Spring* (1962) may be counted among the most influential of our time. It touched off a furor over chemical insecticides, especially DDT. But it also sensitized people to wider environmental issues and quickened the demands for government protection of the environment. A trained scientist and a gifted writer, Carson warned that "the most alarming of all man's assaults upon the environment is the contamination of air, earth, rivers, and sea with dangerous and even lethal materials," including DDT. To a startled audience she carefully explained that "this pollution is for the most part irrecoverable. . . ." Chemical manufacturers attacked her "unfounded, sensational publicity" but could not drown out the clamor for protection against DDT and related insecticides. Ten years later, in 1972, the government outlawed DDT.

President Kennedy appointed a known conservationist to the post of interior secretary: Stewart Udall. His popular book *The Quiet Crisis* (1964) helped draw attention to conservation issues. But the president's preoccupation with foreign policy and his lack of success with domestic legislation stood in the way of reform. Udall came away from a meeting with the president on conservation in 1961 and said, "He is imprisoned by Berlin" (a reference to the Berlin crisis of that year). Kennedy signed legislation authorizing new purchases for national seashores, wildlife refuges, parks, and forests. And he established a Bureau of Outdoor Rec-

reation to better administer federal funds. More useful in the long run was the Clean Air Act of 1963, which allowed the Department of Health, Education, and Welfare to enforce reasonable standards of air purity. The initial effect was minimal, though, as the government decided to let the automobile industry have until 1976 to come up with a "clean" combustion engine.

Kennedy's greatest foreign policy achievement was also a major environmental victory: the Nuclear Test Ban Treaty of 1963. For a decade scientists and aroused citizens had demanded the full disclosure of secret data about the deadly radioactivity released by nuclear testing. While the Atomic Energy Commission continued to insist that nuclear testing was essentially harmless, American chemist Linus Pauling and other prominent scientists warned of the most dire results and demanded the halt of atmospheric testing. In 1956 testing for the first time became an issue in a presidential election. Finally the AEC conceded that the dangers of radioactivity were extensive. In 1963 the major nuclear powers (excluding France and China) signed a treaty agreeing to halt atmospheric tests.

The environmental lobby took the offensive in bringing about the important Wilderness Act of 1964. For years organizations devoted to preserving wilderness had been lobbying for the government to set aside wild preserves in the national parks that would stay free of mass recreation or commercial use. True virgin land—land as seen by the Indians and the early pioneers—was fast disappearing. Only about 2 percent of the country was still wilderness. Beginning in 1957, the wilderness bill ran the gauntlet of congressional hearings. Representatives for oil, mining, ranching, and forestry interests, as well as for many government bureaus and the mass recreation industry, denounced the proposal as too sweeping and economically constricting. Some who testified reminded Congress that the national parks must serve the public, not an elite minority of backpackers and mountain climbers. Proponents of the bill explained the value of wilderness in terms of beauty, recreation, science, and history. They invoked the names of John Muir, Henry David Thoreau, and Aldo Leopold. Their appeal to the memory of the frontier was particularly persuasive. As a result Congress passed and President Johnson signed the Wilderness Act of 1964, which established a network of fifty-four wild areas totaling 9 million acres and earmarked an additional 40 million acres for possible later inclusion.

The new conservation

By now the "quiet crisis" had become noisy. In February 1965 President Johnson issued a landmark message on conservation which dealt mainly with improving the overall quality of the environment. Let us, said the president, protect "our cities and countryside from blight with the same purpose and vigor with which, in other areas, we moved to save the forests and the soil." He proposed new trails for walking, bicycling, and horseback riding, new programs to control billboards, eliminate junkyards, landscape highways, and remove solid waste, and new efforts to preserve historic buildings and sites. Like Theodore Roosevelt's White House conference on conservation half a century earlier, Johnson's White House Conference on Natural Beauty in 1965 brought together state and local leaders to launch a campaign of national beautification.

The "new conservationism" gradually took legislative shape. Senator Edmund S. Muskie of Maine pushed through the Water Quality Act of 1965 and the Clean Water Restoration Act of 1966, which provided for elaborate programs of water pollution control. Congress authorized $3.5 billion for this effort, but Presidents Johnson and Nixon used only a fraction of it. Johnson signed legislation stripping billboards from U.S. highways. In effect, the advertising industry gave up its billboards in scenic areas to save the ones in business zones. Other legislation helped preserve historic landmarks. A nonprofit government corporation, the National Trust for Historic Preservation, got new funds for saving and restoring famous buildings and sites in Boston, Philadelphia, and elsewhere. When the Department of Transportation was created in 1966, it was required to protect the environment at every stage of its work. During the Nixon administration the new agency halted plans for a Florida airport that threatened the delicate ecology of the Everglades.

The Nixon administration supported the manufacture of a supersonic transport (SST) for overseas travel. Production of such a plane by the United States would have bolstered the sagging aerospace industry and met the challenge of a Soviet SST and a joint Anglo-French undertaking. But ecologists objected that the plane's sonic boom would serve as "the national alarm clock" as it thundered to earth. Even worse in the eyes of some, the exhaust from the jet engines would leave soot in the windless region above the atmosphere for all eternity, it was charged. In 1969 only nineteen senators were definitely against the SST. But doubts about its profitability grew, and in 1970, after a vigorous lobbying campaign by conservationists, fifty-two senators cut off federal funds and the big bird's wings.

President Nixon approved the Occupational Safety and Health Act of 1970, a bill sponsored by environmental organizations and organized labor, to clean up the danger and filth of the factory environment. More important, the president also approved the 1970 Clean Air Act, which set tough standards for auto exhaust on new cars by 1975—1976. In 1971 he merged five federal bureaus to create the Environmental Protection Agency (EPA). Its first head temporarily closed

In 1969, oil from an offshore drilling operation washed into a wildlife preserve in Santa Barbara, California. Although conservationists from all over the United States gathered to rescue the oil-soaked waterfowl, many birds died. A year later, Ralph Nader remarked, "It is expressive of the anemic and nondeterrent quality of existing sanctions that offshore oil leaks contaminating beaches for months, as in Santa Barbara, brought no penalty to any official of any offending company."

twenty-three factories in Birmingham until a siege of pollution ended.

Protecting threatened species

By midcentury it was estimated that white civilization in North America had helped destroy over twenty species of birds, animals, and fishes since the earliest European settlement. Hundreds more were immediately threatened by loss of habitat and by pesticides, fire, hunting, and fishing. A new coordinative effort was needed to identify, study, and preserve the threatened species. Preservationists lobbied successfully for the Endangered Species Preservation Act (1966). The law classified and gave protection in three main categories: *Endangered*—some ninety creatures close to extinction from disease, predators, or loss of habitat. *Rare*—wildlife with a small population that could be wiped out by disaster (like the fire that swept Martha's Vineyard in 1916, destroying the last remaining heath hens). *Peripheral*—species that had become scarce in our country, though they still flourished abroad. At least one hundred other creatures were to be watched carefully, simply because little was known of their condition.

"For one species to mourn the death of another is a new thing under the sun," Aldo Leopold once said. "We, who have lost our pigeons, mourn the loss. Had the funeral been ours, the pigeons would hardly have mourned us. In this fact, rather than in nylons or atomic bombs, lies evidence of our superiority over the beasts." Increased concern for endangered species helped some of them markedly. Among protected species which were either holding their own or making a strong comeback were the whooping crane, key deer, Everglade kite (a bird), brown pelican, and elephant seal.

But the "birds and bunnies freaks" who fought doggedly to protect wild species still had their work cut out for them. Whales, for example, were still being hunted into extinction by the fishermen of Russia and Japan, despite laws and treaties to the contrary. The conservationists in 1970 persuaded the Department of Interior to add to the endangered list the names of the eight biggest whales, some of which verged on extinction. Although the addition of these names ended the importation of products made from those animals, it did not persuade other countries to stop hunting for whales. This prompted the United States to ask for a ten-year worldwide suspension on all whale fishing.

For years botanists had warned that many plant species were also threatened with extinction. Their concern was finally beginning to receive attention. The Smithsonian Institution estimated that two thousand of the twenty thousand plants native to the U.S. could disappear forever if steps were not taken to protect them. About thirty thousand plants and flowers the world over are now endangered by modern civilization.

The energy crisis

By the 1970s the country was using seven times as much energy as it had at the turn of the century. Oil alone was consumed at the rate of about 230 billion barrels a year. At such a rate, with the demand for energy rising, most of the world's oil supply would be gone by the year 2000. The U.S. had billions of barrels of oil locked in shale in the western mountain states and fat veins of coal scattered throughout the country—enough for the next two hundred years. But extracting these fuels and putting them to use could exact a tremendous ecological cost. The coal would have a high sulphur content that would befoul the air, and much of it would require strip mining. The processing of oil shale would create blight in some of the nation's most beautiful natural areas.

The discovery of oil in northern Alaska presented other serious problems. Hundreds of miles of pipeline would be required to

Near Prudhoe Bay in northern Alaska, pipes waited while Congress and the courts considered arguments about construction of the pipeline to carry superheated oil across the permafrost. Meanwhile, one effect of civilization was seen in these nearly tame arctic foxes who hung around camp looking for handouts.

bring it to an ice-free ocean port for shipment. Environmentalists warned of the danger of such a line to the permafrost and to migrating caribou, a major source of food for Indians and Eskimos. They also cautioned that a break in the line would threaten the environment. For several years the oil producers were held back. Then, in 1973, the Arab oil-producing nations cut off America's supply, causing shortages of both home-heating oil and gasoline. And when they renewed their shipments, they greatly increased their prices. Suddenly it was clear that the old days of cheap fuel were gone and that the United States must find some way to decrease its dependence on imported oil. The Alaskan pipeline project moved ahead. Environmentalists dug in for a long, hard fight to prevent all their gains of the preceding decade from being reversed in the cause of self-sufficiency.

An intense debate arose as to whether nuclear energy for peaceful purposes was the answer to future energy needs. Was nuclear energy safe enough to use in electrical manufacture without excessively endangering human life? The Atomic Energy Commission claimed that the technology and management techniques had brought it down to the level of "tolerable risk." No serious mishaps had occurred in twenty-five years. Besides, any further delays in developing nuclear power would cause disastrous power brownouts and blackouts in the near future. Environmentalists countered that explosions, fires, hijackings, thefts, and other potential disasters made nuclear energy an intolerable risk. Some proposed a halt, either temporary or permanent, to further building and operating of nuclear plants. They wanted the money spent instead on developing alternate sources of energy such as solar energy.

Survival in the Balance

Was the sky really falling?
In the famous children's tale, Henny Penny, convinced by very flimsy evidence that the sky is falling, proceeds to panic the whole barnyard. Were the environmentalists behaving like Henny Penny, and were their followers like her frightened barnyard friends? The world will run out of just about everything except people, some of them predicted: food, fresh water, plastics, copper, wood, natural gas, and of course, oil. One billion people might die of famine in less than ten years, warned a noted biologist. Major rivers and lakes would "die" in ten to twenty-five years. A combination of dust and carbon monoxide would bring about the deadly "green-house effect" in ten to fifty years. If so, human survival — and therefore not merely the survival of the United States —

was hanging in the balance. And even if the modern-day Henny Pennys were exaggerating, could they be ignored completely?

In another famous animal allegory, the comic-strip character Pogo finds himself with a serious problem. Looking at the bright side, he wonders if maybe the problems are nothing but "insurmountable opportunities." Perhaps the ecology doomsayers were a blessing in disguise, overstating serious problems so that the world could repair them in time.

Perhaps some things could go right, after all. Consider the problem of population. At its 1960s rate of growth the U.S. population would reach almost 300 million by the turn of the century, increasing the drain on diminishing resources. According to Paul R.

Ehrlich, a specialist in population biology and author of the best seller *The Population Bomb* (1968), zero population growth (ZPG) was necessary as quickly as possible. Yet there seemed no practical way to bring it about. Then American adults decided, suddenly and privately, to have fewer children, whether because of inflation, new life styles, or ecological concerns. The birthrate dropped, and the U.S. was well along toward ZPG. The country might stabilize at 250 million inhabitants by the turn of the century.

Saving planet Earth

With a little luck, and intelligent planning, other improvements were possible. Drastic technological change would have to occur. Technology could no longer go by its own logic, without regard for social ends. Materials that were biologically harmful or made of exhaustible resources like oil might have to be curtailed drastically. Materials made of renewable resources like rubber, cotton, and wool might have to be more fully exploited once more. Farmers might have to return to natural, instead of chemical, fertilizers and insecticides. More efficient ground transportation, especially a "clean" automobile, deserved top priority. Recycling of metal, glass, and paper would have to proceed swiftly. To conserve fuel, the country needed smaller cars and better insulated buildings, fewer shopping and vacation trips, better use of

railroads for freight and commuter traffic. There might be less meat and more grain on the dinner table. Perhaps even textbooks should be shortened to conserve paper.

All citizens would have to learn new ways to create less waste. For example, European nations whose living standards were approximately on a par with those of the United States were far less wasteful of their resources.

Many aspects of the environmental crisis were worldwide in nature and therefore required international cooperation for solutions. The first worldwide meeting on ecological problems took place under UN auspices in Stockholm, Sweden, in June 1972. Despite obvious tensions between the developing and developed nations, the 114 national delegations found large areas of common agreement on the environment. The chairman of the meeting, a Canadian, believed that the conference "achieved a heartening consensus to the effect that no fundamental conflict exists between the goal of environmental quality on the one hand and economic social progress on the other." Two prominent participants, Britain's Lady Jackson (Barbara Ward) and France's René Dubos expressed the sentiments of many when they said: "Is it [planet Earth] not worth our love? Does it not deserve all the inventiveness and courage and generosity of which we are capable to preserve it from degradation and destruction and, by doing so, to secure our own survival?"

Review

The quality of earth, air, and water deteriorated noticeably in America, and throughout the world, in the postwar era. Many environmental problems were of relatively recent origin, though the majority were the result of generations of thoughtlessness, wasteful-

ness, and greed. Such new products as plastics, chemical fertilizers, and insecticides put a strain on the ecological balance. As the waste products of human technology polluted air and water, scientists expressed alarm about the effects not only on health and on the quality of life but on human survival itself.

Radioactive fallout from the atmospheric testing of nuclear weapons introduced many people to the problems of environmental pollution. Concern for radiation damage led to a deeper examination of a wide range of ecological issues, including the impact of DDT, of auto exhausts, and of the wastes pouring from industrial plants.

Though less obvious to most citizens than air pollution, water pollution also worried scientists greatly. Farm fertilizers and insecticides and city sewage and refuse damaged land, water, wildlife, and people. Rivers and lakes seemed to be "dying" at an alarming rate as they became garbage dumps for waste materials. In Lake Erie, for example, the dumping was destroying the delicate natural balance of living things and their environment. Even the ocean environment was harmed by oil spills.

The gouging of the land by strip miners was destroying millions of acres yearly. This was a cheaper way to dig coal than shaft mining, but it hurt the environment more severely. The dumping of solid waste was another problem that taxed nature.

For some years after World War II ecology was the concern only of a small, embattled minority. But gradually their struggle to save the environment attracted wider attention. The environmental movement grew and became better organized in the 1960s. New books with ominous titles, especially Rachel Carson's *Silent Spring,* warned the public of severe ecological damage from pollution. Spearheaded by the environmental lobby, voters began to demand, and obtain, more effective legislation.

A fuel crisis jolted the nation in 1973. The sudden scarcity of gasoline and heating oil pointed out the limits of national resources. Congressional approval of the Alaskan pipeline meant some reduction in America's dependence on foreign oil, but the pipeline itself was considered a danger by environmentalists.

Precisely how bad the "ecological crisis" was and what the ordinary citizen could do about it were confusing questions for most Americans. The more extreme predictions of gloom and doom were hard to accept. Yet all but the very young could remember when there was cleaner air to breathe and more room to breathe it in, clearer water to drink, and, more frequently, the sound of silence. Meanwhile, the world seemed to be running out of everything except mouths to feed. The need for drastic austerity measures was predicted throughout the world. In this country the cry was for labor and management, producers and consumers, to rethink priorities. The government must curtail and, if possible, repair environmental damage caused by modern technology. And in a larger context, the environmental crisis had its global dimensions. It was becoming imperative to find global solutions.

Questions

1. Identify and explain the significance of: (a) Endangered Species Preservation Act, (b) "death" of Lake Erie, (c) Test Ban Treaty of 1963, (d) Earth Day, (e) the "quiet crisis," and (f) *Silent Spring.*
2. Describe the environmental approaches taken by Presidents Kennedy, Johnson, and Nixon.
3. In what ways have environmental problems become global?
4. Name some of the ways that land, air, and water have become polluted in recent years.
5. Have environmental damage and shortages of resources affected you directly? What can citizens do to help solve these problems?
6. What part has technology played in bringing about the ecological crisis? Do you believe the crisis is a real one?

Selected Readings

OVERVIEW

Carl N. Degler has written a balanced, scholarly work in *Affluence and Anxiety* (Scott, Foresman, 1975).* Two other useful studies are David A. Shannon, *World War II and Since* (Rand McNally, 1974),* which is the final volume of *Twentieth Century America;* and Arthur S. Link and William B. Catton, *The American Epoch, Volume III, 1946–1973* (Knopf, 1974).*

WEALTH

To determine how wealth is made and distributed consult a basic economics text, such as Robert L. Heilbroner, *The Making of Economic Society* (Prentice-Hall, 1972).* Also useful is *Editorial Research Reports on the Trillion-Dollar Economy* (Congressional Quarterly, 1970).* Brief but systematic and intelligible is Douglass C. North, *Growth and Welfare in the American Past* (Prentice-Hall, 1973).* David M. Potter analyzes affluence in American culture in *The People of Plenty* (U. of Chicago Press, 1954).* Morton Mintz and Jerry S. Cohen, *America, Inc.: Who Owns and Operates the United States* (Dell, 1972)* argue that big business dominates the American economy almost entirely. Roland W. Bartlett, *Modern Private Enterprise: Is It Successful?* (Interstate, 1973)* asserts that small business still has vitality.

On the question of poverty, see Michael Harrington, *The Other America* (Penguin, 1962).* Frances F. Piven and Richard A. Cloward, *Regulating the Poor* (Random House, 1972)* describes the welfare mess in detail. Daniel P. Moynihan, *The Politics of a Guaranteed Income* (Random House, 1973)* discusses his proposal for solving the welfare tangle.

Alvin Toffler in *Future Shock* (Random House, 1971)* and *The Eco-Spasm Report: Why Our Economy is Running Out of Control* (Bantam, 1975)* attempt to explain life in the postindustrial era.

POWER

Two works—C. Wright Mills, *White Collar* (Oxford U. Press, 1956)* and David Reisman, *The Lonely Crowd* (Yale U. Press, 1969)*—offer conflicting theories of power. John K. Galbraith presents his concept of "countervailing power" in *American Capitalism* (Houghton Mifflin, 1962).* See also Richard Gillman, ed., *Power in Postwar America* (Little, Brown, 1971)* and G. William Domhoff, *Who Rules America?* (Prentice-Hall, 1967).*

The postwar presidents have been the subject of numerous works. Truman is dealt with in Alfred Steinberg,

* Available in paperback.

The Man from Missouri (Putnam, 1962). See also *Memoirs by Harry S. Truman* (Doubleday, 1958). Concerning Eisenhower, consult Emmet John Hughes, *The Ordeal of Power* (Atheneum, 1963), written by a member of the administration. On Kennedy see Arthur M. Schlesinger, Jr., *A Thousand Days* (Fawcett World, 1971);* Theodore C. Sorensen, *Kennedy* (Bantam, 1966);* and David Halberstam, *The Best and the Brightest* (Fawcett World, 1973).* Eric F. Goldman, *The Tragedy of Lyndon Johnson* (Dell, 1969)* is but one of many works on LBJ. Theodore White, *The Making of the President 1972* (Bantam, 1973)* tells of Nixon's election.

Studies of Watergate are still in the formative stage. See the historic exposé, Bob Woodward and Carl Bernstein, *All the President's Men* (Simon & Schuster, 1974). Many basic documents are in *The Watergate Hearings: Break-in and Cover-up* (Bantam, 1973),* edited by R. W. Apple, Jr., and the New York Times Staff. A masterful work by a constitutional lawyer is Raoul Berger, *Impeachment: The Constitutional Problems* (Bantam, 1974).*

WAR

For a brief survey of American foreign policy, see Paul Y. Hammond, *Cold War Years* (Harcourt Brace, 1969).* Lloyd C. Gardner, Arthur Meier Schlesinger, Jr., and Hans J. Morganthau, eds., *The Origins of the Cold War* (Xerox, 1970) present differing interpretations of a highly controversial subject. Extremely critical of the revisionist historians is Robert J. Maddox, *The New Left and the Origins of the Cold War* (Princeton U. Press, 1974).* Perhaps the most important revisionist is William A. Williams. His *American-Russian Relations, 1781–1947* (Octagon, 1971) and *The Tragedy of American Diplomacy* (World, 1959) attribute much of American policy to dollar diplomacy and the Open Door. The scariest moment of the Cold War—the Cuba crisis in October, 1962—is dealt with in a fascinating account by Elie Abel, *The Missile Crisis* (Lippincott, 1966).

On Korea see Carl Berger, *The Korea Knot* (U. of Pennsylvania Press, 1964) and I. F. Stone, *The Hidden History of the Korean War* (Monthly Review, 1969).*

The Vietnam conflict has already inspired a number of studies. Marcus G. Raskin and Bernard B. Fall, eds., *The Viet-Nam Reader* (Vintage, 1965)* is an enlightening anthology on the early phases of the war. Contrast *Responsibility and Response* (Harper & Row, 1967) by Maxwell Taylor, a top military policy maker, with *American Power and the New Mandarins* (Random House, 1969) by Noam Chomsky, an academician who was highly vocal in his opposition to the war. The foreign policy goals of the early Nixon administration are presented by Henry Kissinger, *American Foreign Policy* (Norton, 1969).*

RACE
Many facets of the history of race relations since 1945 are presented in a one-volume anthology by C. Snyder, called *Red and Yellow, Black and Brown* (Holt, Rinehart, 1974).

The civil rights revolution can be sampled in James Baldwin, *The Fire Next Time* (Dell, 1970),* James Farmer, *Freedom—When?* (Random House, 1966); Stokeley Carmichael and Charles V. Hamilton, *Black Power* (Random House, 1968);* Martin Luther King, Jr., *Why We Can't Wait* (New American Library, 1964);* and Lerone Bennet, Jr., *What Manner of Man: A Biography of Martin Luther King, Jr.* (Pocket Books, 1968). See also the electrifying *Autobiography of Malcolm X* (Grove, 1965).

On the awakening of the Chicano, see Acuña, cited on p. 337, and the Ortego book, cited on p. 668. Stan Steiner, *The New Indians* (Dell, 1969)* describes the stirrings of native Americans in recent years. Vine Deloria, Jr., *Custer Died for Your Sins* (Avon, 1970)* is a lively statement by an articulate Indian.

Asian Americans are the least well understood of the racial minorities. See Stanford Lyman, *Chinese Americans* (Random House, 1974)* and Victor G. Nee and Brett De Bary Nee, *Long Time Californ'* (Pantheon, 1973), which describes the Chinese experience in modern America.

NATIONALITY AND RELIGION
The white ethnics have found a champion in Michael Novak. His *Rise of the Unmeltable Ethnics* (Macmillan, 1972)* is lively and informative, though not altogether convincing. Perry L. Weed, *The White Ethnic Movement and Ethnic Politics* (Praeger, 1973) is informative. On the ethnic revival see also Andrew M. Greeley, *Why Can't They Be Like Us?* (American Jewish Comm., 1969).* WASPs have also become a minority; see Charles Anderson, *White Protestant Americans* (Prentice-Hall, 1970).* See also Nathan Glazer and Daniel P. Moynihan, *Beyond the Melting Pot* (MIT Press, 1970).* Joseph P. Fitzpatrick, *Puerto Rican Americans* (Prentice-Hall, 1971)* is the most up-to-date treatment of this minority.

For religious history see the works by Ahlstrom and Hudson, cited on p. 519. Dealing with the recent era are James N. Gustafson and Richard D. Lambert, eds., *The Sixties—Radical Change in American Religion* (Am. Acad. Pol. Soc. Sci., 1970); Jacob Neusner, *American Judaism: Adventure in Modernity* (Prentice-Hall, 1972);* Philip Gleason, ed., *Contemporary Catholicism in the United States* (U. of Notre Dame Press, 1969); and Frank S.

Mead, *Handbook of Denominations in the United States* (Abingdon, 1970).

WOMEN AND THE FAMILY
Historians are beginning to make up for lost time in studying the family. See Theodore K. Rabb and Robert I. Rotberg, *The Family in History: Interdisciplinary Essays* (Harper & Row, 1973).* A collection of essays on the younger generation is Erik H. Erikson, ed., *The Challenge of Youth* (Doubleday, 1965).*

Betty Friedan, *The Feminine Mystique* (Norton, 1963) set the new feminism into motion. Another basic work is Kate Millett, *Sexual Politics* (Avon, 1971).* Norman Mailer, *Prisoner of Sex* (New American Library, 1971)* is written by a male whose ideas are not popular with feminists. Elsie Adams and Mary L. Briscoe, *Up Against the Wall, Mother* (Glencoe, 1971)* contains lively selections.

COMMUNITY
Several valuable books on the commune movement have been published. See Richard Fairfield, *Communes U.S.A.* (Penguin, 1972);* Kanter, cited on p. 337; and Keith Melville, *Communes in the Counter Culture* (Morrow, 1972).* Two works of fiction on communes have attracted much attention: Robert H. Rimmer, *The Harrad Experiment* (Bantam, 1973)* and B. F. Skinner, *Walden Two* (Macmillan, 1960).*

Jane Jacobs, *The Death and Life of Great American Cities* (Random House, 1961),* is highly critical of most city planners. Martin Anderson, *The Federal Bulldozer* (McGraw, 1967)* is a devastating treatment of urban renewal.

Presidential commissions on urban life have presented a great deal of information to the public. See the Kerner Commission's *Report of the National Advisory Commission on Civil Disorders* (Dutton, 1968), put together by the New York Times Editors.

Edward Banfield, *The Unheavenly City* (Little, Brown, 1970) irritated many liberals.

ENVIRONMENT
The literature on this topic has mushroomed since the 1960s. As a complement to Rachel Carson's *The Silent Spring* (Houghton Mifflin, 1973),* see Paul Brooks, *The House of Life: Rachel Carson at Work* (Fawcett World, 1974).* *The Population Bomb* (Ballantine, 1971)* by biologist Paul R. Erlich was highly influential despite its doomsday tone. Barry Commoner, *The Closing Circle* (Bantam, 1972)* describes the interaction of technology and biological processes. Many facets of the environmental controversy are covered by Eugene P. Odum et al., in *The Crisis of Survival* (Scott, Foresman, 1970).*

CHRONICLE: MUSEUM OF THE STREETS

o new walls
talking loudly

In the late 1960s public murals began to spring up in
cities throughout the country — big walls with a rugged
imagery of protest and self-identification. The inspiration
of committed artists and the support of local communities
started a mural movement among black, Chicano, Puerto
Rican, and American Indian artists. In executing the huge
paintings, the artist usually would function as director,
carrying out the project with the active help of neighborhood residents. The resulting wall paintings (and the
graffiti which emerged as an outgrowth of the movement)
embodied topical concerns of the city; such works related
directly to the daily life and current interests of the neighborhoods in which they appeared. They were not isolated
monuments; rather, they were brief emblems of the city
which tended to sink back into the texture and mobility of
the street.

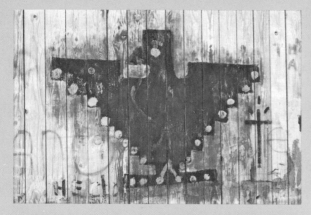

there is no memorial site
in harlem
save the one we are building
in the street of
our young minds
till our hands & eyes
have the strength to mould
the concrete beneath our feet

For Brother Malcolm
Edward S. Spriggs

moving let's go
let's go fast up up up
where
by the candy store   la vieja
la vieja is still alive &
chuchifritos & rice & beans by
la bodega de pepe   by the corner
anti-poverty housing toms
by chelas & the kids yelling & pushing
people down

hey hey
what's happening
que pasa

o new walls
talking loudly

from *Back to / Back to*
Victor Hernandez Cruz

THE DECLARATION OF INDEPENDENCE
In Congress, July 4, 1776

The unanimous Declaration
of the thirteen united States of America,

When in the Course of human events, it becomes necessary for one people to dissolve the political bands which have connected them with another, and to assume among the Powers of the earth, the separate and equal station to which the Laws of Nature and of Nature's God entitle them, a decent respect to the opinions of mankind requires that they should declare the causes which impel them to the separation.

We hold these truths to be self-evident, that all men are created equal, that they are endowed by their Creator with certain unalienable Rights, that among these are Life, Liberty and the pursuit of Happiness. That to secure these rights, Governments are instituted among Men, deriving their just powers from the consent of the governed, That whenever any Form of Government becomes destructive of these ends, it is the Right of the People to alter or to abolish it, and to institute new Government, laying its foundation on such principles and organizing its powers in such form, as to them shall seem most likely to effect their Safety and Happiness. Prudence, indeed, will dictate that Governments long established should not be changed for light and transient causes; and accordingly all experience hath shown, that mankind are more disposed to suffer, while evils are sufferable, than to right themselves by abolishing the forms to which they are accustomed. But when a long train of abuses and usurpations, pursuing invariably the same Object evinces a design to reduce them under absolute Despotism, it is their right, it is their duty, to throw off such Government, and to provide new Guards for their future security.— Such has been the patient sufferance of these Colonies; and such is now the necessity which constrains them to alter their former Systems of Government. The history of the present King of Great Britain is a history of repeated injuries and usurpations, all having in direct object the establishment of an absolute Tyranny over these States. To prove this, let Facts be submitted to a candid world.

He has refused his Assent to Laws, the most wholesome and necessary for the public good.

He has forbidden his Governors to pass Laws of immediate and pressing importance, unless suspended in their operation till his Assent should be obtained; and when so suspended, he has utterly neglected to attend to them.

He has refused to pass other Laws for the accommodation of large districts of people, unless those people would relinquish the right of Representation in the Legislature, a right inestimable to them and formidable to tyrants only.

He has called together legislative bodies at places unusual, uncomfortable, and distant from the depository of their Public Records, for the sole purpose of fatiguing them into compliance with his measures.

He has dissolved Representative Houses repeatedly, for opposing with manly firmness his invasions on the rights of the people.

He has refused for a long time, after such dissolutions, to cause others to be elected; whereby the Legislative Powers, incapable of Annihilation, have returned to the People at large for their exercise; the State remaining in the mean time exposed to all the dangers of invasion from without, and convulsions within.

He has endeavoured to prevent the population of these States; for that purpose obstructing the Laws for Naturalization of Foreigners; refusing to pass others to encourage their migrations hither, and raising the conditions of new Appropriations of Lands.

He has obstructed the Administration of Justice, by refusing his Assent to Laws for establishing Judiciary Powers.

He has made Judges dependent on his Will alone, for the tenure of their offices, and the amount and payment of their salaries.

He has erected a multitude of New Offices, and sent hither swarms of Officers to harass our people, and eat out their substance.

He has kept among us, in times of peace, Standing Armies without the Consent of our legislatures.

He has affected to render the Military independent of and superior to the Civil Power.

He has combined with others to subject us to a jurisdiction foreign to our constitution, and unacknowledged by our laws; giving his Assent to their acts of pretended Legislation:

For quartering large bodies of armed troops among us:

For protecting them, by a mock Trial, from Punishment for any Murders which they should commit on the Inhabitants of these States:

For cutting off our Trade with all parts of the world:

For imposing taxes on us without our Consent:

For depriving us in many cases, of the benefits of Trial by Jury:

For transporting us beyond Seas to be tried for pretended offences:

For abolishing the free System of English Laws in a neighbouring Province, establishing therein an Arbitrary government, and enlarging its Boundaries so as to render it at once an example and fit instrument for introducing the same absolute rule into these Colonies:

For taking away our Charters, abolishing our most valuable Laws, and altering fundamentally the Forms of our Governments:

For suspending our own Legislatures, and declaring themselves invested with Power to legislate for us in all cases whatsoever.

He has abdicated Government here, by declaring us out of his Protection and waging War against us.

He has plundered our seas, ravaged our Coasts, burnt our towns, and destroyed the lives of our people.

He is at this time transporting large armies of foreign mercenaries to compleat the works of death, desolation and tyranny, already begun with circumstances of Cruelty & perfidy scarcely paralleled in the most barbarous ages, and totally unworthy the Head of a civilized nation.

He has constrained our fellow Citizens taken Captive on the high Seas to bear Arms against their Country, to become the executioners of their friends and Brethren, or to fall themselves by their Hands.

He has excited domestic insurrections amongst us, and has endeavoured to bring on the inhabitants of our frontiers, the merciless Indian Savages, whose known rule of warfare, is an undistinguished destruction of all ages, sexes and conditions.

In every stage of these Oppressions We have Petitioned for Redress in the most humble terms: Our repeated Petitions have been answered only by repeated injury. A Prince, whose character is thus marked by every act which may define a Tyrant, is unfit to be the ruler of a free people.

Nor have We been wanting in attentions to our British brethren. We have warned them from time to time of attempts by their legislature to extend an unwarrantable jurisdiction over us. We have reminded them of the circumstances of our emigration and settlement here. We have appealed to their native justice and magnanimity, and we have conjured them by the ties of our common kindred to disavow these usurpations which, would inevitably interrupt our connections and correspondence. They too have been deaf to the voice of justice and of consanguinity. We must, therefore, acquiesce in the necessity, which denounces our Separation, and hold them, as we hold the rest of mankind, Enemies in War, in Peace Friends.

We, therefore, the Representatives of the united States of America, in General Congress, Assembled, appealing to the Supreme Judge of the world for the rectitude of our intentions, do, in the Name, and by authority of the good People of these Colonies, solemnly publish and declare, That these United Colonies are, and of Right ought to be Free and Independent States; that they are Absolved from all Allegiance to the British Crown, and that all political connection between them and the State of Great Britain, is and ought to be totally dissolved; and that as Free and Independent States, they have full power to levy War, conclude Peace, contract Alliances, establish Commerce, and to do all other Acts and Things which Independent States may of right do. And for the support of this Declaration, with a firm reliance on the Protection of Divine Providence, we mutually pledge to each other our Lives, our Fortunes and our sacred Honor.

JOHN HANCOCK	GEO. TAYLOR
BUTTON GWINNETT	JAMES WILSON
LYMAN HALL	GEO. ROSS
GEO. WALTON	CAESAR RODNEY
WM. HOOPER	GEO. READ
JOSEPH HEWES	THO. M'KEAN
JOHN PENN	WM. FLOYD
EDWARD RUTLEDGE	PHIL. LIVINGSTON
THOS. HEYWARD, Junr.	FRANS. LEWIS
THOMAS LYNCH, Junr.	LEWIS MORRIS
ARTHUR MIDDLETON	RICHD. STOCKTON
SAMUEL CHASE	JNO. WITHERSPOON
WM. PACA	FRAS. HOPKINSON
THOS. STONE	JOHN HART
CHARLES CARROLL	ABRA. CLARK
OF CARROLLTON	JOSIAH BARTLETT
GEORGE WYTHE	WM. WHIPPLE
RICHARD HENRY LEE	SAML. ADAMS
TH. JEFFERSON	JOHN ADAMS
BENJ. HARRISON	ROBT. TREAT PAINE
THOS. NELSON, JR.	ELBRIDGE GERRY
FRANCIS LIGHTFOOT LEE	STEP. HOPKINS
CARTER BRAXTON	WILLIAM ELLERY
ROBT. MORRIS	ROGER SHERMAN
BENJAMIN RUSH	SAM'EL. HUNTINGTON
BENJA. FRANKLIN	WM. WILLIAMS
JOHN MORTON	OLIVER WOLCOTT
GEO. CLYMER	MATTHEW THORNTON
JAS. SMITH	

THE CONSTITUTION OF
THE UNITED STATES OF AMERICA

We the People of the United States, in Order to form a more perfect Union, establish Justice, insure domestic Tranquility, provide for the common defence, promote the general Welfare, and secure the Blessings of Liberty to ourselves and our Posterity, do ordain and establish this Constitution for the United States of America.

ARTICLE I.

Section 1.

All legislative Powers herein granted shall be vested in a Congress of the United States, which shall consist of a Senate and House of Representatives.

Section 2.

The House of Representatives shall be composed of Members chosen every second Year by the People of the several States, and the Electors in each State shall have the Qualifications requisite for Electors of the most numerous Branch of the State Legislature.

No Person shall be a Representative who shall not have attained to the Age of twenty five Years, and been seven Years a Citizen of the United States, and who shall not, when elected, be an Inhabitant of that State in which he shall be chosen.

Representatives and direct Taxes shall be apportioned among the several States which may be included within this Union, according to their respective Numbers, which shall be determined by adding to the whole Number of free Persons, including those bound to Service for a Term of Years, and excluding Indians not taxed, three fifths of all other Persons.[1] The actual Enumeration shall be made within three Years after the first Meeting of the Congress of the United States, and within every subsequent Term of ten Years, in such Manner as they shall by Law direct. The Number of Representatives shall not exceed one for every thirty Thousand, but each State shall have at Least one Representative; and until such enumeration shall be made, the State of New Hampshire shall be entitled to chuse three, Massachusetts eight, Rhode-Island and Providence Plantations one, Connecticut five, New-York six, New Jersey four, Pennsylvania eight, Delaware one, Maryland six, Virginia ten, North Carolina five, South Carolina five, and Georgia three.

When vacancies happen in the Representation from any State, the Executive Authority thereof shall issue Writs of Election to fill such Vacancies.

The House of Representatives shall chuse their Speaker and other Officers; and shall have the sole Power of Impeachment.

Section 3.

The Senate of the United States shall be composed of two Senators from each State, chosen by the Legislature thereof, for six Years; and each Senator shall have one Vote.

Immediately after they shall be assembled in Consequence of the first Election, they shall be divided as equally as may be into three Classes. The Seats of the Senators of the first Class shall be vacated at the Expiration of the second Year, of the second Class at the Expiration of the fourth Year, and of the third Class at the Expiration of the sixth Year, so that one third may be chosen every second Year; and if Vacancies happen by Resignation, or otherwise, during the Recess of the Legislature of any State, the Executive thereof may make temporary Appointments until the next Meeting of the Legislature, which shall then fill such Vacancies.[2]

No Person shall be a Senator who shall not have attained to the Age of thirty Years, and been nine Years a Citizen of the United States, and who shall not, when elected, be an Inhabitant of that State for which he shall be chosen.

The Vice President of the United States shall be President of the Senate, but shall have no Vote, unless they be equally divided.

The Senate shall chuse their other Officers, and also a President pro tempore, in the Absence of the Vice President, or when he shall exercise the Office of President of the United States.

The Senate shall have the sole Power to try all Impeachments. When sitting for that Purpose, they shall be on Oath or Affirmation. When the President of the United States is tried the Chief Justice shall preside: And no Person shall be convicted without the Concurrence of two thirds of the Members present.

Judgment in Cases of Impeachment shall not extend further than to removal from Office, and disqualification to hold and enjoy any Office of honor, Trust or Profit under the United States: but the Party convicted shall nevertheless be liable and subject to Indictment, Trial, Judgment and Punishment, according to Law.

Section 4.

The Times, Places and Manner of holding Elections for Senators and Representatives, shall be prescribed in each State by the Legislature thereof; but the Congress may at

---

[1] "Other Persons" being black slaves. Modified by Amendment XIV, Section 2.

[2] Provisions changed by Amendment XVII.

any time by Law make or alter such Regulations, except as to the Places of chusing Senators.

The Congress shall assemble at least once in every Year, and such Meeting shall be on the first Monday in December, unless they shall by Law appoint a different Day.[3]

Section 5.

Each House shall be the Judge of the Elections, Returns and Qualifications of its own Members, and a Majority of each shall constitute a Quorum to do Business; but a smaller Number may adjourn from day to day, and may be authorized to compel the Attendance of absent Members, in such Manner, and under such Penalties as each House may provide.

Each House may determine the Rules of its Proceedings, punish its Members for disorderly Behaviour, and, with the Concurrence of two thirds, expel a Member.

Each House shall keep a Journal of its Proceedings, and from time to time publish the same, excepting such Parts as may in their Judgment require Secrecy; and the Yeas and Nays of the Members of either House on any question shall, at the Desire of one fifth of those Present, be entered on the Journal.

Neither House, during the Session of Congress, shall, without the Consent of the other, adjourn for more than three days, nor to any other Place than that in which the two Houses shall be sitting.

Section 6.

The Senators and Representatives shall receive a Compensation for their Services, to be ascertained by Law, and paid out of the Treasury of the United States. They shall in all Cases, except Treason, Felony and Breach of the Peace, be privileged from Arrest during their Attendance at the Session of their respective Houses, and in going to and returning from the same; and for any Speech or Debate in either House, they shall not be questioned in any other Place.

No Senator or Representative shall, during the Time for which he was elected, be appointed to any civil Office under the Authority of the United States, which shall have been created, or the Emoluments whereof shall have been encreased during such time; and no Person holding any Office under the United States, shall be a Member of either House during his Continuance in Office.

Section 7.

All Bills for raising Revenue shall originate in the House of Representatives; but the Senate may propose or concur with Amendments as on other Bills.

Every Bill which shall have passed the House of Representatives and the Senate, shall, before it become a Law,

be presented to the President of the United States; If he approve he shall sign it, but if not he shall return it, with his Objections to that House in which it shall have originated, who shall enter the Objections at large on their Journal, and proceed to reconsider it. If after such Reconsideration two thirds of that House shall agree to pass the Bill, it shall be sent, together with the Objections, to the other House, by which it shall likewise be reconsidered, and if approved by two thirds of that House, it shall become a Law. But in all such Cases the Votes of both Houses shall be determined by yeas and Nays, and the Names of the Persons voting for and against the Bill shall be entered on the Journal of each House respectively. If any Bill shall not be returned by the President within ten Days (Sundays excepted) after it shall have been presented to him, the Same shall be a Law, in like Manner as if he had signed it, unless the Congress by their Adjournment prevent its Return, in which Case it shall not be a Law.

Every Order, Resolution, or Vote to which the Concurrence of the Senate and House of Representatives may be necessary (except on a question of Adjournment) shall be presented to the President of the United States; and before the Same shall take Effect, shall be approved by him, or being disapproved by him, shall be repassed by two thirds of the Senate and House of Representatives, according to the Rules and Limitations prescribed in the Case of a Bill.

Section 8.

The Congress shall have Power To lay and collect Taxes, Duties, Imposts and Excises, to pay the Debts and provide for the common Defence and general Welfare of the United States; but all Duties, Imposts and Excises shall be uniform throughout the United States;

To borrow Money on the credit of the United States;

To regulate Commerce with foreign Nations, and among the several States, and with the Indian Tribes;

To establish an uniform Rule of Naturalization, and uniform Laws on the subject of Bankruptcies throughout the United States;

To coin Money, regulate the Value thereof, and of foreign Coin, and fix the Standard of Weights and Measures;

To provide for the Punishment of counterfeiting the Securities and current Coin of the United States;

To establish Post Offices and post Roads;

To promote the Progress of Science and useful Arts, by securing for limited Times to Authors and Inventors the exclusive Right to their respective Writings and Discoveries;

To constitute Tribunals inferior to the supreme Court;

To define and punish Piracies and Felonies committed on the high Seas, and Offences against the Law of Nations;

To declare War, grant Letters of Marque and Reprisal, and make Rules concerning Captures on Land and Water;

To raise and support Armies, but no Appropriation of

---

[3]Provision changed by Amendment XX, Section 2.

Money to that Use shall be for a longer Term than two Years;

To provide and maintain a Navy;

To make Rules for the Government and Regulation of the land and naval Forces;

To provide for calling forth the Militia to execute the Laws of the Union, suppress Insurrections and repel Invasions;

To provide for organizing, arming, and disciplining, the Militia, and for governing such Part of them as may be employed in the Service of the United States, reserving to the States respectively, the Appointment of the Officers, and the Authority of training the Militia according to the discipline prescribed by Congress;

To exercise exclusive Legislation in all Cases whatsoever, over such District (not exceeding ten Miles square) as may, by Cession of particular States, and the Acceptance of Congress, become the Seat of the Government of the United States, and to exercise like Authority over all Places purchased by the Consent of the Legislature of the State in which the Same shall be, for the Erection of Forts, Magazines, Arsenals, dock-Yards, and other needful Buildings;—And

To make all Laws which shall be necessary and proper for carrying into Execution the foregoing Powers, and all other Powers vested by this Constitution in the Government of the United States, or in any Department or Officer thereof.

Section 9.

The Migration or Importation of such Persons as any of the States now existing shall think proper to admit, shall not be prohibited by the Congress prior to the Year one thousand eight hundred and eight, but a Tax or duty may be imposed on such Importation, not exceeding ten dollars for each Person.

The Privilege of the Writ of Habeas Corpus shall not be suspended, unless when in Cases of Rebellion or Invasion the public Safety may require it.

No Bill of Attainder or ex post facto Law shall be passed.

No Capitation, or other direct, Tax shall be laid, unless in Proportion to the Census or Enumeration herein before directed to be taken.

No Tax or Duty shall be laid on Articles exported from any State.

No Preference shall be given by any Regulation of Commerce or Revenue to the Ports of one State over those of another: nor shall Vessels bound to, or from, one State, be obliged to enter, clear, or pay Duties in another.

No Money shall be drawn from the Treasury, but in Consequence of Appropriations made by Law; and a regular Statement and Account of the Receipts and Expenditures of all public Money shall be published from time to time.

No Title of Nobility shall be granted by the United States: And no Person holding any Office of Profit or Trust under them, shall, without the Consent of the Congress, accept of any present, Emolument, Office, or Title, of any kind whatever, from any King, Prince, or foreign State.

Section 10.

No State shall enter into any Treaty, Alliance, or Confederation; grant Letters of Marque and Reprisal; coin Money; emit Bills of Credit; make any Thing but gold and silver Coin a Tender in Payment of Debts; pass any Bill of Attainder, ex post facto Law, or Law impairing the Obligation of Contracts, or grant any Title of Nobility.

No State shall, without the Consent of the Congress, lay any Imposts or Duties on Imports or Exports, except what may be absolutely necessary for executing its inspection Laws: and the net Produce of all Duties and Imposts, laid by any State on Imports or Exports, shall be for the Use of the Treasury of the United States; and all such Laws shall be subject to the Revision and Controul of the Congress.

No State shall, without the Consent of Congress, lay any Duty of Tonnage, keep Troops, or Ships of War in time of Peace, enter into any Agreement or Compact with another State, or with a foreign Power, or engage in War, unless actually invaded, or in such imminent Danger as will not admit of delay.

ARTICLE II.

Section 1.

The executive Power shall be vested in a President of the United States of America. He shall hold his Office during the Term of four Years, and, together with the Vice President, chosen for the same Term, be elected, as follows:

Each State shall appoint, in such Manner as the Legislature thereof may direct, a Number of Electors, equal to the whole Number of Senators and Representatives to which the State may be entitled in the Congress: but no Senator or Representative, or Person holding an Office of Trust or Profit under the United States, shall be appointed an Elector.

The Electors shall meet in their respective States, and vote by Ballot for two Persons, of whom one at least shall not be an Inhabitant of the same State with themselves. And they shall make a List of all the Persons voted for, and of the Number of Votes for each; which List they shall sign and certify, and transmit sealed to the Seat of the Government of the United States, directed to the President of the Senate. The President of the Senate shall, in the Presence of the Senate and House of Representatives, open all the Certificates, and the Votes shall then be counted. The Person having the greatest Number of Votes shall be the President, if such Number be a Majority of the whole Number of Electors appointed; and if there be more than one who have such Majority, and have an equal Number of Votes, then the House of

Representatives shall immediately chuse by Ballot one of them for President; and if no Person have a Majority, then from the five highest on the List the said House shall in like Manner chuse the President. But in chusing the President, the Votes shall be taken by States, the Representation from each State having one Vote; A quorum for this Purpose shall consist of a Member or Members from two thirds of the States, and a Majority of all the States shall be necessary to a Choice. In every Case, after the Choice of the President, the Person having the greatest Number of Votes of the Electors shall be the Vice President. But if there should remain two or more who have equal Votes, the Senate shall chuse from them by Ballot the Vice President.[4]

The Congress may determine the Time of chusing the Electors, and the Day on which they shall give their Votes; which Day shall be the same throughout the United States.

No Person except a natural born Citizen, or a Citizen of the United States, at the time of the Adoption of this Constitution, shall be eligible to the Office of President; neither shall any Person be eligible to that Office who shall not have attained to the Age of thirty five Years, and been fourteen Years a Resident within the United States.

In Case of the Removal of the President from Office, or of his Death, Resignation, or Inability to discharge the Powers and Duties of the said Office, the Same shall devolve on the Vice President, and the Congress may by Law provide for the Case of Removal, Death, Resignation or Inability, both of the President and Vice President, declaring what Officer shall then act as President, and such Officer shall act accordingly, until the Disability be removed, or a President shall be elected.

The President shall, at stated Times, receive for his Services, a Compensation, which shall neither be encreased nor diminished during the Period for which he shall have been elected, and he shall not receive within that Period any other Emolument from the United States, or any of them.

Before he enter on the Execution of his Office, he shall take the following Oath or Affirmation:—"I do solemnly swear (or affirm) that I will faithfully execute the Office of President of the United States, and will to the best of my Ability, preserve, protect and defend the Constitution of the United States."

Section 2.

The President shall be Commander in Chief of the Army and Navy of the United States, and of the Militia of the several States, when called into the actual Service of the United States; he may require the Opinion, in writing, of the principal Officer in each of the executive Departments, upon any Subject relating to the Duties of their respective Offices, and he shall have Power to grant

Reprieves and Pardons for Offences against the United States, except in Cases of Impeachment.

He shall have Power, by and with the Advice and Consent of the Senate, to make Treaties, provided two thirds of the Senators present concur; and he shall nominate, and by and with the Advice and Consent of the Senate, shall appoint Ambassadors, other public Ministers and Consuls, Judges of the supreme Court, and all other Officers of the United States, whose Appointments are not herein otherwise provided for, and which shall be established by Law: but the Congress may by Law vest the Appointment of such inferior Officers, as they think proper in the President alone, in the Courts of Law, or in the Heads of Departments.

The President shall have Power to fill up all Vacancies that may happen during the Recess of the Senate, by granting Commissions which shall expire at the End of their next Session.

Section 3.

He shall from time to time give to the Congress Information of the State of the Union, and recommend to their Consideration such Measures as he shall judge necessary and expedient; he may, on extraordinary Occasions, convene both Houses, or either of them, and in Case of Disagreement between them, with Respect to the Time of Adjournment, he may adjourn them to such Time as he shall think proper; he shall receive Ambassadors and other public Ministers; he shall take Care that the Laws be faithfully executed, and shall Commission all the Officers of the United States.

Section 4.

The President, Vice President and all civil Officers of the United States, shall be removed from Office on Impeachment for, and Conviction of, Treason, Bribery, or other high Crimes and Misdemeanors.

ARTICLE III.

Section 1.

The judicial Power of the United States, shall be vested in one supreme Court, and in such inferior Courts as the Congress may from time to time ordain and establish. The Judges, both of the supreme and inferior Courts, shall hold their Offices during good Behaviour, and shall, at stated Times, receive for their Services, a Compensation, which shall not be diminished during their Continuance in Office.

Section 2.

The judicial Power shall extend to all Cases, in Law and Equity, arising under this Constitution, the Laws of the United States, and Treaties made, or which shall be made, under their Authority;—to all Cases affecting

---

[4]Provisions superseded by Amendment XII.

Ambassadors, other public Ministers and Consuls;—to all Cases of admiralty and maritime Jurisdiction;—to Controversies to which the United States shall be a Party;—to Controversies between two or more States;—between a State and Citizens of another State;—between Citizens of different States,—between Citizens of the same State claiming Lands under Grants of different States, and between a State, or the Citizens thereof, and foreign States, Citizens or Subjects.[5]

In all Cases affecting Ambassadors, other public Ministers and Consuls, and those in which a State shall be Party, the supreme Court shall have original Jurisdiction. In all the other Cases before mentioned, the supreme Court shall have appellate Jurisdiction, both as to Law and Fact, with such Exceptions, and under such Regulations as the Congress shall make.

The Trial of all Crimes, except in Cases of Impeachment, shall be by Jury; and such Trial shall be held in the State where the said Crimes shall have been committed; but when not committed within any State, the Trial shall be at such Place or Places as the Congress may by Law have directed.

Section 3.

Treason against the United States, shall consist only in levying War against them, or in adhering to their Enemies, giving them Aid and Comfort. No person shall be convicted of Treason unless on the Testimony of two Witnesses to the same overt Act, or on Confession in open Court.

The Congress shall have Power to declare the Punishment of Treason, but no Attainder of Treason shall work Corruption of Blood, or Forfeiture except during the Life of the Person attainted.

ARTICLE IV.

Section 1.

Full Faith and Credit shall be given in each State to the public Acts, Records, and judicial Proceedings of every other State. And the Congress may by general Laws prescribe the Manner in which such Acts, Records and Proceedings shall be proved, and the Effect thereof.

Section 2.

The Citizens of each State shall be entitled to all Privileges and Immunities of Citizens in the several States.

A Person charged in any State with Treason, Felony, or other Crime, who shall flee from Justice, and be found in another State, shall on Demand of the executive Authority of the State from which he fled, be delivered up, to be removed to the State having Jurisdiction of the Crime.

---

[5]Clause changed by Amendment XI.

No Person held to Service or Labour in one State, under the Laws thereof, escaping into another, shall, in Consequence of any Law or Regulation therein, be discharged from such Service or Labour, but shall be delivered up on Claim of the Party to whom such Service or Labour may be due.

Section 3.

New States may be admitted by the Congress into this Union; but no new State shall be formed or erected within the Jurisdiction of any other State; nor any State be formed by the Junction of two or more States, or Parts of States, without the Consent of the Legislatures of the States concerned as well as of the Congress.

The Congress shall have Power to dispose of and make all needful Rules and Regulations respecting the Territory or other Property belonging to the United States; and nothing in this Constitution shall be so construed as to Prejudice any Claims of the United States, or of any particular State.

Section 4.

The United States shall guarantee to every State in this Union a Republican Form of Government, and shall protect each of them against Invasion; and on Application of the Legislature, or of the Executive (when the Legislature cannot be convened) against domestic Violence.

ARTICLE V.

The Congress, whenever two thirds of both Houses shall deem it necessary, shall propose Amendments to this Constitution, or, on the Application of the Legislatures of two thirds of the several States, shall call a Convention for proposing Amendments, which, in either Case, shall be valid to all Intents and Purposes, as Part of this Constitution, when ratified by the Legislatures of three fourths of the several States, or by Conventions in three fourths thereof, as the one or the other Mode of Ratification may be proposed by the Congress; Provided that no Amendment which may be made prior to the Year One thousand eight hundred and eight shall in any Manner affect the first and fourth Clauses in the Ninth Section of the first Article; and that no State, without its Consent, shall be deprived of its equal Suffrage in the Senate.

ARTICLE VI.

All Debts contracted and Engagements entered into, before the Adoption of this Constitution, shall be as valid against the United States under this Constitution, as under the Confederation.

This Constitution, and the Laws of the United States which shall be made in Pursuance thereof; and all Treaties made, or which shall be made, under the Authority of the United States, shall be the supreme Law of the Land; and the Judges in every State shall be bound thereby, any Thing in the Constitution or Laws of any State to the Contrary notwithstanding.

The Senators and Representatives before mentioned, and the Members of the several State Legislatures, and all executive and judicial Officers, both of the United States and of the several States, shall be bound by Oath or Affirmation, to support this Constitution; but no religious Test shall ever be required as a Qualification to any Office or public Trust under the United States.

ARTICLE VII.

The Ratification of the Conventions of nine States, shall be sufficient for the Establishment of this Constitution between the States so ratifying the Same.

done in Convention by the Unanimous Consent of the States present the Seventeenth Day of September in the Year of our Lord one thousand seven hundred and Eighty seven and of the Independence of the United States of America the Twelfth[6] IN WITNESS whereof We have hereunto subscribed our Names,

GEORGE WASHINGTON,
President and Deputy
from Virginia

---

[6]The Constitution was submitted on September 17, 1787, by the Constitutional Convention, was ratified by the conventions of several states at various dates up to May 29, 1790, and became effective on March 4, 1789.

New Hampshire
JOHN LANGDON
NICHOLAS GILMAN
    Massachusetts
NATHANIEL GORHAM
RUFUS KING
    Connecticut
WILLIAM S. JOHNSON
ROGER SHERMAN
    New York
ALEXANDER HAMILTON
    New Jersey
WILLIAM LIVINGSTON
DAVID BREARLEY
WILLIAM PATERSON
JONATHAN DAYTON
    Pennsylvania
BENJAMIN FRANKLIN
THOMAS MIFFLIN
ROBERT MORRIS
GEORGE CLYMER
THOMAS FITZSIMONS
JARED INGERSOLL
JAMES WILSON
GOUVERNEUR MORRIS

    Delaware
GEORGE READ
GUNNING BEDFORD, JR.
JOHN DICKINSON
RICHARD BASSETT
JACOB BROOM
    Maryland
JAMES MCHENRY
DANIEL OF ST. THOMAS
  JENIFER
DANIEL CARROLL
    Virginia
JOHN BLAIR
JAMES MADISON, JR.
    North Carolina
WILLIAM BLOUNT
RICHARD DOBBS
  SPRAIGHT
HU WILLIAMSON
    South Carolina
J. RUTLEDGE
CHARLES C. PINCKNEY
PIERCE BUTLER
    Georgia
WILLIAM FEW
ABRAHAM BALDWIN

AMENDMENTS TO THE CONSTITUTION

[AMENDMENT I]

Congress shall make no law respecting an establishment of religion, or prohibiting the free exercise thereof; or abridging the freedom of speech, or of the press; or the right of the people peaceably to assemble, and to petition the Government for a redress of grievances.

[AMENDMENT II]

A well regulated Militia being necessary to the security of a free State, the right of the people to keep and bear Arms, shall not be infringed.

[AMENDMENT III]

No Soldier shall, in time of peace be quartered in any house, without the consent of the Owner, nor in time of war, but in a manner to be prescribed by law.

[AMENDMENT IV]

The right of the people to be secure in their persons, houses, papers, and effects, against unreasonable searches and seizures, shall not be violated, and no Warrants shall issue, but upon probable cause, supported by Oath or affirmation, and particularly describing the place to be searched, and the persons or things to be seized.

[AMENDMENT V]

No person shall be held to answer for a capital, or otherwise infamous crime, unless on a presentment or indictment of a Grand Jury, except in cases arising in the land or naval forces, or in the Militia, when in actual service in time of War or public danger; nor shall any person be subject for the same offense to be twice put in jeopardy of life or limb; nor shall be compelled in any criminal case to be a witness against himself, nor be deprived of life, liberty, or property, without due process of law; nor shall private property be taken for public use, without just compensation.

[AMENDMENT VI]

In all criminal prosecutions, the accused shall enjoy the right to a speedy and public trial, by an impartial jury of the State and district wherein the crime shall have been committed, which district shall have been previously ascertained by law, and to be informed of the nature and cause of the accusation; to be confronted with the witnesses against him; to have compulsory process for obtaining witnesses in his favor, and to have the Assistance of Counsel for his defence.

[AMENDMENT VII]

In Suits at common law, where the value in controversy shall exceed twenty dollars, the right of trial by jury shall be preserved, and no fact tried by a jury, shall be otherwise re-examined in any Court of the United States, than according to the rules of the common law.

[AMENDMENT VIII]

Excessive bail shall not be required, nor excessive fines imposed, nor cruel and unusual punishments inflicted.

[AMENDMENT IX]

The enumeration in the Constitution, of certain rights, shall not be construed to deny or disparage others retained by the people.

[AMENDMENT X]

The powers not delegated to the United States by the Constitution, nor prohibited by it to the States, are reserved to the States respectively, or to the people.[7]

[AMENDMENT XI]

The Judicial power of the United States shall not be construed to extend to any suit in law or equity, commenced or prosecuted against one of the United States by Citizens of another State, or by Citizens or Subjects of any Foreign State.[8]

[AMENDMENT XII]

The Electors shall meet in their respective states, and vote by ballot for President and Vice-President, one of

---

[7]The first ten amendments were all proposed by Congress on September 25, 1789, and were ratified and adoption certified on December 15, 1791.

[8]Proposed by Congress on March 4, 1794, and declared ratified on January 8, 1798.

whom, at least, shall not be an inhabitant of the same state with themselves; they shall name in their ballots the person voted for as President, and in distinct ballots the person voted for as Vice-President, and they shall make distinct lists of all persons voted for as President, and of all persons voted for as Vice-President, and of the number of votes for each, which lists they shall sign and certify, and transmit sealed to the seat of the government of the United States, directed to the President of the Senate;—The President of the Senate shall, in the presence of the Senate and House of Representatives, open all the certificates and the votes shall then be counted;—The person having the greatest number of votes for President, shall be the President, if such number be a majority of the whole number of Electors appointed; and if no person have such majority, then from the persons having the highest numbers not exceeding three on the list of those voted for as President, the House of Representatives shall choose immediately, by ballot, the President. But in choosing the President, the votes shall be taken by states, the representation from each state having one vote; a quorum for this purpose shall consist of a member or members from two-thirds of the states, and a majority of all the states shall be necessary to a choice. And if the House of Representatives shall not choose a President whenever the right of choice shall devolve upon them, before the fourth day of March next following, then the Vice-President shall act as President, as in the case of the death or other constitutional disability of the President.—The person having the greatest number of votes as Vice-President, shall be the Vice-President, if such number be a majority of the whole number of Electors appointed, and if no person have a majority, then from the two highest numbers on the list, the Senate shall choose the Vice-President; a quorum for the purpose shall consist of two-thirds of the whole number of Senators, and a majority of the whole number shall be necessary to a choice. But no person constitutionally ineligible to the office of President shall be eligible to that of Vice-President of the United States.[9]

[AMENDMENT XIII]

Section 1.

Neither slavery nor involuntary servitude, except as a punishment for crime whereof the party shall have been duly convicted, shall exist within the United States, or any place subject to their jurisdiction.

Section 2.

Congress shall have power to enforce this article by appropriate legislation.[10]

---

[9]Proposed by Congress on December 9, 1803; declared ratified on September 25, 1804; supplemented by Amendments XX and XXIII.

[10]Proposed by Congress on January 31, 1865; declared ratified on December 18, 1865.

[AMENDMENT XIV]

Section 1.

All persons born or naturalized in the United States, and subject to the jurisdiction thereof, are citizens of the United States and of the State wherein they reside. No State shall make or enforce any law which shall abridge the privileges or immunities of citizens of the United States; nor shall any State deprive any person of life, liberty, or property, without due process of law; nor deny to any person within its jurisdiction the equal protection of the laws.

Section 2.

Representatives shall be apportioned among the several States according to their respective numbers, counting the whole number of persons in each State, excluding Indians not taxed. But when the right to vote at any election for the choice of electors for President and Vice-President of the United States, Representatives in Congress, the Executive and Judicial officers of a State, or the members of the Legislature thereof, is denied to any of the male inhabitants of such State, being twenty-one years of age, and citizens of the United States, or in any way abridged, except for participation in rebellion, or other crime, the basis of representation therein shall be reduced in the proportion which the number of such male citizens shall bear to the whole number of male citizens twenty-one years of age in such State.

Section 3.

No person shall be a Senator or Representative in Congress, or elector of President and Vice President, or hold any office, civil or military, under the United States, or under any State, who, having previously taken an oath, as a member of Congress, or as an officer of the United States, or as a member of any State legislature, or as an executive or judicial officer of any State, to support the Constitution of the United States, shall have engaged in insurrection or rebellion against the same, or given aid or comfort to the enemies thereof. But Congress may by a vote of two-thirds of each House, remove such disability.

Section 4.

The validity of the public debt of the United States, authorized by law, including debts incurred for payment of pensions and bounties for services in suppressing insurrection or rebellion, shall not be questioned. But neither the United States nor any State shall assume or pay any debt or obligation incurred in aid of insurrection or rebellion against the United States, or any claim for the loss or emancipation of any slave; but all such debts, obligations and claims shall be held illegal and void.

Section 5.

The Congress shall have power to enforce, by appropriate legislation, the provisions of this article.[11]

[AMENDMENT XV]

Section 1.

The right of citizens of the United States to vote shall not be denied or abridged by the United States or by any State on account of race, color, or previous condition of servitude.

Section.

The Congress shall have power to enforce this article by appropriate legislation.[12]

[AMENDMENT XVI]

The Congress shall have power to lay and collect taxes on incomes, from whatever source derived, without apportionment among the several States, and without regard to any census or enumeration.[13]

[AMENDMENT XVII]

The Senate of the United States shall be composed of two Senators from each State, elected by the people thereof, for six years; and each Senator shall have one vote. The electors in each State shall have the qualifications requisite for electors of the most numerous branch of the State legislatures.

When vacancies happen in the representation of any State in the Senate, the executive authority of such State shall issue writs of election to fill such vacancies: *Provided,* That the legislature of any State may empower the executive thereof to make temporary appointments until the people fill the vacancies by election as the legislature may direct.

This amendment shall not be so construed as to affect the election or term of any Senator chosen before it becomes valid as part of the Constitution.[14]

---

[11]Proposed by Congress on June 13, 1866; declared ratified on July 28, 1868.

[12]Proposed by Congress on February 26, 1869; declared ratified on March 30, 1870.

[13]Proposed by Congress on July 12, 1909; declared ratified on February 25, 1913.

[14]Proposed by Congress on May 13, 1912; declared ratified on May 31, 1913.

[AMENDMENT XVIII]

Section 1.

After one year from the ratification of this article the manufacture, sale, or transportation of intoxicating liquors within, the importation thereof into, or the exportation thereof from the United States and all territory subject to the jurisdiction thereof for beverage purposes is hereby prohibited.

Section 2.

The Congress and the several States shall have concurrent power to enforce this article by appropriate legislation.

Section 3.

This article shall be inoperative unless it shall have been ratified as an amendment to the Constitution by the legislatures of the several States, as provided in the Constitution, within seven years from the date of the submission hereof to the States by the Congress.[15]

[AMENDMENT XIX]

The right of citizens of the United States to vote shall not be denied or abridged by the United States or by any State on account of sex.

Congress shall have power to enforce this article by appropriate legislation.[16]

[AMENDMENT XX]

Section 1.

The terms of the President and Vice President shall end at noon on the 20th day of January, and the terms of Senators and Representatives at noon on the 3d day of January, of the years in which such terms would have ended if this article had not been ratified; and the terms of their successors shall then begin.

Section 2.

The Congress shall assemble at least once in every year, and such meeting shall begin at noon on the 3d day of January, unless they shall by law appoint a different day.

---

[15]Proposed by Congress on December 18, 1917; declared ratified on January 29, 1919; repealed by Amendment XXI.

[16]Proposed by Congress on June 4, 1919; declared ratified on August 26, 1920.

Section 3.

If, at the time fixed for the beginning of the term of the President, the President elect shall have died, the Vice President elect shall become President. If a President shall not have been chosen before the time fixed for the beginning of his term, or if the President elect shall have failed to qualify, then the Vice President elect shall act as President until a President shall have qualified; and the Congress may by law provide for the case wherein neither a President elect nor a Vice President elect shall have qualified, declaring who shall then act as President, or the manner in which one who is to act shall be selected, and such person shall act accordingly until a President or Vice President shall have qualified.

Section 4.

The Congress may by law provide for the case of the death of any of the persons from whom the House of Representatives may choose a President whenever the right of choice shall have devolved upon them, and for the case of the death of any of the persons from whom the Senate may choose a Vice President whenever the right of choice shall have devolved upon them.

Section 5.

Sections 1 and 2 shall take effect on the 15th day of October following the ratification of this article.

Section 6.

This article shall be inoperative unless it shall have been ratified as an amendment to the Constitution by the legislatures of three-fourths of the several States within seven years from the date of its submission.[17]

[AMENDMENT XXI]

Section 1.

The eighteenth article of amendment to the Constitution of the United States is hereby repealed.

Section 2.

The transportation or importation into any States, Territory, or possession of the United States for delivery or use therein of intoxicating liquors, in violation of the laws thereof, is hereby prohibited.

Section 3.

This article shall be inoperative unless it shall have been ratified as an amendment to the Constitution by

conventions in the several States, as provided in the Constitution, within seven years from the date of the submission hereof to the States by the Congress.[18]

[AMENDMENT XXII]

Section 1.

No person shall be elected to the office of the President more than twice, and no person who has held the office of President, or acted as President, for more than two years of a term to which some other person was elected President shall be elected to the office of the President more than once. But this Article shall not apply to any person holding the office of President when this Article was proposed by the Congress, and shall not prevent any person who may be holding the office of President, or acting as President, during the term within which this Article becomes operative from holding the office of President or acting as President during the remainder of such term.

Section 2.

This article shall be inoperative unless it shall have been ratified as an amendment to the Constitution by the legislatures of three-fourths of the several States within seven years from the date of its submission to the States by the Congress.[19]

[AMENDMENT XXIII]

Section 1.

The District constituting the seat of Government of the United States shall appoint in such manner as the Congress shall direct:

A number of electors of President and Vice President equal to the whole number of Senators and Representatives in Congress to which the District would be entitled if it were a State, but in no event more than the least populous State; they shall be in addition to those appointed by the States, but they shall be considered, for the purposes of the election of President and Vice President, to be electors appointed by a State; and they shall meet in the District and perform such duties as provided by the twelfth article of amendment.

Section 2.

The Congress shall have power to enforce this article by appropriate legislation.[20]

---

[17]Proposed by Congress on March 2, 1932; declared ratified on February 6, 1933.

[18]Proposed by Congress on February 20, 1933; declared ratified on December 5, 1933.

[19]Proposed by Congress on March 24, 1947; declared ratified on March 1, 1951.

[20]Proposed by Congress on June 16, 1960; declared ratified on April 3, 1961.

[AMENDMENT XXIV]

Section 1.

The right of citizens of the United States to vote in any primary or other election for President or Vice President, for electors for President or Vice President, or for Senator or Representative in Congress, shall not be denied or abridged by the United States or any state by reason of failure to pay any poll tax or other tax.

Section 2.

The Congress shall have the power to enforce this article by appropriate legislation.[21]

[AMENDMENT XXV]

Section 1.

In case of the removal of the President from office or his death or resignation, the Vice President shall become President.

Section 2.

Whenever there is a vacancy in the office of the Vice President, the President shall nominate a Vice President who shall take the office upon confirmation by a majority vote of both houses of Congress.

Section 3.

Whenever the President transmits to the President pro tempore of the Senate and the Speaker of the House of Representatives his written declaration that he is unable to discharge the powers and duties of his office, and until he transmits to them a written declaration to the contrary, such powers and duties shall be discharged by the Vice President as Acting President.

Section 4.

Whenever the Vice President and a majority of either the principal officers of the executive departments or of such other body as Congress may by law provide, trans-

mit to the President pro tempore of the Senate and the Speaker of the House of Representatives their written declaration that the President is unable to discharge the powers and duties of his office, the Vice President shall immediately assume the powers and duties of the office as Acting President.

Thereafter, when the President transmits to the President pro tempore of the Senate and the Speaker of the House of Representatives his written declaration that no inability exists, he shall resume the powers and duties of his office unless the Vice President and a majority of either the principal officers of the executive department or of such other body as Congress may by law provide, transmit within four days to the President pro tempore of the Senate and the Speaker of the House of Representatives their written declaration that the President is unable to discharge the powers and duties of his office. Thereupon Congress shall decide the issue, assembling within 48 hours for that purpose if not in session. If the Congress, within 21 days after receipt of the latter written declaration, or, if Congress is not in session, within 21 days after Congress is required to assemble, determines by two-thirds vote of both houses that the President is unable to discharge the powers and duties of his office, the Vice President shall continue to discharge the same as Acting President; otherwise, the President shall resume the powers and duties of his office.[22]

[AMENDMENT XXVI]

Section 1.

The right of citizens of the United States, who are 18 years of age or older, to vote shall not be denied or abridged by the United States or any state on account of age.

Section 2.

The Congress shall have the power to enforce this article by appropriate legislation.[23]

---

[21]Proposed by Congress on August 27, 1962; declared ratified on January 23, 1963.

[22]Proposed by Congress on July 6, 1965; declared ratified on February 10, 1967.

[23]Proposed by Congress on March 23, 1971; declared ratified on June 30, 1971.

PRESIDENTS, VICE-PRESIDENTS, AND CABINET MEMBERS

President and Vice-President	Secretary of State	Secretary of the Treasury	Secretary of War
George Washington (F) .... 1789 J. Adams .... '89	T. Jefferson .... '89 E. Randolph .... '94 T. Pickering.......... '95	A. Hamilton .... '89 O. Wolcott........... '89	H. Knox .... '89 T. Pickering.......... '95 J. McHenry .... '96
John Adams (F)..................... 1797 T. Jefferson (R^J)............... '97	T. Pickering.......... '97 J. Marshall .... '00	O. Wolcott........... '97 S. Dexter .... '01	J. McHenry .... '97 J. Marshall .... '00 S. Dexter .... '00 R. Griswold.......... '01
Thomas Jefferson (R^J) .... 1801 A. Burr (R^J) .... '01 G. Clinton (R^J)................... '05	J. Madison........... '01	S. Dexter .... '01 A. Gallatin........... '01	H. Dearborn .... '01
James Madison (R^J) .... 1809 G. Clinton (R^J).................. '09 E. Gerry (R^J)..................... '13	R. Smith............. '09 J. Monroe............ '11	A. Gallatin........... '09 G. Campbell .... '14 A. Dallas .... '14 W. Crawford......... '16	W. Eustis .... '09 J. Armstrong .... '13 J. Monroe............ '14 W. Crawford......... '15
James Monroe (R^J) .... 1817 D. Tompkins (R^J) .... '17	J. Q. Adams.......... '17	W. Crawford......... '17	I. Shelby............. '17 G. Graham........... '17 J. Calhoun .... '17
John Quincy Adams (NR)............. 1825 J. Calhoun (R^J)................... '25	H. Clay.............. '25	R. Rush.............. '25	J. Barbour........... '25 P. Porter............. '28
Andrew Jackson (D)................. 1829 J. Calhoun (D)..................... '29 M. Van Buren (D).................. '33	M. Van Buren........ '29 E. Livingston .... '31 L. McLane .... '33 J. Forsyth .... '34	S. Ingham .... '29 L. McLane .... '31 W. Duane............ '33 R. Taney............. '33 L. Woodbury......... '34	J. Eaton............. '29 L. Cass .... '31 B. Butler............. '37
Martin Van Buren (D) .... 1837 R. Johnson (D)..................... '37	J. Forsyth .... '37	L. Woodbury......... '37	J. Poinsett .... '37
William H. Harrison (W)............. 1841 J. Tyler (W)....................... '41	D. Webster .... '41	T. Ewing .... '41	J. Bell............... '41
John Tyler (W and D)................ 1841	D. Webster .... '41 H. Legare............ '43 A. Upshur .... '43 J. Calhoun .... '44	T. Ewing .... '41 W. Forward.......... '41 J. Spencer............ '43 G. Bibb.............. '44	J. Bell............... '41 J. McLean............ '41 J. Spencer............ '41 J. Porter .... '43 W. Wilkins , ... '44
James K. Polk (D) .... 1845 G. Dallas (D)...................... '45	J. Buchanan.......... '45	R. Walker............ '45	W. Marcy............ '45
Zachary Taylor (W).................. 1849 M. Fillmore (W).................... '49	J. Clayton............ '49	W. Meredith .... '49	G. Crawford .... '49
Millard Fillmore (W)................. 1850	D. Webster .... '50 E. Everett............ '52	T. Corwin .... '50	C. Conrad .... '50
Franklin Pierce (D) .... 1853 W. King (D) .... '53	W. Marcy............ '53	J. Guthrie............ '53	J. Davis.............. '53
James Buchanan (D).................. 1857 J. Breckinridge (D) .... '57	L. Cass .... '57 J. Black .... '60	H. Cobb............. '57 P. Thomas .... '60 J. Dix............... '61	J. Floyd............. '57 J. Holt............... '61
Abraham Lincoln (R)................. 1861 H. Hamlin (R) .... '61 A. Johnson (U)..................... '65	W. Seward........... '61	S. Chase............. '61 W. Fessenden .... '64 H. McCulloch .... '65	S. Cameron .... '61 E. Stanton .... '62
Andrew Johnson (U) 1865	W. Seward........... '65	H. McCulloch .... '65	E. Stanton .... '65 U. Grant............. '67 L. Thomas .... '68 J. Schofield .... '68

Party affiliations: D, Democratic; F, Federalist; NR, National Republican; R, Republican; R^J, Republican (Jeffersonian); U, Unionist; W, Whig.

Secretary of the Navy	Attorney General	Postmaster General	Secretary of the Interior
	E. Randolph............'89		
Established April 30, 1798	W. Bradford.............'94		
	C. Lee.................'95		
B. Stoddert.............'98	C. Lee.................'97		
	T. Parsons.............'01		
B. Stoddert.............'01	L. Lincoln.............'01		
R. Smith...............'01	R. Smith...............'05		
J. Crowninshield........'05	J. Breckinridge..........'05		
	C. Rodney.............'07		
P. Hamilton............'09	C. Rodney.............'09		
W. Jones..............'13	W. Pinkney............'11		
B. Crowninshield........'14	R. Rush...............'14		
B. Crowninshield........'17	R. Rush...............'17		
S. Thompson...........'18	W. Wirt...............'17		
S. Southard............'23		*Cabinet status since March 9, 1829*	
S. Southard............'25	W. Wirt...............'25		
J. Branch..............'29	J. Berrien.............'29	W. Barry...............'29	
L. Woodbury...........'31	R. Taney..............'31	A. Kendall.............'35	
M. Dickerson...........'34	B. Butler..............'33		
M. Dickerson...........'37	B. Butler..............'37	A. Kendall.............'37	
J. Paulding............'38	F. Grundy.............'38	J. Niles...............'40	
	H. Gilpin.............'40		
G. Badger.............'41	J. Crittenden...........'41	F. Granger.............'41	
G. Badger.............'41	J. Crittenden...........'41	F. Granger.............'41	
A. Upshur............'41	H. Legare.............'41	C. Wickliffe............'41	
D. Henshaw...........'43	J. Nelson.............'43		
T. Gilmer.............'44			
J. Mason.............'44			
G. Bancroft...........'45	J. Mason.............'45	C. Johnson............'45	*Established March 3, 1849*
J. Mason.............'46	N. Clifford............'46		
	I. Toucey.............'48		
W. Preston............'49	R. Johnson............'49	J. Collamer............'49	Thomas Ewing..........'49
W. Graham............'50	J. Crittenden...........'50	N. Hall...............'50	A. Stuart..............'50
J. Kennedy............'52		S. Hubbard............'52	
J. Dobbin.............'53	C. Cushing............'53	J. Campbell............'53	R. McClelland..........'53
I. Toucey.............'57	J. Black..............'57	A. Brown.............'57	J. Thompson...........'57
	E. Stanton............'60	J. Holt...............'59	
G. Welles.............'61	E. Bates..............'61	H. King...............'61	C. Smith..............'61
	T. Coffey.............'63	M. Blair..............'61	J. Usher..............'63
	J. Speed..............'64	W. Dennison...........'64	
G. Welles.............'65	J. Speed..............'65	W. Dennison...........'65	J. Usher..............'65
	H. Stanbery...........'66	A. Randall............'66	J. Harlan.............'65
	W. Evarts............'68		O. Browning..........'66

PRESIDENTS, VICE-PRESIDENTS, AND CABINET MEMBERS

President and Vice-President	Secretary of State	Secretary of the Treasury	Secretary of War	Secretary of the Navy
Ulysses S. Grant (R) ...... 1869 S. Colfax (R) .... '69 H. Wilson (R) .... '73	E. Washburne. . '69 H. Fish .... '69	G. Boutwell .... '69 W. Richardson . '73 B. Bristow ..... '74 L. Morrill ...... '76	J. Rawlins. .... '69 W. Sherman .. '69 W. Belknap . . . '69 A. Taft .... '76 J. Cameron. . . . '76	A. Borie ...... '69 G. Robeson . . . '69
Rutherford B. Hayes (R) .. 1877 W. Wheeler (R) .... '77	W. Evarts ...... '77	J. Sherman..... '77	G. McCrary .... '77 A. Ramsey .... '79	R. Thompson.. '77 N. Goff .... '81
James A. Garfield (R) ...... 1881 C. Arthur (R) .... '81	J. Blaine....... '81	W. Windom ... '81	R. Lincoln ..... '81	W. Hunt ...... '81
Chester A. Arthur (R) 1881	F. Freling- huysen...... '81	C. Folger ...... '81 W. Gresham ... '84 H. McCulloch.. '84	R. Lincoln ..... '81	W. Chandler... '81
Grover Cleveland (D)...... 1885 T. Hendricks (D)........ '85	T. Bayard...... '85	D. Manning ... '85 C. Fairchild.... '87	W. Endicott.... '85	W. Whitney ... '85
Benjamin Harrison (R)..... 1889 L. Morton (R) .... '89	J. Blaine....... '89 J. Foster....... '92	W. Windom ... '89 C. Foster ...... '91	R. Proctor ..... '89 S. Elkins ...... '91	B. Tracy....... '89
Grover Cleveland (D)...... 1893 A. Stevenson (D)........ '93	W. Gresham ... '93 R. Olney ...... '95	J. Carlisle...... '93	D. Lamont..... '93	H. Herbert .... '93
William McKinley (R) ..... 1897 G. Hobart (R)........... '97 T. Roosevelt (R) .... '01	J. Sherman .... '97 W. Day .... '97 J. Hay......... '98	L. Gage .... '97	R. Alger....... '97 E. Root........ '99	J. Long........ '97
Theodore Roosevelt (R).... 1901 C. Fairbanks (R) .... '05	J. Hay......... '01 E. Root........ '05 R. Bacon ...... '09	L. Gage .... '01 L. Shaw....... '02 G. Cortelyou... '07	E. Root........ '01 W. Taft....... '04 L. Wright...... '08	J. Long........ '01 W. Moody..... '02 P. Morton ..... '04 C. Bonaparte.. '05 V. Metcalf ..... '07 T. Newberry... '08
William Howard Taft (R) .. 1909 J. Sherman (R).......... '09	P. Knox .... '09	F. MacVeagh .. '09	J. Dickinson ... '09 H. Stimson .... '11	G. Meyer...... '09
Woodrow Wilson (D)...... 1913 T. Marshall (D) .... '13	W. Bryan...... '13 R. Lansing .... '15 B. Colby ...... '20	W. McAdoo ... '13 C. Glass....... '18 D. Houston.... '20	L. Garrison.... '13 N. Baker ...... '16	J. Daniels...... '13
Warren G. Harding (R) .... 1921 C. Coolidge (R) .... '21	C. Hughes..... '21	A. Mellon ..... '21	J. Weeks....... '21	E. Denby...... '21
Calvin Coolidge (R) .... 1923 C. Dawes (R) .... '25	C. Hughes..... '23 F. Kellogg ..... '25	A. Mellon ..... '23	J. Weeks....... '23 D. Davis ...... '25	E. Denby...... '23 C. Wilbur ..... '24
Herbert Hoover (R) .... 1929 C. Curtis (R)............ '29	H. Stimson .... '29	A. Mellon ..... '29 O. Mills........ '32	J. Good........ '29 P. Hurley...... '29	C. Adams ..... '29
Franklin D. Roosevelt (D).. 1933 J. Garner (D)............ '33 H. Wallace (D).......... '41 H. Truman (D).......... '45	C. Hull........ '33 E. Stettinius ... '44	W. Woodin.... '33 H. Morgen- thau .... '34	G. Dern .... '33 H. Woodring .. '36 H. Stimson .... '40	C. Swanson.... '33 C. Edison ..... '40 F. Knox .... '40 J. Forrestal..... '44
Harry S. Truman (D) ...... 1945 A. Barkley (D) .... '49	J. Byrnes ...... '45 G. Marshall.... '47 D. Acheson.... '49	F. Vinson ..... '45 J. Snyder ...... '46	R. Patterson ... '45 K. Royall ...... '47	J. Forrestal..... '45

Party affiliations: D, Democratic; R, Republican.

Attorney General	Postmaster General	Secretary of the Interior	Secretary of Agriculture	Secretary of Commerce and Labor	
E. Hoar . . . . '69 A. Ackerman . . . '70 G. Williams . . . . '71 E. Pierrepont . . . '75 A. Taft . . . . '76	J. Creswell . . . . '69 J. Marshall . . . . '74 M. Jewell . . . . '74 J. Tyner . . . . '76	J. Cox . . . . '69 C. Delano . . . . . '70 Z. Chandler . . . '75			
C. Devens . . . . . . '77	D. Key . . . . '77 H. Maynard . . . '80	C. Schurz . . . . . '77			
W. Mac- Veagh . . . . . '81	T. James . . . . '81	S. Kirkwood . . . '81			
B. Brewster . . . . '81	T. Howe . . . . . . '81 W. Gresham . . . '83 F. Hatton . . . . . '84	H. Teller . . . . . . '81	*Cabinet status since Feb. 9, 1889*		
A. Garland . . . . '85	W. Vilas . . . . . . '85 D. Dickinson . . '88	L. Lamar . . . . . . '85 W. Vilas . . . . . . '88	N. Colman . . . . '89		
W. Miller . . . . . . '89	J. Wanamaker . . '89	J. Noble . . . . . . '89	J. Rusk . . . . '89		
R. Olney . . . . . . '93 J. Harmon . . . . . '95	W. Bissell . . . . . '93 W. Wilson . . . . . '95	H. Smith . . . . . '93 D. Francis . . . . . '96	J. Morton . . . . . . '93		
J. McKenna . . . . '97 J. Griggs . . . . . '97 P. Knox . . . . '01	J. Gary . . . . '97 C. Smith . . . . . . '98	C. Bliss . . . . . . '97 E. Hitchcock . . . '99	J. Wilson . . . . . '97	*Established Feb. 14, 1903*	
P. Knox . . . . '01 W. Moody . . . . . '04 C. Bonaparte . . . '07	C. Smith . . . . . . '01 H. Payne . . . . . . '02 R. Wynne . . . . . '04 G. Cortelyou . . . '05 G. Meyer . . . . . '07	E. Hitchcock . . . '01 J. Garfield . . . . . '07	J. Wilson . . . . . . '01	G. Cortelyou . . . '03 V. Metcalf . . . . . '04 O. Straus . . . . . . '07	
G. Wicker- sham . . . . '09	F. Hitchcock . . . '09	R. Ballinger . . . '09 W. Fisher . . . . . '11	J. Wilson . . . . . . '09	C. Nagel . . . . . . '09	
J. McReynolds . '13 T. Gregory . . . . . '14 A. Palmer . . . . . '19	A. Burleson . . . . '13	F. Lane . . . . '13 J. Payne . . . . '20	D. Houston . . . . '13 E. Meredith . . . . '20	**Secretary of Commerce** *Established March 4, 1913* W. Redfield . . . . '13 J. Alexander . . . '19	**Secretary of Labor** *Established March 4, 1913* Wm. Wilson . . . '13
H. Daugherty . . '21	W. Hays . . . . . . '21 H. Work . . . . . . '22 H. New . . . . '23	A. Fall . . . . '21 H. Work . . . . . . '23	H. C. Wallace . . '21	H. Hoover . . . . . '21	J. Davis . . . . '21
H. Daugherty . . '23 H. Stone . . . . . '24 J. Sargent . . . . . . '25	H. New . . . . '23	H. Work . . . . . . '23 R. West . . . . '28	H. C. Wallace . . '23 H. Gore . . . . '24 W. Jardine . . . . . '25	H. Hoover . . . . . '23 W. Whiting . . . . '28	J. Davis . . . . '23
W. Mitchell . . . . '29	W. Brown . . . . . '29	R. Wilbur . . . . . '29	A. Hyde . . . . '29	R. Lamont . . . . . '29 R. Chapin . . . . . '32	J. Davis . . . . '29 W. Doak . . . . . . '30
H. Cummings . '33 F. Murphy . . . . . '39 R. Jackson . . . . . '40 F. Biddle . . . . . '41	J. Farley . . . . . . '33 F. Walker . . . . . . '40	H. Ickes . . . . . . '33	H. A. Wallace . . '33 C. Wickard . . . . '40	D. Roper . . . . . . '33 H. Hopkins . . . . '39 J. Jones . . . . '40 H. A. Wallace . . '45	F. Perkins . . . . . '33
T. Clark . . . . . . '45 J. McGrath . . . . . '49 J. McGranery . . '52	R. Hannegan . . '45 J. Donaldson . . . '47	H. Ickes . . . . . . '45 J. Krug . . . . '46 O. Chapman . . . '49	C. Anderson . . . '45 C. Brannan . . . . '48	H. A. Wallace . . '45 W. A. Harri- man . . . . '46 C. Sawyer . . . . . '48	L. Schwellen- bach . . . . '45 M. Tobin . . . . . . '48

President and Vice-President	Secretary of State	Secretary of the Treasury	Secretary of Defense[1]	Attorney General	Postmaster General
			Established July 26, 1947 J. Forrestal[2] .... '47 L. Johnson[2] .... '49 G. Marshall[2] ... '50 R. Lovett[2] ..... '51		
Dwight D. Eisenhower (R)................ 1953 R. Nixon (R)........... '53	J. Dulles........ '53 C. Herter...... '59	G. Humphrey.. '53 R. Anderson... '57	C. Wilson ..... '53 N. McElroy.... '57	H. Brownell ... '53 W. Rogers ..... '57	A. Summer- field .... '53
John F. Kennedy (D) ...... 1961 L. Johnson (D).......... '61	D. Rusk....... '61	D. Dillon...... '61	R. McNamara.. '61	R. Kennedy.... '61	J. Day......... '61 J. Gronouski... '63
Lyndon B. Johnson (D) .... 1963 H. Humphrey (D)....... '65	D. Rusk....... '63	D. Dillon...... '63 H. Fowler ..... '65 J. Barr......... '68	R. McNamara.. '63 C. Clifford..... '68	R. Kennedy.... '63 N. Katzenbach. '65 R. Clark....... '67	J. Gronouski... '63 L. O'Brien..... '65 W. Watson .... '68
Richard M. Nixon (R) ..... 1969 S. Agnew (R) .... '69 G. Ford (R) .... '73	W. Rogers .... '69 H. Kissinger .. '73	D. Kennedy ... '69 J. Connally ... '70 G. Shultz .... '72 W. Simon .... '74	M. Laird ..... '69 E. Richardson . '73 J. Schlesinger . '73	J. Mitchell .... '69 R. Kleindienst . '72 E. Richardson . '73 W. Saxbe .... '74	W. Blount .... '69 *Abolished Aug. 8, 1970*
Gerald R. Ford (R) .... 1974 N. Rockefeller (R) ..... '74	H. Kissinger . '74	W. Simon .... '74	J. Schlesinger . '74 D. Rumsfeld .. '75	W. Saxbe ..... '74 E. Levi ...... '75	

Party affiliations: D, Democratic; R, Republican.

[1]The Department of Defense, established during the Truman Administration, was a combination of the Departments of War and the Navy.

[2]Appointed during the Truman Administration.

Secretary of the Interior	Secretary of Agriculture	Secretary of Commerce	Secretary of Labor	Secretary of Health, Education, and Welfare	Secretary of Housing and Urban Development	Secretary of Transportation
				Established April 1, 1953		
D. McKay .... '53 F. Seaton ..... '56	E. Benson .... '53	S. Weeks .... '53 L. Strauss .... '58 F. Mueller .... '59	M. Durkin .... '53 J. Mitchell .... '53	O. Hobby .... '53 M. Folsom .... '55 A. Flemming . '58		
S. Udall ...... '61	O. Freeman ... '61	L. Hodges .... '61	A. Goldberg .. '61 W. Wirtz ..... '62	A. Ribicoff ... '61 A. Celebrezze. '62		
S. Udall ..... '63	O. Freeman ... '63	L. Hodges .... '63 J. Connor..... '65 A. Trow- bridge ..... '67 C. Smith ..... '68	W. Wirtz ..... '63	A. Celebrezze. '63 J. Gardner .... '65 W. Cohen .... '68	*Established Sept. 9, 1965*	
					R. Weaver .... '66 R. Wood ..... '68	*Established Oct. 15, 1966*
						A. Boyd ...... '66
W. Hickel ... '69 R. Morton '71	C. Hardin ... '69 E. Butz '71	M. Stans .... '69 P. Peterson '72 F. Dent ..... '73	G. Shultz .... '69 J. Hodgson '70 P. Brennan .. '73	R. Finch ..... '69 E. Richardson '70 C. Weinberger '73	G. Romney .. '69 J. Lynn ..... '73	J. Volpe ..... '69 C. Brinegar .. '73
R. Morton ... '74 S. Hathaway . '75 T. Kleppe ... '75	E. Butz ..... '74	F. Dent ..... '74 R. Morton ... '75 E. Richardson '75	P. Brennan .. '74 J. Dunlop .... '75	C. Weinberger '74 F. Matthews . '75	J. Lynn ..... '74 C. Hills ..... '75	C. Brinegar .. '74 W. Coleman . '75

POPULATION OF THE UNITED STATES: 1800–1880

Division and State	1800	1810	1820	1830	1840	1850	1860	1870	1880
UNITED STATES	5,308,483	7,239,881	9,638,453	12,866,020	17,069,453	23,191,876	31,443,321	39,818,449	50,189,209
New England	1,233,011	1,471,973	1,660,071	1,954,717	2,234,822	2,728,116	3,135,283	3,487,924	4,010,529
Maine	151,719	228,705	298,335	399,455	501,793	583,169	628,279	626,915	648,936
New Hampshire	183,858	214,160	244,161	269,328	284,574	317,976	326,073	318,300	346,991
Vermont	154,465	217,895	235,981	280,652	291,948	314,120	315,098	330,551	332,286
Massachusetts	422,845	472,040	523,287	610,408	737,699	994,514	1,231,066	1,457,351	1,783,085
Rhode Island	69,122	76,931	83,059	97,199	108,830	147,545	174,620	217,353	276,531
Connecticut	251,002	261,942	275,248	297,675	309,978	370,792	460,147	537,454	622,700
Middle Atlantic	1,402,565	2,014,702	2,669,845	3,587,664	4,526,260	5,898,735	7,458,985	8,810,806	10,496,878
New York	589,051	959,049	1,372,812	1,918,608	2,428,921	3,097,394	3,880,735	4,382,759	5,082,871
New Jersey	211,149	245,562	277,575	320,823	373,306	489,555	672,035	906,096	1,131,116
Pennsylvania	602,365	810,091	1,049,458	1,348,233	1,724,033	2,311,786	2,906,215	3,521,951	4,282,891
South Atlantic	2,286,494	2,674,891	3,061,063	3,645,752	3,925,299	4,679,090	5,364,703	5,835,610	7,597,197
Delaware	64,273	72,674	72,749	76,748	78,085	91,532	112,216	125,015	146,608
Maryland	341,548	380,546	407,350	447,040	470,019	583,034	687,049	780,894	934,943
Dist. of Columbia	8,144	15,471	23,336	30,261	33,745	51,687	75,080	131,700	177,624
Virginia	886,149	983,152	1,075,069	1,220,978	1,249,764	1,421,661	1,596,318	1,225,163	1,512,565
West Virginia	....	....	....	....	....	....	....	442,014	618,457
North Carolina	478,103	555,500	638,829	737,987	753,419	869,039	992,622	1,071,361	1,399,750
South Carolina	345,591	415,115	502,741	581,185	594,398	668,507	703,708	705,606	995,577
Georgia	162,686	252,433	340,989	516,823	691,392	906,185	1,057,286	1,184,109	1,542,180
Florida	....	....	....	34,730	54,477	87,445	140,424	187,748	269,493
East South Central	335,407	708,590	1,190,489	1,815,969	2,575,445	3,363,271	4,020,991	4,404,445	5,585,151
Kentucky	220,955	406,511	564,317	687,917	779,828	982,405	1,155,684	1,321,011	1,648,690
Tennessee	105,602	261,727	422,823	681,904	829,210	1,002,717	1,109,801	1,258,520	1,542,359
Alabama	1,250	9,046	127,901	309,527	590,756	771,623	964,201	996,992	1,262,505
Mississippi	7,600	31,306	75,448	136,621	375,651	606,526	791,305	827,922	1,131,597
West South Central	....	77,618	167,680	246,127	449,985	940,251	1,747,667	2,029,965	3,334,220
Arkansas	....	1,062	14,273	30,388	97,574	209,897	435,450	484,471	802,525
Louisiana	....	76,556	153,407	215,739	352,411	517,762	708,002	726,915	939,946
Oklahoma	....	....	....	....	....	....	....	....	....
Texas	....	....	....	....	....	212,592	604,215	818,579	1,591,749
East North Central	51,006	272,324	792,719	1,470,018	2,924,728	4,523,260	6,926,884	9,124,517	11,206,668
Ohio	41,365	230,760	581,434	937,903	1,519,467	1,980,329	2,339,511	2,665,260	3,198,062
Indiana	5,641	24,520	147,178	343,031	685,866	988,416	1,350,428	1,680,637	1,978,301
Illinois	....	12,282	55,211	157,445	476,183	851,470	1,711,951	2,539,891	3,077,871
Michigan	....	4,762	8,896	31,639	212,267	397,654	749,113	1,184,059	1,636,937
Wisconsin	....	....	....	....	30,945	305,391	775,881	1,054,670	1,315,497
West North Central	....	19,783	66,586	140,455	426,814	880,335	2,169,832	3,856,594	6,157,443
Minnesota	....	....	....	....	....	6,077	172,023	439,706	780,773
Iowa	....	....	....	....	43,112	192,214	674,913	1,194,020	1,624,615
Missouri	....	19,783	66,586	140,455	383,702	682,044	1,182,012	1,721,295	2,168,380
North Dakota	....	....	....	....	....	....	4,837	2,405	36,909
South Dakota	....	....	....	....	....	....	....	11,776	98,268
Nebraska	....	....	....	....	....	....	28,841	122,993	452,402
Kansas	....	....	....	....	....	....	107,206	364,399	996,096
Mountain	....	....	....	....	....	72,927	174,923	315,385	653,119
Montana	....	....	....	....	....	....	....	20,595	39,159
Idaho	....	....	....	....	....	....	....	14,999	32,610
Wyoming	....	....	....	....	....	....	....	9,118	20,789
Colorado	....	....	....	....	....	....	34,277	39,864	194,327
New Mexico	....	....	....	....	....	61,547	93,516	91,874	119,565
Arizona	....	....	....	....	....	....	....	9,658	40,440
Utah	....	....	....	....	....	11,380	40,273	76,786	143,963
Nevada	....	....	....	....	....	....	6,857	42,491	62,266
Pacific	....	....	....	....	....	105,871	444,053	675,125	1,148,004
Washington	....	....	....	....	....	1,201	11,594	23,955	75,116
Oregon	....	....	....	....	....	12,093	52,465	90,923	174,768
California	....	....	....	....	....	92,597	379,994	560,247	864,694
Alaska	....	....	....	....	....	....	....	....	33,426
Hawaii	....	....	....	....	....	....	....	....	....

POPULATION OF THE UNITED STATES: 1890–1970

Division and State	1890	1900	1910	1920	1930	1940	1950	1960	1970
UNITED STATES	62,979,766	76,212,168	92,228,622	106,021,568	123,202,660	132,165,129	151,325,798	179,323,175	203,184,772
New England	4,700,749	5,592,017	6,552,681	7,400,909	8,166,341	8,437,290	9,314,453	10,509,367	11,847,186
Maine	661,086	694,466	742,371	768,014	797,423	847,226	913,774	969,265	993,663
New Hampshire	376,530	411,588	430,572	443,083	465,293	491,524	533,242	606,921	737,681
Vermont	332,422	343,641	355,956	352,428	359,611	359,231	377,747	389,881	444,732
Massachusetts	2,238,947	2,805,346	3,366,416	3,852,356	4,249,614	4,316,721	4,690,514	5,148,578	5,689,170
Rhode Island	345,506	428,556	542,610	604,397	687,497	713,346	791,896	859,488	949,723
Connecticut	746,258	908,420	1,114,756	1,380,631	1,606,903	1,709,242	2,007,280	2,535,234	3,032,217
Middle Atlantic	12,706,220	15,454,678	19,315,892	22,261,144	26,260,750	27,539,487	30,163,533	34,168,452	37,152,813
New York	6,003,174	7,268,894	9,113,614	10,385,227	12,588,066	13,479,142	14,830,192	16,782,304	18,190,740
New Jersey	1,444,933	1,883,669	2,537,167	3,155,900	4,041,334	4,160,165	4,835,329	6,066,782	7,168,164
Pennsylvania	5,258,113	6,302,115	7,665,111	8,720,017	9,631,350	9,900,180	10,498,012	11,319,366	11,793,909
South Atlantic	8,857,922	10,443,480	12,194,895	13,990,272	15,793,589	17,823,151	21,182,335	25,971,732	30,671,337
Delaware	168,493	184,735	202,322	223,003	238,380	266,505	318,085	446,292	548,104
Maryland	1,042,390	1,188,044	1,295,346	1,449,661	1,631,526	1,821,244	2,343,001	3,100,689	3,922,399
Dist. of Columbia	230,392	278,718	331,069	437,571	486,869	663,091	802,178	763,956	756,510
Virginia	1,655,980	1,854,184	2,061,612	2,309,187	2,421,851	2,677,773	3,318,680	3,966,949	4,648,494
West Virginia	762,794	958,800	1,221,119	1,463,701	1,729,205	1,901,974	2,005,552	1,860,421	1,744,237
North Carolina	1,617,949	1,893,810	2,206,287	2,559,123	3,170,276	3,571,623	4,061,929	4,556,155	5,082,059
South Carolina	1,151,149	1,340,316	1,515,400	1,683,724	1,738,765	1,899,804	2,117,027	2,382,594	2,590,516
Georgia	1,837,353	2,216,331	2,609,121	2,895,832	2,908,506	3,123,723	3,444,578	3,943,116	4,589,575
Florida	391,422	528,542	752,619	968,470	1,468,211	1,897,414	2,771,305	4,951,560	6,789,443
East South Central	6,429,154	7,547,757	8,409,901	8,893,307	9,887,214	10,778,225	11,477,181	12,050,126	12,804,552
Kentucky	1,858,635	2,147,174	2,289,905	2,416,630	2,614,589	2,845,627	2,944,806	3,038,156	3,219,311
Tennessee	1,767,518	2,020,616	2,184,789	2,337,885	2,616,556	2,915,841	3,291,718	3,567,089	3,924,164
Alabama	1,513,401	1,828,697	2,138,093	2,348,174	2,646,248	2,832,961	3,061,743	3,266,740	3,444,165
Mississippi	1,289,600	1,551,270	1,797,114	1,790,618	2,009,821	2,183,796	2,178,914	2,178,141	2,216,912
West South Central	4,740,983	6,532,290	8,784,534	10,242,224	12,176,830	13,064,525	14,537,572	16,951,255	19,322,458
Arkansas	1,128,211	1,311,564	1,574,449	1,752,204	1,854,482	1,949,387	1,909,511	1,786,272	1,923,295
Louisiana	1,118,588	1,381,625	1,656,388	1,798,509	2,101,593	2,363,880	2,683,516	3,257,022	3,643,180
Oklahoma	258,657	790,391	1,657,155	2,028,283	2,396,040	2,336,434	2,233,351	2,328,284	2,559,253
Texas	2,235,527	3,048,710	3,896,542	4,663,228	5,824,715	6,414,824	7,711,194	9,579,677	11,196,730
East North Central	13,478,305	15,985,581	18,250,621	21,475,543	25,297,185	26,626,342	30,309,368	36,225,024	40,252,678
Ohio	3,672,329	4,157,545	4,767,121	5,759,394	6,646,697	6,907,612	7,946,627	9,706,397	10,652,017
Indiana	2,192,404	2,516,462	2,700,876	2,930,390	3,238,503	3,427,796	3,934,224	4,662,498	5,193,669
Illinois	3,826,352	4,821,550	5,638,591	6,485,280	7,630,654	7,897,241	8,712,176	10,081,158	11,113,976
Michigan	2,093,890	2,420,982	2,810,173	3,668,412	4,842,325	5,256,106	6,371,766	7,823,194	8,875,083
Wisconsin	1,693,330	2,069,042	2,333,860	2,632,067	2,939,006	3,137,587	3,434,575	3,951,777	4,417,933
West North Central	8,932,112	10,347,423	11,637,921	12,544,249	13,296,915	13,516,990	14,061,394	15,394,115	16,324,389
Minnesota	1,310,283	1,751,394	2,075,708	2,387,125	2,563,953	2,792,300	2,982,483	3,413,864	3,805,069
Iowa	1,912,297	2,231,853	2,224,771	2,404,021	2,470,939	2,538,268	2,621,073	2,757,537	2,825,041
Missouri	2,679,185	3,106,665	3,293,335	3,404,055	3,629,367	3,784,664	3,954,653	4,319,813	4,677,399
North Dakota	190,983	319,146	577,056	646,872	680,845	641,935	619,636	632,446	617,761
South Dakota	348,600	401,570	583,888	636,547	692,849	642,961	652,740	680,514	666,257
Nebraska	1,062,656	1,066,300	1,192,214	1,296,372	1,377,963	1,315,834	1,325,510	1,411,330	1,483,791
Kansas	1,428,108	1,470,495	1,690,949	1,769,257	1,880,999	1,801,028	1,905,299	2,178,611	2,249,071
Mountain	1,213,935	1,674,657	2,633,517	3,336,101	3,701,789	4,150,003	5,074,998	6,855,060	8,283,585
Montana	142,924	243,329	376,053	548,889	537,606	559,456	591,024	674,767	694,409
Idaho	88,548	161,772	325,594	431,866	445,032	524,873	588,637	667,191	713,008
Wyoming	62,555	92,531	145,965	194,402	225,565	250,742	290,529	330,066	332,416
Colorado	413,249	539,700	799,024	939,629	1,035,791	1,123,296	1,325,089	1,753,947	2,207,259
New Mexico	160,282	195,310	327,301	360,350	423,317	531,818	681,187	951,023	1,016,000
Arizona	88,243	122,931	204,354	334,162	435,573	499,261	749,587	1,302,161	1,772,482
Utah	210,779	276,749	373,351	449,396	507,847	550,310	688,862	890,627	1,059,273
Nevada	47,355	42,335	81,875	77,407	91,058	110,247	160,083	285,278	488,738
Pacific	1,920,386	2,634,285	4,448,660	5,877,819	8,622,047	10,229,116	15,114,964	21,198,044	26,525,774
Washington	357,232	518,103	1,141,990	1,356,621	1,563,396	1,736,191	2,378,963	2,853,214	3,409,169
Oregon	317,704	413,536	672,765	783,389	953,786	1,089,684	1,521,341	1,768,687	2,091,385
California	1,213,398	1,485,053	2,377,549	3,426,861	5,677,251	6,907,387	10,586,223	15,717,204	19,953,134
Alaska	32,052	63,592	64,356	55,036	59,278	72,524	128,643	226,167	302,173
Hawaii	....	154,001	192,000	255,912	368,336	423,330	499,794	632,772	769,913

power of, 380–381, 382–385, 559, 686; privilege, 353
Weaver, James B., 393
Weaver, Robert C., 603
Welch, Robert, 768
Welfare, *see* Poverty, welfare
Welfare state, 366–367, 531, 544, 558–564, 570, 622
West: cattle ranges, 436, 438; cities, 483, 485; dude ranches, 659–660; immigrants in, 373, 448; Indians, 423–429; migration to, 345–346, 373, 423. *See also* Farmers, western
West, Mae, 633–634
Westinghouse, George, 360
Wheeler, Burton K., 624
Whig party, 388
White, William A., 394
Whiteman, Paul, 602
Whorton, James, 807
Whyte, William H., Jr., 701
Willard, Frances E., 473
Willkie, Wendell, 569, 570, 721
Wilson, Charles E., 703
Wilson, Woodrow, 394, 564, 702; administration, 351–352, 373, 387, 395–396, 415, 418, 435, 442, 476–477, 516, 543, 561; foreign policy, 354, 355, 400, 409–413, 415, 577–578, 579; League of Nations, 522–523, 569; and women, 476, 477–478; World War I, 410–413, 477–478, 560, 575, 588
Wister, Owen, 660
Women: abortion, 635, 776, 781, 782–783, 784; alcohol, 472–473, 634; attitudes toward, 472; birth control, 629, 634–635, 770, 777, 779; black, 469–470, 475, 602, 781, 784, 786; careers, 783–784; Chinese, 754–755; conventions, 464, 473, 475, 478; day-care centers, 633, 634,

635, 779, 781; divorce, 465, 466–467, 476, 631, 634, 776, 777–778; dress, 629, 631; earnings, 631, 633, 781, 783, 786; education, 465, 629–630, 634, 781–782, 785; exploitation, 474, 477; farm, 465–466, 631; feminists/-ism, 352, 464–465, 469–478, 545, 628, 630, 634–638, 677, 776, 780–786; Great Depression, 631, 638; immigrant, 465, 466, 473; legal rights, 471; legislation for, 636–638, 781, 783, 785; lesbian, 781; lifespan, 777; middle-class, 629, 630, 631, 777, 779, 781, 786; militant, 780–782; movement, 464, 469–478, 779, 780–786; myths about, 467, 630, 633–634, 777; organizations, 472–473, 475, 476–477, 636–638, 677, 781, 783, 785, 786; pacifist, 472, 477–478; pioneer, 466; in politics, 475–476, 477, 545, 634, 636, 638, 713, 781, 784; power, 631, 777; in prison, 785; professional, 464, 476, 633, 634, 781, 786; and prostitution, 440, 456, 467, 471, 472, 473, 638, 651, 745; property rights, 464, 467, 785; and psychology, 630, 777, 781; radical, 781–782; rape, 472; and religion, 456, 458, 467, 619–620, 784–785; roles, 464, 467, 471, 628, 630–631, 777, 781; and sex, 467, 471, 629–630, 633, 782–783; sexism, 472, 630, 781–782, 783–786; and social work, 496, 634, 638; southern, 474–475, 786; status, 780; suffrage, 352, 391, 393, 396, 464, 467, 469–478, 634–638, 781; and technology, 465, 630–631; welfare, 779, 781; working, 364, 366, 370, 372, 381, 391, 456, 465, 471, 472, 473–475, 477, 552, 631, 633, 634, 637, 638, 777, 779, 781, 783, 786; and World War I, 477; and World War II, 634. *See also* Children; Family; Labor, and women; Marriage

Wood, Leonard, 415
Woodhull, Victoria Claflin, 471
Work ethic, *see* Protestants, Ethic
Workingman's party, 440
World War I: aftermath, 355, 410, 413, 485, 536, 537, 549, 574, 599, 600, 629, 650, 658, 720; battles and generals, 412; beginning, 410; and blacks, 435, 436; and Chicanos, 436–442; end, 413; and labor, 373, 387; mobilization for, 416–418; and women, 477
World War II: aftermath, 574, 585–587, 597, 617, 654, 674, 682, 683, 689, 690, 694, 701, 703–704, 713, 748, 754, 756, 765, 767, 777, 794, 797, 805, 809; battles and generals, 532–533, 585; beginning, 580–581, 721; and blacks, 603–604; casualties, 590, 591; Chicanos in, 606–607; and Great Depression, 549; end, 673, 724; Indians in, 751, 752; and labor, 552, 683; and women, 634, 636
Wovoka, 425
Wright, Frank Lloyd, 525, 647
Wright, Orville and Wilbur, 358, 360

Yahi Indians, 428–429
Yom Kippur War, 771
Yorty, Sam, 709
Young, Whitney, 747
Youth: black, 745; Chicano, 749–750; Chinese, 754–755; in communes, 791–792; disaffection of, 677, 701, 709; and drugs, 768; ethnic, 761–762; and marriage, 761; middle-class, 780; and politics, 712, 713; and racism, 741; rebellion of, 780, 791; religion, 768–769

Zaharias, Babe Didrikson, 783
Zuñi Indians, 428, 438

Index prepared by Dennis Williams